THE
POLITICAL ECONOMY
OF
SOUTH AFRICA

THE
POLITICAL ECONOMY
OF
SOUTH AFRICA

Ralph Horwitz

FREDERICK A. PRAEGER, *Publishers*

NEW YORK · WASHINGTON

BOOKS THAT MATTER
Published in the United States of America 1967
by Frederick A. Praeger, Inc., Publishers
111 Fourth Avenue, New York, N.Y. 10003

Printed in Great Britain

CONTENTS

INTRODUCTION

The political factor, it is suggested, has played a part in the modern economic development of South Africa which may be compared to the role of the imperial factor in its political history. British imperialism or the imperial factor has generally been identified as the continuing instrument and occasion of action and reaction. It was cause and effect. It generated and conditioned the process of interaction that became a major theme of South African political history. The viewpoint here is that there has been a political factor, which has interacted with economic development in South African experience in like manner. It, too, became the determining agency of interaction and a major theme in the country's economic history.

The account of South African social reality, from the time of the mineral discoveries of the 1870's and 1880's and the evolution of a market- or exchange-economy, it will be argued, is most realistically interpreted as the record of a political economy in action. In this respect South Africa is of course not unique but the record has a distinctive character and special interest. The distinctive character arises from the ethos of the political factor with its peculiar dynamism and imperatives, and the special interest from the empirical evidence which the growth of the South African economy from a stagnant society to an adolescent maturity provides for economic development theory.

The political factor in South African history is certainly not a single component of unchanging form. It has had and has, however, a purposiveness and pervasiveness of motivation, that permits of its being given identity. This identity may in the course of time have assumed many guises, sometimes disguises. Yet it remains an always recognizable embodiment of unvarying beliefs and unchanging objectives. It is throughout a consistent, persistent factor of South African reality and its increasingly monolithic quality justifies its description as an ideology. As an identity and an ideology, through the successive guises of trusteeship to segregation to apartheid to Bantustans, the *political factor* remains the unchallengeable, unalterable control of South African society in general and the South African economy in particular by its White peoples.

This is the political factor which is never off the economic stage, where its presence now looms so dominant that it is not only the star but also author and producer. The drama is the record of a political economy, which can be written as economic history because it has a pattern of relationships that are both continuous and interconnected. There is not only chronology of event but a seeming compulsion of choice, which links the polity to the market in a composition of circumstance.

There is no historical inevitability. On the contrary, chance and unforeseen, unscheduled good fortune have marked the entire unfolding of economic events. So much so that a noted South African economist, haunted throughout his academic career by the Cassandra syndrome, was finally driven on the point of his retirement from prophecy of woe to attribute the perennially astonishing economic development of South Africa to a series of miracles [1].

It is not then any inevitability nor any undeviating progressive purpose which provides the record of South African economic history. There is much more happening than planning, more seizure of opportunity than processing of possibilities, more entrepreneurship than management. But political action has been a highly conscious pursuit of idealized and ideological objective by the most politically-conscious, cohesive group in South African society.

Afrikanerdom's awareness of politics and political power may have been the fruit of bitter, earlier experience of lack of power, that drove Afrikaners repeatedly to trek from the confines of others' jurisdiction. Their original drive always to move on, away from political control, was not – at least until the 1870's – restrained by any material benefits deriving from governmental authority. But once economic development caught up with Afrikaner isolationism, once the need for political sophistication overcame the wish and the will to trek beyond into escapism, in brief once gold was found in the Transvaal, then Afrikanerdom's political consciousness became compulsively positive instead of compulsively negative.

Afrikanerdom thenceforth was determined on achieving political authority, indeed unfettered sovereignty – determined not only on rejection of the imperial factor from the Boer republics but on republican status for the whole of South Africa. Afrikanerdom's political consciousness was no less an inflexible assertion of the prerogative of political authority over the course of economic development. As such development intruded into and undermined Afrikanerdom's concept of the South African way of life, so insistence on political sovereignty over the market hardened. As market forces of choice and co-ordination of choice apparently infected the lifeblood of Afrikanerdom, so Afrikanerdom perfected the political purge of foreign impurities.

To Afrikanerdom, the imperial factor was the enemy of its existence and economic development the trouble-maker of its tradition. The imperial factor would enforce unacceptable adjustments from external influences, and economic growth would impose intolerable consequences of market behaviour. The free market would dictate its 'purely economic' values, formed by the exercise of impersonal choice, that ignored the predetermination of Afrikanerdom to personalize White and Non-white as of different biblical origin and hence never to mix 'in Church and State'. Only a politically united, politically dedicated Afrikanerdom could both overcome the imperial factor and also subjugate the apolitical market.

Furthermore, the imperial factor and economic development appeared as Tweedledum and Tweedledee – a twin manifestation of a single threat to Afrikaner sovereignty over South Africa. They were to Afrikanerdom not however the comic figures of an English imagination but the horrific double-image of British inspiration. Impregnable in its Calvinism, Afrikaner nationalism nonetheless saw its being on the South African veldt in terms of Greek tragedy. To Afrikanerdom was given the task of Sisyphus. Only complete political power, a monopoly of authority in every sphere of the nation's life, might enable it to attain the brink of security, and perhaps immunity from being thrust into the extinction of Afrikaner-existence.

It is this compelling political consciousness of Afrikanerdom that constitutes the political factor in both the political and the economic history of South Africa. It did not by any means embrace all Afrikaners in a united wish and will: far from it. Some of the greatest of Afrikaner leaders supported by their personal followers were in almost lifelong opposition, and exercised governmental power for crucial periods. General Smuts, in non-Afrikaner eyes the greatest

3

Afrikaner leader of them all, saw from shortly after the Treaty of Vereeniging[2] – which carried with it the seeds of union while passing on the legacy of disunion – both the imperial factor and economic development in a Holism that transcended Afrikanerdom.

In a larger sense Smuts was a decisive political factor in his own person while political forces and events, much wider than the narrowed designation of the political factor of Afrikanerdom, operated powerfully on the South African economy. It was however those holistic forces to which Afrikanerdom was implacably opposed and in the narrower sense, Smuts was not part of the political factor except inasmuch as he was for long years successful in frustrating it.

The opponents of Smuts indeed soon came to question almost his claim to be an Afrikaner and violently denied his right to represent Afrikanerdom. He was to Afrikanerdom the lackey of British imperalism as much as the handmaiden of Hoggenheimer, that cartoon conception of profit-seeking economic development devoid of all non-economic motivation. The political factor always pictured Smuts and Hoggenheimer in an unholy alliance against it, combining to denature its White nationalism. If White nationalism was to endure and subdue such opponents, then it could only be by way of the political factor – by total control of the polity and, from the 1930's, by a totalitarian concept of the role of the polity.

Afrikanerdom never wavered in its determination to be the polity and never conceded that there was any limitation, legal or moral, on the sovereign power of the Afrikaner polity other than the 'volkswil'[3]. The area of permissible choice, whether by private individual or group collectivity, was to be rigidly delimited by the polity and increasingly the boundaries of such areas were racially demarcated under its direction.

As choice is expressed in and by the market, so the polity came into conflict with the market. In so far as the free market impersonalized choice, in so far as it ignored colour and racial categories and even home-languages and party-political loyalties, inasmuch as it did not acknowledge the authority of the polity's preferences, market choice was a rivalling, and fatally undermining, sovereignty of decision-taking. And in so far as market forces determined economic development, so economic development was suspect – a source of infection of the South African way of life, as evolved by non-economic motivations. The infection could be arrested and a 'healthy'

4

economic development guaranteed only by placing the market under the supervision of the polity.

The market does more, however, than impersonalize choice: it allocates and co-ordinates resources in accordance with such choice. It is a mechanism of linkage. It works through a process of integrating disintegration and disintegrating integration. The social change, thereby effected, conditions the pattern of human relationships – between individuals and among groups. The pattern is never fixed because choice is not fixed, at least in a free society. It is a pattern which is always evolving, but in its evolution, the complexity of linkage intensifies the inter-dependence of its increasing specialization of function and division of labour. Sociologically, the market integrates human relationships more and more widely and more and more intimately.

Economic development need not proceed necessarily nor solely by way of market choice and market forces. The allocation and cordination of the factors of production may not be initiated by private choice and decentralized initiative, but by collective choice and a centralized initiative. If collective choice and centralized initiative prevails, then the economy and its development becomes the increasingly administered economy. The market comes under hierarchical instruction. If Authority – if the hierarchy – is infused with a mission, yet chained to its traditions and engrossed with its ethos, an administered economy will emerge from the administered society.

The drive towards etatism is hastened by the administered society's own inner compulsions. The area of individual choice and private initiative, the freedom of the market, will be increasingly encroached upon by the polity. If, on the other hand, development progresses by way of market forces, it tends to proceed without regard to the motivations that lie behind the political factor. The economy, and economic development, become as it were apolitical. This was the case with South Africa's early economic growth. Development in South Africa came in response to private entre-preneurial effort, and the economy's subsequent market-orientation, structured by the Rand's goldmining industry, progressively integrated all the elements of the South African social system.

The pull and push of the Rand's mining market was exerted intensively and extensively; it was this market whose development dynamic was to make a market-economy out of all the hitherto largely self-contained, self-sufficient sub-systems of South African society. The mining market's choices conditioned the responses in ever-widening sectors of the economy, integrating them out of their self-subsistent isolation. Its decisions and actions were governed by its market-consciousness, by its economic rationality in substituting lower-cost for higher-cost factors of productions. The resultant co-ordination of productive factors aimed at the least-cost combination. The goldmining market worked through and towards economic rationality.

Labour was the critical cost-factor of gold production. It was through its substitutions and its combinations of labour, therefore, that the goldmining industry's co-ordination of its own growth and of the overall expansion of the economy exerted most vigorously the market process of integrating disintegration and disintegrating integration. Its employment and deployment of labour, White and African, in numbers far exceeding those of any other single industry in co-operation with very large sums of capital, and utilizing great quantities of stores, made the Rand goldmines the heart (and the heartland) of the South African market economy – the most significant, single integrating influence in the South African social system.

It was the total social change, which the goldmines of the Rand and their decision-taking, profit-seeking uitlander-entrepreneurs implied for the pattern of human relationships in South Africa, that was wholly unacceptable to the political factor. Hence the long hate between the Chamber of Mines and Afrikanerdom. In the mines' first phase of development, it was their capital imperatives, linked to the imperial factor, that were seen as the mortal enemy of the Afrikaners' way of life. In the South African or Anglo-Boer War, the political factor was nominally defeated though Afrikanerdom found invincible inspiration in defeat. Then, in the later phase of the mines' development, it was the labour imperatives of the Chamber of Mines that came to be seen as the mortal enemy of the White man's way of life. In particular, it was those labour imperatives that pushed the economic rationality of least-cost combination into a crucial challenge to the colour-bar restraints on mining productivity.

Again, it was in the Rand goldmining industry that there originated the second major confrontation between economic development and the political factor. The 1922 Rand Strike, fought on

6

the issue of the colour-bar in mining employment, was the moment of truth for the South African political economy. Economic rationality, the least-cost co-ordination of the factors of production to maximize productivity, won the syndicalist battle against the White trade unions. The Chamber of Mines briefly triumphed against the industrial colour bar but very shortly afterwards lost this minor civil war to the political factor. The Chamber of Mines lost to the unvarying belief and unchanging objective of the political factor – that the unchallengeable, unalterable control of South African society in general and the South African economy in particular should remain with its White peoples, as represented by Afriaknerdom.

In the 1924 General Election, Smuts-Hoggenheimer was pilloried to defeat and Hertzog-Creswell propagandized to victory. White supremacy held henceforth the source of ultimate power and the market economy steadily gave way to the administered society. Hertzog represented nineteenth-century Afrikaner nationalism and Creswell represented nineteenth-century British trade unionism. Their Pact formed a Government in 1924 to represent eternal White supremacy in South Africa.

It was above all a pact against free market co-ordination of resource-utilization and in favour of an administered society. It was against the impersonalized choice of a competitive market that ignored and overruled the raison-d'être of the political factor – that economic development should never be allowed to alter White-Black relationships advantageously to the politico-social status of the Non-Whites and disadvantageously to the politico-social status of the Whites. Economic development might bring material gain to both but market controls were ideologically imperative to perpetuate the differentials of racial status.

This crucial motivation of the polity drove the Pact Government and the post-1948 South African governments towards the etatism that teeters on the brink of totalitarianism. The administered society rigidified wider and wider areas of the market. Only the Second World War and the Smuts Government restored mobility to the labour market and intensified economic development to meet the insatiable demands of war-time markets. But Smuts and the Second World War were the very antithesis of messianic Afrikanerdom in South African history. With the political factor restored to parliamentary power in the 1948 General Election, Dr Malan set his entirely Afrikaner Government to the complete realization

7

of its objective – the unchallengeable, unalterable control of South African society in general and the South African economy in particular by its White peoples, as represented by Afrikanerdom.

The conflict between the polity and the market broadened and deepened. The choices of the market were over-ridden by the preferences of the polity. The linkage mechanism of the market was interrupted at more and more points and it was forced into that process of adjustment to non-market values, which the mechanism's limitless flexibility permits but which inhibits its productivity.

Economic development after 1948 becomes more and more a forced growth, an administered direction of resource-employment and a spreading area of nationalization. In propagandist or leftist description, the South African political economy is so identified with capitalist exploitation that the extent of nationalized enterprise tends to go unperceived. In fact South African governments took possession of the 'commanding heights' of the economy long before the concept was born in British Labour Party pamphleteering enthusiasm.

Railways were state-owned, from the start, and from the earliest days there were voices, sometimes vociferous though never really powerful, that favoured the nationalization of the goldmining industry. The Pact Government of Afrikanerdom and Labour Party under Hertzog-Creswell from 1924 on directed itself, however, not to the take-over of the goldmines but to adminstering the shape and rate of economic development. The re-entrenchment of the colour bar in mining employment by the Mines and Works Amendment Act of 1926 established beyond challenge that the South African ethos and not economic rationality would dictate the ultimate determinants of goldmining costs. In so far as goldmining was then the sum and substance of economic achievement, the Pact Government determined to control the sum and to seek alternative substance.

But if nationalization of the goldmines never became a serious political issue, the Labour tail of the Pact Government was absolutely insistent that the strategic iron and steel industry should be under state control. The political battle to make Iscor, the Iron and Steel Corporation of South Africa, a state undertaking led to the first circumvention, by way of Senate manipulation, of the Act of Union of 1910. Though it was not always the governments of Afrikanerdom that initiated the legislation, it was Afrikanerdom that narrowed

8

the vision and directed the subsequent motivation. It intensified direct and indirect state authority by way of public utilities, massive investment in the public sector, and through the chosen instruments of the Land Bank and the Industrial Development Corporation, the IDC.

State finance promoted agricultural co-operatives and controlled-marketing of crops under bureaucratic direction, and wholly-owned or held majority control of major industrial enterprise. The IDC, after Afrikanerdom had recovered Cabinet authority from Smuts's war-time administration, became the State's financier for such heavily-capitalized undertakings as Sasol (oil-from-coal and petrochemicals) and Foskor (phosphate fertilizers) as public corporations. Nominee directors of the IDC on a number of major industrial companies served to represent government money and government policy.

In South African experience not all farmers were politicians but from the beginning nearly all politicians were farmers. This ensured that collective ownership of the means of production, starting with the land, never became a serious issue of South African politics. It guaranteed, however, that the administration of the market economy was governed by farmer-politicians, acutely mindful of politically-conscious farmers. This reality, too, has been very much part of the political factor in the economic development of South Africa. Forced industrialization, that would expand employment for Afrikaner voters pushed and pulled off the farms by the nature of economic growth, also became a major objective of Afrikanerdom's political economy.

The administered economy did not replace the market economy in South Africa but it steadily displaced it. The market economy is capable of adaptation to non-market interference and will absorb such interference. Actual market collapse or market elimination will take place only with the abolition of private contractual freedom under totalitarianism or the seizure of property under Communism. But the market is otherwise resilient. Given any manoeuvring room, it will manoeuvre. Given any area of freedom for its operations, it will strive to expand that area. Left a breath of life, the market will revitalize. It is then the turn of the political factor to accommodate and adapt to the choices of the market, or be impelled towards an unchallengeable sovereignty, if not a totalitarian dictatorship.

This social process is the general experience of all societies.

It is the common reality because social reality is political economy and not econometrics. There is always the political factor, which economic science may for purposes of classroom analysis usefully ignore but cannot helpfully exclude even in academic debate.

Is it legitimate to identify in South African social reality something called 'the political factor' with Afrikanerdom? Is there an 'ethos' of Afrikanerdom or is this mere jargon? Of course, during all the years there were governments, powerful political parties and politicians, who greatly influenced events and who were not Afrikaners or not accepted as part of Afrikaner nationalism. Of course there were Botha and Smuts, loved and hated by their fellow-Afrikaners, who between them reconciled English-speaking and Afrikaans-speaking to a South Africanism. Of course, there were English-speaking politicians and 'English' groups, especially trade unions, who were as much devoted to White leadership, superiority, supremacy as Afrikaans-speaking politicians and 'Afrikaans' groups.

Of course, therefore, the influence of politics and government in South Africa has not been wholly and exclusively Afrikaner nationalism. Nor is it suggested that other powerful realities, which have had nothing to do with 'politics', have not been of major importance to the country's economic development. But from the vantage point of 1966, has not Afrikanerdom more than any other single influence made contemporary South Africa what it is? Has not Afrikanerdom constituted a 'polity' – a people acquiring a language, a religion, a set of ideas and aims so much in common as to drive them to seek and hold power in every key point of authority: in Parliament, in the civil service, in teaching, in the Universities, in trade unions, in the great state and semi-state enterprises, in every type of separatist organisation from an (Afrikaans) Chamber of Commerce to an (Afrikaans) Boy Scout movement? Do not all such sources of influence and of power add up to a 'polity' and do not the deliberately-sought and consciously-achieved controls become an identifiable 'political factor'?

For almost a hundred years Afrikaner nationalism has written and spoken of its 'lifeblood' – the preservation of what in time it came to call the Christian Nationalism of the volk. May this not be described as something more than a standard manifestation of patriotism – is it jargon to call it 'the "ethos" of Afrikanerdom'?

This thesis argues that there has been such a political factor of Afrikanerdom. It argues that the South African economy of the

1960's has been decisively shaped, and perhaps determined, not merely by the kind of political intervention and increased government activities, which are the common experience of most countries of the Western World, but by an overpowering pursuit of ideals, or ideology. As such South Africa has been made into a very different society from any other in the West or the East. Its way of life arouses passionate world denunciation, so passionate as to attempt its casting out from human fellowship and economic boycott by the United Nations, however representative UN may or may not be of humanity and of world opinion. As such the South African economy – the distinctive features of its economic development – are the outcome and the expression of its way of life. There has been, on this contention, a political factor in the economic development of South Africa which is Afrikanerdom. There has been an Afrikanerdom which relentlessly, if not inevitably, took over the political factor – the exercise of dominant power for the achievement of dominating aims.

This book does not attempt to provide either a political history or an economic history of South Africa. Its aim is a realistic account of the economic development of a country, whose social experience may be as instructive for the theory of economic development as it is dehumanizing for political idealism.

The method of recording may be likened to that of the technique of network analysis, used in the production planning of complex operations. Such production planning or scheduling begins with the ultimate target or objective and then traces back to the starting point all the sequential actions for its achievement. The purpose is not only to envisage from the beginning the full set of production activities but to programme their performance along what is termed the critical path schedule so that the whole operation is completed in the shortest time or by the most economic utilization of resources. This method of production planning is a form of micro-economic programming and its macro-economic counterpart is the economic development programme of the econometrician.

The historical record of modern economic development in South Africa exhibits no such scheduling. Its social process was not programmed. Its chain of interaction was not preconceived. The network of South African economic activities and events, which after the mineral discoveries moved from acquiescent stagnation to self-sustained growth, certainly had no predetermined development conception to give it its particular form. The moves were erratic and often eccentric. There has been no scheduled path of choice, no programmed allocation of scarce resources, nothing indeed resembling an economic plan. Yet there is a traceable network of economic development, in which the self-expression of market forces has come to terms with the motivations of the polity. South African economic development has been very much the response to market forces, external perhaps even more than internal, which after long years of hesitation became increasingly favourable to growth. Market-linkage or resource-utilization adjusted to and combined with administered-linkage. The allocation of resources may in consequence have been less than optimum in terms of output, or, more precisely in consumers' preferred output as reflected in free market choice. Economic development has nonetheless continued. It has continued with an increasing measure of state interference. But it is the argument of this book that the economic history of South Africa is more than an account of state interference into private enterprise. It is a record of the interaction of a political economy in which the political factor, Afrikanerdom, in or out of Government, has always had an ultimate – a way of life to preserve and to promote. The polity has always sought its ideal and its ideology – the White man's supremacy. The network of economic development had to follow accordingly.

THE SOUTH AFRICAN WAY OF LIFE
PART I – CHANGING AND UNCHANGING

The Great Trek of Boer frontiersmen from the Eastern Cape in 1836 may be regarded as an organized withdrawal from all political controls at a time when unchanging economic stagnation exercized hardly any integrating influences at all. As such it may not at first sight seem the most appropriate starting point for an account of the political factor in the modern economic development of South Africa. Yet the network of interaction of a political economy, in which Afrikanerdom as the political factor sought to preserve and promote White South Africa's way of life, reaches back to the exodus from the fringes of a self-subsistent economy – the exodus that in time evoked the national ethos of Afrikanerdom.

It has recently been argued with persuasive evidence by an Afrikaner historian [1] that Afrikaner nationalism was not in fact born until some years after the Great Trek. It was only during the times of trouble for the scattered trekker republics in the years 1868 to 1881 that the 'national self-awakening', first in the Orange Free State and considerably later in the Transvaal Republic, in reaction to British political pressures grew into a clearly identifiable nationalism. Such a political awakening to a shared destiny had been preceded in the old Cape Colony by a cultural awakening to a common heritage.

But the Boer frontiersmen of the Eastern Cape, organizing the first major mass-movement in the long-continuing dispersion of the original Dutch colonist-settlers, had more grievances than cultural mission. It was their grievances that spurred their emigration. Both their grievances and their emigration yielded a group-consciousness, increasingly fostered as a defence mechanism in an unfriendly environment of African tribesmen, British imperialism and economic stagnation. That defence mechanism was sharpened into a positive awareness of nationhood, when the Trekker Republics had to take up arms to safeguard their republican independence.

It took shape when British colonialism seemingly sided with African tribesmen to encircle the republican sovereignty of the Free State beyond the Orange River during the Basuto Wars and the Diamond Fields Dispute in the late 1860's. It took further cohesive form when British Imperialism allegedly intervened to destroy the independence of the disintegrating South African Republic across the Vaal in the late 1870's. It took final form when the Imperial Factor accusedly provoked the Transvaal and the Orange Free State into a common resistance to the extinction of their independent Afrikanerdom in the South African or Anglo-Boer War of 1899–1902, which some Afrikaner historians identify as the Second War of Independence or Second Freedom War.

The Voortrekkers were a group, which legend no less than history forged into a nation. Group consciousness only much later became a national self-consciousness but the former as much as the latter contributed to the Political Factor that conditioned the course of modern economic development in South Africa. The network of the modern South African political economy stretches back to the Great Trek – to more than thirty years before the mineral discoveries of diamonds in the 1870's and gold in the 1880's created the pre-conditions for an economy of increasing division of labour and specialization of activity. It stretches back to a pre-market era, to the long, uninterrupted decades when awareness of land as the only factor of production in a self-contained subsistence was the dominant motivation of both Afrikaner and African conduct.

The group consciousness of the Afrikaner stockfarmers, particularly on the disputed borderlands of self-subsistence of the Eastern Cape, was a bitter, despairing frustration that government, whether the old Dutch East India Company in 1795 or the British Colonial Office of Glenelg in the 1830's, was not willing to support their land-rights and land-claims against the African tribes. Frustration as much as consciousness, grievances as much as if not more than purposiveness sent the Trekkers in search of the White man's untrammeled control over South Africa's only significant, contemporary economic resource. Land for cattle.

In the nearly one hundred and fifty years since the Dutch East India Company had by occupation pre-empted the Cape as a strategic station and supply source on the long route of seventeenth-century European economic development to the East, no significant exchange economy had evolved from the dispersed settlement. Even after the British in their turn of pre-emption by occupation in 1806 had pushed the dispersion into further settlement east and north, no progressively integrating market economy had been generated. The European points of settlement were something more than primitive trading communities and Cape Town itself could count its merchants and craftsmen with its hinterland of wine-growers and produce-gardeners. There were market-oases of concentration scattered over a great expanse of territory but a market economy of developing specialization and increasing capital accumulation could not really be said to have come into being.

No economic development of Schumpeterian entrepreneurship had got under way or was to start on its career of innovating investment until after the mineral discoveries of the 1870's and 1880's uncovered the markets of capitalistic enterprise. Until then the repetition of stagnation was merely carried further and further by the migrant stockfarmers into the territories demarcated by geography and rainfall. Whether the causes of such failure were to be found in the inhibiting isolationism of the country's physical environment, the imposed isolationism of its political neglect or the induced isolationism of its cultural inability to generate capital and capitalists, the vitalizing expansion of markets – sustained by capital accumulation and diversifying innovating-investors – emerged only after those markets had been sparked by the diamond and gold discoveries of the last quarter of the nineteenth century.

Until then cattle-land remained the only meaningful resource to the social systems of White and Black pastoralists. Meeting on the Fish River, for years they disputed for the cattle land up to the Kei River. Confrontation escalated into continuous conflict. Two basically opposed concepts of land ownership – private property and tribal collectivity – could not reconcile two basically similar practices of land utilization.

Land utilization reflected the absence of those crucial determinants of capital and market demand that induce intensive agriculture. Both African tribesmen and Dutch pastoralists were propelled into that never-ending search for more and more territory of less and less productivity. Self-subsistence for men was equated with sustenance for cattle and both, therefore, with land that by these twin tokens constituted the only form of wealth. In consequence though the territorial vastness of South Africa made land plentiful, the virtual failure to develop an exchange economy of income-generating specialization made land simultaneously scarce[2].

Boer stockfarmers and Bantu cattle-raisers met on the frontiers of their chase for the shadowy substance that they both identified as wealth. When the Boers found that the alien English polity, omnipresent whether nearby in the person of Dr Philip of the London Missionary Society or far away in the person of Lord Glenelg of the British Colonial Office, was not prepared to protect and promote their land-needs against the land-needs of Black tribesmen, they departed on their Great Trek. It was a trek in search of uncontained space, free from marauding tribal tradition and of uncontrolled room free from interfering missionary zeal. It was an escape into non-interference.

The Trekkers were seeking not to find a new way of life but to continue an old way of life in what they hoped was unoccupied territory beyond the interest and concern of any polity, other than their own rudimentary organizations for mutual support in their land-occupation. In their penetration of the interior, they took with them this fundamental rejection of outside interference. They also took the unsought possibility that this vast interior would yield other resources than cattle-grazing self-subsistence.

When indeed the land in the undetermined and indeterminate occupation of a Griqua chief, Waterboer, disclosed diamonds, the outside interference of English missionary colonialism avidly aided by capitalists, with and without capital, returned in force. And when the land further north in the absolutely determined occupation of the Boers disclosed gold, outside interference from British imperialism and Uitlander capital was a force, in Afrikaner eyes, to be met with force.

In the half-century reaction from 1850 to outside interference, designated the Imperial Factor by the historians, there was born and bred the nationalism of Afrikanerdom. In the quarter-century from 1875 of the mineral discoveries, there was established the first stages for the take-off into an exchange economy and for the stimulating interactions of a market economy. As economic development in the person of a Schumpeterian colossus, Cecil John Rhodes, wrapped up in his cloak of colonialism, pushed further and farther on to the scene, the political factor of Afrikanerdom reacted and acted. In the political economy of disintegrating integration and integrating disintegration, the ethos of Afrikanerdom began to institutionalize itself.

In that new ordering of the veldt, the South African way of life was compelled to change. But in changing, both Afrikaner and African clung to unchange. Above all, they clung to land and their traditional utilization of land.

Economic development – the mines and their derivative markets – from the 1870's and 1880's began the pull and the push off the land and its extensive exploitation by stockfarmers. The transformation of the South African way of life was under way – the interrelationships of land and labour were beginning their marketmoves and market-motivations. Alongside land-occupation, labour utilization became the source of conflict. Land and labour became the single theme of South African political economy. The network of economic development, under the rationalizing rationality of the White Man, was in the course of being traced. The sequential activities of the market and the consequential responses of the polity were beginning to constitute the modern economic history of South Africa.

And the starting-point was land-utilization and labourdeployment.

In the first days of the Cape, a loan system of land tenure had been tried to settle farmers temporarily on the land as pastoralists moving on to new regions. Later permanent title by perpetual quit-rent or freehold conditioned the settlement of the Cape and Natal. In the case of the trekker republics of the Orange Free State and the Transvaal, each trekker-settler was given permanent possession of as much land as he could ride round in a day. Such a day's ride generally encompassed between 6000 and 8000 acres and if the land did not have natural winter pasturage, then the trekkersettler would also claim and secure title to another holding of land which had such pasturage [3].

Since such land-occupation and utilization was not only the dominant but indeed the only form of productive endeavour of the Afrikaner trekker-settler, and since the self-subsistent exploitation of the land provided almost the only form of life and living for the Transvaal Boer in particular, the major objective of the polity was to preserve scope for future trekking. The Transvaal burghers 'demanded access to new areas where they could live the only kind

17

of agricultural life which they understood.' [4]. Hence the confrontation which Cecil John Rhodes, aided by his imperial factor, and his policy of territorial containment and resource-exploitation, presented in due course to Paul Kruger, president of a trekker republic whose social system – its economy, its polity and its institutionalized culture – was predicated on indefinite trekking.

In the trekker republics there was not only an absence of a market demand but even of a money economy. With coin almost literally unknown, commerical tenancy of land was precluded. New arrivals by way of natural process had a family claim to a portion of the only inheritance – hence sub-division of land holdings was in the course of two or three generations (families of ten to twelve were common) to become a serious cause of indigency. Other new arrivals, who could claim no family ties but had merely started to trek a little later, were accommodated by being given occupation, as distinct from title, rights. They were permitted to occupy part of the 6000 to 8000 acres which the farmer, who had secured title by his day's ride, could not currently use for himself. They became the *bywoners* – those who lived alongside. So long as neither sheep-farming nor crop-cultivation was directed towards production for a market, the bywoner system created no problems. The bywoner indeed provided some human fellowship in a domain of thousands of acres and in a vast land, in which even the rail line when it did come ran single-tracked from coastal ports to the mines of the Witwatersrand.

But the land of South Africa was not so quite unoccupied as its White migrants believed or persuaded themselves. Indeed the very first immigrant from Holland, Jan van Riebeeck, learnt very early on that there were Non-White occupants as well, who could not even be kept out by a hedge of wild almonds[5]. From then on the rights to land, customary, prescriptive and legal, as between Whites and Non-Whites have constituted the warp and weft of South African history. Between the first *plakkaat* of Governor van Riebeeck to the most recent amendment of the Group Areas Act No 41 of 1950, land ownership and occupation have woven the fabric of the South African social system – a fabric so tightly knit today as to make contemporary attempts to unravel that social system by way of segregation, apartheid or separate development a mortal threat to its continuation.

Among the tribalized Africans, there was at an early stage no

18

ownership as such of land 'Land among them was owned by no one: neither by individual nor by family, nor by tribe. It was the duty of the chief to procure the use of land to the natives who, as members of the tribe, were entitled to ask his protection. Although there was no ownership, an elaborate system of rights in land had grown up . . . ' [6].

This highly elaborated system of rights in land constituted the interconnection between the economy and the polity of the tribe. It served as the basic institution for a self-subsistence, mutual-help economy and the key to power in the polity. Thus, writes Goodfellow, the real political power in each tribe rested with the authority who could give natives the right to land; either an individual right to cultivate certain lands or a right to the tribe as a whole to pasture its cattle and to protect them against the claim of other tribes [7]. Loyalty to and acknowledgement of political sovereignty, whether tribal chief or White man's suzerainty, was consequently correlated to the power to underwrite the economic organization by the power to enforce land-rights.

It may be that the gradual acceptance by African tribal chiefs of the authority of the Great White Queen, either indirectly in the case of British Kaffraria or directly in the case of Basutoland and Swaziland, is best interpreted as the unwilling but eventual recognition by the tribalized economy of the ultimate political power of Queen Victoria[8]. Without doubt the preferences of the tribal chiefs for the authority of the Colonial Office 6000 miles away rather than that of the colonists on the spot was their recognition that the former was disposed to continue to guarantee rights in land, while the colonists – and more particularly those who must forever be a-trekking – were resolutely determined on a take-over bid that was composed of very much take-over and very little bid.

The most sophisticated politician among the tribal chiefs, Moshesh, deployed his assets with an unexcelled bargaining skill, so that the successful bidder was the British Crown. Indeed the terms secured by Moshesh provided that though the new board of directors might be nominated in Downing Street, the asset of Basutoland would in the fulness of time revert to the original shareholders – which given the nature of the political economy of the Basuto were co-incident with the original tribal landowners.

In the social system of the tribe, the interconnections between economic organization and political authority also involved the institutions of marriage and family. The rights to land included cultivation of a private garden-path for each wife, who was responsible by her own labour for its cultivation (i.e. agriculture), and rights to pasture cattle, being the responsibility of the man-husband on common land. The more wives a man had, the more garden-patches or privately cultivated land he could lay claim to; but to obtain a wife he required the marriage-custom of lobola or the exchange of cattle to the woman's father. An increase in cattle-ownership increased the capacity to control the number of garden-patches through more wives and thereby the personal share of foodstuffs from the garden-patches. But, because lobola compelled the surrender of a given number of cattle for each wife, the excessively polygamous would have to diminish his private stock of cattle. Hence cattle not only constituted a currency but regulated the terms of trade between agriculture (with private land rights) and pasturage (with common land rights).

Finally the rights of inheritance supported the maintenance of the system. On death the man's lands (i.e. rights in respect of garden-patches or agriculture) were in charge of the widows under obligation to support the sons until the latter should acquire rights to land on marriage and according to custom from the tribal chief, as the source of power in the polity.

Clearly the system not only placed enormous emphasis on institutionalized culture but was critically dependent on tribal authority over an unchecked territorial expanse of appropriate land. Where White authority or ownership, effectively exercised, brought the extension of tribal land holdings to a halt, there was not only a source of Black-White conflict but an inevitable disruption and ultimate destruction of the tribal social system. Broken at any imperative – loss of political power by tribal chief, breakdown of the exchange relationship between private and common land-rights through the terms of trade in respect of wives and cattle, decay of the institutional culture through erosion of lobola – the vital interconnections of the entire system would be disrupted and the tribal social system begin to disintegrate.

In the case of the old Cape Colony and the Natal Colony, it was White authority which increasingly successfully checked the movement of Africans in response to needs of wider tribal lands. In the case of the trekker republics, but more especially the Transvaal, it was trekker occupation of land that compelled a change. Thus in the Cape, the Master and Servants laws (originally a part of the Roman-Dutch law to regulate rights and obligations between apprentices and employers) were applied to Africans to put a stop to their continuous movement and to secure a permanently fixed supply of African farm workers for White-owned farms.

In the Transvaal the White trekker having been confirmed in his title to his 6000 to 8000 acres (sometimes double if both summer- and winter-grazing was necessary) would discover considerable numbers of tribal Africans either already in occupation or moving-in. The White farmer with the assistance of his neighbouring White farmers – and occasionally help from the Veld Cornet as the responsible government official — would attempt to clear his land of the unwanted Africans. This was not always possible since the Africans tended to return repeatedly and, in any event, their presence might on occasions be useful to the White owner. In the Transvaal (and to a lesser extent in Natal) Africans who had lost rights in tribal lands, simply settled without permission on Crown (or Government) or farmer's lands as squatters either to be turned off or made to pay rent at will or, at the other extreme, to be conceded virtually the same status as White bywoners. Whether as squatters or bywoners or as dwellers, the Africans lived on White farms in every kind of informal and undefined way [9]. Many such Africans were unmarried young men who served as migrant farm labourers for part of the year and then returned to tribal lands, perhaps to marry, for the rest of the year. Others were Africans who, with their wives and children, had lost all effective rights and connections with their own tribal lands and became farm labourers.

Such latter groups stayed on farms for long periods, often for life. In return for certain customary rights of cultivation to provide the family with subsistence, the African family as a unit would be obligated to provide the White farmer with whatever farm and domestic labour he required. Occasionally there would be a money wage of £1 per month [10].

The major difference between the White bywoner and the African bywoner was that the latter was required – with his family – to provide some labour service, while the former was very definitely not. Indeed the White bywoner might well expect to be provided with a certain amount of Black labour assistance himself for the harvesting of his crop. This customary attitude to labour was in time to have far-reaching consequences.

The method of land settlement in most of South Africa throughout the greater part of the nineteenth century did not encourage production for a market, and the absence of such market demand prolonged the traditions of a static economy. The newly discovered mineral wealth of Kimberley and the Rand did not have any major impact as a market for South African farming until after the Anglo-Boer War, according to the economic historian D. M. Goodfellow. Goodfellow makes the important point that because there was so slow and so little specialization of farming for market demand, 'the value of nearly all the land was unknown. No agricultural survey had ever been made. The land had never been traversed by skilled farmers of the type which was to be found in Australia and Canada. No official stimulus by way of education, or scientific research, or financial assistance, or scientific land settlement had ever been applied except in a very few minor cases . . .' [11].

Economic calculation only came to be emphasized as the possibilities of commercial farming for markets – initially foreign rather than domestic – began to be recognized through the example of innovators. Paddocking and fencing on sheep farms to make possible selective breeding and recuperative vegetation of fallow lands were only introduced in the late nineties in the more fertile Eastern Cape Province. Financier Cecil John Rhodes with the help of American expertise and the substantial capitalization of his famous Rhodes fruit farms pointed up the potential of the export markets in Britain. The market for ostrich feathers certainly intensified commercial farming near Oudtshoorn, where actual conservation and furrow irrigation were first introduced. The coastal farmlands of Natal were developed under company ownership as tea and sugar plantations to exploit specific market potential, and the unwillingness of Natal's African tribesmen to accept plantation labour service led to the introduction of labour as well as plants and seeds from India. Hence from 1876 to 1900 the number of Indians in Natal increased from 10,000 to 65,000.

In the Free State and in the Transvaal the early effects of gold-mining discoveries were to encourage transport-riding as a form of livelihood among Whites rather than any significant specialization of farming for the new markets [12]. In the Transvaal the landless bywoner class of Whites and the landless class of African farm occupants, bywoners and labourers not only became a source of continuing trouble but from the methods of trying to meet these troubles, there arose certain customary attitudes which have constituted a conditioning factor in South Africa's social system to the present day.

Generally, says Goodfellow, there is no evidence that any of the agriculture in the inerior of South Africa showed any progress in the nineties. The exceptions were certain agricultural regions within easy reach of the Witwatersrand and wool-producing regions in the Eastern Cape Province and some parts of the Free State. In the Transvaal itself, the response to the Rand mining-market by the farmers was to sell their lands to land companies and to take to transport-riding 'which suited their natures better'. It became a commonplace, and a true commonplace, says Goodfellow, that the Transvaal scarcely responded at all to the demand for foodstuffs created by the new industry[13].

The marketing 'system' was the country storekeeper, whose functional significance to both White farmers and Black farmers has never been given due recognition except in the work of the specialist economic historian. At an early stage, the country storekeeper came to provide the vital introduction to an exchange economy, though for many years – and indeed down until recent times – the exchange was a matter of barter. Generally it was a barter transaction of farmer's produce against farmer's needs of coffee, tea, sugar and cloth. The introduction of a money exchange came only with the gradual growth of the export trade, more particularly in raw wool. Not only was the country storekeeper very much part of the South African way of life but he might be regarded as a humble member of the Schumpeterian innovator class and a contributor to the pre-conditions for Rostow's take-off.

Country storekeepers bought the farmers' wool by bale and 'the bale was a collection of wool and dirt and possibly even stones, which was the conventional standard.' The sheep farming districts were not yet highly developed enough to demand a more complex system than that of the storekeepers, and on the other hand, wool producing methods could not hope to improve until some better commercial service was obtained[14]. For many decades South African wool for export was classified either as ordinary or good merino and only within recent times were finer classifications introduced, as part of a developing marketing expertise when wool auction-sales were begun by pioneering private merchants.

Among the tribal Africans the Fingos set the example of cultivating maize for sale to venturesome country traders, who established

23

themselves in appropriate trading stations. Under the stimulation of 'maize exports' from tribal territory, the Fingos began to adopt individual tenure of land. It was however individual life-tenure and not individual ownership. Prompted as much by the Fingo example as by the White traders, the Transkei Africans generally followed this example [15].

But perhaps an even more significant function in the economic development of the South African economy by the country store-keepers was their contribution to the recruiting of African labour for the goldmining industry.

It was the technique of money advances by the White traders to tribal Africans, especially in the Transkei and to a much lesser extent in Natal, which served as a key incentive in persuading young, unmarried males to venture from the relative security of traditional self-subsistence on tribal lands. The traders themselves were almost all recruiters of African labour for the gold mines. Not only did they introduce the stimulation of exchange but also the stirrings of conspicuous expenditure (especially the so-called tribal blanket which was imported from British mills and whose distinctive 'tribal designs' were conceived in those mills by acutely fashion-conscious designers). The critical incentive to the African tribesman to venture into the exchange economy seems to have been the 'advance'.

Goodfellow's account is illuminating and informative:

> The trader-recruiters soon discovered one way in which nearly all natives could be brought under the necessity of earning money and of spending it. This was to make advances in the form of goods or cattle and to tell the native that he could repay by going out to work. The advances system appears to have been the first effective instrument in introducing the new economy to native minds. The traders sometimes found it profitable to advance even more to a native than he could possibly repay by bringing back the whole of his earnings from a period of work in the mines.
>
> The reason for this was that the trader in his other role of recruiter would get a capitation fee which would more than recoup him. Advances to natives, especially of cattle, were quite irresistible, and the system soon became one of widespread grievances. . .
>
> So great did the advances evil become that late in the nineties advances were limited by law, first to a total of £5 and then to a total of £2, being the amount necessary to provide the native with equipment for his journey. This, however, did not prevent the family from running into debt during the boy's absence, and the only real remedy for this was the improvement of native agriculture[16].

The labour tax introduced by the Glen Grey Act, 1894, was probably less important as a stick than was the trader's advance as a carrot. The tax was to be paid by every young, able-bodied African who could not show the magistrate that he had been actively engaged in some economic operation for part of the year. Generally married Africans could evidence such activity and thereby evade the tax. But young adolescents could not and their parents, liable for the tax payment, were in theory supposed to encourage them to go out and seek work in the White man's economy and more particularly on the White man's mines.

However effective the stick or carrot in inducing a supply of African labour for the mines, the whole force of tribal traditional economy operated against a permanent abandonment of land rights by the family as a unit and hence of a settled, permanently resident African labour force in the mining areas. Migrant labour for the gold-mines appears to have met the social system needs of the tribe as much as the political wishes of the White polity – at least until the slow disintegration of the tribal economy began to break up the whole tribal social system.

Africans – the great majority in the beginning being young, unmarried males from the Transkei – accepted a six-month contract period of mining work but very rarely longer without a return home. This return was imperative if the young man was to retain at least a tenuous hold on land rights, which generally involved marriage or on-the-spot inheritance. Hence the success of recruiting in, for instance, the Transkei depended upon the practicable capacity of the tribal chief or headman to guarantee that 'lands would be reserved for the natives returning from the mines, as it already was for natives returning from war or from hunting expeditions' [17].

When Rhodes as premier and minister of Native Affairs of the Cape Colony, as well as mining-entrepreneur, introduced his Glen Grey Act of 1894, his major aim was to encourage the process of westernization among the tribal Africans. The 'way of life' of tribal self-subsistence, under-written and safeguarded – at least until the critical supply of land was directly and indirectly restricted – by the institutional culture and polity of the tribe, was not indeed revolutionized by the Glen Grey Act.

That Act operated to encourage change rather than to delay or to hold up change. Its detail certainly involved almost every aspect of tribal economic life – land tenure, inheritance, agricultural methods, even alcoholic habits. But it did not *create* economic calculation in tribal organization and institutionalized culture. As already made plain, the tribal economy had a high degree of economic rationality, but it was not orientated to wage-earning activities or a money-exchange economy. Rhodes, however, whether as the innovator of new combinations of diamond-marketing through the creation of the central selling organization of De Beers and, with Alfred Beit, of new techniques of gold-mining financing or as the statesman pioneering legislation to transform traditional economic organization, stimulated the opportunities for wage-earning labour and hastened the individualizing of money-motivation in tribal agriculture.

The shadow of Rhodes fell east as well as north in British Africa and under it, whether as lightness or as darkness, the modern habit of mind began its inexorable process of slow disintegration of one social system and slow integration of another social system [18].

The Transkei (and Natal where recruiting of African labour for the mines was at one period prohibited by Natal colonial law) could not however remotely satisfy the labour needs of the gold-mines. This seems to have been due as much to the relatively high recruiting cost as to any other factor. For various reasons, but more especially the effective protection of his capitation fee by the country store-keeper-trader, it proved impossible for the Transvaal Chamber of Mines to apply its new cost-reducing organization of African labour-recruitment to South African sources of supply with the same efficiency as to sources of supply in Portuguese East Africa.

Almost from the beginning of the proclamation of the Witwatersrand gold fields, the mining companies attempted to come to agreed conditions on the recruitment and remuneration of African labour. In the first few years these attempts broke down under the intense competition for labour but as the system of group control of operating mines evolved, a co-ordinating body – the Witwatersrand Chamber of Mines – was established in 1889. Its major objective was to reduce the mining industry's labour cost. This was sought through limiting competition in recruitment (which in the early stages resulted in recruitment cost being perhaps double the actual wage bill) and fixing wages and working conditions, including the length of service-contract, on a uniform non-competitive basis.

Such a monopsonistic position was not completely achieved until about 1913. But recruiting was organized by the Rand Labour

Association (1897), which became the Witwatersrand Native Labour Association (1901), as sole recruiter for mines from territories outside the borders of South Africa i.e. East Africa, including the Portuguese territories, and the British High Commission territories. The sister organization, the Native Recruiting Organization (1912), acted as a centralized body (though without sole rights) for African labour recruitment inside South Africa.

The co-ordination of monopsonistic recruitment and employment conditions proved easiest of accomplishment in respect of Portuguese East Africa. The Portuguese Government exercised totalitarian control and was prepared to deploy it in return for rail traffic guarantees through to its Mozambique ports (as elaborated in the later text). Between 1890 and 1899 the number of African workers on the gold mines increased from 14,000 to 97,000 of which from one-half to three-quarters appeared to have been recruited from extra-South African sources by the WNLA [19].

The early detail of African mine labour supply and demand is germane only to the extent that it finally evolved into the pattern of monopsonistic buying of such labour on behalf of the entire gold-mining industry from about the time of Union. The essence of this unique organizational structure for the supply of labour was that all intra-industry competition was eliminated. In its place was established the industry-wide uniformity of wage and working conditions for contract labourers, who as migrant workers were housed in compounds and who never acquired permanent rights of residence or freedom of association for collective bargaining or even individual choice of occupation.

The Chamber of Mines was and has largely remained an organization for obtaining and allocating undifferentiated labour-units among employers, who are mutually convenanted to the 'maximum average'. This maximum average arrangement appeais to have been introduced in 1902 and fixed the average earnings of all African mine-workers on any and every mine as not to exceed a maximum average. This has meant that where piece-rates have been tried to increase the individual worker's productivity, piece-rates for groups of the more productive workers have had to be cut to restore the average [20]. The maximum average was however also applied, where piece-rates were not the form of remuneration.

A whole series of government commissions has reported on the consequences of the operation of this maximum average method as a barrier not only to the greater use of piece-rates to stimulate earnings of the individual African mine-worker but to increased productivity and concomitant reduced costs of mining gold. Dr van der Horst's conclusion is [21]:

> Actually, a powerful motive preventing the extension of piece-work is fear lest it should lead to increased competition for Native labour between mine managements and to a rise in average wages. This is clearly demonstrated in a memorandum by the Chamber of Mines to the Native Economic Commission (1932) which . . . states that . . . it would lead to a 'certain amount of pirating of natives as between mine and mine' and to 'an increase in the general level of wages without any corresponding advantages'.

The determination of wages, working conditions, range of jobs and fields of employment by custom rather than by competition became from early on the characteristic feature of the labour market. It is the single most important and most enduring fact in the economic development of South Africa.

It was perhaps as much responsible as any other single invariable for the near-static economy of the country from its beginnings in the mid-seventeenth century until the exploitation of mineral wealth in the 1880's. Indeed, as will be shown in later chapters, it continued for another half century to be the inhibiting condition, imposed by the political factor, to the rate of increase in national output per head in South Africa. This measure of economic growth showed little of the growth that might otherwise have been anticipated from the discovery of such fabled natural resources as the greatest diamond- and gold-mines in recorded history. Only when the forces of competition broke through the restraints of custom during the 1930's was the rate of growth especially noteworthy. From then on, and especially from 1948, Afrikanerdom obsessed itself to control competition and to fix for all time the socio-economic differentials of White-Black status. But competition for labour was too powerful to be entirely frustrated by the political factor and such competition in the labour market energized the economy to unprecedented rates of development.

Because of the domination of custom over labour-utilization, and the related land-utilization, the kind of 'economic development' which Schumpeter defined i.e. only such changes in economic life as are not forced upon it from without but arise by its own initiative from within [22], was for a generation curtailed in South Africa.

Customary allocation of labour-supply and utilization was for generations the unchanging condition of the labour market. But competitive forces released by war-time demand pressures penetrated the hard crust of custom to bring about new combinations of productive resources, more especially in manufacturing industries. Until that happened, development was slow and growth of output per head (and income per head) unremarkable.

The immobilizing of the resources of African labour as determined by tradition and custom was at an early stage reinforced by the polity. The first pass laws may be dated back to 1857, when the Colonial Government of the Cape in Act No. 23 of 1857 made it an offence, under penalty of up to twelve months' imprisonment with hard labour, for a native from British Kaffraria to enter the Cape Colony without a pass. The mining industry was especially concerned to secure the power of the law to reinforce its short-term contractual recruitment of migrant labour. In 1895 the Volksraad of the Transvaal passed Law No. 23 of 1895, drafted by the mining employers, which provided that on entering a gold-field proclaimed a labour district, an African had to secure a District Pass authorizing him to seek employment for three days and subsequent extension on fee payment. When employed, the employer held the District Pass and retained it until the African was discharged. The African himself had to carry an Employer's Pass without which he was liable to arrest and imprisonment. It was an offence for employers to engage Africans without a District Pass.

The history and complexity of the pass laws and regulations governing the movement of Africans in South Africa probably defy complete recording. Their general purpose and significance have however remained fundamentally unchanged – to re-inforce custom by law in restricting the competitive forces of supply and demand for African labour so as, firstly, to curtail and direct its mobility and, secondly, to control the range and terms of its employment.

The early pass laws may be regarded as primarily concerned with directing the supply of African labour, the later pass laws from the 1950's with directing the demand for African labour. They are so pervading, however, as to constitute not only one of the major influences on economic growth but the administrative *deus ex machina* for the perpetuation of the stratified South African social system under the control of the White polity. They were to become the Frankenstein of political economy.

3

POOR WHITES AND BLACK
PROLETARIAT

The interaction between land- and labour-utilization was the conditioning determinant for ultimate power and status relationships and hence the continuing concern of the White polity. The point has already been made that the South African way of life in respect of its White peoples grew out of its isolation and insulation from change. The extraordinarily extensive character of its land settlement – particularly when it is remembered that the Dutch forbears of the Afrikaners came from one of the most intensively cultivated countries in Europe – perhaps as much as any other single circumstance explains why Afrikaners so steadily and ultimately so completely differentiated themselves from Hollanders.

The most striking feature of this differentiation was for centuries and as late as the 1920's the attitude to work and effort. The compulsive dictation of the environment expressed in the very name, the Netherlands, created the special character of economic development of the Dutch distinguished by their extraordinary exertion. Between the interconnections of environment and economic development in a territory of 30,000 sq. kms already inhabited by about 2,000,000 Hollanders in mid-seventeenth century and the interconnections of environment and economic development in a territory of 472,000 sq. miles inhabited by less than 750,000 Afrikaners in a total South African population of 6,000,000 as late as 1910, there was a difference which readily explains a radically divergent value-orientation towards work and effort by the former Dutch who became the present Afrikaners.

The crucial significance of this factor is stressed not in any sense of derogation of the Afrikaner people. Indifference to physical work and effort with its implications of unwillingness to change certainly became part of the Afrikaner character but that character has repeatedly shown an indifference – perhaps not unrelated – to hardship and danger which has made the Afrikaners most tough and daring fighters. The Afrikaners never lost Dutch courage though, settling in the vast territory of South Africa and among great numbers of tribal peoples offering virtually cost-less labour, they lost Dutch tenacity for economic exertion and entrepreneurship.

In consequence from the 1880's indigency among the Afrikaans-speaking White population proliferated into the national problem of the 'Poor Whites', which only began to yield to the amelioration of the rising tempo of economic growth in the 1930's. Not only did the 'Poor Whites' constitute the country's number-one sociological problem for a half-century but the problem and the votes of their overwhelming numbers have conceived and controlled the course of the White polity through the history of the South African Republic (which was the nineteenth-century Transvaal) until it re-emerged, revolutionized in its economy but hardly changed in its institution-alized character, sixty years later in the Republic of South Africa.

The absence of a money economy, the failure to evolve a com-mercial tenancy for agriculture, the slow response of farming to market demand in the Trekker Republics have already been noted. It was in the Transvaal, even more than in the Orange Free State, that resistance to change – in land-cultivation, land-tenure, land-inheritance – began to produce a problem of over-population which expressed itself in rural indigency and, then, urban indigency.

The Report of the Transvaal Indigency Commission T.G.13–1908 is the classic documentation of early indigency. It recorded the facts – so effectively pointed-up by Goodfellow in his Economic History – of farms averaging 7,700 acres, the failure even to farm to supply a home-grown rounded diet, the late-coming bywoners, the excessive sub-division of land among children, the preference for hunting for food rather than crop-cultivation, the alienation of patrimony to companies in return for easy option-money.

This Report, too, makes it clear that the Anglo-Boer War, while it may have aggravated, certainly did not originate the indigency of the Transvaal Afrikaner. 'Even before the outbreak of war in 1899 a great portion of the agricultural population were declining into indigency and from this date begins the drift of poor whites into outlying parts of larger towns . . . . In itself the war was not, as many witnesses have thought, the primary cause of the existing indigency . . . the second effect of the war was that it swept into the towns from the country, in a destitute condition, a very large number of those who did not possess land of their own, and who had previously been sinking into poverty' [1].

The Transvaal Bushveld and Lowveld was a large area of poor vegetation and unfavourable climate. But it contained plenty of game and opportunities for free-booting among resident and migrant African cattle-owners. White inhabitants of this part of the Transvaal early developed a taste for the life of the pioneer rather than the settler and became wholly unable to adapt to regularity of any occupation whatsoever, even of farming.

A large proportion of the indigent developed from among the group, originally known as bywoners. The bywoners, it will be recalled, were the late-comers among the trekkers, who found that the farms had already been taken up by those who had spent the day riding around their domains as the qualifying title to ownership or who were too shiftless even to exert themselves to take up a land-holding. So long as the original farmer-owner had no wish nor incentive to develop his estate, bywoners were undisturbed in their occupation. But as the desire or the opportunity showed itself to improve the land-holding by paddocking for sheep or cultivation of a money-crop (or where sub-division to meet the claims of inheritance operated), so the bywoner became a liability.

This was especially the case of the White bywoner as compared with the African occupier, who might have almost a bywoner status. The Black man and his family owed an obligation to contribute labour. But no Afrikaner acknowledged an obligation to labour for a fellow Afrikaner in return for occupying a portion of his lands. Even more unthinkable was that his wife and children should render any labour-service. Economic rationality – the substitution of cost-reducing factors of production – clearly dictated that while the African bywoner might for a while be an asset, the White bywoner and his often-numerous family had no use-value at all.

Hence the displacement and dispossession of the White bywoner became part of a people's tragedy. It was not only the bywoner who lost his place on the land. Often the owner himself was only too willing to be dispossessed by the offer of ready cash as option-money by the land-acquisition companies, which in a remarkably short time after gold was first found came to control a major part of the Transvaal. These companies tended to accept the continued presence on the land of those willing to work rather than those who regarded all manual labour as 'kaffir's work' [2].

So the 'kaffir' at least was offered and generally accepted work, while the White man drifted into idleness in between the occasional opportunity to earn a little as a transport-rider or keep himself by his beloved rifle by shooting either game or, during 1899–1902, British 'rooi-neks'. His shooting capacity was undoubtedly highly developed but hunting animals or hunting the enemy is not really a form of economic development. There are people who certainly make money out of war, and war often promotes economic growth. But the money-makers are not the soldiers in the field and the Boers turned guerillas came back to find their farms a very much wasted asset, if they possessed any scrap value at all.

The Anglo-Boer War made its contribution to human misery as all wars do. And, again, like all other wars, it produced its fighters who could not or would not re-adjust when they found, like so many Othellos, their occupations gone. No doubt the years of hardship and exhilaration of veld-vegters induced even more firmly the belief of what was White man's work and what was 'kaffir's work'.

The Transvaal Indigency Commission listened to predikant after predikant and social worker after politician tell the same story of the Afrikaner's aversion to manual work as beneath his dignity.

The early settler in the Transvaal and, indeed, the whole South African-born white population up to nearly the middle of the nineteenth century, had grown to maturity in the belief that the normal and proper relation of White to Coloured (i.e. Non-White) was the relation of master to slave or serf. They regarded it as the natural province of the White man to supervise the native and to direct his energies, and the duty of the native to perform for the White man the rough manual labour, which was required for cultivating his land and tending his stock. Despite the abolition of slavery this tradition remained, and has continued to govern the relations between White and Coloured races to this day[3].

And a little later in the same Report:

The system of slavery has simply given way to the system of caste . . . We have been impressed with the frequency with which it has been stated in evidence that the unskilled labour was 'kaffir's work' and as such not the kind of work which a White man should perform . . .. This attitude of the white man has greatly affected his efficiency as a labourer. He has never regarded unskilled labour as an ordinary field of employment . . . .[4].

33

On the land the White bywoner refused to become a farm labourer and in the towns 'any white man . . . who has not the knowledge or the training to qualify him for doing skilled or semi-skilled work is almost certain to become indigent'.

The Commission commented at length on 'the very high standards of living adopted by the white man in the Transvaal as compared with the ordinary standards of white working men in similar positions elsewhere . . . ' [5]. The establishment of this customary standard of living and related wage-expectation by White men was a prime cause, in the Commission's opinion, of urban unemployment and resultant indigency among White – and especially Afrikaans-speaking with little or no education and training – persons in South Africa and in the Transvaal in particular. This foreshadows Keynes's distinction between voluntary and involuntary unemployment. No 'small rise in the price of wage-goods relatively to the money-wage' would have brought about any increase in the 'aggregate supply of [white] labour willing to work for the current wage'.

The voluntary unemployment in South African economic history must be regarded as not so much unique but as an unusually pervasive preference or motivation, which has probably been a significant factor in the relatively slow rate of economic growth of output (and income) per head until very recent decades. It is well characterized and classified by Professor Hutt in his *Theory of Idle Resources* as 'preferred idleness'. In respect of the tribal Africans and Coloureds (though possibly not among the Indians), there has always been a marked leisure-preference which for many decades inhibited their productivity (and the co-operating capital) but which seems now to be changing with growing consumption-consciousness. In respect of the 'Poor Whites', the acceptance of a category of work or a wage-level identified with 'kaffir's work' was so deeply wounding to racial pride as to be one of the major influences in the special character of the country's political economy [6].

As early as 1908 the Transvaal Indigency Commission was to be only the first of repeated Commissions, which rejected either minimum wage legislation or special job protection as the solution to the White man's (and woman's and child's) value-orientation to kaffir-work. The relevant passage from the Report merits quotation at length because it expresses the non-political viewpoint that despite its reiteration down the decades by almost all similar non-political opinion was always rejected by the politicians:

. . . the second suggestion for protecting the position of the white man in the economic world is that legislation should be passed fixing a ratio between the number of white and coloured (i.e. Non-White) men engaged in any industry employing more than a certain number of hands. This proposal we also think impracticable. No uniform ratio could be laid down which would suit every industry. Moreover, if the state did attempt to fix a uniform ratio for all trades either the ratio would have to be put so high as to be of no practical use, or so low as to result in the closing down of many industries now giving employment for white men.

On general grounds, however, and apart from the difficulties in the way of carrying out these proposals, we are opposed to any Government action which is designed to protect the white man against reasonable competition from the Coloured races. In the first place, we are opposed to it from the point of view of the native . . . it would, in effect, be an attempt to protect the position of the white man by preventing the native from making full use of those qualities and powers with which he is endowed . . . the white and black races have to live together in South Africa, and time and their respective qualities and capacities alone will determine the relations which are to subsist among them . . .

To protect the white man from native competition at this stage is simply to bolster up the aristocratic tradition for a few years longer, without doing anything to qualify the white man for the ultimate but inevitable struggle for economic superiority with the native . . .[7].

But to 'bolster up the aristocratic tradition' not merely for a few years longer but for all time was the sovereign motivation of the Whites to which all else, especially economic rationality, must be subordinated. The ideology of the unbridgeable gulf between kaffir's work and White man's work was steadily institutionalized not only through custom-thought and power-thought but in a body of elaborated legislation and regulation unique to any industrial nation in the twentieth century.

Legal enforcement of the aristocratic tradition, this categorization of kaffir's work and White man's work, this peculiar form of preferred idleness or voluntary unemployment, this institutionalization of the dominant motivations of the dominant is of course achievable through the polity. And only through the polity. Necessarily, therefore, the polity had to be and remain for all time a White polity.

Furthermore, though such concepts of 'work' and 'non-work' were held as tenaciously by English-speaking trade unionists as

35

by Afrikaans-speaking Poor Whites, it was the imperatives and power of English capitalists that pushed economic rationality to the point of least-cost substitution of labour resources. The political economy that pursued productivity in disregard and disruption of the past was the creation and the creature of Smuts-Hoggenheimer, as anathemized by Afrikanerdom. Its politics was 'imperialist' and its economy was 'capitalist' and a White polity of imperialistic profit-seekers (of Smuts-Hoggenheimers) could not be entrusted to safe-guard the South African way of life.

As early as 7 December 1912, General J. B. M. Hertzog, walking out of the first Cabinet of the first Union Parliament to found the National or Nationalist Party, declared at De Wildt:

> The time has come when South Africa can no longer be ruled by non-Afrikaners, by people who have no real love for South Africa . . . that I place so much emphasis upon the feeling of nationality of my Dutch-speaking fellow-Afrikaners is because they have a deeper realisation of it than the majority of the English, and that is because their ancestors came here two hundred years earlier. . . .

The more economic rationality acted, the harder the political factor reacted. In its first phase, the nationalism of Afrikanerdom was anti the capitalists but the sacrosanctity of land ownership ensured that it never became anti-capitalist. Afrikaner nationalism eagerly embraced the work-fund theories and restrictionist practices of English trade-unionists and readily entered a Pact with an English-led South African Labour Party against Smuts-Hoggenheimer – against imperalist capitalists who linked the City to the Chamber of Mines by way of Downing Street. In the later phase, after the embrace with English trade-unionsts had become a take-over of the trade unions by the Blankewerkersbeskermingsbond[8], the political factor pursued an exclusive Afrikanerization of power.

Power was not only control over the polity but control of the instruments of economic development – over state direction of capital investment but not socialization of the means of production. The process of proletarianization[9] was the direct and most powerful consequence of such politico-economic change. Proletari-anization is a concept so over-toned in Marxist and agitationist literature as almost to have lost all objective usefulness. Yet it is a social process clearly recognizable in respect of the detribalization of Africans in South Africa.

36

The chief causes for proletarianization, as elaborated by either Marx or Sombart, is exclusion of the masses of the peasants from the land. Marx stressed the expropriation of peasants from their individual holdings by the statutory enclosure of commons land, forced sales and bankruptcies. Sombart, while critical of the Marxian interpretation which would make proletarianization a purely English phenomenon, also found land spoliation and land restrictions as a major factor.

The interconnection between land-utilization and labour-supply in respect of tribal Africans has already been examined, but it is so much cause and effect in the network of changing activity in South African political economy that it must be further elaborated. The reports and evidence of numerous official commissions of enquiry are invaluable source material. Such government commissions and the testimony tended to them reflect as clearly as any other evidence the characteristics of custom-thought and power-thought contemporaneously dominant in a society. They highlight motives and aims, the value-orientations of sociological classification, in a manner which make such reports and testimony primary reference material.

One of the most noteworthy and 'fundamental' of such commissions, accepted by South African historians, is the South African Native Affairs Commission, 1903–5 (Cd. 2399–1905, Vols. 1–5). The Commission was appointed, after the British defeat of the Boers, by Lord Milner, British High Commissioner, at a time when the four colonial governments were nominally and legally wholly separate authorities. Its membership comprised the nominees of all the colonial governments (including Rhodesia and Basutoland) and its policy clearly signified that there should be a *common* policy on the relationships of Whites and Africans in Southern Africa, irrespective of political boundaries. Furthermore the Commissioners, under the chairmanship of Sir Godfrey Lagden, were almost all Native Administrators of great experience and not politicians [10]. Rights to land were the prime concern of the Commission. The first item of reference, and perhaps the most important, it reported, is land tenure. 'From it there is a common origin of many serious Native problems. It dominates and pervades every other question, it is the bedrock of the Native's present economic position, and largely affects his social system. It was clear from the mass of evidence tendered that the public attention to a great extent centred round it [11].

37

The facts, as established by the Commission, were: in the Cape Colony, Africans lived in reserves or locations set apart for African occupation; as servants in continuous employment of landowners; as holders of individual titles in freehold or leasehold or under quitrent tenure; or in urban locations. There were 13,440,000 acres of land reserved for Africans with a population of 1,057,610 or 50 per sq. mile. In Natal, the greater portion of land was vested in the Crown and occupied by Africans communally but more Africans lived on private lands under White ownership than in locations and mission reserves combined. In the Orange River Colony, Africans lived in locations or reserves set apart for African occupation, as servants in continuous employment of landowners, as squatters and labour tenants periodically employed as farm-workers, and in urban locations. In the Transvaal similarly the Africans lived in locations or reserves set apart for African occupation, on lands owned by Africans, on other private lands, on Crown lands and in urban locations. It was estimated that in the Transvaal about one-half of the Africans were domiciled on occupied and unoccupied lands under White ownership.

The Commission expressed itself in favour of encouraging individualization of land tenure where 'natives exhibit in sufficient numbers a desire to secure and a capacity to hold and enjoy individual rights to arable plots and residential sites on such lands . . .' [12]. But the Commission was much more concerned with the two critical issues of 'free traffic in land' and 'squatters'.

It asked what effects could be expected to follow if the Africans were allowed free traffic in land. And this was the answer the Commission supplied:

No emphasis is required in stating that, wherever Europeans are living, repugnance is shown to the invasion of their neighbourhood by Natives for residential purposes. Farmers resent the intrusion among them of Native owners of land . . . . The capacity (of Natives) to purchase (land) by collective process if necessary is to-day in excess of what it was formerly. Furthermore, there is a manifest effort on the part of Natives to-day being made to possess land, which is not counteracted by any reluctance on the part of European holders to dispose of it, so long as the sellers are not themselves bound to live in proximity . . . [13].

And then follows the classic assertion of ideological motivation against market realities:

If this process goes on, while at the same time restrictions exclude Europeans from purchasing within Native areas, it is inevitable that at no very distant date the amount of land in Native occupation will be undesirably extended. Native wages and earnings are greater than they used to be, their wants are few, and their necessary expenses small. They will buy land at prices above its otherwise market value, as their habits and standard of living enable them to exist on land that is impossible for Europeans to farm on a small scale. There will be many administrative and social difficulties created by the multiplication of a number of Native lands scattered through a White population and owning the land of the country equally with them.

It will be far more difficult to preserve the absolutely necessary political and social distinctions, if the growth of a mixed rural population of land-owners is not discouraged. . . [14].

It is hardly possible to over-emphasize the crucial significance of this finding by the Commission – and its consequent recommendation and the subsequent legislation – to the political history and myth of South Africa in the following half-century. Throughout these fifty years, the major (White) political parties[15] have held as an incontrovertible truth that the Union's land legislation preserved the Africans from being dispossessed of their land by the superior economic power of the Whites. Yet the reality, as established by the South African Native Affairs Commission, was that the process of economic development was facilitating African acquisition of White-owned land.

At the time the Commission was investigating, 1905, only a minority of White land-occupiers had effectively responded to market-demand for foodstuffs or industrial crops. This was especially the case in respect of the Transvaal, despite the coming into being of the Witwatersrand mining-market for foodstuffs twenty years back. Africans in sufficient numbers, according to the Commission's concern, had however reacted to the new tempo of economic development by acquiring the appropriate liquid resources through saving to be able to invest in European-owned land in the belief that they, the new African owners, could obtain a return on their investment.

Perhaps the Commission over-stated the contemporary realities yet their conclusion permits of no other inference but that the Africans showed a keener insight into the function of capital and the market under the process of economic development than did the Whites. Whether or not there was an accurate estimate by the

Commission of the relative rates of response by Africans and Whites to the new market economy, ushered in by the discovery of gold and investment in the gold-mining industry, the Commission was flatly opposed to leaving the working-out of land-ownership and -utilization to the forces of competition.

The Commission preferred to place its faith in the very personal force of the White polity and not in the impersonal anonymity of the market economy. It therefore unanimously recommended:

that it is necessary to safeguard what is conceived to be the interests of the Europeans of this country, but that in so doing the door should not be entirely closed to deserving and progressing individuals among the Natives acquiring land . . .

and resolved:

(a) that purchase (of land) by Natives should in future be limited to certain areas to be defined by legislative enactment
(b) that purchase of land which may lead to tribal, communal or collective possession or occupation by Natives should not be permitted[16].

It was not only in relation to land-utilization that this key Commission was to propose a political solution to what seemed to the highly-principled Commissioners an essentially administrative problem of the social system. A similar non-awareness, perhaps even more than an ignorance, of the economic aspect distinguished their analysis of the related labour-utilization [17].

The Commission attempted to establish the 'total number of male [natives] who may be expected to work at any one time' and arrived at a figure of 350,177. On the other side, it 'estimated the number required' at 752,000 for the four colonies of South Africa. Hence the shortfall between supply and demand was some 400,000 [18].

It then noted that labour had to be imported from other parts of Africa, from India and from China. The Commission's calculations of demand and supply make no reference to and show no recognition of wage-rates as the price of labour. Demand for and supply of Native labour are treated as absolutes. This unconscious or conscious calculation of numbers of African workers without regard to the wage or price factor of their labour might fairly be noted as part of the South African tradition.

The reasons for labour 'difficulties', the Commission concluded, were not idleness (which it rejected) but that the African population had always been pastoral and agricultural people; that the rapid increase in demand for labour found the Africans to a great extent unprepared to meet the new conditions which surrounded them; that the traditional mode of life of Africans unaccustomed them to the regularity of daily labour; that the inexpensiveness of their living and limited wants led to a comparative absence of incentive to labour; and, lastly, the terms on which occupied land was worked did not encourage work-seeking.

The supply available from local sources is capable of being increased and the Commission has given attention to suggestions as to how this is to be done. Any recommendation as to higher wages is quite out of place. In the first place, any departure from the principle that the rate of wages must be a matter of free contract between employer and employee is unsound, nor is any relief from present difficulties to be found in such a measure. To raise the rate of wages in one locality might have the effect of attracting labour to that particular quarter at the expense of other industries, but that would not alter the general situation. Further, it has been stated, and the Commission feels there is a measure of truth in the suggestion, that while increased wages might have the effect of tempting a larger number of labourers in to the market, on the other hand, such increased gains would enable them to remain for a longer period at their own homes[19].

The Commission, therefore, made no recommendation on the subject of African wages. It also rejected any measures of compulsion on the African including the indirect compulsion of a labour tax. It favoured rather the general creation of a climate of opinion favourable to the Africans becoming more industrous.

Specifically, and significantly, it recommended positive implementation of existing laws against 'squatting', the imposition of rents on Africans living on Crown lands, the enforcement of anti-vagrancy laws, the encouragement of higher standards of wants through education and training.

The Report of the South African Native Affairs Commission of 1905 has been examined at some length. Not only is the view justified that this Report has provided the blueprint for much subsequent Native policy [20], but it reveals strongly the continuing characteristics of the operation of the South African social system. Always there is the determining influence of custom, consummating the motives of the Whites, in directing the power of the White polity to restrain and inhibit the working-out of the market economy as the determinant of economic development. It expresses and exemplifies the persistent subordination of market choice to ideological imperative.

It is instructive to compare the Commission's views on the causes of difficulties in respect of African labour-utilization with Sombart's analysis of proletarianization. Sombart, as already noted, regarded land spoliation and restrictions as a major causative influence but he also emphasized other factors leading to the break-up of medieval society[21].

At the same time, observed Sombart, that complaints of 'universal vagabondage' were being voiced, the early capitalist entrepreneurs were lamenting the fact that they could not procure enough labour. Sombart traced this 'curious coincidence' of abundance and shortage of labour to three causes: the bad organization of the labour market, which prevented interlocal and interregional adjustment between supply and demand; the empirically traditional and non-rational character of production, which was inimical to the migration of labourers from overcrowded to less crowded occupations; the hostility of the early proletarians to the needs of capitalist production.

He further noted the static, corporate character of medieval economic life with production for traditional demand instead of for unlimited gain as revealed in the numerous holidays and the many rest periods during the working day. This sharply contrasted with the workers in the early factories with uninterrupted labour for intolerably long hours, severe discipline and restriction to one detail of the production process. There is a good deal of agitational misrepresentation of the facts of later factory employment in the Britain of the Industrial Revolution[22]. But urbanizing change undoubtedly caused severe problems of adaptation for the influx of landless poor, as capitalistic organization first undermined and then overwhelmed the medieval self-sufficiency.

The parallels between this process of proletarianization in Western Europe, more particularly Britain, between say 1650 and 1850 and the process of proletarianization in South Africa from 1880 on are close and suggestive. Furthermore in respect of South Africa, the impact of change was concentrated into a much shorter period of time in an era of extraordinarily intensive and extensive change.

The traditional economy of the African tribal society has obvious resemblances to the static economy of medieval Europe with its pronounced leisure-preference and corporate rather than individualist motivation for effort and gain. Similarly economic development which simultaneously promoted an urbanized-industrialized market and intensified population pressures on land brought about an internal migration from country to city, which in South Africa reflects in striking detail the similarity of process in Europe and Britain. Both landless Whites and landless Blacks in South Africa were drifting into the towns and cities from the early phase of economic stimulation through investment sparked by the mining discoveries.

But while the 'Poor Whites' could use their votes to compel action by the White polity to mitigate the effects of their proletarianization, the 'Poor Blacks' were from the beginning denied virtually any influence in the polity. The Africans' proleterianization proceeded apace and indeed the White polity actively – though not always consciously – promoted the process among the Blacks in the mistaken conviction that this was the path of salvation for the 'Poor Whites'.

The credo and catechism of the Whites, as the country acquired increasingly the motivations of a market economy under the rising tempo of economic development, were fastened on, firstly, that no White man shall do 'kaffir's work' and, secondly, those who 'squat' do not serve society.

4

NEITHER SQUATTER NOR SKILLED

With a paternalism perhaps even more affected than that of Polonius, the White polity advised its Black step-son neither a squatter nor a skilled man be. Squatting undoubtedly dulls the edge of husbandry and skill will lose both 'die kaffer sy plek'[1] and most certainly the White man as friend. But whereas Laertes was voyaging out of Polonius' vision, the Black man was venturing into the White man's control – and a control which the latter was totally resolute to maintain and extend.

The term 'squatter' was generally applied to Africans living on Crown land, to Africans renting White-owned land, and often also to labour tenants. In Dr van der Horst's study of Native labour in South Africa, the first reference to legislation against squatting is Ordinance No. 2 of 1855 of the Natal Legislative Council (significantly one of the earliest legislative enactments of the partly-elected White settler polity). It was an 'ordinance to prevent the unlicensed Squatting, and to regulate the Occupation of Land, by the Natives'[2]. The owner or occupier of any land on which more than three African families resided was required to make a return of the numbers and a subsequent hut-tax law exempted Africans in effective employment of the White farmer.

This appears to have been the earliest of the Squatters Laws, and like all its successors it very soon became a dead letter. Natal made repeated attempts to impose rents and taxes on Africans squatting on Crown land, while in the Cape the Location Acts had partly the same purpose. In the Trekker republics the burghers had acquired practically all the land by virtue of the claim to title in a day's encompassing horse-ride or other assertion of right. The Cape Labour Commission Report of 1894 noted the complaints against the squatting system which, it was said, reduced the supply of labour by enabling Africans to live without working for Whites. In the Transvaal Law No. 21 of 1895, the 'squatters' law' was passed

44

limiting to five families the number of Africans allowed on any farm or portion of farm. It proved unenforceable from the beginning. In the Orange Free State a similar 'squatters' law' of 1893 repeated the sacrosanct number of five African families permitted per White-owned farm. It too could not be effectively enforced.

White opinion was largely in agreement as to the causes of the failure of African labour supply to measure up to (White) demand. The views of the South African Native Affairs Commission have already been quoted. In the Transvaal Labour Commission of 1903 (majority report), farmer witnesses were unanimous that Africans living on Government farms, on unoccupied farms and on locations could not be induced to come out to work and favoured strict enforcement of the Squatters' Law and a break-up of the locations. This latter Commission reported:

After hearing the evidence of a great number of witnesses, we have formed the opinion that the scarcity of labour is due, first and mainly, to the fact that the African native tribes are, for the most part, primitive pastoral or agricultural communities, who possess exceptional facilities for the regular and full supply of their animal wants, and whose standard of economic needs is extremely low . . .. Sitting in 1894 the Labour Commission of the Cape Government stated that 'the fundamental cause for the insufficiency of supply available for farm work and, to some extent, for all other work, including that of domestic servants, lies in the condition of life and population in South Africa. The mere necessaries of existence are few and obtainable with little exertion in this new and sunny country. . . [3].

And again:

The rise of industries in South Africa has in fact created a demand for industrial workers among nomadic or pastoral peoples, who until the Europeans came into contact with them were ignorant of the uses of money and who therefore cannot be dragged suddenly into the industrial labour market by the operation of the ordinary law of supply and demand . . . the only pressing needs of a savage are those of food and sex, and the conditions of native life in Africa are such that these are, as a rule, easily supplied . . .[4].

'Squatting' is not a logical categorization of scientific sociology; it is patently the kind of symbolization of rationalization, which can evoke emotional response and justification. The image projected by 'squatting' – almost onomatopoeically – suggests hundreds of thousands of Africans sitting on their haunches in the sun on the lands of the Europeans, while these latter are working away to build a modern market economy for the benefit of all. What were the realities – the social and economic realities?

The 'ethical' justification for private ownership of land is beyond the scope of this analysis. The 'economic' justification would appear to be optimization of productivity in response to market demand. The disposal of common- or Crown-land has throughout history taken place under all kinds of land-settlement and land-tenure arrangements. Those already detailed in an earlier chapter in respect of the several states of South Africa can be duplicated in the experience of many other countries – including the day's ride on a horse as a title to ownership of the relevant number of God's acres.

Whether the Whites or the Africans of South Africa have the 'better' title to the land can be determined in one of two ways – by superior power or superior productivity. This implies allocation either by the polity or by the economy. If allocation and title are to be determined by the economy – or more specifically by the social control of the market – this of necessity means 'the free traffic in land'. Such a 'free traffic in land' or, in more familiar terms, the continuing marketability of land by sale and purchase might be expected to tend towards an allocation, and continuing re-allocation, of available land among those current occupier-owners, who believed themselves able to optimize its productivity as determined by prevailing market factors.

Skin colour of the occupier-owner would as such be irrelevant. Also irrelevant would be the occupier-owner's customary standard of living or reserves or low level of wants in determining the market price of land[5]. It was indeed the awareness, or perhaps more accurately the fear, of the South African Native Commission that in a growing number of instances the Africans, at this stage of capitalistic development in South Africa, were being motivated by the market more than Whites. The awareness and fear led the Commission to make its epochal and decisive recommendation against the 'free traffic in land' as between White and Black.

In due course this recommendation was to be given the force of law, so that henceforth land-occupation as between White and Black was to be determined by the polity and not the market. The manner of such division will be examined later. For the moment the critical consideration is that the shape of the country's economic development in respect of land-utilization was determined rather more by ideology and rather less by economic rationality with the probable consequence that the rate of economic growth was significantly slowed. Since it is part of the South African credo that Whites *per se* employ land more productively than Africans *per se*, it is clearly heretical to suggest that the contrary might be true.

The only market support for such a heresy is that the South African Native Affairs Commission established that in the first decade of this century, tribal Africans were buying land from White owners and White owners had to be stopped by law – by the action of the polity – from alienating land to the Africans.

But prohibiting the sale of land to the Africans was only one arm of the pincers movement aimed at restricting land-utilization by the Africans so as to increase labour-utilization of the Africans. The other arm was positive action on squatting. The South African Native Affairs Commission had gone on record that 'unrestrained squatting of Natives on private farms, whether on terms or otherwise, is an evil and against the best interests of the country' and should therefore be energetically controlled.

This, however, was an assertion. At the time there was no evidence that African 'squatters' were less beneficially utilizing the land on which they 'squatted' than were the White 'bywoners' utilizing the land on which they 'lived-alongside'. Some evidence indeed suggests the contrary and from one aspect of relative productivity, African 'squatters' occasionally contributed labour while White bywoners on principle did not.

Few (White) witnesses to the various commissions that repeatedly investigated ways of increasing the number of African work-seekers in and on the White man's mines, industries, businesses, railways and farms, failed to press strongly for rigid enforcement of the pro-visions of the squatters' and related laws. Generally five African families per White farm came to be regarded as the fair and proper number and all those in excess of five were somehow to be forced off to find work with some other White employer. It will be noted that throughout these decades there was never any suggestion – at least from the White men – that there should be 'separate develop-ment' or 'segregation' or 'apartheid' between the two races, which might in any way make it more difficult for more White 'masters' to have available more Black 'servants'.

On the contrary the Transvaal Labour Commission of 1903 noted that a considerable part of its time was taken in listening to witnesses making suggestions to improve labour supply which 'generally fall under the head of compulsion, either direct or indirect, modifications of the native tribal system or changes in native land tenure'. The Commission duly reported that '. . . the testimony of many witnesses . . . indicate that they were in favour of measures which would compel the natives to work either by requiring from him a certain measure of labour annually or by such drastic changes in his condition as would have the same effect' [6].

The Commission itself opposed such ideas as impractical and also pregnant of 'social problems of the utmost magnitude'. Though it, like all the other Commissions that busied themselves with the 'Native labour problem', advocated strongest application of the laws against squatting, such direction of labour against the South African realities of land-settlement and land-utilization proved about as effective as price controls in a period of continuing inflation.

Land restrictions and squatting curtailments aimed at exercising a push effect on African labour supply. What was the White man's opinion and policy in relation to the pull factor of wages? It will be recollected that the South African Native Affairs Commission could be said not to have acknowledged that wage rates were a factor. The Transvaal Labour Commission of 1903 showed greater sophistication at least on this aspect.

It recorded the painful awareness of the Transvaal Chamber of Mines that African labour-supply exhibited a degree of elasticity at least as between one mine and another, which showed up a marked economic rationality or acquisitiveness (according to semantic sensitivity) among persons not supposed to be acquainted with a money economy or having more than animal wants. It quoted from the annual Chamber of Mines Report for 1889 that eager competition between mine managers for labour:

has in some cases taken the regrettable form of overt attempts to bribe and seduce the employees of neighbouring companies to desert their employers. Even without resort to actual attempts to bribe, a manager finding himself short of labour which is urgently required, has, standing alone, scarcely any other remedy than that of raising his rates of pay. The result has been a steady rise of wages all round, which is adding a very heavy additional expense to the working of the mines. . .[7].

The Commission then went on to record one of the minor articles of belief among White employers, and more particularly mining

employers, on the so-called backward-sloping demand curve for
African labour:

. . . it was held by many witnesses that the effect of high wages is,
ultimately, to re-act disadvantageously on the supply, as the limited nature
of the natives' wants enabled them to be more easily satisfied when wages
are good, thus inducing them to withdraw from employment at an early
date. It was however maintained by others that high wages improved the
supply, the majority stating that the reduction of wages on the mines after
the war had prejudicially affected the supply. This conclusion appears to be
well-founded. . .[8].

Two members of this Commission in a Minority Report made some
highly pertinent comments on African labour. After sixty years the
shrewd thrusts of Mr J. W. Quinn and Mr P. Whitside have a ring
of reality which even now is too discordant for the harmony of
myth. They noted that the first major demand for industrial labour
was following the discovery of diamonds and added '. . . it seems
to your Commissioners a remarkable fact that to-day, after a lapse
of less than 40 years, in addition to those engaged as herds and in
agriculture, at least 250,000 [natives] are engaged in industries
to a large extent unknown to them prior to the commencement of
this period . . .' [9].

The same two Commissioners observed there was no evidence
that the Kimberley diamond mines were ever short of labour and,
further, that '. . . the Native's wants are so few that unless special
inducements are held out to him, he has no desire to enter the labour
market; and certainly one of these inducements and, perhaps, the
most effective, is a high rate of wage . . .' [10].

The incontrovertible fact is that, after most strenuous effort, the
gold-mining companies through the Chamber of Mines finally
adopted its unique monopsonistic policy in respect of African labour
with the sole purpose of eliminating market competition on the
demand side. It is a reasonable inference that what the mining
employers really feared was too keen rather than too blunt a sensitivity of tribal labour to differential wage-rates and too highly
developed a consciousness of money as a medium of exchange [11].

Indeed almost simultaneously with the never-ending complaints
about the unwillingness of the Africans to acquire the working habits
and wants of the industrial and industrious world of the White man,
other and increasingly violent protestations were being voiced

that the rising tide of African workers were depriving White men of their inherent right to the jobs which 'civilization', not to say custom and trade unionism, assigned to White men only.

This fear, which in a short time was to become the distinguishing national phobia, pervades much of another landmark Report in South African political economy – that of the Mining Industry Commission, 1907–8 [12]. The chairman was Andries Stockenstrom but its most important commissioner was Frederic Hugh Page Creswell. Col. Creswell as aide to General Hertzog fifteen years later was to help establish a rarely challenged mastery of the polity over the economy and to compel the social system of South Africa to cling more tenaciously, and ultimately perhaps fatally, to the credo of nineteenth-century British trade-unionism and the ethos of Afrikaner isolationism.

This Mining Industry Commission of 1908 was broadly charged with investigating the possibilities of mechanization and other means which would increase the employment of White labour in the mines. Its Report is a document of great significance and interest, sharpened by a pungent repudiation of its objectivity by a dissident minority of one Commissioner.

Indeed the emotive intensity of the Majority Report's peroration suggests some doubt as to whether the Commission had not already reached its recommendations in advance of hearing the evidence [13]. Nonetheless that evidence got to grips with the realities of colour competition in mining labour in a manner that half a century of subsequent misrepresentation now makes difficult to recognize.

The Report noted – but emphatically did not accept – the 'accepted view' and 'orthodox theory' that there was and is something permanent and stable in the demarcation of the respective spheres of the White man and the African and in the dependence of the White man on the African. 'The native was, according to the orthodox theory, a muscular machine doing unskilled work only. He was not in any sense a competitor with the White man, who was to have a monopoly of all skilled work; and he was regarded as a necessary adjunct to enable White men to be employed at remunerative wages' [14].

But, it went on, such views and theories must 'be set aside as inconsistent with the facts . . . . The theory that the native is a "mere muscular machine" must be discarded . . . experience has shown that he can no longer be looked upon as debarred by lack of brain and industrial training from interfering with the White man's opportunities of employment and as merely an aid to enable the White man to earn wages to keep him in contentment. It is clear from the evidence that the position as between White man and native is one of very unstable equilibrium . . . and the tendency to-day is for Coloured labour to be employed in an increasing proportion and with the effect of displacing White labour' [15]. The Commission repeatedly stressed that there were no natural limitations to the competitiveness of African labour at almost any level of occupation – at least in those parts of its Report, where it wished to drive home its conviction that White and Black labour were in no wise complementary but directly competitive. Thus:

Upon the evidence before us we can come to no other conclusion than that the generally accepted idea that by increasing the supply and efficiency of coloured labour the country is at the same time increasing the field of permanent employment for white labour on the mines, is founded upon a quite erroneous conception of the limitations of the natives and of his industrial position in relation to the white man. . . .

The truth of the matter is, probably, that the capacity of the average unskilled native as he comes to the mines is very limited, But it is undoubtedly the case that among the large numbers of natives working upon the mines under existing regulations and control, an increasingly large proportion of them are, by long service and continued practice, acquiring all or nearly all the skill required to do a very great deal of work which in the past has necessitated the employment of white men. . . .

. . . . the mines authorities are fully alive to this fact; and that, as is but natural, every effort will be made to train the natives to do more and more skilled or semi-skilled work, and to take full advantage of each increase in the capacity of low-waged 'selected' natives to do such work. . . [16].

Opinions and experience of the skill potential of African (coloured) labour understandably differed widely. Generalizations are patently unwise and illegitimate, though of course the human proclivity to generalize in this field of (very) human relations is not to be inhibited by any doubts of competence.

Thus Mr Webber, general manager of Rand Mines, said: Having skilled, or rather experienced, coloured labour we have been able to go on and man our drills and do fairly decent work – about as good as before – and it proves the whole matter to our view that it is possible to run our mines with much less labour and cheapen our working costs . . . [17]. And a sub-committee of the

Chamber of Mines General Committee in their evidence on underground transport said: In some cases where mechanical appliances
have been introduced, we find them erected and run entirely by
natives and so satisfactorily as to obviate the extended employment
of white labour on economic grounds. . .[18].

Followed by Mr Petersen, general manager of the Geldenhuis
Estate Gold Mining Company, who said *inter alia*: We have some
of the Kaffirs who are better machine men than some of the white
men; I have boys who have been working on the mine from 12 to
15 years, and they are better machine men than many on the Rand
nowadays . . . they can place holes, fix up the machine and do
everything that a white man can do, but of course we are not allowed
to let them blast . . . I do not think [that they could blast with
safety], I feel sure about it. I have had experience with natives since
1879, and I know what a native can do. . .[19].

There was indeed even the proof of operational experience that
the Africans' skill-potential could, when circumstances demanded,
be readily deployed. The Report noted that the coal mines offered
a striking object lesson as to the degree to which the African could
render unnecessary the services of White men.

In one mine where the manager informed us that he has natives who have
been with him in every case for over ten years, we found that practically the
whole of the work was done by these natives, who may be looked upon to all
intents and purposes as being Kaffir colliers . . . we found that underground
the only white men employed were six overseers, while on the surface
natives were employed driving such engines as the law permitted and requiring in fact hardly any white supervision. . . [20].

The Commission disclosed a widely-known but rarely-acknowledged
practice – that the actual operator of the drill machines was, and
always had been, the 'kaffir labourer'. This was stressed by a number
of mine managers and engineers, who observed that the White
machine-operator has always been merely a supervisor and urged
that the cheapest work would be got by increasing to the practicable
limit the number of machines under each White man's supervision[21]. In another context the Commission referred to 'an object
lesson . . . furnished by the miners' strike in May, 1907, when
although 50 per cent of the underground white workers were on
strike for several weeks the operations of the industry were hardly
at all hampered thereby . . . . They [the owners] were able to do

this because the bulk of the work was and is done by indentured coloured labour, which could be kept at work for the time being by utilizing as supervisors the members of the permanent white staffs of the mines, and a number of skilled and unskilled white men hastily recruited' [22].

The Commission made a resolute attempt to establish in which direction economic rationality, or least-cost combination and allocation of productive resources, lay. It set out to provide actual cost data in respect of, for instance, (a) the utilization of coloured labour for all classes and categories of mining work from the unskilled roughest tramming and shovelling of broken rock and carriage to the shaft, to the semi-skilled job of operating underground machine drills for breaking ground, including shaft sinking, development and stoping (one of the critical cost-operations) to skilled artisan-type jobs both underground and on the surface, (b) the utilization of White labour for all similar classes and categories of mining work but proceeding from the most skilled to the most unskilled, (c) varying combinations including machine drills of different capacities ranging from one miner to one machine to one White (or 'selected' Coloured) supervisor per ten machines.

It is beyond the scope of this context to examine the detail [23] but it was a thorough-going effort at analysis of perhaps the single most important factor determining the rate of economic growth of South Africa then (and now). Given the overwhelming significance of the gold-mining industry to South African economic development – on any theory of economic development – nothing could, and even now no doubt can, compare with establishing the current least-cost combination of factors of production in mining. Patently the optimization of productivity in gold-mining affects profit-rates, hence savings-investment rates, in all sectors of the economy.

It can be argued that all a priori calculation in working costs is invalidated by the subjectivity of the very concept of cost as the lost, alternative opportunity [24]. Nonetheless the Majority Commissioners tried their best and the 'facts' they report range widely.

Mr Ross Browne of Rand Mines Ltd made his 'estimate of Rand costs on the basis of the most favourable conditions' i.e. carrying the coloured labour employment to practicable limits and arrived at a figure (for the year 1907) of 15s. per ton against a ruling 21·3s. per ton, or a reduction of 30 per cent [25]. The Commissioners after re-interpreting Mr Ross Browne's assumptions conceded that working costs might be reduced by 27 per cent as 'the average . . . for the whole industry which . . . may possibly be arrived at, by persistence in the coloured labour policy under ideally favourable conditions and for no increase in output above that of 1906–7'.

Then the Commissioners proceeded to establish their estimates of working costs on the basis of the adoption of the White labour policy, a policy of employing White unskilled and skilled labour in virtual total replacement of Non-White labour throughout the mining industry. Their comparative standard of labour rates and efficiency was the 'all-white' labour in the Californian mines [26]. On that key assumption (and others in regard to reduced rail and customs costs) which implied that the total working force, Whites only, would be one-fourth of the then working force of Whites and Coloureds, the working costs of the mining industry would be reduced by an almost identical 27 per cent as in the proposal by Mr Ross Browne.

But perhaps the modern management accountant would finally identify himself with Mr C. H. Spencer, in his minority of one, who scathingly commented:

> The Majority Report goes on to discuss at some length the relative benefits accruing to the country from the employment of White or Coloured labour on the gold mines, but I do not intend to follow them into this academic discussion . . . I should like in the first place to refer to an answer given by one of the engineering witnesses . . . to the effect that a mine cannot be worked according to arithmetic formulae. This is in fact, and it seems to me that it is a fact which takes away most of the value from such calculations as those contained in the Majority Report, until they have been confirmed by practical experience.
>
> In the second place, I should like to point out that nearly all the evidence quoted by the Majority Report in order to show that the costs of working with White labour would be no greater, or less, than those of working with coloured labour is obtained by picking certain parts of the evidence of practical men, mine managers and engineers, who had themselves come, in their whole experience, to exactly the opposite conclusion [27].

And then Mr Spencer becomes even more pointed:

> It seems to me a very dangerous method of reasoning, to take isolated pieces of evidence on isolated departments of mining work, given by mine managers who all affirm that the substitution of white for coloured labour would mean a great increase in working costs, and to endeavour to prove from these pieces of evidence, and from nothing else, that the witnesses were

wrong in their main conclusion. This could only be justified if it was assumed that all the technical witnesses were either incompetent or dishonest. . . . But unless some such assumption is made, the use which this part of the Majority Report makes of the technical evidence seems to me to be, from a practical point of view, absurd[28].

Although the Majority Report proved to its own satisfaction, if not to Mr Spencer's and in due course to the Government of the day, that 'assuming the most favourable conditions for low working cost, whether on a coloured or a white labour basis, the figures show that so far as can be at present foreseen the ultimate attainable level of cost is for all practical purposes the same in both cases [29], the Commissioners were more concerned to prove that the extra-economic case for an all-White labour force in the mining industry was overwhelming and decisive.

With which policy (continuation of the Coloured labour policy or White labour policy) does the balance of advantage lie, the Commission asked itself. It detailed at length[30] all the manifold and manifest gains from a White labour policy, claiming that its full application would be 'of the nature of a chemical addition affecting the whole industrial organization and changing many of the facts and possibilities of the position'. The Commission itself was opposed to any statutory demarcation of work or job classifications as between White and Black. It dismissed all such *specific* colour bar reservations as impracticable and undesirable. It stood completely for 'the adoption of the white labour policy [which] necessitates the final and complete abandonment of the coloured labour policy' and (as already quoted) 'upon this may be said to depend . . . whether the vast expanses of South Africa . . . shall be the home of a great white people or be the habitation and breeding-place of masses of natives and other coloured people of mixed races, in all degrees of semi-barbarism and semi-civilization'[31].

The emotive echo rings responsively and contemporaneously across the divide of the decades.

Despite the ideological appeal, backed with as much economic calculation as could be pressed into service, of the Majority of the Mining Industry Commission of 1908, the Botha Government of the Transvaal Colony did not accept its unequivocal recommendation of an all-White labour force for the mining industry. Perhaps an exhaustive examination might establish why Botha and Smuts (who had appointed the Commission, selected its members and drafted its terms of reference) turned it down. Conjecture can however provide reasoned guide.

The Commission had proposed that its all-White policy could be made effective by the simple action of fixing forthwith a maximum limit to the number of Africans from outside British South Africa, who might enter the Transvaal to serve indentures on the mines. This maximum should be diminished automatically and periodically, say, every six, or, at the outside, twelve months, 'until importation is entirely stopped at a date not later than three years ahead' [32].

But Botha, now prime minister of the Transvaal Colony, was no doubt still mindful of the key weapon which the railway agreement with the Portuguese gave him in relation to the governments of the Cape and Natal, with whom he must soon sit down at the table of the National Convention. Smuts, right-hand man of Botha and now supercharged with his vision and mission of unification, assuredly would not have countenanced the scrapping of his bargaining bludgeon over all other representatives at the Convention by tearing up the *modus vivendi* with Mozambique.

The Mining Industry Commission was obviously being unrealistic in expecting the Botha-Smuts combination to prohibit the indenture of Portuguese African labour, wreck their rail-link to Delagoa Bay and sit down – stripped of the four aces and joker – to play the the poker-game for the unification of South Africa [33].

Perhaps, too, Botha and Smuts, whose contacts with the Transvaal-born Whites were much closer than those of the members of the Commission (and their trade-unionist supporters from Britain), were unpersuaded by all the assurances that some thousands of Whites were only too eager to accept manual labour underground in the mines. Some of the most doubtful rationalizations of the whole argument of the Mining Industry Commissioners, and of former mine-manager Creswell in particular, relate to the willingness of Whites to undertake 'kaffir's work'. Thus, *inter alia*, they said:

We cannot regard any of the general objections, based rather upon a dying local prejudice than upon any reasoned argument, as being sufficient justification for continuing a policy otherwise undesirable.

The future leader of the South African Labour Party, Col. Creswell, was not however able to persuade two future prime ministers, Generals Botha and Smuts, that the fate of South Africa as 'the home of a great White people' would be decisively determined by the adoption of his passionately recommended White labour policy for the mining industry. To have hazarded the profitability of the Transvaal Colony's greatest industry at this pre-Union climactic would have been to hazard unification itself. Botha, and assuredly Smuts, had a larger vision of what would secure the position of the White man in South Africa. It was control of the new greater polity of the Union of South Africa.

Reporting, however, some five years later the Economic Commission, 1914, found the local prejudice far from dying. On the contrary one of the most disturbing realities this Commission noted was an unwillingness of White youths to enter the employment of the mines in either a skilled or unskilled capacity. It wrote:

Very few of the younger generation seem to seek employment in the mines. The supply of men underground, apart from immigrating miners, is largely kept up by learners who do not go through a regular apprenticeship and are not all young . . . In view of the very high earnings on the Witwaterstrand, the fact that so few of the younger generation seek employment there may cause some surprise. No doubt the miner's phthisis disclosures form the chief item in the explanation. But probably another item of some weight is the almost universal South African prejudice against manual work, which extends even to the work of directing and supervising manual labour[34].

5

LEGACY OF DISUNION

The integrated society, which the mining market of the Witwatersrand was forcing on the peoples of South Africa, had indeed no political entity in South Africa in the 1890's. From 1886 when the Witwatersrand goldfields were proclaimed until 1910 when the Union of South Africa was proclaimed, it is possible to see clearly the compulsion exercised by the economy on the polity. Resistance to economic integration into a unified South Africa by Kruger's republican polity escalated into the Anglo-Boer War. But the Anglo-Boer War was itself only an interruption in the compelling process of integration consequent upon a market that was being centred on the goldmining industry through the developmental consequences of that industry.

The history books have named it the Anglo-Boer War of 1899–1902. This tends to obscure the real element of civil war, which manifests the failure of a single society to subsist as an entity. Politically there were four separate governmental units in South Africa in the last quarter of the nineteenth century – the Cape Colony, the Colony of Natal, the Transvaal Republic and the Orange Free State. But from 1886 the Rand's gold was forcing the single society into being. It was the Rand market which made separation of political authority unrelated to the new integrating phase in social process exerted by the mining industry.

The element of civil war was the consequence of political responses to market reactions, as South Africa was pushed and pulled into a single society. The war was not only between the Boers and the British, not only between Kruger and Steyn on the one side and Chamberlain and Milner on the other. It was also between the Transvaal-Free State and the Cape-Natal and the quarrels were as much over railway and customs revenues of the several governmental units of South Africa as over the strategical imperatives of Downing Street. The clash between the patriarchal Kruger and the financier

Rhodes is not really comprehended by the stereotypes of economic imperialism of Marxist orthodoxy or of Afrikaner nationalism.

The British historian A. J. P. Taylor asserts that the British problem in South Africa was essentially strategic and political, not economic. The British, he writes, needed a united white South Africa in order to have strategic security at the Cape – the lynch-pin of the British Empire [1]. The naval station at the Cape was doubtless more important to the 'imperial factor' in the 1890's than Simonstown in the 1960's. Doubtless, too, as the South African historian, J. S. Marais, puts it, 'in the eyes of British statesmen a united South Africa – like a united Canada and a united Australia – would be a source of additional strength to the British Empire instead of a source of expense' [2].

Yet the 'causes' of the Anglo-Boer War, however exhaustively sought in the moves and motives of Chamberlain, Milner, Rhodes and Kruger, should not exclude the critical examination of railways and customs policies of the four South African governments from 1886 on [3].

The duality of political power, or will, in South Africa was, says Professor Marais, the real origin of the Anglo-Boer War [4]. The political federation of South Africa may not have been an 'historical necessity' and historical determinism may not explain the War, as Marais argues. It is undeniable that new urgency was given to the problem of duality of power by the proving of the vast potentialities of the Witwatersrand goldfields by 1895. But the political unification of South Africa, henceforth, was the manifest destiny of an ineluctable customs union and separately nationalized railway systems [5].

In 1896 Lord Selborne, the then Under-Secretary wrote to Joseph Chamberlain, the Colonial Secretary, as follows:

In a generation the South African Republic will by its wealth and population dominate South Africa. South African politics must revolve around the Transvaal, which will be the only possible market for the agricultural products or the manufactures of the Cape Colony and Natal. The commercial attractions of the Transvaal will be so great that a Union of South African states with it will be absolutely necessary for their prosperous existence. The only question in my opinion is whether that Union will be inside or outside the British Empire.

The prescience of Lord Selborne is reflected by the outcome in 1961 of all the twists and turns of six decades of subsequent South

African history and social process. Before the Transvaal's dominance of the South African political economy would some sixty years later come to reconstitute the Union as the Republic of South Africa outside the British Commonwealth-Empire, the republican Transvaal (or South African Republic of the 1890's) was first to be defeated in the Anglo-Boer War. The extraordinary rapidity, however, with which the post-war colonial Transvaal re-asserted its dominance over the political relationships of the four states of South Africa, was proof that the economic development the Rand generated from its goldmining industry exercised an irresistible compulsion on the economies of the separate units to accept the Transvaal's political leadership, first in the Union of South Africa and then decades afterwards in the Republic of South Africa.

The tough seed of Krugerism flowered into the political factor of Afrikanerdom. Afrikaner consciousness had scattered and sown itself in the wilderness, which the uncovered gold transformed into a market – the first truly dynamic, integrating market in Southern African geopolitics. The interacting stimulation given by the mining industry of the Transvaal Republic to the railways and ports of the Cape Colony and the Colony of Natal became the most powerful factor in the economic development of the whole territorial complex of South Africa. Inescapable problems of political sovereignty arose.

Perhaps because it tends to disfigure some of the emotional images of the 1899–1902 South African conflict, for which the significant preferred name in some Afrikaner writings is The Second Freedom War, the element of civil strife as among South Africans themselves is generally minimized. But Dr Jean van der Poel's examination of the railway and customs policies of the four separate governments, after the gold discoveries of the Transvaal magnetized the inland market for the coastal colonies, makes it plain that there were irreconcilable conflicts of material interest among South Africans themselves.

The nature of capitalization of a railway system, particularly on its inauguration and initial development, with its very large investment in absolutely specific track-laying and long-lived assets, makes it crucially important for the investors correctly to forecast future demand for the rail services. The significance of such capitalization on the costing and pricing of rail services and on competitive forms of transport will be examined in a later chapter. The decision, which is not only crucial but may even prove crucifying for the promoter-investors in a railway system, is what certainty attaches to the projected demand. In a sense they seek a guarantee of progressive stability in the market which their railway is planned to serve.

The importance of established expectations in respect of market demand and of large lumps of initiating and developing capitalization explains why most railway systems are monopolies, generally with official sanction and often encouragement. The implications of risk are both economic and political. Market demand may fail to meet projections in that the purely market factors determining growth may change adversely. But in addition to this market or economic risk, there is also the political risk. The official, i.e. governmental, sanction and encouragement of monopoly expectations may be amended adversely.

When a railway system is state-owned, the market risk and the political risk may be minimized *within the territory of state sovereignty*. If the state-owned system serves a territory *outside* its jurisdiction and subject to *another* state's sovereignty, both market risk and political risk may be maximized. The particular market conditions and capitalization conditions of the railway systems of geographical South Africa in the last quarter of the nineteenth century exacerbated both market and political risks to the point of being a critical cause of the civil war element in the Anglo-Boer War.

After the first 60 miles of rail track had been pioneered by private initiative under official financial guarantees, they were 'nationalized' by the Cape Government in 1873 as the starting point for a developing Cape Railways to serve the growing dry diamond-diggings of Kimberly both from Cape Town and from Port Elizabeth. Not to be outdone in linking its port to the interior which now glittered from the mounting diamond excitement, the Natal Railways also under government ownership set out from Durban.

So both Cape and Natal treasuries began to raise loans in Europe, the debt servicing of which was to be their major preoccupation for years to come. The cost of 'economic development' comes high, if economic development is measured in replacing ox-wagons with steel rails and engines, to serve vast expanses – more particularly if the oxen find their consumable stores always to hand, while iron monsters have to be fed on coal that has to be shipped all the way from Wales.

By the beginning of 1884 Cape railway debt was £12,000,000

and 50 per cent of a half-million pounds of interest had to come from a revenue which fell below expenditure by £672,000. Not to be outdone, the Legislative Assembly of Natal raised its public debt to a total of £5,000,000 when its total revenue for all governmental purposes was £700,000 [6].

This however was nothing to the intensification of 'economic' or railway development, and its cost in debt-servicing, when the market-demand moved further into the interior and began to glitter with Witwatersrand gold and not merely Kimberley brilliants. Both the Cape and Natal governments recognized that incipient bankruptcy could be forestalled only when their respective rail lines reached right into the heart of the Witwatersrand, that market which by the 1890's already so dominated the whole of South Africa as to establish a *de facto* economic unity.

In the Transvaal Republic, however, the government was President Paul Kruger. Isolationist and tradition-minded, Kruger was very much more concerned with his *de jure* political sovereignty. He was determined to maintain it against outside economic development, whether originating from Uitlanders, or Cecil John Rhodes, or the Afrikaner Bond in the Cape, or even his fellow-Afrikaners in the neighbouring republic of the Orange Free State. The social system of the Transvaal Republic was not going to permit its way of life to be changed by any external entrepreneurial dynamism. So Kruger, frustrated in his attempts to extend his polity geographically to secure his own link to the sea at Kosi Bay, was resolute in his turn to frustrate both the Cape and Natal. His answer to encirclement was a competitive rail line which, with the nerve-wracking co-operation of Portugal and of some of Europe's trickiest financiers, would run from the Rand to Delagoa Bay in Mozambique.

Kruger, moreover, could at least in this instance claim that economic rationality and ideology ran parallel in the more direct and shorter rail line between the Rand and Delagoa Bay as compared with the longer rail line from the Rand to either Port Elizabeth or Cape Town or to Durban.

But railway costing – and rating – has its own imperatives. A rail line to reach its market hundreds of arid miles away costs millions to lay. And a rail line which, by fiat of the government in political control of that market, is then stopped short only 50 miles of that market, imposes even more compelling imperatives. Waiting for Kruger's authority to extend the Cape Railways and the Natal

Railways into Johannesburg itself did not encourage goodwill. Only when Kruger was sure that his Netherlands Company which he controlled would finally achieve the competitive link to Delagoa Bay did the Transvaal President allow the Cape Railways to close the gap of the last 50 miles over Transvaal territory and also extended his indispensible sanction to the Natal Railways to complete its service from Durban to the Rand itself.

For a brief year during which the Cape Railways was the only line with a terminal in Johannesburg itself, by now the centre of a golden reef extending 30 miles either side of it, this monopoly position proved that even a high-cost railway line could pay. With 85 per cent of the lucrative Transvaal trade in 1893, the annual reports of the general manager of the Cape Railways reported gratifying traffic records. By 1895 total imports through the Cape's harbours reached R13¼ millions and the Cape Railways made a profit of £800,000 after paying about £730,000 interest on £20,000,000 capitalization [7].

Durban, however, was much nearer Johannesburg than Cape Town or than Port Elizabeth. By permitting a rail line from Durban, President Kruger had ensured that customs tariffs on imports finally destined for his own political territory – and the Rand's propensity to consume anything from mining stores to the conventional necessities of Randlord plutocracy was gratifyingly high – would be the subject of bilateral competition between the Cape Government and the Natal Government. He also ensured that his Transvaal government would indirectly benefit from the rail revenues accruing to the longer section of railway line under the administration of the Netherlands Company [8], which completed the vital link from the Natal terminal, than from the equally vital link of the Cape terminal.

The Railway convention between the Transvaal and Natal in February 1894 acknowledged Natal's interests *vis-à-vis* the Cape and simultaneously acknowledged the economic realities of the shortest rail link and least-cost railway charge of them all, i.e. from Portuguese Delagoa Bay to the Rand's market-heart of Southern Africa. Natal agreed to share the Transvaal traffic with Portuguese Delagoa Bay. The appropriate railway rates to provide for such a division were written into the railway convention between the Transvaal and Natal concluded in February, 1894. Meanwhile the Orange Free State and the Cape Colony had already after much difficulty set up a Customs Convention in 1889, which gave the Free State a fiscal stake in channelling its imports through the Cape ports and hence over the Cape railways to the Free State section of the line.

The confrontation of the Transvaal-Natal railway convention and the Cape-OFS customs convention, with an agreement between the Transvaal and Portuguese East Africa to provide a labour supply from Portuguese East Africa for the Rand mines in exchange for a guaranteed share of the rail market demand of the Rand to Portuguese East Africa, and with a defensive political alliance between Kruger's Transvaal and Reitz's Free State in anticipation of a future republican federation (that also made provision for certain duty reciprocity on transit trade) provides some highly instructive material for the economic theory of monopolistic competition for a single, dominant market.

But the bewildering tactics of pricing of rail-transport services and customs-duty entry that constitute the story of Dr Jean van der Poel's *Railways and Customs Policies of South Africa* had their extra-economic impact. The political ploys of monopolistic competition introduced their overtones of ideological irreconciliation. A 'final conference' in April, 1895, of all governments was held in Cape Town to reconcile politics with economics and both with market realities. The Cape Railways substituted alternative ox-wagon transport to carry goods off-loaded at the Drifts, 50 miles short of Johannesburg, to counter Kruger's tactic of sharply raising the rail rate on this last 50 miles (which came under his controlled Netherlands rail company). The slide towards civil war became slippery indeed [9].

President Kruger responded to the Cape Railways economic Oliver with his own political Roland. The Cape Railways, as noted above, had countered Kruger's highly discriminatory rail rate on the last 50 miles from Viljoensdrift and Zand Drift into Johannersburg by off-loading their rail freight at the Drifts for ox-wagons to complete final delivery. *Ceteris paribus*, such a transhipment from iron horse to ox-train was undoubtedly a least-cost substitution in a highly politicalized economy.

The counter-action to such economic rationality from the polity was not long delayed. Kruger promptly ordered the closing of the Drifts as ports of entry for goods into the Transvaal. From this deliberately hostile act against the Cape to the even more deliberate and more hostile Jameson Raid against the Transvaal, the tragedy moved to ultimatum and to war.

Whether the causes of the Anglo-Boer War are to be found in the strategic needs of Britain and the determination of the British Colonial Office to impose its supremacy over the Transvaal Republic, or whether they are to be found in the ideological imperatives of Krugerism and Kruger's *kragdadigheid* never to accept less than complete sovereign republican independence, the economic development set off throughout the territorial area of South Africa by major capital investment in the Rand mining industry was patently promoting a single economic system.

This indeed was recognized – and perhaps by none more clearly than President Brand of the republican Orange Free State – in the attempt to establish a customs union. Such a customs union represented undoubted economic rationality and the outcome logically was some form of federal or unifying political authority.

An economic heartland exercises political magnetism. A zollverein, a customs union, a common market must go forward to an empire, a federation, a community of centralized authority – or the single market will be broken up.

Because the motivations and aims of the political actors in South Africa in the bedevilled situation of the 1890's could not be accommodated to the imperatives of the economy, a single polity could not be established until a war had been fought, lost and won. The Anglo-Boer War in a sense settled nothing. Political authority was of course transformed. President Kruger departed to die in Switzerland and the British High Commissioner, Milner, moved from Cape Town to Pretoria. The 'imperial factor' was now in unfettered political authority. But even imperial ideology consummated in a Milner-Chamberlain joint-will had to adapt itself to the even more imperious adaptive demands of economic rationality.

Despite Milner's pressing desire to federate all four territories under the temporary control of the war-time British High Commission Authority, he was hardly in Pretoria before he was compelled to take even more pressing action to start up the gold mines as the prime mover of the total South African society. As early as December, 1901, before even the guerilla stage of the War had been ended and peace signed at Vereeniging, Milner signed his *modus vivendi* with the Portuguese Government. It allowed the mining companies to recruit African labour from Mozambique in return for a railway rating agreement, which would guarantee a minimum 50 per cent to 55 per cent of the Rand 'competitive area' through Lourenco Marques on Delagoa Bay.

Delagoa Bay by the facts of economic geography remained as much the 'rational' port of importation for the Transvaal as a colony as it had been for the Transvaal as a republic. Constitutional changes sometimes change little more than constitutions. The rail lines of the Netherlands Company were now government property and the interests of the Transvaal colonial treasury were still best served by the revenues from the rail line of longest route within its territory and under its own state ownership.

Even more compelling were the labour needs of the mines. From 1890 to 1899 it was estimated that the number of Africans employed on the gold-mines rose from 14,000 to 97,000. In 1897 about half of these were from Portuguese East Africa, according to estimate. In 1904 the percentage of African labour from Portuguese East Africa on the Transvaal gold- and coal-mining was officially put at 66⅔ per cent increasing to just short of 70 per cent through the next four years and fluctuating around 50 per cent right down until 1929[10].

The Peace of Vereeniging ended the hot war between republican independence and the imperial factor but the cold war of railway rates and customs tariffs continued to presage an economic debacle and a renewal of the civil war. Even replacement of the hated Milner[11] by the conciliatory Lord Selborne as the 'imperial factor' could not dissolve the 'railway factor' as an integrator of economic development and the disintegrator of political separatism.

Indeed the dominance of the Transvaal mining-market was strengthened by Milner's fusion of the pre-war republican inland railway systems (of the Transvaal and Orange Free State) into the Central Railways. The maritime colonies of Natal and the Cape attempted to overcome the to them financially disastrous drain on the Transvaal's railway traffic market from the competitive rates of Delagoa Bay. They offered rebates to Transvaal merchants importing through their respective ports of Durban, Cape Town and Port Elizabeth and transporting over their respective Natal and Cape rail lines. But the Natal and Cape railway and political authorities were met by a threat from Lord Selborne of countervailing rail rates over the inland Central railways under the latter's control.

The Cape and Natal were forced to yield to His Majesty's High

Commissioner Selborne's bargaining strength – deployed in a manner hardly different from its use by Republican presidential Kruger before him. The basic problem of accommodating the adaptive exigencies of economic development within a non-unified polity remained. Either the civil war would break out anew or some form of political federation would have to be brought about. As Dr Jean van der Poel put it:

A commercial crisis which might easily have ended in civil war had thus been temporarily averted, but the danger of such a violent outcome of the prevailing quarrels was by no means over. One circumstance above all others had given the contestants pause and tempered their jealousies with a discretion that was three parts fear, namely, the imminent grant of self-government to the wealthiest colony in South Africa . . . South African statesmen, contemplating the probable results of a separatist policy on the part of the new Transvaal, shrank from the prospect of chaos which it threatened. Bitter experience of a recent past made such a course unthinkable. Once that conviction had been reached, the realization that nothing but political federation could ensure the future peace of South Africa began to impress itself more and more strongly on the minds of thinking people. . .[12].

Meanwhile economic growth itself appeared to have ground to a halt. After the usual inflationary war-time boom, a trade depression beginning in 1902 went on year after year. The depression itself both encouraged the political separatism of the ideologically-motivated and, on the other hand, the recognition by influential business interests that the return of prosperity awaited a political settlement of unification.

Statemanship in the persons of Smuts, Botha and Merriman now began to operate decisively in favour of a unified political system for the four separate polities. Thompson's definitive account of the birth of the Union of South Africa[13] leaves a strong impression that it was an act of political will achieved by men who were essentially concerned with politics – and their farms[14]. The unifying influence of economic development had hitherto been unable to produce a zollverein or customs union or common market as the precursor of a political federation. The aspirations of the Boers and the British respectively were too conflicting to contribute towards the realization of a single polity until the tragedy of war and its aftermath had exercised its leavening influence on that élite which directs social change.

67

Botha, Smuts and Merriman among the South Africans and Lord Selborne and the Milner Kindergarten (especially Lionel Curtis) among the 'imperialists' constituted just such an élite. But they were men of politics. That is politicians, not in the now pejorative sense of 'fixers', but as practitioners of Aristotle's 'master-science' among men. They saw politics, as Bernard Crick well puts it, as arising from accepting the fact of the simultaneous existence of different groups, hence different interests and different traditions, within a territorial unit under a common rule [15]. To Smuts especially politics was the master-science in the sense 'not that it includes or explains all other sciences but in that it gives them some priority, some order in their claims on the always scarce resources of any given community' [16].

So when the next and crucial Intercolonial Conference was called at Pretoria in May, 1908, of the four South African governments with the avowed object of arriving at a definitive railways and customs agreement, before even the details of economic negotiation were tabled, Smuts moved his unopposed motion in favour of a National Convention to draft a constitution for a united South Africa. And Smuts, as Thompson's history makes clear, was the principal architect of the Act of Union of 1910. On its last day, this Intercolonial Conference passed Merriman's resolution admitting 'it was a practical impossibility under existing conditions' to reconcile 'the financial requirements and economic policies of the various South African Governments' [17].

From the time that the gold-rich market of the Rand was first proved in 1886, the economic development it generated began to unify all South Africa and all South Africans – English-speaking and Afrikaans-speaking, White and Non-White, urban and rural, financial and farmer, merchant and manufacturer, republican and colonialist, poor White and poor Black – in a single social system. But the economic development was not in itself capable of reconciling beliefs, motives and aims. Only political will could bring into being the single polity that would henceforth interact with economic development to sustain a single social system – and when almost exactly half a century later the never-subdued ethos of Afrikanerdom compelled republican independence, it was the political factor that imposed the Republic of South Africa.

At the National Convention to bring about Union, the political will was expressed primarily through Smuts and Merriman. The motivating ambitions of the man who in due course was to give new intensified purposiveness to Afrikanerdom, General J. B. M. Hertzog, key delegate of the Free State, were for the present concentrated on language recognition. Hertzog indeed was one of those who saw clearly – more clearly than most – that the keys to the control of the polity were possessed by teachers as much as by politicians, and by both combined more effectively than by business men.

Chapter III of Thompson's *The Unification of South Africa* is headed: the origins of the principal features of the South African constitution. He discusses (i) the personal factor (ii) the form of the constitution (iii) political rights (iv) the electoral system (v) language. These indeed were the issues of the National Convention and it was their political aspects and not their economic aspects that absorbed the time and thoughts of the Convention.

The constitution that emerged was decisively shaped by the political philosophy of Smuts and Merriman. The two critical questions of their concern related to the form of the constitution – flexible or rigid; unitary or federalistic. Merriman favoured an unitary constitution because he thought four federal parliaments an unnecessary extravagance and he was opposed to the idea of judicial review. Smuts, after exploring a modified form of federalism in his first 'Suggested Scheme' [18], became convinced of the need for a concentration of centralized power in a union that would adapt itself to future change.

Nothing in Thompson's study suggests that either Merriman or Smuts, or indeed other critical thinkers such as Lionel Curtis and R. H. Brand, gave much thought as to which form of constitution – unitary or federal, flexible or rigid – would promote the most rapid rate of economic growth. Even R. H. Brand seemed to accept that the coming in a single polity – and not the form of that polity – was the essential condition for the resumption of economic growth. It is not possible to consider this interesting point but the thought may be ventured that while federalism may have curtailed state interventionism and thereby promoted economic growth, it may also have made the political settlement of the railways and customs factor in the financial and fiscal problems of the several former colonies more stubborn and have served as a continuing source of future conflict.

It is true that the National Convention was to leave railway and tariff policy part of the legacy of disunion that carried on beyond the Act of Union. But the actual settlement of the economic factor that had so bedevilled political relationships, from the moment that the Rand's mining-market had exerted its integrating irresistibility, was disposed of with remarkably little difficulty.

The financial and railways chapters of the Constitution were largely those provided for in the programme which the Transvaal delegation (expressing the chief bond between Government and Opposition members of the Transvaal delegation) took to the National Convention [19]. Significantly these proposals had been worked out by the members of the Milner Kindergarten, who constituted the civil service of the Transvaal Colony [20]. The Union acquired colonial government assets and colonial government debts. More particularly all railways and harbours became the nationalized property of the Union Government, administered by a specially constituted South African Railways and Harbours Board.

Of the total public debt of all four colonies as at 1910 amounting to £113 millions, 46 per cent was the burden of the Cape, 27 per cent of the Transvaal, 19 per cent of Natal and 7 per cent of the Orange River Colony (or Orange Free State). The net debt per head of White population was, in round figures, £90 in the Cape Colony, £73 in the Transvaal, £221 in Natal and £47 in the Orange River Colony.

Table showing Ordinary Revenue, Ordinary Expend

All figu

	CAPE COLONY				NATAL			
Year	Ordinary Revenue		Ordinary Expenditure Total	Surplus or Deficit	Ordinary Revenue		Ordinary Expenditure Total	Surp or Defi
	Railway Receipts	Total			Railway Receipts	Total		
1902–3	5·617	11·701	11·197	+0·503	2·286	4·334	5·102	−0·
1903–4	5·120	9·913	10·862	−0·949	2·499	4·160	4·071	+0·
1904–5	4·033	8·472	9·149	−0·677	1·884	3·384	3·814	−0·
1905–6	3·940	8·236	8·231	+0·005	2·085	3·665	3·673	−0·
1906–7	3·662	7·701	8.349	−0·648	1·881	3·471	3·681	−0·
1907–8	3·094	6·981	7·973	−0·991	2·019	3·510	3·689	−0·
1908–9	3·065	7·312	7·681	−0·369	1·989	3·569	3·530	+0·
1909–10	3·143	7·747	7·611	+0·136	2·409	4·293	3·530	+0·
Cumulative				−2·991				−0·

SOURCE: Compiled from various tables in Append

The principal capital assets for which the major portion of this indebtedness had been incurred were the railways and harbours, which were valued at £84 million in respect of the four colonies. But the valuation of capital assets, especially such highly specialized assets as railway systems and harbour installations, is very directly related to their net earning capacity. The table below is therefore informative of the bargaining strength and weakness of the representatives of the assembled treasuries at the National Convention.

The weakness of the Cape and of Natal is obvious from the major proportion of total receipts that came from their railways (and customs) and the ominous re-occurrence of annual deficits on their current budgets in an era when budgetary arithmetic was interpreted with Gladstonian nicety rather than Keynesian contempt. Not only did the railway and customs receipts of the Cape (and to a lesser extent Natal) fail to come up to the expectations on which the original capital investment decisions had been made but the real capital valuation of the assets was much more related to the market authority of the Transvaal Volksraad than to the accounting procedures of the Cape Parliament.

The financial cards at the Convention table were certainly stacked against the coastal colonies of the Cape and Natal. The

Net Balances of the Four Colonies 1902/9 to 1909/10
ns of pounds

	TRANSVAAL			ORANGE RIVER COLONY (O.F.S.)			
Ordinary Revenue		Ordinary Expenditure Total	Surplus or Deficit	Ordinary Revenue		Ordinary Expenditure Total	Surplus or Deficit
ning ation	Total			Customs Receipts	Total		
508	5·427	4·273	+1·154	0·288	0·956	0·839	+0·116
720	5·333	4·318	+1·014	0·419	0·875	0·807	+0·067
791	4·411	4·018	+0·393	0·298	0·786	0·780	+0·005
083	4·670	4·236	+0·433	0·305	0·759	0·759	+0·000
236	4·651	4·415	+0·236	0·310	0·787	0·774	+0·012
068	4·670	4·118	+0·551	0·285	0·740	0·727	+0·012
436	5·735	4·553	+1·182	0·283	0·915	0·952	−0·037
340	5·585	4·792	+0·792	0·342	0·952	0·957	−0·004
			+5·758				+0·173

ompson's *Unification of South Africa.*

assumption of liabilities of the individual colonies by a Union Treasury more than counter-balanced the take-over of colonial assets in so far as the Cape and Natal were concerned, and they readily acquiesced in the not ungenerous proposals of the Transvaal. As far as the Transvaal was concerned, the quid *pro quo* for accepting the major share of financial obligation for the Union's finances was the acceptance of the Transvaal's proposals for the future administration of the South African Railways and Harbours.

These – largely drafted by Philip Kerr as a supplement to the Selborne Memorandum – provided for the Railways to be administered as 'commercial undertakings' and not used 'as instruments of taxation', while rates were to be kept as low as possible with no unreasonable preferences. Commercial and industrial interests in the Transvaal strongly favoured these principles. With minor modifications, they formed the relevant sections of the Act of Union.

The actual wording of Sections 128, 129, 130, 131, 132 and 133 provided, however, for just that degree of ambiguity which enabled subsequent politicians to render nurgatory the intentions of the Selborne Memorandum to free the future railways of Union and its rating policy from political jobbery and influence. The removal of all impediments to internal free trade was, of course, implicit in unification. In the course of time the Union's external customs tariff policy was to become a major cause of dissension but the conflict of interest was not inter-colonial or inter-provincial.

In the financial and railway discussions of the National Convention, it was recognized that the Transvaal held all the aces. Trouble started only when the Transvaal produced the joker in the pack. This was the guaranteed share of the Rand railway traffic for the rail line through Lourenço Marques at Delagoa Bay. The Transvaal Government had been negotiating with the Portuguese authorities for a new Mozambique Convention to replace the old *modus vivendi* of Milner. The new treaty provided that Lourenço Marques would be assured of at least 50 per cent of the gross tonnage of commercial seaborne traffic destined for the Witwatersrand.

The reaction of the Natal and Cape delegates, when Botha requested that the Mozambique Convention be accepted as binding on the forthcoming Union of South Africa, was one of the keenest disappointment that unification was not to confine the lucrative Rand imports to Union ports only.

Once again, however, it was the turn of the economic factor to exercise its imperatives over the newly emerging polity. The continued supply of African labour from Portuguese East Africa was vital to the gold-mining industry, more especially as the last of the indentured Chinese labour were being repatriated. Over 50 per cent of the unskilled – African – labour employed by the Transvaal gold-mining industry in 1910 came from Portuguese territory by agreement with the Portuguese Government. By 1910 the gold output of the Transvaal mines had reached the then post-war record figure of over 7½ million ounces, valued at nearly £32,000,000 and representing 34·20 per cent of total world output.

Without the labour supply from Portuguese Africa, which kept the average African mine-worker's monthly wage at 48s. 7d. and the average White mine-worker's monthly wage at 456s., gold-mining costs would have critically reduced the marginal grade of ore and therefore total gold output. A substantial reduction in gold output would have heavily cut the volume of imports into the Witwatersrand and hence the total quantum of the vital traffic market for Natal's and the Cape's railways and harbours. In addition Natal's and the Cape's own agricultural trade with the Rand would have fallen *parri passu* with the Rand's diminishing gold output.

The coming constitution of the single polity of the Union of South Africa did not give absolute power to that polity to minimize gold-mining costs through the continued supply of the appropriate numbers of unskilled African workers. This depended no less on the external polity of the Portuguese, who would exercise it in favour of the Transvaal gold-mines only in return for the minimum guaranteed 50 per cent share of the Witwatersrand rail traffic through Lourenço Marques.

Hence the Cape and Natal had no alternative but to accept that the Mozambique Convention in its entirety was in the interest of the Union of South Africa and all its provinces – as much indeed as it always had been in the interests of the four separate colonies, though the coastal colonies had not hitherto realized the obvious. The Transvaal – Mozambique Convention, now binding on the Union, had its related undertakings to secure a minimum 50 per cent of the Witwatersrand traffic through Lourenço Marques, 30 per cent through Natal ports and the remaining 15–20 per cent through Cape ports by appropriate modification of railway rates. This was to add one more insoluble problem to the task of the Union's Railway and Harbour Board in its constitutional injunction to administer its state-owned undertakings 'on business principles' and to fix railway rates at a vaguely-defined cost.

The interpretation and misinterpretation of these sections of the Act of Union have from 1910 onwards been one of the main restrictive influences on the economic development of the new political economy of South Africa; a political economy at last unified, after previous abortive attempts, in a definitive instrument of the polity.

The finance and railway provisions of the Act of Union of 1910 are of special significance. Finance is patently one of the key sources of power. Under the Act of Union that power was secured completely and virtually exclusively to the central government of the Union of South Africa. The provincial governments of the Cape, Transvaal, Natal and the Orage Free State – dependent on grants from the Union Treasury and with very limited direct taxing authority – have through their total financial dependence on the central government no real autonomy at all. The centralization of sovereign power in the Union Parliament was far-reaching and, ultimately, to prove beyond limitation.

Those sections of the Act of Union which specify in great detail how the railways and harbours of the Union are to be administered, and how their rating principles determined, are unusual – and perhaps unique – in constitutional law. In one respect they might well be regarded as the peace terms of the civil war between the separate states of South Africa, whereas the peace terms of the same war between the Boers and the British had been concluded eight years previously at the Treaty of Vereeniging.

In another respect those particular sections were an acknowledgement of the crucial importance of transportation to South African economic development. For the common market of South Africa to progress as a political economy, it was necessary for its conflicting elements to be brought within a single polity that would promote the inter-relationships and inter-connections of a unifying market. Mobility of resources is a function of a market price-system. Transportation not only gives movement to resources but its intensification of mobility progressively optimizes the productivity of market-linkage.

It is efficient transport which indeed gives meaning to a common market and reconciles resource-utilization within the market. It is an effective polity which conciliates human relationships. Without efficient transportation there can be no linkage of economic activities and without effective political sovereignty there can be no rule of order. Both are fundamental to the network of a political economy evolving as a peaceful society.

The constitution of an expanding, enterprising market from out of the vast separations of South Africa – the divisions of its human relationships no less than the dispersions of its natural resources – required an Act of Union that would incorporate the instruments of cohesion. A unifying political authority as well as a unifying transportation service was essential for a developing social system. The Union's Parliament and the South African Railways and Harbours were the chosen instruments.

Unfortunately the Act of Union bequeathed its legacy of disunion. The political factor of Afrikanerdom was unsatisfied by its inheritance, while the new White polity almost immediately addressed itself, first, to limit and, finally, to eliminate the inheritance of the Africans.

THE WHITE POLITY
TAKES CHARGE

The White's divine right to rule in the market depended on White control of Parliament and that in turn necessitated guarantee by the ballot box. Land-rights, employment-rights and voting-rights have in consequence been as much part of South African economic history as of South African political history. Once the Whites of South Africa had agreed at their National Convention on the terms on which they would constitute the Union Government for the common market of South Africa, much subsequent parliamentary and administrative energy was taken up with extending land-benefits and employment opportunities for the Whites and in diminishing the voting benefits and opportunities of the Non-Whites.

To entrench the preferential position of the Whites against any egalitarian changes coming from economic development was ultimately dependent on the total disenfranchisement of the Non-Whites. To have the vote was to exercise influence through the polity, not to have the vote was to incapacitate potentiality in the market. The vote conferred economic status and economic status was an open door to social status. Hence the political factor never rested until it had undone what the imperial factor had done. Afrikanerdom came to power on its twentieth-century mandate to disenfranchise those whom the 'outside interference' of the nineteenth century had enfranchised.

The pre-Union position had been long-established. In the Cape Colony a 'citizenship' status had been given to Non-Whites of the Cape by Article 8 of the Cape of Good Hope Constitution Ordinance of 1852. That article contained no reference to race or colour as disqualifications and the *principle* was maintained when responsible government was granted to the Cape in 1872, in the Parliamentary

Registration Act of 1887 and the Franchise and Ballot Act No. 9 of 1892. Despite the steady stiffening of voting qualifications, by 1909 there were in the Cape 142,367 voters (all male) of whom 121,336 or 85·2 per cent were White, 13,611 or 9·5 per cent were Coloured, 783 or 0·6 per cent were Asiatic and 6,637 or 4·7 per cent African [1].

In Natal Colony, the Charter of Natal, 1856, granted the vote to all adult males on property and income qualifications without reference to race or colour. But the early Natal legislators – anticipating by a century the Union legislators in using the letter of the law to annihilate its spirit – passed Natal Law No. 11 of 1865 which disqualified all Africans, except those exempt from Native law, from exercising the vote. Consequently, since the White Natal legislators decided who might be 'exempted from Native law', it comes as no surprise that in 1907 there were in Natal 23,686 registered voters of whom 23,480 or 99·1 per cent were White, 150 Indian, 50 Coloured and 6 African. Conjuring tricks that yield 99·9 per cent electorates of appropriate supporters for 'controlled democracy' are not really a twentieth-century totalitarian invention.

The old Transvaal or South African Republic had been even more fundamental. Its Grondwet of 1858 stated clearly: the people desire to permit no equality between Coloured people and the White inhabitants, either in Church or State. This was repeated again and again in for instance Law No. 4 of 1890, which declared: persons of colour, bastards, persons of openly bad behaviour and unrehabilitated bankrupts were ineligible for either Volksraad. In the Orange Free State, the Bloemfontein Convention, 1854, gave voting rights to burghers defined as 'all white persons' born in the State or with residential qualifications.

The so-called northern principle of the Transvaal-Free State was written into the Treaty of Vereeniging, 1902, that ended the Anglo-Boer War. When responsible government was granted to the Transvaal in December, 1906, political rights were given to White adult males only and in June, 1907, when the Orange River Colony was granted similar responsible government, clause XI laid down that voting qualifications were 'for every White British subject of the age of 21 upwards'.

The National Convention had been convened to forge a new, single polity from the Cape, Natal, Transvaal and Orange Free

State. And although the franchise provision was of course a crucial hurdle, it presented no really difficult barrier to such skilled negotiators of constitutional obstacles as Smuts of the Transvaal and Merriman of the Cape. Before the Convention started both had – reluctantly – reached the conclusion that if the Union of South Africa was to be achieved at all the then-existing franchise laws of the several provinces would have to be left unchanged. The obstacle was overcome by the relatively-easily reached agreement not to put the particular hurdles up at all.

It would be left for the Union Parliament to find out, firstly, how high a hurdle did exist and, secondly, that its circumvention would require decades of circumlocution and ultimately subversion. At the National Convention itself, the Africans were not of course represented directly. Botha as prime minister of the Transvaal made it clear that the first duty of the Convention was to bring about the union of the White races of South Africa and any extension of the 'southern principle' of a civilized franchise into the northern provinces was utterly unacceptable. The committee appointed duly proposed that the existing franchise provisions in each of the individual provinces should continue and without much debate, this recommendation became the relevant clause of the Act of Union, entrenched against simple amendment by the requirement of a two-thirds majority of both houses of Parliament sitting together to secure a lawful change [2].

Another critical aspect of the future Union's electoral system, that was to have crucial consequences on control of Parliament and hence on economic development, was the value to be attached to the individual vote. One vote, one value had never prevailed in any of the constituent colonies or republics. The old Cape Colony had substantially favoured the rural as against the urban voter – the extreme being Victoria East with 445 voters to a parliamentary member and urban Woodstock in the Cape Peninsula with 2,691 voters to a member. In Natal the only truly urban constituencies of Durban and Pietermaritzburg were so under-represented – Durban with 1,500 voters returning one member against Alfred County with 389 voters returning two – that the farming element always had the decisive say in Natal politics. In the Transvaal or old South African Republic the complete determination to ensure that political power was always retained by the 'volk' or Afrikaner farmers as against the Uitlanders of Johannesburg, had been a real factor in both the Jameson Raid and the Anglo-Boer War [3]. In the Free State alone, the Boer predominance throughout the all-White, almost wholly non-urban, electorate was so pervasive that no artificial aids were required to support the farm vote.

Among those who gathered at the National Convention, farming interests were well to the fore with the majority of delegates occupationally identified as farmers. Over and above the balancing of the rural-urban voting values, there was perhaps the even more delicate balancing of the representative strength of the former colonies-republics, now provinces, in the Union Parliament. Discussion was heated and occasionally threatened the collapse of the Convention. Section 40 settled an *ad hoc* division which over-represented the smaller provinces of Natal and the Orange Free State and provided for regular delimitation of constituencies that would allow, *inter alia*, for an under or over-loading of 15 per cent either way.

Although some members of the Convention intended that the loading provision would favour the urban rather than the rural vote, the reverse application was equally possible. Over the years the range of discretion of an overall 30 per cent proved distinctly advantageous to the rural constituency. The First Delimitation Commission certainly interpreted Section 40 to justify over-weighting of sparsely populated rural districts so that, according to Thompson, the main urban areas of the Union were given 40 seats and the rest of the country 81; whereas if each province had been divided into equal constituencies those main urban areas would have had 43 seats and the rest of the country 78 [4].

The election for the first Parliament of the Union of South Africa was won by General Botha's Party – only formally constituted as the South African National Party in 1911 and known as the Nationalists, until this label was taken over by General Hertzog when he broke away to form his separate Party in 1913. In the Cape, Botha's Party won 29 seats – all rural and the mainly English-speaking Unionists secured 12 urban and 9 rural seats with one Independent (urban); in the Orange Free State, Botha's Party (known as the Orangia Unie) won 16 out of 17 seats; in the Transvaal Botha's Party (known as Het Volk) won all the rural, 17, seats and 3 urban with the Unionists securing 12 urban and the Labour Party 4 urban seats; in Natal most seats were won by so-styled Independents.

Thompson, after noting the impossibility of trying to estimate the strength of the parties because of the many unopposed seats and the numerous independents, concludes:

What the results did show was that, notwithstanding the 'non-racial' platforms of all the parties, there was a very loose correspondence between 'race' and politics throughout the Union. Every division won by a Nationalist (i.e. Botha's Party) contained a large number of Afrikaners; every non-Nationalist division contained a large number of British South Africans. The overwhelming majority of the Afrikaner electorate had certainly voted Nationalist; the overwhelming majority of British South Africans had certainly voted non-Nationalist. All the Nationalist divisions were rural except three – one in Pretoria and three on the Witwaterstrand, which reflected the beginnings of a townward movement of Afrikaners; all the non-Nationalist divisions were urban except seventeen, which were the only areas where British settlement had taken root on an effective scale[5].

The dominant and dominating representation of Afrikaans-speaking farmers was to give a very particular character to Parliament from 1910 on; and throughout the decades the farmer element, no less than the Afrikaner element, was to exercise a powerful and often decisive influence on the shape – and pace – of the development of the now formally unified economy.

The new Parliament – and all-White polity – very soon turned its attention to land- and labour-utilization and their interconnections. On November 14, 1910, the Minister moved to appoint a Select Committe on Native Affairs (S.C. 3/1910) to investigate the question of African land settlement with reference to the problem of Native squatters on White farms; in the second session of the First-Parliament the Mines and Works Regulation Act No. 12 of 1911 and the Native Labour Regulation Act No. 15 of 1911 were passed.

In an earlier chapter, the South African Way of Life, the manner in which the mining industry of the Witwatersrand achieved the almost unique monopsonistic position in the unskilled (African) labour market was briefly considered. In essence the collective aim of the mine-owners, the Chamber of Mines, was to control the recruitment and remuneration of African labour so as to eliminate inter-mine competition. In respect of labour from outside the borders of South Africa, the WNLA from as early as 1901 by securing sole rights of recruitment was able to effect major economies in the cost of recruitment. This had required the indispensable co-operation of the governments of the supply-territories or supply-sources. Such 'rationalization' of supply through 'one-channel' control had not however been so readily achievable in respect of African labour recruitment from within South Africa. At one period, recruitment costs had been double the actual wage bill.

In order to apply inside the South African polity the cost-reducing, centralized recruitment organization operated outside the South African polity by the WNLA, legislation was necessary. What had not been possible under four separate governments, each recognizing its African labour supply as its most valuable resource, became practical politics with the establishment of the single Union Parliament.

The Native Labour Regulation Act No. 15 of 1911 legislated the conditions under which the supply of African labourers to various centres of work in South Africa would take place. In introducing the second reading [5a] the Minister of Native Affairs (Mr Henry Burton) declared that the South African Government 'in no sense whatever would make itself responsible for the recruiting of natives'. But an Act was necessary to consolidate existing laws to achieve a simple, uniform method and to eliminate malpractices – especially in respect of advances – by licensing labour agents and runners, who would be authorized to recruit labour for mining and all other activities other than farming, irrigation and of domestic service. That malpractices existed, which the Act would eliminate, was true and substantiated by the welcome given in the debate to its provisions by T. L. Schreiner, the member for Tembuland and unquestioned friend of the Africans, who acknowledged in refuting accusations of 'slave labour' by Creswell, the member for Jeppe, that 'on the whole, the goldfields and diamond fields had been beneficial to the Africans'. The Act however not only helped to end some of the abuses of the advances-contracting system and safeguarded unsophisticated tribal labourers against the misrepresentations of the unscrupulous (who on occasions included tribal petty chiefs and headmen to whom concession 'fees' for permission to recruit were often irresistibly lucrative). The Act also contained clause 13(c) which provided that:

No person (whether the holder of a licence or permit under this Act or not) shall by offering higher wages or greater benefits or other inducements, persuade or attempt to persuade any native who has been lawfully recruited to desert or repudiate having been so recruited or to break or repudiate any then existing and binding contract of service, whether or not the contract be in writing. . . .

81

The intention of this may have been the legitimate one of preventing an African labourer from breaking a contract into which he had knowingly entered and being induced to do so by another labour-recruiter or prospective employer. But it also served as a powerful legislative re-inforcement of custom in inhibiting competition among employers from increasing wages and related benefits. In particular, it made completely effective the application of the 'maximum average' in the mining industry [6].

Very shortly after the Native Labour Regulation Act of 1911 became law, the Native Recruiting Organization (NRO) was set up in 1912 by the Chamber of Mines to act as a centralizing body for the mining industry for African labour recruitment inside South Africa. It was the sister organization to the Witwatersrand Native Labour Association (WNLA) which had for some years carried out a similar (and solely authorized function) in respect of recruitment outside South Africa. No doubt the NRO by diminishing imperfections on the market supply side for African tribal labour from, say, the Transkei did secure a real reduction in labour costs. But, armed with the legislative prohibition clause 13(c) on using competition from the demand side to bring about increased wages or benefits among recruited African labourers, the NRO as the instrument of the Chamber of Mines could legally enforce the inter-mine or inter-mining-employer agreement not to increase African wages above the calculated 'maximum average' of earning.

Whether or not the 'maximum average' clause promoted or retarded the economic development of South Africa through frustrating attempts to improve the productivity of the individual African mine-worker must be left to a later chapter. The point here is that though the Native Labour Regulation Act of 1911 may have contributed to 'perfection' of the African labour market on the supply side, it underwrote the grossest imperfection of that market on the demand side.

Almost concomitant with the above Act, the first Parliament in its early session also passed the Mines and Works Act No. 12 of 1911. In this particular case General Smuts was in charge as Minister of Mines. His biographer, Sir Keith Hancock, whose reference to the rapid *rapprochement* between Smuts and the mining capitalists has already been noted, write as follows:

In the debate on the Mines and Works Bill, 1911, which Smuts himself piloted through Parliament, Clause 15 of the Bill, when one views it in the long perspective of South African history, was explosively political, for it provided the means of embedding the industrial colour-bar in the law of the Union. Yet Smuts told Parliament that the Bill was purely technical. That, no doubt, was how he saw it. No speaker arose to point out his mistake. It may well be that the members of the other provinces looked upon this Bill as the domestic concern of the Transvaal, while the Transvaal were so used to the colour bar they took it for granted . . . . The clause which Parliament did not think worth debating contained the seed of revolution[8].

It must be accepted that nothing in Smut's private papers nor other available evidence discloses that the normally highly percipient Smuts, already known as Slim Jannie, perceived that his technical measure was providing for the administrative application of the colour bar to skilled and semi-skilled work in the mining industry. Yet Clause 4 (l) (n) authorized regulations to be made by the Governor-General in respect of the grant, cancellation and suspension of certificates of competency to mine managers, mine overseers, mine surveyors, mechanical engineers, engine drivers, miners entitled to blast and such other classes of persons employed in, at, or about mines, works, machinery as the Governor- General may from time to time deem it expedient. . . .

The exercise of such administrative jurisdiction to implement a *de facto* restriction of skilled and semi-skilled categories of mining work to Whites had already been practised in the Transvaal. It is somewhat difficult to credit that Smuts with his knowledge and experience of pre-1910 conditions on the Transvaal gold mines did not recognize that he was at least legalizing the continuation of the customary colour demarcations of mining jobs. It is rather more likely and more in character that Smuts was indulging in his proclivity for not letting the left hand of the legislator know – or at least publicly acknowledge – what the right hand of the administrator proposed to continue to do.

Certainly Hancock is correct that Smuts did not see he was sowing the seeds of his own downfall, and of the complete conquest of the polity by Afrikanerdom. But Smuts, however much the political realist, is not accorded by any of his biographers with an intellectual interest in economic analysis. He was unlikely to waste time thinking through the possible future course of economic rationality or least-cost substitution of labour in the light of unpredicted world price-cost relationships of gold – and to weigh the impact of such unknown developments on current political pragmatism.

Neither Smuts nor Botha, as already noted, had been prepared to accept the recommendations of the Transvaal Mining Commission (now being pressed with vehemence in the parliamentary debate itself by Creswell) to bring about an all-white labour force for both unskilled and skilled work on the mines. But Smuts certainly did not intend at this stage that the Africans should take on the customary range of job categories, which superior White know-how had obtained for itself. The Minister of Mines surely knew that no formal colour bar reservations of work were necessary in the Mines and Works Act so long as the more informal, and flexible, use of regulations could achieve the same purpose.

The Act, clause 4 (2), empowered different regulations to be made in respect of different Provinces or mining districts of the Union. In the Transvaal and the Orange Free State, accordingly, Regulation No. 285 prohibited the grant of certificates of competency to 'coloured persons', and certificates granted to 'coloured persons' in Natal and the Cape were not valid in the northern Provinces. Other regulations laid down that many types of work were to be done by White men only. In 1920, the Low Grade Mines Commission found the employment of White men was prescribed in thirty-two occupations on the mines employing over 7,000 persons, while trade union influence had added another nineteen reserved occupations employing over 4,000 Whites [9].

Consciously and unconsciously, Smuts was allowing the Chamber of Mines to take charge and the White trade unions to take more than charge of the course of economic rationality with an impact on ideology that was to bring about his own political defeat. Almost simultaneously with the enactment of laws to prevent free competition from advancing the wages and work opportunities of tribal Africans, the Botha Government and Parliament moved to stop market forces from extending land-ownership and land-utilization opportunities among the Africans.

The third select committee appointed by the Union Parliament, S.C. 3 of 1910, was charged with examining the question of African land settlement with special reference to the 'squatting' problem. It recommended a uniform policy throughout the Union for the settlement of Africans on private property and appropriate legislation 'broadly on the lines of the resolutions arrived at by the South African Native Affairs Commission'.

That Commission, it will be recollected, had adopted as its

fundamental proposal legislative control against 'the free traffic in land'. It had expressed itself of the conclusion that if this process (the manifest effort on the part of the Africans to possess land not counteracted by any reluctance on the part of European holders to dispose of it) goes on, while at the same time restrictions exclude Europeans from purchasing within Native areas, it is inevitable that at no very distant date the amount of land in African occupation will be undesirably extended [10].

At a late stage of the third session of the First Parliament, the Government unexpectedly introduced the Native Lands Bill [11]. The debate, of exceptional length, makes most interesting reading [12]. It reflects the consciousness – indeed self-consciousness – that this was the most important legislative act since the Act of Union itself. Speaker after speaker drew attention to the non-representation in the House of those whose major interest was being decided and the great need to have the understanding of the Africans and their co-operation, if not their complete acceptance of the vital proposals.

Yet despite the protestations of good faith and of the honour of the White man, of the consequences for our children and our children's children, of the necessity for the goodwill of the non-represented, the fundamental principle of the Bill goes through. The purchase of land in the open market by Africans over the major part of South Africa is halted. The distribution of wealth, as it was most deeply and emotionally identified by both Whites and Africans – land, is not to be the subject of competition between the Whites and the Africans. That is too impersonal, too risky in allowing the 'undesirable extension of the amount of land in Native occupation' (as the South African Native Affairs Commission had concluded). Instead the broad and indeed detailed distribution of rural South Africa is handed over to that indispensible instrument of polity, the nominated Commission.

As evocatively perhaps as on any later occasion, this early debate reflects the motivations and aims of the White polity and more especially of the spokesmen of the Afrikaner-farmer. Thus E. N. Grobler (member for Edenburg):

It was impossible to delay the solution of the native problem . . . to be sure the Bill did not go so far as he (the speaker) would have desired but at any rate it affirmed the principle of the separation of whites and blacks . . . . At the same time he did not like the system of allocating reserves for natives

. . . the farmers would suffer from lack of labour, and that deficiency would be a growing one. At the present time the farmer had to take off his coat, his children had to go to school, and now his workmen would be taken from him, and he would stand alone. . . . Neither could he agree to the principle of the expropriation of land belonging to whites in order to increase the size of the native reserves . . . there were enormous reserves where the natives could go and live, and if they refused to go there, they should be required to pay a stiff tax. Then they would go and work for white people. . .[13].

And J. van der Walt (member for Pretoria District, South):

When they came to examine history they would see that all whites must stand together, and together draft a law. Johannesburg had been established as a town in 1886, without having any natives in its neighbourhood. To the north of that town they now found thousands of natives on the farms. The men were working on the mines and the women did the farming. The Kafirs no longer dwelt in the bushveld but in the vicinity of the goldfields. Eight miles outside Johannesburg, they could drink as much beer as they wanted. Not only sheep were stolen but also cattle, and when these were sold the money was used for the purpose of buying ground. . . . To the east of Pretoria also they bought ground, and it was said that the money of the natives was as good as that of the whites. But the money of the natives was stolen money. The natives came from Basutoland to the Rand, stole and slaughtered cattle, and then bought land with the money. Should not such things be brought to an end? . . .[14].

Another interpretation was given by P. G. W. Grobler (member for Rustenburg):

The hon. member for Fordsburg had stated that he did not believe there were many natives who would personally buy land for themselves . . . . the natives first as a tribe bought the ground, and after that three or four of them made a plan to buy a farm, for a Kafir was the most absolute communist that existed. Individual natives were now beginning to buy ground for their own use. The hon. member had stated that the economic condition of the native was of such a character, that he could not compete with the white. But did the hon. member know that a native was able to offer a higher price for ground that the white? A native was ready to pay much more because the ground became in fact inalienable. His needs were not very great, and he could easily exist with many others on one farm. That was why the native was able to pay a higher price. . .[15].

What an extraordinary 'economic man' is this tribal African! He is the most absolute communist that ever existed but he finances his capitalistic purchases of White man's land by stealing his cattle as a source of funds. He competes with the White man by paying *more* for land because his needs are not very great, and he competes with the White man by taking *less* for his labour also because his needs are not very great. Undeniably the African competes.

Market competition was indeed forcing the pace of economic development and its shape was already beginning to assume that integrating character to which the ethos of Afrikanerdom now instinctively reacted with: Halt. The *cri de coeur* had already come from Afrikanerdom's newly proclaimed champion, General J. B. M. Hertzog. Breaking with Botha and Smuts, Hertzog declared his faith at De Wildt on December 7, 1912: The time has come when South Africa can no longer be ruled by non-Afrikaners, by people who have no real love for South Africa . . .' [16].

And it was Hertzog, now no longer a member of Botha's Government but already committed to the formation of his opposition National Party at Bloemfontein in January 1914, who entered the Native Lands Bill debate to express the fear of where competition was leading and might ultimately end:

. . . the real danger lay in the strong competition there was today and which there was going to be in the future between the native and the white man. The white man began to feel this more and more, and unless other measures were taken he would eventually, if the present state of affairs continued, be pressed out of South Africa or out of a large part of South Africa. No one could deny that as regards unskilled labour there was no room here at all for the white man. . . . They might attribute this to laziness or to lack of skill, or to any other cause, but the fact remained that the native was the unskilled labourer here, and there, where the white man was still the unskilled labourer in this country, it was where the native had not yet been sufficiently trained. Their [the white man's] foundation had been taken away from them, because the great foundation always lay in the unskilled labourers and those closely related to them. . . . In these circumstances, he emphatically declared that it was their duty, the duty of the white race to preserve themselves, to see that the pressures were not exercised any further. . . .

It was just as much, if not more, in the interests of the natives. It would take the natives not another hundred or two hundred years, but at least five or six hundred years before they had attained the same stage of civilization which the Europeans had attained today. And should they in that time allow the Europeans to sink down or be driven out of the country? They would have to admit that immediately the white man left these shores, the native would go back immensely. Therefore it was essential for them to take up a strong stand, and see to it that the white man kept his ground . . . .

Many people wanted the native to have the vote. He emphatically repeated what he had said before, that in years and years to come the native would not have more votes than he was allowed today under the Act of Union. Why not? Simply because they must take into account the feelings of the people and these feelings would not change. . .[17].

Hertzog's specific introduction of the African franchise issue into this Land debate as early as 1913 is significant. Originally it had been intended by the Government and by the Minister, Mr Sauer, that the key principle of the Native Lands Bill – the prohibition of market competition for land as between White and African – should be applied to all four provinces of the Union. But the constitutional experts pointed out that to prohibit the free traffic in land in the Cape Province would strike at the property qualifying provision in respect of the Non-discriminatory colour franchise of the Cape, entrenched against alteration except by the two-thirds majority of both Houses of Parliament sitting together.

To prevent the Cape Africans from buying and selling land would make it impossible for them to hope to achieve the minimum requisite property ownership, which might qualify them to vote on the common roll of the Cape. Hence the entrenchment of the Cape African franchise in the Union made it possible to apply the restraints of the Native Lands Act of 1913 to the Transvaal, the Orange Free State, and Natal – but not to the Cape[18]. General Hertzog was in due course to make this nexus between the Cape African vote and the land, and the cutting of the Gordian knot, the fixed star of his subsequent premiership[19].

THE WHITE POLITY TAKES CONTROL

General Hertzog was, however, not yet prime minister though he had taken the first step by breaking with Botha-Smuts and forming his own political party at Bloemfontein. There, in January 1914, the political factor of Afrikanerdom was given organizational structure and the National or Nationalist Party launched on its ultimately triumphant career. The evocative magic of Paul Kruger passed to James Barry Munnik Hertzog.

In Kruger's time, the explosively adaptive forces of economic development exerted by the Witwatersrand mining industry produced such tensions that the social system of South Africa disintegrated into the war of 1899–1902. Throughout the next twenty years the tensions coming from the Rand mines continued to be barely manageable until the pursuit of an economically organized mining industry so strained the patterns of established expectations and status as to explode in another, minor, 'civil war'. General Hertzog had been on the losing side in 1902. He was to emerge with ruling authority and power in South Africa in 1924.

Economic exploitation of the extensive but low-grade, gold field uncovered in the virgin veldt at a time when neither the political system nor the economic system, nor hence the social system, of Southern Africa had reached any measure of sophistication, was not to be achieved in a hurry. But neither the capriciousness of capital supply nor the inconstancy of labour supply slowed the urgency of producing profits. On the contrary they aggravated the problems in an era when entrepreneurial zest generally exceeded managerial zeal.

The economic detail of the attempts to maximize productivity on the goldmines through the application of least-cost combinations of labour will be examined later. The Witwatersrand mining industry was patently structuring the country's political economy. It related party politics to welfare economics in a society in which White politicians spoke for White voters. It forced the labour mobilities of integrating industrialization on the social rigidities of disintegrating agrarianism. It was the political reaction of British trade-unionism and Afrikaner nationalism, the combination of work-fund restrictionism and grass-roots isolationism, to such economic rationality that enabled the White polity to move from being in charge to being in control of the South African economy.

Poor labour relations erupting into violence seem almost pandemic to the world's mining industry. The Rand mines from an early stage showed no immunity. Mining employers on the Rand – as elsewhere – strenuously resisted recognition of trade unionism as a legitimate bargaining organization. By 1913 only one craft union was recognized. Because of this or in spite of this, industrial unionism made rapid headway among White workers under the leadership of non-South Africans, many of whom were syndicalists.

The motivating aspirations, or value-orientations, of such leadership in the contemporary environment of colour-conscious South Africa were starkly displayed by the evidence of the general secretary of the Miners' Union to the Dominions Royal Commission:

The Kaffirs ousted the aboriginals ahead of him, and the Bantu ousted the Hottentots, and the Dutchmen ousted the Kaffir, and we are now trying to oust the Kaffir from those spheres of industry which we maintain are the proper sphere of the white man. . . . Seeing that the average Kaffir is bred as a slave, he has no right to usurp our position as a free man, or drive us from these mines – we have a right to the colour bar. I hold that the Kaffir should be allowed to get free, but in the interim, as he is here only as a semi-slave, I have a right to fight him and to oust him as the Australians ousted the Chinamen and the Kanakas. . . .

Question: Then you would fight and exterminate the Kaffir?

Answer: No, I would drive them down to where they came from. . . . He robbed the land from the Hottentot, and he should be allowed to stay on the land. What we say is that he should not be brought here to compete with the white man on the economic conditions at present existing. . .[1].

The character of industrial violence on the Witwatersrand during 1913–4 is grimly told in the pages of the Witwatersrand Disturbances Commission appointed to inquire into the disorders of June/July 1913[2]. This was the strike which began at the New Kleinfontein Mine and ended in the Carlton Hotel, Johannesburg, where Botha and Smuts met four armed delegates of the Federation of Trade Unions supported outside by thousands of strikers and hooligans. On police information that the mob might sack Johannesburg and permanently destroy the mines, Smuts agreed to the reinstatement of the strikers, a judicial committee to inquire into grievances and the recognition of their trade unions.

In January 1914 there was a violent eruption of industrial militancy, beginning on the Natal coal mines, spreading to the railways and the Rand and followed by the proclamation of a Union-wide general strike. The classic instrument of syndicalist revolution was now being tested in South Africa, writes Sir Keith Hancock in his biography of Smuts. But Smuts, who had used the intervening six months to establish the Union Defence Force, responded with martial law, trained cannon on the Trades Hall, the strikers capitulated and the syndicalist bubble was pricked. The general strike collapsed and Smuts incurred parliamentary rebuke for summary deportation of the strike leaders.

The immediate reaction of the White electorate of the Transvaal was to give the South African Labour Party its first and only (provincial) political majority. This was in the Transvaal provincial election in March 1914. The intensity of conflicting emotions about 'true South-Africanism', but in a context unrelated to 'colour', manifested itself in the abortive and easily-suppressed rebellion against the Government in September 1914, after Botha and Smuts 'took England's side' in the First World War [3]. Though the rebel leaders – who included a former Cabinet Minister and very senior defence force officers – received little support in the field, it was from this time on that Botha-Smuts were with increasing bitterness and effectiveness represented as 'traitors to their own people' in party political propaganda [4].

Significantly in the 1915 general election Hertzog's National Party, beginning with five seats in the House in 1912, won 27 constituencies and every seat except one in the Orange Free State. The Botha-Smuts party got 95,000 votes but Hertzog already had 77,000 of the electorate behind him. The political dynamism behind Afrikaner nationalism was obvious, though during these years of the Great War its anti-English venom precluded an overt political alliance with the South African Labour Party of largely English-speaking trade-unionists led by Col. Creswell, who served with distinction under General Smuts himself.

But the Great War over and the beloved Botha dead, the now world-statesman Smuts had already a vision and awareness of holistic humanity that fatally exposed his philosophic and political detachment from the South African *veldt* to the remorseless emotionalism of Hertzog's isolationism and colour-consciousness. In the March 1920 general election Hertzog's Nationalists with 44 seats out-ranked Smut's own South African Party of 41 and only a working agreement with the almost entirely English-speaking Unionists enabled Smuts to survive as a minority government.

In that same general election the Labour Party of Creswell achieved its high-water mark total of 21 seats. This success as much as anything pointed to the future course of South African politics and to the conflict between ideological tradition and economic rationality. In the South African environment of colour the former was undefeatable at election time.

The post-war world-wide inflation struck critically, and potentially catastrophically, at the generator of the South African economy – the gold-mines of the Witwatersrand. The political impact was a resumption of pre-war industrial strife but now even more ideologically identified with the war between the classes and the 'clash of capitalism and communism'. A few weeks before the election of 1920, the White mine workers came out on strike and three days after it was settled, 30,000 to 40,000 African mine-workers followed their example but with less success in securing increased wages. African industrial unrest continued and a Native Labour Union's demands in Port Elizabeth led to violence with serious loss of life. Shortly after police action against a religious sect of Black Israelites at Bulhoek in the Cape ended in the death of 300 Africans.

Turbulence was producing growing violence in South Africa. An appeal by Smuts for all 'moderate South Africans to join him' at a Conference in Bloemfontein, which went unanswered by Hertzog's Nationalists, resulted in a coalition of the South African Party and the Unionists. This combination plus growing concern at labour syndicalism gave Smuts the overall majority of 71 against the Nationalists 45 and Labour 9 in the election that Smuts forced in February 1921.

The potentialities of Black Peril [5] campaigning had however already shown themselves in the 1920 election, when the faked picture of a Griqua or Hottentot soldier with a French bride and a related poem allegedly by Smuts welcoming the pair to South

Africa was widely publicized in the anti-Smuts press and in leaf-lets[6]. Such obvious electoral exploitation of the most deeply hidden complexes of racial emotions was enhanced by the compara-tively slow growth of the economy since Union. In human terms this showed itself by the continuing decline of a frightening propor-tion of the population into poor Whites and poor Blacks.

The Transvaal Indigency Commission of 1908 had found it impossible to arrive at an estimate of the numbers of indigent Whites but it was firm on the main underlying causes – a deep-rooted aversion to manual labour and the unprogressive farming tradition. It had written that indigency in the Transvaal was due to two main causes – to the attitude of the people towards manual labour and to certain traditional ideas with regard to the use and ownership of land; and it had stated that no cure for indigency which neglected those two fundamental causes could really be effective.

Poverty will remain, and will grow worse so long as the white man con-tinues to regard manual labour as beneath him, and to remain content with the traditional methods of dealing with the land. . . . It is not in the parti-cular law or institutions that its roots lie, but in the habits and outlook of the South African people. . . . If health is to be restored to society in any part of South Africa, it must be because the white people have become alive to the necessity of becoming more vigorous in its habits and of changing the ideas which have dominated it for so long[7].

In its second intermin report, the Unemployment Commission of 1921 dealt with measures to prevent the influx into the larger centres of those Whites without skilled training which, said the Commis-sioners, amounted to an inquiry into the 'poor White' problem. It stated there was no reliable estimate of numbers but put the figure at 120,000. The Commission wrote:

Its essential characteristics have not changed since the publication of the Report of the Transvaal Indigency Commission of 1908, that of the Select Committee of 1913, and of the Relief and Grants-in-Aid Commission Report of 1916; the only change being that it has become more pressing than ever before, and it is now so serious a social and economic evil that immediate and comprehensive measures should be taken effectively to deal with it[8].

Ten years later, in 1930, so little improvement had taken place that a special grant from the Carnegie Foundation was obtained through the influence of an American sociologist appalled by the social problem of Poor Whiteism he had found in South Africa. The result was perhaps the most exhaustive, and sympathetic, sociological study to be undertaken in South Africa. The Carnegie Commission on Poor Whites reported in five volumes. From question-naires sent to almost half the white schools in the Union, covering 72,844 families, 17·5 per cent of families were classified as 'very poor' i.e. supported largely by charity in cities or existing in dire poverty on farms.

'If we apply the same percentage to the total European population – just over 1,800,000 in 1931 – more than 300,000 (as a conserva-tive estimate) of the white population were 'very poor'. These figures were obtained in 1929/30 before the effects of the present depression were so noticeable' [10]. The joint observations declared that the problem was primarily a failure of adjustment to modern conditions – due in a measure to inadequate education in the rural areas and went on:

With many of the poor, a very marked tendency to dependance, especially on the State, has been created. This attitude was not formerly characteristic of the people. The sense of dependence is very noticeable in such matters as: the gratis provision for the board and education of children, sometimes even of books and clothing; child welfare; providing the unemployed with work; provision of food for housing; provision of land and stock on easiest terms; gratis care of the sick and aged; relief of distress due to catastrophic events; advances on farm produce; protection against the competition of the Non-European, especially of the native, on the labour market[10].

The Commission declared itself to be convinced 'that much of the assistance is given in such a way as to have a demoralizing effect on poor Whites and so increases the difficulty of their rehabilitation. It causes loss of independence and may imbue them with a sense of inferiority, impairs their industry, weakens their sense of re-sponsibility, and helps to make them dishonest' [11].

But the poor Whites had votes. And the Carnegie Commission, especially Professor Grosskopf who was responsible for the volume on economic aspects, had the academic integrity to state baldly what was common knowledge but normally neither polite nor politic to acknowledge:

Since 1910 party politics have brought about more and more harmful results. Practically all the White indigents have the vote, and in several constituencies they hold the balance. Public men, who do not realize their responsibility or only consider election chances, have increasingly created wrong ideas and foolish expectations in the minds of the poor. Men who are returned on the strength of election promises are obliged to use all their personal and political influence to obtain something.

The dangers and temptations are greater in a country like ours where the constituencies are small (in 1929 on an average 3057 electors for each member of the Legislative assembly). Instead of a healthy sense of civic duty, a tendency seems to develop to make use of the vote for personal interests. Nearly every parliamentarian should be able to cite cases of men threatening to vote for his opponent, if he could not procure this or that for them.

And then, goes on Professor Grosskopf:

A large proportion of the poorer settlers on state land in the northern Transvaal are firmly convinced that they owe their land to a definite political party, and therefore consistently vote for the party under whose rule the allotment took place[12].

The insuperable difficulties, which faced the Commission appointed under the Native Lands Act of 1913 in acquiring additional land by purchase for Africans in fulfilment of specific Parliamentary promises (which is elaborated in the text later), arose from this critical interconnection between the Poor White value-orientation towards land and his highly persuasive vote.

In his Sociological Report, Part V of the Carnegie Commission on Poor Whites, the Rev. J. R. Albertyn of the Dutch Reformed Church was if anything more blunt:

The Poor White Commission in almost every one of hundreds of interviews with the poor throughout the whole Union put the following question to the man after hearing his grievances: 'Well, what in your opinion is the solution of your troubles?' And in almost every case the reply was 'The Government must do this or that', until the matter became almost ludicrous. . . . So conspicuous is this habit of expecting too much from the State, that even visitors from other countries have been struck by it. A well-known sociologist from America after a visit of some months to our country expresses himself as follows: 'With the possible exception of Russia, I know of no country where dependence on the Government is greater than in South Africa. . .'[13].

In a special section on the Influence of the Poor Man's Vote on the State's Policy, the Rev. Albertyn said:

If it were the law that any indigent person receiving a certain measure of State relief, would automatically lose his vote, the efforts for his rehabilitation would be less prejudiced. The fear of disenfranchisement would also act as a wholesome deterrent against the seeking of State aid and as incentive to self-help. At present, however, even the person who is totally dependent on the State for his existence, has the vote, and so at least one of the means of breaking down the spirit of dependency remains inoperative.

But the law did not so exclude any White male, however poor, while Parliament was already moving towards the exclusion of every Non-White, however rich. The disenfranchisement of all Non-Whites was to occupy Parliament more than thirty years and it was only in 1956 that the Cape Coloured voter was to lose his hundred-year old right on the common roll. But by 1924 the White polity had taken unchallengeable control of economic development of South Africa – certainly of its shape if not of its pace.

The combination of the voting power of the poor rural White and the urban skilled White presented their respective leaders, Hertzog and Creswell, apparently widely differentiated by their ideologies, with the prospect of power. It required only their Pact to convert the prospect into the prize. The increasing failure of the poor Whites, almost entirely Afrikaans-speaking, to adapt to change strengthened every year the minority influence of the Nationalist party and its leader Hertzog; the increasing resistance of the urban skilled Whites, mainly though not entirely English-speaking, to the consequences of change extended the marginal political influence of the Labour Party and its leader Creswell. In due course the combination of minority with marginality added up to majority.

An anecdote of the time tells more than chapters of elucidation. Hertzog and Creswell 'were too busy hating Smuts to worry about such trifles', i.e. Labour's views on the socialization of the means of production. Creswell had addressed in English a meeting on the Platteland on socialism and trade unionism and at the conclusion of his speech Mr Louis Karovsky, a Labour extremist but a great personal friend of Tielman Roos (leader of the Nationalist Party in the Transvaal), rose to give a short summary in Afrikaans of what had been said: He stated as follows: 'The Leader of the Labour Party has just explained that his policy is to put the nigger in his place and to repatriate all Asiatics'. There was wild cheering and Col. Creswell, who knew insufficient Afrikaans to understand his interpreter, was carried shoulder-high to his car' [14].

Such a bald interpretation of the motivations of the leadership of the South African Labour Party would be unfair. But the degree of physical violence with which White labour on the Rand was only too prepared to resist a competitive market in mining labour, or the application of least-cost substitution by an industry in a price-cost squeeze, could leave no politician – as distinct perhaps from a statesman – in doubt of what would secure the plaudits and votes of a White electorate.

The Department of Mines and Industries in its annual report for 1913 had drawn attention to the syndicalist character of the trade union movement of the time. It quoted from a study of the trade union movement in South Africa and of leadership 'views' as follows:

Labour produces all capital . . . whereas capital is entirely dependent for its existence and use on labour . . . the Labouring Class is now educated and combined sufficiently to take the place in the world to which its majority entitles it, to reverse the former position, to rule the country and the civilized world, and to dictate conditions of service, justice and life to the 'Upper Class', who will then be reduced to their proper position of servants to the masses . . . the above facts being demonstrably true and axiomatic, it follows that it is the moral and religious duty of every workman to be discontented with his present lot, and in every way aid the exertions of his leaders in overturning the existing order of things by any means in their power, in order that the new structure of society may be built on its ruins[15].

The Mines and Industries Report commented: 'The above creed, which is not over-stated, represents what is believed to be the ruling motives of many Labour leaders . . . . A similar feeling is undoubtedly moving everywhere in the world, but it is extraordinarily accentuated in this country, [both] by the aristocratic feelings produced in the white workers by their social superiority over the coloured workmen . . .'[15].

The most graphic account of the 1922 Rand Strike appears in the biography of Smuts by Sarah Millin[16]. Its revolutionary character is most authoritatively evidenced in the Martial Law Inquiry Judicial Committee appointed by the Smuts Government after it had been intensely criticized in Parliament. The chairman of this Committee, T. Lynedoch Graham, noted that his examination was inhibited by the simultaneous judicial proceedings against many strikers. The Judical Committee found that the coal mines stopped work on 1 January 1922, and work ceased on the gold mines, power stations and town engineering shops on 10 January[17].

A resolution of the Central Strike Committee of the South African

Industrial Federation (in an undated circular), the Judicial Inquiry reported, read:

Whereas it is desirable and imperative that Commandos of the following three sections of the white community, inhabitants of the Union of South Africa, be immediately formed and raised with the object of protecting the interests of all white workers namely (a) Strikers' Commandos, (b) Unemployed and (c) Employed.

And whereas it is essential and the time has arrived to fundamentally establish this country as a white man's country: it be resolved:

That Commandos of all sections of (a) strikers (b) unemployed (c) employed of the white community of the Rand be immediately formed with branches in each township under officers to be elected by each platoon . . . [18].

Following this, the Judicial Inquiry found that:

The Movement spread like a flame and upon the outbreak of the Revolution in March there was scarcely a township along the Reef without its Commando [with elected officers with rank badges, signalling corps, exercises in bombing]. By the 9th of March a General Staff had been established. . . . It is stated that as the movement grew the personnel of the force also changed . . . the moderate element amongst the strikers . . . withdrew from it. . . . It is also stated that at the outbreak of the Revolutionary phase of the srike, the bulk of the men forming the rank and file of the Command and practically all the Commandants, were Dutch South Africans who have adopted the politics of the Nationalist Party [19].

Percy Fisher, a member of the South African Communist Party and the leader of the Council of Action, indulged in numerous inflammatory speeches, which included:

'A man had suggested that General Smuts should be shot. He told that man to go and kill him himself. . . . We are out to win this fight and by God we will, if we have to raze Johannesburg to the ground [20].

Towards the end of February a secret meeting was held in the Town Hall, Boksburg, of all the Commandants on the Rand at which he (Percy Fisher) was present. At this meeting . . . the Commandants were instructed to report how many men had arms and had explosives, and at the same meeting a proposal was unanimously carried that a South African Republic be formed and that the present Government be overthrown.' Mr. Waterston M.L.A., the Judicial Inquiry found, associated himself with the movement and was styled General O.C. Commanding Brakpan Commando. On the 5th February Mr. Waterston had attended a meeting of some 3000 persons in the Town Hall of Johannesburg and proposed the following resolution: 'That this mass meeting of citizens is of opinion that the time has arrived when the domination of the Chamber of Mines and other financiers in South Africa should cease, and to that end we and the members of Parliament assemble in Pretoria to-morrow to proclaim a South African Republic and immediately to form a Provisional Government for this country'. The resolution was carried practically unanimously and the meeting terminated with the singing of the Red Flag and the Volkslied [21].

. . . On the 10th of March the Brakpan Commando, now under the command of another officer, since Mr. Waterston was attending Parliament, marched to the mine, attacked it and killed four of the officials, as well as the commanding officer and three special police and one native . . . [22].

Throughout the disturbances the casualties numbered 153 killed and 534 wounded.

The Commission said it was informed that, of the labour forces employed upon the Rand at the outbreak of the strike, 75 per cent were Dutch South Africans, a considerable majority of whom were stated to belong to the political party known as the Nationalists. To these men, went on the Commission, the cry of a White South Africa made a profound impression; for in the Northern Provinces of the Union the prejudice against the black races of South Africa is still extreme. Encroachment by coloured men upon any form of work which has hitherto been performed by Europeans, in any industry, is jealously safeguarded . . . .

The cry of a White South Africa, and the feelings it aroused amongst a large body of workers, were skilfully exploited by the Trade Union leaders and by certain political parties. . . . Whether the leaders of the strike movement were genuine in the belief that under the proposals of the Chamber of Mines, the future of the white workers in South Africa was threatened by the black man is open to grave doubt, but that most of the followers were under this impression is beyond question . . . [23].

Even the Church added fuel to the smouldering fire. On January 19 the Rev. Oosthuizen addressed a meeting at Brakpan estimated at 2000 and is reported to have said: 'Their forefathers had fought for a White South Africa but upon the 15th December, the Chamber of Mines had declared there should be a black South Africa [24].

Again on 3 February, at a meeting in the Town Hall, Johannesburg, the Rev. Hattingh is reported to have said:

The Government is only prepared to do what the Chamber of Mines told them. In order to fill their pockets, the Chamber of Mines were murdering the workers; if the colour bar was abolished, the souls as well as the bodies of the workers would be murdered and the authority of the White race in South Africa come to an end [25].

The Inquiry Commission also reported evidence of deliberately organized attacks on Africans designed 'to stampede them and to give the impression that a native rising on the land was imminent' but the Commission found that 'the behaviour of the natives before and during the disturbances was most exemplary, and that there is no evidence, upon which any reliance can be placed, that any of them gave any occasion for the assaults made upon them, notwithstanding the wanton and unprovoked attacks to which they had been subjected on numerous occasions' [26].

Martial law and vigorous action by Government forces restored law and order. Percy Fisher and H. Spendiff, professed Communists and the leaders of the Council of Action whose object was 'the abolishment of capitalism', both committed suicide in March. The details of this crisis phase in South Africa's economic development are analyzed subsequently. The account here, with its extensive quotations from official and non-official sources, is not intended to over-emphasize the excitability of language and political extrovertism but to give an authenticated impression of the interactions between racial feelings, the uninhibited struggle for political power and the crunch of economic stagnation [27].

The economic malaise and its tensions are reflected in the Report of the Unemployment Commission of 1921 appointed to inquire into the extent, causes and remedies for unemployment, and means of preventing the influx from country to towns of persons without skilled training. It found that Whites from the country were attracted to towns by money wages which 'appear almost fabulous . . . he [the rural poor White] has no notion of house rent and the increased cost of living that awaits him, and is, therefore, not deterred by any such considerations. Letters from irresponsibles in the urban centres to their relatives and friends in the country telling them of high wages, pleasant life, plentiful opportunity, play no small part in attracting from the country simple folk to whom they are addressed' [28].

This Unemployment Commission found that a push effect was being exerted in the country-side by the lack of educational and training opportunity, the want of suitable land for cultivation and the insecurity of tenure, the natural conditions of adverse climate and sub-division of farms resulting in population pressure [29]. Although the Commission was to recommend that the State should facilitate land purchases for and by this class of White bywoners, there was no question of applying those measures of 'influx control', which later became the key feature of government policy to prevent the almost identical pull-push effect on landless poor Africans entering the 'urban areas'.

The poor Whites might not have training nor even education nor still less property. But they did have votes. No actor on the local political stage knew more instinctively how to interact with the emotions of Anglo-Boer War defeat and despair, of Black Peril fears and competitive frustrations, no one was more sincerely and completely convinced that the White polity must take charge of South Africa than General Hertzog, Nationalist Party leader[30]. This last conviction was undoubtedly held by many other leading political actors, including Col. Creswell, the Labour Party leader and long-time champion of all-White labour policies.

The political implications of the Rand Strike of 1922 had indeed been perceived clearly enough by the Secretary of the Communist Party. W. H. Andrews in a letter to another Communist Party member in Australia wrote: 'The political aspect of the strike is disclosed by the *rapprochement* between the Labour and the Nationalist Parties, loose and unofficial at present, but it is possible it may develop into a working agreement on the lines of complete autonomy and independence for South Africa'[31].

Perhaps because he had so recently occupied a leading role on the much greater stage of world politics, Smuts was more conscious of the larger social system in which South Africa and the Rand goldmines were but a part. His experiences in the British War Cabinet and at the Peace Conference in Paris had clearly convinced him of the vast interconnections of human society and especially of the interconnections of the British Commonwealth, including India. He could comprehend the relationships of the City (of London) and the Rand, and indeed of the Rand goldfields and a collapsing world order. He – unlike any other South African statesman before or since – had also had an on-the-spot view of Communism and a disintegrating society under Red or syndicalist leadership, when sent on a mission by the British Government to Hungary and to meet with Bela Kun[32].

In such an atmosphere, the politically fateful by-election of Wakkerstroom was held on 5 April 1924. No constituency in South Africa at that date perhaps mirrored more clearly the working-out of social process. 'It is noteworthy that at the Census of 1921', wrote Professor Grosskopf in his economic analysis of Poor Whiteism in South Africa, 'Wakkerstroom probably the most important sheep district in the Transvaal was the only district in that Province which showed a decrease in European rural population. Between 1911 and 1926 the white rural population of Wakkerstroom decreased by more than 26 per cent' [33]. Sheep, and their more effective shepherding by fencing, displaced people in Wakkerstroom, Transvaal, as they have done elsewhere during the centuries and the White rural population declined from 5,047 in 1911 to 3,988 in 1926.

As a campaign-ground for vote-catching, it was ideal country for the exercise of ideology. The story of the battle is crisply and frankly told in the biography of Hertzog by O. Pirow:

Smuts put up his strongest candidate, Mr. Alfred Robertson, a local man and Administrator of the Transvaal Province. This gentleman was Afrikaans-speaking and a popular and successful farmer. He had only one vulnerable spot viz. his record in the Anglo-Boer War. The Nationalists decided to hit him where he would feel it most and put up against him Mr. A. S. Naude, an unknown farmer but a man who had been shot to pieces in 1900 and lost the use of both legs. Every newspaper in the country took part in the campaign and the South African Party money flowed like water. But nothing could stop the crippled veteran: he won by a majority of over 200 [34].

On 7 April 1924, Smuts dissolved Parliament and in the June 1924 election his South African Party was overwhelmingly defeated. The Nationalists won 63 seats, the Labour Party 18 and the Smuts supporters 53. Smuts himself, and three of his Cabinet Ministers, were defeated at the polls.

Hertzog's Nationalists and Creswell's Labourites formed their Pact Government and from the very beginning left no doubt that the White polity was now in control of the economy and intended to take a very firm hand with the exercise of economic rationality or least-cost substitution in the labour market. The application of least-cost substitution in the mining industry, which led to the 1922 Rand Strike, had been made possible by a Court decision declaring *ultra vires* the clause in the Mines and Works Act of 1911 that had reserved certain occupations for Whites only. The Mines and Works Amendment Act of 1926 restored the legality of the colour bar in the mining industry and the 'civilized labour' policy of the Pact Government established the letter and spirit of the new political economy of labour in South Africa [35].

Prime Minister Hertzog showed soon and clearly his understanding of the legitimate limits of political labour in South Africa. As part of the electoral agreement between Hertzog and Creswell, the South African Labour Party was initially to be given two Cabinet seats and a third as soon as a separate Department of Labour should be established. In due course Mr Walter Madeley, chosen as its nominee by a Labour Party Council vote, was accepted by Hertzog as the third Minister but given the apparently innocuous post of Minister of Posts and Telegraphs. When Madeley however showed more interest in dabbling in trade union matters and – against the specific request of Hertzog – received a deputation from the African trade union, the ICU, the Prime Minister dismissed the errant Madeley [36].

This hastened the break-up of the South African Labour Party into Creswellite and Councilite factions [37]. It was however more than a factional squabble. It was already clear that Afrikaans-speaking workers would find their political identification with Afrikaner nationalism, which had given legislative and administrative proof of its intention and its ability to promote the interests of White workers, who were voters against non-White workers, who were not voters.

The next general election campaign of 1929 made this evident. Smuts in a speech at Ermelo, Transvaal, in January 1929, indulged in that kind of visionary exercise which won him world stature but made it only too easy for Hertzog to knock him off his local pedestal. Smuts thought forwards to the creation of a vast African federation of states, of which the Union would form one. The response of Hertzog was swift and politically annihilating. He countered with his famous – or notorious – Black Manifesto. Smuts was attacked as a man 'who puts himself forward as the apostle of a black kaffir State, of which South Africa is to form so subordinate a constituent part that she will never know her own name no more'.

Hertzog's Nationalists with 78 seats had an overall majority over Smuts's South African Party, 61, and both wings of the Labour Party, 5. Although Hertzog honoured his old alliance with Labour by giving Creswell and another English-speaking Labourite two Cabinet seats, there was no doubt of the triumph of Nationalist ideology in 1929.

In a critical respect, however, 1929 was not 1924. At the earlier date Hertzog's first victory coincided with the end of the world depression following World War 1 and his Finance Minister, Mr

Havenga, was to enjoy an exceptional run of fortune's favours. The rate of economic growth, though not outstanding, was nonetheless adequate to carry the extra costs of, for instance, 'civilized labour' on the South African Railways and also the special basing-point price system to launch the high-cost public utility of the Iron and Steel Corporation.

But late in 1929 economic development was running out in the world at large. The subsequent impact of the Great Depression on South Africa's export industries – gold-mining, wool, fruit, sugar, maize – was so severe that the polity would have to acknowledge the adaptive coercions from the economy. The 'gold standard crisis' not only exposed the very vulnerable interconnections between South Africa and the City (of London) but also that the ideology of White South Africanism had a strong streak of materialism.

The party political intrigue that ensued makes a fascinating chapter in politics as the art of the possible. When Smuts with the magnanimity of the philosopher rather than the pride of the politician agreed to serve under the premiership of Hertzog, the fusion of the warring factions of the White polity was consummated in the United Party. Dr Malan, drawing ever closer around himself the mantle of Afrikanerdom, took Ideology into Opposition there to sit like patience on a monument until yet again the strains of economic growth on institutionalized culture should result in another interchange of power in the White polity.

For the time being, however, this extraordinary political response to the economic pressure of the Great Depression gave the new United Party of Hertzog-Smuts for the first time the critically strategic, more than two-thirds parliamentary majority. With four-fifths of the seats in the House of Assembly, Hertzog as United Party premier was at last able to break through the entrenched enfranchisement of the Africans in the Cape. This is the objective to which he seems to have been committed from the time the provisions of the Land Act of 1913, that established the framework of segregation, could not be applied to the Cape Province because of Section 35 of the South Africa Act, 1909.

The first Union Parliament of 1910 had forthwith superimposed the law over the market for land and for mining-employment. To the extent that the law was initially ineffective in appropriating the land-market and the employment-market for Whites, the political factor sought and gained White votes to strengthen the law and weaken the market. In every parliamentary election, throughout the years, Afrikanerdom sought a mandate for segregation, for apartheid, for separate development – for the extension of the administered society over the market economy so that the structure of the South African social system should never be defined and conditioned by the rate of economic development and the concomitant social progress of the Non-Whites.

To the degree that the franchise rights of the Cape Africans protected their freedom of contract in the market for land and jobs, so the political factor in the person of General Hertzog and the Nationalist Party he founded set itself to diminish those rights. To the extent that the franchise rights of the Cape Coloureds, on the common roll, similarly protected their freedom of contract in the market for – more particularly urban – land and jobs, so the political factor of Dr Malan and his Re-united, or Purified, Nationalist Party set itself to nullify those rights. To the extent that representation of the African peoples by their own communally elected three Houses of Assembly, and four Senate, members secured a voice in the polity, so the political factor of Mr Strijdom and *baasskap* nationalism set itself to eliminate those Native representatives.

To the extent that Smuts from time to time tried to give some token of parliamentary recognition to the Indians of Natal, so his own political influence in his own Party diminished until it contributed to his electoral eclipse in the critical post-war 1948 General Election. The decades of the political factor in action had enabled the Union Parliament to take up and eliminate the tenuous, attenuated franchise rights of the Non-Whites. And to do so in a manner that had the National Convention of 1909, to constitute the Union, then foreseen, would have made a unified South African polity and Union Parliament still-born. The Whites by way of the vote first took charge and then unchallengeable control of the polity.

But what had happened to the network of economic development all this time?

ECONOMIC GEOGRAPHY AND
UNECONOMIC TRANSPORTATION

Even if it is accepted that economic development is a consequence of interaction, it remains a constant non-academic – even perhaps academic – belief that there must be a philosopher's stone which starts the process of transmuting dross into gold. It was South Africa's remarkable, if not indeed unique, good fortune that it could start quite literally with the gold.

What came to be regarded as South Africa's special problem in economic development was how to prevent the gold from reverting to dross.

Entrepreneurial investment, capital accumulation, technological and social change began with the finding of gold. Here was surely the most strategic variable of all for a model of economic growth. But the very dynamic of the Rand goldmines never ceased to plague the expectations of the élite of South Africa – whether those expectations were stimulated and tortured by either ideology or economic rationality.

Those, whose combinations of ideology and economic rationality were politically represented by Hertzog and Creswell, saw the goldmines as attracting to the Rand a vast number of the 'semi-civilized'. These African tribesmen by their very presence and willingness to work for 'uncivilized' wages, would make it impossible for South Africa to survive as a 'White man's country'. Others, who took a more hopeful view of what had been accomplished by van Riebeeck's 1652-boatload of Europeans in peopling a sub-continent, were more concerned to safeguard against the day when all the payable gold ore was symbolized as distinctly unpayable mine-dumps. Their view of the future working relationship between White and Non-White was from the economic development aspect more rationally economic.

If the maintenance of White civilization in South Africa haunted the nightmares and dreams of the ideologically political, so the maintenance of mining marginality haunted the dreams and nightmares of the rationally economic. That one group's nightmares may be another group's dreams has already been touched on in the previous chapter. The fears that least-cost substitution in the gold-mining industry would begin by destroying the economic colour bar and thereby open the possibility for the elimination of social and political colour bars enabled Hertzog-Creswell to win political power from Botha-Smuts.

A more consistent fear was the need to find a substitute for the goldmines as the dynamic of sustained economic growth. Patently the gold provided the energy for take-off – but how ensure that the country stayed taken off? Undoubtedly the almost complete approval of White South Africa for unification was the conviction that, over and above the vital need for 'White unity', a single political control could more effectively promote the growth of the economy through diversification.

Anxieties about how to promote the well-being of the peoples of the newly constituted Union of South Africa were well-founded and serious. Viewed as at 1910, the economy of South Africa must have presented to disinterested and interested observers a pretty problem in skewed development.

Unfortunately to write a detailed economic geography of the new polity is not possible. As the Dominions Royal Commission on Natural Resources and Trade declared feelingly in 1914: 'Another . . . difficulty which meets those who are concerned with agriculture conditions in the Union is that there are no adequate statistics to help them' [1]. Indeed as one reads the two volumes of evidence to this Commission, doubt grows as to the validity of almost all contemporary data other than for the mining industry. No agricultural survey had been undertaken and the so-called agricultural census of 1911 was admitted by officials to be 'most unreliable'. Though a hydrographic survey was under organization in 1914, the Union Director of Irrigation, guessed to the Dominions Royal Commission that 'only 5 per cent in all' of the land of South Africa was suitable for agricultural crops, whether under irrigation or as dry-farming, and that the balance of 95 per cent was essentially pastoral land [2].

The Union Secretary for Agriculture was unable to say and

unwilling to guess at 'what extent of land would be available for closer settlement within the next ten years' [3]. No soil survey had as yet been started. No statistical data whatsoever was available in respect of manufacturing industry [4]. In regard to mining, there was a great deal of detail on operating performance and results but in fact the potential of the mineral deposits and even of the gold ores was largely guesswork, where it was known at all [5]. The frustration which the Dominions Royal Commission repeatedly experienced in trying to give factual content to South Africa's resources must be regarded as in itself a serious obstacle to economic development. Statistical and factual knowledge is a critical part of the infra-structure and the neglect and parsimony of South African Governments in relation to gathering and publishing basic data was one not unimportant factor in the slow rate of resource utilization [6].

The illumination which follows is therefore as much impressionism as realism. The first Union Parliament was taking political direction of 5,973,394 people of all races of which 1,276,242 were White, 4,019,006 were African or Bantu, 152,309 Asiatic and 525,837 Coloured, according to the census of 1911. The White population had evidently increased by about 150,000 only since the previous census of 1904. There were in 1911 only 12·63 persons to the square mile of South African land-area, of whom 2·70 were White and 9·93 Non-White. Only five towns had more than 20,000 White persons each – they were Johannesburg with 119,953 Whites (237,104 total), Cape Town 85,443 Whites (161,759 total), Durban 34,880 Whites (89,998 total), Pretoria 35,942 Whites (57,674 total), Port Elizabeth 20,007 Whites (37,063 total).

One-quarter of the White population was nevertheless occupied in these five towns. The 1911 census gave the occupational classifications – of doubtful accuracy – of the White population throughout the country to be professional 59,721; domestic 290,560; commercial 81,627; agricultural 192,424; industrial 143,255 and indefinite 10,745; dependants 492,959 and unspecified 4,951. The very great majority of Non-Whites were shown as engaged in agriculture or as domestics or as in industry (i.e. mining).

There were in 1911, too, 163,257 White scholars in 3,873 schools and 136,000 Non-White scholars in 1999 schools. The number receiving higher education amounted to 1,171 and total expenditure on education was £1,597,062.

No attempt was made to obtain any complete data for the Union's agricultural production until 1918 and before then figures were admittedly 'incomplete, inadequate and in some respects misleading'. Sheep and wool was perhaps the oldest and certainly the most important source of income from the land. Woolled sheep increased from 11,800,000 in 1904 to 21,800,000 in 1911 and the weight of the wool clip exported had grown from about 40 million lbs in 1875 to over 100 million lbs in 1909 – values of course fluctuated widely. As at the time the Dominions Royal Commission was reporting, ostrich feather exports were second only to that of wool but this somewhat esoteric pastoral pursuit had an obvious high risk factor associated with the fashion preferences of Europe's aristocracy. Mohair, maize, hides and skins, fruit, wine contributed more promise than performance to the country's export trade.

Mineral exports dominated, being in 1913 over 80 per cent of the total. The significance of gold and diamonds to the living standards of South Africans is indicated by the failure of this vast expanse of land as late as 1910 to feed even its sparse population. There were relatively large imports of mutton (nearly $3\frac{1}{2}$ million lbs in 1911) and of pig products (nearly $5\frac{1}{2}$ million lbs in 1911). Although the domestic wheat crop was put at 350 million lbs in 1911, more than 210 million lbs of wheat and wheaten products was being imported to feed the White population. Though sugar cane cultivation had begun in Natal as early as 1850, in 1911 imports still totalled more than 36,000 tons. Tea, too, though grown in Natal, was imported to about 75 per cent of consumption. Viticulture which had begun with the Huguenots in the Western Cape nearly 250 years ago had, through many vicissitudes, declined in quality standards until in 1914 the wine and brandy exports amounted to less than £10,000 while imports of £100,000 were needed to satisfy superior tastes.

In Schumpeterian terminology, it could almost be said that in more than two and a half centuries no 'development' at all had taken place in agriculture. If 'by development we shall understand only such changes in economic life as are not forced upon it from without but arise by its own initiative from within' [7], then most of South African agriculture had not developed. Rather South African agriculture 'in itself without development, is dragged along by the changes in the outside world' [8]. Some growth perhaps there may have been but virtually no development through the carrying out of new combinations of productive means, in Schumpeter's concept of the mechanism of change.

The Schumpeterian entrepreneur or innovator of development is the one who carries out these new combinations – the introduction of a new product or the addition of a new quality to an existing good, the introduction of a new method of production or marketing, the opening of a new market whether or not it existed heretofore, the conquest of a hitherto unexploited though perhaps known source of supply of raw materials, the carrying out of a new organization for any activity [9].

The role of the external entrepreneur and foreign capital – the 'Uitlander' – in the development of South Africa's mineral resources from 1870 is of course well known. What is not generally recognized is that the carrying out of new combinations in land-utilization – both pastoral and crop-cultivation – in South Africa almost from the earliest times until at least 1910 was also very largely the innovating effort of newcomers to South Africa.

As Goodfellow had emphasized in his study of agriculture in South Africa during the last quarter of the nineteenth century, the almost complete absence of contact with either markets or scientific agricultural practice meant that the value of nearly all the land was unknown. According to Goodfellow the Karro in its natural state had been able to develop resources of soil through vegetation appropriate to the action of water on its surface but its great potential had been destroyed or ignored by failure to control the movement of sheep over the steadily denuded veldt. A Mr Southey by experiments on Karroo land in paddocking sheep so as to give different parts of the land rest periods had decades before, about 1870, pointed to the possibilities of a form of pasturage-rotation to allow the vegetation to recuperate [10]. Fencing and selective breeding of sheep was introduced in the late nineties into the more fertile Eastern Province also by newcomers.

Almost without exception those giving evidence to the Dominions Royal Commission on South Africa's agricultural resources and potential were 'Uitlanders'. Whether a Mr Stephen, managing director of the South African Milling Co., speaking confidently of wheat cultivation on the Zak River Estates of the south-western Cape and of supplying in 1912 more than half of the country's current wheat demand, or a Captain H. Noyes reporting on the prospects of euphorbia tirucalli, or a Dr William MacDonald propagating with great enthusiasm the enormous possibilities of dry-farming techniques, or a Mr Howe Browne on his hopes for cotton cultivation near East London, or a Mr F. T. Angus on his early shipments of wattle bark exports, or a Mr H. E. V. Pickstone with formidable assurance on his pioneering success of a fruit export trade from the famous Rhodes Fruit Farms, the overwhelming impression is of the critical contribution of the newcomers as Schumpeterian innovators.

On the marketing side, too, it is largely immigrants with little or no initial capital, who set up country stores and introduced the beginnings of a money-exchange system as an adjunct to a bartering of farmers' needs against farmers' produce. The economic historian will acknowledge the indispensible pioneering role of the immigrant storekeeper and produce-dealer in gathering, distributing and financing marketable produce [11].

But even if it is felt that Schumpeter's interpretation and definition of economic development is too rigorous and circumscribed, the economic growth of South Africa by 1910 was not encouraging to those who saw it either as the latest of His Majesty's Great White Dominions or as the only home of a new White Independent Nation. It was perhaps even more than discouraging to the many millions who, though described as 'natives', were virtually excluded from a vote in the new polity of their native land. To contemporary observers, it must have required neither the non-availability of statistical data for national income calculation nor the depressing evidence of the Transvaal Indigency Commission nor the report of the Economic Commission of 1914 to see that gross output and income per head in the Union of South Africa were unacceptably low.

With the never-stilled Cassandras to draw attention to the 'wasting assets' of the mines, the compulsion to force agricultural and industrial growth by changes from without must have been powerfully strengthened in the minds of the polity by the scarcely evident development coming from within.

Given the economic geography of South Africa at the time of Union, it was believed by some acute observers that transportation could make a positive, even decisive, contribution to development and diversification [12]. The negative contribution which the separate railway systems as the instruments of political autonomy had made to pre-Union conflicts has already been examined. Recognition of the negative past and the positive potential lay behind the great care given by the Milner Kindergarten to try to ensure that a unified railway system for a unified South Africa would serve as a critical factor in preventing development relapsing into underdevelopment.

The non-political control and operation of the South African Railways seemed of the essence. Hence the unusual incorporation of certain basic principles of railway management into the Act of Union itself. The constitutional guarantees to provide for the business operation of the key instrument of the country's economic growth aimed to entrench a non-political management against a likely political interference. Hence section 126 of the South Africa Act provided:

Subject to the authority of the Governor-General-in-Council, the control and management of the railways, ports and harbours of the Union shall be exercised through a board consisting of not more than three commissioners, who shall be appointed by the Governor-General-in-Council, and a minister of State, who shall be chairman

And the very next section 127 proceeded:

The railways, ports and harbours of the Union shall be administered on business principles, due regard being had to agricultural and industrial development within the Union and promotion, by means of cheap transport, of the settlement of an agricultural and industrial population in the inland portions of all provinces in the Union . . .

While to spell out 'business principles', this section 127 went straight on:

. . . So far as may be, the total earnings shall be not more than are sufficient to meet the necessary outlays for working, maintenance, betterment, depreciation, and the payment of interest due on capital not being capital contributed out of Railways and Harbours revenues, and not including any sums paid out of the Consolidated Revenue Fund in accordance with the provisions of sections 130 and 131. . . .

With hindsight and perhaps foresight of the ingenuity of South African politicians in circumventing the spirit of the law, Sections 130 and 131 tried valiantly to provide its letter. The potential divergence of interpretation between (a) determining total earnings not to exceed necessary outlays and (b) promoting development through the settlement of the interior was anticipated. Section 130 provided:

Every proposal for the construction of any port or harbour works or of any line of railway before being submitted to Parliament shall be considered by the Board, which shall report thereon, and shall advise whether the proposed works or line of railway should or should not be constructed. If any such works or line shall be constructed contrary to the advice of the Board, and if the Board is of the opinion that the revenue derived from the operation of such works or line will be insufficient to meet the costs of working and maintenance, and of interest on the capital invested therein, it shall frame an estimate of the annual loss, which, in its opinion, will result from such operation. Such estimate shall be examined by the Controller and Auditor-General, and when approved by him the amount thereof shall be paid over annually from the Consolidated Revenue Fund to the Railway Fund . . .

And to make proof positive, Section 131 said:

If the Board shall be required by the Governor-General-in-Council or under any Act of Parliament or resolution of both Houses of Parliament to provide any services or facilities either gratuitously or at a rate of charge which is insufficient to meet the costs involved in the provision of such services or facilities, the Board shall at the end of each financial year present to Parliament an account approved by the Controller and Auditor-General showing, as nearly as can be ascertained, the amount of the loss incurred by reason of the provision of such services and facilities, and such amount shall be paid out of the Consolidated Revenue Fund to the Railway and Harbour Fund.

These sections of the South Africa Act were devised and virtually written by non-South Africans – by the Milner Kindergarten and more especially Philip Kerr and R. H. Brand. As R. H. Brand had put it: 'A single idea, the prevention of political jobbery and the administration of the railways and harbours . . . on commercial principles runs through all the railway provisions of the constitution . . . it is an attempt to save democracy from itself'.

But the problem of safeguarding South Africans from other South Africans was not so readily accomplished. Neither the attempt to entrench 'business principles' in the management of the railways and ports nor the attempt to entrench the franchise of the Non-Whites was to survive the remorseless erosion by political action.

In respect of the administration of the South African Railways and Harbours, the detail and manner of political manoeuvre is elaborated in S. H. Frankel's study of *The Railway Policy of South Africa* [13]. The first tactic beginning with the appointment of the original railway commissioners in 1911 was to dispute the interpretation of Section 126. This would seem to have had the clear intent that the control or management of the S. A. Railways and Harbours would be by a Board of Commissioners. On that Board the Minister of Railways would be *ex officio* a member but with no more authority other than that of chairman. It was surely intended to be a fully responsible executive Board.

From the outset, however, the Cabinet and the Minister of Railways claimed that the real legislative purpose was that the Board should advise the Minister. The Minister would have complete control of policy and implementation of a solely ministerial evaluation of the conflicting doubts between Administration on 'business principles' and the 'due regard . . . to agricultural and industrial development . . . in the inland portions of all provinces in the Union'.

In 1916 the Railway Board Act provided this characteristic clarification by the polity: Section 126 of the South Africa Act, 1909, as well as every other provision of that Act and every provision of any other law which related to the Board shall be interpreted so that 'the railways, ports and harbours of the Union . . . shall be administered and worked under the control and authority of the Governor-General-in-Council to be exercised through a Minister of State . . . who shall be advised by the Board'. And furthermore that 'the management and working of the railways and harbours shall, subject to the control of the Minister, be carried on by the general manager, who shall be governed by such regulations as the Minister may from time to time frame, after consultation with the Board . . .'

This did not so much open the way to political jobbery as remove any restraint on a ministerial interpretation of what constituted business principles and appropriate development of the economy by the instrument of the state-owned transportation system. The party political abuse of the S. A. Railways & Harbours was probably no worse – it was certainly no better – than is the inevitable fate of any major nationalized undertaking. Indeed the abuse did not have to await the legal demotion of the Board of Commissioners to the creature of the Minister. It began with the first session of the Union Parliament when nearly fifty 'petitions' for branch rail lines were presented, and a great may more for rate reductions.

Nor was the Government itself slow to adopt that flexibility of definition of capitalization, depreciation and renewals which permitted the evasion of the formal obligations of the Act of Union not to overburden the S. A. Railways & Harbours with excess debt charges or unload from the Central Government the responsibility for finding necessary capital. According to Frankel, the excess capitalization of the S. A. Railways & Harbours amounted to about £13,000,000 or an annual excess debt charge of £450,000 by the Central Government against the S. A. Railways & Harbours[14].

Dubious procedures in respect of depreciation allowances and the renewals fund permitted excess depreciation provision to be diverted for the purchase of new rolling stock, which would otherwise have had to be met from additional capital funds subject to parliamentary scrutiny[15]. Ministerial unwillingness to face Parliament with requests for desirable additional capital not only curtailed appropriate development but the Minister of Railways intervened continuously to direct the expenditure of voted capital.

Flagrant parliamentary bargaining in respect of branch line extensions resulted in the Railway Board submitting 'to Parliament reports on proposed new lines of railway couched in the vaguest possible terms, and containing astoundingly inaccurate estimates ... In 1926, out of 70 branch lines, only 10 showed a net profit, 32 paid working expenses but were unable to meet full interest payments, while 28 showed earnings which were not even able to cover working expenses. The total losses on these lines, after the payment of interest, amounted to £526,596'[16].

Opportunism and jobbery in the fifty-year-old administration of the S. A. Railways & Harbours can no doubt be paralleled from the experience of other state-owned transport systems. Venality in vote-buying was not the prerogative of any South African political party. In a Parliament elected by an almost exclusively White electorate and with a distribution of seats heavily loaded in favour of farming areas, no party was ignorant of or immune to the possibilities. Since, for example, both parties when in power carried drought-stricken stock to fresh pasturage without charge, neither had any particular interest in reminding the Minister of Railways of his statutory obligation to recover the costs from the central revenue.

In respect of employing White workers for unskilled labour in place of lower-paid Africans, the Botha-Smuts administration did ensure that the Central Government paid over the differential cost to the S. A. Railways & Harbours. But with the uninhibited implementation of the civilized labour policy by the Hertzog-Creswell Pact Government, the excess cost was evidently too embarrassing to be reflected in a direct charge against the Central Government.

By 1927 the Railway Board itself had minuted to the General Manager of the S. A. Railways & Harbours that the additional cost of the civilized labour policy was not required to be recorded separately even by the S. A. Railways & Harbours itself.

Despite the petty and not-so-petty jerrymandering, the problem of what would constitute the objective realization of managing the South African Railways in accordance with business principles and of giving due regard to the agricultural and industrial development of the interior was a very real and very complex one. The failure of South African farmers and manufacturers to meet the demands of the Rand market was generally attributed to the want of the indispensible communication-transportation system.

The pre-Union railway construction had – for good and obvious reasons – concentrated on linking the ports with the diamond fields and the gold mines. But it had in consequence failed to link potential South African sources of supply with the existing market. To encourage the potentiality of such supply into the actuality of demand was now open to the unified South African Railways Administration. Not to embark on the additional rail-line building and not to adopt the appropriate railage rates might well have seemed to ignore the constitutionally-imposed responsibility to manage the rail system on business principles with due regard to agricultural and industrial development.

Given the difficulties of raising the necessary capital for new construction and equipment, the optimisation of invested capital was a complex responsibility of management. Interference by successive Railway Ministers, excessively aware of party politics, resulted in major wastage and leakage. But the theory of railway rating itself raised most complex principles on which to base the practice of the S.A. Railways even without such vote-motivated complications.

At 1910 what would have been the most appropriate and desirable rates structure? To begin with there was the pre-Union rating structure, which had been evolved by the separate colonial administrations to preserve their respective market positions in a decidedly imperfect market. There was the *modus vivendi* undertaking with Portuguese East Africa to be observed. To ensure a continuation of the vested-interest division of traffic was clearly in the spirit of Union and an obligation that no management, however animated by business principles, could have ignored. But what are business principles in railway rating?

In fairness it must be acknowledged that no theoretical unanimity has probably been achieved even to-day – and in the early part of the century a thoroughly business-like management could have found much academic support for the value-of-service principle or charging what-the-traffic-will-bear. Though the worst mal-practices of discriminating monopoly in railway operation in the U.S.A. had already brought anti-monopoly legislation, it still seemed a powerful argument that by allowing the railways to charge what the traffic would bear, *more and not less* traffic would be carried.

The argument rested on the economics of overhead costs and the consequent economies of spreading such overheads over the maximum demand that could be generated by differential prices related to different elasticities of demand. If demand for rail transport would continue from particular railway customers at however high a rate, whereas no demand for railage would come into being from other customers except at a much lower rate, would not *both* groups benefit by charging different rates? A low rate to bring into being – or allow to continue – the demand for railage from the latter group, who could and would pay only that low rate, did nonetheless generate this additional rail traffic. This additional rail traffic made a contribution to overheads of the railways, which therefore did not have to charge the full total of those overheads against the first group of railway customers, who would continue to demand railage at however high a rate. Hence, because the overheads could be spread, the high rate would at least be less high [17].

By differential or discriminating rates, both groups of rail users – those who could afford high rates and those who could not afford those rates – would benefit. The total reveneues of the railways would be greater and the railways would *presumably* earn greater profits.

For the S.A. Railways Administration the significance of this theoretical case for differential or discriminating rates to the con-stitutional obligation to operate on business principles *and* to promote the development of agricultural and industrial South Africa was clear. Good theory for once seemed to go hand in hand with good politics. Elaborating the classification of goods so that each class of traffic would fall into the rating group which it could and would pay served everybody's best interests – each group of railway customers as well as the national interest of development of the economy through diversification.

A measure of co-incidence between, say, farmers and the low rate group on the one hand and, say, the Rand gold mines and the high rate group on the other hand was, from the Government's view, an even more gratifying coincidence of good practical politics and sound theoretical economics. But was the economic theory as good as the practical politics?

One had only to study the composition of all South African Parliaments and the delimitation arrangements for constituencies agreed to at the National Convention, and subsequently retrogressively modified, to know that to classify all agricultural products and needs in the low-rate groups was good politics. To classify all the needs of the mining industry in the high-rate groups was certainly not bad politics. To classify South African manufactured goods at special rates below the rates charged for railing the identical imported goods over exactly the same mileages was also better politics than charging non-preferential rates.

To devise a scheme of distribution rates so that goods railed 700 miles from an inland centre, such as Johannesburg, to a destination only 300 miles from a port, such as Port Elizabeth, would pay the same railage bill whether sent 700 miles from Johannesburg or 300 miles from Port Elizabeth, was also good politics. Very low rates to promote the export of beans, barley, compressed fodder and forage, kaffir corn, oats, peas, potatoes, milled kaffir corn and maize, wheat, and fruit ranked as exceptionally good politics. Was this highly complicated classification of rates, however, sound railway economics?

The theory is that differential pricing in the case of a monopoly is in the interests of all groups of consumers of the monopoly product, if its supply is subject to decreasing average costs. Under such circumstances discriminating monopoly may, it is argued, yield a larger output than non-discriminating monopoly.

A railway system was long regarded by some economists as the classic example of such a monopoly. Rail rates based on the value-of-service to the rail-user as distinct from rail rates based on the cost-of-service to the railway company would, it was argued, increase the total amount of rail transport supplied and bought. It would permit full utilization of the capacity of the South African Railways, for instance, so that this State-owned enterprise earned the maximum revenue from its existing rail-system at any given time. Simultaneously it would enable all current and prospective rail-users to make use of that rail-system to the limit of the individual user's ability to pay for railage.

The value-of-service rating or charging what-the-traffic-will-bear meant – according to this theory – that no traffic paid more than it was able to pay. No traffic was not offered or not accepted because it was unable to pay the rate charged against it.

If the theoretical argument for such a rating system was valid, then it was indisputably a highly desirable method for the development of the agricultural and industrial interior of South Africa. It would facilitate a flow of goods from dispersed sources of supply to concentrated markets of demand. It would help to link the vast expanses of grazing and crop-lands, especially, with the highly centralized consuming market of the Rand and, by way of the ports, with the world's greatest consuming market at the heart of the British Empire.

Hence the economist in 1910 who accepted the theory of value-of-service railway rating might, all politics set aside, reasonably have seen the South African Railways and a differential rating system as the most important instrument for the simultaneous development and diversification of the underdeveloped and skewed-development economy of the new polity.

Was he right in his theory?

In his *Economics of Welfare*, Pigou seems effectively to expose the fallacies on which the theoretical case for discriminating railway rates had been based by 'railway economists' [18]. Among the latter, Taussig had argued that whenever a very large fixed plant is used for varied purposes, the influence of joint costs or joint supply exerts itself. The initial capital sunk in the railway system and the largest part of the operating expenses, according to Taussig, represent outlays that are common to all or most of the traffic – these costs are regarded as equally incurred to aid in carrying every item of traffic.

Taussig's case was that joint supply operated wherever a large mass of supplementary costs exists together with the fact that the plant is used for varied purposes. While Taussig admitted that joint supply, and hence joint costs, cannot appear where the plant is used to produce a single homogeneous product, he asserted that, in regard to the conditions of demand, the railage of tons of different goods (and even the railage of the same goods for different ultimate use) are different, non-homogenous services or 'products'.

But Pigou emphasized that 'true' or economically significant jointness of supply, such as to result in differential prices even under competition, depended not only on large, common supplementary costs. It was also of the essence that each additional unit of investment must be such that it could not increase the supply of one product without simultaneously and necessarily increasing the supply of the other product or products. If the additional investment could be used to increase the supply of one product *or* the supply of another product, then the products were in *alternate* and not joint supply.

If investment in increasing transportation services is such that it can be made to increase or facilitate the supply of transport for one market or another market i.e. for one class of transport-users or another class of transport-users, then a particular supplier of (i.e. investor in) transport will offer his service to the higher-priced rather than to the lower-priced market. If there is more than one supplier of transport, if there is competition and not a monopoly, the competition between these suppliers will tend to bring transport rates or prices in the higher-priced and lower-priced markets towards a single, uniform price covering the long-run cost of service.

The elaboration of detail of this complex argument is not immediately relevant [19]. What is relevant is that the theory of railway rating did not lend quite the indisputable economic argument claimed for the discriminating rating policy adopted and intensified over the years by the South African Railways Administration. What is even more relevant is that when technical progress made available cost-reducing road motor transport, a dubious railway rating theory had been so compounded by politics as to result in an extraordinary price-diversification between high-rate and low-rate rail traffic. This in turn brought about such a delicate balance in the financial viability of the South African Railways that the Government, with the immense and intricate political stakes vested in monopolistic railway rating and railway operating, found itself compelled to restrict competitive road motor transport to an extraordinary extent.

To operate the South African Railways on business principles with due regard to the agricultural and industrial development of the interior was not to be achieved by the SAR Administration, beginning in 1910, charging what the traffic would bear. Charging the Rand gold mines high rail rates on all their stores and needs, charging Transvaal and Orange Free State farmers low rail rates on all their supplies and requirements, charging manufactured goods high rates and raw materials low rates certainly brought about a re-distribution of the country's resources. But did that re-distribution optimize the rate of economic development as distinct from influencing the shape of development?

It is not a social gain, as Pigou had pointed out, if a railway company by temporary low prices develops the traffic from one district at the expense of destroying the traffic from another equally well-situated district. In this respect low-rate development rail rates have the same justification or lack of justification as protective tariffs. A re-distribution of the utilization of existing resources is not development in the sense of net growth. Even if hitherto unemployed resources are given employment by the protection either of preferential rail rates or customs tariffs, it is the optimization of the deployment of all resources which promotes the most rapid rate of development.

It is not possible *ex ante* quantitatively to prove optimization of resource-deployment and *ex post* judgment must be even more qualitative. In the absence of all political considerations, it would still have been an exceptionally complex task to invest very scarce capital in the SAR & H system so as to optimize the rate of over-all development of the resources of the Union of South Africa. The single most important resource was the gold of the Rand. Gold-mining was both the magnet for the investment of foreign capital and the generator of domestic savings. Capital accumulation and capital investment was highly correlated with *profitable* gold output. Cost increases that diminished current or prospective *profitable* gold output would seem to have reduced the rate of over-all development of resources; cost decreases that increased current or prospective *profitable* gold output would seem to have optimized the rate of over-all development.

The exact 'excess burden' which Frankel calculated was placed on the Rand goldmines by the monopolistic railway rating policy of the SAR, in its pursuit both of political advantage for governments and of promotion of the agricultural and industrial development of the interior of South Africa, may be a matter of dispute. What can hardly be doubted is that South Africa's economic development had waited for decades and perhaps for two centuries on the dynamic of an expanding market. Capital investment in diamond and goldmines brought such markets into being, first in Kimberley and then, much more significantly, in Johannesburg.

The market of the Rand was the integrating factor of South Africa's social system – of its economic relationships no less than of its political relationships. It was the overwhelming factor in integrating the relationships between White men and Black men. It was indeed the patent integrationist implications of the Rand in respect of the Africans that led to so much consideration of and concern for railway development as a more acceptable alternative of linking the country's supply-potential with market-demand, whether in domestic or export markets.

The Dominions Royal Commission, reporting in 1914 on South African agricultural prospects, suggested that the most promising line of advance was in scientific stock-raising. It looked to the time when 'South Africa will at least be freed from the reproach of being unable to supply its own wants in the way of butter, milk and meat (and) it may even be enabled to enter the world's markets as a competitor with Australasia and the Argentine' [20]. The Commission noted the large increase in numbers of woolled sheep and the prospects of a growing export of fleece of improving quality. It recorded the many optimistic expressions of opinion that the maize-growing potential of South Africa was unexcelled by any other country in the world, the admirable opportunities for the development of fruit-farming in many regions, and the prospects of wine and brandy exports if quality standards could be improved and maintained. It seemed especially interested in promoting an extension of cotton cultivation to which it devoted much detailed consideration. Tobacco-growing also had favourable prospects subject to quality-improvement. The outlook for extended tea-cultivation was in the Commission's opinion unfavourable, but it looked forward to Natal's sugar industry meeting the Union's total domestic needs within a few years, though 'it does not appear that South Africa will ever compete in the world market' [21].

Finally, the Commission desired 'to add one general observation. ... We were struck with the comparative indifference, or want of enterprise, which prevails in bringing the various agricultural products, particularly wine, tobacco, and fruit to the notice of consumers outside the Union, or preparing them in such a fashion as best to meet the requirements of importers overseas. ... We notice that only £850 appears in the estimates for 1914–15 for the High Commissioner's Office, for advertising and exhibitions' [22].

In its general programme of new-line and branch-line construction and in the classification of farming needs and agricultural produce in the very lowest-rate groups, the S.A. Railways heavily subsidized the distribution costs of the South African agricultural industry to help it in achieving its contribution, the potential of which had been sketched in the Dominions Royal Commission Report, to the country's economic development [23].

What was the statistical record ten to fifteen years after Union – about 1920 to 1925, at which latter date a major change in the control of the polity had taken place with the advent of the Pact Government?

The country was certainly less dependent on imported foodstuffs. The progress towards greater outputs from pastoral – and crop-farming would seem to owe much to the major impetus given by the First World War. The 1914–18 War both forced the domestic market to seek its supplies from domestic-grown produce and, also, powerfully stimulated the external demand from Britain for critical supplies of food and agricultural raw materials. But the table below indicates that post-war price declines brought substantial setbacks, suggesting that South African farming broadly had not yet secured its competitive position through increasing productivity.

Imports of beef valued at £30,553 in 1910 and over £80,000 in 1913 had by 1919 become exports of £1,138,000 but rapidly falling away to £118,000 in 1924. Butter production which in 1910/1911 was about 11¼ million lbs had nearly doubled to 21½ million lbs by 1918/1919 and then fell back slightly to under 21 million lbs by 1923/1924. A small amount of net importation of butter continued to reflect adverse years of drought. Imports of bacon fluctuated from £220,000 in 1910 to under £2,000 in 1918 and back to £67,000 in 1924 with imports dwindling except again in bad seasons. Total wheat grown at home increased from 362 million lbs in 1910/1911 to over 500 million lbs in 1918/1919 and fell back to 358 million lbs in 1923/24. Imports of wheat were still substantial – in 1910/1911 being 193 million lbs and 287 million lbs in 1923/1924. Maize production and exports – analysed in greater detail in the next chapter – fluctuated widely in consequence of climatic conditions.

Wine exports were in 1911 96,000 gallons valued at £21,944, in 1919 452,021 gallons valued at £121,897 and in 1924 about

No. of Livestock and Crop Production on Farms and Holdings occupied by Europeans, Asiatics and Coloured Persons (including Stock and Production of Natives on such Farms but excluding Stock and Production of Natives in Native Reserves, Locations, Mission Stations and Native Farms) :

Year	Cattle No.	Woolled Sheep No.	Other Sheep No.	Wheat 1000 lb.	Maize 1000 lb.
1904	3,500,553	11,820,635	4,501,868	141,739	722,319
1919	5,575,488	23,548,130	4,943,370	478,734	1,734,118
1924	6,664,059	24,187,914	4,526,160	352,698	1,666,426

Year	Cotton Unginned lbs.	Tobacco 1000 lb.	Sugar Cane Tons	Tea Leaf 1000 lb.	
1904	—	—	—	—	—
1919	1,418,611	14,183	1,258,302	5,744	
1924	10,003,285	10,676	1,918,560	3,515	

(N.B. The above figures are taken for the Union Year Book No. 8 for 1910/1925. The accuracy of these agricultural censures is questionable and no agricultural census data are available as at Union c. 1910. It must also be remembered that figures for 1904 are shortly after the Anglo-Boer War and are at a low-point, tending to over-state increases in later years.)

500,000 gallons valued at £75,000. Brandy exports fluctuated similarly and in 1924 were £46,192. Fresh fruit exports grew from £60,000 in 1911 fairly steadily to £464,000 in 1924.

The broad picture emerges that progress was slow and only the long established wool-farming sector was making gains significant in both relative and absolute terms. It would seem fair to contend that many years of subsidized transportation costs for agriculture had not enabled it to reach the point of take-off into sustained growth. Certainly heavy continued dependence on the Government land bank and the commercial banks for both mortgage financing and short-term crop financing suggests little net capital formation in South Africa's agricultural industry.

In his pioneering calculation of national income, which of necessity involved a large element of estimate from inadequate data, R. A.

Lehfeldt put the net income from the agricultural sector at £29,000,000 in 1918 – a period of peak prices – giving a figure of £174 per head of economically-active rural Whites but substantially less if wives and dependants are included[24]. Lehfeldt though sympathetic to the role of farming in the South African economic development and optimistic about its prospects, nonetheless acknowledges the generally unprogressive tradition and character of farming as late as the nineteen-twenties:

Unfortunately for the history of this country the settlers, living isolated lives and with no educational facilities, and morally weakened by dependence on the labour of a subjugated race, have failed to adapt themselves at all readily to changed circumstances. The descendants of the early pastoralists should have adopted new methods of farming which produce more from a given area; but usually they know no method of farming except what their fathers practised. Attempting this on inadequate pieces of land, many have been reduced to destitution[26].

Indeed the alarming visual evidence of rural poverty, reflected in the continuously growing numbers of Poor Whites, led W. M. MacMillan to publish *The South African Agrarian Problem and Its Historical Development* to warn that South Africa was repeating in the twentieth century the social process of eighteenth-century England. The 'cash nexus' was turning South African farming away from subsistence production and giving it a market orientation and in the course of this development, many tens of thousands of the bywoners were transferring their landless poverty to urban unemployment[26].

Whatever the detail of railway rating theory and practice, the general conclusion is inescapable. After fifteen years of effort by the polity through the instrument of the South African Railways Administration to make the South African economy less dependent on the Rand gold mines and to diversify its income-producing sources, South Africa was in 1925 decidedly more rather than less a mono-economy of gold. In absolute terms, the production figures for agriculture are unimpressive with the single exception of woolled-sheep farming[27].

Low-cost – often below-cost – railway rating for the farming sector had not encouraged the agricultural and industrial development of the interior. MacMillan, indeed, noted that 'neither Natal nor the Western Province . . . has either much of the bijwoner tradition or of the peculiar "Poor Whites" problem, but both of them are great producing centres' [28]. It was the interior where the process of rural de-population among the Whites was yielding an alarmingly increased rate of social degradation.

Indeed the essential characteristic of the S.A. Railways rating differentiation may well have retarded rather than promoted resource-utilization in the farming interior. By classifying agricultural raw materials, and raw materials generally, in the lowest tariff classes and made-up or manufactured goods in the higher-tariff classes on the so-called value-of-service principle, manufacturing tended to locate itself adjacent to urban-consumer markets rather than rural-supply areas.

Industrialists were induced through least-cost rationality of minimizing railage rates on their high-rated, made-up products to establish their factories in Cape Town, Johannesburg and the Reef towns, and in Durban. It was relatively cheaper to rail the low-cost raw materials from the farms and the coal mines. It was only many decades later that the centralizing rather than the decentralizing consequences of the S.A. Railways rating policy came under examination and criticism from a Government, now alarmed by the entrenched economic power of the concentrated urban-industrial regions of South Africa to attract tens of thousands of Africans from their rural homes.

THE POLITICAL ECONOMY
OF LAND

There are six key propensities, generalizes W. W. Rostow, which operate on the process of economic growth. They summarize, he claims, the effective response of a society of its environment. They are the propensity (i) to develop fundamental science (ii) to apply science to fundamental ends (iii) to accept innovations (iv) to seek material advance (v) to consume (vi) to have children [1].

A sketch of the environment in which the society of South Africa struggled and stagnated has been given in earlier chapters. What is most striking in respect of those who occupied the land or went trekking in search of more land was the absence of five of Rostow's six key propensities. Only in respect of the sixth – to have children – did South Africa's agrarian population, White and Non-White, have a high propensity. But this in face of the low and almost non-existent propensities to develop and apply science, to accept innovations and to aspire to increasing material consumption was an unfavourable rather than a favourable factor for economic growth [2].

In a paper given to the S.A. Association for the Advancement of Science, 1908, F. B. Smith, the then director of the Transvaal Department of Agriculture and later first secretary of the Union Department of Agriculture, gave a penetrating survey of prevailing 'propensities' [3]. He noted that the past seventy-five years had been characterized by a remarkable development of the agriculture of the majority of the countries inhabited by Europeans, particularly in the newer countries like the U.S.A., Canada, Australia, New Zealand, the Argentine. Not only, he said, had the yield of the soil been enormously increased but the range and variety of products had been greatly extended and quality vastly improved.

Unfortunately, he found that South Africa had not shared in this general advance:

For various reasons the Europeans who settled in South Africa did not apply themselves to the development of the soil with the same zest and dogged determination that they had displayed in acquiring it. . . . Consequently, while agriculture was making such great strides elsewhere, here it moved so slowly as to appear almost stationary . . . Without wishing to be unjust to the farmers or to reflect upon the natural resources of the sub-continent, it may be safely asserted that there are few parts of the world occupied by Europeans which are so little understood from an agricultural point of view or in which farmers are exposed to so many risks and difficulties as South Africa, or where judged by the standards attained elsewhere, both as regards the science and the art, agriculture is in such a backward condition. . . .

In many respects our farmers are in a worse plight now than they have ever been . . . a collection of pests has been accumulated that for variety and virulence could scarcely be equalled, and certainly not surpassed, by any country in the world . . .

Smith, as others had done before, referred to the failure of a large and thinly populated country like South Africa to feed itself, importing in 1907 nearly £5½ million of meat, poultry, eggs, butter, cheese, condensed milk and like produce. Although he argued that the urgency of the problems confronting agriculture, above all the control of contagious diseases, was in itself sufficient justification for bringing about a closer union of the sub-continent, Smith emphasized that there had been no lack of monetary aid to the farmers of South Africa in the past:

Taken together, it is probable that during the past twenty years more money per head of the rural population had been devoted to the relief of the farmers in South Africa than in any country in the world . . . not only is there little to show for this expenditure as regards advances in the theory and practice of agriculture or in other directions that make for progress, but it is to be feared that in some respects actual harm has been wrought, for instead of fostering a spirit of independence and initiative and thrift amongst the farmers, they have been induced to rely upon the Government for everything. . .[4].

Undoubtedly it was the non-scientific habit of mind and approach which, added to the want of communications and marketing awareness, made the great majority of South Africa's rural population land-occupiers rather than farmers. The essential stimulation of the key propensities to develop and apply science, to promote innovation and consumption standards would have to come from the polity [5]. Even the critical savings for productivity-generating investment did not until a much later stage come from within farming itself.

As early as 1858 the federation-minded Governor, Sir George Grey, had recognized that the inertia, ignorance and inefficiency of a population, which had deliberately isolated itself from the external world, could be overcome only by the efforts of a centralized government. The task of modernization could however be tackled only when unification was finally achieved in 1910. The input from the polity from then on was continuous, comprehensive, material, and massive – but in terms of increased net output from the land elusive and illusive.

Between 1910 and 1935, eighty-seven bills relating to the land were enacted by Parliament – a Parliament in which farmer-members were a high proportion in all political parties. Almost all these acts aimed at giving permanent assistance by way of scientific environmental improvements, land grants, land acquisition and improvement, finance, furtherance of co-operation [6]. Every one of these acts was in practice for the beneficial aid of White farmers and would-be farmers. The financial input from the polity for permanent capital improvements (irrigation schemes, land settlement schemes), loans from the Land Bank for private capital improvements, short-term farm credit, assistance by expertise through agricultural research colleges and stations was overwhelmingly, if not exclusively, confined to land under White ownership.

South Africa, as de Kiewiet noted, came increasingly to be farmed from the legislative capital of Cape Town and the administrative capital of Pretoria. The titles of the first six of the eighty-seven acts of permanent assistance were the Agricultural Pests Act No. 11 of 1911, the Diseases of Stocks Act No. 14 of 1911, the Dipping Tanks (Advances) Act No. 20 of 1911, the Irrigation and Conservation of Waters Act No. 8 of 1912, the Land Settlement Act No. 12 of 1912 and the Land Bank Act No. 18 of 1912. They express the recognition that the task of modernization of South Africa's social system related to land-utilization was dependent on the external political factor.

Innovating entrepreneurship from within the farming community, or collectivity of land-occupiers, was patently ineffective in promoting agricultural development in Schumpeterian terms. The propensities to develop and apply science for material advance of land productivity were confined to perhaps a dozen cheque-book, part-time farmer-financiers. The determinants and variables of capital accumulation and investment, that would increase the economic output of the land in Arthur Lewis's 'old fashioned sense', were also dependent on governmental intervention.

While undoubtedly farmer-representation in Parliament 'made agriculture the favourite and special charge of the State'[7], the stream of legislative and administrative effort to place men upon the land, to conserve water and finance water conservation, to conquer environmental and entomological adversity, to promote co-operative marketing, was in principle supported by most White men. They voted for it as the apparently logical pursuit of securing the future of the White man in South Africa, which the Native Land Act of 1913 had fundamentally identified with guaranteeing the ownership in perpetuity by Whites of most of the land of South Africa.

That Act laid down that no African, except with the special sanction of the Governor-General, may purchase or even hire land other than in certain 'scheduled areas'. The scheduled areas included only the Native Reserves long secured to Africans by old Treaty rights or other express enactment. This land area was essentially the minor fraction of South Africa, which tribal agglomerations had succeeded with the last-resort intervention and support of Downing Street in preserving against the more powerful pressures of the White man. The fraction was virtually unanimously acknowledged in the parliamentary debate of the Native Lands Act to be manifestly inadequate and unjust. This epoch-ending and -making 1913 Land Act was duly passed with fervent solemnity as an interim measure to maintain the *status quo* of land ownership 'until the passing of a definite, comprehensive and final measure based upon the report of the Commission for the appointment of which provision was made in Section 2 of the Act'. The function of this Natives' Land Commission was to delimit the areas to be set aside for White and African occupation, recommending what equitable 'further provision' of land for African settlement should be released. But it was to be nearly a quarter-century before Hertzog's Native Trust and Land Act of 1936 proposed to add to the 1913 scheduled areas significant further areas known as the 'released areas', within which the restrictions upon the purchase of land for African settlement would be removed[8].

Although the Natives' Land Commission under section 2 of the Act of 1913 was strictly limited to delimitation of areas, the chairman

Sir William Beaumont addressed a minute on policy issues to the Minister of Native Affairs [9]. A reading of the Beaumont Minute reveals the extent to which both Whites and Africans looked to the polity rather than to the market as the decisive determinant in the allocation of the scarce resource of land:

A very general impression prevails that the Act contemplates a segregation – complete or partial – of the Native races throughout the Union. The impractibility of such an idea makes it difficult to understand how it has come to be entertained. It probably owes its origin to the free use of the term segregation without any definite idea as to what is meant by the term. The error, unfortunately, has led to considerable misconceptions in the minds of the public, and more especially among the Natives, as to the nature and scope of the work of the Commission. . . .

The views taken of the Act by Europeans vary very considerably. Some altogether disapprove of the principle of the Act, and consider that Natives should be free to purchase land where they like, allowing economic forces to take their way. Others think that the Native Reserves are quite sufficient, and are averse to Natives being allowed to acquire more land. Between these extreme views, there are many modifications. Farmers are chiefly interested in the supply of labour . . . they view with apprehension the establishment of large Native areas, where Natives could easily obtain land and so free themselves from the obligations which attach to residence on private farms.

Some are in favour of reserves, provided they are under Government supervision, with some sort of compulsory obligation to work; others fear that unless the natives' requirements are reasonably met, the Natives will migrate from the locality or Province, and their labour will be lost; others think that provision should be made only for those Natives who have raised themselves to a position of independence; most, though by no means all, even in the Orange Free State, view the Act as a necessity, and regard it as designed to do away with the share-system which has so largely adopted in many parts of the Union. . . .[10].

The Commission also met large deputations of chiefs, headmen and Africans at every centre:

. . . Some have been under fear that the areas already reserved to them would be taken away or at least curtailed; others, that the Government intends to extend the reserved areas; others, that there is to be a general segregation of Whites and Blacks so as to entirely separate the two races, involving, as it would, a general movement of peoples; others, again, regard the Act as violating promises made to the Natives by the Imperial Government, and as depriving them of rights which they had hitherto exercised and enjoyed, and they claim the right to buy land anywhere.

The light in which the Natives of the Orange Free State regard the Act requires special mention, because in that Province there is a considerable body of Natives who have for years – some of them all their lives – lived as independent tenants under the share system on private lands, and who are now threatened with sudden and summary ejectment. These Natives complain bitterly of the enforcement of the Act before they have had time or opportunity to consider how it is likely to affect them or to make representations respecting it to the Government. They consider it unfair to subject them to ejectment before provision has been made for Native areas to which they might remove or to find places where they might go. . . . But the great mass of the Native population in all parts of the Union are looking to the Act to relieve them in two particulars—the first is to give them more land for their stock, and the second is to secure them fixity of tenure. . . [11].

The intensity of the value-orientations attached to land by both Whites and Africans is impregnated throughout the Beaumont Minute.

It is not too much to say that the Act has been misinterpreted and misrepresented by Europeans and Natives alike; and that, so far as the Natives are concerned, this had the effect of creating suspicion, distrust and anxiety in every part of the Union[12].

Although the Commission tried hard to allay the misapprehensions of the Africans, the Beaumont Minute recorded that unfortunately a considerable number of White landowners had since the coming into force of the Act ejected Africans from their lands.

Some have done so under the impression that the Act necessitated it; others because the Act offered a good opportunity to get rid of Native tenants who were not rendering sufficient labour. A large number of Natives have been so removed both from Crown lands taken up by Europeans and from private lands, and many more are under notice to quit, especially in centres where farming is more intensive. Many of the Natives so ejected have been led to believe that it is the duty of the Commission to set apart lands to which they might remove[13].

Between the passage of the Act in 1913 and the report of the Native Land Commission in 1916, the outbreak of World War 1 had patently exercised an exogenous stimulant to land-utilization. Rising market demand for food-stuffs and agricultural raw materials, especially wool, was making land more valuable and monetary inflation was steadily increasing land values. Furthermore the

White farmers already had some first fruits of 'making agriculture the favourite and special charge of the State'.

Under such conditions it was obvious that the 'further provision' of land for African purchase, enjoined by the Act through the recommendations of the appointed Commission, would not be made on any significant scale. Where further African land purchases were sanctioned under the special powers given to the Government in areas suggested by the original Beaumont Commission or the subsequent local committees, the prices paid reflected the contrived scarcity of supply. The 'further provision' recommended by the Beaumont Commission amounted to an additional 17,700,000 acres which would have brought the total area of 'Native land' to 38,685,000 acres in all. But between 1916 and 1936, when the Native Trust and Land Act was passed together with the measure finally dis-enfranchising the Africans of the Cape Province, the actual extent of additional land provided was negligible.

The intervention of the political factor into the allocation of land as between the Whites and the Africans does not of course begin with the Native Land Act of 1913. For three-quarters of a century before then, either the British Crown in the Cape and Natal or Trekker Volkraads in the Transvaal and the Orange Free State had added right to might.

In the Cape Province the Natives were driven further and further back until they finally became consolidated in the region of the Kei River (in the Crown lands known as the Ciskei and the Transkei), although the Africans' legal right to acquire land in the Cape was maintained by the special factor of their entrenched franchise rights until 1936. In Natal, Crown locations and mission reserves were set aside for exclusive occupation by Africans in accordance with the reserve policy first introduced by Shepstone in 1846–47 and climaxing in 1897 with the annexation of Zululand, of which about three-fifths was placed under the Zululand Native Trust.

In the Orange Free State, the Volksraad from the beginning took the view that the whole state was exclusively a White area with Africans prohibited by law from purchasing or hiring land – the Native areas of Thaba 'Nchu and Witzieshoek not being originally part of the Orange Free State. The superior military and diplomatic skill of the Basutos secured for themselves the Protectorate of Basutoland. In the Transvaal the Africans were driven back from the localities in which the Trekkers settled but were allowed to continue in occupation where the Boers could not, or would not, develop. The Volksraad under prodding from British 'suzerainty' provided legal ownership of reserves in the northern fringes amounting to some 3 per cent of the total Transvaal land area. Bechuanaland was retained primarily for African ownership by the proclamation of a British protectorate and similarly with Swaziland, though in the latter cases large-scale alienation took place to White concessionaires.

At the time of Union, 1910, the land area reserves for Africans (excluding the protectorates) amounted to 23,500,000 acres or some 7·13 per cent of the total area of the country. This constituted roughly the scheduled area in terms of the Native Land Act of 1913 – the territorial extent of African ownership of the rural land of South Africa as delimited by the political factor. It could not be extended except in so far as 'further provisions' might be recommended by a Commission and accepted by a Parliament elected by an exclusively White electorate, other than in the Cape Province where Africans might qualify for the franchise. It was this franchise qualification in the Cape, in part dependent on land-ownership, that prevented the legal extension of this Act of 1913 to the Cape.

For almost a quarter-century Parliament virtually never implemented any 'further provisions' of land. The political argument was that so long as African franchise rights in the Cape were linked legally to the right to buy land anywhere in the Cape (i.e. in 'White' areas), no Parliament would honour the undertaking of 1913. That undertaking had been, once the *principle* was adopted that the racial ownership of land was a political and not a market decision, to implement an equitable and just allocation through a Commission as the instrument of the polity. Although land ownership might be determined by legal enactment of political power, land-utilization and land-occupation continued to be no less influenced by economic rationality or the pursuit of optimizing productivity as interpreted by land-owners.

A graphic pen-picture of the land of South Africa as it evolved in socio-economic terms down until about 1930 is given by W. M. MacMillan in his *Complex South Africa* [14]. MacMillan made one of the first independent statistical surveys of the broad interconnections between land-ownership, land-utilization and land-occupation and between land and labour. His general conclusion was that 'the wholesale appropriation of what was once Native land enormously increased the dispersal of the European population, thus killing any hope of really sound white agriculture, while the "extermination" of Natives yet left such masses of them at the beck and call of farmers as to perpetuate the ill effects of earlier colonial dependence on slave labour'[15].

The encouragement given by land-acquisition sanctions to basic environmental factors of soil and water made extensive agriculture the entrenched White tradition; the compulsion exerted by White land-acquisition on the Africans was to force the adoption of such intensive, non-traditional, agricultural practice within the limited tribal territories as to result in a degree of malnutrition that some-times approximated starvation. Extensive agriculture in the White areas contributed to the alarming increase of Poor Whites, intensive agriculture in the tribal reserves to the proliferation of Poor Blacks – though this alarmed only the 'kaffir-boeties'[16].

The Beaumont Land Commission estimated, in 1916, that of a rural total of 3,880,554 Africans, there were slightly more than half or 2,290,000 who lived on Reserves, mission reserves, Crown lands or on their own privately-owned farms. Of this total rural African population, 1,264,593 lived on land occupied by Europeans and 325,179 on land owned but unoccupied by Europeans[17]. Mac-Millan calculated certain densities of population from the 1921 census. The average for the Union as a whole was 14·64 to the square mile, and for predominantly or exclusively Native areas: Transkei as a whole 58·59; Glen Grey 46·13; Herschel 53·54; Kingwilliamstown 70·01; Zululand 24·06; rest of Natal 35·76 ranging from 51·37 in Camperdown to 150·65 in Inanda.

Thus at that time the essentially African, and almost completely non-urbanized, districts of the Transkei and Natal had a density of population hardly exceeded by even the highly-urbanized Rand.

On 'the most generous showing' the density of the 3,387 sq. miles (out of a total 110,540 sq. miles) of designated Native reserves in the Transvaal was from 70 to 90 the sq. mile. For the Orange Free State, the adjoining Basutoland – sometimes regarded as its 'Native Reserve' – had for its inhabitable area from 42·44 to 120 persons to the sq. mile; while in the Free State itself only 244 sq. miles out of the total 50,000 sq. miles was 'reserved' for the African population. who in fact numbered over 440,000 and lived as share-farmers –

illegally or under legal exemption – or as labourers on Free State White-owned farms [18].

Since mining was regarded as a wasting asset and since the land was identified as the only permanent asset, it seemed irrefutably logical to tax the income-stream from the gold-mines – so long as it lasted – for investment-funds to develop the productivity of the land, owned and farmed by the White man [19]. In twenty-five years from 1910 to 1936, Frankel estimated that the State spent over £71,000,000 from loan funds and over £41,000,000 from revenue for (White) agriculture. Furthermore, nearly £20,000,000 (a large part of which was spent on irrigation) of that £71,000,000 had to be written-off or classed as irrecoverable, while another £20,000,000 of the loan fund expenditure was in fact for farmers-assistance, farmers' special relief measures and relief of distress. Nearly £33,000,000 of the total loan fund expenditure came from mining revenues credited to loan account with the balance coming from State borrowing [20].

On the other hand, the assistance given by the Union Government for agriculatural development in the Native Reserves in the period 1910–34 was limited to a grant of £49,000 from loan funds and £346,000 from revenue for fencing and dipping-tanks, together with a sum of £228,821 for land purchases [21]. In respect of communications development, the South African Railways had built by 1930 for the Native areas one single line of railway running to a dead-end at Umtata and at St. Johns there was a port open to a very small coasting steamer at favourable spring-tides [22].

The attempt by the State to influence the economic geography of the country through railway development and railway rating has been analyzed in an earlier chapter. The efforts of the State to control land-ownership and direct land-utilization have been indicated above. What had the political factor achieved in respect of the economic development of the country at about 1929, that breaking-point in world economic growth?

The heavy expenditure on veterinary science and agricultural education had undoubtedly transformed the potentialities of the land, though resistance to change and innovation inhibited the translation into actualities. Thus, for instance, sheep-farming – one of the oldest and the most important source of income from the land – as late as the 1920's remained attached to practices that threatened irreversible destruction of vegetation and resultant soil

TABLE I

SOUTH AFRICA

*Value of Output of Certain Branches of Production, 1918,
1922, 1926, 1930*

	Farm Produce Estimated Open Market Value £000	Gold Exports £000	Manufactures Census Value Gross Output £000
1918	75,514	35,312	29,914
1922	67,989	31,845	37,346
1926	81,000	43,223	44,466
1930	60,000	47,460	55,787

(Table taken from E. Davis: S.A. Journal of Economics Vol. I. 1933, p. 168.)

erosion. The Drought Investigation Commission of 1922 noted that, though a large portion of South Africa was dry long before the arrival of the White man, since the White man has been in South Africa enormous tracts of country have been entirely or partially denuded of their original vegetation with the result that rivers, vleis and water-holes described by old travellers have dried up or disappeared [23].

This Commission concluded that stock losses due to drought could be fully explained without presuming a decline in mean annual rainfall, for which it could find no evidence in recent historical times. From 'the vast amount of evidence placed before it . . . only one conclusion can be drawn, namely, that the severe losses of the 1919 drought were caused principally by the faulty veld and stock management' [24]. The Commission found that kraaling or concentration of sheep at certain fixed places at night was practised by most White farmers, with the rare exceptions of those few who permitted their stock to run free day and night in suitable paddocks or in jackal-free country.

Kraaling results in reversing the natural timing of feeding and resting times, necessitating much driving of stock and increased food requirements with resultant stock-debilitation aggravated during drought. Kraaling and concomitant over-stocking leads to mechanical destruction of vegetal covering due to trampling and the consequent soil-erosion. But kraaling remained decade after decade the standard practice and few small-stock farmers in South Africa had by the time of the Drought Commission adopted paddocking, which permits essential grazing control and veld management under arid conditions[25] as pioneers in South Africa had demonstrated more than fifty years back.

The 'most promising line of advance' for South Africa's agricultural development was 'scientific stock-raising', as the Dominions Royal Commission in 1914 had endorsed the expert evidence and its own observations. From the time of Union, the State had undoubtedly made its contribution to the development and application of science but the slowness with which the majority of stock-farmers accepted innovation was hardly consolidating the advance. Although land-values were rising for extensive pasturage in consequence of State assistance, sheep and cattle were displacing people on the land rather than realizing the hopes of the Dominions Royal Commission that South Africa's pastoral production might begin to rival and challenge that of Australasia and the Argentine.

It will be recollected, too, that the same Commission had recorded the many optimistic expressions of opinion that the maize-growing potential of South Africa was unexcelled by any other country in the world[26]. State assistance had particularly concentrated on aiding this sector of the country's interior agricultural development by an export-development railage rate. As early as 1907 a flat railage rate of 10s. per 2000 lb of maize was patently below average-cost and probably below marginal-cost. But it served to promote an export trade in maize and provide a freight-load for a large number of rail trucks returning empty to the coast, after their forward journal of delivering imports from the coast to the Rand.

This return-journey movement is indeed a genuine example of joint-supply, which justified the charging of differential prices or rates. A low-rate for the export-maize traffic was defensible so long as the rate covered the avoidable or prime costs of maize-transport; it was even desirable so long as (a) there was no better or more remunerative alternative freight to provide traffic for otherwise empty truck-movements and (b) the volume of maize traffic was not so stimulated by the below-cost transportation that the S.A. Railways were led to incur additional capital investment to handle the resultant maize tonnage.

In the course of time neither of these latter conditions was satisfied. A railage rate for bulk-maize that was maintained at an effective rate of 10s. per ton for decades fell further and further below average- and even marginal-costs. In 1925/26 it was calculated that the actual average earnings on all maize for export amounted to 0·27 pence per ton per mile [27]. This near-elimination of transport costs from maize-marketing naturally encouraged an increasingly-dispersed and extra-marginal cultivation of maize. In addition the State gave other direct and indirect financial encouragement so that maize cultivation, except when drought or pests intervened with near-catastrophic results on production, expanded greatly and was financially uncontrollable. Parliament from time to time had to authorize large sums through the Land Bank to write off over-advances made to maize-farmers when world prices slumped.

Within a few years maize-production for export had been so 'developed' that it no longer merely filled otherwise empty freight-trucks returning to the coast. More and more trucks had to be diverted from other net-revenue producing freight, and then the basic movement of forward- and return-freight reversed itself so that the S.A. Railways had to accept the costs of the continuous return haulage of empty trucks from the coast to the interior maize triangle. Finally the S.A. Railways was led to incur the heavy capitalization of an extensive elevator system for bulk-handling of the maize crop [28].

Sheep- and maize-farmers were not, of course, the only sections of agriculture to be increasingly farmed from Cape Town and Pretoria. Dairy-produce, meat, sugar, fruit, wheat, wine and spirits, tobacco may perhaps be more appropriately included in the political economy of food discussed in the following chapter.

How did the political economy of land-utilization affect the long-term distribution of population?

The population movement out of agriculture into so-called secondary and tertiary occupations is of course part of the process of economic growth [29]. South Africa was fortunately to follow this social process. It was, however, the unsought and unappreciated consequence of State policy which contrariwise for decades clung tenaciously to its avowed objective of promoting a 'back to the land' development policy for the Whites. State contributions to land-acquisition and land-improvement aimed at increasing the number of Whites on the land, but the working-out of the measures had the reverse results. Poor Whiteism as a malady of rural un-employment and depopulation was being deepened by the process that stimulated land-values. Concurrently the State aided the relative financial strength to increase their land-holdings of those farmers, who were able and willing to implement improved techniques.

Thus jackal-proof fencing and paddocking of sheep gradually supplanted kraaling among the more progressive farmers, often helped by State grants and loans for fencing and water-conserva-tion. Economic rationality then dictated that White bywoners should lose customary rights to 'run' their own animals on the farm-owner's controlled grazing lands. The displaced were indeed the White bywoners who contributed no labour rather than the African 'squatters', who by custom and enforced immobility did render labour (often on a non-cash basis).

The decline in the White rural population from 1910 was most marked in the sheep-rearing and, to a lesser extent the maize-growing, districts. From 1911 to 1921, the whole of the Central and Eastern Cape and the adjacent Southern and Western Orange Free State showed an absolute decrease in the numbers of Whites, while in other districts of the Orange Free State, Natal and the Transvaal only the shift from the farm to the local dorp or village avoided a total decline of the rural White population.

The tempo of urbanization and rural depopulation was consider-ably increased from 1921 to 1936, when capital investment in mining and manufacturing industry began to speed the rate of economic development – more especially after 1932 – and urban employment. Out of the 104 magisterial, i.e. census districts, of the Cape Province, no less than 61 districts showed an absolute decline in their rural population; in the Orange Free State, 26 of the 33 rural districts showed absolute decreases in rural population. In Natal only 9 out of the 33 districts and in the Transvaal only 7 of the 41 districts recorded absolute losses in rural population.

H. A. Shannon made a careful analysis of trends, trying to reach behind the essentially legal differentiation between urban (possessing any form of local government) and rural (not having any form of local government) [30]. He found for the whole period 1904 to 1936 the rise in White population possessing local government had been greater (100:232) than in White population not possessing local government (100:131); and the rise in the really large urban areas of over 10,000 Whites still greater (100: 296). On a basis of differentiating as an urbanized area those local government areas with more than 2000 Whites and as non-urbanized areas those with less than 2000 Whites, Shannon constructed the table below:

'*Urbanized*' and '*Non-urbanized*' *Population Trends, 1904–1936:*
South Africa (excluding Native Territories and Zululand)

	'*Urbanized*'					'*Non-urbanized*'			
	E	N	C	A	T	E	N	C	A	T

(a) Total Population = 100

	E	N	C	A	T	E	N	C	A	T
1904	10·7	5·9	3·3	1·0	20·8	15·6	54·5	7·2	2·0	79·2
1921	11·5	7·9	3·2	0·8	23·3	14·7	53·6	6·2	2·1	76·7
1936	13·1	11·2	3·7	1·5	29·6	11·5	52·0	5·7	1·1	70·4

(b) Each Racial Group = 100

	E	N	C	A	T	E	N	C	A	T
1904	40·3	9·8	31·0	35·0	—	59·7	91·2	69·0	65·0	—
1921	43·8	12·7	34·1	27·2	—	56·2	87·3	65·9	72·8	—
1936	53·3	17·7	39·3	57·2	—	46·7	82·3	60·7	42·8	—

(c) 'Urbanized, and 'Non-Urbanized' Each = 100

	E	N	C	A	T	E	N	C	A	T
1904	51·0	28·4	15·7	5·0	100	19·7	68·8	9·1	2·4	100
1921	49·3	33·7	13·7	3·3	100	19·3	70·0	8·0	2·7	100
1936	44·4	38·0	12·4	5·2	100	16·3	73·9	8·1	1·6	100

(d) Each Section in 1904 = 100

	E	N	C	A	T	E	N	C	A	T
1904	100	100	100	100	100	100	100	100	100	100
1921	151	185	136	102	155	131	137	119	147	134
1936	242	372	220	288	278	144	186	154	116	173

(N.B.   E = Europeans or Whites; N = Natives of Africans;
C = Coloureds; A = Asiatics; T = Total.)

These basic and substantial population shifts of all races from non-urbanized agriculture into urbanized mining-industry, and at the most rapid rate of all into the Witwatersrand area, ran counter to the most deeply-held beliefs and wishes of Afrikanerdom. The confrontation by an urbanized Black proletariat was increasingly regarded as a mortal threat to the institutionalized culture of the Afrikaner people. More immediately there was competition between Poor Whites and Poor Blacks for unskilled jobs, while the operation of least-cost substitution in mining and manufacturing was striving to reduce the exceptional spread of 5 (or more): 1 between skilled (White) wages and unskilled (African) wages.

Through these decades economic stagnation was slowly quickening into economic growth, as indeed mirrored in the geographical and occupational shifts of the population. But the economic development was producing motivations and aspirations regarded as increasingly foreign to the South African way of life. To manage the tensions of economic change and to maintain the social patterns of the past, the Pact Government of Hertzog-Creswell had been voted to political power. Then the world economic depression had imposed such a crisis on South Africa's economic growth as to compel the new party political combination of Hertzog-Smuts in a United Party. Now Prime Minister Hertzog was quick to recognize how the fortuitous local political working-out of the world's economic misfortune provided his decisive policy opportunity. In one combined exercise of parliamentary power he would bring segregated land ownership in the Cape within the Native Lands Act of 1913 and secure the final elimination of the Cape African common franchise.

Almost from the Union's first parliamentary session, Hertzog had seen the social system of South Africa not as an unacceptable unity of European and African but as the segregation of White man's land and Black man's land. Hence the manner of his intervention into the debate of the Natives Land Bill as far back as 1913 with his emphatic warning against any extension of the African vote and his prophetic awareness of his own mission to bring the Cape Province within the Land Act by destroying the common franchise rights of the Cape Africans.

The Native Administrative Bill of 1917, introduced by Botha, aimed to validate the Beaumont Commission's recommendations for the lines of permanent territorial land-allocation. It was aborted by the Government's law-adviser's opinion that in making it impossible for an African to acquire and hold land in the Cape Province, on which land-holding the Cape African's entrenched franchise qualification depended, a two-thirds majority of both Houses of Parliament sitting together would be necessary. In the debate on the withdrawn Bill, Hertzog made it clear that the Cape franchise, which stood in the way of 'final' territorial segregation, would have to go.

In July, 1926, Prime Minister Hertzog published his four 'Native Bills' embodying his solution of the 'Native Question'. They provided for the repeal of section 35 of the South Africa Act and removal of the Africans (though not the Coloured) from the ordinary voters' rolls, the disenfranchisement of the Cape African voters, special African representation in Parliament through seven (White) members in the House of Assembly – elected by Government nominees of prominent Africans – with restricted rights except on scheduled African matters. A General Native Council was to be constituted for the whole of the Union with 50 members – 15 nominated and 35 elected by the same government-nominated electorate.

Simultaneously the Native Land Act Amendment Bill was to provide the final solution to the land question with the addition to the existing scheduled areas of released areas, in which Africans and non-Africans might acquire ownership subject to such acquisition being land adjoining land already held by members of the same race. Generally the aim was to prevent White islands of land in Black areas, and vice versa. Any land held by Africans outside the scheduled or released areas could be exchanged for Crown land within scheduled and released areas. A Native Land Purchases and Advances Fund was to be created to assist Africans in land improvement and land-acquisition from non-Africans [31].

The four bills were made inter-dependent in respect of enactment. The Natives Land Act (1913) Amendment Bill of 1926 aimed to make final throughout the Union the principle of territorial segregation as the sovereign law of the land rather than allow the land to remain the continuing subject of the sovereign, colour-blind market. The promise of additional released land to the Africans was the major inducement to the Africans to surrender voluntarily their entrenched franchise [32].

The Africans rejected out of hand all proposals that might involve surrender of the Cape African franchise in the inter-locking of the four proposed bills, which did not indeed get beyond the first reading stage in Parliament. Hertzog spent from 1927 to 1935 implementing the essence of his bills which were considered by numerous elect committees over eight years [33].

When Hertzog won his 'Black Manifesto' general election in 1929 to secure an over-all majority of the Nationalist Party, the Women's Enfranchisement Act, 1930, enfranchised all adult White women (but not Coloured women despite Hertzog's repeated assurances) without qualifications [34]. Enfranchisement of adult White women of course diminished the African male vote, then numbering 15,780, from 3·5 per cent of 452,472 voters to 1·4 per cent of 889,173 voters [35].

From 1930 to 1935 the Joint Committee sat to work out agreed, non-party legislation governing land allocation and African political representation. In his book, already cited, Tatz gives valuable and illuminating detail of the preceedings of the Committee from the unpublished records of Senator Nicholls [36]. Senator Nicholls of Natal was convinced that Natives would trade the Cape franchise for the £30 million fund proposed for African development in the Reserves and additional land purchase. His proposals formed the basis of the 1936 legislative settlement.

The 1936 legislation combined the Representation of Natives Act and the Native Trust and Land Act. The first, No. 12 of 1936, removed all Africans from the common roll, existing African voters being placed on a separate, special register which would elect three members of Parliament (the Native Representatives). It also provided for the election of four Senators for four Native electoral areas by indirect communal vote, and for an advisory Natives Representative Council.

The Native Trust and Land Act, No. 18 of 1936, established a Trust with funds to be provided from time to time by Parliament for the objects of land-purchase in the released areas, land-improvement in the scheduled and acquired released areas, and generally to promote the well-being of Africans in the scheduled, and released areas. The Act ended 'free traffic in land' in the Cape Province, since the entrenchment of the old franchise rights of the Africans of the Cape had now been expunged. The Native Land Act of 1913 had originally scheduled about 21,000,000 acres and the Native Trust and Land Act of 1936 proposed to release a further 15,000,000 acres in which Africans might acquire land-ownership rights – always provided the purchase funds were made available [37].

From 1937 until 1940, when all further land purchase was suspended because of the Second World War, Parliament had voted £5 million and the Trust had spent about £4¼ million on land purchase of some 2¾ million acres. But the war created financial and administrative difficulties and further land acquisition by the Trust practically ceased. Once again, under war-time demands for foodstuffs and agricultural raw materials and war-time inflationary finance, land-values rose so that White land-owners became increasingly unwilling to sell. In 1944 the Chairman of the Natives Representative Council responded to increasingly vehement criticism by African members of non-implementation of land-purchase by declaring that the price of land was too high and 'it was an absurd thing' to purchase land at that stage.

The polity had decreed the division of the land between the Whites and the Africans, from 1913 when 'free traffic in land' was prohibited except in the Cape Province until 1936 when the prohibition was effectively extended to the Cape as well. In 1913 the areas scheduled for African ownership amounted to some 7 per cent of the total area of the country: in 1936 the polity proposed to release about another 6 per cent so that the final share of the land of South Africa under African ownership would be about 13 per cent.

But the market still operated in the released areas until the land was actually purchased by the S.A. Native Trust, and by 1940 onwards the market had practically compelled the Trust to cease its purchases on behalf of the polity [38].

THE POLITICAL ECONOMY
OF FOOD

While land-hungry, disenfranchised Africans waited for the Greek kalends, White farmers voted for manna this day. Manna from a polity is however apt to show its origin as a mixed blessing and to be of such unsatisfying quantity and quality as not to sustain its recipients out of the wilderness. Entry into the Promised Land normally requires more votes for future-offering and more manna for spot-delivery.

At what desirable point the process of intervention, sought and unsought, by the polity into the economy ends is a matter of much opinion [1]. The process undoubtedly has a special dynamism when it operates on the marketing of agricultural produce. The development may be traced as follows.

The invididual farmer selling to a perfectly competitive (or sovereign) market supplies as much as he can produce in the expectation that the market-demand price will not be influenced by the amount he supplies. Under certain conditions of relative inelasticity of market-demand, these expectations of all the farmers together supplying their total produce results in such a fall in market-demand price as to make the price received by the individual farmer a sad disappointment to his hopes.

At this stage the help of the polity will be sought to separate the demand-price from the market-price and to fix the former higher than the latter. At this stage, too, however the individual farmer selling to the now imperfectly competitive market still supplies as much as he can produce in the expectation that the polity-fixed price will not be influenced by the amount he supplies. These expectations (unless the conditions of relative inelasticity of demand have unpredictably changed) of all the farmers together supplying their total produce results in more being supplied than the market will now demand at the polity-price. The unsold quantities now become a sad disappointment to the individual farmer's supplies.

At this next stage the aid of the polity will be needed to separate the amount supplied to the market from the amount produced for the market. This will usually involve segregating one market from another market – the home market in which the domestic polity has sovereignty and the foreign polity in which the export market has sovereignty.

In the home market under the sovereignty of the polity the amount supplied to that market will be not more than will be demanded at the polity-price. The balance of the supply, which is the remaining amount produced, will then be sold in the foreign polities at their (sovereign or perfectly competitive) export-market demand prices.

Separating amounts supplied to the domestic market from amounts supplied to export markets so that the higher polity-price in the domestic market compensates for the lower market-price in the export markets, means telling the individual farmer how much of his total produce is to be sold on the domestic market and how much on the export markets. The telling is then followed by compelling.

Whether the process can be halted at this stage of sales-compulsion will depend, once again, on the course of development of the inelasticities of demand in the domestic market and the export markets. If the inelasticities should be inappropriate, then the final and now unsought aid of the polity will be reached in instructing the individual farmer how much he may produce [2].

The process of market-demand prices evolving into polity-fixed prices by its very nature proceeds through delegated legislation to administrative jurisdiction (so that polity-fixed prices are sometimes called administered-prices). The instrument of the polity typically is the board of control, whose objective is orderly marketing – the more order, the more control, then more disorder, so total control. In its earliest phase, the polity may exert no more influence on market-demand price than to suggest voluntary quality-standards and then to impose compulsory quality-standards. The subsequent stages towards a polity-price system of total control, as outlined above, may be a slow or a fast process, depending on how wide is the divergence between the ruling market-price and the desired polity-price – and how much influence farmers have in Parliament.

In South Africa, although White farmers had a dominant influence from even before Union this was concentrated initially on land-acquisition and labour-availability. After Union the farmer-vote was also exercised to powerful and far-reaching effect in establishing polity-rates for rail transport [3]. It was in the nineteen-twenties that polity-price fixation began and culminated in the agricultural marketing-board controls of the nineteen-thirties – these latter years being when the times of trouble in world agriculture escalated into (or were aggravated by) the times of trouble of the world economy as a whole.

A paper read to the Economic Society of South Africa by J. G. van der Horst in 1932 traced the course of South African legislation, with its origins in Roman-Dutch law concepts of property-rights, as it set out to compel the conditions of farming in South Africa to obey the law rather than the market and the consequent implications for those property-rights [4].

The earliest legislation for the control of an agricultural industry was passed in 1914. It imposed quality-grading standards on export fruit and in 1922 *minimum such standards* were extended, culminating in the entire regulation of export fruit coming under the Fruit Export Board in 1925 and its instrument the Fruit Exchange. No export fruit could be sold except as sanctioned by this Board. In 1926 a Perishable Products Control Board assumed the powers of both the Fruit Export Board and the Fruit Exchange and no export of fruit could be effected unless in accordance with a contract made by or with the consent of the Board, whose administrative costs were to be met by a compulsory levy on all export fruit.

Similarly in respect of dairy produce, control began in 1917 with quality standards for export butter followed in 1918 by registration of all creameries and cheese factories with powers to close sub-standard factories to conform to quality- and health-regulations. In 1925 the Agricultural Industries Advancement Act provided for a levy on all butter produced – the proceeds being available to the Minister to any purpose for promoting the dairy industry. In 1926 only those creameries and cheese factories were registrable which obtained their cream from other persons unless such factories belonged to co-operatives or incorporated associations. Simultaneously export of dairy produce was placed under the entire control of the Perishable Products Export Board, with all export contracts to be made through or with consent of this Board. This was then followed by a 1930 law to establish the Dairy Industry Control Board.

This last Board was empowered to control not only those exports that the producer wished to export but to determine what proportion of dairy produce must be exported compulsorily by every producer. Price-fixing powers were now conferred in addition to quality-quota export controls. Minimum prices to be paid for cream and milk by a creamery or cheese factory were made legal minima. The Board could compel any cheese or butter factory to hand over to it specified quantities of its output for export; it was authorized to make a levy on all dairy produce produced and use the funds for subsidy of export.

Subsequent 1932 legislation extended in detail the administrative jurisdiction of the Dairy Industry Control Board to pay bounties on all exports and establish compulsory export quotas to be handed over at prices and places for delivery by the factory to the Board. The Board exported the delivered produce, paying net proceeds to the factory owner. Should proceeds not cover expenses, the Board could recover the deficiency from the factory owner by legal action. Furthermore, should the factory owner not deliver for export his assigned quota, the Board had authority to purchase a similar quantity elsewhere, export it and recover cost and loss from the defaulting owner.

Meat marketing followed the pattern. It began in 1917 with legal quality-export standards and in 1923 a bounty was paid on exported beef to the producer. In 1932 a board was given 'almost unlimited powers' of control of the meat trade. The Meat Industry Control Board got powers to fix the number of slaughter animals lawfully sold on any day, or during any period, at any place. The Board might fix the number of slaughter animals for lawful transport from one place to another and fix arbitrarily the highest price for which meat could be sold in any area.

In 1924 Cape Provine wine farmers were prohibited from selling and manufacturers from buying any wine for distillation except through the co-operative K.W.V. Such authority extended to non-members of the K.W.V. During 1931 and 1932 statutes required compulsory exports of maize- and tobacco-quotas as determined and authorized by the Minister of Agriculture. Every trader-dealer in maize and tobacco must be licensed, make returns of his transactions and execute any compulsory allocated export quotas.

An amending Act extended the compulsory export-quota to any farmer-producer with 1000 bags of his own mealies left on his hands after a given date.

Legal powers fixed the price of wheat to be paid by wheat-buyers to producers and imports of wheat and flour might be allowed only at appropriately higher-price or prohibited entirely. Sugar followed its own course of detailed regulation with absolute controls over sugar-cane areas for cultivation.

As van der Horst concluded, in respect of the principal agricultural products 'the rights left to the owner of property are the right to consume it himself and the right to destroy it. The rights which give rise to its value in exchange have been, or are about to be, taken away from him, and for the most part vested in boards subject to the control of a minister' [5].

Though considerable numbers of South African farmers had handed to the polity crucial powers, their objective was of course the reverse of diminishing their ownership rights in their land – the overall division of which as between White South Africans and Black South Africans had preoccupied much of their history and parliamentary time. The South African farmers had indeed now called upon their local polity to save them from the world market. The Western World's technological developments of mechanized large-scale farming and the scientific contributions of biology and chemistry were interacting with a wave of industrial and agricultural protectionism to bring about apparently irreversible price declines for foodstuffs and primary raw materials. Economic nationalism so narrowed the world market for agricultural produce that national polities tried unilaterally to isolate their own landowners and peasants from the deflationary chain-reaction by self-defeating export dumping to maintain a consequent disappearing international trade in such produce.

For reasons that are the very stuff of White-Black relationships in South Africa, the home market for South African farmers – especially of food crops – appeared unchangeably undynamic. No voice of authority (economists of the time having voices but no authority) suggested that African demand for food might be elastic. Only export dumping in combination with virtual import prohibition suggested itself as an answer. At least as the answer, in terms of political economy, to save an unacceptably large number of White land-owners from being compelled to yield their ownership

not to the Africans, a fate from which their polity had already preserved them, but to the mortgagors, an eventuality from which they
hoped passionately their polity could rescue them.

The Carnegie Commission had calculated the long-term mortgage
indebtedness for South African agriculture as a whole in the period
1930 to be about 35·8 per cent of the land value. In 1933 J. G. van
der Horst, when putting forward his van der Horst Plan of Govern-
ment-funding of long-term farming debt estimated mortgage debt
not to exceed £120,000,000 [6]. The Government Commission to
Inquire into Co-operation and Agricultural Credit regarded
£100,000,000 as a more fair figure but this did not of course include
an unknown amount of short-term debt, much of it unsecured to
maligned country-storekeepers [7].

The chairman of this Commission was P. R. Viljoen, the Secretary
for Agriculture and subsequent chairman of the National Marketing
Council. Dr P. R. Viljoen was to become the most influential
practitioner of 'planned agriculture' and also the central figure of
the highly controversial debate over the complete elimination of
market-demand prices and its replacement by a polity-fixed price
system, as it culminated in the Marketing Act of 1937 [8].

This Co-operation and Credit Commission of 1934 may be looked
upon as the last official attempt to see self-help rather than etatism
as the source of economic development of the land and its utilization.
It concluded that agricultural co-operatives, despite inhibiting
stubborn individualism of non-co-operators and past poor management, were necessary and essential for the sound promotion of
agriculture in the Union. It nevertheless went on record:

Compulsory co-operation or compulsory sale through one channel by means
of a board of control, both of which have as object the fixation and control
of prices, is economically unsound and socially unhealthy and while it may
temporarily benefit producers it will inevitably lead to over-production,
maladjustment of supply and demand and an ultimate collapse of prices.
Price control schemes in other countries have proved that price levels
cannot be artificially maintained since increased prices mean increased
production and increased production means lower returns.

The experience in the Union with price control measures in two of its
major agricultural products, tobacco and wine, substantiates the view that
this form of control is undesirable and not in the best interests of agriculture.
Further, price control schemes have characteristics which are harmful to
that independent spirit of self-help which is so essential in the building up of
a virile and viligant nation [9].

But even brave words have sometimes to be eaten in a later humble pie. The compulsive pressures of political economy – those pincers of farmers' votes and farmers' diminishing incomes – were very soon to compel Dr Viljoen as Secretary for Agriculture to detail the recipe for the pie to be digested by Parliament as the Marketing Act of 1937. This Act was the enabling measure for compulsory sale through one channel marketing-control boards with unrestricted price-fixing powers [10].

For reasons analysed above, when farmers look for manna from the polity because the market no longer provides plenty, it is nearly impossible to stop polity-pricing from totally replacing market-pricing or to leave the smallest area of sovereignty to the market, from which it might mount a counter-movement for the recapture of a larger freedom. Hence the political struggle to enact 'orderly marketing' of food, despite intense academic and consumer opposition, ended inevitably in legislation for total control of the market, exercised by bureaucracy on behalf of the farmers.

The Marketing Act No. 26 of 1937 established a National Marketing Council with officials of the Department of Agriculture *ex officio* chairman and deputy chairman and three other government-appointed, full-time members. The powers of the Marketing Council were virtually unlimited to secure the unstated objectives of the Act but objectives implicit in the powers. Hence the Council could examine, report, draft and submit any scheme, defined as a set of rules for regulating the marketing of any product within the Act. It could examine and amend any existing scheme. On the Minister's instructions, it could investigate or have investigated marketing conditions in any province or in general or the conditions relating to any particular product or ruling on any market. It could recommend the prohibition or the regulation of the importation of any product generally or from any particular country; it could recommend the prohibition or regulation of the exportation of any product generally or to any particular country.

The Council had appropriate powers to enforce its decisions and though required to ascertain views of, for instance, the Board of Trade and Industries, and take note of the advisory and consultative Consumers' Advisory Committee and of the advisory and consultative Producers' Advisory Committee, the Marketing Council was in fact subject to no limitations on its legal authority other than to the Minister of Agriculture.

A marketing scheme, which might also be initiated by any association of farmer-producers or regulatory board in addition to the Marketing Council itself, must detail the product, area, class of producers and traders covered by the scheme. Full powers to impose levies on any basis determined by a regulatory board permitted unrestricted variations as between different classes of producers and traders, all of whom could be made subject to levy-payment. Subject to audit, the administration and control of the levy fund was entirely under the control of the regulatory board.

The scheme might provide that no producer or trader might sell the controlled product unless registered with the regulatory board in accordance with its requirements. The regulatory board might determine the maximum quantity of any product that, during any period fixed by the board, could be brought into or removed out of any area defined by the board; the maximum quantity which might be sold or offered for sale on any day or during any period at any market or other place specified by the board. The board, furthermore, had complete powers to trade, acting as agent for receipt and sale of the related product; to conduct a pool for the sale of the product on any terms of grading, packing, storing, processing, marketing, advertising and transporting; to finance the operations of the pool; to exercise detailed, compulsory powers of export with rights to impose special export levies and operate equalization funds.

The regulatory board might call for any information in respect of the product from any producer, trader or processor. It might finance on any terms any undertaking for marketing or processing the product concerned. It might advise on any aspect of grading, standardization, packing, brand; it might advise the prohibition, control or regulation of import or export of the product and – for good measure – on all matters relating to the marketing or processing of the product. The board had powers of physical investigation of premises and of examination of records of producers.

But the powers of the regulatory board might be even further extended to ensure, if needs be, complete control of the market of the product to which the scheme related. The board might buy the product from any source and treat such purchase in any manner as it deemed fit. It could then sell in its original form or after processing or it could refrain from selling. With the Minister's approval, the board might prohibit any producer from selling that product or any class, grade, quantity or percentage except as determined by the board to any purchaser or through any channel other than that determined by the board.

The board with the approval of the Minister might from time to time prohibit any producer from selling the regulated product he has produced or any trader in any grade, class or quantity (whether in its original form or partly or wholly processed) at a price other than a price fixed by the board or below or above that price for any particular class, grade of quantity of such product. The board might even prohibit entirely the sale of the product except under permit issued by the board.

The Minister in respect of any proposed scheme might at his discretion submit such a scheme to be voted on by producers (not traders or consumers) concerned. Although the scheme related to all producers or farmers, White and Non-White, only White farmers had legal voting rights and Non-White producers or farmers were compelled to accept the terms of the adopted scheme. A three-fifths majority of White farmer-voters producing more than half of the total quantity of the product during the preceding three years for a scheme was sufficient to extend the scheme to all.

The Marketing Act was thus a consolidating measure of the past and an enabling measure for the future. Though the academic economists were moved to intense disapproval[11], the political economy of food was determined by the over-representation in Parliament of the rural vote (for which the large, relatively wealthy farmer was by the nature of party political finance and organization the influential spokesman), the under-representatation of urban consumers and the non-representation (other than token) of the millions of African poor.

What can be said of the exercise of the political factor in this particular sector on the country's economic development? Whatever is said has an admittedly major element of subjectivity – perhaps more in this sector of economic development than in any other. Objective assessment lacks statistical meaning in the absence of agreement even on what is to be measured.

Polity-pricing by way of controlled marketing brought about large increases in areas under cultivation and, irregularly, large increases in output. Many agronomists, both inside and outside the Department of Agriculture, condemned the resultant balance of land-utilization alleging that soil erosion was seriously aggravated.

The application, even the awareness, of comparative costs to the optimization of the country's resources disappeared from intelligible consideration in official policies which increased the costs of gold-mining, imposed differential taxation of investment-categories, and simultaneously aimed to stimulate the 'primary industry' of agriculture and the 'secondary industry' of manufacturing by countervailing tariff protection.

The most deeply-hidden and incalculable cost of all was in reducing the demand of the very great majority of Non-Whites for protective foodstuffs by deliberate restriction of supplies to the domestic market in order to ensure that the polity-prices were effective. Malnutrition was and remains the heaviest burden on economic growth from the political economy of food [12].

S. H. Frankel claimed it could be shown that, from 1930 to 1934, the taxed incomes from all farming were actually less than the cost of the artificial measures (subsidies, relief and related measures) incurred by the Central Government to the agriculturists. In 1933/34 farming incomes subject to tax were only 1·6 per cent of the total taxed incomes of the Union, due both to special exemptions and to the low net incomes obtained from agriculture[13]. C. S. Richards made an attempt to calculate the cost of subsidies, quotas, tariffs and special assistance to agriculture in South Africa for the year 1933. He put the figure at between £7½ million and £8½ million [14].

As a Schumpeterian innovation in marketing, the entrepreneurial achievements of the control boards remain at best unproved. Academic opinion was exceedingly critical. By the nature of the dynamic process, it is difficult if not impossible to prove that the marketing boards increased or reduced the costs of marketing. Costs, which are the reflection of foregone opportunities or alternatives, cannot be established if the other opportunities were inhibited or the alternatives prohibited.

The so-called rationalization of marketing did not, as the chairman and deputy-chairman of the National Marketing Council in their alter ego as Secretary and Under-Secretary of the Department of Agriculture were subsequently to report[15], achieve or even contribute to 'farming in accordance with the natural controls'. It encouraged a high degree of restriction and near-monopoly in some classes of food distribution and processing. In the early years of operation of the control boards, fluctuations in market supplies were so accentuated as occasionally to compel panic corrective action to secure imports for totally-exhausted stocks.

Perhaps the most interesting judgment on land-use in South Africa under White ownership was made, however, in the Report of the Reconstruction Committee of the Department of Agriculture[15]. This 1943 Report undertaken at the request of the Cabinet Committee on Post-War Reconstruction sought 'to focus attention on matters which are of importance not only to the present generation but more particularly to generations to come'. It may therefore be regarded as expressing the basic convictions of the Department of Agriculture – its aspirations for the future and towards the role of the polity in respect of the economy in general and agriculture in particular.

The Report noted that in 1936 the Union's population was about 10,000,000, of which the Whites numbered some 2,000,000. The 1936 census had classified about 35 per cent of the White population as rural and about 77·5 per cent of the Non-White population (including the Africans in the Native Reserves) as rural. In 1939 it estimated that there were 104,000 White-owned farms, comprising an acreage of some 100 million morgen (and an acreage of Native Reserves of some 10 million morgen). At an average of £3 per morgen the White-owned farm land was valued at £300,000,000 plus stock valued at £107,000,000 plus movable assets of £20,000,000 or a total of £427,000,000 (or £457,000,000 if the Native Reserves are included). The average net income from agricultural production for the years 1936/37 to 1938/39 the Report calculated at £44,270,000 per year.

It commented that in the light of the fact that approximately 64 per cent of the gainfully employed population was then engaged in farming, 'it is disconcerting that since 1934 the contribution of all branches of South African agriculture to the total national income has not exceeded 13 per cent'[16].

But the benefits accruing to the nation from agriculture cannot be assessed in terms of money . . . the farming population also makes a most valuable psychological and spiritual contribution to the essential elements of the nation. There is a great difference between town and country, both sociologically and economically. By having a fairly large percentage of people whose mental outlook embraces a love for the soil and livestock, for rural pursuits and outdoor life, in fact for things stable and permanent and for the whole biological process which is unfolded on the farm every day, a steadying influence of great value is exercised on the economic and social life of the nation. . .[17].

Unfortunately, went on the Report, wrong and unbalanced methods of using the country's basic agricultural resources had arisen because of the commercialization of agriculture since the development of urban demand after the mining discoveries.

The activities of the farming community have been guided largely by market demands and not by soil demands, with the result that over wide areas land has been greatly exhausted . . . Unstable farming practices are manifested in various ways, chief among which are: the abuse of the natural veld by injudicious burning, overstocking and improper management . . . the extensive and often indiscriminate ploughing up of veld for the production of grain and other cash crops, without due regard to the maintenance of tilth and fertility, particularly to be condemned in marginal areas where crop production is at best a gamble; the over-concentration on cereal farming areas not naturally suited to this type of farming; and the neglect of systems of diversified farming in which stock play a more prominent part[18].

The whole question of land abuse is closely linked up with economic considerations . . . It is true that wrong or bad farming is a very important contributory factor, but a fundamental difficulty is the fact that the man on the land has been caught in the vortex of an economic system not of his making, which in a large degree compels him to exploit the agricultural resources in order to enable him to meet his commitments and at the same time to maintain a reasonable standard of living[19].

In brief, the senior officials and directing minds of the Department of Agriculture – who were also the senior officials and directing minds in the National Marketing Council – rejected production in response to market-demand as the aim or justification of land-utilization. Food would not appear to be a function, or at least the main function, of farming. The motivations of farming could only be directed by the values of market-demand at an unacceptable cost in the erosion of the natural soil and the human soul.

Indeed as the Report exhumed South African agriculture, it became more and more obvious to its authors that the reconstruction of its remains could be entrusted to the polity alone[20]. After cataloguing the dismal disabilities – the low, uncertain, extremely variable rainfall, the frost, the denudation of soil aggravated by dust storms succeeding torrential rains; the less than six per cent of cultivated land area and less than fifteen per cent that ever could be cultivated; no inland waterways; droughts that cause enormous losses; stock diseases, insect pests and plant diseases of malignant variety; the poor prices; the unsatisfactory marketing and distribution; the over-capitalization of land from the farmer's love of land and the non-farmer's love of tax-evasion; the uneconomic subdivision of land; the unbeneficially occupied land; the inadequacy of the State agricultural services and the apathy of farmers towards such services – the Report concluded:

It is clear from the foregoing that farming in this country is one long, hard struggle against heavy natural and economic odds[21].

Others, including academic economists, had over the years observed – in perhaps less lugubrious language –the factors making for relatively high-cost farming in South Africa and had been led to recommend investment policies to facilitate a movement from the land. The Report however, after noting that the Marketing Act of 1937 might well be looked upon by producers as their 'magna charta' [22], declared that 'what is wanted is a new charter for agriculture in the light of the experience gained . . .' [23]. It then proceeded to write the new charter for Cabinet approval [24].

The march of veld deterioration, fertility depletion, erosion and desiccation over all parts of the country points unmistakably to the wide prevalence of unsound or exploitive farming, which is ill-adapted to the natural controls and characterized by inefficient or abusive methods of using the land. A great deal of exploitation follows as an inevitable result of economic pressure on the land. . . . Appropriate action has to be taken to deal with these economic issues . . . [but] the crux of the problem, however, lies in the actual systems and methods of land use. . . .

The imposition of certain restrictions in regard to land use and the prohibition of definitely injurious practices will obviously have to be considered in this connection, as also will positive measures for the encouragement or enforcement of sound land use. . . .

Within certain broad limits the system of farming practised has depended largely on the predilection and financial standing of the particular farmer and the markets and prices available for the products. The temporary success of systems, that in the long run prove to be ill-judged, has led to a fairly general belief that, where the natural controls are not completely inhibitive, any type of farming can be practised if the farmer is efficient. The point missed is that . . . one is dealing with long-term effects which may not show up until many years and even generations have passed. . .[25].

In addition to the positive soil, veld and water conservation measures by subsidization of individual farmers, selected by and under continuous control of Departmental officials, special legislation was recommended for restriction or prohibition of erosion-promoting practices. Harmful practices listed for Departmental field restriction and prohibition included (i) veld-burning timing and frequency (ii) over-stocking (iii) categories and techniques of slope-cultivation (iv) grain monoculture (v) drainage and ploughing of vleis for crop production. For possible Departmental decision, the Report listed in addition (vii) limitation of goat and sheep farming in particular regions and (viii) limitation of cultivation, not only in marginal and sub-marginal but also in recognized crop-production areas, to ensure efficient management. As the final complement of conservation, there should be powers for the expropriation and permanent protection of selected areas 'which, for one reason or another, are considered unsuitable for farming'.

Reclamation measures 'by the Department should without doubt be the main method of approach. While private initiative should not be discouraged, landowners are often at a serious disadvantage . . . . This implies in effect the establishment of a new reclamation scheme under which the Department would supply all the necessary labour, equipment and supervision for the carrying out of approved works on private farms as well as town lands' [26]. The capital cost would be financed by the State but 'the landowner would be debited with a definite percentage of the working cost, say 25, $33\frac{1}{2}$ or even 50 per cent' [26]. It is essential, the Report considered, 'that the Department should exercise its own initiative in the choice of areas where reclamation works are to be undertaken' [26].

A truly fearsome picture of loss of natural fertility of the land, and even of the foreseeable desiccation of South Africa, was built up in this Report. There is, however, no hint that land-utilization as it had developed had anything to do with (a) the division of the land by the polity as between White and African so that one-fifth of the population had secured something more than 100 million morgen and four-fifths of the population something less than 10 million morgen and (b) the polity-price system evolved by the control boards and the National Marketing Council.

Market demand for foodstuffs and agricultural raw materials was indeed regarded as a fundamentally malignant factor:

For centuries the farmer had been subject to the whims and caprices of consumer demand. If nature blesses his lands and flocks, he finds that his products are not wanted; if he turns to something for which there is an apparent demand he is faced with consumer apathy and low prices. . . . During all the years the farmer has had no assurance that the food and raw materials wrung from the soil by his energy and labour would bring in sufficient for a living[27].

Small wonder that the Report noted 'in the Union, the Marketing Act of 1937 may well be looked upon by producers as their 'magna charta'[28]. The Department of Agriculture however was unpersuaded that State price fixation was in itself sufficient authority or effective power for the economic development of land.

Price fixation, as a security measure to the farmer, logically pre-supposes control and direction of production. . . . Dependent as agriculture is upon natural forces which may give plenty in one season and little in the next, strict control of production becomes difficult if not well-nigh impossible, especially when international demand also enters. Control can only take the form of direction. Here the control board system will be able to lend itself to direct the production of a particular product. . .[29].

While the Report was not quite prepared to recommend outright nationalization of the land (though evidently much impressed with Soviet-type powers to control and direct production), it had no such inhibitions in regard to food-distribution and food-manufacture.

But control should go further than the mere raw product and should extend to the food processing industries which are vital to the needs of the nation. Price control alone will prove insufficient and ultimately the food processing industries themselves should be state-owned or at least owned and operated by public bodies. Private ownership of mills, creameries, canneries and other food processing plants has led to wasteful utilization of resources and exploitation of the public. . . . Food processing is a national matter which should be dictated by the needs of the people and the necessity of such processing to avoid wastage, as in fruit and vegetables, and cannot be left to private initiative where a monetary gain is the main consideration[30].

The classical view of etatism[31] is in respect of South Africa nowhere more fascinatingly evidenced than in this Report of the Reconstruction Committee of the Department of Agriculture.

Starting in the first decade of the century to provide a state, scientific-educative service (a generally unquestioned function of government), the Department of Agriculture assumed increasing powers over marketing and – when required to report on fundamental policy for the post-war future – proposed state-manufacturing of food products. This basic rejection of private initiative in marketing and manufacturing was in essence a claim that the polity should replace the market as the sovereign influence over economic development. It was pursued to the most remarkable recommendations of this whole revealing Report – the proposals for the valuation, occupation and ownership of farm land [32].

Since agricultural production for the market has become predominant, farming has largely been commercialized. . . . Land too, is thus evaluated by the farmer on the prices now ruling for the products he intends to raise on the land he is buying. . . . It is generally accepted that over capitalization of the land is one of the greatest evils, on the economic side, of our agriculture. The difficulty, however, is to find effective means of preventing it . . . whether the fixing of a mortgage limit by law is contemplated or not, a Bureau of Farm Values appears to be essential for any really constructive social and economic agrarian policy . . .

Such a Bureau of Farm Values would have to build up a card index (carefully catalogued) . . . in which would be collected all relevant facts pertaining to every piece of land privately held under separate title. . . . Any material changes affecting the productive value of a given piece of land would have to be currently noted. The preliminary card data would be obtained from various existing official sources, and would gradually have to be expanded and made more complete, particularly by reports from field officers of the Department.

The Bureau of Farm Values should be conceived as an impartial scientific institute for the collection of the most accurate and complete information on the fundamental facts connected with the true farming value of every piece of land used, or usable, for pastoral, agricultural, and forestry production. As such it would soon become indispensable to Departments like those of Agriculture, Lands, Irrigation, Social Welfare and Finance (particularly in connection with the activities of the State Advances Recoveries Office and the Land Bank). The Bureau would bring up a staff of trained and experienced valuators of agricultural land . . . (and) the valuations of land in different regions would soon be reduced to uniform criteria and measures of value.

Such a conception of valuation of all agricultural land, card-indexed and cross-referenced, might well come from a text-book on Soviet agricultural planning. It is certainly somewhat startling to encounter it in an official policy white-paper of a South African government department. But the ruling minds in the Department of Agriculture had clearly come to a total rejection of the market as a determinant of economic development.

Although at first sight the proposal that the State should be the sole mortgage creditor may appear somewhat radical, there is under our conditions only one really effective way of checking inflation of land values and preventing excessive mortgage indebtness; that is by expanding the present Land Bank into a National Mortgage Loan Bank having the sole right of granting loans against mortgage on agricultural land. . . .

If a National Mortgage Bank were to have the sole right of advancing money against farm bonds, and if in fixing the amount of the loan the Bank were obliged to work on the assessments of the Bureau of Farm Values, the existing evils of overcapitalized farm enterprises could be practically removed. . . . Moreover, it should be possible to lay down a rule that a person buying land outright at a higher price than that assessed by the Bureau of Farm Values, will thereby be restricted in subsequently partici-pating in any other form of Government financial assistance to farmers.

Finally, while the Report concluded 'as far as the Union is concerned, it is considered that the system of private land ownership should be retained as the basis of our agricultural production', the Report recommended legal restriction of unbeneficial occupation of farm land, in the sense of large holdings which are not effectively used in the national interest, or land that is held idle for speculative purposes. It further proposed nationalization of land on a voluntary basis, and also expropriation in the case of land unsuitable for farming by Europeans and of land which should be reserved by the State as grazing areas only [33].

This curious combination of fundamentalism and collectivism had, however, already been overtaken by the intensified rate of economic development, which was the concomitant of war-time change and resource-utilization. Prices of foodstuffs and agricultural raw materials soon reflected the intensified pressures of war-time de-mands. Long-term purchase contracts by the British Government for all South Africa's exports of wool, sugar, maize, and much of its citrus-crop reduced the marketing problem to one of physical shipment.

Even more significant was the rapid expansion of domestic war-time employment and increased wages so that a substantial increase in total and *per capita* consumption of most agricultural produce had by early 1942 transformed the entire problem [34]. It was no longer a question of limiting supplies to force prices up but of limiting demand to keep prices down. The Minister of Agriculture became Controller of Food and the Secretary for Agriculture acquired in addition to the chairmanship of the National Marketing Council the alias of Deputy Food Controller [35]. Such dual-personalities imposed severe strains and Smut's War Cabinet was finally induced by consumers' clamour to separate the Food Control Organization from the Department of Agriculture.

The Government, however, resisted pressures for food-rationing[36]. It remains a Cabinet secret whether it was the formidable administrative difficulties or the perhaps greater embarrassment of the highly-discriminating points-allocation to Whites and Non-Whites that led to ration books being printed but never implemented. But these years from 1940 to 1948 had made it very evident that the reconstruction of agriculture along the lines of bureaucratic collectivism, as proposed by the Department of Agriculture, would frustrate the new dynamic of economic development that had the potential of carrying the South African economy and its social system from its completed take-off into its drive to maturity.

The Smuts Cabinet discreetly sought the support of other authorities, inclined to a more holistic view of the place of agriculture in the post-war economy. Under the chairmanship of Dr H. J. Van Eck, the Social and Economic Planning Council was invited to state how it envisaged 'The Future of Farming in South Africa'[37].

It provided dismaying but hardly-contestable evidence of the

TABLE I

Yield in Quintals per Hectare

Maize	1928–32 (ave)	1933	1934	1935	1936	1937	1938
Argentine	19·3	15·9	20·1	19·6	18·9	15·0	—
Australia	16·3	15·5	17·2	15·7	19·3	13·4	—
U.S. America	15·5	14·2	9·9	15·1	10·2	17·8	17·4
South Africa	5·0	7·0	5·7	5·4	8·2	5·7	8·9

Wheat	1928–29 1932–33 (ave)	1933/ 34	1934/ 35	1935/ 36	1936/ 37	1937/ 38	1938/ 39
United Kingdom	21·9	24·1	25·2	23·4	20·6	20·6	25·6
Germany	21·1	24·2	20·6	22·1	21·2	22·6	27·4
U.S. America	9·7	7·5	8·2	8·2	8·2	9·1	8·9
Argentine	8·8	10·7	9·4	9·4	10·6	8·2	11·8
Australia	7·8	8·0	7·2	7·2	8·3	9·2	7·2
South Africa	5·4	6·5	5·9	5·9	5·1	3·9	5·5

(South Africa: White crops only – overall crops lower.)

TABLE 2

Cattle Products, 1937, in 'ooo Cwts.

	Cattle ('ooos) Nos.	Beef/Veal	Butter	Cheese
Australia	13,078	11,025	2,853	397
New Zealand	4,506	3,390	3,358	1,768
South Africa (White and African)	11,407	2,870	413	103

TABLE 3

Sheep Products, 1937

	Sheep ('ooos)	Sheep slaughtered	Wool-Greasy ('ooo,ooo lb)
Australia	113,373	18,536	983
New Zealand	32,379	13,920	304
South Africa (White and African)	41,033	5,000	219

relative high-cost, low productivity of South African land-utilization, both arable and pastoral, reflected in the comparative tables.

The Planning Council's Report asserted that the policy of self-sufficiency and forced-export pursued by the Department of Agriculture had not only failed to optimize land-utilization but introduced serious distortions that delayed adjustments to increase output *per capita* in farming.

The 1941 population census gave the cash incomes of White farming families. Almost half the owner-occupiers had money incomes of less than £200 per year; of the tenants more than half had money incomes of less than £100 per year, while among the bywoners more than half earned less than £50 cash per year. The earnings of African farm-labourers in the immediate pre-1939 years, *including* payment in kind, ranged from £13·2 to £27·6 per year. Coloured farm-workers in the Western Province wheat-areas at the same period earned between £40 to £60 per year, including payment in kind.

The position of agriculture in the Native Reserves was even worse. No reliable calculations are available but an official Commission (1944) suggested a figure of just over £17 annual income for a family of five in the Transkei.

Fifty years after important consumer-markets had come into being in the mining areas, thirty years after the unification of South Africa and the sustained financial assistance of every kind, the productivity of farming in South Africa made it patently 'the sick organ of the country's economic body'. The intervention of the polity had equally patently inhibited for two generations the intensified mobility and employment of both White and Non-White population.

The re-deployment of the country's White labour resources slowly shook off the constraint of its 'back-to-the-land' complex. The growth factor of urbanization exerted increasing influence. From 1926 to 1936, 150,000 Whites of rural origin moved to urban areas. The capital investment in South Africa's gold-mining and manufacturing industry that stimulated the mobility of both Whites and Africans was also the solvent for the fuller employment of the Whites. But the polity, reluctant to accept that the same process was also inexorably urbanizing the Africans, was committed by the whole institutionalized culture of its White electorate to resist with rigidity fossilizing into inflexibility the fuller employment of the Non-Whites.

THE POLITICAL ECONOMY
OF LABOUR

The political economy of land conditioned the political economy of food and the political economy of food was frustrated by the political economy of labour. The unified polity, setting out with renewed resolution in 1910 to promote the wealth of White farmers, never recognized nor even understood that this was related to increasing incomes of Non-White consumers as a function of their growing productivity as workers. The impersonal co-ordination of resource utilization through the market to promote economic development was uncomprehended[1]. But its influence on colour-class relationships became increasingly suspect so that economic development itself came to be questioned as the destroyer of the institutionalized culture of the 'volk'.

The electoral weight of rural Afrikanerdom was deployed to secure control of the polity for Afrikanerdom, so that Afrikaner nationalism might direct the executive and administrative authority within the polity to shape the adaptive compulsions of economic rationality.

The agents of production, wrote Alfred Marshall in the classical tradition, are commonly classed as Land, Labour and Capital. In respect of land, legislative enactment established that legal ownership of about 87 per cent of the national territory was secured for members of the White electorate. In respect of the second agent, Labour, the division of the labour market so that the Whites secured a leasehold in perpetuity on all better-paid jobs was a more complex task of frustrating economic rationality. In respect of the third agent, Capital, though nationalization of the gold mines was espoused by some influential leaders of the Nationalist Party (apart from earlier slogan-makers of the South African Labour Party), the most deep-rooted, almost-emotional Afrikaner attachment to land-ownership inhibited the socialist heresies though it did not preclude a growing extension of state-capitalism.

So long as the economy continued almost untouched by or unresponsive to market determinants, that is for nearly two hundred years after the establishment of the supply-station at Cape Town, the pursuit of productivity through least-cost substitution was desultory. The dynamism of economic rationality in the allocation and employment of the scarce resource of labour became disruptive of institutionalized culture, of the Africans first and the Whites subsequently, only when the country's economy was energized out of its near-stationary self-sufficiency.

As the economy was projected by the mineral discoveries and related capital investment into a progressive interaction within an exchange- or market-economy, the pursuit of productivity exercised increasingly far-reaching adaptation on the whole social system. In the earlier stage, non-monetary, customary terms of labour service[2] persisted even after the gradual introduction of a cash or market economy – more particularly in the Transvaal, where monetary media of payment hardly existed until the gold discoveries. Capitalistic forms of economic activity henceforth emphasized economic rationality with the concomitant specialization and division of labour. The consequent clash with tradition, traditionalism and ideology centred on the utilization of African labour.

The gold-mining industry was the focus of this conflict of value-orientations. It was here, predictably, that economic dynamism became political dynamite. It was here, inevitably, that the integrating effects of economic development, of Schumpeterian change and innovation, exerted their critical challenge. And it was here that the challenge was taken up by the political parties so as to maintain the social system in accordance with the institutionalized culture of the dominant White electorate. It is the detail of economic rationality, as implemented and frustrated in the gold-mining industry which provides the most significant chapter in the record of the political economy of labour in South Africa – both for the political scientist and for the economic analyst.

By the time of Union, the pattern of labour utilization in the Rand gold-mining industry had been established in its essentials[3]. Those essentials reflected the realities of the labour market – the economic and the extra-economic. The profitable exploitation of low-grade, goldiferous rock-earth under contemporary conditions of low-grade mechanization necessitated massive application of low-grade human energy. Such low-grade human energy was present in Southern Africa in the form of tribal Africans – present but inhibited in its availability by the social system of tribalism. Conjunct high-grade human skill was not present virtually at all in Southern Africa. Hence gold-mining management had, in addition to attracting capital, to concentrate on attracting labour – unskilled labour from Africa, which was Black, and skilled labour from Europe, which was White. The market determinants of demand and supply operated to establish the frame of wage-rates and the institutionalized culture of trade-unionist Europeans and tribalized Africans hardened the matrix of expectation-frustration.

A gap was formed between the wages and working conditions of skilled artisans, largely immigrants from Europe and consequently White and relatively few, and the wages and working conditions of unskilled labourers, migrants from Africa and consequently Black and relatively numerous. It was *formed*, it must be emphasized, in accordance with the market realities of demand, supply and marginal productivity. It was these market realities which in 1894 employed on the Transvaal gold-mines about 40,000 Africans at an average wage of 61s. per month (plus the cost of compound feeding of about 10s. per month) and about 5,400 Europeans at an average wage of about £21 per month [4].

But the gap that was formed by market realities became the gulf of insitutionalized culture and, finally, the chasm of the South African social system. Skilled workers for the new mining and manufacturing activities were recruited from overseas, mainly from Britain. Branches of British craft unions were soon formed. In 1881 the Amalgamated Society of Carpenters and Joiners was established, between 1886 and 1893 branches of the Amalgamated Society of Engineers, the Ironmoulders' Society in 1896 and in 1902 the S.A. Engine Drivers' and Firemen's Association for mine- (not railway) employees. A strike on Crown Reef Gold Mine in 1902 was successful under the leadership of a Joint Mechanics' Committee and from this Committee was launched the Witwatersrand Trades and Labour Council with political as well as industrial aims. In 1911 a Transvaal Federation of Trades affiliated most of the Transvaal employees' associations [5].

Membership of these trade unions and political organizations of labour was exclusively White. Though their operations and activities extended of course beyond the gold mines and beyond the Witwatersrand, the concentration of collective bargaining and of political agitation by trade union action was on the gold-mining industry and in the Rand. The Chamber of Mines both as employers and as 'capitalists' was the focus of labour-market variables and constants, which encompassed among others the world price of gold, yields on the international market for risk capital, trade unionism and social convention.

Hence the Economic Commission of 1914 was directed by the Botha Government to inquire into wages and working conditions and the cost of living more particularly on the Rand, and also into the general question of establishing minimum or subsistence wages[6]. The Report of this 1914 Commission with its illuminating data on contemporary conditions brings out clearly the extent to which 'conventional necessities', 'involuntary employment', 'preferred idleness' exercised their effects on the supply-price of White labour.

The Commission noted that '. . . working class life in South Africa is rendered unavoidably expensive in numerous ways . . . the white man is expected and expects to be domiciled in a fashion unmistakeably superior to that of the Non-White . . . a man must ride daily to work since he rarely lives near it, cost of amusements and recreation is high, education is costly . . . medical expenses are exceedingly high . . . the cost of a native (servant) must be reckoned as a part of the artisan's actual cost of living in South Africa – one might say as a part of his necessary cost of living in a not overstrained sense' [7].

After stressing the limitations of such statistical calculations, the Commission published the data below for *circa* 1913 [8].

Index Numbers of Money Wages of Skilled Artisans

Johannesburg	100	Germany	26
South Africa (elsewhere)	80	Belgium	20
England & Wales	31	U.S.A.	72
France	23	Australia	60
	New Zealand 58		

It calculated that '. . . a family which migrated from Johannesburg to England and maintained its old standard of house-room and consumption on food would find the cost of food and housing reduced in the ratio of 100 to 52' [9]. 'The wages (for White miners i.e. supervisors) paid on the Witwatersrand' the Commission concluded 'are unquestionably very high, but it does not follow that they are excessively high when the nature and conditions of the work are allowed for. . . .' [10] It found that 'social convention has set its seal on customs'.

The gap between White skilled and Black unskilled wages and working conditions was established by the market realities of demand, supply and marginal productivity. It became the gulf, buttressed by social convention, barricaded by militant White trade unionism and increasingly fortified by the White polity after 1924, when the South African Labour Party became the minor partner in the Pact Government of General Hertzog. Hence when the Economic and Wage Commission of 1925 came to its conclusions (some ten years after the first Economic Commission) on comparative wages and living costs, it wrote:

To sum up – our comparison of money wages in different countries showed the level of urban skilled rates to be high in South Africa – far higher than in any European country, higher than in Australia, about as high as in Canada, and exceeded only by the United States of America. When we allow for differences in the purchasing power of wages and compare real wages the advantage of South Africa over Europe is reduced, but remains considerable; real wages being about 40 per cent above the highest European level, namely, London. . . . Taken in connection with the capacity to pay of industry in the different countries, the rates of wages in South Africa are relatively far higher than in any other country.

The explanation is obvious: the rates of wages that we selected for comparison . . . were the rates of a small minority of workers . . . they were the rates of white workers, while the great majority of wage-earners in South African industry and agriculture are natives, coloured or Asiatic . . . In other words, the explanation of the remarkable fact that the rates of wages which we took are above the average income per occupied person, while in other countries the corresponding rates are usually about half the average income, is to be found in the characteristic of South African wages that we noted first – the wide spread, a spread several times as great as in any other country, between the highest and the lowest rates of wages. The rates of mechanics, building artisans, miners and printers are the rates of a small skilled class of urban white labour[11].

The early scarcity of skilled workers on the Rand undoubtedly helped to add a powerfully conventional concept of White man's money-wage to the even earlier and stronger social convention of 'kaffir's work'. Furthermore, while White trade unionists applied all the pressures of militant collective bargaining so as to secure a monopolistic position in the skilled labour market, the Chamber of Mines had through the centralization of its recruitment and application of the 'maximum-average' wage agreement for African workers established a monopsonistic position in relation to its unskilled labour force.

Within the gold-mining industry, consequently, the imperfections in its labour market from an early stage made it increasingly unlikely that wage-rates reflected marginal productivity of labour. It was these imperfections that critically influenced working costs and, through such working costs, the marginal grade of ore it was profitable to mine at ruling, fixed gold-price.

Repeatedly during the history of the South African gold-mining industry, commissions of inquiry were appointed to consider working costs as a seemingly inexorable break-even crisis threatened the early closing of marginal mining [12]. The major issue was labour-costs, though other aspects such as the 'burden' of discriminatory railway rates, customs tarffis and taxation made their regular appearance. In the next chapter the significance of gold output to the rate of the country's economic development will be examined but, from 1886 until at least 1940, that it was the decisive and over-whelmingly important variable seems hardly disputable.

What has, however, been hotly debated for sixty years with no consensus is the effect of the Chamber of Mines policy of centralized recruitment and wage-fixation of its African labour [13]. Centralized recruiting by the two official agencies, the Witwatersrand Native Association and the Native Recruiting Corporation, as elaborated earlier, was intended to reduce costs of recruitment. As an organizational method, it was doubtless more efficient and therefore less costly than the heterogeneous recruiting techniques it replaced. But recruitment costs are patently a function of the attractiveness of wage-working conditions to prospective workers [14].

The Native Recruiting Corporation, apart from operating the monopsony on behalf of the Chamber of Mines for the Rand gold-mines in South Africa and the then British Protectorates, also laid down the wage-rates applicable to *all* Africans employed on the gold-mines. Times-rates for different categories of work could not be exceeded by any mine-employer, and earnings from piece-work were limited to a *maximum average* not to be exceeded under penalty of a fine to the 'black-leg' mine.

In brief, there is a single buyer of African labour for the gold mines, who by agreement exclude wage-rate competition among themselves for such labour. The labour-market for African workers in goldmining is thus monopsonistic – furthermore as opposed to this 'single buyer', African mine-workers are prohibited from any form of trade-union combination on the supply side and in terms of the pass-laws are subjected to criminal prosecution for any breach of labour-contract.

Since there is no permissible alternative to this monopsonistic condition, its effect on labour productivity, working costs and gold output must therefore be a matter of opinion [15]. Only subjective evidence is necessarily available on this important factor or deter-minant of the rate of South Africa's economic development.

The Chamber of Mines viewpoint from the earliest days (though individual mining industrialists have differed) is that the Africans' demand for money income is inelastic. The amount of work the African-miner is prepared to offer is a function of his earnings but since his earnings are pre-determined by his fixed income-target, he will work only for the time necessary to secure that fixed income-target. Thus the Native Recruiting Corporation told the Economic and Wage Commission of 1925:

The social and economic position of the native is such that he is able to satisfy his needs by intermittent periods of service. Generally speaking, the native postpones going out to work until the last possible moment, and the possession of additional funds merely enables him to remain in idleness a further period. . . . The Corporation is convinced that any increase in the level of native wages would be followed, to only a small extent, by an increase in the native standard of living; that the main result would be that the native would work for a shorter period than at present; and that consequently the native labour available to industry in the Union would be reduced[16].

It will be noted that the Chamber of Mines was contending that the *reduction* in the supply of African labour in response to an *increase* in wage-rate (i.e. the so-called backward-sloping supply curve) applied not merely to mine labour but to the over-all supply of African labour in response to the demand by industry in general. Undoubtedly White farmers were even more firmly convinced that to increase the African farm-labourer's wage was to reduce the supply [17].

The implications of such a backward-sloping supply curve for African labour, if it conformed to the facts, for the rate of economic development of South Africa were patently highly significant and far-reaching. It implied that a competitive market on the demand side for African labour would through higher wage-rates contract the total supply of African labour, and hence diminish gross national product. It justified the monopsony formally operated by the Chamber of Mines as well as the 'tacit-understanding' on non-competition for labourers among White farmers in that *lower* wage-rates for African workers *expanded* the total supply of such labour, and hence presumably increased gross national product.

It implied, further, that until the critical change in income-leisure preference could be effected among the great mass of the African population, the inelasticity of their demand for money-income inhibited (or even prohibited) an expansion of a major sector of total market-demand for South African manufacturing industry and agriculture[18]. If the White polity desired to stimulate the rate of economic development, then it became a desirable objective of polity to stimulate money-earning among the Africans. The spokesmen for manufacturing industry, anxious to promote the domestic production of manufactured goods, were indeed persistent and consistent critics of the (low) wage-policies of the mining and agricultural industries.

There is evidence that the tribal Africans did not lack money *consciousness*. In the absence of such money-consciousness there would, for instance, have been neither purpose to nor need for the abortive attempts by the mining companies in the eighteen-nineties, to eliminate wage-competition for African labour between the mines[19]. In fact the reports of numerous Commissions confirm that money-consciousness among African mine-workers was percipient to a degree.

The Economic Commission of 1914 analysed the piece-work system as applied to African labour on mines, classified as hammer-boys, machine-drill boys, lashers and trammers and surface boys. It reported that nothwithstanding the strenuous nature of hammer-work, it was eagerly sought after because 'hammer-boys make much more than the average rate of wages and are paid according to capacity'. It noted how machine-drill boys responded to a bonus-system and also the response of lashing-tramming gangs to a task-bonus.

But the maximum average-penalty compelled the mines not to exceed the average of 2/3d. per shift and the Commission commented:

Your Commissioners feel no doubt that the productive powers of the native are being held in check, while at the same time a sense of injury is being generated by the device of the maximum average in particular, and in general by a failure on the part of the gold mines to pay natives more frequently on a system which furnished an incentive. To the system of piece rates for White workers there may not infrequently be objections, but these objections do not carry the same weight in the case of the native. He is at that stage of industrial development in which the crude incentive of gain is an important, if not indispensable, educational instrument. . . . The native desires to be paid according to his strength; and he complains of the small amount he earns. Your Commissioners understand that the question of an extension of piece-work for natives is closely engaging the attention of the gold-mining industry, and are convinced that much can be done in this direction to increase the efficiency of native labour.

They agree with Mr. Taberer (of the Native Recruiting Corporation), who stated he preferred piece-work (for natives) in the interest of the mine, of the native, and of the industry.

The same Commission further reported that the maximum average day's pay of 2s. 3d. is 'especially felt by the natives as a grievance' and that there were 'general and bitter complaints of rate-cutting and other methods of reducing earnings, and of under-payment for superior work as clerks and boss-boys'. Indeed from the Report of the Native Grievances Inquiry of 1914[20], it is patent that tribal African labour showed acute perception of the detail of work-organization that affected piece-work earnings.

Hammer-boys, paid at piece-rates for every inch-depth of hole drilled, complained that they were required to do lashing, i.e. clearing the working-place of broken rock produced by the previous blast before they could begin their own piece-rate work of boring holes for the next blast. 'I have', said the Commissioner while rejecting most complaints as exaggerated, 'come across a mine where 90 per cent of the natives employed were hammer-boys. There can be no doubt that, in that case at least, practically all the lashings must be done by hammer-boys. It is observed that the employment of hammer-boys to do lashing is, in a very large number of cases, a plain breach of contract'[21]. He also quoted from circular No. 55 of the Native Recruiting Corporation that 'it has always been considered inadvisable to insert a clause in the native contract having reference to the (lashing work) . . . as it is feared it may needlessly alarm them as to what they may be compelled to perform, and so adversely affect our recruiting operations'.

The Commissioner noted that on mines where labour was organized so that lashing was scheduled adequately in advance of hammering, there were no complaints. 'Again, at the City and Suburban, the lashing boys go down an hour before the hammer-boys and clear out the stopes, so that the hammer-boys do no lashing at all. This has been going on for the last four years and has given no rise to difficulty. . . . It may be worth noting that this mine succeeds in doing without recruited labour; it has no difficulty in filling up with voluntary boys. . . .' [22].

There were complaints of insufficient drills to accomplish hole-drilling either through poor stores-organization or deliberate under-issue of drills to save steel; of insufficient candles to perform tasks thereby forfeiting pay. A perpetual source of complaint was that the White miner-supervisor had sole, unfettered authority for marking or non-marking of tickets which served as basis for the African labourer's wage-calculation and record of number of shifts worked so that there might be partial or total loss of pay [23].

African mine-workers patently showed no lack of money-consciousness in relation to the operation of piece-work earnings. Such money-consciousness was not necessarily incompatible with the Chamber of Mines contention that the tribal African's demand for money-income was inelastic and that they were target-workers. Keen awareness of piece-work incentives may have implied a desire to achieve target-earnings earlier rather than later, and thereby satisfy their leisure-preference. Since the African miner contracted to complete a specific number of shifts before he could legally return home, maximizing his earnings from greater productivity during the time-period of his contract did not enable him to reduce time-spent at the mine in that particular contract. But experience of higher-earnings to be achieved through his greater productivity might possibly influence him to contract for fewer shifts in subsequent service-contracts.

Such nicety of calculation implies a fairly high degree of sophistication in work-attitudes [24]. The Africans made complaints to the Commissioner on the general level of earnings and their rates of pay. According to the evidence of the Chamber of Mines, the then (1913) schedule of wages showed a general increase of underground rates but with little change in surface rates since their agreed uniform schedule of May 1897. However the Commissioner commented: 'On the other hand I am told that the schedule of 1897 represented a reduction of approximately one-third on the scale previously in force; if so wages were higher in 1896 than they are now (1913)' [25].

The common complaint, said the Commissioner, was there was no increase of pay for long service with its accompanying increased efficiency. 'The real grievance of the native on this point is the colour bar, which blocks practically all his opportunities for promotion. He argues – and I see no flaw in his reasoning – that if he can do the same work as white men, there is no reason why he should not receive the same remuneration. That in many instances he can do it and in some instances is actually doing it, admits of no doubt' [26].

It was indeed the approach of the Chamber of Mines to this crux and crunch of the colour bar that suggests some equivocation on 'the backward-sloping supply curve' for African mine labour. Under a gold price-working cost squeeze that from time to time threatened the very life of marginal mining, the Chamber of Mines moved purposefully and resolutely towards least-cost labour utilization. It aimed to advance some Africans to higher categories of labour, that is to realize the potential of their productivity. At such increased marginal productivity, African mine-workers would have merited and received higher wage-rates. And at such times, the Chamber of Mines does not appear to have advanced the argument that the Africans' alleged inelasticity of money-income demand would have made it impossible or difficult to find a supply of Africans for advancement.

The White miners in their trade-unions assuredly had no doubts about a supply of African miners being forthcoming for jobs of higher marginal productivity at related pay. The pressure of trade-union collective bargaining, occasionally exploding in pre-1914 strikes, was continuously exerted against 'dilution of labour' through attempts to widen the range of African-performed jobs. During World War 1, such pressure was relaxed when large numbers of White miners enlisted and by common consent some semi-skilled underground jobs, such as drill-sharpening, were no longer exclusively demarcated as White.

The more extensive employment of Non-Whites, particularly Africans, in the gold-mining industry during the First World War years led to the July, 1918, *Status Quo* Agreement between the Chamber of Mines and the South African Industrial Federation to maintain the then prevailing job-demarcation between Whites and Non-Whites. The potentialities of least-cost substitution were evident to mining management. As war- and post-war inflation of costs embarrassed exploitation of increasing areas of low-grade, goldiferous rock-earth, the pursuit of economic rationality by the Chamber of Mines became an imperative. Such pursuit would patently be resisted by the whole force of trade union tradition supported by Afrikaner ideology [27].

The political conflict and challenge that led from the 1922 Rand Strike to the 1924 Nationalist-Labour Pact Government has been related in an earlier chapter. The realities of gold-mining operation and its significance to the rate of economic development of the country at this period emerge clearly from the Report of the Low Grade Mines Commission 1919/20, appointed as a matter of great urgency by the Government. It was to inquire into gold mines currently working at a loss or small, diminishing profit; the effect of their closure and what action could be taken by the Government; the position in the mining industry of the Native and Coloured workmen and the more efficient utilization of the available Native labour force [28].

From mid-1914 to 1919, working costs rose from 17s. 5d. per ton milled to 22s. 9d. A parliamentary select committee had reported that in the last quarter of 1917, 14 mines were working at a loss or working profit of 2s. per ton or less. The Low Grade Mines Commission Interim Report of September, 1919, stated that three of these mines had already closed and a further 11 mines had become marginal. The marginal mines 'constitute, from the employment and expenditure point of view, roughly one-half of the Witwatersrand gold-mining industry' [29].

The detail of work-organization as given by this Commission is highly instructive in relation to the problems and prospects of re-organization, which had least-cost substitution as the objective.

The White miner is the first to enter his working place in the morning. His last act on the previous shift was to light up his fuses for blasting, and it is now his duty to see that the place is safe enough for his gang to work in before letting them commence their tasks. He enters with a few natives, dresses down pieces of rock which might fall and endanger life and limb, and generally makes the place secure. . . . He then admits the remainder of the natives, points out the position and direction of the holes to be drilled, assists in the rigging up of machine drills, and gets the work well under way.

When he feels that he can safely leave the natives to continue their tasks, he proceeds to the place where his explosives are stored, prepares his cartridges, fuse and detonators for blasting, returns to the working place to see the finish of the process of drilling, fetches his explosives, sends the natives out, charges up his holes, places guards to prevent persons entering by mistake, lights up his fuses, either in person or by means of natives acting under his immediate eye, and proceeds up the shaft to be hoisted to the surface. The natives in his gang will have rigged up the machine drills, done the drilling, and shovelled the rock, broken by the previous day's blast, to the bottom of the stope to be transferred to the trucks, and generally done all or nearly all the manual work required. . . .

The white trammer, waste packer and timberman, similarly will do the supervision of the native's work, lending a hand where required and being generally responsible for the safety of the native . . . . There is a good deal of elasticity in the extent to which native labour is utilized in the actual operations to be carried out. One White man will do a good deal of the manual work himself, where another would content himself with directing.

One principle is, however, practically universally observed and that is that every native or coloured person has to work under the supervision of a White man who is not an official. A shift boss, for example, is not permitted to set half-a-dozen natives on any job, such as tramming or shovelling, but must place them in charge of some White man, who is responsible for their safety and for the due performance of their work. This restriction is due primarily to custom and partly to mining regulations which, although primarily intended for the preservation of safety, have in course of time come to be regarded by White workers as their bulwark against the demand of the natives to be allowed to do work now only entrusted to whites. Those regulations and customary restrictions constitute what is generally known as the 'colour bar'. . .[30].

It is patent that in respect of underground operations, the White 'miner' was essentially a supervisor and that he was totally opposed to any work re-organization which, in the process of reducing working costs, would 'dilute' the customary demarcation of White supervision. As the Commission reported: several witnesses representing the views of White workers have said that rather than give way on the colour bar, they would prefer to see the low grade mines closed down, despite the resulting unemployment and misery which such a calamity would cause. . .[31].

Such opposition extended even to the detail of operations which, while in the Commission's opinion not involving 'any diminution in the number of skilled or unskilled underground White workers', would allow for 'experienced natives to charge up and blast' or for 'special blasting gangs of Whites with native assistants'. Customary practice, for example, dictated that Africans proceeded underground first and came up last and that they must work within the time limits and supervision of White gangers. Hence the Africans' effective shift was much shorter than the 8 hours shift of White workmen and was estimated to amount to not more than an average of about five hours [32]. No estimate seems to have been made of the significance of this single factor to total output but its substantial reduction of work-output hardly requires the nicety of calculation by latter-day 'operations-research'.

It is highly significant, however, that the viewpoints expressed on the one side by the majority of the Commissioners and on the other side by the minority (the trade-unionst members of the Commission) gave as much weight to the extra-economic as to the economic [33].

The majority, after noting the opposition to the legal colour bar in the Mines and Works regulations by earlier Commissions (the Transvaal Indigency Commission, 1908, the Economic Commission, 1914, the Relief and Grants-in-Aid Commission 1916, the Native Grievances Inquiry Commission, 1914) said:

While not agreeing entirely with the reasoning of our predecessors we are of the opinion that the legal restrictions now in force should be abolished. From the point of view of abstract justice as between man and man, there is nothing to be said in their favour. . . . It may be argued that, if the larger section of the people wish to and are able to enforce the effective colour bar, this may as well be incorporated in legal enactments. . . . It is, however, doubtful whether the majority of white South Africa supports the colour bar, and even if it did, it might yet hesitate to incorporate this feeling in a statute or other legal provision which conflicted with its sense of justice. . .[34].

The trade-unionist minority members said:

The Commission should have as its aim the adjustment of outstanding views, so as to arrive at the maximum amount of all round satisfaction rather than at a pronouncement of just and equitable theory, hopelessly inapplicable to existing circumstances. . . . To give something to the Native with which he is in the main little concerned about, but which takes from the white workers something which will certainly excite their feelings beyond dangerous limits, is surely lacking in wisdom, however possessed of theoretical justice. . .[35].

This Low Grade Mines Commission of 1919/20 was also greatly concerned about 'the serious shortage of native labour'. According to the Chamber of Mines another 40,000 African workers were necessary to ensure that all mines could be worked to the full capacity of their reduction plants, i.e. that average costs per ton milled would be significantly reduced by employing more labour on the existing fixed-cost capacity[36]. The Commission therefore examined the view that 'the insufficiency of wages paid . . . is one of the principal causes of the serious shortage of native labour. . . .'

Since 1911 the Commission found the average earnings per shift of all Africans employed in the Witwatersrand gold-mining industry to have been:

1911	1/11·3	1916	1/11·1
1912	1/11·6	1917	1/11·1
1913	1/11	1918	1/11·5
1914	1/11·7	1919	2/0·3 plus a long-service
1915	1/11·4		bonus of 5/- per month.

The Commission noted that from 1914 to 1919, the remuneration of White miners was at least 40 per cent higher with reduced working hours. A similar percentage increase for African workers would have involved the mining industry in an increased cost of over £2 million per annum. 'While such a large increase is out of the question, even a smaller one has been rendered more difficult by the concessions to White employees and other increases in costs . . .' [37].

The Commission was in no doubt about the money-consciousness of the African mine-workers. The wage question, it wrote, is a matter of acute concern to the native worker and his demand is insistent that he should be placed on a footing which will compare not unfavourably with the purchasing power of his pre-war earnings. The equity of this demand bears close scrutiny . . . [38].

But the Commission, and the Chamber of Mines, was still haunted by the belief that increased wages could not induce an increase in the total supply of African labour. 'It is true that the wages paid on the gold mines have increased only to a slight extent since 1911 but unless a sufficient supply of unemployed natives is obtainable from present sources of supply, an increase in wages on the gold mines would merely divert natives from other industries'. These would then increase their rates of pay, and, in the long run, although natives' wages had been increased all round, and the distribution of the natives among employers perhaps altered, the total number of 'natives employed by the industries of South Africa would not have increased appreciably, and an industrial crisis might result . . .' [39].

So the Commission unanimously recommended 'the temporary modification of the existing prohibition on employment of natives from north of latitude 22° South'. After 1913, the Government had prohibited the employment of such Central African migrants because of the extraordinarily high mortality rate but it was now argued that medical advances made previous mortality experience 'extremely unlikely' [40].

The expectation-frustration matrix of labour utilization and labour organization was indeed coming under stress and strain in gold-mining industry. The compulsions of change were being exerted on the industry and the South African economy as a whole, now under the severest pressures from the world's post-war depression of the nineteen-twenties. The sharp deflation in the general price-level was felt especially by the farmers, whose burden of indebtedness became increasingly onerous. The period from mid-1920 to mid-1922 was a major downward swing in the South African trade cycle [41].

It was the fluctuations in the gold premium that caused the most serious alarm regarding the country's economic development. Up to 1914 the gold price had held steady at 84s. 11d. an ounce but in the years just after the First World War it moved between 130s. and 95s. The working costs of the Rand gold mines rose from 55s. 1d. per oz in 1913 to 65s. 11d. in 1918 and by 1921 were 76s. 5d. Working profit of £12·1 million in 1913 fell in each successive year to a record low of £6·7 million in 1919, recovered in the next two years but with the drop of the gold price to 95s. per oz in December 1921, the working profit of the gold mines fell again to an ominous £7·8 millions for 1922 [42].

In his annual address in March, 1920, the Chamber of Mines President had foreshadowed that if the gold premium disappeared 31 mines, employing 14,400 Whites would become unpayable. In an anticipatory Keynesian calculation, the Chamber's President put the indirect effects as: '. . . it would probably be correct to say that the Rand with a spending power in South Africa of about £28,000,000 per annum and a productive value of about £36,000,000 per annum supports a quarter of a million Whites and a million Natives'[43].

In November, 1921, a series of conferences between the Prime Minister, the Minister of Mines and workers' representatives proposed certain amendments to the mining regulations, which would increase the effective working time underground of the African work force. The Chamber of Mines, sensing strangulation by the price-cost squeeze, urged on the South African Industrial Federation (recognized by the Chamber in 1915) a more flexible work-reorganization including modification of the *Status Quo* agreement. The Chamber undertook to maintain a fixed ratio of one White to 10·5 Non-Whites but the workers' Federation replied with a demand for a ratio of one White to 3·5 Non-Whites applied to the gold-mines and to all other industry except agriculture.

When negotiations failed, the White miners struck on 10 January 1922. A general strike was called on 7 March and was ended on 16 March. The detail of this 'minor civil war' and its political consequences have already been related. The strike itself failed and work-reorganization followed. A Mining Industry Board appointed on 15 April 1922, concluded that there was no necessity for continuance of the *Status Quo* agreement and that its abolition after the strike was fully justified; that it was not desirable to establish by law the ratio of White to African labour in the Transvaal goldmines; and that it could not recommend that differential systems of wages and overhead charges should be brought into practice on the gold mines. There followed a (temporary) elimination of a number of White miners, a substantial reduction in wage-cost, an increase in the scale of operations and in the mining of lower grade ore[44].

THE POLITICAL ECONOMY
OF LABOUR
continued

The year 1924 was indeed a high point of achievement in the operating experience of the Witwatersrand gold-mining industry. Working profit of £14·6 millions was the highest recorded from 1911 until 1932. Though the complexity of the determinants of the profitability of an industry like gold-mining must caution against conclusions, the profit performance that accompanied relaxation of colour-bar restraints on appropriate deployment of labour is suggestive. The 1924 peak of total working profits, £14·6 millions, was achieved on the basis of a profit of 31s. 4d. per oz and 10s. 4d. per ton milled. From 1911 until the major increase in gold price in 1933, such indices of profitability were not exceeded.

Despite this empirical evidence in relation to the rate of development in the industry, which clearly operated as the prime mover of the country's economy, it was organized White labour and not the Chamber of Mines who successfully laid claim to be the Fourth Estate. Col. Creswell led the White political wing of the White trade unions into the Pact Government under General Hertzog, as Prime Minister and leader of White Afrikaner nationalism. With the White polity taking firm control, both the maximization of productivity in the mining industry and the shape of economic development generally were soon subjected to the motivations of the White electorate.

The Hertzog-Creswell Government served immediate notice that least-cost substitution in mining operations was unacceptable in principle and in practice. The Mining Regulations Commission was appointed in October, 1924[1]. Its terms of reference covered the implications of the more flexible working-regulations of the mines on the immediate and long-term relationship of White worker to African worker on the mines.

The Commission addressed itself to regulation No. 102 (1) which had replaced the old regulation 106(7)(a). The essential difference, it found, was that the new regulation enabled any competent person, including an African boss-boy, to make safe underground working-places. In consequence African miners need not have to wait for the supervising White ganger or miner before starting effective working of their shift, which according to the Government Mining Engineer was thereby increased from five or six hours to the full eight-hours. '. . . Though evidence . . . does not in its entirety support the conclusion that the amendment has brought about an increase in accidents . . . the risk is somewhat greater with the new regulation' [2], declared the Commission which accordingly recommended a revision of the new regulation to ensure that making-safe a working place was to be entrusted only to certified miners. And, therefore, it recommended a definite limitation of the number of such working places required from the examining miner.

The extended passages below indicate the general line of approach of this Commission:

On the evidence therefore as to the working of the regulations . . . we have come to the conclusion . . . that they are frequently, and in some case habitually, contravened. In entertaining it, we regret to find ourselves in disagreement with views expressed by the Government Mining Engineer and Senior Inspectors, but the grounds on which those views are based appear so unsubstantial and the evidence against their acceptance so cogent, that we are compelled to reject them. We think too that the primary cause of the contraventions that occur lies in a practice, to which we shall repeatedly have to refer, of extending the sphere of the European miner's responsibility beyond what we conceive to be its justifiable limits. . . .

This tendency results from the obligation to increase output at a minimum of working costs. Combining with another viz. the marked advance during recent years in the efficiency of the native boss-boy, it has been instrumental in so far extending the European miner's responsibility as virtually to reduce his control over the work of his natives in many cases to a mere shadow, they looking upon their boss-boy rather than upon him as their real supervisor. . . .

The process of gradually enlarging the scope of the European miner's responsibility must needs bring in its wake another viz. an increasing employment of native labour in spheres formerly occupied exclusively by Europeans, and this we think exercised an equally baneful influence in the direction in which we are endeavouring to examine. . . .

There are certain specific occupations on the mines such as winch-driving and loco-driving in which it is possible to perceive in the clearest light the displacement of Europeans by native workers, but apart from this, general widening of the European miner's sphere of responsibility has resulted in many natives i.e. boss-boys, being entrusted with duties that were formerly performed by Europeans. . . . Throughout the mines, natives are being set to do work that for its efficient carrying out requires on the part of its performers a regard for safety, a sense of responsibility and a capacity to exercise control over others, with which not even the most exceptional among their numbers are endowed; and secondly that in course of time the supply of competent European miners is substantially reduced, a circumstance which is naturally utilized for continuing the system. . .[3].

What aroused the urgent concern of the Commission was the empirical evidence from the Messina Copper Mine, which in July 1922 had been exempted by the previous Smuts Government from regulations which restricted certain mining occupations to certificated miners.

The ground upon which the application for such exemptions . . . was solely the economic one that in their absence all operations on the mines in question would have, by reason of excessive working costs, to be discontinued . . . the effect of the exemptions being granted was in the space of a few months considerably to increase the ratio of native to European workers on the Messina Mines (for years 1915/21 the average ratio was 13 to 1, and from 1922 to 1924 it rose to 29 to 1).

The comparatively enormous displacement of Europeans by natives in actual breach, as we think, of the regulations which is reflected in these figures has not been proved to have had any adverse effect upon the safety or health conditions in the mines where it has occurred. This circumstance, however, we do not think falsifies the conclusions already set forth with reference to the general effect on safety and health conditions of the employment of native in place of European workers, and is to be accounted for by an abnormal degree of vigilance exercised both by the Inspectors and mine officials to avoid accidents during what was naturally regarded as an experimental period[4].

To this Commission such evidence permitted of only one conclusion, which it proceeded to draw:

Of such conditions (transgression of regulations) the one that cries out most insistently for rectification is the practice of assigning to the European miner an area of supervision and responsibility too wide for him effectively to control. . . . As to the form modification should take, we would suggest that the average limits of the European miner's area of responsibility should be considerably curtailed and that, in the interests of health and safety, the employment of natives be restricted to the lower grades of mining occupations, all posts involving any exercise of supervision over others being confined to European workers, since mine natives in the present state of their development and the terms of their relationship with Europeans are unfitted to occupy them[5].

It was, however, when the Mining Regulations Commission turned to its second category of terms of reference – the changing ratio between Europeans and Africans in mining – that its arguments most clearly reflected the viewpoint that 'the interests of White civilization in South Africa are not to be sacrificed to profits'.

Table showing Employment Ratios on Rand Gold Mines [6]

Year	No. of Europeans employed	No. of Natives employed	Ratio	Tons Treated (millions)
1911	23,272	181,100	7·7	24·0
1912	23,196	188,252	8·1	25·6
1913	22,388	179,563	8·0	25·7
1914	20,403	164,009	8·0	25·7
1915	21,738	193,007	8·9	28·4
1916	21,857	200,582	9·1	28·5
1917	22,079	180,777	8·2	27·3
1918	22,328	177,800	7·9	24·9
1919	22,529	168,181	7·4	24·1
1920	21,672	173,598	8·0	24·2
1921	20,542	170,365	8·3	23·4
1922	13,556	158,306	11·6	19·6
1923	17,357	176,180	11·1	26·8

(1922 – Year of major strike)

The association of high tonnage treated with high ratio of Africans to Whites will be noted. The Chamber of Mines in its evidence attributed the 1923 output to the improved efficiency of machinery achieved during the years and to the discharge of a 'considerable number of redundant and inefficient men' following on re-organization after the 1922 strike[7].

The Commission accepted that drill-sharpening and rock-drilling machinery had improved but did not 'admit' that the elimination of considerable numbers of European workers 'has been a necessary consequence'[8]. The argument of the Commission was developed as follows:

. . . before 1914, in which year drill-sharpening machines began to come into use, one white man, assisted by two natives, would . . . sharpen approximately 100 machine drills . . . with advent of drill-sharpening machine it was possible within the same time to sharpen 600 such drills. Instead, however, of the European being placed in charge of the machine, his services, being considered superfluous, were frequently dispensed with, and those of one native assisted by two others brought into operation. . . . In justification of the dismissal of the European drill-sharpener, it has been urged by the Chamber of Mines that 'drill-sharpening is now in no sense a skilled occupation justifying the employment of Europeans', but with this contention we cannot agree, and venture to think that such employment would have been attended by better results than are at present being obtained. . .[9].

The Commission declared that there was the same trend in respect of rock-drilling machinery with 'the previously unskilled native converted into the semi-skilled native working a machine, and the retrenchment on the ground of redundancy of the European supervisor'[10]. It noted that the main development had been the extension of the European miner's sphere of responsibility and 'his dismissed co-worker cannot truly be said to have become redundant . . . the decrease in the number of European employees, which has gone hand in hand with an increase in the quantity of ore handled, while the number of natives has remained practically constant, we are unable to attribute to any other cause than a deliberate policy, consistently pressed during the period under review, of displacing Europeans in favour of cheap coloured labour[11].

After analysing the categories of semi-skilled work, the Commission summed up:

The substitution of native for European workers, which we have attempted to show, has proceeded along the directest lines in connection with rock-drilling, drill-sharpening, winch-driving and loco-driving, we have no doubt will tend to spread to many other mining occupations of even a skilled nature. We find ourselves unable to share the view of several witnesses, who gave evidence on behalf of the Chamber of Mines and of a previous Commission (the Mining Industry Board, 1922) that a process which has flourished for years back in the sphere of semi-skilled occupations is going suddenly and immediately to stop at the highly artificial line, which is drawn to separate these from what we may call the skilled.

Experience of the rapidly advancing efficiency of the natives, culled from every other region of industrial activity, it is impossible to believe will be unconfirmed in that of mining alone. . . . The circumstances, that have paved the way for the inroad of natives upon Europeans in what has been termed semi-skilled work, are to be found in the enormous advantages the

former possess over the latter and the natives' almost phenomenal advance
in efficiency during recent years. . .[12].

And finally:

Infinitely the most serious result, however, of the policy pursued during
recent years, and far transcending all others in importance, is the elimination it seems bound, if unchecked, to bring about of the European worker
from the entire range of mining occupations[13].

These extensive passages from the Mining Regulations Commission of 1925 are not so frequently referred to as the more familiar
denunciations of the 'economic colour bar' in the oft-quoted
Commissions of enquiry into South Africa's economic problems and
performance. Better known, thus, are:

It has been clearly proved to us that the restriction of the native to the
sphere of unskilled work cannot be permanent . . . we are opposed to any
Government action which is designed to protect the white men against
reasonable competition from the coloured races . . . any action on the part
of the State which would have the result of suddenly throwing large numbers
of natives out of employment in order to ease the position for the white man
would, in our opinion, be unjust . . . (Transvaal Indigency Commission,
1906–8).

But in our opinion any measure which seeks to place a permanent
artificial barrier by legislation in the way of a coloured man improving his
position according to his capacity is very difficult to justify or maintain.
Further, we feel assured that no such measure could by itself be permanently effective . . . so long as conditions are permitted to exist which cause
natural laws and economic forces to be operating in the opposite direction
(the Mining Industry Commission, 1907–8);

He (the native) is increasing in working efficiency, obtaining education
and advancing in material wants. . . . Your Commissioners are of opinion
that there should be no legal barriers to prevent natives, or others of the non-
white population, from engaging in any work above the grade of unskilled
(the Economic Commission, 1914).

We also agree . . . in rejecting the proposals that the Government should
assist to improve the white man's position by . . . fixing the ratio between
the number of white and coloured labourers in all employment . . . such
artificial methods will do more harm than good. So far from remedying the
evil they aggravate it; they encourage the white man to rely upon artificial
aids rather than upon his own resources. They also interfere with the operation of the economic principles on which alone a true and lasting solution of
the problem must depend (the Relief and Grants-in-Aid Commission,
1916);

The real grievance of the native on this point is the colour bar . . . . He argues – and I can see no flaw in the reasoning – that if he can do the same work as white men there is no reason why he should not receive the same remuneration (Native Grievances Inquiry Commission, 1913–14);

. . . we are of the opinion that the legal restrictions now in force should be abolished. From the point of view of abstract justice as between man and man there is nothing to be said in their favour. . . . It may be argued that if the larger section of the people wish to and are able to enforce an effective colour bar this may as well be incorporated in legal enactments, since, whether it is just or not, it is the will of the people. It is, however, doubtful whether the majority of white South Africa supports the colour bar, and even if it did it might yet hesitate to incorporate the feeling in a statute or other legal provision which conflicted with its sense of justice (the Low Grades Mines Commission, 1920)[14].

The legislation of the next forty years, that is from the accession to power of the Pact Government in 1924 until to date, leaves no doubt as to which was the canonical voice of the White polity. Whatsoever the scripture of the labour colour bar to be found in all the texts of economic analysis (interpreted so faithfully, irrefutably and prophetically in so many commissions of enquiry), the White polity found its authorized version in the Mining Regulations Commission.

The Mines and Works Amendment Act was passed as Act No. 25 of 1926[15]. It re-established the Mines and Works Act of 1911, as one of the earliest expressions of the polity's objectives. The minutiae of work-organization in the mines, provided by legal rule and administrative decision, secured for the White mine-workers a leasehold in perpetuity (as perpetuity was interpreted by their trade-union organizations) on the job-categories designated as White (by the same trade-union organizations) [16].

The 1922 Rand Strike and the Mines and Works Amendment Act of 1926 did more, however, than determine the future of labour utilization and allocation in the gold-mining industry. The manifest motivations of White labour, whose numbers and composition increasingly reflected the absorption of 'Poor Whites' as Afrikaner industrial workers, made it evident that the maintenance of the patterns of the past would at all times complicate the management of the tensions of the future.

However much economic development might interact with change, not competition nor least-cost substitution, nor economic rationality nor economic development itself was ever to be accepted as either the dominant value-orientation or the decisive determinant of the South African labour market. Indeed the polity never accepted that there *should* be a single labour market of both White and Non-White labour, all reality to the contrary[17].

Though the polity in 1910 had rejected the majority recommendation of the Mining Industry Commission of 1908 to adopt its White-labour policy as the *sine qua non* of the maintenance of White civilization in South Africa, from 1924 onwards labour legislation and administration had two basic objectives. The first was that the White worker should be safeguarded against what the Mining Regulations Commission had described as 'the enormous advantages' of the African worker. The second was that the 'inter-dependence' of White and Non-White labour should not imply a non-differentiating integration. The separate identities of White and Non-White labour categories should never be so amalgamated in or by a single labour market that separate racial categories, as legally classified on the Population Register[18], should be fused in or by a single social system.

It will be recollected that Creswell had been the main protagonist of the 'White-labour policy' on the Mining Industry Commission of 1908[19], but that first Botha and then Smuts had as prime ministers made policy until Smuts was defeated by the combination of Hertzog-Creswell. It was Creswell now, as Minister of Labour from 1925, who fashioned the letter and imbued the spirit of industrial-wage legislation.

The letter and the spirit of the Industrial Conciliation Act No. 11 of 1924, of the Wage Act No. 27 of 1925, of the administration of the Apprenticeship Act of 1922 have been acutely analysed a number of times[20]. Their operation on the South African labour market (and *ipso facto* on the rate and shape of South African economic development) is a lengthy and complete study in itself. Interaction between administered wages, labour demand and labour supply must probably defy even mathematical precision.

The general consequences of such interaction were perceived as early as 1925 in the Majority Report of the Economic and Wage Commission[21]. The wisdom is still wise, whatever later sophistication of either micro-economics or macro-economics might add:

While definite exclusion of natives from the more remunerative fields of employment by law was not urged upon us, the same result would follow a certain use of the powers of the Wage Board under the Wage Act of 1925, or of other wage-fixing legislation. The method would be to fix a minimum rate for an occupation or craft so high that no native would be likely to be employed. Even the exceptional native, whose efficiency would justify his employment at the high rate, would be excluded by the pressure of public opinion, which makes it difficult to retain a native in an employment mainly reserved for Europeans.

The significance of such a policy is that it would extend still further, to all skilled and responsible work, the conditions observed in the mining and some other industries where there is a skilled white class, receiving a relatively high rate of pay for their work accompanied by the payment of a low rate for all other work. . . .

The effect of such a policy would depend on the level of minimum rates fixed, and on the range of employment brought within its scope. If the rates fixed were on a level with the skilled rate fixed for builders and printers by the recent agreements enforced under the Industrial Conciliation Act, the effect would certainly be to exclude all natives, but also to exclude many Europeans, since industry with its present output cannot afford to pay more than a small minority of its personnel rates as high as these, and it is unlikely that the forcing up of wage rates would lead to anything like a corresponding increase in efficiency . . .

The precise effect of fixing legal minimum rates in occupations at present followed by natives at a level much above the present native rates is difficult to predict in detail. The general tendency, however, would certainly be to restrict the field of native employment, and so to crowd the natives into the already restricted fields in which they have a monpoly of employment. In these fields the low rates ruling would be still further depressed, and the gap between the rates for skilled work (done by Europeans) and unskilled work (done by natives), between rates in industry and rates in agriculture, would be still further widened. . .[22].

Interaction within the South African labour market was of course subjected to interaction between the labour market and the markets for all other variables of the production function – and to interaction between the production function and the consumption function. Furthermore, all such endogenous and exogenous interaction has taken place in an economy which, so far from being 'closed', is generally recognized to be as involved in international trade as heavily and as sensitively as any other country in the world. International trade during these four decades, from 1924 to date, has in itself come under cataclysms of change. Any resemblance, therefore, between the predicted consequences of attempted control by the White polity of the market for labour on South Africa's rate of economic development and the actual course of development would indeed be co-incidental.

Yet the later course of the political economy of labour utilization and organization has followed a pattern, which was foreshadowed.

Collective bargaining by White labour and frustrated combination by African labour produced the characteristic rigidities of monopolistic competition in the labour market. As the power of monopoly intensified inflexibility in wage-categories, so the power of competition substituted adaptibility by work-categories. The earnings gap between skilled high-paid White and unskilled low-paid Non-White, and especially unskilled tribal African, became a gulf. In that gulf the tens of thousands of Poor Whites floundered, their productivity not even approaching the forbiddingly high marginal line which the Industrial Conciliation Councils' wage-rates fixed for skilled work.

To connect a gap by a bridge of semi-skills at semi-skilled earnings is the function of a flexible labour market but to bridge a gulf may require a more complex, more roundabout capitalistic process.

South African economic development had indeed to proceed by way of the Great Depression, the epochal rise in gold-price, the forced industrialization of the Second World War and its aftermath before the gulf was bridged. Being White and enfranchised, political economy eventually ensured that the Poor Whites crossed the bridge and ceased to be 'Poor'. Being Black and unenfranchised, political economy strove to ensure that the Blacks were immobilized along the way and stayed 'Poor Blacks'.

The violence of industrial conflict on the Rand gold-mines was not only decisive for the re-legalization of the colour bar in the Mines and Works Amendment Act of 1926. It was that violence which led to the establishment of formal conciliation machinery to adjust labour disputes. Though initiated by the Smuts Government, the Industrial Conciliation Act No. 11 of 1924 was given its essential administrative interpretation by the newly formed Ministry of Labour under Creswell of the Pact Government[23]. Such interpretation carried the pattern and related earnings of work-organization in the gold-mining industry into manufacturing industry.

The Act applied generally to industrial activity, except Government undertakings and farming and domestic service, where labour is organized. It provided for the setting-up of industrial councils, subject to ministerial approval, to regulate wage-rates and working-conditions in the specific industries by negotiation, conciliation or arbitration. An industrial council is composed of representatives of registered employers' associations and of registered employees' associations in the particular industry. An industrial council agreement, once approved by the Minister of Labour, becomes legally binding on all employers and employees (not merely the contracting parties) in the industry and area specified.

Within the terms of a particular industrial council agreement, strikes are illegal and even outside the terms of an agreement, no strike is legal until appropriate conciliation and arbitration procedures have failed. On the evidence, this Act has maintained a favourable record of industrial peace in South Africa. It is however a matter of highly subjective opinion whether this is the direct or the indirect consequence of the Act. The industrial councils may be regarded as making peace between employers and employees on opposite sides of 'the capitalist system', or as the machinery for the establishment of a bilateral monopoly of White employers and White trade-unionists within the industry to the more or less effective exclusion of new entrants, who might as interlopers or as dilutees upset agreed price- and wage-structures [24].

Henceforth the potential disturbers of industrial peace were the unskilled. In so far as they were African, their *de jure* rights to collective bargaining have generally been curbed by the *de facto* frustration of their effective combination. A legal right to form trade unions is not faciliated by no legal claim to *recognition* as registered trade unions. It was further fettered, when a *de facto* inhibition of strikes by African workers became a *de jure* prohibition in the Native Labour (Settlement of Disputes) Act No. 48 of 1953.

But the significance of the Industrial Concilation Act to economic development lies more in its effect on labour mobility, and to the resistance to change in the labour market.

In essence the industrial council system was intended to protect White workers against the competition of African workers. The original Act of 1924 aimed to limit the benefits of bilateral bargaining between employers and employees by the definition of persons declared *not* to be employees within the meaning of the Act and who therefore could neither participate in nor share the fruits of 'industrial self-government'. In effect all Africans, other than those of the Cape Province, were declared *not* to be employees. Africans in the

Cape Province could not be treated on the same legal basis as Africans in other provinces until they lost the potentiality of the franchise in Hertzog's 1936 native legislation.

The inevitable adjustments by some employers to the consequent high-wage industrial council agreements was to substitute 'non-employees' i.e. unskilled Africans for 'employees' i.e. skilled Whites [25]. Hence the Department of Labour in due course provided amended definitions of employee in the various amending Acts to prevent such substitution and the undermining of the fundamental aim of protecting White workers from competition[26].

'Industrial self-government', more particularly as interpreted by the 'labour-aristocracy' of skilled workers, naturally concerned itself with the conditions of admission to this upper house of craft unions. Enfranchisement was generally by way of apprenticeship.

Even before the industrial council system was established and before the coming to office of the Pact Government, the Unemployment Commission of 1921 had yet again drawn urgent attention to the problem of the Poor Whites – the influx of those 'whose lack of training and education, having closed the door to every other pursuit . . . drift to the towns and/or are driven to unequal competition with the natives in unskilled labour' [27]. The deep, wide fear that such 'unequal competition' would debase White living standards led to the expressed need for a system of apprenticeship, which would both regulate training facilities and ensure that White youths obtained the standards of skill to secure them against the competition of Non-Whites.

The Apprenticeship Act No. 26 of 1922 provided for no formal, legal colour bar. But the specification of minimum educational standards, which few Coloured and Indians and almost no Africans then possessed, plus the requirement for technical school training, facilities for which for Non-Whites did not exist outside Cape Town, was effective preservation of the skilled trades for Whites [28]. In due course the apprenticeship committees set up under the Act to determine conditions of admission and training came in effect to be sub-committees of the industrial councils administering 'industrial self-government'.

Wage-rates in the skilled trades could be maintained at their relatively high levels and be the more readily incorporated in industrial council agreements by appropriate limitation of the numbers of apprentices. The combination of industrial council system and apprenticeship regulation gave to the White trade unions a power of restrictionism, which the inner-workings of party politics and its inter-connections with trade union politics underwrote with minimum risk.

These inner-workings and inter-connections undoubtedly provide one of the key chapters in both the political history and the economic history of South African from 1924 until the present day. The importance of this kind of intrigue is not to be underestimated in its impact on the labour market, and through the labour market on the production function and the rate of economic development. The struggle for power within the White trade unions cannot be recounted here but it merits study [29].

To evaluate with any precision the contribution of 'industrial peace' by way of 'industrial self-government' to economic growth is impossible. It would be unrealistic not to give due acknowledgement to the encouragement of capital investment, particularly foreign investment in South Africa, from the relative absence of strikes and lost man-hours. But this enviable record has undoubtedly its opportunity cost – the lost opportunities of all those excluded from the high-paid skilled trades and whose inhibited productivity was and is incalculable. No realistic assessment is possible but it nonetheless constitutes a 'record' of restrictionism in comparative industrial relations to be set against the other, more 'enviable' record of industrial peace.

The political factor had certainly been exerted powerfully and effectively to ensure that economic rationality should not be pursued in South Africa beyond the boundary, set by White men's prescription on skilled jobs [30]. To attempt to maximize productivity by optimising the allocation and employment of labour without regard to its colour was to transgress this boundary and to try to impose an unacceptable adaptation on the social system. From 1924 the polity, as stated above, never accepted that there should be a single labour market of both White and Non-White labour, all reality to the contrary.

That part of the labour market which 'organized labour' claimed as its preserve, either in terms of the Mines and Works Amendment Act or the Industrial Conciliation Act, was henceforth its reserve. But 'organized labour' did not include all White workers. On the contrary 'organized labour' was so organized as to limit its membership and related pre-emption of skilled jobs to that restricted supply, which ensured money-wages and real-wages for artisans in South Africa to be among the highest in the world. This necessarily excluded at that time a major proportion of White workers – and especially the 'Poor Whites'.

So the incoming Pact Government included in its concern the unorganized labour – or, more, particularly, the unorganized 'civilized' labour. Creswell, the new Minister of Labour, had never doubted that White men could and should do unskilled work, always provided they were paid as 'civilized' men. His Department of Labour was made responsible forthwith for the 'civilized labour' policy. An official circular defined 'civilized labour' as:

the labour rendered by persons whose standard of living conforms to the standard of living generally recognized as tolerable from the usual European standpoint. Uncivilized labour is to be regarded as the labour rendered by persons whose aim is restricted to the bare requirements of the necessities of life as understood among barbarous and undeveloped peoples[31].

The Creswell letter clearly expressed the Creswell spirit and the spirit hardly concealed that 'civilized labour' had votes, while 'uncivilized labour' had not.

Again the preferential placement of White 'civilized labour' at higher wage-rates in unskilled jobs in Government undertakings did not begin with the Pact Government. But it was most vigorously promoted by the new Minister of Labour. Between 1924 and 1933 the proportion of White labourers employed, for instance, by the S. A. Railways & Harbours rose from 9·5 per cent to 39·3 per cent and the proportion of Africans fell from 75 per cent to 48·9 per cent – the number of Whites increasing from 4,760 to 17,783[32]. In due course a departmental directive made it unnecessary for the extra wage cost of this policy of substitution to be calculated for publication. Though the Department of Labour on occasion asserted that the definition of 'civilized labour' did not *per se* exclude 'Natives', inspectors of the Department however stated that under no circumstances would Natives be regarded as civilized labourers.

Despite more or less vigorous work-creation in Government undertakings and official employment, the influx of Poor Whites from rural South Africa was far too large to be so absorbed. The Pact Government unimpressed by warnings from, for instance, the Economic and Wage Commission[33] or the Chamber of Mines, of the impact of tariff protection on mining costs and on the country's exports, introduced its Customs Tariff Amendment Act of 1925. An avowedly protectionist policy to develop manufacturing or secondary industry was part of the new Government's solution for the Poor White problem by expanding employment opportunities in private industry.

One of the qualifying conditions for a favourable tariff application was an assurance by the industry that it would employ an appropriate ratio of 'civilized labour'. Continuation of tariff protection was to be contingent on the maintenance of such a ratio, and Government buying also favoured the 'civilized labour' content in successful tenders.

It was, however, in introducing on behalf of the Pact Government the Wage Act of 1925 that Creswell evoked the nineteenth-century to safeguard the twentieth-century – and 'unorganized labour' of 'higher civilization' from the 'bare requirements' of 'barbarous and undeveloped peoples':

It is common knowledge that the tendency of modern industry unless controlled and checked simply leads to larger and larger sections of the population being sweated down below the level of dignified life. In South Africa we have not got a homogenous population. We have two races separated by the wide gulf of history and civilization; a gulf of difference in material wants which are considered necessary for life. The same process which leads to sweating in another country gives a tendency in this country to eliminate those who require the higher standard of life. . . . In the competitive wage production system in a situation such as we have here in South Africa, the lower civilization will gradually drive out the higher civilization.

I believe there is room in South Africa for all of us . . . (but) if our civilization is going to subsist we look upon it as necessary that our industries should be guided so that they afford any men deserving to live according to the European standards greater opportunities for doing so, and we must set our face against the encouragement of employment merely because it is cheap and the wage unit low. . . .

It is mainly, at all events in its earlier years, in regard to unorganised labour of the sweated industries, and where men can hardly look after themselves, that this Act will find its main field of work in the earlier years of its existence . . .[34].

The Wage Act No. 27 of 1925 was thus intended to take over what the Industrial Conciliation Act No. 11 of 1924 left out – the administrative determination through a Wage Board of the wages- and working-conditions of unorganized labour, i.e. those who as workers lacked as yet the capacity or the organization to engage in 'self-government in industry'.

There was no mention of 'colour' or 'race' in the Wage Act and the first chairman of the Wage Board, F. A. W. Lucas, declared: 'The first (underlying aim of the Act) is to safeguard civilized standards of living for all classes of workers irrespective of race or colour; the second is that the productive energy of the community is not to be hampered, so that full scope can be given to that productive energy subject to the securing of the first aim'[35].

Nonetheless, as detailed by Dr van der Horst in her *Native Labour in South Africa*, in one case only between 1926 and 1932, was the Wage Board directed to make a recommendation exclusively for unskilled workers; in five cases up to 1935 where the Wage Board found it could not recommend 'civilized standard' rates, it was directed to make no recommendation by the Minister of Labour; and in 1929 an amended regulation, requiring *all* persons supporting an application to the Wage Board for an investigation to sign it themselves, made it impossible for any large body of Africans, the least organized and the most illiterate, effectively to apply.

Although by 1934 the increased sterling price of gold had begun to exert an accelerator-multiplier dynamic through the gold-mining industry on South Africa's economy, the labour market seemed unresponsive to change. Could it be that the system of wage-rewarding was imposing the rigidities and barriers against which the Economic and Wage Commission had warned a decade back in 1925? Could it be that these rigidities and barriers were exacerbating rather than ameliorating the income-distribution between the 'haves' and the 'have-nots'?[36].

The political solution to the gold-standard conflict, which fused Hertzog and Smuts into a new United Party[37], tended also to diminish the doctrinaire appraisal of 'capitalism' and 'socialism'. A booming Johannesburg Stock Exchange induced a rosier in place of a redder appreciation of 'the profit-system' in many quarters. And a new Minister of Labour appointed an Industrial Legislation Commission[38] to undertake, in effect, a review of the workings of the country's industrial legislation and its effect on employment and the labour market.

This Commission began by stating that the labour situation in South Africa had since the earlier days 'undergone a radical change'. It found that in every race 'the existence of different grades of labour and of difference in ability must be admitted', that this applied to Whites 'many (of whom) are only capable . . . of doing manual labour' and that Whites 'in increasing numbers are, therefore, entering the ranks of unskilled labour in the towns where they have to compete with the growing numbers of non-Europeans'.

The labour supply, it said, thus no longer consists of a small skilled White labour force superimposed upon a mass of Non-White unskilled labour with a low standard of living. Economic forces, it went on, have now drawn Whites into the unskilled group, while some of the Non-Whites had elevated themselves into the semiskilled and skilled groups. 'But notwithstanding this radical change in the structure of the labour supply, the South African wage structure in the meantime remained steadily unaltered' [39].

Despite legislation and some progress in the provision of semiskilled rates, the Industrial Legislation Commission found that the gap between skilled and unskilled wage levels had not significantly altered [40] from 1925 when it had drawn such severe strictures from the Economic and Wage Commission. The gap was still very much wider than in the U.S.A., Australia, Britain, France – where as a rough guide unskilled earned from one-half to two-thirds of the skilled.

Apart from differences in natural ability, vertical mobility had been so conditioned that the Commission claimed the higher groups of skills had to all intents and purposes become 'non-competing groups'. The existence of artificial barriers to the free movement of labour from one sphere of work to another had resulted, it stated, in the maintenance in many industries of the wide gap originally brought about by the realities of the labour market. The country's apprenticeship legislation ruled out the majority of the Non-Whites, who could not penetrate the contrived educational obstacles. Above-age Whites, too, were in practice excluded and 'there is reason to believe that in several trades apprenticeship is quite unjustified under existing productive methods while in others the period of apprenticeship would seem to be unnecessarily long' [41]. Racial prejudice, it found, backed to some extent by legislation constituted a barrier for Non-Whites:

These examples of impediments to the free movement of labour from occupation to occupation explain in part the tremendous divergence of existing wage rates from those which would probably have existed if everyone was free to choose his own occupation and weigh up the advantages and disadvantages of the various types of employment. These barriers block the outflow from the large reservoir of unskilled labour into channels of employment where skill or training is a necessary factor. While it is difficult to climb the ladder, it is always easy to descend and to fall into the ranks of the unskilled masses and wage regulation itself may result in a sifting and elimination process and even in positive unemployment[42].

Indeed the more this Industrial Legislation Commission pursued its terms of reference into detailed examination of the Industrial Conciliation Act, the Wage Act, the Apprenticeship Act and their workings, the less enamoured it was of their operation.

Despite difficulties of interpreting 'adequacy' of wages for standards of living generally regarded as 'decent', it had no hesitation in asserting that large numbers of persons of all races were compelled to eke out an existence on bare subsistence standards and that under 'present conditions have no prospects of improving their position' [43]. In many instances, the Commission declared, representatives of industrial councils and of trade unions admitted that they were not catering for the interests and needs of the less privileged labour groups and 'they are, therefore, creating a situation where outside interference with the self-government of industry may become imperative' [44]. In respect of the apprenticeship system 'the evidence points to the necessity for reviewing the lists of designated trades in all scheduled industries with a view to eliminating those in which apprenticeship can no longer be justified or reducing the prescribed periods when the necessary skill can be acquired in shorter periods. We recommend that the whole position be examined at the earliest possible date and that thereafter it can be reviewed from time to time' [45].

Twenty-five years after the White polity had taken charge and ten years after it had taken control, this Commission could find no comfort in the living standards achieved for the great mass of the population, whether Poor Whites or Poor Blacks. It was unconvinced that wage- and work-regulation by the polity had achieved significant benefits but rather that restrictions on labour mobility had depressed standards and limited opportunities for Whites no less than for Non-Whites. It was persuaded that further control of labour mobility and the labour market was not a satisfactory answer [46].

It is the duty of the State, the Commission declared, to ensure that the protection afforded by existing legislation is not abused, before there is an outcry from those who are less privileged, who, although fully competent for semi-skilled work, are being forced to be satified with unskilled work. 'The time has, in our opinion, arrived for a full investigation to be made of the different industries with a view to ascertaining to what extent the failure to make reasonable provision for semi-skilled labour is retarding further industrial development' [47].

The Industrial Conciliation Act was redrafted in Act No. 36 of 1937 and the Wage Act in Act No. 44 of 1937. Though the Industrial Conciliation Act of 1937 permitted any of the provisions of industrial council agreements to be extended to persons excluded by the statutory definition of 'employee' [48], i.e. to Africans, such Africans were not permitted any representation on the industrial council except by an 'inspector'. Such an 'inspector' may be appointed by the Minister of Labour but he has no 'vote' in the Industrial Council. As S. T. van der Horst commented, 'Such meagre representation is not likely to prevent the wages and conditions of work of Natives from being used as a pawn in the game of collective bargaining conducted in the supposed interests of Europeans' [49].

The Wage Act of 1937 seemed to have resulted in a more vigorous effort to extend minimum wages to larger numbers of the unskilled, including a small fraction of urban African workers but it remained questionable whether the consequence was indeed not to restrict employment opportunities for Africans through wage-rates that were above marginal productivity [50]. No legislative changes were made as at that time in the apprenticeship system.

The 1937 revision of legislation did not intensify racial rigidities in the labour market in the manner of the post Second World War revisions (Industrial Conciliation Act No. 28 of 1956, Native Labour Settlement of Disputes Act No. 48 of 1953, the frequently amended Native Urban Areas legislation, the Wage Act No. 5 of 1957 and the Bantu Laws Amendment Act No. 42 of 1964). But the 1937 industrial legislation certainly did not provide for nor encourage the 'drastic alteration in the wage policy of the country'. Such change, the Industrial Legislation Commission of 1935 had said 'is demanded if for no other reason than the fact that the grounds on which the unusual disparity was tolerated in the past have changed and the labour situation has altered' [51].

It was a wider political factor that was to introduce and indeed compel a greater flexibility into the South African labour market. The determinism of the Second World War imposed the values of a competitive labour market. The value-orientations of that section of the White electorate, whose every tradition rejected the colour-blind values of such an 'unregulated market', were perforce contained in nine years of frustrated Opposition. From 1939 to 1948 Afrikaner nationalism and Afrikanerdom had to accept a mobility of labour – geographical, vertical, racial – unique in South African social process. It transformed the shape and rate of economic development, stimulating industrialization to a dynamism that restructured the country's economy. It pulled tens of thousands of Africans from rural slums into urban slums but simultaneously pushed them from a declining self-subsistence into a broadening exchange of productivity. It broke down the contrived division of skill and unskill to establish the lebensraum for semi-skill. It made widening opportunities for so many Whites that they ceased to be categorized as 'Poor'. It made categories of operatives into which the Coloured and the Indian entered with gratifying facility.

So much compulsive adaptation exerted by the economy on the total social system was intolerable. In the post-Second World War general election, the White electorate gave a majority of parliamentary seats, though not of votes, to Afrikaner nationalism. From 1948 the Nationalist Government made it repeatedly clear that such uncontrolled adaptation was not indeed to be tolerated. Nothing in the social system of Afrikanerdom, of its interpretation of the political economy of labour organization, would adapt itself to mobility of labour and competition – unregulated, uncontrolled and colour-blind – in the labour market.

THE POLITICAL ECONOMY
OF LABOUR
continued

If competition in the labour market threatened unacceptable change to White workers, the competition of the labour market posited no more tolerable transformation for South African farming operations and costs. The manner in which White farmers ensured that the polity and not the market should be the decisive determinant in regard to their rights to land and to income from that land has already been elaborated. The political economy of land ownership conditioned the political economy of agricultural marketing and the political economy of agricultural marketing compelled farmers to clamour that the polity should provide them with farm labour [1].

The more market demand for African labour induced responses in supply, the more White farmers insisted that the elasticity of supply should be countermanded by legally imposed immobilities. Many farmers indeed could not understand and would not accept that change should influence labour supply – at least to move away from their farms. Control over the movement of Africans by pass laws of increasing stringency was imposed. The early Natives (Urban Areas) Acts of 1924 and 1930 aimed to limit the numbers of pass-bearing Africans entering towns and villages in the hope that the excluded would seek farm-work.

When economic change operated strongly – for worse or better – then farmers pressed harder to restore custom as the invariable in their labour factor. Numerous attempts were made to regulate the system of labour tenancy and to increase the period of labour service, despite general criticism that the system had 'outlived its usefulness' and involved 'a serious waste of labour units'. Employment in farming (as in domestic service) was invariably excluded from the scope of industrial legislation. In so far as it was subject to law, it was governed by the Masters and Servants Acts[2]. The essence of these Acts, which originated in the Cape in 1856 and were subsequently enacted in all provinces during the nineteenth century, was to make desertion of service a criminal and not civil offence. The object was to limit labour mobility[3].

By the nineteen-thirties, labour tenancy as a concomitant of the squatting system or so-called 'kaffir farming' had disappeared in areas of commercial farming or intensive cultivation – that is from the Cape, the Orange Free State and parts of Natal. Such labour-tenants had been replaced by wage-paid labourers[4]. But where cash-farming remained sluggish, that is in most parts of the Transvaal, northern Natal, and the eastern and north-eastern boundary of the Free State, labour tenancy persisted. It permitted the continued reality of African occupation (though not of course ownership) of the land and of labour service to be provided, remunerated not in cash but in cultivation and stock-grazing rights. Such rights and obligations were varying and vague but they were essentially customary.

With economic development in other sectors of the economy – in mining and in manufacturing, in the urban areas but not the rural regions – labour-tenants (and especially the young) went in search of cash in the exchange-economy[5]. Farmers and landowners however clung to custom. When the aid of the polity was invoked, it was not that of the Minister of Labour. Working conditions, rights and obligations in South African farming had never been accepted as the subject of industrial legislation. Indeed the objective of control and regulation was to exclude the intrusion of the competitive market.

It was the Minister of Justice, therefore, who introduced the Native Services Contract Act No. 24 of 1932 to amend the law relating to Masters and Servants in the Transvaal and Natal[6]. The Act, which provided for written labour service contracts of three years duration, aimed at preventing Africans from evading their labour service obligations by prohibiting the employment of labour tenants in towns (or by other farmer-employers) during the period that they should be fulfilling labour service to their landowner-employer. Furthermore the parents or guardians could enter into labour service contracts on behalf of their minor children without their consent and it was illegal for such minors to seek alternative employment or to be so employed or even to enter into an outside labour service contract without prior permission of the landowner of the parental labour-tenant. The landowner-farmer also acquired the right to cancel a contract with a whole family or kraal-group, that is to deprive them of their rights of tenancy or occupation on his land, should one member of the family or kraal-group fail or evade his personal labour-service obligations.

Laws to prevent the movement of agricultural labour, of course, go back centuries and the same centuries also evidence the failure of the law in the face of economic development. It is not therefore surprising to find the Report of the Farm Labour Committee, 1937–39, recording that 'notwithstanding the regulatory provisions of the Native Services Act, there appears today to be even greater dissatisfaction than formerly. Farmers now complain that the Government is failing in its duty in that it does not ensure that the provisions of the Act are carried out' [7].

The complaints of the farmers to this Farm Labour Committee, appointed to enquire into the shortage of African farm labour and its remedies, went further. The reasons for the shortage as given by the farmers [8] were that farming was economically unable to compete with other industries so that cash wages on farms were generally low and juveniles unable to obtain cash; that there was an uneven, wasteful and uneconomic distribution of farm labour owing to the labour-tenant system, squatting and African share-farming; the superior attractions of urban opportunities and life especially to the young; that the favourable economic position of Africans in some reserves, as well as their low standard of living, made it unnecessary for them to work regularly or to work at all; that there was a strained relationship between farmer and farm labourer owing to continual propaganda against farm work; intensive competition from the mining industry owing to its tremendous expansion and also of government departments at all levels; liberal and ill-advised assistance during times of drought and crop-failure by the Government to Africans making it unnecessary for them to seek employment. The Africans' reasons, according to the Committee, were that farm wages were generally low, and in some cases there was an entire absence of opportunity to earn cash wages; objections to the system of the kraal head contracting to bind all kraal members to enter into service; no clarity in contractual arrangements; no educational or medical facilities on farms; poor food, housing and treatment; inadequate land and time for own farming operations; eviction from farms and share farming no longer allowed[10].

Although individual farmers who had successfully developed commercial farming for the market experienced little or no difficulty in obtaining wage-paid labour at market wages, it is clear that the rate of development in agriculture as a whole was lagging behind that of other sectors of the economy. The shortage of labour was indeed most marked where custom most predominated. Hence the Committee recognized the labour tenant system as a critical factor which 'had not only made the gradual evolution of a distinct class of farm-labourers impossible, but, on the contrary, educated Natives over a long period of years to look to the towns as the places where they were able to obtain high wages, congenial conditions and many other amenities'[11].

Nonetheless the Committee recognized 'that labour tenants represent a most valuable potential labour supply, which should be properly conserved, utilized and distributed to meet the reasonable requirements of a much larger number of farmers than at present'. It therefore recommended the Union-wide proclamation of the relevant provision of the Natives Trust and Land Act No. 18 of 1936 (the *quid pro quo* of Hertzog's native legislation disenfranchising Africans in the Cape Province). Such proclamation would make a labour service period of six months in the case of the Cape, Natal and the Orange Free State, and a minimum period of 122 days in the case of the Transvaal compulsory for an African to qualify as a labour tenant.

The significance of this proposal was that, as originally provided in the Native Services Contract Act of 1932, a prohibitive tax of £5 per annum per able-bodied male African became payable by the landowner-farmer for every 'squatter' on his farm unless a minimum labour service to the landowner-farmer was rendered. Such labour service exempted the landowner-farmer from the tax[12]. The Committee consequently hoped that an appropriate redistribution of African farm labour could be achieved but farmer-opposition appears to have rendered the provision and the proclamation nugatory.

From the time of the Native Land Act of 1913 through to the Natives Trust and Land Act of 1936 and subsequent legislation, the polity has aimed at the administrative determination of farm labour supply through intensifying restrictions on land-holding and land-occupation by Africans. But market forces consistently operated against the effectiveness of such administrative controls. In particular the pull or urbanization and its cash-nexus could not be permanently obstructed, though such obstruction was to occupy much of the White polity's legislative and administrative machinery from 1948 onwards.

It is perhaps of significance that throughout the nineteen-thirties, and even earlier, the farmers' complaints were particularly directed against the attractions of urban life for African youth. Juvenile desertion of the land and its subsistence-stagnation for the cash economy of the cities was, however, as much the irresistible response of young Africans as of young Whites. Among young Africans, it had the added importance for economic development that it tended to break down the dragging influence exercised by the extended family system, and to intensify the acquisitive incentives of individualism.

Because the farmers pressed for rigid enforcement of administrative control under existing legislation, the Farm Labour Committee examined the administrative machinery in much detail[13]. It summed up:

Repeated demands were made for the introduction of more stringent laws to bring Natives into farm employment by the use of coercion. We have endeavoured in this report to show that many of the restrictions asked for are already in existence and to explain the procedure necessary to set in motion the administrative machinery to obtain a remedy. At the same time we have endeavoured to show the futility of employing force to compel Natives to accept employment not desired by them[14].

Perhaps the clearest picture of the belief among the most traditionally minded section of the electorate, the White farmers, that the polity should and could rescue them from the adaptive compulsions of economic development came in the Committee's concluding paragraphs:

The despondent, indeed despairing, attitude of the farmers in regard to their labour supply was only too apparent to your Committee. The enormous migration of farm labour to the mines and urban industrial areas which, consequent upon the unprecedented industrial development in this country, has taken place in the last few years and which is undoubtedly on the increase, developed with such alarming rapidity as to bring about a very difficult situation.

Farmers can see relief only in action by the Government and that only in the direction of compulsion on the Natives to accept farm work and the imposition of further restrictions upon the movements of those already so employed. Your Committee is convinced that such measures are among the factors which have made farm labour unpopular, and it sees no prospect of any relief being obtained by accentuating them[15].

The point has already been made that the political economy of labour frustrated the political economy of food. Neither Say's Law nor Keynes's Law penetrated the consciousness of the White polity and certainly not the White farmers. Relationships between production and consumption or between consumption and production never constituted part of the function of economic development in the minds of those with *power* in South African society down until the Second World War. After that War the relationships were evident – so clear that Prime Minister Verwoerd in October 1963 declared to a Nationalist Party meeting: We would rather be poor and White than rich and multi-racial[16].

In the nineteen-thirties, however, so stark an ideological dichotomy did not present itself. The dialectical materialism of the Chamber of Mines and of the White farmers and of White trade-unionists was more immediately materialist. The wage-fund theory and the labour theory of value had that measure of meaningfulness for an economy and a polity, which was still looking for the key to development. As Schumpeter observed, 'Although it is not true that a greater number of workers must share the same wage fund as a smaller number, it is correct that if the number of workers increases while the methods of production remain the same, the level of wages cannot increase proportionately but only to a lesser extent'[17].

Capital accumulation was growing and methods of production were changing but slowly. Too slowly to win recognition from skilled White workers that they shared a complementary relationship with non-skilled, Non-White workers, which in the long-term outranked and overweighed a competitive challenge of short-term sharpness. Too slowly for the great majority of farmers who were not concerned with Engel's Laws. They sold their wool, their wine, their fruit mostly to the British. They sold their maize mostly to the Chamber of Mines and not to African mine-workers, who lived largely on the mealie-meal. It was the industrialists who, converting agricultural raw materials into manufactured goods, saw that their self-interest might lie in more productive employment of Africans at related rising wages.

As for the Chamber of Mines, most of all it feared a rising wage-bill. This as much as any other factor periodically threatened to kill the goose that laid the low-graded, golden eggs.

THE GOLDEN GOOSE

The general theoretical model of a growing economy is of an expanding circular flow. The activators or agents of such growth are usually identified as the innovator-entrepreneurs, who might be private individuals or state bureaucrats. Acting either as capitalists or communists, they will need a source of either private or public savings. Their entrepreneurial decisions will invest such capital with the co-operating factors of labour, natural resources and technology so as to yield profits as the source of new savings for further investment.

This will explain the expanding circular flow – in theory. In practice there remain two key questions – what starts the flow and what sustains the flow? How does a stagnant pool convert into a circular flow? How does a circular flow open a succession of sluice-gates to higher and higher water?

These are large questions for economists and economic historians. For the poor toiler who found the golden goose, there was really no need to ask questions. All he had to do was to take rational care of his goose and not permit any outsider to make destructive demands on its productivity system. For South Africa, too, there is no problem in establishing the critical impetus that shocked stagnation into growth. The search for the golden goose was an unorganized but nonetheless purposeful lone-prospecting exercise carried on intermittently for almost twenty-five years until success came to the Struben brothers in 1884. Once found, the gold-bearing reefs of the Witwatersrand provided the golden eggs – though rational care of the goose certainly demanded highly sophisticated entrepreneurial management.

With the discovery of gold at the far end of the stagnant pool of the South African economy, entrepreneurship could begin its conversion into a circular flow. The circular flow started, entrepreneurial management could open the succession of sluice-gates that led to higher and higher water. To bring together the capital, labour and technology initially and then continuously so that the Witwatersrand reefs in the course of fifty years from 1886 produced three-quarters of the amount of gold which the whole world had produced during the previous four hundred years, ranks the mining-finance-house group system of Johannesburg-London as an outstanding operation in the history of entrepreneurial-management.

An economic development plan may be regarded as a plan to raise productivity per unit of factor of production used[1]. The mining-finance houses evolved by Cecil John Rhodes, Alfred Beit, Julius Wernher, J. B. Robinson, Barney Barnato, Adolf Goerz, George Albu, Samuel Marks, Abe Bailey, and George Farrar[2] had little apparent resemblance to the modern United Nations team of experts moving into an underdeveloped country. But these mining-finance houses in reality provided precisely the expertise of entrepreneurial management, which pursues productivity or economic rationality. The reason why the mining-finance houses succeeded in South Africa, unlike the UN expert-teams elsewhere, was not only the existence of a golden goose but that its rational care was under private parentage for profit.

The interaction between minerals discovery-exploitation and capital investment in Africa is the major subject-matter of Professor Frankel's study of economic development in Africa[3]. For South Africa, it is a particularly informed interpretation. It establishes empirically many significant realities about theoretical assumptions in respect of the strategic variable of capital.

Mining investment is high-risk enterprise. High profit expectations will at particular times more than off-set low-profit or even net-loss secular performance. This seems to be true not only with the specialist class of large capitalists but of the much bigger numerical class of small savers, unable to resist the psychological excitement of a speculative share-market boom irrespective of past disappointments. Hence the long-term supply of capital for mining ventures has exceeded what long-term, actual interest- or dividend-receipts would have called forth, if hindsight mirrored foresight. The supply of capital for high-risk mining is a variable of experience and expectation, rather more exaggerated by psychological behaviour and rather less influenced by arithmetical calculation.

This results in periodic interruptions and stoppages to the supply of capital. This in turn adds significance to timing-expertise in mining-company promotion and also to self-financing through re-investment of non-distributed profits. The role of the financier is therefore a strategic factor in its own right in the mining-production function [4].

According to Frankel, the class of investors who was prepared to interest itself permanently in speculative mining investment in Southern Africa has always been relatively small. Frankel found that, except during booms, the type and number of shareholders in mining, financial and exploration companies both in and outside South Africa had altered surprisingly little. Though such investors might change their investments in particular companies, they remained gold-mining investors.

For the fifty years preceding 1936, claimed Frankel, gold mines had been the main attraction for investment in Africa by Europe's money markets. Nearly one-half of the private listed capital from abroad had been directly invested in the Rand gold mines. If related investment in social structure is added in, then, said Frankel, one-half at least of the total foreign capital had entered South Africa 'as a result of the exploitation of its mineral wealth' [5]. The close connections between the Rand's financiers and the City of London were especially important, giving favoured access to and comparative advantage in the world's greatest money-market at perhaps the zenith of its venturesomeness. It is also worth noting the German origin of some of the key Rand financiers at the thrustful time of the First German Empire.

The Rand gold-mining industry was and is capital-intensive. Hence its capacity to attract steadily and relatively large amounts of foreign investment capital virtually underwrote the continued contribution of capital to the production function of South African economic development. Furthermore the capital-output ratio in South African gold-mining and diamond-mining was exceptionally favourable, while profits – though fluctuating widely and yielding a comparatively low-net for the entire time-period of capital investment – followed a pattern favourable for substantial re-investment.

From the time of the diamond discoveries in Kimberly in the 1860's, the subsequent mineral resource discovery and exploitation of such resources in South Africa provided an exceptional sequence of investment-opportunity favourable to optimizing the capital input in its direct and indirect development consequences. The significance of conjuncture of favourable factors for economic development, emphasized by Benjamin Higgins in his study of Economic Development[6], will be examined in a later chapter. What needs to be noted here is the organizational structure of the mining-finance houses and the personal relationships of leading financiers in South Africa. It enabled a relatively small group of key decision-takers to ensure the generation of an appropriate flow of capital through the crucial stages of the pre-conditions for take-off into take-off of the South African economy[7].

In this respect the importance of profits as the source of capital re-investment is to be found not in the global, long-term rate of return on risk-investment in mining in South Africa but in the particular profit performance of companies under group control. The identification of such group controls with especially venturesome individuals, to whom in time the esteem or magic of success attached, is another realistic consideration in the record of capital investment in South Africa.

The most outstanding example of the practical consequence in the above paragraph comes from the diamond industry and De Beers Consolidated. According to Frankel, from the date of the discovery of the diamond fields until 1936 the value of diamond production of the Union of South Africa (excluding South-West Africa) exceeded £320,000,000 and this sum in turn was in excess of the total value of minerals produced up to the time of his calculation (c. 1936) for the whole of the rest of Africa. Net dividends of the South African diamond-producing companies, of which De Beers is the giant, for the whole period exceeded £80,000,000 whereas, says Frankel, the total amount of foreign capital invested in the diamond industry up to that date was probably not in excess of £20,000,000 [8].

Further development capital for this flush diamond industry came largely from profits and dividends, which were subsequently invested to a very considerable fraction in the Rand goldfields. The connections between Rhodes-Beit of De Beers and Rhodes of Consolidated Goldfields and Beit of Wernher, Beit and Company in the pre-1914 period, and of the Oppenheimers (father and son) of De Beers and the Oppenheimers of Anglo-American Corporation in the post-1930 period (as well as the now nearly century-old connection of these great companies with the City of London) made a tactical contribution to capital supply for South Africa's economic development, that is very much part of capital as the strategic variable for the South African model.

The diamond industry achieved an exceptional output in relation to the comparatively small capital invested. The gold mining industry absorbed much more absolute capital. It will be suggested below that in respect of the country's economic growth, the gold-mining industry has a definitive two-era stategic significance – from its beginnings in 1887 to the world gold standard 'crisis' of 1932, and from the major rise in world gold-price in 1933 until to date. For the first period, from 1887 to 1932, Frankel put the gold-mines capital utilization at £148,000,000 subscribed plus another £63,000,000 of re-invested profit appropriations. Some of this re-investment of profits was in respect of depreciation and obsolescence but there was also redemption of about £9,000,000 debentures from profits.

Broadly speaking, writes Frankel, the Rand thus absorbed some £200,000,000 of capital until the end of 1932, of which roughly £120,000,000 can be regarded as having been invested from abroad [9]. The total value of gold output for the same period, 1887 to 1932, was £1,145,000,000 with a total dividend payment for the period of £255,000,000 [10].

The structural significance of such sustained capital investment for economic development hardly needs emphasizing. Furthermore, the major portion of investment amounting to £125,000,000 was made from 1887 to 1913; from 1913 to 1932 capital investment was only about £23,000,000. It is clear that the first phase was decisive in its contribution to energizing the growth of the South African economy. Figures for investment in the non-mining sectors of the economy are not available but, in a sense, the pre-statistical era and non-statistical area of the country's economy is indicative of its unsophisticated development and even of its stagnation [11]. Contemporary calculations of gross national product are not of course available and despite the usefulness of recent statistical researches into the past, it seems unrealistic to use them for precise comparative interpretation [12].

The Rand gold-mining was not only the most capital-intensive industry in Africa, it was also the most labour-intensive. In the previous chapter on *The Political Economy of Labour*, the implications of the colour bar between skilled and unskilled in general and in the mining industry in particular were analysed. It undoubtedly constitutes the critical parameter of the political factor in the economic development of South Africa. But the scale of the Rand gold mines in providing employment, irrespective of the colour bar, matches its strategic significance as the magnet for capital in the production function.

The Witwatersrand gold-fields were proclaimed in 1886. By 1889 there were forty-five companies producing gold and a population of 25,000 Whites and 15,000 Africans on the Rand [13]. By 1899, just prior to the outbreak of the Anglo-Boer War, African workers on the gold mines had risen to 97,000. For almost the next ten years, during the war-time interruption and the subsequent Chinese labour-indenture phase, there was a substantial drop in the numbers of African workers. By 1908, almost 150,000 Africans were again employed on the gold- and coal-mines of the Transvaal. From then on, though there were annual fluctuations, the numbers rose steadily.

From 1911 the Rand gold mines provided work for about 22,000 Whites and the numbers of Africans are given in the following table.

Number of Africans Employed on Gold- and Coal-Mines of W.N.L.A. [14]

1911	174,000	1916	191,000	1921	188,000	1926	203,000
1912	191,000	1917	176,000	1922	183,000	1927	215,000
1913	155,000	1918	158,000	1923	196,000	1928	213,000
1914	156,000	1919	177,000	1924	199,000	1929	205,000
1915	198,000	1920	173,000	1925	192,000	1930	222,000

For an econometric analysis of development, it would be of consequence to give detailed consideration to the geographical composition of this African labour force. The changing numbers coming from South Africa proper, from the British Protectorates of Basutoland, Swaziland and Bechuanaland, and from Portuguese East Africa have a patent relevance to the production and consumption functions of the separate tribal economies and to the exchange economy of twentieth-century South Africa. For a study of the political factor in the economic development of South Africa, interpreted with the insights of social system theory, broader considerations are appropriate[15].

Underdeveloped natural resources and an economically or technologically backward people within a single territory will theoretically aggravate, and have historically aggravated their interaction in a vicious circle of stagnant decline[16]. A unique aspect of the Rand gold-mining industry permitted a break-out of that vicious circle – at least for the geopolitical area of the Union of South Africa. *The unique aspect of the gold-mining industry was that it was capital-intensive, labour-intensive and export-intensive.*

The econometrician-planner of underdeveloped economies, Dr Jan Tinbergen, has pointed out that both highly capital-intensive and highly labour-intensive activities 'seem to turn out products that do not readily enter into international trade'[17]. But the Rand gold mines were producing the very medium that financed international trade. Gold exports from South Africa – and virtually the total production was exported – did far more than earn foreign exchange to pay for the Rand mining industry's essential imports; such exports financed the crucial flow of imports for the secondary and tertiary sectors of the South African economy. These secondary (that is manufacturing) and tertiary (that is commerce, communications, urbanized services) activities are recognized as the key to the transformation of the social structure, which is identified with economic maturity.

The Witwatersrand complex of urbanization, centred on Johannesburg, within fifty years became qualitatively and quantitatively (with the possible exception of Cairo) the most advanced in Africa. Its integrating impact on the political divisions of republican and colonial South Africa has already been elaborated in earlier chapters. Its integrating consequence for the labour-relationships of White and Black South Africans and concomitant segregationist impulse for the political-relationships of White and Black South Africans have also been noted.

The labour factor in the pursuit of productivity within the gold mining industry can indeed be understood only as an interaction between this integrationist compulsion and segregationist impulse. From the viewpoint of the Chamber of Mines (as the organizational expression of majority policy of the gold-mining companies and their directorates), maximization of the production function of the gold-mines depended critically on full utilization of the strategic variable of African labour.

Qualitatively, this was to be achieved by a non-discriminatory application of labour productivity irrespective of skin-colour in a flexible combination with available capital and changing technology. Quantitatively, it was dependent on obtaining the very large numbers of unskilled labourers to ensure that fixed, specific mining capitalization (in goldiferous rock and extracting plant) was operated to full capacity.

The qualitative aspect – the adjustments to and modifications of the colour bar on employment – occupied the Chamber of Mines down until the decisive change in the polity in 1924, which followed on the supreme challenge of the 1922 Rand strike. Economic 'victory' for the Chamber of Mines in the epochal strike ended in political 'defeat' when the Nationalist-Labour Pact Government came to power in 1924. Nothing expresses the character and acceptance of the superior power of political ideology over economic rationality as the post-1924 labour policy by the Chamber of Mines.

From 1924 onwards, there is a virtual end to serious labour disputes in the Rand mining industry. In total contrast to the previous quarter-century of almost continuous turbulence and frequent syndicalist violence on the Rand mines, the forty subsequent years have been marked by an industrial 'peace' probably unparalleled in labour relations in the world's mining industry. The Chamber of Mines acquiesced in a collective bargaining agreement with the White Trade Unions, that from 1924 onwards recognized the written and unwritten rules of White-Black job demarcation as simply not an agenda item. Year after year the presidential address of the Chamber of Mines from 1924 refers to the cordial relations with its White organized labour and only after 1937 is there the occasional disturbing reference to the impact on wage- and working-conditions emanating from party political intrigue in the White mining trade unions [18].

Accepting the political realities of the qualitative aspect, the Chamber of Mines turned its undivided attention to the quantitative aspect of labour supply. To secure the numbers of African unskilled workers which would optimize the tonnage of ore milled (that is, ensure full capacity operation of fixed, specific mining capitalization), becomes the never-ending task of what the Chamber now accepts as its prime aim. Every presidential address from 1924 has its extended reference to the supply of African labour.

Once the Chamber acknowledged that no South African Government from 1924 onwards would regard the qualitative combinations of labour utilization as a subject for discussion, it concentrated its negotiating objectives on obtaining Government authority for the employment of 'foreign' Africans – that is, from outside the Union of South Africa and the British Protectorates. 'Foreign' Africans were identified as those from Portuguese East Africa, portions of British

East Africa and the territories north of 22° South latitude – 'tropical' Africa.

Between 1924 and 1930, the supply of African labour which the Chamber of Mines could secure was inadequate to operate the gold-mining industry at its full then-capacity. The Chamber never publicly questioned its own article of faith that a backward-supply curve for tribal labour made it economically disadvantageous to increase African wage-rates; and hence it never departed from its monopsonistic policy of buying labour at an unvarying wage-rate. Since the Chamber denied the possibility of higher wages securing South African labour, it consistently sought permission from the South African Government to bring in more 'foreign labour'. When it became evident that the Portuguese were not prepared to revise the terms of the long-standing Mozambique Convention except to reduce the permitted-quota of Portuguese East African worker-migrants for the mines, the Chamber pressed hard for a relaxation of the bar to admission of Africans from north of 22° South latitude.

The Chamber argued that environmental conditions of underground mining work and new medical advances made it most unlikely that the earlier disastrous mortality rate in respect of such tropical African underground-workers would be repeated. The Government's concern however was not so much with the empirical health factors, as with its policy-objection to importation of 'foreign Africans'. From 1924 until the new Coalition Government of 1933, furthermore, the Minister of Labour was Creswell. He had never abandoned his belief that the exclusion of all foreign African labour from the gold-mines was the means of achieving by stages his all-White labour policy. In 1933 under a new Minister of Labour in the new United Party Government and with the irresistible prospects created by the greatly-increased world price of gold, the Government agreed to relax its opposition to 'foreign' Africans and more particularly to the admission of numbers of those from hitherto excluded territories of Africa.

In the absence of the political factor, both qualitative and quantitative aspects of labour supply would undoubtedly have increased the productivity of labour as a key co-operant factor in gold-mining output. The significance of this not merely to the production function of gold-mining but to the rate of South African economic development is incalculable[19]. Some observations on non-econometric aspects are perhaps of interest.

The absence of a colour bar on the gold-mines would have introduced a fundamental new condition into the social system of South Africa through its radical impact on the production-consumption function. The accelerator or spread effect of increased *per capita* income for a growing class of detribalized Africans, living as urbanized families and not as 'bachelor'-migrants in mining compounds, can only be an estimate. As a subjective speculation, the writer believes that the gross national product and rate of annual increase in GNP which South Africa achieved from, say, 1948 might have been anticipated by perhaps a quarter-century.

The quantitative aspect is open to perhaps more objective academic or theoretical argument. In the absence of South African Government opposition to the uncontrolled employment of 'foreign' Africans, the position might have approximated to that envisaged by Arthur Lewis in his consideration of economic development with unlimited supplies of labour [20]. The gold-mines of the Witwatersrand were the greatest natural resource of Southern Africa, if not of Africa. As such, in the absence of government-imposed restraints on the mobility of Africans in Southern Africa, the total supply of African labour for the gold-mines would have been 'unlimited'. That is, as defined by Arthur Lewis, the population of Southern and Tropical Africa was so large relatively to capital and natural resources in the same geographical area at that historical period, that the marginal productivity of such labour was contemporaneously negligible, zero or even negative.

Under such conditions, says Arthur Lewis, the price of labour is a wage at the subsistence level. So long as the supply of labour exceeds the demand for labour at this price, he continues, the supply is 'unlimited'. Under such conditions, old industries could be expanded or new industries could be created without limit at the ruling wage. The ruling wage is, of course, part determined by the alternatives open to the workers. If such alternatives are either negligible or the potential earnings in the subsistence sector, then the actual wage-levels established in the industrial sector will be those which the employing industry regards as appropriate to customary standards of subsistence for the category of 'unlimited' labour.

That such a situation may permit of economic development through facilitating capital-accumulation in the employing industry is acknowledged by Lewis and will be taken up again later. The analogies between his model of unlimited labour and the South

African reality are evident, but the political factor in South Africa did not operate unconditionally nor even unilaterally to bring about the position of 'unlimited' labour supply at subsistence price for the Rand gold-mines. South African Governments certainly did tolerate monopsonistic determination of African wage-rates by the Chamber of Mines and did impose poll-taxes to push tribal Africans into the labour market of a money-exchange economy, while simultaneously limiting African land-ownership to 13 per cent of territorial South Africa. Such action by the polity in conjunction with the pass-laws for migrant mine-labour brought about a position of a 'subsistence' wage-level for African mine-workers, which remained virtually unchanged for sixty years [21].

But there was not an unlimited supply of African labour at that rate. If South African Governments had not obstructed the flow of 'foreign' Africans to the mines, there is little reason to believe that – in the absence of such politically-imposed restrictions – there would not in fact have been an unending stream of African work-seekers from their subsistence economies in Southern Africa to the Rand gold-mines. Indeed 'foreign' Africans have illegally entered South Africa to participate in the South African labour market in very large numbers [22]. For decades the Chamber of Mines was anxious for the legal authority to recruit and employ such 'foreign' labour but the Chamber did not have the political influence to obtain such sanction until after 1933.

Although the standardized myth of Marxism presents the Chamber of Mines as the most powerful capitalist group exercising political diktat, the Chamber throughout has been politically ineffective if not impotent. There is only one major instance at the time of the gold-standard crisis in 1932, when a crucial policy decision favourable to the gold-mining industry was taken by a South African Government [23]. Apart from this admittedly critical occasion, the Chamber of Mines throughout the decades has had great difficulty in dissuading the polity from making destructive demands on the productivity of its golden goose.

Though the goose maintained a gratifying golden regularity (the consistency and persistency of the goldiferous reef being of unique uniformity), it nevertheless had a genetic tendency to lay eggs of lower and lower grade. The presidential address of the Chamber of Mines from 1889 has never failed to draw attention to the inherited low-grade characteristic and of the consequent relationship of production costs to reproductive vitality.

The constant concern of these presidential annual accounts of egg-laying performance are the improper inputs that diminish and sometimes threaten to destroy the proper output. The improper inputs of excess labour costs, transportation costs, stores costs and taxation are identified with the decisions of the polity. Functional and geographical immobilities of labour – the colour bar and the barrier to foreign unskilled labour – were imposed by the Government. Railway rating of a highly discriminating kind added to the delivered cost of mining machinery and materials [24]. Tariff protection and state-sponsorship of manufacturing industry increased the costs of stores. Mining taxation – technically a complex issue – certainly did not facilitate the delicate timing of raising capital at ruling interest-rates in Europe's money-markets [25].

The essential criticism is that all such policies, that is the political factor, through shifting upwards for the whole industry the marginal cost curve of goldmining – facing a fixed price of gold – must diminish the total output of gold [26].

As far back as 1908, the Transvaal Mining Commission had noted that the Chamber of Mines in its evidence had claimed as a fundamental postulate for testing every policy-proposal that working costs must be reduced, not increased. Furthermore the Chamber invariably asserted that any course of action which tended to increase working costs without a more than compensatory increase in profits was economically inadmissible [27].

But that Commission of 1908 took the view which, 'only putting into words the general feeling and conviction', was 'that the chief value, and indeed the only real or permanent value, of the mining industry to the State is the means it affords of building up and maintaining a large and prosperous white population in this country . . .' [28]. Specific recommendations of that Commission that aimed to off-set its key proposal of an all-White labour policy by reducing railway rates and customs tariffs on stores for the gold-mines were not accepted by either the then Transvaal or later South African Government.

A decade later, immediately after the first World War, when inflated costs threatened the closure of more than half the operating mines, the Low Grade Mines Commission of 1919 recommended unanimously a temporary modification of the ruling prohibition on employment of Africans from Tropical Africa. This was in response to an urgent appeal from the Chamber of Mines to ensure a labour supply essential to maximization of tonnage of ore milled and therefore of minimization of working costs. Despite the strong case of reducing marginal costs by such full-capacity operations to prolong the extraction of low-grade ore, the Government would not change the prohibition imposed in 1913.

Yet another decade later in August 1930, when the working revenue-working cost margin was foreshortening the life of the gold-mining industry, another Low Grade Ore Commission was appointed. It had a single term of reference – to report upon the mining of low grade ore and matters connected thereto. Before it was a calculation made by the Government Mining Engineer, Dr. Hans Pirow, dated December 1929. Dr Pirow was providing for the Gold Delegation to the League of Nations an estimate of the value of the future annual gold production of the Union on a basis of ruling mining development and developing areas and ruling costs of production. His estimate, as given in the following table, was indeed dismaying.

Fortunately mining engineers are normally no better prophets than economists, but to the South African government mining engineer the data available of ore-grades, mining costs and assumed fixed gold price permitted only of an extrapolation which would almost eliminate gold output from the South African GNP in a generation. Moreover this was at a time when no other sector of the economy – certainly not an almost-prostrate, debt-loaded agriculture – looked in the least likely to carry forward or even maintain the rate of economic development.

Estimated Value of Gold Output of South African Mines [29]
(by Dr Hans Pirow, December 1929)

	£		£
1930	43,500,000	1940	25,500,000
1931	42,600,000	1941	25,500,000
1932	43,800,000	1942	20,100,000
1933	42,500,000	1943	20,100,000
1934	40,700,000	1944	15,500,000
1935	39,000,000	1945	15,500,000
1936	34,250,000	1946	11,700,000
1937	34,400,000	1947	10,100,000
1938	34,400,000	1948	10,000,000
1939	27,400,000	1949	10,000,000

The Low Grade Ore Commission of 1930 issued an interim report as a matter of urgency to secure what it described as a permanently adequate supply of African labour for the gold mines. This Commission significantly noted that the recommendations of its 1919/20 predecessor had been followed by the Chamber of Mines in so far as 'they did not require the co-operation of the Government'. In regard to those major policy changes which, however, needed Government approval – importation of tropical African labour from north of 22° South latitude and the abolition of the legal colour bar – such official support had not been forthcoming.

African labour supply was, in the judgement of this 1930 Commission, the key variable for gold output. It concluded that on all the evidence submitted, including the Underground Officials Association and the South African Mine Workers Union, and other bodies representing mine workers, 'there is no possibility of doubt as to the vital bearing . . . of the provision of a permanently adequate native labour supply for the gold mines' [30].

The 1930 Commission accepted the evidence of the Chamber of Mines that only in most exceptional circumstances (such as crop failures) could South Africa, including the British Protectorates, provide more than 115,000 Africans in the early part of the year falling to 100,000 at harvest time out of a total labour requirement of 208,000 for capacity production. The complement from Portuguese East Africa was scheduled in terms of the revised Mozambique Convention to a progressive reduction to 80,000 by the end of 1933.

The weight of evidence, the Commission wrote, was overwhelmingly in favour of the employment of Africans from north of latitude 22° South. All the workers' bodies were in favour of it, with the exception of the Transvaal executive committee of the S.A. Labour Party, Creswell's section. The reason for this unusual consensus of opinion, asserted the Commission, lay in the recognition of the enormous value of the industry to the Witwatersrand and to the Union and the belief that the maintenance of the current scale of operations depended on a larger supply of African labour than was available from the Union and the Protectorates [31]. It also accepted as established that the Chamber of Mines left 'no stone unturned to obtain Natives from the Union and the three Protectorates'.

Other than, of course, wage-stones.

In fact, almost at the very time that the Committee was reporting, a major change was coming over the African labour supply position.

The world and South Africa entered the Great Depression, aggravated for South African tribal agriculture by severe, prolonged drought. Productivity in the tribal territories of British South Africa [32] approximated that zero or negative-level which, as Arthur Lewis's model suggested, would call forth an 'unlimited supply' of labour.

Thus the forty-first annual report of the Transvaal Chamber of Mines for 1930 began by reporting that the outstanding feature of the past year had been the excellent African labour supply, rising to 211,600 in Feburary 1931. Due, in the words of the Report, 'to exceedingly low prices now ruling for agricultural products, he (the Native), temporarily must obtain from service with an employer, a larger income than he usually finds necessary, and, as a result, not only have more Natives offered themselves for work on the mines, but those who are employed are staying longer'.

The next presidential review for 1931 again was able to report not only that African labour supply had been ample that, with alternative opportunities almost non-existent, 'indeed, we have been embarrassed by its abundance. In consequence of the severe depression of all other industries, the low prices obtainable for Native produce, and famine conditions in certain areas, workers are flocking to the mines – with the result that we are now employing about 216,000 Natives. The large accretion to our Native labour force consists entirely of British South African Natives, as in order to assist the Union Government and to relieve the necessities of British South African Natives, we have considerably restricted the immigration of East Coast Natives'.

The Chamber's long-held conviction that the required labour supply was not obtainable from South Africa and the Protectorates, i.e. British South Africa, endorsed by so many authorities including Government commissions, was readily disproved. It was so disproved by a reduction in the supply price of that labour. The subsistence and alternative wage was in effect diminished because conditions in tribal areas and other sectors of the economy reduced the numbers who could subsist in such areas and sectors. It would seem logical that the Chamber of Mines could have called forth a similar increase in labour supply at any time by an increase in its wage-reward that would have established a similar differential between mine-employment and ruling subsistence or alternatives.

The Chamber was, however, able to substantiate the functional relationship between African labour supply and gold output. In that same year of 1931, the Transvaal gold mines milled a then-record tonnage of 32,426,220 tons with a yield of 10,707,805 fine ozs and related record value of £46,000,000 [33]. Two years later, for 1933 when the scale of operation was increasing consequent on the gold-price rise, the annual report noted that the African labour force had increased to 240,000 of which no less than 191,000 Africans were from the Union of South Africa and the Protectorates and only 49,000 from Portuguese East Africa. 'In five years the number of British South African Natives employed has virtually doubled' but with the major development prospects for the gold-mining industry and the related accelerator-multiplier effects on the rest of the economy, the Government (in which Creswell was no longer a minister) agreed to the experimental employment of 2000 Africans from north of 22° South latitude.

It has been asserted above that the South African gold-mining industry, in its strategic significance for the country's economic development rate, shows a definitive two-era contribution. In the first era from 1887 to 1932, the major variables might be regarded as the quantum of capital and the quantum of labour employed. In the new era, opened up by the world rise in the price of gold after 1932, the strategic emphasis shifts to profits.

Obviously capital invested and labour employed have an inverse or two-way functional relationship to profits, but a new magnitude of absolute profits generated by the gold-mining industry after 1933 had in itself important psychological spread effects. An ebullience which characterized Johannesburg from its earliest days as a mining-town expressed itself in a capitalistic zest of venturesomeness that transformed the Johannesburg skyline into what Johannesburgers were particularly fond of describing as a 'little New York'.

The so-called gold standard 'crisis' of 1932 as the prelude to a 'finding of a second Rand' was in itself one of the most dramatic episodes in South African financial and political history. It is worth recalling some of the circumstantial background of the gold-mining industry, as it illustrates so effectively how favourable conjuncture of events can be a real determinant of growth in the life of a national economy as in the experience of an individual business.

Although the fortieth annual report of the Chamber of Mines for 1929 had opened with the gratifying statement that the gold production valued at £44,236,000 was a record, the high global figure obscured the position of the constituent parts. The Far East

Rand mines had milled about 40 per cent of the industry's total tonnage, returned over 80 per cent of total profits and distributed 86 per cent of total dividends of the industry in that year. The remaining mines, which contributed only 20 per cent of total profits and 14 per cent of distributed profits or dividends, had handled 60 per cent of the industry's full tonnage and produced 49 per cent of the total gold output, spending 65 per cent of total wage bill and 60 per cent of total bill for stores. Ten producing mines, with a total wage bill of about £5,000,000 and total working costs of £9,500,000 paid no dividends at all.

The Low Grade Ore Commission of 1930, whose publication of the Government Mining Engineer's dismal projections of future gold production appear above, estimated that of the total White employment and total stores-purchases of the gold-mining industry in 1930, 30 per cent was by mines earning less than 2s. per ton working profit and 40 per cent was by mines earning less than 3s. per ton working profit.

Such gloomy projections were deepened in their economic development consequence by estimates of the contemporary contribution of the gold-mining industry to the economic structure of the country. Professor Frankel had ventured a calculation that one-half of South Africa's total population obtained its livelihood directly or indirectly from the industry. Dr. J. E. Holloway, then director of Census and Statistics and subsequently Secretary for Finance, while disagreeing with the practicality of such statistical precision, bluntly stated, 'the single fact that it (the gold mining industry) has a gross output of about £45,000,000 per annum is sufficient proof (that) if South Africa were suddenly deprived of its gold mines, it would be a stupendous disaster, resulting in the smashing up of its economic system' [34].

The contribution of the gold-mines to the contemporary production function, as well as what the mineral resource-exploitation of the last fifty years had meant to an underdeveloped economy, was expressed by the Chamber of Mines president in his 1931 report. At the depth of the world economy's Great Depression, he said:

I think I am justified in pointing out the enormous benefit resulting to the State from this huge annual expenditure in South Africa (wages and salaries for the year £16,000,000 plus another £16,000,000 stores of which £12 million expenditure on South African stores and railways and customs dues), especially in view of the very grave depression prevailing as far as most other industries are concerned. It would be difficult to overstate the immense importance of the operations of our mines to the stability and well-being of South Africa. . . .

I should like, if I could hope to reach them in this address, to impress upon the people of the country that it is evident on every hand that the gold and diamond mines have been the chief means of transforming South Africa from a group of small territories (as measured by their White populations and activities before the discovery and subsequent development of diamonds and gold) into a considerable and important Dominion. If from an apparently arid soil, it is possible to extract enormous riches in the way of precious stones and precious minerals over a very long period of years, that is a wonderful and almost unlooked-for accession to the wealth of the country fortunate enough to contain them.

In this respect South Africa has indeed been exceptionally fortunate. Although at the moment the diamond industry is in a difficult position . . . the gold mining industry of the Transvaal is in an exceptional position as regards to its stability. . . . It is hardly necessary to explain that the main source of prosperity in South Africa during the last forty years is that, of something over one thousand million pounds value of gold produced in that period from the mines of the Transvaal, by far the greater portion has been expended in this country in working costs, such as wages and stores, and in capital expenditure on construction work and local manufacture.

While the Chamber's President was felicitating the South African public on its golden goose and while the Low Grade Ore Commission was lamenting its future reproductive vitality, the British Government left the gold standard and thereby increased the sterling price of gold from 84s. per fine oz to 125s. per fine oz. The Low Grade Ore Commission had issued its interim report on 13 March 1931, as a matter of urgency to secure Government action on African labour supply for the mines. Its Final Report of 24 February 1932 did not express an opinion on the now violent political controversy as to whether or not the South African pound should align itself with British sterling to obtain the higher sterling price of gold. This Final Report merely noted that a reduction of 2s. per ton in working costs would probably add at least 50 per cent to the future average life of the Witwatersrand and a reduction of 4s. per ton would more than double life [35].

It was indeed highly-opinionated expectations as to the future level of working costs which added academic fuel to the political flames now raging round the burning issue whether South Africa should 'follow Britian' and abandon the gold standard. Some academic opinion felt strongly that a devaluation of the South African pound to secure the higher sterling price of gold would be followed rapidly by a countervailing inflationary increase of costs. This was also the opinion of the Nationalist Government's public service advisers, especially Mr Postmus, Governor of the S.A. Reserve Bank. But other academic opinion and other political leaders, especially in Smuts's South African Party Opposition, felt the reverse.

Over and above the issue of mining-costs, there was the near-ruinous position of South African agricultural prices. With Britain taking about 90 per cent of South African agricultural exports (more particularly wool, dairy produce, maize, fruit), the farmers' produce was threatened with near-total exclusion from the British market unless export-subsidies compensated for the exchange-differential so long as 'South Africa refused to follow the British pound'. This was swinging the South African rural vote away from Hertzog's Nationalist Government to Smuts's Opposition South African Party, where such voters were not climbing on the bandwagon which Mr Tielman Roos, resigning as the Union's Chief Justice, was now flamboyantly driving through the South African countryside with all the exuberant injudiciousness of a former politician delighted to be an ex-judge [36].

The Chamber of Mines initially approved the wait-and-see policy of the South African Government. But the Chamber was very shortly powerfully motivated by the profits-production consequence of the substantial gold-price increase in terms of South African currency to match the gold-price increases in other currencies, as world devaluation proceeded. Such motivation became irresistible when to it was added speculative visions of the bonanza awaiting repatriated funds sent in mounting millions to London, there to fiddle while Hertzog's Nationalist Government burned [37].

At a special meeting of the Chamber on the Gold Standard, held on 13 November 1931, the president, Mr John Martin, declared that the assumption that a departure from the gold standard and the accrual of a premium on gold would be followed by a corresponding increase of costs was unfounded. There would, he said, be no necessity for, and scarcely the possibility of, a corresponding, or anything like a corresponding, increase of costs. The premium on gold that would follow the departure of South Africa from the gold standard and the linking of currency with sterling would, the Chamber's president claimed, however, be much more than sufficient to meet any justifiable claims involving an increase of working costs and other charges. The net benefit to the mining industry and to the country, he insisted, would be immediate and great [38].

At a meeting of the Chamber on 27 June 1932 Mr John Martin emphasized the insupportable decline of the country's non-gold exports. There had been a 'colossal contraction' of external trade, notwithstanding that gold production had been increasing.

South African Exports-Imports for first Five Months Only
1929-1932

	1929	1930	1931	1932
Exports gold, bullion	£19,000,000	£19,700,000	£20,200,000	£20,800,000
Other exports	£19,800,000	£15,300,000	£11,200,000	£8,500,000
Imports	£34,200,000	£27,800,000	£22,400,000	£13,900,000

With an economy contracting so violently, the polity would on this occasion have to do the adapting to realities. South Africa devalued its currency and the country's first 'national government', burying – temporarily – the Afrikaans-English antagonism of the past, was formed. It was not however the eclipse of the political factor. On the contrary, Hertzog as prime minister of the United Party now had the essential two-thirds parliamentary majority and was able at long last to carry the articles of his segregationist faith in his Native Bills. But concurrently entrepreneurial management could pursue productivity in a political economy so propitious to profits that in eight years the gold mining industry achieved a total working profit greater than the total for the previous twenty-two years.

From 1933 until 1940, the working profits of the gold-mining industry amounted to £275·3 millions as compared with £263·3 millions for the period from 1911 to 1932, inclusive.

The effective price of gold for the mines moved from just under 84s. per oz in 1932 to about 125s. from the date of linking South African currency with British sterling, 28 December 1932, and then to 140s., when the U.S. dollar-price of gold was adjusted to $35 per oz in 1934. Working costs of the mines benefitted from the unique conditions that world and South African prices were broadly stabilized by the continuing unemployed and underemployed capacity until the outbreak of the Second World War [39]. Wages, as a major component of mining costs, did not significantly rise. From 1933 the S.A. Labour Party was a spent parliamentary force and in the new United Party with its overwhelming parliamentary majority, the Mineworkers Union could exert virtually no leverage.

When the White miners in 1933 demanded increases ranging from 20 per cent to 35 per cent and a reduction of the working week to 40/36 hours, the only concession from the Chamber of Mines was a provident fund. The Chamber could establish that living costs had not significantly risen and that 'it was not in the national interest' to concede even higher differentials in wages to the highest-category of wage-earners in the country. A strongly conservative government with a very orthodox Finance Minister, Mr Havenga, enjoying a mining-tax yield that had risen from a pre-1933 average of about £3½ million to a post-1933 average of nearly £14 million, saw no political reason to take sides in the collective bargaining.

As for the African labour, the continuation of negligible, nil or negative marginal productivity in tribal agriculture maintained an 'unlimited labour supply' at unchanged subsistence wage-levels. By the end of 1935, African labour had increased to 287,000 of which three-quarters was coming from South Africa and the Protectorates. For 1936, the numbers rose to 310,000.

The final conjuncture of favourable factors was the capital market. From the beginning of 1933 to the end of 1936, according to the statistics of the Government Mining Engineer, about £45,000,000 new capital was invested in the gold mines. Under prevailing conditions, profit prospects in gold-mining were relatively attractive and more than half of the above investment came from foreigners. A sustained 'bull' Johannesburg share market also naturally assisted the very large capital needs of feverish mining activities.

From 1933 to 1936 mining development, in addition to the deepening-level activities of the large companies, was taking place over an area nearly four times as large again as the whole of the Rand in 1932. In the fiftieth Chamber of Mines Report for 1939, the point was made that the disposable profit per ton of ore in the hands of the mines was only slightly greater than before the Union left the gold standard in 1932. The expansion of development was therefore primarily responsible for the increase in total dividends distributed. During seven years, from 1933 to 1939, investors had put £80,000,000 into gold-mining, a significant fraction coming from re-invested dividends.

The profits realized and the profit expectations, following the major gold-price increase in December 1932, transformed the volume and rate of capital investment in the industry. The above figure of £80,000,000 in seven years compares with Frankel's estimates of £148,000,000 for the whole period from 1887 to 1932. But the increased concentration of the capital input in the post-December, 1932, era is emphasized by the facts that, of the £148 millions, £125,000,000 had been invested prior to 1913. From 1914 to 1932, only about £23,000,000 had been invested.

For the nineteen years prior to 1933, the average annual new capital raised was about £1,217,000; from 1933 for the next seven years the average approximated £11,430,000.

The detail of performance data by the gold-mining industry for the period 1911 to 1942 is given in the table appended to this chapter. The magnitudes of change in working profit from 1933 are clear. From 1923 to 1932 inclusive working profits fluctuated narrowly around the ten-year average of £13·4 millions. In 1933, they jumped to £31·5 millions and for the next decade, from 1933 to 1942, working profits averaged £36·48 millions.

The multiplier effect on consumption and the acceleration effect on extra-mining investment [40] brought the level of GNP to a new order of magnitude. According to a recent re-calculation of gross domestic product (see table below), the total in 1921 was R482·1 million (or £241·5 million) for a 1921 census total population of just under 7,000,000 South Africans; in 1940, the total was R988·9 million (or £494·5 million) for an estimated population of about 10,500,000. These calculations of gross domestic product appear to be at market prices but the official South African retail price index (base 1914 = 1000) was exceptionally high at 1451 in 1921 and from 1933 until the Second World War price movements remained steady at between 1170 to under 1200.

From the early twenties to the early forties, gross domestic product can be reasonably regarded as having doubled in real terms. The author remains a sceptic about the precision of national income accounting, more particularly on the basis of statistical reporting for South Africa. By the very nature of the South African social system with its imposed immobilities and gulf between the living standards of its racial components, calculations of income *per capita* are – in the author's view – without useful purpose.

Gross Domestic Product of South Africa – Selected Years [41]
(Calendar year and at market prices)
in millions of rands

Year	Total	Agriculture Forestry & Fishing	Mining & Quarrying	Manufacturing
1911	299·2	62·3	83·9	11·4
1920	561·6	122·1	108·7	40·4
1921	482·1	86·7	80·9	36·5
1929	591·5	95·1	100·1	53·5
1932	463·5	59·7	80·3	45·5
1933	530·8	69·2	116·4	53·3
1939	887·6	114·0	176·3	99·3
1940	988·9	119·8	203·4	114.5

The above figures are in millions of *rands*, the new post-1960 unit of currency of the Republic of South Africa. For an appreciation in more familiar pounds, they should be halved throughout. The years selected show 1911, the first year after unification of South Africa; 1920, the post-World War 1 boom year and 1921, the succeeding slump year of deflated prices; 1929, the peak year of boom and 1932, the year of Great Depression; 1933, the first year of gold-price at 125s. per oz and 1939/40, the years of peak gold-mining expansion at the outbreak of World War 11.

The broad trends are clear. From unification of the country's economy down until the world-wide increase in the price of gold, rate of growth is unexciting. Neither agriculture nor manufacturing has fulfilled anything like their expectations. Agriculture especially has shown no contribution commensurate with its highly favoured legislative attention. Mining, too, has fluctuated to end in 1932 much where it began in 1911.

Twenty years of the political factor from the time of Union have made no spectacular impression on the rate of economic development. The political pre-occupation with ensuring that the polity and not the market determined the distribution of land, labour and wealth as between White and Black had achieved no impressive increase in gross national product – the total wealth for distribution.

But an external impetus from 1933, the world-wide increase in the price for South Africa's greatest natural resource – from 84s.

per oz of gold to 125s. and then to 140s. – adds a dominant influence to the side of economic rationality. From 1933, the pursuit of productivity ignores the polity. The years between 1933 and 1939 may well be distinguished as the period in which the polity and the economy were so intensely immersed in their internal objectives as to have neither time nor desire to interfere with each other.

The Prime Minister, General Hertzog, having abandoned a gold standard (to him an uninteresting mystery) and gained a two-thirds parliamentary majority (a far more vital elusive interest) was free to concentrate on his life-long ideology – the search for segregation by ending the remnant of the Africans' common roll franchise and their related rights, to 'traffic' in the common land of South Africa. The Chamber of Mines, having for perhaps the only time in its history exercised effective influence on the polity to bring about the abandonment of the gold standard, was free to concentrate on its life-long ideology – the pursuit of profits.

Such a climate of confidence, unprecedented in the country's political and economic history, was highly favourable to the rate of economic development. During the subsequent years of the Second World War, irreconcilable emotional sympathies split Parliament and the electorate into revived, intensified political conflict. But the overriding demands of War gave a decisive freedom to productivity, uninhibited by the labour colour bar for the duration of hostilities.

STATISTICAL APPENDIX

OF

GOLD-MINING OPERATIONS

SOUTH AFRICA : 1911–1942

Year	Tons Milled	Yield ozs	Gold Price per oz £	Working Revenue		Working
				Total £ millions	Per Ton milled s. d.	Total £ millions
1911	24,075,502	7,967,198	4·715	33·8	28 1	21·7
1912	25,695,837	8,883,847	4·715	37·5	29 2	24·1
1913	25,842,692	8,512,359	4·715	36·2	28 0	23·2
1914	25,900,789	8,111,288	4·715	34·5	26 7	22·2
1915	28,522,499	8,852,433	4·715	37·6	26 4	25·0
1916	28,757,532	9,061,799	4·715	38·5	26 9	26·1
1917	27,507,680	8,822,431	4·715	37·5	27 3	26·5
1918	25,040,063	8,274,174	4·715	35·1	28 1	27·1
1919	24,158,688	8,182,909	4·715	34·8	28 9	27·8
1920	24,217,177	8,022,010	5·590	42·7	35 3	31·1
1921	23,519,805	7,992,858	5·342	41·5	35 4	30·4
1922	19,614,414	6,876,163	4·614	30·9	31 7	23·2
1923	26,649,675	8,974,838	4·544	39·4	29 7	26·8
1924	28,336,073	9,428,414	4·673	42·5	30 0	27·9
1925	28,431,508	9,428,468	4·673	39·8	28 0	27·3
1926	29,624,072	9,778,173	4·673	41·3	27 11	28·2
1927	29,361,617	9,951,301	4·248	42·1	28 8	29·0
1928	30,327,500	10,170,723	4·248	43·2	28 6	30·2
1929	30,797,300	10,233,321	4·248	43·4	28 2	30·5
1930	31,477,000	10,550,701	4·248	44·6	28 4	30·9
1931	32,426,220	10,707,805	4·248	45·4	28 0	31·6
1932	34,906,450	11,378,064	4·306	48·8	28 0	33·5
1933	36,860,900	10,841,054	6·236	67·3	36 6	35·8
1934	39,722,850	10,304,923	6·901	70·8	35 8	38·6
1935	44,234,650	10,564,904	7·103	74·4	33 8	41·8
1936	48,221,120	11,117,327	7·103	77·4	32 1	45·3
1937	50,725,750	11,445,087	7·035	79·7	31 5	48·0
1938	53,834,150	11,839,077	7·127	83·6	31 1	51·7
1939	58,340,200	12,495,111	7·765	92·3	31 8	56·6
1940	64,515,350	13,683,418	8·400	114·2	35 5	66·7
1941	67,255,450	14,039,912	8·400	117·0	34 9	71·1
1942	66,979,700	13,761,035	8·400	114·5	34 2	70·8

Costs				Working Profits					Total Government Revenue from Gold Mines
Per Ton milled s. d.		Per oz s. d.		Total £ millions	Per Ton milled s. d.		Per oz s. d.		Income Tax & All Other
									£ thousands – fiscal years
18	1	55	3	11·5	9	6	29	2	1448·0
18	9	55	1	12·7	9	11	29	2	1450·0
18	0	55	1	12·2	9	7	29	0	1499·0
17	2	53	6	11·6	9	0	27	11	1412·0
17	6	56	10	12·0	8	5	27	3	1681·0
18	2	58	1	11·7	8	1	25	11	1881·0
19	3	60	6	10·3	7	6	23	7	1914·0
21	7	65	11	7·6	6	1	18	6	1622·0
23	0	68	4	6·7	5	6	16	5	2058·0
25	8	78	0	11·6	9	7	29	0	2570·0
25	10	76	5	11·2	9	6	28	2	2360·0
23	7	67	11	7·8	8	0	23	0	1964·0
20	1	60	3	12·6	9	6	28	4	2777·0
19	8	59	8	14·6	10	4	31	4	3471·0
19	3	58	6	12·5	8	9	26	10	3183·0
19	1	58	2	13·1	8	10	27	1	3687·0
19	9	58	8	13·1	8	11	26	7	3517·0
19	11	59	8	13·0	8	7	25	9	3500·0
19	10	60	1	12·9	8	4	25	5	3510·0
19	8	59	3	13·6	8	8	26	1	3623·0
19	6	59	5	13·7	8	6	25	10	3768·0
19	3	59	3	15·3	8	9	27	1	4587·0
19	5	66	5	31·5	17	1	58	6	14915·0
19	5	75	6	32·3	16	3	63	2	13541·0
18	11	79	11	32·6	14	9	62	5	14598·0
18	9	82	3	32·1	13	4	58	2	14029·0
18	11	84	9	31·7	12	6	56	0	13990·0
19	3	88	4	31·9	11	10	54	6	12930·0
19	5	91	8	35·7	12	3	57	9	17017·0
20	8	98	6	47·5	14	9	70	3	26740·0
21	2	102	6	45·8	13	7	66	1	27328·0
21	2	104	4	43·7	13	0	64	4	27703·0

UGLY DUCKLING INTO
PROTECTED SWAN

What's good for the Chamber of Mines is best for South Africa's economic development.

This was not only the article of faith of the mining-finance houses but was, and remains, the objective conviction of much highly regarded academic opinion. When the Mills-Clay-Martin membership of the Economic and Wage Commission of 1925 wrote:

Now protection in its early stages, whatever its ultimate effects, does nothing to increase the resources of total wealth of a nation. It may lead to the development of new industries, but it cannot create these out of nothing and, in fact, creates them by diverting to them labour, capital and enterprise, that, but for the protective policy, would have been applied elsewhere.[1]

it was not merely calling Adam Smith to witness but invoking almost all respectable authority. Such a version of economic development in general and of the Union's economic growth in particular was emphatically endorsed by most South African economists. Intervention by the polity to alter the shape of the country's economic development had and would manifestly diminish the rate of growth. S. H. Frankel had made a formidable case against one key state-controlled enterprise, the South African Railways; C. S. Richards had made another against the other key state-controlled Iron and Steel Corporation (Iscor). They and other South African economists made the general case against the protection of manufacturing or secondary industry.

The evidence that the gold-mining industry was the crucial, if not the sole, strategic variable in the GNP function and the critical determinant of national income per capita was powerfully argued by Frankel in a signposting study. In 1944, a date which permitted him to look back to the pre-war break-through into expansion and to look forward to post-war hopes and fears, he published *An Analysis of the Growth of the National Income of the Union in the Period of Prosperity Before the War* [2].

Frankel's calculations of total national income at current prices showed an increase from £234·7 million in 1932/33 to £394·8 million in 1938/39 or an increase of 68·2 per cent. Acknowledging the doubtful validity of the retail price-index as a price-deflator, he gave a 'real' national income per head of the gainfully-occupied population of £56·2 in 1932/33 and £77·3 in 1938/39 or an increase of 37·5 per cent. The table which follows suggests that national income per head doubled from Period I, 1911/12–1919/20, to Period II, 1922/23–1928/29 and then doubled again in Period III, 1932/33–1938/39.

Annual Percentage Rates of Growth of the National Income of South Africa for Three Selected Periods [3]

	Period I: 1911/12– 1919/20	Period II: 1922/23– 1928/29	Period III: 1932/33– 1938/39
National Income at current prices	7·0	4·6	8·8
National Income at constant prices	3·0	5·0	7·5
National Income at constant prices per head of gainfully occupied population	1·4	2·5	5·3

Period III from 1932/33 to 1938/39 was designated by Frankel as one of 'Great Prosperity'.

What especially concerned Frankel was that 'the great rise in the national income, and the further rise subsequently engendered by the exceptional circumstances of the war, should not be permitted to obscure the fundamental economic factors from which it has resulted or the basic conditions on which the growth of the national income depends'.

He found that fundamentally those standards had been achieved by a high degree of specialization of the country's economic activity, and by the export of certain specialized valuable products in order to obtain the benefits arising from the import of a large variety of goods and services. It is this operation of international trade, he asserted, based on specialization which has led to the existing real income standards of the community. The exceptional rate of growth in Period 111 was to be explained by (a) the growth in real income yielded by export production, particularly of gold exports and (b) by the great stimulus which such increased export activity gave to new capital investment, financed from both domestic savings and foreign capital.

So great were the windfall gains from the gold-price increase, that Frankel claimed the rate of growth in the post-1933 period was not only much greater than in the other two periods analyzed but also exceptional, when compared with the experience of most other countries in the world over comparable periods.

From this statistical evidence, Frankel asserted inescapable inferences for government policy. He found 'dangerous and fallacious' those suggestions which believed that in the post-war period full employment at increased income standards could somehow be achieved merely by maintaining net investment from domestic savings and by stimulating new manufacturing production for the home market. He was greatly perturbed at what seemed to him autarchic thinking and insisted that with the existing natural resources and population, South Africa was so fundamentally dependent on the maintenance and expansion of international trade that 'all future economic and fiscal policies must be based on the realization of this inescapable fact'.

There can be no underestimating the empirical substance nor analytical penetration of Frankel's well-timed study. Nonetheless, did it in fact provide the last figure and the final word?

In the previous chapter, the post-1933 gold-mining expansion era was assessed. Such expansion was the acknowledged decisive contributor to a structural change in the South African economy that generated a critical impetus towards the drive to maturity. The increased inputs of African labour and of capital were undeniably major. Frankel's calculations of total new investment in his Period 111 of 'Great Prosperity' are impressive. He put the figure at £261·9 million, an average of £37·4 per year from 1932/33 to 1938/39 – nearly double the period of the previous upward swing in the South African trade cycle from 1922/23 to 1928/29.

Furthermore, while Frankel found gold mining investment from 1922/23 to 1928/29 to be negative, i.e. new investment not replacing capital obsolescence and closed-down mines, from 1932/33 to 1938/39 total net new investment in gold-mining contributed the 'extremely large' sum of £55·5 millions. For this latter period, the total investment for the private sector was £154·4 millions and for the public sector £107·4, together amounting to £261·9 million.

But the generative effect of massive gold-mining investment was taking place in a political-institutional framework that had its own unique constraints. It was taking place in a social system that exhibited at least some Marxist features within Talcott Parsons's general theory of social systems [4].

Those years in which, to the pleasureable astonishment of the annual presidential address to the Chamber of Mines, African labour supply increased from 211,000 in 1930 to 367,000 in 1940, were the decade in which the subsistence tribal economies of South Africa 'pushed' their 'unlimited labour supply' into the mines. They were the years in which the process of making millions of Africans legally landless was fermenting its urbanized proletariat. The Africans' economic life was being compelled to adapt to the White man's polity.

In such a social system, are not the calculations of 'real' national income per head of gainfully occupied population the abstractions of arithmetical averaging? It is patent that Frankel was acutely aware of the immobilities in the South African social system and intensely sympathetic to its consequent poverty-creation. But to derive a description of 'Great Prosperity' from averaging national income estimates over the quantum of the South African population, however justified by econometric values, was to imply a misleading reality [5].

It was misleading in that a mass of contemporary evidence suggests the proletarianization of the African people under the land-labour controls imposed by the White polity was adding nothing to their net wealth and little to their net income. An examination of the country's social system did suggest certain features of under-employment and under-consumption, that were not solely the inbuilt characteristics of a slow rate of economic development. The political process was a real determinant of the interacting under-employment and under-consumption; and the under-employment and under-consumption were real determinants of the social process.

Landlessness among the Africans was a creation of the polity. The decade of Frankel's 'Great Prosperity' by econometric measure was also the decade in which the political economy of South Africa was bringing the Africans' marginal productivity on the land to the point of nil or negative yield, while the colour bar on the mines imposed an insurmountable ceiling to their marginal productivity in mining.

The under-consumption of such a social system would not necessarily be solved by no interference with the specialization of the country's economic activities, in order that maximum gold output might bring the optimum gains of international trade. Such under-consumption might be a permanent trap so long as the land-labour utilization of resources in South Africa was a function of the polity rather than of the market.

The study of the realities of the South African political economy might yield a different answer than the unchallengeable logic of international trade theory. The pursuit of productivity in the South African social system might under such compelling reality justify some intervention into the productive system of the golden goose.

However ugly the duckling of an infant industrialization looked to those who had such legitimate admiration for the golden goose, was there not a *special* case for nurturing a protected swan?[6]

The general case of international trade was of course fully and almost completely stated by Adam Smith a long time ago[7]. It remains the classical statement of the problem of free trade and protection and the argument of Adam Smith is almost as valid today as when he deduced it. This general case, to run over it very briefly, is that under the assumptions of general economic theory (that is, free competition, mobility of resources and a certain political-institutional framework), the unrestricted international exchange of goods and services increases the real incomes of all the trading countries concerned – both those who export and those who import.

In classical terms free trade maximizes the social product through automatically ensuring that each country specializes in the production of those goods and services in which it has relative advantage and imports those goods and services which it can obtain more cheaply than it can relatively produce itself. As a general theory it remains virtually unchallengeable.

Some economists have attempted, however, to examine this classical theory in terms of other assumptions, which are not the assumptions of free competition or mobility of resources. They have questioned how far the classical doctrine of comparative costs, based on equilibrium theory, is entirely satisfactory for a poltical economy in which the institutional factors present a different picture from the assumptions of general economic theory. How far is the classical argument conditioned by the dis-equilibria of the South African political economy? How far is the general comparative cost doctrine modified by the particular social system of South Africa?

The constitutional and institutional immobilities of South Africa resulted, it has been contended above, in a degree of under-employment and under-consumption that was chronic and might through neglect become congenital.

Haberler in his *Theory of International Trade* reviewed the arguments for protection advanced to reduce unemployment. He categorized the arguments as relating to (*a*) unemployment which is general and enduring (*b*) to unemployment which is cyclical and (*c*) to the unemployment specific to an industry. He conceded a very limited possibility to such a special case as Britain's unemployment after Word War 1, when Keynes had argued for protection as an alternative to devaluation just before the 1930's[8]. But Haberler's general argument is that protection merely shifts employment as between different activities. In the case of South Africa, however, the general unemployment of the Africans was an *imposed* underemployment.

The manner in which the polity imposed such underemployment meant that neither in agriculture nor in mining was there any likelihood of a tribal society of non-differentiated labour emerging from a stagnant pool of self-subsistence and merging into the circular flow of an exchange economy based on division of labour.

Haberler did not indeed deny the contention of those who argued that it is not invariably true to assume that the available factors of production are given and fixed in quantity so that they cannot be increased, but only redistributed, through protection. He conceded that protection may bring previously idle resources into utilization and that tariffs may attract factors of production, through the import of capital and immigrant labour, from other countries. But, according to Haberler, the effects of such industrialization must be short-lived because the import of capital sets up obligations to repay that capital in the future. The balance of payments problem is merely postponed and the obligations to redeem foreign investment ultimately necessitates additional exports in future years for the execution of payment.

Empirical evidence in the case of South Africa, however, lends itself to another interpretation. Although much of South Africa industrialization has been brought about by foreign or imported capital and entrepreneurship, protection (whether by way of tariffs or import controls) has attracted a transfer of permanent capital and scarce know-how to co-operate with unutilized or under-utilized African labour. This aspect will be taken up again later in the text but it must also be acknowledged that world events combined with further natural resource exploitation in South Africa to provide for the continuation of South African 'miracles', which miracles greatly expanded the country's exports.

The special case for the protection of South African manufacturing is implicit, it is suggested, in the general infant-industry exception of free-trade theory. The infant-industry argument is of course an aspect of industrial *development* by way of protection. Because the South African economy had by the end of the Second World War acquired certain special features of what may be termed an *adolescent* economy, protection of industry after 1945 could and has in fact increased the rate of economic development.

Such an analysis, however, requires the support of historical fact and a brief account of South African industrialization therefore follows. After the factual account has been filled in, it will be more intelligible to return to the examination of the special case for the protection of South African industry.

From even before Union in 1910, there had of course been non-academic enthusiasts for the fostering of manufacturing or secondary industry by customs tariff protection [9]. Their enthusiasm did not then match their political influence. Thus an editorial article in the August 1907 issue of the *South African Commerce and Manufacturers' Record* noted that a few importers have been the merchant princes of the country, 'looked up to as oracles on every question under the sun and their influence is almost absolute', while 'manufacturers as a class, have occupied a very different and less influential position'. The first Congress of South African Manufacturers was held in Cape Town in October 1909, and a proposal made for a fund to support candidates for election to Parliament in the interests of industry. The first Union Parliament was an opportunity for William J. Laite, pioneer of the chamber of industry movement in South Africa, to press on Lord Gladstone, the Governor-General, a claim for one of the unallocated seats in the first Union Senate to be given to a 'direct representative of manufacturing interests'.

Although the occasional customs duty helped a local manufacturer, industrialists exercised virtually no political influence in the early

Union Parliaments. On the other side the redoubtable J. W. Jagger, the greatest merchant of the Cape Colony and the Union, imposed a Gladstonian free trade orthodoxy on pre-Union and post-Union cabinets until the political downfall of Smuts in 1924. With the Nationalist-Labour Pact Government an avowed protectionist policy was adopted. The Customs Tariff Act of 1925 and the reconstitution of the Board of Trade and Industries with extensive powers and advisory duties for the protection of secondary industries (agriculture and mining by South African tradition being classified as 'primary') did not, however, imply a suddenly acquired major influence by manufacturers and organized industry in the polity.

Such influence was rather a necessary administrative by-product of the new Government's basic social objective – increased employment opportunities for Whites. In the gold-mining industry, the Mines and Works Amendment Act ensured the regulations that re-established an unchallengeable category of Whites-only jobs. In government undertakings, more particularly the South African Railways and Public Works Department, the 'civilized labour policy' was forthwith implemented directly to increase the numbers of White employees in labouring categories. Tariff protection of secondary industry *politically* was intended to ensure that this 'civilized labour policy' was made effective in what was thought of as a secondary field of economic activity.

Manufacturing industry, indeed, remained secondary to the primary industries of agriculture and mining – in political influence even more than in economic significance until after the Second World War. The public attention aroused by the vociferous free trade-protectionist argument, academic and non-academic, has tended to exaggerate the extent of protectionist policy in promoting South African industrialization until the Second World War [10].

A memorandum by the Board of Trade and Industries to the Customs Tariff Commission of 1934 claims a gradual evolution of a revenue measure into a device used to an appreciable extent for the encouragement of industrial development. The first Union Customs Tariff Act No. 26 of 1914, itself based on pre-Union colonial tariffs, was primarily revenue in character though it contained an appreciable number of protective duties and had provisions against dumping. The 1925 Customs Tariff Act No. 36 of 1925 has generally been regarded as the inauguration of a more positive or definitive protective policy, though it was an outgrowth of the 1914 Tariff.

The Board of Trade and Industries itself now acquired a purposively protectionist responsibility.

In its Report No. 51 on Tariff Revision, the newly charged Board announced these general principles as fundamental considerations for its directive:

    (i) the interests of primary industries, farming and mining, whose costs of production had to be kept as low as possible;

   (ii) the interests of consumers, including protection against undue increase in the cost of living; and

  (iii) provision of increased scope of employment for civilized labour, tariff assistance to be partly dependent on satisfactory labour conditions and, where possible, on the employment of a larger proportion of civilized labour.

The Board's memorandum to the 1934 Tariff Commission declared that since 1925 the Government's policy of encouraging the employment of civilized labour had become a distinct and important feature of the Union's industrial and commercial life. As far as encouragement of industry through the means of the Customs Tariff is concerned, the Board said, it was definitely expected that efforts at promoting the employment of civilized labour should not be relaxed.

On the contrary, when it was discovered that evasions of wage determinations and agreements were taking place in individual industries which were entitled to some form of tariff assistance, the remedy was sought in the Tariff Act. Thus a new clause governing Class XV of the Tariff has been introduced into the regulations, which provides for the exclusion of particular manufacturers from the privilege of free admission of raw materials and requisites under rebate, after investigation by the Board of Trade and Industries had shown that such manufacturers were maintaining unsatisfactory labour conditions.

The 1934 Customs Tariff Commission itself, under the strong chairmanship of Dr J. E. Holloway, in its introduction indeed declared that it did not wish to be understood as advancing the view that no alternative development of the country's resources was possible in 1925. 'We have regarded', it asserted, 'the adoption of a protectionist policy as being primarily influenced by social rather than economic considerations, and this view underlines the whole of our report' [11]. It made an attempt to establish the magnitude of protected secondary industry and estimated employment of 26,000 to 28,000 Whites and 21,000 to 23,000 Non-Whites earning a combined wage bill of just over £5,000,000 and with a gross output of £19,300,000 as specifically attributable to protected secondary industry for the year 1933. For the same year, private industrial establishments as defined in the Industrial Census employed a total of nearly 69,000 Whites and about 96,000 Non-Whites, who together earned a wage bill of £17,500,000 and had a gross output valued at about £80,500,000 [12].

It seemed clear, said the Customs Tariff Commission, that the ratio of employment of Whites was higher in protected than in economic secondary industry. 'In 1933 the ratio of Whites to total employees in all the classes covered by the Industrial Census was 41·9 per cent while in a number of fully protected secondary industries, for which separate data are available, the ratio was 57 per cent' [13]. From an analysis of employment in three sheltered industries and seven protected industries, and acknowledging that the former were particularly vulnerable to the depression, 'it is yet clear . . . that the protected industries showed a much greater increase in employment than the sheltered industries (and) it will be noticed, for instance, that the seven protected industries accounted for just over 50 per cent of the total increased employment of Whites in all private industries' [14].

That the White labour-employment potential was a guiding, if not determining, consideration of protectionist policy is unequivocally acknowledged by the long-term chairman of the Board of Trade and Industries, A. J. Norval, when he wrote after his retirement [15]:

From 1925 up to the outbreak of the Second World War in 1939 the Government's policy of encouraging the employment of civilized labour became a cardinal feature of the country's economic policy. . . . As far as the encouragement of industry through customs tariff protection was concerned it was definitely expected that efforts to promote the employment of civilized labour would not be relaxed. In this regard the Government's efforts were crowned with great success. The Poor White Problem, a tragic feature in the country's economic and social life, was virtually wiped out in a comparatively short period through the absorption of the Poor Whites in industry.

Footwear, clothing, motor assembly, tyre and saw-milling industries in centres such as George and Port Elizabeth contributed much to alleviate this distressing problem by attracting whites from the countryside to the factories. The Government's policy of maintaining and promoting healthy labour conditions in industry was further carried into effect by withholding, through a provision in the Customs Tariff and Excise Duties Act, the privilege of importing under rebate of duty raw materials and requisites, from manufacturers who maintained unsatisfactory labour conditions.

Norval also makes it clear that in this phase the protectionist policy was labour-intensive and not capital-intensive. He claimed that the customs tariff contributed very materially to the development of expansion of industries in respect of which a nucleus existed in 1925, such as blankets, clothing, footwear, canning, confectionery, soap, cigarettes and tobacco and others, but that during the period 1925 to 1939, the tariff failed to stimulate capital intensive industries.

Throughout this period, Norval elaborates, it was avowed Government policy not to increase the customs duties on capital goods or on the requirements of agriculture and mining, even where such articles could be satisfactorily produced in South Africa. The special requirements of agriculture and mining, in consequence, bore either no duties at all or only low revenue duties. 'Since 1925 the customs tariff was so framed and applied as to avoid as far as possible, the penalizing of primary industries in respect of their special requirements' [16].

Down until the Second World War it was the primary industries of agriculture and mining which commanded the interest of the polity. The exercise of influence by manufacturers was, as befitted their classification, essentially secondary and indeed exerted at administrative rather than at legislative level [17]. The continuous, close and zealous concern of the polity with agriculture has been documented in an earlier chapter. If the protectionist policy of the South African Government until 1939 is closely examined, it will in fact be found that it was as much directed to the protection and encouragement of 'primary' agriculture as of 'secondary' industry.

It might even be argued that until 1939 the tariff protection given to secondary manufacturing was not so much the promotion of industrialization as the consequence of a virtual import prohibition to safeguard primary agriculture against foreign competition. While wool, milk and fruit were unprotected, the heavily protected wheat, maize, sugar, butter, condensed and powdered milk, leather and tobacco leaf constituted the raw materials for the important food and drink industry group.

The Board of Trade and Industries in its Report No. 282 pointed out that confectionery manufacturers must buy highly protected sugar, glucose made from maize, condensed milk and milk powder at relatively high prices and that agricultural protection must be followed by industrial protection, if local factories are to use South African raw materials. Export subsidies, it wrote, direct or indirect, on local products, such as sugar, fruit, maize, meat, eggs and butter, place local manufacturers at as great a disadvantage as do comparable import duties on imported raw materials [18]. What the Board of Trade and Industries did not elaborate was that the dumping of many of these agricultural raw materials under forced-export policies enabled foreign manufacturers to obtain *their* raw materials at below cost to the even further disadvantage of their South African competitors.

The interest of the polity in the gold-mining industry was somewhat different. As the Chamber of Mines saw it, the polity's concern was to keep the industry in being in order to milk it for the 'protection' of others. The tax yield, at discriminatory rates, from the gold-mining industry was thus an interest of first priority to the Minister of Finance. Mr Havenga in those years of his bounding budgetary surpluses after 1933 gave a special kind of consideration to those gold-mining companies which made such a gratifying, to Mr Havenga, contribution.

The Finance Minister was not disposed therefore to impose on this primary industry a *direct* burden of increased machinery and materials costs through related customs tariffs for the benefit of the secondary industry of manufacturing. He did not however oppose an *indirect* burden consequent from the protection given for the other primary industry of agriculture.

Both these aspects were acknowledged by the spokesman of the Chamber of Mines in his evidence to the Customs Tariff Commission, 1934–35:

Mr Gemmill (of the Chamber of Mines) expressed the view that owing to the freedom from duties of a large part of the materials used by the mines, protection can have had only a slight *direct* effect on the costs of production. He was, however, emphatically of the opinion that *indirectly*, in its effect on the level of prices, it materially influenced the cost of gold production through the general wage level. . .[19].

The Customs Tariff Commission was satisfied that, whatever the exact incidence of the additional cost of the products of protected industry, a considerable share must ultimately fall to be paid out of the proceeds of the largest economic industry of the country.

Regard for the productivity of the golden goose was perhaps understandably wider and keener in the light of its contemporary record-laying output. Such heightened appreciation extended beyond enthusiastic, non-discriminating share-dealers and more discriminating though equally enthusiastic economists[20]. Gold-mining investment was multiplying income for a growing number of White South Africans, including those who supplied stores and those who supplied labour. The consequential chain of expenditure accelerated investment so that a sizeable market for domestic manufactures was for the first time establishing the possibility of economic production, if safeguarded against foreign 'dumping'.

Certainly the majority of the Customs Tariff Commission, whose chairman Dr J. E. Holloway was the Secretary for Finance, concluded that mining was primary and manufacturing secondary – in terms of the concern of the polity:

It was represented to us in evidence, not only by many industrialists but also by the Board of Trade and Industries, that it is necessary in this country to develop secondary industries to take the place of the gold mining industry when it finally disappears. Without commenting on this matter *we desire to emphasize most strongly that if secondary industries are to take the place of the gold mining industry they must themselves become economic. The fulfilment of this condition is absolutely essential*; for otherwise when the gold mining industry does disappear the resulting adverse effect on the country's economy will be much greater than if secondary industries had not been developed at all[21].

The majority report (with a strong dissentient minority) indeed concluded, in its own words, that South Africa has reached a stage where her economic system can bear the burden of further protection only at the cost of a lower national income and that, one of the main requirements of the country being to reduce its level of costs . . . one of the first essentials is to reduce the cost of protection wherever it is possible to do so without detriment to the industries concerned[22].

Indeed in its rejection of protection as a policy to promote economic development, it went further:

We desire to add to these conclusions that if we had considered it possible to call a halt to the process of extending protection *without detriment to the work which has already been undertaken under the protective policy*, we would have preferred to recommend that no further protection be granted, except when room is made for it by protected industries no longer requiring the protection granted to them[23].

The discussion at the opening of this chapter stressed characteristics of the political economy of South Africa which, it was contended, might give theoretical validity to a special case for the protection of South African industry. They were the constitutional and institutional framework of a social system imposing chronic, and possibly congenital, underemployment and under-consumption on the African population. Industrialization, it was suggested, might have been the only way out of the under-consumption trap and protection a theoretically valid practical policy to increase productivity from unutilized resources.

The empirical examination has shown however that the polity accepted and applied a protectionist policy only because it promised increased, improved employment of Whites, otherwise described as 'civilized labour'. That this was the *raison d'être* of industrialization, if needs be under the encouragement of protection, is brought out unequivocally by the Customs Tariff Commission of 1934 as well as by the launching of a state-controlled iron and steel industry by the Pact Government.

One of the reasons for the adoption of a policy of development of protected industries, the Commission explained, was the difficulty of securing employment for a larger number of Whites, 'on account of the fact that the two major natural industries of the country employed a relatively low percentage of Whites and offered only slight employment for women' [24]. The Commission was much impressed by the evidence of the Chamber of Mines that in the past the Chamber had claimed a reduction in mine-working costs would have generated additional employment of substantial numbers. 'We consider, however, that it is open to doubt whether at the time the protectionist policy was framed the possibility of this alternative employment becoming available could have been entertained or even envisaged', said the Commission. But, it went on, the facts about available reserves of low-grade ore were now known and although it could not agree to supporting the Chamber of Mines in its plea for the gradual 'elimination of the protective tariff policy', the Commission was opposed to its extension as 'the biggest economic problem which faces the country is reducing costs' [25].

The Tariff Commission had no doubt as to what and who were being protected by the fiscal policy introduced by the Pact Government in 1925:

The greatest competitive drawback of South African industry is the high cost of White labour, and the protection which exists is to a large extent a protection of the wage rates payable to Whites in industry in South Africa [26].

This aspect is well exemplified from the early record of the state-controlled iron and steel industry. The exhaustive analysis of Iscor by C. S. Richards must be read in its voluminous detail to gain a full impression of the political factor in the development of this key industry [27]. War-time pride and post-war propaganda have so overlaid pre-war performance of Iscor that only the diligent student of Richards will learn some of the facts.

Briefly the iron and steel industry in South Africa was *not* a creation of Government enterprise after 'private enterprise had failed'. The State took over existing efforts from private entre-preneurs. The Government did not step in because it could raise the capital from the public when private financiers had flopped. In those years of world-wide excess capacity in the steel industry and of general depression, the 'public' would not put up the capital. The Government, after its failure to obtain the equity from private share-holders, then 'subscribed' the public's money on the strength of parliamentary approval obtained only after the first of subsequent devious amendments of the Act of Union. The public's money being unwilling to volunteer was drafted for service in the iron and steel plants as a matter of nationalized interest.

Despite absolute parliamentary assurances that Iscor would require no protection nor subsidization, high-cost railway branch-lines were provided by the South African Railways without the customary undertakings against initial losses; dumping duties were imposed against imported steel and in 1936 an agreement entered into with the International Steel Cartel which determined minimum c.i.f. prices depending on 'fair average prices of steel on world markets'. This agreement gave Iscor an unfettered discretion to apply its own basing-point price system (modelled on the American technique declared illegal under anti-monopoly legislation) so that Iscor could ensure that the South African market, that is the South African Railways and the booming gold-mines, took up its full capacity. The early financial results of Iscor were 'most disappointing' – which suggested that private prospective shareholders had shown no lack of foresight. Following the Agreement with the International Steel Cartel gazetted on 1 March 1937, the high profits made and dividends declared provided, however, the proof of the prescience of the politicians.

Again, labour costs played a key part in Iscor's costs [28]. The government-appointed chairman forthwith announced: 'It is the intention to man the works with white labour with possibly a few exceptions. We believe that this policy will yield better results in a modern highly mechanized works such as are being built at Pretoria and our estimates of production costs are based on white labour entirely. The experience so far gained with the employment of white labour on the construction work is encouraging'.

But the encouragement did not last long. In the subsequent labour-disputes leading to the appointment of a Conciliation Board and on its failure to the appointment of two Arbitrators, the submission was:

The Management engaged European labour (many taken over from the contractors constructing the works) to a much larger extent than it would have done under normal economic conditions . . . on operations generally performed by non-Europeans . . . on humanitarian and not economic grounds . . . and at wages much higher than . . . usually paid to non-Europeans for the same class of work.

The Arbitrators described the wages of White unskilled and semi-skilled labour as 'extraordinarily high' and that in the beginning there was definite over-staffing so that employees in the past had not worked to full capacity. In due course Iscor modified its all-White labour policy as its White labourers found alternative opportunities in the mining boom of 1936 and replaced them with African general labourers.

It is evident that the post-1925 interest of the polity in industrialization, either by way of customs tariff protection or by way of extended state-controlled enterprises such as expanded railway transport, iron and steel manufacture and electrical power supply, was related to the need and desire to find employment for the Whites now migrating by the thousands from a depressed agriculture. It is easy to relate the need and desire of the Poor Whites for jobs to the need

and desire of the Pact politicians for votes. Yet the obvious inferences of obvious vote-catching politics have a more fundamental
explanation in the realities of the country's total social system.

The fact that in the early nineteen-thirties there were millions
of under-employed poor non-Whites does not refute the contemporaneous gravity of hundreds of thousands of underemployed poor
Whites. The complementary relationship was not however clear
except to a few social analysts. The Nationalist-Labour Cabinet
taking charge of a static, even stagnant, economy might understandably be more perceptive of and responsive to the aggravated
short-term competitive relationship of Poor Whites and Poor Blacks
for a non-expanding work-wage fund. It was also understandable
that in seeking to expand that work-wage fund by the encouragement
of industrialization, it should accord a preferential priority to the
Poor Whites.

It is a political fact that the Poor Whites were the concern of
the polity; it was an economic consequence that the Poor Blacks
were also caught up in the process of forced industrialization to solve
the problem of Poor Whiteism. Hence though 43,000 Whites were
employed in private industrial establishments in 1924/25 compared
with about 101,000 in 1939/40, the numbers of Non-Whites had
increased from 88,000 (55,500 Africans only) to 182,000 (130,500
Africans only) over the same period [29].

Once again, however, it was the turn of history for an external
social process rudely to interrupt the internal social system of South
Africa. Hitler and September, 1939, broke into the Union's political
economy with shattering effect. Hertzog and his nationalist supporters, unconvinced that they would be fighting for South Africa's
interests and unreconciled to fighting even up to the *limes* of Africa
for 'British Imperialism', re-joined their nationalism to the official
Nationalist Opposition. Smuts taking charge as prime minister
once again linked South African destiny to a one-world holism.
Political power was transformed, and the imperatives of the Second
World War were steadily to re-structure the South African economy.

The Industrial and Agricultural Requirements Commission was
forthwith constituted, under the influential chairmanship of Dr H. J.
van Eck, to facilitate the re-structuring – both to meet the urgent
needs of war and to anticipate the compelling pressures of the post-
war. Its famed third interim report addressed itself to Fundamentals
of Economic Policy in the Union [30].

It began with a review of realities. The generalizations are informative in giving sociological perspective to econometric derivatives. Although large in size, 472,000 sq. miles, South Africa had a 1940 estimated population of about 10,000,000. Probably two-thirds of it was still rural. Authorities had shown that of this population, small in relation to land-area, probably as many as 400,000 Whites and the bulk of Non-Whites were underfed, badly housed and poorly educated.

The van Eck Report repeated what had been said at the time of Union. The summer rainfall falls in a semi-arid area and only one-third of all South Africa receives more than 25 inches a year – a precipitation required for successful crop production in most of the country. Winter crops are confined to a small winter rainfall area. The country's soils lacked phosphates and areas of good soils are patchy so that restricted mechanization retards higher yields and cost reductions; rivers are neither navigable nor suitable for large-scale hydro-electric power generation.

Save in certain areas, the Union's physical features, therefore, do not combine to give the moisture, temperature and soils required for successful crop cultivation, and today less than 6 per cent of the total area of the country is cultivated. The maximum irrigable area is very restricted – possibly 2,000,000 acres – and in all these circumstances at most 15 per cent of the Union is ever likely to be cultivated. Agriculturally, the greater portion of the country is, therefore, suited only for livestock farming. . .[31].

Over and above the physical controls which compelled recognition that South Africa was poor crop-raising country, improper pasture management was resulting in an almost general deterioration of natural grazing, culminating in further denudation and moisture loss. The most durable of South Africa's natural resources, the van Eck Commission was led to warn, was being dissipated extensively and at a cumulative rate.

While the country was extremely poorly wooded with timber-producing plantations of less than 2 per cent of total area, surveys of the Union's lengthy coastlines were disclosing enormous potential fishing grounds. Contemporaneously, however, as against an agricultural production of over £60 million a year, only 70 million lbs of fish worth £600,000 were being landed. Mineral resources, apart from gold disclosed and undisclosed, were highly encouraging.

Available data showed beyond doubt, said the van Eck Commission, that the potential underground wealth was impressive. Several of the key minerals are plentiful – iron ore, steam coal, limestone, asbestos, chrome and manganese. In the Transvaal, Natal and the northern Free State, easy mining conditions and low-wage African labour gave a then pithead price of coal at an average 4s. 9d. to 6s. 9d. against a British pithead price of 15s. per ton. The Union of South Africa, the Commission declared, could thus rank with the limited number of countries in which the essential minerals for heavy industry are present in large quantities.

Human resources were even more than natural resources a potential of unutilized, if not unknown, capacity. The very great majority of the Non-White population, and many Whites, were poorly educated and had no vocational training or qualifications. The country had no comparable supply of highly skilled labour as was available to the leading industrial countries. Nonetheless the van Eck Commission discerned that the growing urbanized Non-White population was suited by temperament to the standardized processes of modern mass production and that there was a highly adaptable complement of White, and Coloured, workers for more skilled operations.

But, the Commission declared, with few exceptions South African factories were working on a small scale, not highly mechanized and were largely dependent on tariff protection. In consequence they were adapted neither to make the best use of the labour supply nor the fullest use of the ample cheap power available.

The analysis of the van Eck Commission established that South Africa possessed the potential of materials and men. What it did not have were the markets. Professor Frankel and other authoritative academic opinion was convinced that the markets should be conceived as those developed by international trade. The van Eck Commission, while conscious of the interdependence of foreign and domestic markets, was more disposed to use the instruments of the polity to develop the domestic market. Neither the Commission nor the academics were doctrinaire enthusiasts for free trade but both, though much more strongly the academic economists, opposed a fostering of manufacturing industry that would increase gold-mining costs and thereby inhibit its critical contribution to post-war economic development.

Again the quantitative-qualitative assessments of both the van Eck Commission and of Frankel's national income analysis established that by the early 1940s, the South African social system had produced a skewed development. The problem of preventing gold reverting to dross remained. It is the special merit of the van Eck Report that, in making a plea for the use of government as a catalytic agent, it turned away from the alchemy of party politics.

The van Eck Report saw the future not as a projection of the party political intervention from the time of Union to the outbreak of the Second World War. It rejected back to the land for the Whites, the concept of civilized labour narrowly interpreted as a work-wage fund for Whites, railway rating as an instrument for extra-economic aims, indiscriminate encouragement of manufacturing industry.

It pressed strongly that the polity face the responsibilities arising from the realities. The most unacceptable reality was that in 1936 just under two-thirds of the total working population was still dependent on farming, which was contributing about one-eighth only of the national income and that from 1927–8 to 1936–7 the amount so contributed had remained static at about £49,000,000. It saw the limited local market was a fundamental obstacle to the establishment of new industries and that the gap in wages – in mining White earnings currently 8 times and in manufacturing 4–5 times, respectively, as high as Non-Whites' wages – was being widened. It acknowledged the practical monopoly of skilled work by well-organized Whites and the restricted collective bargaining rights of Non-Whites, confined to unskilled grades, with all the consequences for the earnings-differentials.

It saw some of the implications of a monopolistic South African Railways, whose discriminating rates had contrived to secure 60 per cent of its total revenue from 16 per cent high-rate traffic tonnage, and the relationship to restrictions on competitive, cheaper road transport. It faced the facts of goldmining's significance – its contribution of one-fifth of the nation's net income and two-fifths of the State's annual revenue, of gold exports of £110 millions out of then total yearly exports of £140–£150 millions. It urged the formulation of a long-term goldmining policy so that State action affecting costs and revenue should henceforth aim at optimising productive life.

It took a particularly realistic look at South African manu-facturing industry. It found a rapid increase in output concomitant with the expansion of goldmining since 1933. But it declared that the bulk of the country's manufacturing structure was not self-supporting and was dependent upon protection, estimated at costing £10,000,000 a year. The high industrial cost structure indicated a low level of efficiency, with insufficient mechanization to obtain the full benefit of cheap power and operatives' semi-skills. The inordinately restricted use of lower-paid Africans for the benefit of very much higher-paid Whites inhibited a cost-reducing rationalization. It was convinced of the potential of industrial expansion subject to the replacement of rigidities in labour-organization by the flexibilities that would favour the non-skilled [32].

This van Eck Report, prepared for the Smuts Government by a number of independent minds with no party political connections or political interests in the narrow sense, at a low-point of the Allied fortunes in the Second World War and at the time of the Atlantic Charter, introduced its own aspirations for the post-war South African social system:

The Commission considers that the low-income groups at present receive an inequitable share of the national income and this both limits the local market for industrial and agricultural products and is the cause of serious social degeneration through malnutrition. This is a consequence of the present labour policies regarding wages and employment. There is much social injustice and the resulting economic position of the low-income groups is so parlous that malnutrition is rife amongst them and their efficiency is impaired. It is, therefore, imperative that the position of the low-income groups be improved[33].

The Commission, in brief, brought before the politicians what had long been known to the economists. The rigidities that the polity had fastened on the economy in the supposed interests of economic growth in general and of the Poor Whites in particular had achieved neither the rate of growth of which the optimum use of the country's resources, human and natural, aided by domestic and foreign capital and technology, was capable – nor the social justice acceptable to the new thinking of welfare economics.

Underconsumption and underemployment after thirty years of political unification, centring on the great Witwatersrand gold-mining industry, was seemingly unmalleable. But the Second World War was on – providing its own grinding, pounding flexibilities.

War-time protection of domestic manufacturing by the forced exclusion of imported competition may prove nothing about the theory of peacetime international trade, though Adam Smith of course allowed for defence needs in his 'exceptions'. But the rapid build-up of South African industrial production after 1940 was important and impressive. The iron and steel industry certainly proved itself to be strategic to national defence and the key-supplier to a growing engineering industry. The food manufacturing factories and the clothing factories fed and clothed civilians and armed forces. Raw material imports still came in – largely paid for by gold as before – but South African secondary industry proved of primary importance to the war-time economy.

What war-time protection does however prove is that war mobilizes more than armies. It mobilizes resources – utilized, under-utilized and unutilized. It breaks down entrenched positions in factories as well as on battle-fields. It brings fluidities into institutions and geography. It introduces risk-taking behind the lines and in the lines. It brings forward 'new men' into command of resources, military and civilian. It deploys manpower and employs woman-power. It attacks all barriers – including colour bars. It operates through a disintegrating integration.

In essence, to repeat, war-time protection mobilizes resources. In pre-war South Africa there were unutilized resources in abundance waiting for mobilization. The underemployment and undercon-sumption of the Poor Whites had less quantitative but no less qualitative significance than the underemployment and under-consumption of the Poor Non-Whites. Industrialization, forced by the protection of war, did not under such conditions merely mean a redistribution or diversion of workers already at work.

The theory of free trade, however, does not accept that the exis-tence of unutilized labour is in itself sufficient case for protection. Such unutilized labour still requires the co-operant capital, entre-preneurship and material resources. A valid case for protection would have to substantiate that the economic development achieved is a greater social product than the economic achievement sacrificed by a diversion of the co-operant capital, enterpreneurship and material resources.

War-time experience is by the nature of things not a satisfactory test of maximizing the 'social product'. Victory is more a war-aim than a definable 'social product' either for econometrics or welfare economics. Yet the war-time industrialization of South Africa has empirical significance. There are suggestive magnitudes to be read into the figures of the Table of Industrial Growth in South Africa, appended to this chapter. Apart from the unutilized labour, there were unutilized material resources and there was unsuspected or unproved entrepreneurial management. But whether the inspiration of the war-created industrialization, which brought together the unemployed labour-raw materials-entrepreneurial management, was newly created markets or newly created money is unanswerable.

Either way, if it was capital formation by way of monetary inflation or domestic demand creation by way of non-available imports, the war years meant a rapidly growing market for South African manufactured goods. Infant industries were being forced to grow up, while new infants were steadily born [34]. Haberler in his *Theory of International Trade* acknowledged, as many others including Adam Smith had done before him, the possibility that protection may help an industry to survive the weaknesses of infancy [35]. He also repeats the familiar argument that this is an advantage only if the 'nursing' through the infant stage attracts workers into employment where their marginal employment will be greater than it was in their previous employment.

Haberler's argument that, in a modern industrial country well supplied with skilled workers, trained technicians and enterprising leaders of industry, tariff protection can fulfil a nursing function in exceptional cases only is not readily deniable. Nor is his contention that the alleged advantages of mass production following on the nursing, depend on certain conditions of decreasing costs flowing from external economies, which are the 'curiosa of theory' rather than the realities of practical policy.

But South Africa was not such a 'modern industrial economy' – certainly not at the beginning of the Second World War nor even at its end. It was an economy of mass underemployment and mass underconsumption. Yet neither in 1939 nor in 1945 was it an *underdeveloped* economy, at least as defined by Bauer and Yamey in their *Economics of Underdeveloped Countries* [36]. South Africa, though not necessarily unique, was unusual. It was, it is suggested, an adolescent economy.

An adolescent economy might be said to have some of the features of an underdeveloped economy and some of the features of a fully developed economy. The interesting theoretical and practical issue is whether protection or forced industrialization can add to the social product of an adolescent economy. Is there a protectionist case, not only for the infant industry, but for the adolescent economy? Were there real possibilities of external economies flowing from expanded industrialization in respect of South Africa? Further consideration is left to a later chapter [37].

South African experience of industrialization, it is submitted, indicates that an ugly duckling may grow up into a protected swan – with greater self-assurance if, of course, it can do so in the maternal care of a golden goose. And self-assurance might excuse boastful conceit, if Mother Golden Goose should suddenly start to inject uranium into her golden eggs just when the world becomes infatuated with atomic energy. While boastful conceit might even with impunity indulge in chauvinistic assertions, if Mother Golden Goose decides in her declining years to have offspring of golden goslings [38].

The Second World War unquestionably acted as highly stimulating protection for South African manufacturing industry. When war-time exclusion of competitive imports was soon followed, in 1948, by post-war foreign-exchange controls that continued such exclusion of competition, industrialization developed rapidly indeed. Such very complete protection of secondary industry did not, however, curtail the rate of economic development through diminishing essential gold output. A unique joint-product of uranium and gold in the older Rand goldfields and some of the world's richest goldmines brought into production in the newer Orange Free State goldfields, all on top of a sterling devaluation in 1949 to raise the sterling price of gold to 250s. per oz, ensured that from the early nineteen-fifties gold-mining profits and production soared annually.

A ten year record of increased performance by the gold-mining industry yielded for the operating year of 1963, 27,000,000 fine ounces of gold valued at R677,500,000 or £339 millions (apart from the proceeds of uranium sales). It must, therefore, remain an academic question whether the protection of manufacturing industry has been 'at the expense' of the gold-mining industry. The non-academic might well feel that Mother Goose could afford the cost.

When he was analysing the growth of South Africa's national income in 1944, Frankel had written: 'Unless the Union becomes the fortunate recipient of new favours, owing, for example, to an exceptional turn of the currency wheels of the world economy, which may yield another windfall increase in the value of its exports, it will have to increase the efficiency of its labour force both in export and home industry.'

The windfall favours for gold-mining exports were to come in flowing measure in the post-war period. The years of war were more decisive in increasing the productivity of the country's labour force. They were the years of crucial institutional change. As the Whites went off to battlefields and war-factories, the Non-Whites entered into the urban workshops by the tens and tens of thousands. The colour bars did not disintegrate nor were they abandoned. They remained barriers but the pre-war gulf was now bridged by the new industrial class of operatives, Coloured, Indian and – more slowly – Africans. Between the skilled and unskilled, the semi-skills were increasingly inserted.

These institutional changes were such as to revolutionize the South African social system – what had passed and what lay ahead. It propelled change into the economy so radically that the demand for unchange by the polity became irresistible [39]. The network of economic development was enveloping South African society in a manner which the political factor of Afrikanerdom saw as the extirpation of its ethos. It reacted with nationalist potency.

STATISTICAL APPENDIX
OF
MANUFACTURING INDUSTRY
SOUTH AFRICA

(i) Only private undertakings i.e. excluding government undertakings, are shown. Establishment in this period i.e. prior to 1954/1955 and 1955/56: an 'establishment' included any business using motive power and in which three or more persons employed whole time on work of an industrial nature – hence it included large numbers of in effect non-manufacturing activities.

(ii) Gross output represents gross value of production and value of work done – hence it includes element of duplication where finished product of one industry (e.g. tanning) is the material processed in another industry (e.g. footwear).

(iii) Net output, or net value of production, is gross value minus cost of materials and fuel, light and power used and the amount paid for work given out. It represents value added to cost of materials etc. by process of production. Broadly speaking, it comprises salaries and wages, overheads and profits.

(iv) From 1954/55 and 1955/56 new definitions and classifications make comparibility with previous period of limited significance.

Year	Establish-ments Number	Value of		Employment	
		Land Buildings £1,000	Machinery £1,000	Total	Whi
1924–25	6,009	16,125	14,721	114,876	40,7
25–26	5,957	15,888	14,732	120,928	43,9
26–27	6,012	16,594	16,286	126,922	47,1
27–28	6,162	17,399	16,070	132,184	50,4
28–29	6,238	18,331	16,722	140,689	53,6
29–30	6,472	18,857	17,010	141,616	54,8
32–33	6,543	18,901	15,796	132,503	57,0
33–34	7,232	21,205	18,336	159,611	68,7
34–35	7,636	23,120	20,042	181,755	77,1
35–36	8,152	25,954	22,536	206,430	84,9
36–37	8,416	29,375	23,758	224,014	91,3
37–38	8,581	31,552	24,925	231,986	92,6
38–39	8,614	33,529	26,103	236,123	93,0
39–40	8,505	34,723	27,978	245,457	92,5
40–41	8,599	36,362	30,270	273,779	96,5
41–42	8,608	39,273	32,700	291,248	97,4
42–43	8,639	41,477	34,779	308,657	99,1
43–44	9,166	46,183	38,973	332,528	104,5
44–45	9,316	50,565	40,814	361,004	112,2
45–46	9,642	56,825	46,466	379,022	120,4
46–47	9,999	64,968	55,251	396,940	129,6
47–48	11,376	80,871	66,471	433,756	140,4
48–49	12,060	90,420	88,801	473,373	152,4
49–50	12,517	104,294	104,747	497,887	157,1
50–51	12,983	140,653	122,512	543,252	168,2
51–52	12,887	154,959	137,912	575,866	173,4
52–53	13,260	173,867	143,289	595,855	177,8
53–54	13,811	191,671	167,972	622,682	183,1
54–55	13,725	216,563	218,254	652,635	184,3

Salaries and Wages		Materials used £1000	Value of Output	
Total £1000	Whites £1000		Gross £1000	Net £1000
1,060	7,404	30,846	57,304	24,746
1,962	8,017	35,188	63,766	26,791
2,831	8,668	36,634	67,219	28,676
3,887	9,476	42,324	75,642	31,292
4,865	10,130	45,075	80,648	33,776
5,603	10,742	42,435	78,425	34,194
3,356	9,646	35,037	67,332	30,700
6,318	11,891	43,959	82,448	36,401
9,264	14,063	50,411	95,373	42,637
22,230	16,090	56,255	108,412	49,542
25,081	18,095	66,365	126,036	56,743
26,948	19,325	70,142	134,142	60,769
27,848	19,821	73,213	140,587	64,068
29,546	20,794	87,088	161,671	70,851
33,943	22,983	102,413	189,849	83,288
41,007	26,911	112,440	212,298	95,229
48,253	30,578	121,148	230,962	104,833
56,481	34,459	143,275	267,839	119,281
57,353	40,233	160,453	304,083	137,810
74,818	44,945	175,965	334,554	152,476
84,181	51,733	209,434	390,222	173,717
97,691	60,471	252,859	461,234	200,451
13,103	70,283	293,580	531,195	228,524
22,442	76,265	342,119	608,486	256,011
41,239	87,741	467,929	791,604	310,860
54,006	102,916	538,480	904,494	350,246
82,577	114,727	547,802	954,259	387,729
98,121	124,090	554,627	1,006,553	430,211
16,416	135,056		1,110,388	482,101

e: Union Statistics for Fifty Years – Bureau of Census and Statistics, Pretoria.

THE SOUTH AFRICAN WAY OF LIFE – CHANGING AND UNCHANGING PART II

Industrialization, more forced by war than protected by customs tariffs, had given suggestive evidence of the latent productivity in the South African economy, hitherto institutionalized into immobility. It had perhaps given too obvious indications of the 'shock effect' of integrating industrialization on the segregating ethos. The 'big push' had sent hundreds of thousands of Africans from tribal territories and the now thoroughly commercialized White agriculture into the cities and the 'shock effect' was felt more deeply by those who believed 'the struggle of the past was the struggle of the present, and the struggle of the present the same as that of the past'[1].

It was however the Boer General Smuts, now the British Field-Marshall Smuts, who, in taking South Africa into the Second World War, had confused the struggle of the South African present with the struggle of the Afrikaner past. It was Prime Minister Smuts whose holism 'held that all entities tend to seek larger groupings within which to realize themselves', who refused to understand that the Afrikanerdom was an entity to itself and whose nationalism could never seek a larger grouping, if it was to realize itself.

It was Dr. D. F. Malan, the former Dutch Reformed Church predikant, who had withdrawn Afrikaner nationalism into the desert of a 19-strong opposition fifteen years ago, and who could look more deeply into the Afrikaner heart[2]. It was Malan who, through all the years of his monumental patience, had always understood that Afrikaner nationalism would never realize itself by voting United Party instead of *Hereenigde Nasionale of Volksparty*.

It was Smuts' United Party, too absorbed in change by the war-economy, which failed to perceive the urge towards unchange from the pre-war polity. It was Malan, therefore, who in 1948 became Prime Minister of his triumphant Nationalist Party and it was Smuts who was defeated in his own constituency by an opponent who had resigned from the civil service rather than withdraw, as ordered, from the Broederbond [3].

The most striking aspect of the 1948 election, wrote an American political scientist, Professor Carter, was the degree to which it reflected national origins and sentiments [4]. Malan's Nationalist Party, together with its soon-to-be absorbed, coalition-partner Havenga's Afrikaner Party, won virtually every seat in the pre-dominantly Afrikaans-speaking areas; the United Party and the Labour Party (which in 1946 had once more split and begun again with a declaration on 'fundamental rights for all races in the Union') won every seat in the English-speaking areas.

According to a careful analysis by Professor Gwendolin Carter, only about 20–25 per cent of the Afrikaans-speaking people voted for Smuts's United Party although it had an equal number of Afrikaans-speaking and English-speaking candidates. The Nationalist Party had not a single predominantly English-speaking candidate and Malan's Cabinet was consequently exclusively Afrikaner.

For the first time in the history of the Union, the Government was composed of only one of its two European peoples. Moreover, the party in power was one which had gone through a long period in the wilderness for the sake of its convictions. . . . Politically, then, the year 1948 marks a watershed in South African politics[ ].

In 1910, as chapter seven of this thesis expressed it, the White polity had taken charge; in 1924, as chapter eight put it, the White polity had taken control. Now, in 1948, the Afrikaner polity had taken over.

At each point, the polity expressed the value-orientations of the South African social system – or, more precisely, of its contemporary electorate. If the significance of these value-orientations for post-war economic rationality, that is for the pursuit of productivity through a colour-blind market, is to be appreciated, a brief account of the formative agents of Afrikaner nationalism is necessary.

The polity is more than the government. It comprehends the interacting, interlocking organizations and persons which are both the source and the expression of party political power that is in control of the government of the nation.

The cohesion of nationalistic Afrikanerdom comes in part out of the vividness of its memories and grievances; the way in which the British imperial factor pursued the Afrikaners who had trekked North to free themselves from its influence; the Anglo-Boer War; the concentration camps for women and children; the one-time discrimination against Afrikaners. In large part, however, its closely knit unity is the creation of a host of organizations which have more or less consciously sought to overcome the traditional divisions within Afrikanerdom, and develop political, economic and cultural fronts which reflect its common ideals and purposes. The National[ist] Party is one of the most influential of these organizations. At the same time, it is only one – though now the most important one – amongst an interacting series of groups covering all aspects of life and knitting nationalistic Afrikanerdom together[6].

Without doubt the most important influence on Afrikanerdom was, and possibly still is, the Dutch Reformed Church. The Dutch Reformed Churches have provided the comprehensive philosophy of life for a *volk*, more church-going perhaps than any other Protestant-professing people. Though urbanization undoubtedly brings other values and mores, the institutionalized culture of Afrikaans-speaking peoples – and especially in the rural areas – is evoked by its distinctive interpretation of Calvinist faith and is focused on the church. The constitutional law, the *grondwet*, of the Trekker Republics insisted on racial separation in Church and State and herein is the link between Afrikaner faith and Afrikaner government.

Nonetheless, a constant questioning of the appropriate relationship between State and Church and consciousness of its divisive intimacy led Afrikaner intellectuals to establish a secular authority for the 'ideal of total apartheid'. The South African Bureau of Racial Affairs, known as Sabra, was inspired at Stellenbosch University as the intellectual front of Afrikanerdom and infused with its total apartheid concepts by Dr W. W. M. Eiselen, son of a Dutch Reformed Church missionary. Dr Eiselen was to be brought into the key civil service office of Secretary for Native Affairs by the 1948 Nationalist Government in a unique non-careerist appointment.

It was Dr Eiselen who spoke of

separating the heterogeneous groups from the population of the country into separate socio-economic units, inhabiting separate parts of the country, each enjoying in his own area full citizen rights, the greatest of which is the opportunity of developing such capabilities as its individual members may possess to their optimum capacity[7].

And it was Dr Eiselen who, as the *machina ex dei* of Dr H. F. Verwoerd, also summoned from Stellenbosch University to non-elected appointment as Minister of Native Affairs in 1950, spelt out the administrative detail of Verwoerd's legislative programme of Apartheid. The Dutch Reformed Churches and Sabra are, however, influences of Afrikaans thought and not instruments of Afrikanerdom.

The earliest and probably the most effective of such instruments has been the Broederbond. It was conceived in 1918, constituted in 1920 and expanded into a secret society in 1922. The exact role of the most controversial band of non-consanguineous brothers in South African politics is unlikely ever to be established[8]. Following the 1944 ban by Smuts on Broederbond members continuing as civil servants, the Broederbond secretary published four articles in *Die Transvaler*. The articles declared *inter alia*:

The Afrikaner Broederbond is born out of a deep conviction that the Afrikaner nation was put in this land by God and is destined to continue in existence as a nation with its own nature and calling.

Its highest aim is honourable service to Afrikanerdom
(a) To bring about a healthy and progressive unanimity amongst all Afrikaners who strive for the welfare of the Afrikaner nation
(b) To arouse the Afrikaner's national self-consciousness, and to implant a love for his language, tradition, country and people
(c) The furtherance of all the 'interests' of the Afrikaner nation.

The Broederbond, though disavowing party politics, laid down a seven-fold 'ideal' for which Broers should strive in 'their political action'. These included: Putting a stop to the exploitation of the resources and population of South Africa by strangers, including the more intensive industrial development; the nationalization of the money market and the systematic co-ordination of economic policies; the Afrikanerization of our public life and our teaching and education in a Christian National spirit while leaving free the internal development of all sections of the nation insofar as it is not dangerous to the State[9]. Though disclosure of membership of the Broederbond is prohibited (at the present time of 1966), it is generally believed that about four-fifths of the Nationalist Members of Parliament are Broers and most, if not all, the Cabinet members including the Prime Minister, Dr H. V. Verwoerd. It is also believed that most of the top-ranking civil servants and the present chairman of the South African Broadcasting Corporation are members. A considerable fraction of university and school teachers at Afrikaans institutions are members. Professor Carter sums up:

Whether or not is is more than a close association of like-minded persons dedicated to the advancement of Afrikanerdom, the Broederbond has contributed strongly, and perhaps dangerously, to the natural isolation of nationalist Afrikanerdom, as well as to its power[10].

On the initiative of the Broederbond, the Federasie van Afrikaanse Kultuurvereenigings or FAK was established in 1929 to co-ordinate Afrikaner cultural, religious, educational and economic societies [11]. In 1939 The Economic Institute was founded by the FAK and remained under the latter's jurisdiction while the Reddingsdaad-bond, also founded by the FAK, became an autonomous body. The FAK was also responsible for bringing into being the Afrikaanse Handelsinstituut (or Afrikaans Chamber of Commerce), the National Council of Trustees to promote Afrikaner labour organizations (which under Dr Albert Hertzog's chairmanship was instrumental in securing Afrikaner-National control of the Mineworkers' Union) and the Institute for Christian National Education.

In 1938 the Reddingsdaadbond or RDB was established at the time of Great Trek centenary celebrations 'to train the Afrikaners to take their place in industrial society'. Apart from help to the individual worker, the RDB aimed at mobilizing the capital resources of the Afrikaner people. Dr Dönges, subsequently to become the key Cabinet Minister in effecting the withdrawal of the Cape Coloured voters from the common roll, claimed: We have the purchasing power. We have the capital power. We have the money power. The question is: have we the will power and the power to act?

The RDB is generally accorded recognition for stimulating Afrikaner institutional finance. During the war- and post-war years, it effectively encouraged farmers to invest their savings in Afrikaans insurance, banks, building societies and savings institutions instead of the traditional plough-back into further farm-lands, The return flow of investment-capital brought about a major take-over of small business enterprise in the dorps or country towns by Afrikaners. The RDB, while a valuable catalytic agent, was soon surpassed by the self-generating growth of the major Afrikaans financial institutions. Unquestionably the inter-connections of purposive Afrikaner consumer-buying, clientèle-support and capital-generation proved effective in a generally favourable business climate.

A Christian National Education Conference was organized by the FAK in Bloemfontein in 1939. In the course of ten years the Institute for Christian National Education formulated a complete system of Christian National Education for all levels of primary, secondary and higher education. The chairman was subsequently to claim that the policy had the support of the 'whole of Afrikanerdom' and in the course of time became quasi-official educational policy [12].

In due course, other distinctive Afrikaner organizations were founded ranging from automobile clubs to Boy Scouts (Voortrekkers), from Red Cross (Noodhulpliga) to university students (Afrikaner Nasionale Studentebond).

Professor Carter puts it well:

The very fact of describing these groups may, in a sense, exaggerate their importance. . . . Yet they represent something almost unique in modern Western society. Other countries and peoples, in particular Americans, have developed a network of associations to bridge the divisions caused by shifting populations, and social mobility. But the groups described . . . do much more than this. Consciously or unconsciously, they have sought or seek to create out of nationalistic Afrikanerdom an integrated whole which can assume what is looked on as its 'destiny', the direction, if not domination of all other peoples within the Union, and possibly beyond.

The intensity of purpose of these groups, and the effectiveness of their actions, provide an essential underpinning for the drive and power of their political spokesman and leader, the National Party[13].

It is evident that the culture of the Afrikaner volk was institutionalized with increasing emphasis and impetus from about the time that Dr Malan took his 'Purified' Nationalist Party into seemingly hopeless Opposition in 1934. It is equally evident that this intensively institutionalized culture carried Dr Malan and his Nationalists to parliamentary power in 1948 [14].

It is no fanciful academic abstraction to identify the interactions of polity and institutionalized culture of Afrikanerdom from 1948 onwards. The Afrikaner polity had taken over to preserve the charisma of the *volk*. It directed itself with extraordinary intensity of concentrated, dedicated parliamentary purpose to bring about the unchange of its institutionalized culture and to erect an impenetrable defence of that culture against the adaptations of compulsive change coming from the economy.

In consequence, a mounting tide of legislation and a flood of regulation engulfed the social system of the Non-White South Africans.

The essence of Apartheid was that Whites and Non-Whites did not, could not and must not constitute a single social system. The self-existence of the Whites subsisted in excluding Non-Whites from a shared reality of human relationships, however much the existence of the Non-Whites proved an economic entity. The parliamentary programme of Afrikanerdom directed itself accordingly [15].

Among the earliest bills were those that, significantly, dealt with sex-contacts. The Prohibition of Mixed Marriages Act, 1949, though only 100 mixed marriages had been solemnized between 1943 and 1946, was followed by the Immorality Amendment Act No. 21 of 1950, which prohibited all illicit carnal intercourse, even with consent, between a 'European' and a 'non-European'. The debates stressed on the Nationalist-Government side that the special urgency for legislation arose from the process of industrialization and consequent increasing urbanization of the population with its cosmopolitanizing demoralization.

Customary contact-relationships were subject to increasingly rigid legal regimentation and administrative jurisdiction. An Appeal Court ruled that 'separate but equal' facilities was a fundamental civil right and invalidated unequal facilities as manifestly unjust and oppressive [16]. This was followed by the Reservation of Separate Amenities Act, 1953, to separate physical contacts between Whites and Non-Whites in post offices, railway entrances and stations, trains, bridges, buses, public parks, benches, beaches, swimming pools, libraries [17]. The law specifically provides for the principle of inequality, leaving no discretion to the courts to place limitations on its extent.

Identification of colour-classification became an obvious administrative necessity for a social system based on Apartheid. The key Population Registration Act of 1950 provided for identity certificates for every South African inhabitant with specific categorization of colour-group [18].

Throughout these debates and years, the governing Nationalist

Party and its press repeatedly emphasized that they were doing no more than give legislative authority to hallowed social practice and customary mores. It would indeed be totally inaccurate to suggest that either the major political opposition, the United Party, or many English-speaking White South Africans wished to see an end to social discrimination based on colour. Throughout his political career, Smuts had been bedevilled by the problem of Indian 'penetration' in Natal and the bitter resistance of English-speaking Natalians to unrestricted property-ownership by Natal's rapidly-growing Indian population. The former's insistence on residential segregation in Durban forced Smuts to enact the Pegging Act of 1943 to make illegal inter-racial property transactions in Durban. The subsequent – aborted – Asiatic Land Tenure and Indian Representation Act of 1946 coupled land ownership and occupation restrictions on Indians with a limited communal representation in Parliament and local authorities.

Smuts's Indian legislation split the South African Labour Party. Its stormy petrel Madeley, former Cabinet Minister and trade unionist leader, declaring himself 'to be a white man before he was a socialist', left the Party. The Labour Party was then reformed and its 1946 statement marked the beginning of subsequent declarations on 'fundamental rights for all races in the Union'. This too was the period of cleavage within the trade union movement itself, with a bitter taking-of-positions on White workers' opposition or support for Government action to entrench and extend the labour colour bars. Smuts's policy towards Natal's Indians also led to the hardly papered-over cracks in his own United Party and to a confusing split in the Dominion Party formed from an earlier split from the United Party. In particular Smuts's destined successor, the liberal-minded, brilliant Jan Hofmeyr, became the bogeyman of anti-integrationist value-orientations among White opinion generally and in all political parties [19].

The determination of English Natal to secure legislative restraints on Indian property-ownership and residential-penetration of 'European areas' was a stage in the long sequence of residential segregation. The policy culminated in the Group Areas Act of 1950, described by Prime Minister Malan as 'the kernel of the apartheid policy . . . the most crucial for determining the future of race relations' and by Dr Dönges, its ministerial author, as 'the cornerstone of positive apartheid'. Its fundamental principle was to extend residential segregation to colour groups of White, Coloured and African – the Act itself providing for subdivision of category of Coloured into 'any ethnical, linguistic, cultural or other groups of persons'. The ultimate goal, according to the responsible Minister, Dr Dönges, was to restrict each defined group to its own particular area as far as ownership, occupancy and trading are concerned[20].

Despite the patent emphasis on minimizing physical human contacts between Whites and Non-Whites in such legislation, its basic expression was to control the integrating influences of the market. This is most clearly brought out by the concentration of legislative and administrative attention on the *urban areas*.

It was the process of urbanization, speeded up by the gold-price increase of the 1930s after which Johannesburg 'grew more in four years than in the previous forty', and the accompanying industrialization of post-1940 that gave seemingly irresistible impetus to market forces. Urbanization is in one respect essentially a market-process – a mechanism for centralizing human contacts to achieve economies of space and time. The village, the town, the city, the megapolis, the conurbation each in its turn evinces the compulsive co-ordination of the market. The intimacy of inter-relationships, increasingly impersonal as urban-market forces interact to generate growth, is unendingly disruptive of individuality.

The cry of the Nationalist backbencher in the Group Areas Act debate that mixed residential areas are 'the deathbeds of the European race'[21] and of another that they lead to 'loss of colour sense'[22] expressed the depth of revulsion against the impersonality of the market and the loss of group-consciousness from its urbanizing concurrency. While the Apartheid legislation, outlined above, was the obvious method by which Afrikanerdom after 1948 aimed to manage the tensions and maintain the patterns of the South African social system[23], its Bantu Education Act of 1953 and Native Laws Amendment Act of 1957 were the clear demonstrations of intent to preserve its institutionalized culture[24]. Subsequent legislation to control the *geographical and functional mobility* of the Non-Whites in general, and the Africans in particular, manifested the determination of the polity to resist adaptation coming from the economy.

Government policy was concerned with resistance to change from the exercise of economic rationality. So-called 'total apartheid' in

the sense of two totally-separated social systems was indeed disavowed as an 'impracticable ideal' by successive Nationalist Prime
Ministers[25]. But the pursuit of productivity in the economy was
never to be allowed to challenge the institutionalized culture of
Afrikanerdom, which was specifically identified with total control
of the polity of Afrikanerdom.

Hence the long, bitterly-fought constitutional measures that
finally eliminated the Cape Coloured voters from the common
franchise roll and the ultimate exclusion of direct representation of
Africans by their elected-representatives in the Union Parliament.
Hence – though this would not necessarily be widely-agreed – the
inevitable break-away from the Commonwealth and the reconstitution of the Union of South Africa as the Republic of South
Africa.

The detail of this constitutional crisis of 1951–6 moved between
Parliament and the Supreme Court. The initial unconstitutional
less-than-two-thirds majority for the Separate Representation of
Voters Act of 1951 was followed by a too-ingenious, if not ingenous,
High Court of Parliament Act of 1952 to substitute Parliament for
the Supreme Court. Finally the Constitution and the Supreme
Court were out-flanked by the Senate Act of 1955 to create the
requisite number of senators for the two-thirds majority to eliminate
the century-old franchise rights of the Cape Coloureds. The full
story is exceptionally interesting constitutional law – and party
political ploymanship.

The significance of these measures, and of the subsequent act
that finally excised any form of indirectly elected parliamentary
representatives of the African peoples from the Union Parliament –
the Promotion of Bantu Self-Government Act of 1959 – was the clear
and present purpose of Afrikanerdom to deny the reality of a single
social system of White and Non-White South Africans.

Both the 1953 and the 1958 general election made it evident that
this clear and present purpose had a growing support among the
White electorate.

House of Assembly Membership – General Elections

	1948	1953	1958
Nationalists	79	94	103
United Party	65	57	53
Labour Party	6	5	Nil

But while Afrikanerdom was taking over the polity[26], the entrepreneurs were taking decisions. While party politics was winning votes, enterprise was winning markets. While the Nationalists entrenched unchange, productivity pursued change. While Dr Verwoerd master-minded counter-revolution in South Africa, Sir Ernest Oppenheimer consummated the Schumpeterian revolution that Cecil John Rhodes had begun.

From 1940 onwards the South African economy became market-orientated in extent and in depth. The break-away from subsistence and under-capitalization gave critical impetus to that division of labour and specialization of function, which in the remarkably short period of fifteen years virtually eliminated Poor Whiteism. The years of the Second World War sharply stimulated the geographical and social mobility of the rural White population, already being pulled into the Witwatersrand by post-1933 mining investment[27]. War-time demand for the output of farms and factories at prices which were in effect cost-plus at all levels of output meant favourable incremental capital-output ratios in money terms. Markets which could readily absorb the total yields of agriculture and the total capacity of manufacturing plants meant an increasing rate of domestic capital formation, though inadequate provision for depreciation at replacement prices over-stated true profits.

The high level of war-time demand for food crops and agricultural raw materials continued into the post-war years. The gross value of agricultural production at current prices, which had fallen to a near-nadir of £37 millions in 1933, achieved £73 millions in 1940, reached £295 millions in 1951 and climbed to £384 millions in 1957. The country's long-time major pastoral export, wool, showed the most spectacular price increases – an index of 100 for the base 1935/36–1938/39 was 176 in 1946/47, jumped to 445 in 1949/50 and to an unparalleled 950 during the Korean War phase of 1950/51. Wool sales valued at an annual £8,500,000 in 1939 rose steadily to about £14,500,000 in 1947 and then began the spectacular climb for the next fifteen years into the 1960s with an all-time peak of £91,000,000 in the exceptional year of 1951.

The tables on pages 278–80 highlight changes in South African farming from about the outbreak of the Second World War[28].

The broad indicators are clear.

South African agriculture in the White farming areas – the data are for all practical significance the statistics of White-owned farms – was becoming completely commercialized. After long decades, and even centuries, South African agriculture found its markets or the markets found South African agriculture. From 1940 it became market-integrated. The Second World War years were decisive. Internal consumption of food complemented by bulk-purchasing governmental contracts (including the highly lucrative British Government contracts) ensured prices that guaranteed profitability, except in the most reckless instances of over-capitalized indebtedness. In the post-war years, rising monetary incomes both inside South Africa and in the country's major export market of the United Kingdom maintained remunerative price-levels.

The indexes of physical volume of agricultural production suggests unremarkable increases in productivity. There is no striking evidence of 'scientific farming'. Neither in area cultivated nor in yields is there a break-through in Rostow's one key propensity – the application of science to fundamental ends. But in respect of two other key propensities – the seeking of material advance and the acceptance of innovation – there is patent progress. Farm mechanization is reflected in tractors, which increased: 1937, 6,019; 1947, 22,397; 1957, 100,420; in stationary engines, which increased from 10,573 in 1937 to 53,674 in 1955; in the number of farm motor-lorries that rose from 8,568 in 1937 to over 52,000 in 1955. Evidence to a Commission reported that total investment in farming machinery and implements before 1939 was approximately £30,000,000, which figure had risen to over £150,000,000 by 1955, without allowing for price increases [29].

Changes in census classification inhibit comparisons but there is no doubt that in the crucial measure of population-shift out of primary agriculture, the figures for White South Africans establish a key to material advance both in respect of White farming as a sector and the economy as a whole. The number of White males, classified as economically active in 'Agriculture, forestry, hunting and fishing' fell from about 178,000 in the 1936 census to about 160,000 in the 1946 census and to about 141,000 in the 1951 census. Figures for the numbers of White farm workers, i.e. not self-employed, are not available earlier than 1947 but a total of 14,470 in 1947 steadily declined to 9,255 in 1956 (a subsequent figure of 11,071

Selected Data of Agricultural Statistics for South Africa

		GROSS VALUE AGRICULTURAL PRODUCTION £1000								
Season ending in	Grand Total field and livestock products	Maize	Wheat	Slaughter Cattle and sheep	Wool	Fresh Fruit	Vineyards	Sugar	Tobacco	Dairy Produce including fresh milk
1911	28,933	4,031	1,553	4,812	3,179	832	304	499	249	3,090
1931	42,534	5,731	3,020	6,154	6,530	2,829	598	2,457	457	4,763
1941	78,504	12,960	5,142	12,361	9,895	5,179	1,669	4,151	1,137	7,641
1951	294,929	42,273	17,313	31,247	79,656	19,438	5,504	8,939	5,090	28,027
1952	258,018	32,267	17,424	39,319	44,115	19,598	4,134	7,972	3,535	29,836
1953	320,902	53,875	15,351	48,730	56,563	23,293	4,838	11,029	3,583	34,671
1954	340,593	59,978	15,399	49,552	59,879	26,928	4,860	12,865	3,727	37,958
1955	334,956	55,965	17,489	48,765	53,974	26,450	5,837	13,814	3,447	39,257
1956	347,859	54,499	22,329	51,946	47,833	29,581	5,692	15,934	5,613	40,540
1957	383,809	60,177	23,728	56,846	66,869	34,278	5,564	14,390	6,477	42,174
1958	359,544	51,326	19,767	60,775	47,917	33,507	5,711	16,133	9,423	43,165

Index of Physical Volume of Agricultural Production

1936/37–1938/39 = 100

Season ending	Grand Total field and livestock products	Maize	Wheat	Slaughter Cattle only	Wool	Fresh Fruit	Vineyards	Sugar	Tobacco	Dairy Produce and milk
1911	47	34	42	39	50	24	27	18	66	39
1931	83	63	65	81	120	55	61	86	63	81
1941	106	95	109	108	103	85	145	120	99	115
1951	140	118	177	152	93	147	196	129	237	174
1952	130	84	165	151	95	136	158	108	196	174
1953	147	132	139	154	103	167	181	129	178	179
1954	154	153	135	163	108	187	182	140	152	190
1955	160	147	155	146	115	196	203	166	134	198
1956	170	147	201	157	117	221	226	180	195	205
1957	179	166	213	158	121	268	200	170	242	213
1958	174	144	202	163	114	245	202	194	282	217
1959	181	154	168	155	118	247	201	231	301	220

Index of Producers' Prices of Farm Products
1936/37–1938/39 = 100

Year	Combined Index	Summer Cereals	Winter Cereals	Slaughter Stock	Wool & Mohair	Dairy Products
Weights	100	19	13	17	32·3	6
1912–13	101	116	101	108	—	110
1931–32	72	76	110	65	47	91
1941–42	124	120	144	135	102	131
1951–52	355	302	258	310	501	280
1952–53	411	320	277	329	620	312
1953–54	411	333	282	339	612	320
1954–55	378	323	277	351	519	318
1955–56	360	320	273	358	464	317
1956–57	409	312	275	379	610	318
1957–58	365	300	275	393	459	319
1958–59	328	296	276	371	368	319

for 1957 probably indicating a change in statistical designation of 'farm worker').

Proportionately but not absolutely in terms of respective population totals, Non-Whites too were less employed as farm employees and domestic servants on White-owned farms. The absolute numbers increased from about 831,000 in 1947 to about 953,000 in 1957.

From the viewpoint of South African agriculture, the consequences of the Second World War were hardly less revolutionary than for the country's manufacturing industry. A factor the full import of which may still lie ahead is that world demand for foodstuffs and agricultural raw materials gave much-increased capitalized values to that fraction of arable and pastoral South African land to which environmental conditions lent productive significance[30].

The socio-economic consequences of change in South African agriculture have been far-reaching. The transformation in the marketability of its products has carried land-values totally out of the context of Goodfellow's earlier observation that, farming in South Africa for market demand having proceeded so slowly and with such little specialization, 'the value of nearly all the land was unknown'. The same marketability and related land-capitalization had also finally pushed the White bywoner out of his traditional context. Indeed from about 1945, the tax consultant became a more frequent presence on the farm than the White bywoner [31].

Another socio-economic consequence of changing marketing practice made its indirect contribution to increased entrepreneurship in South Africa – perhaps more in the capitalized structure of entrepreneurship than in the arduousness of its risk-bearing. The early Jewish-immigrant *smous* or itinerant pedlar often settled down to carry out his no less vital marketing function as the country store-keeper. From after the Second World War, the pull of more profitable, urbanized retailing, wholesaling and consumer-goods manufacturing – perhaps even more than the push of Reddings-daadbond finance for Afrikaner take-over of the 'algemene handelaar' (or country general-dealer) – stimulated a shift in distinctive Jewish entrepreneurial expertise. Country-storekeeping experience, market observation and accumulated capital often inspired large-scale, heavily capitalized manufacturing and merchandising after the 1940s [32].

The war and early post-war exclusion of foreign competition and resources was responsible for a more far-reaching structural change in two other factors of production – raw materials and labour. It was the crucial contribution of entrepreneurial management to being about this shift. With the market clamouring for supplies, manufacturing outputs responded. Entrepreneurship abhors a vacuum and profits are the mother of innovation. South African industrialists moved in to fill the pipe-lines of profits.

During this period there was a major increase in the proportion of raw materials of South African origin utilized in South African manufacturing. During the First World War, the proportion of South African materials used had increased from 44·9 per cent in 1915–6 to 53·5 per cent in 1918–9 and then declined to 45·5 per cent in 1921–2. By the early part of the Second World War in 1941–2, it had risen to 57·4 per cent. By 1944–5, in respect of private industry only, the percentage was 64·9 per cent; it fell away to 55·5 per cent in 1948–9 and from 1954–5 the proportion was approximately two-thirds [33].

The most notable, and significant in terms of structural change, increase is in respect of the metal-using industries. The account that appears later in the text and which goes behind the unsatisfactory statistical data [34] brings out some of the facts, and the government policies behind those facts, that have characterized South African industrial growth since the 1940s. The 'facts' also provide empirical substance for even some of the theoretical queries, raised in the previous chapter, whether the special circumstances of South Africa's adolescent economy justified a special case for forced industrialization.

The era of forced industrialization by way of more positive intervention from the polity had been foreshadowed both in the Board of Trade and Industries Report, No. 282, Investigation into Manufacturing Industries in the Union of South Africa of 1945, and the van Eck Report into Fundamentals of Economic Policy in the Union of 1941.

The van Eck Report had perhaps placed more emphasis on restructuring the country's labour resources in conjunction with the rationalization, i.e. increased mechanization, of industries based on the available resources of base minerals, especially cheap coal and iron ore, and agricultural raw materials for textile-manufacturing and food-processing. The Board of Trade had stressed the practical importance of demonstrated Government 'goodwill' towards industrialists. The risk-factor of capital investment in manufacturing industry was progressively minimized by such Government 'goodwill'.

From early in the 1939–45 War, as the chairman of the Board of Trade and Industries writes in his account of industrial progress in the last quarter-century[35], the Government adopted a policy of giving an assurance in advance that customs tariff protection, under clearly defined conditions, would be granted to specific essential industries, such as agricultural implements, electric motors, spinning and weaving, pulp and paper, and certain chemicals. The technical instruments ranged from anti-dumping duties and suspended duties to exchange-import controls.

In the earlier phase of protectionist policy from 1925 to 1940, the general policy of the Government was (a) before granting tariff protection to require the establishment of an industry to the extent of supplying a given fraction of South African market demand and (b) to admit raw materials (other than agricultural produce for food processing) duty-free or under rebate. After 1940 Government policy was (a) to give direct and indirect assurance of appropriate tariffs prior to the commencement of manufacturing and (*b*) to apply tariff protection to increasingly earlier stages of materials-processing and semi-manufactures.

Indeed the general rule could be formulated on the empirical evidence of actual *administration* of government industrial policy from 1940: the greater the risk and the larger the scale for capital investment in an industrial undertaking the more complete the *advance* assurance by government of the minimum domestic market-share by the appropriate measure of protection.

This policy was not altered when in 1948 the Smuts war-time government gave way to Malan's Afrikanerdom polity. On the contrary the year 1948 was, if anything, an even more critical date in the history of forced industrialization. Not only was 'Made in South Africa' identified in the Nationalist Party credo as sound nationalism but the balance of payments crisis attendant on its accession to power gave it a new imperative.

The combination of hot-money inflow from Britain after the 1945 advent of Attlee's Labour Government and hot-money outflow from South Africa after the no-less panic reaction to the advent of Malan's Nationalist Government in 1948 (plus the uninhibited restocking imported spree arising from grossly inflated personal expenditure and manufacturing expansion in South Africa after war-end in 1945) made foreign exchange control a practical certainty [36]. With a majority of six the new Nationalist Government, despite the return of the conservative Havenga to the Ministry of Finance, was hardly likely to try the deflationary alternative.

Foreign exchange control meant and must mean control of foreign imports, all ministerial assertions and protestations notwithstanding. Economic policy administration moves through the looking-glass into the Wonderland of Alice with no more contrived confusion between pretence and reality than in the regulation of exchange-import controls. No major manufacturing group and no heavily-capitalized undertaking from 1948 in South Africa was delayed in its capital-expansion programme by other than a few additional meetings with more rarified levels of hierarchial authority before it obtained practical demonstration that foreign exchange control was restraint of foreign imports [37].

The partial or total exclusion of competitive imports by the realities of the Second World War, post-war shipping and supply bottlenecks, and by post-1948 exchange-import control administration resulted in a massive increase in the gross output of manufacturing industry. The related increase in net output was not necessarily as uninterrupted. Correlation between gross output and net output is of course interfered with by numerous contemporary conditions[38]. The overall actions of the polity on the prospects for economic development in general and industrial growth in particular were such as to lead to ebb-tides of confidence, while the shots fired at Sharpeville were indeed to reverberate around the world until they near-shattered confidence in South Africa itself. Withdrawal from the Commonwealth shortly afterwards sent capital into such flight that foreign-exchange control became capital-movement prohibition except as authorized[39].

But import control of foreign competition pushed the infant industry argument for protection to its logical, or illogical, conclusion. The customs tariff that is urged to give the infant industry the chance to achieve the alleged economies of scale is in fact a claim to a specific share of domestic market demand. The external economies of growth, analysed so perceptively by Alfred Marshall, are a function of the size of the market. Industrialists have generally argued that their case for protection turns on this particular key consideration.

Protection, such industrialists often insist, does not necessarily lead to higher prices for domestic-manufactures provided that the market share acquired by local industry permits 'the economies of mass-production'. It was this argument with its variations that their experience of the South African market from 1940 onwards seemed to confirm. When imports were restricted or prohibited, South African manufacturers were confident of their ability to supply the total needs of the domestic market at competitive prices. The unanimity of such confident opinion was broken only when the manufacturers were not themselves given the desired quantum of import permits for their own raw materials from foreign suppliers at world price.

Government policy was however increasingly persuaded of the polity's interest in import-substitution. Such import-substitution served as a powerful inducement to persuading shy foreign capital, instead of listening to Afro-Asian threats of boycotts, to safeguard its share of the South African market by intensified investment in South African-located capacity. It also served as a vital national-defence interest in the face of threatened boycotts and United Nations interference.

An analysis of policy, in the contemporary context of the conditions for economic progress, by the Viljoen Commission [40] reflected the more pragmatic approach towards forced industrialization in the balanced development of the country's resources. This Commission, proceeding from recognition that (i) the marginal productivity of much African labour was low or nil and (ii) the statistical support of massive unemployment among tribal Africans, Durban's Asiatics and Non-White women, was persuaded that the protection would not necessarily involve a diversion of labour. Indeed the Commission saw the stimulation or creation of the appropriate employment opportunities for a rapidly growing population projected for the year 2000 at about 5,000,000 Whites or Europeans, 23,000,000 Africans, 4,000,000 Coloured and 1,250,000 Asiatics as the crucial task of balanced economic development. Since neither agriculture nor mining promised significant increased employment, secondary industry would perforce have to expand.

Future Government policy towards forced industrialization was most clearly fore-shadowed in a section on The Psychological Effect of Protection. This variation of Marshall's external economies or the 'Big Push' of later theorists was expressed by the Viljoen Commission as follows:

The inducement to invest is determined by the expectations of businessmen in regard to the prospective yield of investments. The outstanding fact in regard to these expectations is the extreme precariousness of the basis of the knowledge on which the estimates of current yields have to be made. The willingness of entrepreneurs to risk money in industrial development, therefore, depends not merely on probable forecasts but on the confidence with which these forecasts can be made. . . .

It was maintained by the representatives of organized industry that entrepreneurs would not be prepared to invest capital, to an extent sufficient to ensure the renewed rapid development of the country's economy, unless they were assured of a sufficient share of the limited South African market, so that production could be planned and unit costs reduced to a level comparable with that of overseas manufacturers with much larger home markets. The assurance that the Government would be prepared to extend adequate protection and sympathetic treatment to South African industry would, it was maintained, act not only as a spur to the development of industries that cater for the domestic market, but would also encourage overseas firms that at present export to African territories to establish their factories in the Union, in order to be in close proximity to their markets. . . . [41]

It is noteworthy that the official attitudes towards the protection of secondary industry by the primary industries of agriculture and gold mining, as reflected in the Viljoen Commission's Report, had almost completely swung round. The South African Agricultural Union in evidence expressed the opinion that protection had exerted no appreciable adverse effect on agriculture [42], while the mining industry was said to have 'benefited greatly from the development of certain local protected industries, which supply the mines at prices well below those ruling in world markets' [43]. The Gold Producers' Committee of the Chamber of Mines said the mining industry benefited especially from the development of the iron and steel and metallurgical industries, the heavy chemical industry, the cement industry, the rubber industry and the heavy footwear manufacturing industry [43]. Some opinions in South Africa had certainly changed!

An even more decisive change of opinion, with the power to give effect to that new viewpoint, came from the new Prime Minister himself. Dr H. F. Verwoerd, from the time of assuming office as Minister of Native Affairs in 1950, had repeatedly expressed his ethos that industrialization-urbanization of South Africa was too high a price to pay for its concomitant integration of the Africans in the White Man's economy and social system. Much of the legislation for which he was directly and indirectly responsible had aimed to stem the tide and then reverse it. It was Dr Verwoerd who gave 'influx control' a new meaning and a new magnitude so that legislative and administrative control over the mobility of African labour, geographically and occupationally, acquired a completeness and complexity unique in the modern industrial world, with the possible exception of Stalinist Russia.

Dr Verwoerd became prime minister in September 1958. On 21 March 1960, at Sharpeville, 69 Africans were killed and 186 wounded in this charismatic tragedy. On 5 October 1960, there took place the Referendum for a Republic in which the Whites only of South Africa and South West Africa were allowed to vote and 850,458 said Yes, while 775,878 said No. The application by Dr Verwoerd to the Commonwealth Conference in London that South Africa should retain its membership of the British Commonwealth, after it became a Republic, was withdrawn on 15 March 1961. The bill for the Republic of South Africa was enacted by Parliament on 31 March 1961.

The Minister of Finance, Dr Dönges, after the customary avowals of uncontemplated and unthinkable action, imposed a prohibition on capital withdrawals from the Republic and severed free transferability of securities between the Johannesburg Stock Exchange and the London Stock Exchange on 17 June 1961. The break with the City had followed the break with the Commonwealth. Perhaps only the economic historian would recognize that it was a single break [44].

At this particular moment South Africa's political and economic isolation seemed near-absolute. Though the drama of the event suggested a climacteric in the country's political economy, it was part of the continuing process in an unchanging-changing South African way of life. The attempts by Afro-Asia's new nations to force an economic boycott of South Africa had been in progress for some while with little outward effect. The break with the Commonwealth and the City merely intensified the characteristic reaction of Afrikanerdom to outside interference – escapism into the laager of self-sustaining effort.

Dr Verwoerd was either persuaded by Dr Dönges of the desirability of the deliberate creation of a favourable monetary climate to restore confidence and induce investment or the Prime Minister believed with the Finance Minister that the largest proposed capital investment programme in South African economic history in both public and private sectors could be accomplished within the proposed restructured framework of the South African social system. That restructuring was implicit in the new image now given to Apartheid as 'Separate Development', in the envisaged polities of the Bantustans to be created in due time under the Promotion of Bantu Self-Government Act of 1959, and in the proposed programme of industrial re-location in 'border areas' [45].

In either event, a skilful deployment of monetary expansionism, announcements of vast public sector development projects such as the Orange River Project and of mammoth capital expenditure by such State-controlled, commanding-heights of the economy as the S. A. R. & H., Iscor, Sasol, Foskor, plus the exuberance of capital investment in constructional industry certainly produced the favourable Psychological Effect for industrialization of unlimited horizons [46].

Import control ever since 1948 had served to force industrialization. As Afro-Asian hostility threatened increasing pressures on

287

South African import-export trade and, ultimately, on the country's sovereignty as a political economy, import-substitution became almost a national rallying-cry. Self-sufficiency was however hardly attainable or even sought by a nation now boasting and determined on an annual rate of growth, that would compel recognition of the Republic's economic viability from all critics and respect for the progressive strength of its political economy from all-comers.

Moreover, despite an increasing percentage of local raw-materials inputs yielding a growing quantum of domestic gross outputs, the South African propensity to consume imports was exceptionally high. The Viljoen Commission referred to an inter-war calculation of income elasticity of demand for imports of between 1·5 and 2. With, therefore, a 1 per cent increase in national income associated with a 1·5 to 2 per cent increase in the value of imports, economic growth targets of 5 or 6 per cent patently carried with them a high volume of imports – and the exports to pay for them.

For many decades South African exports had meant the Rand's gold – and not much else of comparable significance. This fact indeed was the essence of the economists' long-time support of What's good for the Chamber of Mines is good for South African economic development. The increased industrialization, by way of customs tariff protection in the nineteen-thirties with its consequent increased imports, had been nurtured and nourished by the crucial post-1933 gold-price increase and hence value of gold exports. The Second World War years of shipping priorities pushed up merchandise exports and cut down imports. The post-war back-log in both consumer goods and capital goods – luxuries, durables, plant and equipment, semi-manufactures – brought an upsurge of imports that lagging exports could not sustain. The balance of payments deficit on current account was temporarily financed by an unprecedented inflow of capital escaping from Socialist Britain until in 1948 the escape route of capital reversed itself out of Nationalist South Africa. Import Control became a politico-economic necessity.

The more import control, the more imports; the intensified import-substitution, the increased imports. This, though it may have surprised the politicians, would not surprise the economists. A rapidly developing economy – especially one being 'developed' by an expansionist monetary policy – produces its own developing needs for more imports. The composition of the imports will of course change but the quantum will steadily grow. Indeed the shift

288

from consumer goods to raw materials to semi-manufactures to capital equipment in response to a more capitalistic structure of industrialization will almost certainly increase the money-costs of the imports.

Hence the case to be made that exports and not imports, or exports at least as much as imports, are the determinant of a country's rate of economic growth and of rising national income *per capita*. Hence, in respect of South Africa from the end of the Second World War, the case to be made that its history was at least as crucially determined by Sir Ernest Oppenheimer as by Dr Hendrik Verwoerd. Export-creation perhaps more than import-substitution was the key variable in the GNP function. And it was the entrepreneurial decisions of Oppenheimer that generated the massive exports.

The 'architectonic and creative achievement' of a Schumpeterian colossus is recorded by Sir Theodore Gregory in his *Ernest Oppenheimer and the Economic Development of Southern Africa* [47]. It is of more than passing interest that Sir Ernest's critical entrepreneurial contribution was in marketing. It was this expertise that took over the chairmanship of De Beers on 20 December 1929, only a few weeks after the historic crash of the New York Stock Exchange on 29 October heralded the Great Depression, together with over £13,000,000 of virtually unsaleable stocks. It was marketing and financial skill of the highest order that prevented a total collapse of sales becoming the total extinction of the diamond market. It was Ernest Oppenheimer's Diamond Corporation that absorbed through the next five years stocks from sources beyond the fiat of De Beers to close down and then years later disposed of such accumulated stocks in the midst of the greatest boom the diamond trade had ever seen, so that in 1952/53 the Diamond Corporation's cash resources rose to £40,000,000 [48]. It was his epochal decision that ploughed back the mammoth once-for-all windfall profits from De Beers and the Diamond Corporation into the further financing of a major chemical industry and the Anglo-American Corporation goldmining ventures in the Far West Rand and the Orange Free State. However open to criticism from disappointed De Beers shareholders and opponents of self-financing, diversification of this magnitude not only was to bring a golden harvest in due course to staunch shareholders but to launch the golden goslings that may yet surpass the golden goose.

Oppenheimer's Anglo-American Corporation did not indeed

initiate the search for the golden goslings in the Far West Rand and the Orange Free State. The 'West Wits Line', the Klerksdorp field and the penetration south of the Vaal River into the Orange Free State were largely pioneered by New Consolidated Gold Fields Limited, Rhode's old company. Anglo-American Corporation followed on closely. Sir Theodore Gregory points out that the search for gold is historically stimulated during times of relatively low prices, such as in the nineteen-thirties and it was then that the first steps were taken to prove the golden goslings. The new gold price added of course a further incentive but, despite the new technological development of geophysical surveying, it was only the West Wits Line and the Klerksdorp field which had been proved by the outbreak of the Second World War. The Free State still lay fallow.

During the war years, gold production after increasing initially to a maximum of 14,039,000 fine ounces in 1941 fell successively to 11,936,000 fine ounces in 1945 with the realized value of gold sales falling by £15,000,000. With increasing costs, labour shortages and tight capital controls, the war and immediate post-war years were discouraging except to the venturesome in new techniques of expensive scientific, systematic exploration, new methods of financing and new measures of co-ordination between mining-finance houses. It was the achievement of Sir Ernest Oppenheimer to inspire decisive effort in each area of innovation so that his Anglo-American Corporation by 1945 was clearly destined to dominate the exploitation of the Free State goldfields. The story and the significance of the new goldfields to the economic development of South Africa are well summed up by Sir Theodore Gregory:

By 1955, the development of the Orange Free State field as a whole had involved the provision of some £200,000,000. For the seven mines of the Anglo American Corporation Group alone over £63 million had been found by 1954 and Anglo American Corporation also provided part of the funds for mines under the control of other groups. Of this amount, over £18 million had been put up by De Beers Investment Trust (out of a total investment outside the diamond industry of over £28 million). London and the Continent had also contributed heavily. In sum, 40 per cent or more of the total investment was furnished by the Anglo-American Corporation Group alone, and nearly 10 per cent of this amount came from the profits of the diamond industry. . . . Without Ernest Oppenheimer it is doubtful whether the diamond industry's contribution would have been possible at all, and the prestige of his name must have powerfully contributed to the willingness of London and the Continent to put up the very large sums actually forthcoming[49].

A single sentence, continues Gregory, can sum up the contribution of the Far West Rand, Klerksdorp and the Orange Free State fields to South African mining. In 1959 these three fields furnished 60 per cent of the total output of the gold which contributed 79 per cent of the working profit from gold. Out of the dividends paid, 75 per cent came from companies in these areas. The Free State alone, percentagewise, contributed 28 per cent of the total output of gold, 37 per cent of the working profit and 36 per cent of the dividends paid from gold[49].

What then had happened to the South African way of life in these years in which Afrikanerdom prepared for the transformation of the Union into the Republic? If the politicians had striven to impose unmoveable unchange, the entrepreneurs had promoted irreversible change. The clash between the polity and the economy was continuous though increasingly concealed by mutual consent. A single socio-economic fact shows however the absolute determination of the polity to remain in charge of change and, hence, of the social system.

Appropriately it is evidenced in a parliamentary question by Mr Harry Oppenheimer, son and successor of Sir Ernest, and answered by the Minister of Native Affairs, Dr Verwoerd. It was an answer too, that foreshadowed that Dr Verwoerd had in due course to become Prime Minister, if Afrikanerdom was to retain control of the unchanging-changing South African way of life.

The question to the Minister was: 'Whether he would be good enough to define his attitude in regard to the experiment which is being made on certain of the new gold-mines in the Orange Free State by the establishment of villages on the mines for married Native employees'.

Dr Verwoerd's reply was: 'In regard to married quarters on the mines on the Free State gold-fields I want to state quite unequivocally that I am opposed to that development . . . my department has been instructed to investigate the position very thoroughly and to stop the development of such villages as far as possible. . . . Within that Free State gold-mining area every mine can then establish its own Native town with married quarters. That will then mean a series of Native towns . . . . Now we must bear in mind that, when the mines stop working one day, large numbers of towns will remain there spread out over that area. That may amount to 20 or 30 or 40 within that area! In addition it must be borne in mind . . . that the Natives who work on the mines . . . are usually Natives who have been recruited by agents in the reserves, but usually their children who grow up on those mining towns do not want to work on the mines . . . . They will disappear from those mining towns in the course of time . . . [and] So it means that those married quarters become a channel through which the rest of the non-European population in the cities become greater and greater. . . .'

APPENDIX OF STATISTICS

OF SIGNIFICANT CHANGE AND GROWTH

SOUTH AFRICA

TABLE I

Distribution of the Working Population of the Union between the Different Sectors of the Economy: 1921–1960

	Farming Forestry & Fishing	Mining	Secondary Industry(I)	Services(II)	All Sectors
Whites—% ages					
1921	31·6	6·3	12·3	49·8	100
1936	24·5	6·3	17·9	51·3	100
1946	18·9	6·0	21·4	53·7	100
1951	14·8	5·8	26·1	53·3	100
1960					
			Number 1960		
	117,599	62,171	311,614	649,085	
Asiatics—% ages					
1921	34·9	4·3	14·1	46·7	100
1936	27·2	1·3	17·2	54·3	100
1946	17·3	0·8	24·8	57·1	100
1951	13·7	0·6	25·9	59·8	100
1960					
			Number 1960		
	9,587	466	35,338	60,529	
Coloureds—% ages					
1921	36·5	1·3	13·5	48·7	100
1936	34·2	1·2	16·8	47·8	100
1946	27·9	0·8	22·0	49·3	100
1951	24·2	0·9	27·4	47·5	100
1960					
			Number 1960		
	119,203	4,153	139,049	285,877	
Africans—% ages					
1946	*43·7	15·2	8·4	*32·7	100
1951	*40·3	14·4	12·1	*33·2	100
1960	*37·5	13·9	13·1	*35·5	100
			Number 1960		
	*1,454,569	539,210	510,286	*1,377,414	

*Almost certainly a very large fraction of Africans classified as 'Services' are resident and 'gainfully occupied' in farming.

TABLE I NOTES

1 Source for Whites, Asiatics and Coloureds – Viljoen Commission, U.G. 36 – 1958 with figures for 1960 added from Statistical Yearbook 1964, of Bureau of Statistics, Pretoria.

2 Source for Africans – Statistical Year Book, 1964, table H–6. There would seem to be significant variations in definition over the years, requiring caution in interpretation.

3 (i) Secondary industry includes manufacturing, construction, electricity, gas, water and sanitary services.

(ii) Services include commerce and finance, transport and communication, services and 'unspecified including presumably unemployed'.

TABLE 2

Gold Production and Total Imports 1929–1963

Year	Imports A £ millions	Gold Production B £ millions	B as percentage of A
1929	83·5	44·2	52·9%
1930	64·6	45·5	70·4
1931	53·0	46·2	87·2
1932	32·8	49·8	151·5
1933	49·3	68·7	139·1
1934	66·3	72·3	109·0
1935	75·3	76·5	101·6
1936	86·3	79·5	92·1
1937	103·4	82·5	79·9
1938	95·9	86·7	90·4
1939	91·3	98·9	108·3
1946	215·1	102·8	47·8
1947	300·4	96·6	32·2
1948	353·5	99·9	28·3
1949	313·1	114·8	36·7
1950	304·1	144·8	47·6
1951	466·8	142·9	30·6
1952	416·9	147·1	35·3
1953	424·3	147·6	34·8
1954	439·0	164·7	37·5
1955	482·2	182·7	37·9
1956	494·9	198·5	40·1
1957	550·6	212·6	38·6
1958	555·5	220·0	39·6
1959	488·5	250·0	51·1
1960	556·0	268·0	48·2
1961*	1006·0 (Rands m.)	575·0 (Rands m.)	57·1
1962	1028·0	637·0	62·0
1963	1252·0	686·0	54·8

*From 1961 figures in Rands i.e. £1 = R2.

Source: S. A. Reserve Bank, Quarterly Bulletin of Statistics.

TABLE 3

*Value and Proportion of Local to Imported Materials Used in
Secondary Industry.*
(*All Industries – Private and Public Sectors*)

Year	Total Cost of Materials Used A £1000	Cost of Local Materials Used B £1000	B as Percentage of A
1938–39	101,472	52,488	51·69
39–40	110,251	48,880	53·41
40–41	125,742	67,712	53·85
41–42	136,835	78,543	57·40
42–43	142,352	88,972	62·50
43–44	166,748	105,031	63·02
44–45	188,587	119,634	63·44
45–46	211,873	126,791	59·84
46–47	255,212	140,303	54·98
47–48	310,240	170,749	55·04
48–49	361,859	196,038	54·18
49–50	422,296	247,147	58·52
50–51	542,246	320,336	59·08
51–52	619,990	382,005	61·61
52–53	637,931	412,800	64·71
53–54	649,297	408,497	62·91

Source: Bureau of Census & Statistics: Industrial Census.

TABLE 4

Changing Pattern of Gold Production in South Africa

Period	Witwatersrand & Extensions oz fine	Total Transvaal oz fine	Orange Free State oz fine	South Africa oz fine
1884–1889	531,643	630,499		
1890–1895	6,636,055	7,310,310		
1896–1901	11,934,200	12,837,176		12,838,083
1902–1907	24,722,448	25,611,973		25,614,089
1908–1913	46,119,519	48,033,791		48,044,063
1914–1918	42,674,936	44,221,218		44,226,211
1919–1923	39,702,430	40,776,739		40,777,747
1924–1928	47,942,013	40,603,869	59	49,604,149
1928–1933	51,961,758	54,576,581	1,163	54,478,698
1934–1938	52,394,985	56,482,255	2,447	56,486,029
1939–1942	50,405,739	55,400,609	403	55,402,510
1943–1947	59,412,036	60,435,434		60,436,083
1948–1952	57,114,219	58,045,408	242,955	58,288,741
Year				
1953	11,332,095	11,509,353	431,262	11,940,616
1954	11,929,919	12,114,505	1,122,606	13,237,119
1955	12,243,639	12,411,821	2,189,574	14,601,404
1956	12,565,112	12,715,124	3,181,560	15,896,693
1957	13,114,777	13,261,424	3,769,313	17,030,737
1958	13,186,755	13,334,669	4,321,773	17,656,447
1959	14,334,945	14,483,597	5,581,881	20,065,515

Source: Report Government Mining Engineer for year ended 31/12/59, p. 31.

THE POLITY VERSUS THE MARKET

The point has been made[1] that the early years of the polity in action in the new Parliament of the Union of South Africa had made it clear that economic change expressed through the competitive market would never be allowed to alter the status-differentials of White-Black relationships advantageously to the Blacks and disadvantageously to the Whites. The polity would never accept that the distribution of wealth (land) and wages (labour) as between White and Non-White should be determined in the last resort by the market.

Nearly forty years and two World Wars after Union, the dynamic of economic development through the intensification of the market economy was exerting the most far-reaching adaptationist impact on the social system. The impact was necessarily strongest in the urban-industrial regions where White capital investment was progressively concentrated and in the rural-Reserves (or so-called Native Territories or Bantustans) where White private capital investment had been virtually prohibited and where Government capital investment had been relatively negligible. Hence the emergence of the so-called dual economy in a plural society[2]. It is, of course, essential to appreciate the co-ordinating influence of the *market* on such a dual economy in a plural society.

From the time of the large-scale mineral-resource development by private capital investment in South Africa, that is from the last-quarter of the nineteenth century, the exchange economy and related market co-ordination of factors of production penetrated deeper and wider into the South African social system. Simultaneously and concomitantly it exerted its integrating disintegration on the rural-Reserves of the Native Territories[3] with their collectivist ethos and its disintegration-integration on the urban-industrial regions with their capitalist ethos. Co-ordination of such basically opposed social systems by the market could be expected to proceed with friction. The nature and extent of such friction would be determined largely by whether the value-orientations, as manifested in the actions of the sovereign polity of the social groups, accepted or rejected a *single* social system. If the sovereign polity, that is the White Parliament of the Union of South Africa, had as its goal a single social system then it would have intervened only to promote the effectiveness of market co-ordination of the dual economies of the plural society.

But, if the White polity's goal was to resist the reality of a single social system and to reject its desirability, then it would oppose and frustrate ever more vehemently and extensively the purely market forces of co-ordination. In the familiar terms of South African political usage, trusteeship aiming at guiding the transition towards a unified economy would be followed by segregation determined to restrain the process of bringing together. In its turn as the power of market co-ordination penetrated more completely – as under war-time pressures to dissolve contrived frictions – so segregation would give way to apartheid, resolved on reversing the processes of the market and aiming ultimately at two totally separated social systems.

This has been the course of South African political economy from the birth of Union to the coming of the Republic.

The special features of the South African economy – migrant labour and the linkage-mechanism by way of administrative direction of change rather than market adjustment to change – have consequently been the subject of continuing conflict between the polity and the market. Increasingly, too, the conflict expressed itself in and centred on the urbanized-industrial regions of the country.

It is these urbanizing-industrializing regions which, of course, have throughout been the magnets for migrant tribal Black labour. The diamond field of Kimberley and the gold field of the Rand provided the impetus for cash-seeking pilgrimages and established urbanizing growth-points in the interior. It was the rapid development of Johannesburg as the market stronghold for the entire South African economy that brought a new order of urbanization not only to the Witwatersrand but to the original defence-trading settlements of Cape Town, Port Elizabeth, Durban.

It was the Rand's gold-mining industry, too, which made migrant African labour both the basic, critical cost factor in its operations or production function and also a national policy. The overwhelming concentration of private capital investment, mainly from external sources, was on the Rand and much of public capital investment, such as in harbours and railways, was to serve the market of the Rand. Simultaneously private capital investment by Whites was virtually prohibited in the reserved tribal territories, which became thereby totally dependent for technological advance on the relatively negligible fraction of Government investment. The flow of labour was consequentially towards the essential co-operant capital.

Migration from the tribal economies of the Reserves was pushed both by the absence of capital investment and by the continuation of the traditional shifting cultivation. However appropriate to the earlier phase of apparently unlimited pasturage and extensive agriculture, the system was forthwith escalated into diminishing returns by the White polity's legal reservation of 87 per cent of the country's land-area for White ownership. Simultaneously, the imposition of taxes to be paid in money and the encouragement to buy Western goods 'imported' into the tribal Reserves by authorized White-owned trading-stores necessarily created a demand for cash by the tribal inhabitants. Specialization by the tribal economy to produce saleable produce or merchandise to trade with or export to the exchange economy of the White man's polity was frustrated as much by the traditional tribal social system with its resistance to individual land-ownership title as by the obvious superior alternative labour-productivity associated with capital investment in resource-exploitation in 'White' South Africa.

Labour in consequence was 'exported' from the tribal economies as their only saleable product and 'imported' by those regions, where its utilization yielded the highest returns. This latter meant dominantly the mining areas and then the related industrializing regions, which were linked to and by the Rand market. The location of manufacturing industry in four industrial regions – the Witwatersrand, Greater Cape Town, Durban-Pinetown and Port Elizabeth-Uitenhage was further encouraged by the discriminatory railway rating and restrictionist transportation policy adopted by the State, largely in support of the Poor White and rural vote.

The characteristic features of proletarianization in South African social experience have been previously remarked upon, as well as those special conditions of labour-organization by the Chamber of Mines to secure the largest quantum of marginal ore at the ruling fixed price for its gold content. The compound system of housing for its short-term contracted labour force adopted by the gold-mining companies had in its early decades serious defects, exposed to strong criticism in public enquiry from time to time. It did however involve a rudimentary organized provision, however inadequate. In respect of Africans attracted to non-mining employment in the urban centres by the push of negligible or negative productivity in their own limited territories, following the legal prohibition of further land-ownership rights in agriculture, virtually no organized accommodation for living was made by municipal authorities until the nineteen-twenties. Such facilities as the Africans could establish for themselves out of non-existent capital and primitive skills were fashioned largely from second-hand corrugated iron, hessian sacks and paraffin tins.

The Tuberculosis Commission of 1914 reported: The majority of such urban locations are a menace to the health of their inhabitants and indirectly to the health of those in the towns . . . it is with the character of the dwellings that the greatest fault must be found. With few exceptions they are a disgrace, and the majority are quite unfit for human habitation . . . altogether one could hardly imagine more suitable conditions for the spread of tuberculosis [4]. The influenza epidemic of 1918 which caused an exceptionally high mortality rate among White and Non-White South Africans of all social classes gave the general public a shocking revelation of the urban living conditions of Africans and the standing menace to the health of all. The Native Affairs Commission, established by the Native Affairs Act of 1920, had as its first, most important, designated consideration the urban African.

A memorandum [5] of conclusions between the Native Affairs Commission and the Transvaal Local Government Commission, known as the Stallard Commission, of 1922 formed the content of the Native (Urban Areas) Act No. 21 of 1923. This was the first of a long series of amending acts which, in addition to imposing uniform legislation for the country and increasing Central Government supervision of municipal authority and responsibility for housing and administration, established what has come to be known as the Stallard dictum of principle. It was:

We consider that the history of the races, especially having regard to South African history, shows that the commingling of black and white is undesirable. The Native should only be allowed to enter urban areas, which are essentially the White man's creation, when he is willing to enter and to minister to the needs of the white man, and should depart therefrom when he ceases to so minister[6].

That the cities and urbanization in South Africa were 'the white man's creation' has remained a fundamental article of faith of the White, and above all the Afrikaner, polity. From this, indeed, has flowed the whole complex of law and administration to fix the contacts and inter-connections of White-Black relationships in South Africa for the foreseeable future. Furthermore the unending flow of enactment and regulation has aimed at containing the influence of the market relationships between persons based on private contractual freedom and private rights to property. Inevitably, the end-result of the determination of the polity to impose beyond challenge its will on the market was (*a*) to disenfranchise and abolish all representation of the Africans in the sovereign Parliament and (*b*) to end all private contractual freedom and private property rights of Africans in 'White' South Africa.

Urbanization in South Africa was not 'the white man's creation'. It was, as elsewhere, the response to economic development and the reflection of market-foci. The mineral-ore exploitation of the Witwatersrand, which set off significant urbanizing in South Africa, was as much the indispensible contribution of immigrant African labour as it was the indispensible contribution of immigrant European capital, technology and skills. The centripetal force of urbanization to economize human relationships is not unlike the process to economize a single medium of exchange for monetary payments or relationships[7]. The more marketable a particular money becomes because of its increased acceptability, the more such acceptability increases its marketability. The more exchangeability of human activities to obtain the benefits of specialization and division of labour promotes decentralization, the more marketability for such specialized, divided human relationships encourages centralization.

The process of decentralizing-centralization that is a function of the size of the market is patently common to every type of human society, in which human inter-relationships are promoting economic development. South African experience was naturally in conformity with this broad process. It was not unique nor fundamentally different. But the South African polity's response to urbanization has become increasingly distinctive because of the increasing rejection by that polity of the implications of such all-encompassing urbanization on the total social system.

Although it is customary to present economic development as a cause of urbanization, urbanization might be as properly regarded as the stimulant of economic development. This is as true for the Poor Whites migrating from a stagnant agriculture as it is true for the Poor Blacks, seeking a temporary and then a permanent escape from a decaying tribal collectivism.

The massive injection of capital investment into the Rand that followed the 1933 gold-price increase, after which 'Johannesburg grew as much in four years as it had in the previous forty', was accompanied by an equally massive injection of people. The total numbers of Africans employed on the Witwatersrand gold-mines increased from 246,000 to 340,000, 1933 to 1937, without which increase gold output could not have risen, even allowing for the gold price increase, from £46 million to £82 million. Between the 1921 census and the 1951 census, the total population of the Witwatersrand increased from 537,000 to 1,670,000: the Whites over that period rising from 233,000 to 573,000; the Non-Whites, mainly Africans, increased from 304,000 to 1,036,000. Between 1936 and 1951 the White population of the Witwatersrand grew by about 224,000 and the Non-White, mainly Africans, by about 414,000.

Despite the large and increasing numbers of Africans permanently employed in the urbanized areas, the legal permanence of their domicile was not admitted nor their legal right to freedom of movement conceded. With the exception of Alexandra Township outside Johannesburg, Eerste Rust, Riverside and Lady Selborne outside Pretoria and Korsten near Port Elizabeth, ownership-title to residential land was never granted to Africans in urban areas. Africans at this time were not legally precluded from buying land in the urban areas of South Africa but the Urban Areas legislation could prohibit their *occupation* of such purchased land. Free title in effect was negated and ultimately totally eliminated even in the areas here listed. The fundamental basis for home-ownership by Africans being witheld, the provision of housing accommodation had necessarily to be financed from public funds. On the assumption that the African workers were migrants whose 'homes' were in their own Native Reserves, municipal authorities were reluctant to incur indebtedness financed from local rates on what for many years they continued to regard as temporary housing. The volume of housing accommodation was severely restricted from any given capital expenditure by White trade union insistence that the customary colour bar in the building trades should be maintained in such housing schemes for Africans. With houses being built by White skilled workers at wage-rates some six times greater than the average wage-earnings of the African tenants, the rent-subsidation became a formidable burden on municipal rates.

It was only after 1950 that the new Nationalist Government, while extending the fundamental non-recognition of the legal permanence of Africans' urban domicile and imposing additional legal contraints on the geographical and occupational mobility of Africans (and non-White groups generally), could begin a major slum-clearance programme[8].

Whereas the heavy capital investment in the key market strongholds or four major urbanizing-industrializing regions of the country was pulling in the co-operant African labour from the tribal economies, an alarming failure even to maintain the literally vital capital of the soil intact in those tribal economies was breaking up the social system based on that controlled inter-connection of land-cattle-marriage described in an earlier chapter[9]. The export of able-bodied male labour was the inevitable consequence. Though tribal custom, as much as the White polity's movement-controls through the pass-system, operated to keep in being the migrant basis of African life and labour, the relentless realities of the market were permanently urbanizing millions of Africans.

They were being urbanized at those points of the production function, where the combination of capital, entrepreneurship, technology and labour were yielding increasing gross outputs.

As far back as 1930, the Native Economic Commission had been appointed to study: the economic and social conditions of Natives especially in the larger towns; the application to Natives in urban areas of existing industrial legislation; the economic and social effect upon the European and Coloured population of the Union of urbanized Natives and measures to prevent increasing urbanization. At the first meeting of the Commission, the Minister of Native Affairs emphasized that the Government wanted the facts and conditions of Africans in the larger towns to be investigated.

The Commission, however, was convinced that the '. . . the Native economic question is not primarily a problem of a small, vocal, dissatisfied, semi-civilized group of urbanized Natives: it is primarily a problem of millions of uneducated tribal Natives, held in the grip of superstition and of an anti-progressive social system. The former group must be fairly considered, and room must be found for them in the body economic. But their articulateness must not obscure the fact that they represent a less important part of the problem; the real problem lies with the non-vocal millions and in many respects the approach to the problems of the former must proceed by way of the latter[10].'

This Native Economic Commission hence concentrated on an elaborate review of the tribal background, placing great emphasis on its unprogressive character, its ancestor worship, the special status of cattle in the social-religious system of the Abantu; the strategic authority of the tribal chief and parental authority which it said was breaking down; the absence of diversification in economic activities; the primitive methods of husbandry and generally the underdeveloped condition of the Native Reserves. Its greatest stress was on over-stocking as the root of all the evils[11]:

The effect of the impact of Western civilization on the condition of the Bantu-speaking people was in time to change all the essential conditions on which their social system was founded. Particularly was this so in regard to land. The Native system postulated plenty of land for grazing and for culti-vation. The Europeans put limits to the factors which diminished the pres-sures of both population and animals on land. . . . At the same time the White man, accustomed to a higher standard of living, occupied large territories on which the Natives had hitherto fallen back in case of need. . . . Over-population became an evil in the Native territories because numbers increased and knowledge of how to make the land 'beget' itself did not increase among the Natives or was neglected. Overstocking followed the same path, because while the application of veterinary science prevented animal diseases from taking their full toll, next to nothing was done to teach the Natives to husband their grazing resources.

The result is that we now have throughout the Reserves a state of affairs in which, with a few exception, the carrying capacity of the soil for both human beings and animals is definitely on the downgrade: a state of affairs which, unless soon remedied, will within one or at the outside two decades create in the Union an appaling problem of Native poverty.

The European rapidly changed the environment of the Native: but inside the Reserves he did very little to teach the Natives how to adjust himself to the new environment . . . the natural result has been that the Native continued working his lands largely as he had done before, continuing practising animal husbandry after the ways of this fathers.

To what has this led? To a state of affairs in which, with the exception of a few favoured parts, a Native area can be distinguished at sight by its barrenness. Overstocking is now so general in the Reserves as to have become an evil of the first magnitude. Your Commissioners wish to stress the fact that unless some limit can be placed to the familiar overstocking, the very existence of large numbers of Natives in the Reserves will, in the near future, be impossible . . .

It would be idle, however, the Native Economic Commission went on, to blame the Native for all this [11]; 'He acts according to his lights. He knows only his traditional methods, and nothing or little has been done to teach him others. In his primitive state, his mind is held by a superstition and animism, which makes it dangerous to depart too freely from the habits of his ancestors; his body is held by the agreeable *dolce far niente* which, with limited material needs in an equable climate, he regards as a sufficiency for a good life'.

Though the Holloway Commission clearly identified the source of the economic decline of the Reserves in the White polity's limitation of land-acquisition and -usage by a growing tribal population, the Commission showed perhaps less appreciation of other aspects of reality in the economic development of South African society as a whole. Tribal Africans had failed to 'accumulate' to provide the domestic capital for intensive agricultural cultivation under individualized land-tenure. The non-provision of education inhibited almost any technological development. Furthermore the sovereign White polity had (a) in effect prohibited all private capital investment in the Reserves and (b) had made a negligible investment of social capital, above all in education [12]. White South Africans, too, had until the massive importation of *outside* capital, *outside* entrepreneurship, *outside* skills in the development of its mineral resources made unimpressive progress.

At the time the Native Economic Commission was reporting, in 1932, varying estimates of the numbers of the Poor Whites went as high as 300,000 in a total White population of 1,800,000. A future Prime Minister, Mr Strijdom, opposing the 1936 Hertzog land legislation to carry out the promised provision of tribal land made in the Native Lands Act of 1913, asserted that 500,000 Poor Whites had a prior claim to land in 1936. In earlier chapters some indication has also been given of the tens of millions of pounds of State expenditure on White farming and White farmers, and of the special work-creation policy for 'civilized' i.e. White labour in direct State employment and forced industrialization.

The Commission too, with the notable exception of commissioner Dr Roberts, was not disposed to acknowledge that the White polity's control of the labour market was holding back both the growth of gross national product and the share of the Africans in the net output, which they were helping to produce. The Commission saw the solution to the economic conditions of the urbanized Africans, which it was specially charged to investigate, in social investment by the State to rehabilitate the Reserves and not in any removal of the contrived frictions of the total labour market.

Despite its perspectives of the past, the Native Economic Commission's insights into the future were – like most commissions of social enquiry – largely conditioned by the context of the present. The early nineteen-thirties in world economic and South African conditions were the years of catastrophic decline, in which competition appeared as a cause of contraction rather than the incentive to expansion. It was perhaps asking too much, therefore, to expect the Commission to recognize that market co-ordination of the tribal social system and the 'White' social system, by removing the restraints on competitive mobility of factors of production, would generate growth. Inevitably the Commission saw the problem and the solution rather in direct intervention to improve the environment of the tribal territories so as to minimize the push of nil or negative productivity in the Reserves on its only export of labour.

In the *economic* development of the Reserves, the Commission declared, must inevitably be sought the main solution for the Native economic problem. It transcended in importance, in its judgment, every other phase of the Native economic development and indirectly it found it to be at the root of the whole Native economic question. The undeveloped state of the Reserves, which it believed inherently capable of supporting a much larger population, was largely the cause of the universal demand for more land coming from the Africans and the consequent 'dead uniformity of life in the Reserves results in emigration of a large number of Natives who desire to follow occupations other than primitive pastoralism and peasant farming . . .' [13].

Your Commissioners have given long and serious thought to this question (the urbanization of the Africans and its effect on the Europeans), which lies at the root of the whole Native economic problem, and, in a wider sense, of the South African economic problem. We wish to express our conviction that in the past the Native has been given an entirely mistaken economic orientation . . . the recruiting of Natives for European industries and the need for cash had before this brought out large numbers to the European areas (so that) the developed European areas began to support part of the Native population of the underdeveloped Reserves.

As long as the Native was 'raw', fit only for the crudest manual labour – which was wanted in plenty by the mines – the flow was looked upon by the European as a necessity and was even encouraged. We can go further and state that while this stage lasted it was beneficial to the European, in giving him labour, always scarce in a new country; and to the Native, in giving him an income and accustoming him to European methods of industry[14].

As the Africans sought higher wages to satisfy increasing tastes, they started to migrate permanently to the towns there to compete with less skilled Europeans and also with their fellow-Africans who had migrated before them.

Hence the Commission emphatically insisted: '*The cure, the proper economic synthesis of our wealth producing factors, lies in a wise, courageous forward policy of development in the Reserves*'. A large proportion of the Reserves, it was satisfied, possessed agricultural potentialities which were not exceeded elsewhere in the Union. 'It would be wise to develop the wealth-producing capacity of these excellent areas and thus secure a larger amount to go round, rather than to allow a continuance of the present struggle between Black and White for a larger share in the wealth being produced from the developed areas. With these areas developed to a reasonably productive level there would be enough to make possible friendly co-operation between the races [15].

Once again a Government Commission of Enquiry saw the market as a place of racial strife and not as a mechanism of racial co-ordination, leading to an ultimate non-racial division of labour, limited only by the size of the market and by its very specialization of function extending the size of that market [16].

Handicapped by the cancellation, on grounds of economy, of the 1931 African census, the Native Economic Commission had little factual information on the main subject of its investigation – the urbanized African. It acknowledged that there was a permanently urbanized group of Africans who had been born in the towns and who had lived there all their lives. The urbanized Africans, the Commission argued, had no source of income other than wage-employment and had already adopted living standards in which there were no limits to personal expenditure. Such a social group had to meet the competition of tribal Africans whose 'tribal assets supply at least a portion of primary needs' and 'who will frequently prefer a congenial job at lower wages to a harder and more distasteful job at a higher rate of remuneration'[17].

The continuing influx of Africans from the tribal territories and the White farms, the Commission believed, was the main cause of the chronic state of chaos of the urban labour market, in which the wage-rates of the permanently urbanized were constantly being forced below subsistence level.

In the matter of wage-rates, he (the urbanized African) cannot get away from his tribal brethren on the labour market. They come into the towns in their thousands to supplement the living which they obtain from their tribal lands or from labour tenancy on the farms. They create a plentiful labour supply for urban occupations other than mining. Being purely casual labourers, they seldom give rise to even reasonable efficiency. Supply plentiful, efficiency low, and we have the natural corollary of low wages . . . the pressure of their numbers far exceeding those of the urbanized Natives makes the competition very severe for the latter, who seeks on the one hand to sustain a higher standard of living, and on the other hand do not possess those assets which make the former less dependent on wages . . .

The labour market is, therefore, in a chronic state of chaos. No regular class of urban labour gets a chance to develop because those Natives who remain permanently in town are always subjected to the disturbing influence on wage rates of a large supply of unskilled labour. . . .

These evils must be attacked in the Reserves. This will have the effect of stemming the flow of labour to the towns, and of reducing the town labour problem to manageable proportions. . . . In order to encompass this it is essential that no time shall be lost both in developing the Reserves, and in reducing the present pressure on land, by making available more areas for Native occupation. While present conditions last the flow to the towns will continue, the pressure on the urbanized Native will increase, and the problem of Native wages in towns will become worse. State policy should be directed to reducing this pressure, in the interests of a class of Natives who have made considerable progress in civilization, and with whose aspirations for conditions in which better living is possible, one cannot but have the fullest sympathy[18].

The Commission believed the solution, however, to be in its positive proposals of development of the tribal Reserves rather than in additional negative restrictions to the existing Urban Areas Act controls to 'stop the drift to the towns'. While the Commission was not prepared to add to the White polity's power to control directly geographical movement of the Africans, it saw in the contemporary market realities only competitive chaos. The majority of the Commissioners either did not acknowledge or were not prepared to concede that the polity's imposed imperfections on the market might be the more crucial determinants of, firstly, the slow rate of over-all economic growth and secondly, the stagnant and probably declining income *per capita* of the African population.

The effective prohibition of the alienation of land by White men to the Africans must have had a sociological significance, the influence of which on market demand is almost impossible to assess. Thus home and property ownership, surely one of the most powerful incentives towards intensifying consumption and personal capital accumulation in all societies, was denied to the urbanizing Africans. Colour bar legislation, and trade unionist barriers to expanding job opportunities for Africans, combined with collective and imposed wage-determination to confine Africans to unskilled categories of employment. In the mining industry, by far the largest single field of employment, a monopsonistic labour-recruitment system gave permanency to an undifferentiated, migrant labour force.

The view of the majority of the Native Economic Commissioners, Dr Roberts and Mr Lucas excepting, was that State policy could not allow free competition between peoples living on such widely different levels of civilization as the Africans and the White population of the Union and that such free competition would not lead to the ultimate benefit of the Africans. 'Differentiation is recognized in other spheres and differentiation in industry is necessary to prevent the lowering of White standards of living, which is sure to be followed by a lowering of the standards of efficiency and of culture. Should this be allowed, it will be necessary, after the process has worked itself out, and a new society has been created on a lower level, to start rebuilding what has been destroyed in the process' [19].

But almost at the moment of publication of the Report of the Native Economic Commission, market forces were bringing about a structural change in the South African economy. The sustained, heavy capital investment in post-1933 gold-mining and the great increase in the country's exports were introducing a new magnitude of urbanizing-industrialization and an unstoppable inflow of African labour. Using the not very satisfactory urban-rural definitions of the Census, from 1921 to 1936 the percentage of White population classified as urban increased from 55·78 to 58·18; the percentage of African population increased from 12·50 to 17·31. Counting all Non-Whites together, the urbanized percentage rose from 16·42 in 1921 to 22·44 in 1936. There were 847,000 urban Whites in 1921 and 1,307,000 in 1936; in 1921 there were 587,000 Africans classified as urban-resident and in 1936 the number was 1,142,000. In the fifteen years the Whites had shown as 54·26 per cent rise of urban inhabitants, and the Africans a 94·49 per cent.

The trend was clear. Even in the absence of census figures, the popular impression among the White electorate, who saw more and more squatters' shanties mushrooming in the peri-urban areas, was that the Africans in great numbers were leaving the safe refuge of their Reserves to follow the lure of the apparent wealth of the towns, where they overloaded the labour market; and then, to the detriment of themselves and the whole community, fell into misery and crime[20].

So the polity again moved against the market. A Departmental Committee of 1935 was instructed to draft legislation (1) to enforce the principle of limiting the numbers of Africans in urban areas to the labour requirements of such urban areas; (2) to provide for controlling the entry of Africans into urban areas; and (3) to provide for the withdrawal of superfluous Africans from urban areas. Though this Young-Barrett Committee[21] was highly critical of and rejected as a 'highly immoral line of reasoning' the Stallard dictum, that the Native should only be allowed to enter urban areas to minister to the needs of the White man and should thereafter depart, the Committee dutifully provided the Natives (Urban Areas) Amendment Act of 1937, in turn amended and consolidated repeatedly in subsequent years.

The detail of urban area legislation in respect of Africans is so prolix and has been subjected to such complexity of amendment that it well-nigh defies understanding and recording. The essence of the extended controls has, however, been to limit progressively rights of entry, rights of continued employment and rights of continued residence in urban areas of all Africans whether rural-born or urban-born. The ultimate apologia for all such legislation was that Africans, wherever born or however long domiciled, could never acquire citizenship status outside the land-areas assigned in terms of the Natives Lands Acts and would for all time be migrant labour into White South Africa. Furthermore the kinds of jobs and categories of employment for Africans were in terms of the revised Industrial Conciliation Act Number 28 of 1956 subject to ministerial control and discretion.

The administrative control document to govern the movement of all Africans, men and women over the age of 16, is the reference book [22]. Urban areas legislation defines urban and proclaimed areas to include in effect all urban and peri-urban centres (other than the Native Territories subject to other legislation) of South Africa. Within these areas no African may remain for more than 72 hours unless (a) he or she has resided there continuously since birth (b) he or she has worked there continuously for one employer for 10 years, or has been there continuously and lawfully for 15 years and has thereafter continued to reside there, and is not employed outside the area and while in the area has not been guilty of certain minimum penal contraventions (c) he or she is the wife, unmarried daughter or son under 18 years of age of an African falling into classes (a) or (b) and ordinarily resides with him or (d) he or she has been granted a permit, by an employment officer in the case of work-seekers, or by local authority otherwise, to remain [23].

As at 1960, in terms of regulations issued over the years under the Native Regulation Act of 1911, a work-seeker is any African over the age of 15 years who is unemployed, is not a full-time student, is capable of being employed and is mainly dependent on employment for subsistence. The burden of proof that he or she is not a work-seeker, if he or she is living in an urban or proclaimed area, is on the African to avoid arrest and expulsion on allegations of 'idleness'.

All work-seekers must obtain employment only by way of official labour-bureaux and subject to the sanction of such official bureaux. Employers may not employ an African without a reference book and unless such African work-seeker has been registered by the employment officer of the labour bureau. All details of such employment – employer's name, African worker's name, identity number, date of engagement, nature of employment and rate of pay – must be recorded and endorsed in the reference book. A monthly fee, to be receipt-stamped, in the reference book records continued employment.

Any unemployed work-seeker within 72 hours of becoming unemployed (and any youth reaching the age of 15 and any full-time student within 14 days after ceasing to be a full-time student) must report to the employment officer of the labour bureau, who has far-reaching powers to authorize or not authorize permission to seek re-employment. No one may engage for employment an African in an urban or proclaimed area, for employment in mines and works in non-proclaimed areas (in effect in all forms of employment other than farm-work), unless the African has been registered by a State employment officer.

No African may proceed to or enter in an urban or proclaimed area for the purpose of obtaining employment without first obtaining permission from the district labour bureau or employment officer in which he or she normally lives. The local employment officers in the urban or proclaimed areas *must* register (but see subsequent post-1960 amending legislation increasing discretionary authority of the State official to register) Africans, who qualify to remain in such urban or proclaimed area or who have been authorized to proceed there for employment, or who apply to re-enter the area after an absence of not more than twelve months in order to return specifically for employment in the same class of work with their previous employers. In the last instance, the right of the African to return to his previous employment is subject to the fact that his previous permission to be in the area was not for a specified period only.

Apart from such limited class of Africans who, as of 1960, had as of right to be registered for employment by the local employment officer of the urban or proclaimed area, registration of all other Africans in the area is at the discretion of the appropriate local employment officer. An African legally in the area who becomes unemployed may be registered, if there is a vacancy in the class of work in which he or she was previously employed or in some other class of work approved by the regional labour bureau and if he or she is prepared to accept such work. If there is no such vacancy, or if the African is not prepared to accept the work offered, he or she may still be registered for a period not exceeding seven days provided that the African reports daily and lives in a depot if such accomodation is available.

Registration will not be granted if there is a 'surplus' of labour in the area, or if the African has not complied with the laws relating to the carrying of documents, or for other administrative reasons. No man under 18 and no woman under 21 will be registered, unless the guardian's consent has been given to enter the area to seek employment.

When an employment officer registers an African, he must complete an index card of personal data and records the African's industrial classification. The employment officer then tries to place the African in employment. An African, who does not qualify to remain in an urban or proclaimed area and is placed in employment, will have his reference book endorsed with permission for that specific employment only.

From the above account, it will be observed that the legal contractual freedom of the African in respect of his personal rights to employment has been narrowed almost to nil and his practical contractual rights to a nullity. The reality of freedom of contract subject, except in certain categories (subsequently further limited by later legislation), entirely to administrative discretionary authority, must furthermore be related to a 72-hour permit to seek employment and possible 'endorsement out' of the area in the event of unemployment for whatever cause [24].

While the right of choice of employment by the African was thus subject to extraordinary restraint and interference by the polity, it must also be stressed that the employer's freedom of choice was *per contra* limited. The legal right of the employer to choose his own African labour was subjected to the same discretionary administrative authority to accept or reject that choice; the practical power of the employer to choose his own labour complement is determined not by the supply and demand operations of the labour market but by administrative decisions of what the supply and demand *ought to be*. If it is the unfettered authority of hierarchical administration to control the numbers of permitted work-seekers at all times in a particular labour-demand area and to decide arbitrarily what constitutes a 'surplus' of available labour, with total disregard of what employers may be willing to pay for the labour quantum, categories of labour and individual workers or of what employees will be willing to accept, then a 'labour market' in ordinary usage cannot be said to exist.

Although it must be repeated that the continuous free market mechanism is capable of almost limitless adjustment to administrative intervention and interference and will adjust prices and wages appropriately[25], the effect of etatism on resource-allocation in South Africa and on the consequent rate of economic development must clearly have been restrictive. The fact that the State's monetary management may run completely counter to its direct controls of the labour market is, of course, the key reason for the *practical* breakdown of its direct controls. This monetary factor made its explosive impact in the post-Republic phase of forced expansion and of planned growth. But even before, the Government's unwillingness to proceed to compulsory controls of private capital investment (while maintaining its prohibition of private capital investment in the Native Reserves or re-named Bantustans) was stretching the *de facto* urbanization of the Africans in 'White' South Africa beyond containment of the most absolute *de jure* limitations and denials[26].

It is of interest that the clearest acknowledgement of market reality and legal unreality should have officially come from a former Chief Justice and a former Minister of Native Affairs in Hertzog's Government. Justice H. A. Fagan[27], Chairman of the Native Laws Commission 1946–48, was appointed by Smuts's wartime Administration to examine the laws controlling the movement of Africans with particular reference to urbanization and the socioeconomic significance of the migratory labour policy of the goldmining industry. This Commission reached the conclusion:

From what we have already said it should be clear, firstly, that the idea of total segregation is utterly impracticable; secondly, that the movement from country to town has a background of economic necessity – that it may, so one hopes, be guided and regulated, and may perhaps also be limited, but that it cannot be stopped or turned in the opposite direction; and thirdly, that in our urban areas there are not only Native migrant labourers, but there is also a settled, permanent Native population.

These are simply facts which we have to face as such. The old cry, 'Send them back!' – still so often raised when there is trouble with the Natives – therefore no longer proffers a solution. A policy based on the proposition that the Natives in the towns are all temporarily migrant – or can be kept in the stage of temporary migrance – . . . would be a false policy, if for no other reason, then because the proposition itself has in the course of time proved to be false. It is, however, precisely this proposition of the Stallard Commission which, as has already been noted by the Young-Barrett Committee of 1935, lies near the root of many provisions of the legislation relating to Natives in urban areas and has had far-reaching effects in the administration of that legislation throughout the Union.

An admission, therefore, that it is an untenable proposition – and that is an admission which is simply forced upon us by hard facts – makes it necessary for us to find a new formula which may serve as a guide in respect of our suggestions for revision of the existing legislation[28].

But the Fagan Commission was already reporting to a changed Government and a new Minister of Native Affairs. Malan's 1948 Nationalist Government and his Minister of Native Affairs from 1950, Dr Verwoerd, were not disposed to regard any proposition as 'untenable', more particularly as their whole institutionalized culture now to be formulated in Apartheid put a totally different construction on the 'hard facts'.

The frequency and emotive intensity of the references in a text-book *Apartheid*[29] to the relationship between African urbanization and the apartheid idea established clearly that the Fagan 'admission' would have struck at the very roots of Afrikanerdom.

The large-scale urbanization of the Bantu during and after the First World War brought the new Black stream into direct conflict with the Afrikaner in the city. The socio-economic struggle transformed this conflict into a veritable struggle for survival. As will be shown, there is a direct link between this struggle for survival and the apartheid idea. Without the stimulus it provided, it is doubtful whether apartheid would ever have crystallized into its present form. . . . The economic integration of the Bantu and the chaotic racial conditions in the cities threatened the existence of the Afrikaner people, hence the consolidating effect of this danger. The socio-economic struggle in the cities became to the Afrikaner a national struggle.

The differentiation policy of the National(ist) Party after 1924 was therefore a true deliverance to them. . . . The economic integration and national awakening of the Bantu reached a climax during and after the Second World War (and figures) show the extent to which economic integration had already taken place by the end of the war. The report of the 1946 census revealed in particular the enormous concentration of Natives in the Union's four most important industrial areas. . . . The multi-racial urban areas became a Second Eastern Cape frontier to the Afrikaners. The dangers attendant upon the urbanization of the Bantu provoked lengthy discussions at the various People's Congresses. At a Congress in Bloemfontein in 1944 it was even stated that the urbanized Native constituted a threat to the Afrikaners. . . .

The cities formed the terrain on which the two forces (Black nationalism and Afrikaner nationalism) would oppose each other, while the socio-economic struggle for survival, waged simultaneously, served only to aggravate the conflict. *It was therefore in the urban areas that the so-called Native problem took on its present-day alarming character*. Afrikaner and Bantu were thrown into contact with each other in, so to speak, every sphere of life. The two racial groups took their stand ranged against each other as units, and the numerically weaker Afrikaner realized that only drastic steps could guarantee his continued existence as a separate entity. . . . It was in this manner that a favourable climate was created which led to the 'crystal-lizing-out' of the apartheid idea. Self-preservation could be reconciled with Bantu development by means of apartheid: 'He (the white man) has then at least the chance of preserving himself, a chance which he would under no circumstances have in a multi-racially controlled state – Dr Verwoerd pointed out in Parliament in 1959.

When they are judged objectively, it becomes crystal clear that the changes which took place during the years from 1939 to 1948 in the field of colour relations reshuffled the old and familiar racial patterns in South Africa in a manner which was quite revolutionary. The result was inevitable: A new approach by the White towards the non-White – in action as well as thoughts[30].

The 'hard facts' of urbanization following on accelerated economic development, and more particularly industrialization, which the Fagan Commission had found so irresistible even by ideology, were analyzed in greater detail by the Industrial Legislation Commission of Enquiry of 1951 [31]. The tables which follow are taken from that Commission's Report[32].

TABLE I

Urban and Rural Population of South Africa, 1911–46

Race	Urban				Rural			
	1911	1921	1936	1946	1911	1921	1936	1946
A: Total Population-thousands								
Europeans	658·3	847·5	1307·4	1740·8	618·0	672·0	696·5	631·9
Africans	508·1	587·1	1141·6	1810·5	3510·9	4110·7	5455·0	6021·4
Asiatics	311·4	51·2	145·6	210·8	366·7	114·5	74·1	83·5
Coloured		250·0	414·9	546·7		295·6	354·8	381·8
All Races	1477·9	1735·8	3009·5	4299·8	4495·5	5192·8	6580·4	7118·6
B: Percentage of Total of Each Race								
Europeans	51·6	55·8	65·2	73·4	48·4	44·2	34·8	26·6
Africans	12·6	12·5	17·3	23·1	87·4	87·5	82·7	76·9
Asiatics	45·9	30·9	66·3	70·7	54·1	69·1	33·7	29·3
Coloured		45·8	53·9	58·9		54·2	46·1	41·1
All Races	24·7	25·1	31·4	37·7	75·3	74·9	68·6	62·3

(Source: Population censuses with 1946 re-computed to include in 'Urban' certain African townships in Southern Transvaal classified as 'rural' by Census definition)

TABLE 2

Distribution of African Population in Various Areas 1936 and 1946

Area	1936 thousands			1946 thousands		
	Male	Female	Total	Male	Female	Total
Native areas	1236·3	1726·1	2962·3	1369·3	1897·9	3267·2
White-occupied farms	998·9	1054·6	2053·4	1107·3	1079·8	2187·1
All farms*	1062·7	1133·1	2195·7	1238·0	1219·9	2457·9
Other areas- mainly urban	1013·7	424·9	1438·6	1389·8	717·0	2106·8
Total Union	3312·7	3284·0	6596·7	3997·2	3834·8	7831·9
	percentages			percentages		
Native areas	37·3	52·6	44·9	34·3	49·5	41·7
White-occupied farms	30·2	32·1	31·1	27·7	28·2	27·9
All farms*	32·1	34·5	33·3	31·0	31·8	31·4
Native areas & farms	69·4	87·1	78·2	65·2	81·3	73·1
Other Areas	30·6	12·9	21·8	34·8	18·7	26·9

*All farms but excluding tribal farms owned by Africans
(Source: 1936 Official Year Book, 1946 Official Census Report)

TABLE 3

Urban Population of South Africa and Four Principal Industrial Areas

Area	1946				
	Whites	Africans	Asiatics	Coloured	Total
	A: Total urban population-thousands				
South Africa	1740·8	1810·5	201·8	546·7	4299·8
Western Cape	264·7	43·4	7·2	255·8	571·1
Southern Transvaal	708·4	985·8	27·0	46·1	1767·3
Durban/Pinetown	132·0	119·8	118·1	11·5	381·3
Port Elizabeth	66·0	50·8	3·5	35·0	155·2
	B: Proportion of total population				
Western Cape	15·2	2·4	3·5	46·8	13·3
Southern Transvaal	40·7	54·4	13·4	8·4	41·1
Durban/Pinetown	7·6	6·6	58·5	2·1	8·9
Port Elizabeth	3·8	2·8	1·7	6·4	3·6

(Source: Industrial Census – Western Cape: magisterial districts of Cape Town, Bellville, Wynberg, Simonstown, Somerset West, Stellenbosch, Paarl, Wellington, Malmesbury. Southern Transvaal: Witwatersrand, Pretoria, Vereeniging)

TABLE 4

Racial Composition of Urban Population in Four Industrial Areas, 1946

Area	Whites	Africans	Asiatics	Coloureds	Total
	%	%	%	%	%
1: Western Cape	46·3	7·6	1·3	44·8	100·0
2: Southern Transvaal	40·1	55·8	1·5	2·6	100·0
3: Durban/Pinetown	34·6	31·4	31·0	3·0	100·0
4: Port Elizabeth	42·5	32·7	2·2	22·6	100·0

TABLE 5

Employment in South Africa and Principal Industrial Areas, Manufacturing Industry, 1947/48; Racial Composition and Total No. Employees

Area	Whites		Africans		Asiatics		Coloureds		Total	
		%		%		%		%		%
1.	33,038	32·6	22,768	22·4	209	0·2	45,428	44·8	101,443	100
2.	99,289	36·4	164,802	60·4	1,058	0·4	7,614	2·8	272,763	100
3.	18,851	27·7	34,262	50·4	12,197	17·9	2,649	3·9	67,959	100
4.	13,967	44·7	10,670	34.2	239	0·8	6,365	20·4	31,241	100
Union	210,355		308,080		18,812		74,795		612,042	

TABLE 6

Racial Composition of Total No. Employees in Manufacturing Industry, by Industrial Areas, 1932/33–1947/48

Year	Whites	Africans	Asiatic	Col'd	White	African	Asiatic	Col'd
	1: Western Cape				2: Southern Transvaal			
	%	%	%	%	%	%	%	%
1932–33	47·6	10·3	0·8	41·3	46·3	51·7	0·3	1·7
1938–39	43·6	13·9	0·2	42·3	41·1	57·1	0·3	1·5
1944–45	33·0	21·3	0·2	45·5	36·2	60·4	0·4	3·0
1947–48	32·6	22·4	0·2	44·8	36·4	60·4	0·4	2·8
	3: Durban/Pinetown				4: Port Elizabeth			
	%	%	%	%	%	%	%	%
1932–33	39·5	35·6	20·6	4·2	60·5	22·4	1·0	16·1
1938–39	34·6	41·5	20·4	3·6	57·3	24·2	0·5	18·0
1944–45	26·4	49·9	20·0	3·8	46·6	31·2	0·9	21·3
1947–48	27·7	50·4	17·9	3·9	44·7	34·2	0·8	20·4

(Source of data for above tables: Industrial Census)

The trend of these figures is evident. Urbanization was proceeding among all racial groups and had gone furthest with that group, whose educational and cultural attainments interacted with the specialization of labour characteristic of increased marketability – that is, the Whites. With nearly three-quarters of the White population already urbanized by 1946 and heavily concentrated in the industrial region of the Southern Transvaal, the honey-pot of profits in Southern Africa, the co-operant labour of all other groups would necessarily follow a related flow of urbanization. The Asiatics virtually confined to Natal were pulled into Durban-Pinetown; the Cape Coloureds gravitated from their regional birthplaces into Greater Cape Town; the Africans were pushed and pulled into the urban workshops in all four major industrial regions but especially into the Southern Transvaal.

By 1946, some three-fifths of the labour force of manufacturing industry in the Southern Transvaal was already African. No less significant was the rapid percentage increase of the African proportion of industrial labour from about 10 per cent in 1932/33 to more than 22 per cent in 1947/48 in the Western Cape, where the Cape Coloureds were steadily becoming the operatives of more and more mechanized manufacturing.

It was the restructuring of skill by such mechanized manufacturing which, from the Second World War onwards, launched South Africa into its own industrial revolution. The pre-war, small-scale, under-capitalized work-premises using a high-cost combination of journeyman skills at collective-bargaining wage-rates comparable to North American standards and of wholly unschooled, totally untrained, unskilled workers steadily gave way to the post-war, expanded-scale, adequately-capitalized factories employing increasing numbers of operatives on modern, mechanized plant. From 1924 to 1940, fixed capital per employees grew neglibly, if not negatively in some years. From 1939 to 1944, it grew at an annual rate of 5·01 per cent, from 1948 to 1953 at 10·79 per cent, in the next industrial census years of 1953/54 to 1954/55 at 14·47 per cent.

Process-simplification and job-reclassification, the potentialities of which were dramatically demonstrated by the Cott war-time scheme of artisan-training, was management's response to the rigid, increasingly non-functional apprenticeship-journeyman system of the craft unions. In the Western Cape, particularly, food- and clothing-manufacturing rapidly expanded the employment of semi-skilled Cape Coloureds, including large numbers of women. Textile manufacturing, one of the major industries of post-war capital investment, was developed with semi-automatic plant utilizing African and Coloured and Asiatic operative labour. Generally South African manufacturing, which from 1945 employed an entirely new magnitude of capital available both from a high rate of domestic capital-formation and foreign investment in South African subsidiaries, equipped itself with plant designed for operative labour. An industrial council agreement for the important metal industry negotiated in 1944 on a national scale, which allowed for more flexible job-classifications utilizing operative-class labour and incentive payments, facilitated the growth of metallurgical and engineering manufacture in place of the pre-war engineering repair-shops and jobbing foundries.

Consumer-goods manufacturing, greatly encouraged by the Government's policy of forced-industrialization, provided exceptional employment potential for Non-Whites. The total number of workers in eleven such industries, more particularly textiles, clothing, foot-wear, food, canning and furniture, increased from 44,769 in 1935 to 190,529 in 1959 – the number of White employees grew from 25,296 to 36,091, whereas the increase in Non-Whites was from 19,473 to 154,438.

Apartheid, which saw in the permanent urbanization of the Africans so mortal a 'threat to the survival of Afrikanerdom', was equally apprehensive at this restructuring of labour [33]. It was another manifestation of market change which Afrikanerdom felt bound to subject to the over-riding control of the polity. The Industrial Conciliation Act No. 28 of 1956, ostensibly a consolidating measure to improve the machinery of the industrial council collective-bargaining system and provide for a greater measure of co-ordinated national labour policy, was the legal instrument [34]. This Act, its key provisions in total contradiction to the evidence of almost all employer- and employee-organizations to the preliminary Industrial Legislation Commission of Enquiry [35], was passed against bitter parliamentary and extra-parliamentary opposition after two years of debate and select-committee analysis. The Minister of Labour, Senator de Klerk, in fact made no concession of political principle in respect of its racial clauses.

The Act removed all hitherto legal doubts by absolutely excluding

'Native' from the definition of 'employee' in terms of the Industrial Conciliation Act so that Africans may not belong to a registered trade union nor take part in industrial council or conciliation board proceedings. The Native Labour (Settlement of Disputes) Act of 1953 had prohibited Africans from any kind of strike action. Though Africans are therefore not covered by nor may participate in collective bargaining machinery, industrial council agreements can still be declared binding on African workers to prevent circumvention of such agreements.

In respect of recognition of registered trade unions, the Act introduced the vital new principle of compulsory racial segregation as between 'White' and 'Coloured' persons. After the Act's commencement, no trade union could be registered (a) in respect of both White persons and Coloured persons; or (b) if membership of such union is open to both White persons and Coloured persons. Existing trade unions with a mixed membership, the so-termed 'mixed-unions', must provide for separate branches of White and Coloured persons to be established with separate meetings and the executive committee of the mixed trade union shall consist of White persons only. No member of one racial branch (other than an official) may attend a meeting of the other racial branch; no Coloured member of the trade union will be allowed to attend the executive meeting of the mixed union except for interrogation or explanation[36]. Subsequent amendments to the 1956 Act further restricted the extension of the area of the operations of mixed-unions and facilitated the registration of small, break-away White unions for particular trades and areas.

The party political background, and implications of such compulsory separation of trade unions, was the activities of the National Council of Trustees to promote Afrikaner labour organizations and whose major success was the capture of the powerful Mineworkers Union[37]. The splintering confusion introduced into the trade union movement with its consequent five major co-ordinating bodies, ranging from the 'right' to the 'left', may have weakened the over-all effectiveness of collective bargaining by organized trade unionism[38].

On the other hand, the power of certain all-White unions to secure Government action on the job-reservation clause 77 of the 1956 Industrial Conciliation Act has doubtless been strengthened. The total exclusion of Africans from registered trade unions and the substantial derogation of status of Coloureds in organized, recognized trade unionism clearly extended the potential coercive power of White trade unionism. It was, however, the job-reservation clause 77 of the 1956 Act that gave legal sanction to the polity to impose a virtually limitless colour bar on all categories of employment.

The relevant clause 77, as amended, provides that the Minister of Labour may instruct his appointed Industrial Tribunal, to investigate any undertaking, industry, trade or occupation or class of work and for any area for the purpose of a job reservation determination. Normally the Minister must gazette such instruction but, if in his opinion such public notification is unnecessary, he may inform by letter those whom in his opinion should be consulted.

The Minister may then issue any terms of reference he so wishes, not being bound by the gazetted notice, to the Industrial Tribunal and shall appoint assessors or not at his discretion. After consideration of any representations and consultation with industrial councils, registered employer and employee organizations and the Central Native Labour Board [39], the Industrial Tribunal may issue a recommended determination, which the Minister of Labour, after consultation with the Minister of Economic Affairs, may or may not gazette as the legal determination under clause 77 of the Industrial Conciliation Act (though he cannot vary the Industrial Tribunal recommendations, which includes recommendations for exemptions).

A job reservation order may reserve wholly or to the extent detailed the reservation of work or any specified class of work or work other than a specified class of work in the undertaking, industry, trade or occupation or any portion thereof for persons of a specified race (or for persons belonging to a specified class of such persons or for such persons other than a specified class of persons). The order then prohibits the performance of such work by any other persons.

The order may then provide for the minimum, maximum, or average number or percentage of persons of a specified race employed by an employer generally or for any time-period, in proportion to the total number of employees or the total number of a particular race.

The order may then relate these specified numbers or percentages to work generally or any class of work in the undertaking, industry, trade or occupation. The order may prohibit the replacement by an employer of employees of a specified race by employees of another

323

race. The order may prohibit the employment of a smaller per-centage of a particular race-group than the percentage which existed or may exist.

The clause further provides that the powers of the Industrial Tribunal to make a recommended job reservation order shall not be affected in any way by the extent to which persons of any race are presently employed or available for employment or are likely to become available for employment.

It will be appreciated that this legislation gives total powers of arbitrary decision to the Minister of Labour. This no doubt was necessitated by the very fact of theoretical limitless substitution and combination of work-persons, work-categories and labour-capital structure. The polity must take totalitarian powers over the market because the mechanism of market-price co-ordination has virtually infinite adaptability. Indeed if such a wholly arbitrary measure was to be put into force in any instance, its very arbitrariness compelled unrestricted powers to the Minister to grant exemptions form all or any provisions of a job reservation order so that he might escape from his own arbitrariness.

Nevertheless, even if the technical compulsion of such total authority is acknowledged, legally *all* private contractual rights in respect of employment in South Africa have been abrogated. The objective of the Government in introducing its job reservation powers for labour-quota allocation may be, as the official statement declares: 'work reservation is merely the maintenance of the tradi-tional labour pattern which progressively developed between differ-ent racial groups in South Africa according to and based on their respective standards of living, background and spheres of employ-ment' [40]. In order, however, to achieve that purpose of the polity, the labour market had to come under the authority of potential ministerial allocation of *every single job in the economy*.

The legal elimination of private contractual rights applied not only to one race group but to all race groups, not only to employees but to employers, not only to one category of employers and em-ployees but to each individual employer and employee.

Such a legal reality *ipso facto* becomes a legal unreality. This is reflected in the actual work reservation orders promulgated.

Job reservation No. 1 reserved for Whites all except the lowest-paid jobs in the clothing industry throughout South Africa. From 1938/39 to 1952/53, according to the Industrial Tribunal's own report submitted to the Minister, the number of clothing factories had increased from 280 to 566. The total number of workers in that period had increased from 18,250 to 45,837 and the value of articles manufactured at current prices from £5,866,000 to £49,182,000. During that time, the number of male White workers had increased absolutely from 1,620 to 2,998 and female White workers from 9,494 to 10,085. But total employment of all races having grown from 18,250 to 45,837, the *percentage* of White workers had fallen from 60·9 to 28·5.

The interpretation placed upon these figures was not that an expanding industry had expanded employment so substantially for Non-Whites as to maintain a constant work-force of White females and increased work-force of White males. The interpretation was that there had been a replacement of White workers by Non-White workers, despite evidence submitted that White workers were simply not available having accepted more favourable, alternative employment opportunities in a growing economy.

Since the ministerial order would have closed down the entire clothing industry of the Western Cape, in which Coloured workers supplied most – indeed almost the total – work-force in the reserved jobs, a blanket exemption was accorded to the Western Cape. This particular registration ran into certain legal invalidities which led to an amendment to the Act and a revised order was promulgated in May 1960. By then, the total number of workers had increased to about 50,000 and gross output to about £66,000,000, while the percentage of White workers seemed to have fallen below 20 per cent.

The new order broadly froze the percentage distribution of workers by racial groups for each category of designated employment[41]. But different percentages are provided for different areas, while in the so-called uncontrolled or border-areas to the Native Reserves a totally different wage-structure prevails. The job reservation order could not control the movement of a factory from one area to another nor the investment decision in establishing new factories.

What originated in a party-political campaign to help a separate, small group of White clothing workers (in the then Minister of Labour's personal constituency stamping-ground of Germiston) split the multi-racial Garment Workers Union[42], ended in a nation-wide job reservation order to maintain the particular employment of those White worker-voters. This produced an unworkable set of regulations. It also produced a steady shift of clothing manufacture out of Germiston to other locations.

Another kind of tradition was responsible for determination No. 2. This reserved the occupation of motor vehicle driving in the cleansing department of the Durban municipality for Whites, the Industrial Tribunal Report establishing *inter alia* that the removal of a yearly 2,000,000 pails of 'night soil' from the African locations being by custom a White man's job. The Government's official over-all defence of Apartheid that 'each race should serve its own community' apparently was not apposite to human excrement.

Other determinations reserving work have applied to window-manufacturing, traffic constables, fire brigade and ambulance services, lift attendants, electrical-goods manufacture, the building industry, motor transport driving, the wholesale meat trade and the liquor and catering trade.

The most recent work-reservation, at the time of writing, has a special significance for the production-function of a major industry of large-scale capitalization in specific plant-motor-vehicle assembly and manufacturing. This industry has shown a typical South African development pattern. Originally completely assembled motor vehicles, packed in boxes, were imported. The first-stage tariff protection encouraged importation of unassembled components so that progressively shipments of 'completely-knocked-down' components were assembled in South African assembly plants. Extended tariff protection favoured domestic manufacture of components. Then from 1960 an import-replacement programme to increase the 'local content' of a 'South African-made car', by way of import-permit allocation that would in time virtually eliminate from the local market any car with a less than 55 per cent by weight 'local content', became a major feature of official forced-industrialization policy.

The capital-structure of motor assembly and component manufacture changed accordingly. Non-specific warehouses of relatively small-scale gave way to purpose-designed layouts of medium-capitalization. In the period since 1961, the declared intention by such world-wide companies as General Motors, Ford, British Motor Corporation, Chrysler and other European and Japanese organizations provides for multi-million rand investments in highly specific manufacturing plants.

Necessarily the labour-structure changed in relationship to the capital-structure, technological process and, of course, the labour market. At the beginning so-termed 'civilized-labour' of unskilled and semi-skilled Whites were employed in plants located at Port Elizabeth, as the import-port and area of a large Poor White problem. With changing domestic-content of the assembled car, location of assembly plants responded to market facts and transport costs so that new plants were located in Durban, the Western Province, East London and the Witwatersrand.

From 1949 to 1963 the labour-pattern in the industry – or more accurately assembly industry – is reflected in the table below [43]:

Employees in the Motor Assembly Industry (South Africa)
1949 to 1963

Year	White		Coloured		African	
	Number	% of Total	Number	% of Total	Number	% of Total
1949	2370	82·0	142	4·9	379	13·1
1950	2231	74·0	350	11·6	435	14·4
1951	2395	72·5	450	13·6	459	13 9
1952	2019	65·0	560	18·0	527	17·0
1953	1747	58·1	584	19·4	678	22·5
1954	1629	54·0	755	25·0	663	21·0
1955	1932	48·4	1131	28·3	933	23·3
1956	2231	44·8	1231	24·7	1516	30·5
1957	4796	49·7	2726	28·2	2132	22·1
1958	4781	52·9	2285	25·3	1965	21·7
1959	4687	52·3	2284	25·5	1984	22·2
1960	5025	52·4	2708	28·3	1849	19·3
1961	4555	52·1	2416	27·6	1777	20·3
1963	5675	41·7	5525	40·6	2416	17·7

(Source: Industrial Tribunal Report, p. 8)

The interpretation placed upon these figures by the Industrial Tribunal Report was to note the absolute increase in employment in each racial group but to concentrate its conclusions on the percentage drop of the number of Whites to total number of employees. By excluding from the total number of workers in all categories of employment those employed either as administrative office staff or as labourers, the Industrial Tribunal found that for the remaining production workers the Whites were only 34·2 per cent of this last category as compared with 41·7 per cent of total employees.

	All Employees	Production Workers
Whites	41·7%	34·2%
Coloureds	40·6%	49·0%
Africans	17·7%	16·8%

The Tribunal Report therefore concluded that job-reservation in respect of the category of production workers was desirable and so recommended. It noted and accepted employers' assurances that administrative work was exclusively White and found no problem in the category of labouring work in which the 'physical strength' of the African was necessary.

Work reservation Determination No. 16 accordingly reserved for the Republic as a whole, excepting the area of Blackheath, for Whites only supervisory and control work and welding work; throughout South Africa no replacement of a White worker currently employed by a Non-White worker and no replacement of a Coloured worker by an African worker. Furthermore, in addition to the just-mentioned reservations, the minimum percentage of White workers to total workers was fixed at 45 per cent for Bellville in the Western Province, 45 per cent for Port Elizabeth, 65 per cent for Uitenhage, 25 per cent for East London, 20 per cent for Durban and 25 per cent for the Witwatersrand. The particular area of Blackheath, where the British Motor Car Corporation had established a plant employing Coloured, was in effect excluded from these provisions except that no Coloured worker could be replaced by an African. A motor-assembly plant for Japanese vehicles, a joint venture of Japanese and Afrikaner capital, established as a so-called border area industry at Rosslyn near Pretoria, was exempt from the job restraints on African workers.

This example of job reservation has been elaborated for its patent implications of the minutiae of an administrative decision affecting the development of an industry of major importance to the Government's vision of the economic development of South Africa.

Motor vehicle manufacture and assembly is the Government's chosen instrument for achieving the crucial sophistication of industrialization in South Africa over the next decade, when gold-mining is expected to decline in significance [44]. An import-control technique was perfected to ensure that the great car-manufacturing companies of America, Britain and Europe either abandoned their existing investments in South Africa or made additional investments probably exceeding R100,000,000 in the immediate future in an expansionist programme of increased local manufacture.

With this vast capital-expenditure programme committed, a White trade union unrecognized by the employers but registered by the Government instigates a job-reservation enquiry. The Tribunal ignores the factual figures of a growth in total employment, from 1949 to 1963, of 2,891 to 13,616 workers of all races, and of 2,370 White workers to 5,675 White workers but finds evidence of 'replacement' of White workers in certain grades as in conflict with early employment practice of the industry. It further ignores that White workers have been upgraded and that in the year 1963, in which 'there was a serious drop of over 10 per cent' in the percentage of White workers, an industry achieving a record level of sales from its capital investment completed (and planning much greater future investments) had found additional White workers for production categories unobtainable at current wage-rates.

A work-reservation determination, despite the critical importance of flexibility and interchangeability of workers to keep mass-assembly productional lines operational, provides for rigidities of non-replacement by one racial group by another and fixes percentages, varying from one area to another, of employment by a minimum White quota. One of the major plants employing Coloured workers is in effect excluded. There is no reference in the Report, i.e. no inclusion in the Determination Order, to planned investments by Japanese-Afrikaner finance in assembly of Japanese vehicles at a plant-location conforming to the Government's border-area policy, which policy provides for state-aided finance and tax-concessions and comes under a differential wage-agreement highly favourable to work-simplification of processes performed by Africans.

The practical significance, immediate and ultimate, of job reservation as an instrument of control over the labour market is not readily assessed. In theory it eliminates entirely the market-price mechanism or market-wages as the basis of allocation of labour resources in the production function. Choice of labour, by categories and as individuals, by the employer in accordance with its combined productivity potential with any given capital structure is no longer determined or determinable by its marginal productivity. Choice of job by the worker is no longer a response to comparative evaluation of competitive wage and opportunity. Private contractual freedom in the labour market, by both employer and employee, becomes in theory entirely subject to administrative direction and discretion.

The general belief is that managements' real-life decisions in respect of labour have been made without taking into account the restrictions either on the geographical mobility of African labour by way of influx-controls or on the occupational mobility of racial categories of White, Coloured and African labour by way of job-reservation orders. Concessions and exemptions in respect of such controls and orders may be assumed before decision-taking and resource-allocation, and hence such controls disregarded from the outset.

On the other hand, the practical importance of such far-reaching controls on the labour market may go largely uncomprehended even by practical management as distinct from economic analysis. Location of factory-site and choice of factory-plant may well be made in anticipation of the *probable* response of the Labour Department to the consequential implications for geographical and occupational labour controls[45]. There are a number of instances where it is public or private knowledge that major capital investments have been made only after obtaining advance rulings of Government reaction[46].

The opportunity costs involved in administrative-linkage in place of market-price co-ordination are necessarily incalculable, since the foregone opportunities cannot be assessed. From the side of labour, the quantum of lost-opportunities is even more a question-mark. How much total productivity has been and is lost through restraints on the geographical and occupational mobility of millions of Non-Whites? Even the most confident econometrician might baulk at a calculation.

If lost opportunities and concomitant costs of Apartheid policies cannot be computed, only the official data of continuing trends in urbanization and employment categories can be offered. Some relevant figures are given in the final chapter.

In 1948 the Afrikaner polity took over parliamentary power to implement its institutionalized culture, which it identified with Apartheid. It eliminated all direct representation of the African peoples in the sovereign Parliament and the Cape Coloureds from the common electoral roll – and hence from any political influence. It introduced the most comprehensive measures of actual and symbolical separation between different groups of colour. It repeatedly and emphatically denied the validity of 'economic considerations and motivations' in decisions and matters of policy affecting 'the survival of White civilization in South Africa'. It declared that the ultimate ideal must be 'total separation of the races' so that 'each might be free to develop separately to the maximum of its potential'. Nothing could or should be allowed to stand in the way of the realization of that ideal – other than 'because government is the "art of putting into execution that which is practicable" the Government's Apartheid *policy* cannot at any given moment be the precise embodiment of the Afrikaner's Apartheid idea', *vide* Dr D. F. Malan, the man who achieved the 'miracle' of the Nationalist Party victory in the 1948 General Election [47].

In 1958, ten years later, the Viljoen Commission into South Africa's industrialization policy was to write:

The development of secondary industry in South Africa has been greatly facilitated by the existence of a large and elastic supply of labour, and international comparisons would seem to show that the number of people drawn into this sphere since the cessation of hostilities has, with the exception of Western Germany, been proportionally greater in the Union than in any other major western industrial country[48].

For Germany as a whole and for South Africa as a whole, the barriers set up by the polity somehow were overcome by the market economy. Africans escaping from tribal collectivism, like Eastern Germans from their tribal collectivism, preferred to elect with their feet.

SPRINGS OF DEVELOPMENT

Economic development is patently a process of social interaction. A favourable confluence of capital, labour, resources, technology and entrepreneurship starts the increasing flow. Schumpeter identifies the source of the perennial spring with the initiating-innovating entrepreneurs. But the inspiration of individual effort clearly needs a social framework[1]. The argument then turns on whether the constitution of order or the constitution of liberty, as the conditioning political milieu, provides the more propitious framework.

South African economic development, as observed in the introduction, is not unique but it has certain special features of interest. This is particularly true of its social framework. In this social framework, the constitution of order has always taken precedence over the constitution of liberty. Furthermore as the structure of economic development has grown more capitalistic, that is in the sense of both the intensification and sophistication of capital employed in production, so the constitution of order has appeared to the White polity to be the overwhelming priority in the social system. Freedom of choice extended to the Non-Whites in general, and the Africans in particular, however intrinsic to the constitution of liberty – one man, one vote – seemed incompatible with the continuation of order – White control into the foreseeable future, and therefore of progressive economic development.

The constitution of order may appear to be reflected in the administered economy and the constitution of liberty in the market economy. But the proper constitution of liberty may well in the ultimate be inescapable, for the continuation of order and the conscious perfection of the market economy may equally be basic to the continued optimization of resource-allocation and -utilization. Both Hayek in the *Constitution of Liberty* and von Mises in *Human*

Action provide insights into the market economy of individual initiative that will perhaps yet have to be re-learnt by those who see a superior orderliness in collectivist compulsion. The South African record, as the previous chapter elaborated, has been increasingly to subordinate the market to the polity as the defender of the Whites' institutionalized culture.

The constitution of order in South African experience has been manifested in an expanding bureaucratization of the direction of economic resources. This stamp of the administered economy is the more real expression of the White South African's will, however strikingly Apartheid has evinced the avowed purpose of Afrikanerdom. The opportunity cost of the administered economy is the market economy – the foregone opportunities of market co-ordination of economic development; the opportunity cost of the constitution of order is the constitution of liberty – the forgone opportunities of establishing the consensus for the continuation of order.

As at 1870, despite or because of the attempts of the imperial factor to impose a federated South Africa[2], no single social system had come into being and no signs of self-generating economic development in any part of the country. South Africa exhibited the characteristic institutional and structural framework of a dormant economy, which Henry J. Bruton [3] describes as becoming so alien to growth that the social organization is a more fundamental obstacle to the process of development than simply a low rate of capital accumulation. The shock, which introduces a vitalizing change into one sector of the economy so that henceforth it grows more rapidly than others, was of course the impact of the mineral discoveries, first at Kimberley and then on the Witwatersrand.

As Bruton notes, several writers [4] have emphasized that periods of sustained growth are normally dominated by one or a very few industries exhibiting a rate of growth greatly in excess of that of the whole economy. It is the performance and behaviour of the rapidly growing sector which begins to exert its influence on the more slowly growing sectors until their rate of development begins to catch up. It was in the South African goldmining industry that the uncharacteristic institutional and structural changes began so that an intensity of integration of the South African social system brought about not only the Union of South Africa but a new complexity of interrelationships between White and Non-White, between the men of Europe and the men of Africa. Performance and behaviour in the mining industry, which first dragged and then pushed other sectors of the economy into sustained activity, became the determining influence.

The Rand goldmining industry served both as geographic and economic frontier in South African economic development. It yielded increasing returns both to capital and to labour with contemporaneous techniques and population as well as increasing returns with changing techniques and population. Dynamic changes, coming from the time of the proclamation of the Witwatersrand goldfields in 1886 have yielded increasing returns from and in the Witwatersrand for generation after generation. Mining technology and the periodic decisive gold-price increases ensured the exploitation of an expanding frontier, with its productive shifts of labour and capital from old, settled areas of geography and occupation, that constitute continuing national economic development [5].

It was in the goldmining industry, however, that market determination of labour-resources aroused the most powerful ideological resistance and where the acceptance of the administered direction of labour-utilization became most complete. From the 1924 accession to power of the Nationalist-Labour Pact Government, as related earlier, the Chamber of Mines ceased to press for a least-cost rationality of labour organization and concentrated its influence to secure the co-operation of the State in the administered wage- and working-structure of its essential, unskilled labour force. The wage- and working-structure of its unskilled labour force had been throughout the key factor in the mining industry's production function. After the 1922 Rand Strike when it was made clear beyond further challenge that organized White mining labour would dictate job-demarcation and -reservation, the optimization of profit and maximization of output became critically dependent on the administered direction of the quantum of unskilled labour.

A theoretical and pragmatically formidable case can be made that this last factor became *the* strategic variable in the development of the goldmining industry and, hence, of the South African economy as a whole.

The financing of a prospective goldmine and the cost-structure of a producing mine, i.e. the capital structure of very large monetary sums in highly specific and fixed assets of incalculable earning life, place a premium on maximum utilization of the mining plant. Optimum exploitation of the whole body of mining ore of the Witwatersrand goldfields depended on such critical unknowns as the extent and grade of ore bodies and the future price of gold. Future finance for profitable ore-bodies, consequent on new discoveries or favourable changes in the unknowns, was largely dependent on successful redemption of past equity investment. This was pragmatically important since the provision of share capital for risk-taking in goldmining had been shown by experience to come from a limited number of 'specialists' in such risk-investments. All these factors made the *availability* of the optimum complement of the co-operant factor of labour the vital consideration of mining management [6].

It might consequently have been expected that market determinants would have evolved a highly stabilized labour force of appropriate structure of skilled and unskilled.

In respect of both skilled and unskilled labour, however, cultural and institutional influences were resistant to such market determinants. Earlier chapters have elaborated the problems of attracting skilled (White or European) immigrants and unskilled (African) immigrants. Both groups were subject to a high degree of labour turnover. Among the skilled, the high incidence of destructive occupational disease and in the early period the lack of family life contributed to a 'restlessness' that was the subject of repeated comment by commissions of enquiry into industrial relations and labour troubles. Among the unskilled, tribal traditions in respect of land and marriage-custom similarly operated against permanency in the labour force.

Superimposed on the contemporary realities of skilled and unskilled labour supply, the wants and wishes of White skilled labour secured the support of the unchallengeable authority of the polity. It became from the viewpoint of mining management, that is the Chamber of Mines, the undeniable reality that the skilled labour would have to be White; and if such White labour was to be available without disruptive strikes, its stability would have to be ensured by collective bargaining arrangements judiciously acknowledged.

The availability of the co-operant unskilled African labour also became subject to the overriding authority and power of the polity rather than to the market. There was, firstly, the absolute racial demarcation of job-evaluation and work-organization imposed by the White skilled workers in their trade unions, entrenched beyond even dissent from 1924 onwards, and, secondly, the whole weight of White 'feeling'. Such opinion, reflected in the early 'Black Peril' agitation over sexual assaults in mining areas, was totally opposed to a permanently urbanized mine-labour force of many tens of thousands of Africans.

This labour force would necessarily have had to be recruited initially from tribal societies throughout Southern Africa – not only inhabitants from 'British' South Africa but from East and Central Africa. It may have been that in the course of time a resident, family-based African labour force could and would have been called into being by market factors, more particularly market wages. But the White polity was absolutely resistant to the implications of progressive integration of primitive Africans, including great numbers of foreign-born Africans. Furthermore, it would have taken much time and effort in skilled human management (at a time when industrial relations was not even a discipline) to have persuaded tribal Africans to have abandoned all tribal links to land rights through bringing marriage-partners out of the tribal lands, and thereby destroying all claims to such land-rights.

Though the resistance of Africans to the process of permanent, urbanized wage-employment and consequent detribalization has patently been exaggerated by White opinion, it was certainly a real factor which mining management would have had to overcome. Moreover in overcoming it, mining management would have had to raise the additional capital for the more costly family accommodation housing in place of the bachelor-compounds of minimum amenities [7]. Alternatively wage-rates would have had to reflect the supply-price of Africans accepting the higher opportunity costs of detribalization of themselves and their families. Finally, there was the major problem of silicosis – the extremely costly occupational disease of mining. Legal-provision for silicosis-compensation to Whites was a substantial operating cost but said to be unnecessary in the case of Africans. As short-term, contract workers, the latters' non-permanence in mining employment and their frequent return to tribal environment allegedly reduced their incidence to this destructive disease. The system of migrant, unskilled workers provided the 'excuse' for not extending to Black men the silicosis cost-obligations legally demanded for White men [8].

The *availability* of White skilled labour involved acceptance of its polity-backed, unionized collective bargaining power by the Chamber of Mines. The *availability* of African unskilled labour involved (a) centralized recruitment of a never-permanent, migratory

tribal labour force which, though subject to an almost continuous turnover of its individuals, would nonetheless be stabilized as
a total complement of ever higher numbers, and (*b*) the monopsonistic wages and working conditions applied to that labour force.

Finally, when the Chamber won the fight but lost the battle for
the elimination of the legal-customary colour bar during the
'minor civil war' of the 1922 Rand Strike, the future pattern of the
migratory labour system of African workers was rigidified by the
Chamber of Mines as much as by the authority of the White polity
itself. This is fully reflected in the evidence of the Chamber of
Mines to the Lansdown Commission.

After armed-intervention ended a one day strike in 1942 by African mine-workers in protest against war-time price increases and
unadjusted wages, the Witwatersrand Mine Natives' Wages Commission[9] was appointed under the chairmanship of Justice
Lansdown to investigate the wage- and working-conditions of
African goldmining workers. The Lansdown Commission was
particularly concerned to emphasize the continuing crucial importance of the goldmining industry to the South African economy in
the face of contemporary estimates of its diminishing role and what
it regarded as uncritical over-estimation of the potential of manufacturing industry[10].

Partly as an act of deliberate high policy and on American insistence, the South African Government and the Chamber of Mines
had accepted a virtually static production of gold during the
Second World War. Nonetheless the Lansdown Commission stressed
that payments by the goldmining industry to all its beneficiaries, i.e.
workers, suppliers, shareholders and Government; for the year 1942
amounted to £115 millions. Even to the casual reader, said the
Commission's Report, these figures could not fail to indicate the
enormous importance to the Union of an industry which had produced since the year 1884, gold to the value of over £2,000,000,000.
'This steady flow of wealth from the Witwatersrand has spread over
the whole of the Union, of which it would be hard to find any corner
unaffected thereby . . . many urban communities of the Witwatersrand are almost entirely dependent for the continuance of a
prosperous existence upon the operations of mines in the vicinity'[11].

The functional relationship of African unskilled manual labour
to gold output and profitability was expressed by the Lansdown
Commission in these terms:

The goldmining industry of the Witwatersrand has indeed been fortunate in having secured, for its unskilled labour, native peasants who have been prepared to come to the Witwatersrand for periods of labour at comparatively low rates of pay. But for this fortunate circumstance, the industry could never have reached the present stage of development – some mines would never have opened up, many low grade mines would have been unable to work with any prospect of profit; in the case of the richer mines, large bodies of ore, the milling of which has been brought within the limits of payability, could never have been worked, with the result that the lives of the mines would have been considerably reduced.

That the results accruing from this cheap native labour supply have had a profoundly beneficial influence on the general economic development of the Union is a matter that needs no demonstration. Not only has the earth yielded up a great body of wealth which would have remained unexploited, but vast amounts of money have been paid away in wages and put into circulation for the acquiring of equipment and stores necessary for the working of the mines and this, in turn, has had the beneficial effect upon the development of secondary industries[12].

The significance of 'unlimited' supplies of labour to economic development, which Arthur Lewis analyzed[13], has already been referred to. Although Lewis was highly critical of those imperialist policies in Africa, which had deliberately impoverished the subsistence tribal economies to maintain the 'unlimited' labour supply forced into the capitalist sector by negligible, nil or negative marginal tribal productivity, he unequivocally identified the developmental contribution of the resultant profits accruing to the capitalist sector.

In actual fact, writes Lewis, the record of every imperial power in Africa in modern times is one of improverishing the subsistence economy either by taking away the people's land, or by demanding forced labour in the capitalist sector or by imposing taxes to drive people to work for capitalist employers[14]. This may not be literally true of every colonial authority in Africa but it is supported in broad generalization in South African experience, at least until very recent times when a recognizable and definitive effort in terms of capital and expertise has been made by the Government at encouraging productivity in tribal agriculture. Lewis, too, does not in this article perhaps give due acknowledgment to the real practical difficulties in overcoming traditional agricultural practices among primitive pastoral-nomadic peoples.

Since the process of capital accumulation must begin somehow, somewhere in the system before the progressive increase in output per head can be generated, it is critical that profits be generated out of which savings can be made. In a system under total bureaucratic direction, that is under totalitarian collectivism, the state itself will ensure the forced or compulsory savings by the appropriate real wage policy of restricted wage- or consumer-goods. In a system of private capitalism, the source of savings must be primarily private profits. The share of current national income must be altered in favour of the saving capitalists and against the spending workers. Only in this manner is capital accumulation, which is indispensible to increasing total productivity, achievable in any significant measure.

It is, says Lewis, the inequality which goes with profits that favours capital accumulation and the central fact of economic development is that the distribution of income should be in favour of the saving class. Hence, since the major source of profits is savings, the share of profits in the national income must increase for capital accumulation to increase.

In the Lewis model of 'unlimited' supplies of tribal-peasant labour from a subsistence economy, the assumption is:

that practically the whole benefit of capital accumulation and of technical progress goes into the (capitalist) surplus; because real wages are constant, all that the workers get out of the expansion is that more of them are employed at a wage above subsistence earnings. The model says, in effect, that if unlimited supplies of labour are available at a constant real wage, and if any part of profits is re-invested in productive capacity, profits will grow continuously relatively to the national income, and capital formation will also grow relatively to the national income[15].

The monopsonistic recruitment and contractual employment of tribal African labour within the goldmining industry of South Africa together with the appropriate legislation prohibiting (a) individual desertion of service and (b) collective withdrawal of labour, as well as Government support for treaty-arrangements to obtain additional tribal labour from East and Central Africa, ensured constant money – and probably real – wages for such labour for nearly half a century. Unchanging wages of African mine-workers with increasing supplies of such labour over the decades underwrote the profitability of the goldmining industry.

Whether re-invested as undistributed profits by the mining-finance houses or re-invested as unspent dividends by the small class of mining shareholders [16], the annual flow of mining profits was the source of the capital accumulation that maintained and then expanded South African economic development. From 1911 to 1940, the working profits of the goldmines amounted to about £538,000,000 and more than half of this was earned during the period 1933-40 following the increased gold price and during which highly prosperous seven years, the 'unlimited' supply of African labour continued at virtually unchanged wages.

The Mine Natives' Wages or Lansdown Commission of 1944 found that ninety-nine per cent of the unskilled workers on the Witwatersrand mines were tribal Africans 'who, for the most part, have their lands and stock left in charge of their families, while they are away at work on the mines[17].' Only less than ten per cent of the total African labour force, employed as clerks and related categories, were detribalized. Conditions in the 1890's, which resulted in average wages of Africans being bid up as high as 63s. a month, had been made subject increasingly to the controls of an administered rather than a market economy.

The labour force which averaged 68,000 in 1898 reached a figure of over 370,000 in 1942 [18]. Whereas, said the Lansdown Report, the Native in the Reserves, either on account of higher productivity of his lands or because of his simpler tastes, was reluctant to leave his home, he is today forced by economic pressure to seek employment which will enable him to support his wife and family, and this pressure is so great that the goldmining industry is able, in spite of the competition due to increased demands of secondary industries, to recruit native labour for underground work at a cash wage of 2s. per shift [19].

The cash wages of African mineworkers in 1943 are reflected in the table on page 341 from the Lansdown Report[20]. Apart from a small number of long-service and supervisory workers, the mean cash remuneration was 2s. to 2s. 3d. per shift with 300 shifts per year. This gave annual cash earnings of between £26 15s. 6d. to £30 12s. od.

Although the Low Grade Mines Commission of 1920 had reported that the 'maximum average' clause, condemned by the 1914 Native Grievances Enquiry Commission, had been amended so as not to be 'open to the same serious objection as previously', the Lansdown Commission of 1944 found that in fact the maximum average or ceiling to earnings – originally applied to piece-workers – was now general over the average earnings of all African labourers [21].

Distribution of Wage Rates over Native Labour Force – 1943

		Surface	Under-ground	Total
Numbers earning less than 1/9d a shift		4,658	—	4,658
„	1/9 to 1/11d	30,360	—	30,060
„	2/0	17,488	107,690	125,178
„	2/0 to 2/3	7,993	61,648	69,641
„	2/4 to 2/6	5,742	26,247	32,169
„	2/7 to 2/9	1,922	12,026	13,948
„	2/10 to 3/0	1,562	5,741	7,303
„	3/1 to 4/0	2,003	6,541	8,544
„	4/1 to 6/0	1,402	5,258	6,660
„	6/0 and over	135	1,181	1,316
		73,265	226,512	299,777

The maximum average, fixed up to the end of 1942 at 2s. 3d. was increased to 2s. 3¾d. per shift in 1943. In addition to cash earnings, the remuneration in kind coming under (i) rations (ii) quarters and (iii) medical treatment was valued by the Lansdown Commission at 1s. 1·4d. per worker per shift.

The case for the African mineworkers was that there had been no significant increases in wages in the course of thirty years since 1914, despite an increased cost of living including the increased costs of their families in the tribal Reserves and the decreased income from the lands on the Reserves. The case against any increase in wages made by the Chamber of Mines was the adequacy of the existing cash wage, having regard to remuneration in kind, the additional means of subsistence available from the migratory labourer's Reserve-income, the cost-price structure of the industry at a time when inflation was steadily encroaching on marginality of ore.

Significantly, reported the Lansdown Commission, 'the Chamber of Mines has based its case very largely on the argument that, in fixing the wages of the mine labourers and in determining whether the wages so fixed are adequate, it is entitled to take cognizance of the full subsistence which a native is able to obtain from his holding in the Reserve' [22]. The Chamber of Mines contended that the average stay of the tribal migrant worker at his home in the Reserves was something over twelve months with fourteen-month contract working-periods at the mines. The Commission found the average Reserve home-living to be between seven to eight months, and in the case of perhaps 16 per cent of the labour force three months or less.

The Commission put the value of the Reserve income (1943) at £17 15s. 2d. per year, cash earnings for the mine surface worker at £26 15s. 6d. per year and for the underground worker at £30 12s. od. per year against a family budget for a tribal family of five (with man at work) of £57 12s. od. per year. Based on an 18-month mine-work and 6-month Reserve-home period, a surface worker's estimated needs exceeded his income by £34 1s. 2d. and an underground worker's by £32 11s. 11d. for a two-year period [23].

The evidence for the Arthur Lewis argument that wage-payments by the capitalist sector will be a function of subsistence in the tribal economy is underlined by the statement of the Chamber of Mines to the Mine Native Wages Commission:

The basis of employment of native labour by the mines is in complete accord with the balanced South African native policy laid down practically unani-mously by Parliament after thorough investigation and discussion in 1936–7, and embodied in legislation (in particular the Native Trust and Land Act, 1936, and the 1937 amendment to the Urban areas Act) and re-affirmed by the Minister of Native Affairs in the House of Assembly on February 26, 1943. In brief, that policy is the enlargement and planned development and improvement of the Native Reserves and the concurrent restriction on the number of natives permitted in the towns, coupled with the proper housing of those so permitted. It aims at the preservation of the economic and social structure of the native people in native areas where that structure can be sheltered and developed. The policy is a coherent whole, and is the anti-thesis of the policy of assimilation and encouragement of a black proletariat in the towns, divorced from its tribal heritage.

The ability of the mines to maintain their native labour force by means of tribal natives from the Reserves at rates of pay, which are adequate for this migratory class of labour but inadequate in practice for the detribalized urban native is a fundamental factor in the economy of the Gold Mining Industry[24].

The implications, commented the Commission, of the Chamber's interpretation of South African Government land-labour policy were, firstly, that the Native Reserves should be kept at just such a stage as not to prevent tribal Africans from seeking employment because they had too much land or the land was too productive and, secondly, that if the Reserves could afford the African family an extra subsistence then the mining industry would be justified in reducing the African worker's wage still further.

It was the further submission of the Chamber of Mines which established the extent to which political rationalization had replaced economic rationality. The Chamber did not raise before the Lansdown Commission any reference to legal or customary restrictions on the employment categories of Africans, the critical issue of least-cost labour utilization or the 'colour bar', which had led to the 1922 Strike [25]. But the Chamber's representative. Mr W. Gemmill, took up and answered the argument that the position of the tribal African 'in enjoyment of Reserve subsistence income from his lands' was similar to that of a White worker with a private income and that the wages of both should be determined without reference to their 'reserves' – that is, by market competition:

This argument ignores the fact that the ability of the native to earn a Reserve's income is largely due to the fact that he is granted by the Union Government land to cultivate, and pasturage, with practically free occupation of both; in effect he receives in this way a substantial subsidy from the Government which enables him to come out to work in the intermittent fashion which suits him and which accords with his historic background and tribal circumstances. The subsidization of the tribal native by way of free land is a basic factor in the economy of the Union and in any estimate of the economic requirements of that class of native, and I submit that it comes into account under the Commission's terms of reference as a provision made apart from wages materially related to the tribal needs of the native[26].

This assertion by the spokesman of the goldmining industry, perhaps as much as any other obiter dicta ever expressed by 'White South Africa', establishes the inter-connections between land and labour in South African economic history and the crucial significance of such land-labour inter-connections to the economic development of South Africa. It also establishes the continuing reality of White control of the social system as a political economy.

Though the Commission made no specific comment on the historical accuracy of this version of land-distribution as between the Whites and the Africans, its own estimate of the Reserve annual income of a tribal family was, in 1943, between £16 18s. 6d. and £17 7s. 8d. against the £30 estimate of the Native Affairs Commission and submitted by the Chamber of Mines. The Lansdown Commission's final recommendation was a minimum wage for surface workers of 2s. 2d. per shift and for underground workers of 2s. 5d.

per shift, yielding a cash income of £36 19s. 6d. and £42 6s. 7d. respectively [27].

But the emphatic conclusion of the Commission was that the migratory labour system could not be replaced by a permanent body of unskilled labour – 'any other policy would bring about a catastrophic dislocation of the industry and consequent prejudice to the whole economic structure of the Union . . .'

Economic theory and empirical evidence seem, then, to demonstrate beyond denial that, firstly, the economic development of South Africa was above and beyond all else a function of the profitability of goldmining investment, and, secondly, that such profitability was a function of the migratory labour system applied to unskilled, tribal African labour.

If the first point is conceded to economic theory and empirical evidence, is the second point equally unchallengeable?

It is unchallengeable only on two assumptions of political realities of power. The first assumption is that White mining workers, supported by the White polity, would always impose their colour bar differentials on labour-utilization and -substitution in the mining industry (i.e. an unalterable political parameter in the production function of goldmining in South Africa). The second assumption is that the White polity would never accept that employers of mine labour (individual mine managements even more than the employer-organization of the Chamber of Mines) be allowed to bid competitively for unskilled labour beyond the territorial limits of South Africa.

Had the goldmining industry been permitted to 'import' its unskilled labour, without political restraints, from the whole geographical area of Southern and Central Africa i.e. the territory of which the goldmines of the Witwatersrand was the economic heart, then it is possible that the market-wages of such labour would not in fact have significantly diverged from the monoposonistic-wage established. It is arguable that the monopsonistic-labour policy was 'forced' on the Chamber of Mines because the several mining companies were not free (a) to attract labour from all possible 'natural' sources of supply and (b) to train Africans to higher productivity because of the rigidities of colour-bar work-organization.

Not only did the diamond- and gold-mining industries greatly stimulate the whole scale of autonomous and subsequent induced capital investment, first within and then without mining, but they inspired and then accomplished the transformation of a hitherto subsistence economy into a market or exchange economy for South Africa. This essential condition [28] for economic development beyond a primitive level emerged with the resource-exploitation by capital and by technology of mineral wealth. But the political factor resisted and restrained the shifts and specialization of the population, which are the essence of a market or exchange economy.

Afrikanerdom had, as previously elaborated, always identified itself with the land. Its cultural no less than its political roots, its spiritual no less than its material strength, were at least down until after the Second World War emotively linked to farming as the 'only' way of life. When excessively optimistic expectations of agricultural exports were repeatedly disappointed by world market realities, except in war-time demand schedules, parliamentary power was more and more deployed to extend the authority of the administered economy to maintain Afrikaners on the land rather than accept the mobilities of the market economy.

The philosophy and practice of administered marketing by the official Department of Agriculture, culminating in the Marketing Act of 1937, conceived the maintenance of White numbers on the land as an end in itself. It was held to justify, apart from the subsidized transportation in the form of below marginal-cost railway rates, a state expenditure of £25,000,000 in the ten years from 1931/32 to 1940/41 in direct financial assistance to White farmers and price-raising measures to consumers, estimated at an excess consumer-cost of over £6½ millions in respect of sugar, wheat, maize, butter and cheese and leaf tobacco for the year 1939–40. Furthermore, the massive state-aid was primarily for labour-intensive agriculture rather than livestock farming.

At the outset of the Second World War in 1940, hence, the Van Eck Commission claimed that, taking into account casual farm labour and Non-White farming, almost two-thirds of the South African population engaged in farming was producing only one-eighth of the national income. Even if some 1,750,000 Africans over the age of 10 in the Native Reserves and about 750,000 Non-Whites undertaking casual farm labour were assumed not to share in the farming income, one-third of the remainder of the South African population permanently on the land were producing only one-eighth of the national income.

Despite the extensive drift to the towns, the residential population permanently dependent upon farming and the number of casual farm labourers are, therefore, far in excess of the proportion warranted by the unimpressive contribution of this industry to the national income. This feature of the occupational distribution of the Union's population is indicative of a major maladjustment in the economic structure[29].

Within the mining industry and within the farming industry, the productivity of the great majority of the country's African population was massively inhibited by the actions of the White polity. Such inhibitions on specialization were intensified by the Native Land Acts which by their barriers to additional land-ownership among Africans and prohibition of private (White)investment capital in the Native Reserves, aggravated the diminishing returns of self-subsistent tribal agriculture.

Given that the absolute priority of the White polity was to ensure that economic development did not 'undermine the White man's supremacy', i.e. alter White-Black relationships advantageously to the politico-social status of the Non-Whites and disadvantageously to the politico-social status of the Whites by narrowing the economic differentials, a low-level trap of under-consumption and massive disguised unemployment could not readily be evaded. There was an absolute political bar or institutional barrier on the development of the country's resources of its Non-White peoples within mining and agriculture.

With such far-reaching rigidities imposed on four-fifths of the South African labour force, the aggregate demand of the Non-White peoples was institutionally inhibited with increasing restraints from the time of Union – from when the White polity took charge of a unified economy to promote a rate of economic development 'to guarantee White civilization in South Africa'. Dominant economic philosophy and policy in South Africa was, until the Second World War, not only pre-Keynesian but held fast in the lump-of-labour conviction. The short-term existence of a work-fund, in which every Non-White employed was one job less for a White unemployed, gained in the appearance of reality because the key income determinants of full employment were so obstructed from exerting the reality of their appearance in the long-run.

A fundamental, and increasingly ideological, master-servant viewpoint of contact-relationships between White master and Black servant, imposed critically limiting conditions on the production function. Nowhere were such conditions more critical and more limiting than on the production function of goldmining, which South African academic economists almost without exception identified as the key determinant of the country's overall level of activity. It was indeed beyond question that gold-mining as the main source of capital investment and wage-payments, as well as being the major producer of exports and foreign-exchange earnings, made a contribution to the quantum of employment so strategically important that any policy diminishing the profitability of gold-mining seemed logically indefensible.

Yet, despite the secular increases in the gold price which 'uncovered' more and more unprofitable earth to transform it into profitable ore, goldmining was and is an 'extraction' industry. It was and is for South Africans an industry that must 'exhaust' itself, so that the day comes when it makes a diminishing and ultimately nil contribution to income and income-generation. Hence opinion remained concerned with promoting alternative sources of income and income-generation.

The comparative costs argument of the benefits from international trade seemed most undeniable in the case of a country like South Africa, whose economic emergence from stagnation is so patently identifiable with mineral discoveries and whose drive towards economic maturity is also so readily related to the increasing rate [30] of mineral-resource discovery.

The facts of South African economic growth appeared so self-evident that continuous political pressure and industrialists' agitation for the tariff protection of so-called secondary or manufacturing industry seemed the most obviously unjustifiable and unjustified arguments of self-interest. The classical case for free trade has rarely seemed to be more irresistibly demonstrated than in the history of South African economic development. The comparative advantages of resource-investment in the gold mines made it undeniably the country's primary industry, which made any diversionary investments – that increased mining costs unnecessarily or artificially – subtractions from gross national product.

Yet were the 'practical' manufacturers, who argued their case for the tariff protection of their struggling factories against foreign competition, so demonstrably wrong? Their self-interest in opposing free trade hardly needs refutation – but the self-interest of the Chamber of Mines in supporting free trade also needs no demonstration.

347

Myrdal[31] has been most critical of the classical international trade theory to explain the realities of economic development and under-development. His theory of circular causation, more especially related to White prejudice and low Negro standards in his *American Dilemma*, argues that the cumulative process of interaction will cause any change in one factor to be continuously supported by the reaction of the other factor in a circular way.

As applied to regional economic development, the cumulative process of interaction might result in a continuous improvement in the measures of development (i.e. output per head or standards of living) in the entire region or it might reproduce the vicious circle of disparate stagnation. While assumptions of perfect mobility of resources (implicit to classical international trade theory) would ensure that the gains of growth from a widening division of labour in extending markets are diffused throughout, there are unquestioned awkward historical realities of population shifts, capital movements and trade which have operated 'with a fundamental bias in favour of the richer and progressive regions against the other regions' [32].

In South African experience, too, for nearly half-a-century after the proclamation of the Witwatersrand goldfields, the continuation if not aggravation of poverty among the Poor Whites and the Poor Blacks in rural South Africa alongside the advancing prosperity of the goldmining regions affords confirmation of Myrdal's general thesis. Persistence of regional and sectoral underdevelopment outside the goldmining industry for decade after decade may indeed have been due more to non-economic inhibitions on social and geographical mobility rather than to defective arguments in the comparative costs theory of inter-regional economic activity.

The under-consumption and under-employment trap was, however, a reality of South African life. The political factor of Afrikaner-dom was dedicated to breaking out of the vicious circle on behalf of the 'boerevolk' (i.e. the 'original' Afrikaans-speaking inhabit-ants of the land) and it was not to be convinced by any economic analysis of the spread-effects of goldmining prosperity. The Nation-alist Party was increasingly won over to support of State interven-tionism – the more so since it identified itself with the State and the State exclusively with the Volksparty.

Forced industrialization, whether by way of tariff protection for manufacturing industry or by direct and indirect state ownership of 'key' industries, was to be the solution for the Afrikaner rural poor. In its pre-1939 phase, the concern of the polity was exclusively with the Poor Whites and not the Poor Blacks. The widening opportunities of industrial employment were to be reserved for 'civilized labour'. Partly because of this policy with its related high-cost inflexibilities but perhaps even more because of the barriers, economic and non-economic, to the realization of the 'external economies' of large-scale industrialization in South Africa, pre-1939 state encouragement of manufacturing industry could not realistically be said to have either diversified the South African economy or achieved a self-sustaining, dynamic stage of industrial growth.

This whole pre-1939 phase of 'forced' industrialization was, as related in an earlier chapter, only incidentally a contribution to increased mobility of resources. The almost religious fervour, with which Afrikaner-identification with the land was regarded as the source of its spiritual strength and the related conviction that 'civilized labour' in urban employment was the preserve of White men and women, imposed inflexibilities which when weighed in the balance against the mobilities induced by industrialization may or may not have produced a shift.

The Second World War contributed the 'Big Push' [33], both in technical economic development and in social system change. The record of industrialization in South Africa from 1940 strikingly confirms the indivisibilities-arguments of Rosenstein-Rodan [34]. The virtual guarantee of the home market, through diminution and ultimate disappearance of foreign competitive supplies, provided the critical assurance of demand. The elimination of uncertainty in investment-decisions in domestic-manufacturing was further underwritten by the general use of cost-plus contracts in mounting government purchases and price-control legislation which permitted increased costs to be passed on.

With only brief interruptions, during which industrial investments altered, this elimination of uncertainty in market-absorption of output has exhilarated industrial investment from 1940 onwards in South Africa. It has probably been the crucial condition for the excessive but not grossly exaggerated assertion that 'in no other country has there, within the brief compass of 25 years, been a more complete metamorphosis of the economy and a more spectacular development of its industries, with such an absence of industrial disturbance by way of labour strikes, than in South Africa' [35].

The Second World War years not only removed all risk-taking from consumer-goods manufacture but, perhaps even more importantly, removed the market-risks in the more technologically-advanced-goods manufacture. This was especially the case for the strategically-significant metal-industries. Until 1939 the goldmining companies, despite their large and continuously increasing consumption of metals-engineering, gave no encouragement to the domestic metals-engineering industry. Engineering was almost entirely a service-and-repair industry but with the outbreak of the War, and almost total deprivation of imported supplies, the mining industry and munitions-manufacture assured the demand for specialized metals-manufactures of continuing diversification and sophistication.

The end of the War in a world starved of peace-time metal-goods brought no resumption of imports of competitive significance. The introduction and operation of exchange-import control from 1948 contemporaneously with the massive development stage of the great Free State goldfield, in a capital-concentration expenditure programme unique in mining investment, ensured a text-book example of risk-eliminating complementarity of demand. A sustained investment programme in the sophistication of capital-intensive engineering plants was consequentially undertaken by private entrepreneurship. The scale of this investment by private initiative was of the strategic lump-sum magnitude, which some economic-development models would attribute only to the potentialities of government-enterprise and state-financing.

It not only made a related contribution to gross national income but accomplished the critical changes in inputs-outputs within the engineering industry, which may be regarded as the restructuring of the economy in the key phase of the drive towards maturity. In the pre-1939 period this industry was largely restricted to jobbing shops, serving as adjuncts to the gold mines. During the Second World War, the complete dependence of the mines on locally made and repaired plant and equipment began the transformation, which after the introduction of import-exchange controls in 1948 might be described as a minor revolution in development.

In 1943, the total number of workers in the metal industries (steel, engineering, constructional and consumer-goods) had risen to 70,000 with a total wage bill of R29,000,000. Twenty years later, in 1963, this had become 225,000 workers with a wage-salary bill of R250,000,000 and a gross output of R950,000,000. The metal industries currently comprise raw materials manufacture: ferrous (iron and steel), and non-ferrous (copper, brass, zinc, aluminium); heavy engineering; constructional engineering; foundry industry; electrical and electronics, heavy and light; light engineering; light fabricating and consumer goods.

Heavy engineering by 1965 had reached the stage where, apart from turbines and specialized machine tools of limited demand, it was able to undertake the manufacture of almost every type of plant and machinery. Electric locomotives are a current manufacture. The constructional engineering industry meets South African needs from power stations to mining plants. Railway wagons and coaching stock for the SAR Administration are entirely locally produced, and small ocean-going craft are fabricated. The foundry industry, iron, steel, and non-ferrous, produces general castings up to twenty tons. Rolling-stock wheels and all the heavy castings necessary to rolling stock and locomotives are locally made. At the other end of the range, components and consumer goods, plumbers' requisites and all cast articles suited to production methods are regularly made.

Light engineering products range from rock-drills to automotive components, brass-ware to small-tool manufacture; on the fabricating side a wide range from agricultural implements to steel windows.

In the quarter-century since the outbreak of the Second World War, the backward linkage from consumer-goods manufacture progressed steadily. Basic and intermediate material processing industries were established in range and depth so that industrial development has achieved the growth stage of supplying inter-industry demand. Iscor, the publicly-controlled iron and steel industry, in 1938 was producing at a rate of 344, 300 tons of ingot steel a year. By the end of the War in 1945 a production figure of 503,000 ingot tons was established. In 1946 a second fully-integrated steel works was planned and by 1951, Iscor's two works had a capacity of 1 million ingot tons. The continuously rising demand for steel products led in 1956 to a further expansion project with a target of 2,350,000 ingot tons and, before its completion, in 1960 yet another increase was planned – the largest expansion scheme in Iscor's history at an estimated cost of R506,000,000. The envisaged goal for 1969/70 is 4·5 million ingot tons.

The gross value of the output of South Africa's metal and engineering sector for the calendar year 1965 was estimated at about R1,550,000,000. Although in the case of many industrially underdeveloped countries the textile industry begins at an early stage, South African experience was different. The make-up end or clothing manufacture was one of the first consumer-goods industries to be given tariff protection in the 1925 customs tariff – mainly because it was labour-intensive and at that time the employment of 'civilized labour' was the *quid pro quo* for the protective duties on imports. As clothing manufacture – including army clothing – greatly increased in the period of the Second World War and subsequent years, the cost of textile imports rose to a volume and value which was one of the immediate bills responsible for the introduction of import-exchange controls in 1948.

In addition to the aim of reducing the import-bill for textiles by encouragement of local manufacture, a major post-1948 expansion of a South African textile industry became a key instrument of the new Nationalist Government's race relations policy. It was seen as the most suitable for mass-employment of Africans with mills located in proximity to the Native Reserves or Bantu homelands or Bantustans, as these areas came to be named in accordance with changing semantic fashion, and perhaps constitutional significance.

The policy of partial state financing and decentralization of the textile industry as a growth-industry for African employment was in point of time introduced by the United Party Government, which preceded the Nationalist Party victory of 1948. As a state industrial banker, the Industrial Development Corporation was in fact the brain-child of General Smuts. Established by the Industrial Development Act of 1940, the IDC has from the beginning taken a major initiating role in textile manufacturing in South Africa. The War resulted in a vast stock-accumulation of grease wool awaiting shipping space, while urgent large-scale demands for South African army blankets required related material-supplies of scoured and mixed wool. The first IDC-financed and -managed venture was in wool scouring and mixing. Subsequently in technical and financial partnership with British firms, a cotton spinning and doubling plant was shipped out, worsted manufacture was begun at Fine Wool Products in Uitenhage in the Eastern Cape and South Africa's first integrated spinning, weaving and finishing mill for cotton fabrics was started at Kingwilliamstown also in the Eastern Cape.

Apart from such state-financing, textile development was encouraged by an import-substitution policy progressively programmed to increase the domestic manufactured share of a rapidly expanding market. Whereas in 1939, a few wool processors, blanket makers and underwear-hosiery knitting mills represented the oddments of this industry of bewildering specialization, range and variety of product, by the middle of the 1950's the industry was making medium-price, mass production lines of increasing range and moving into double jersey cloth, nylon hosiery, stretch nylon stocks, warp knitted fabrics. By the early 1960's, the industry was producing plain fabrics and spreading into the specialities of fancy cloths for the makers-up in the clothing industry. In the mid-sixties, expansion was proceeding both in increasing capacity of medium-price piece-goods and higher-price quality ranges.

Backward linkage has resulted in mills for industrial textiles for tyre manufacture, a nylon spinning plant, plans for polyester yarns and a rayon fabrics mill. From 1940 when the share of the domestic mills of the domestic market was less than 5 per cent, this share is currently in the mid-sixties estimated at 45 per cent of market demand. Domestic textile production in the mid-sixties has a gross output of R180 millions but, significantly, the concurrent textile import bill remains at the high figure of R150 millions.

The textile industry illustrates many of the possibilities and problems of the varying strategies for promoting development. State finance has been effectively used for large-scale, capital-intensive plants. Apart from such a source of finance capital, foreign expertise and capital has been encouraged to participate in joint-owned enterprises by the foreknowledge that the IDC-equity interest and personal contacts of IDC directors with the Cabinet and civil servants of key influence could underwrite appropriate import-protection as required. But effective protection to promote import-substitution is complicated in the case of textiles by the almost limitless product-substitutability.

Tariff categories and definitions for protective duties of specific items of domestic manufacture are easily evaded by modifications of specifications through collaboration between foreign exporter and domestic importer to evade the categories and definitions, and thereby escape duty. In consequence, tariff protection is progressively extended by ever more comprehensive category-definitions which then include whole ranges of textiles not locally manufactured at all.

Expanded protection for the intermediate or materials-supply industry clearly increases costs in the finishing industry. In consequence, rising costs of clothing manufacture in South Africa either make imported clothing more price-competitive or compel higher tariff duties on imported clothing. Both alternatives tend to raise clothing prices with a tendency to curtail demand for clothing, and in consequence for the textile materials-supplies from domestic mills. It has been established that clothing demand shows a significant degree of income elasticity, becoming more marked at the low-income categories. A study of African household expenditure shows that the percentage of income spent on clothing rises from $5\frac{1}{2}$ per cent for the lowest income group to 12 per cent for the highest income group. The textile industry is a growth industry in that real consumption *per capita* rises with a growing proportion of the increase in national income accuring to Non-Whites. But expansion of textile manufacturing may be checked by higher clothing prices.

The underdeveloped economy gives substance to Say's Law in that production does create its own demand. Among the Africans (moving out of marginal, nil or negative productivity in their diminishing-return peasant, pastoral and agricultural lands – subject to legal prohibition on their enlargement – into industrial employment in, for instance, textile mills) greater capacity to produce provides its own greater capacity to buy. Greater capacity to buy clothing provides the demand for increased supplies of textiles, and also growing employment potential for Africans in textile mills. The development strategy should work but its effectiveness may be inhibited by higher-priced clothing consequent on higher-cost textile-supplies.

The problem can be illustrated from contemporary experience of the newest Industrial Development Corporation venture. Shirt manufacture was one of the earliest sections of clothing manufacture to be started in South Africa and, following moderate tariff protection, the shirt-making factories greatly expanded to ensure one hundred per cent capacity for the domestic market – a market steadily expanding with the growing demand from African males entering wage-employment in industry generally. Imports of shirting-poplins grew in step until the Board of Trade and Industries in its import-substitution studies clearly identified domestic shirting-poplin manufacture as 'particularly promising'.

The Nationalist Government also saw the establishment of a

poplin-producing mill as the demonstrative example of a border-area industrial policy, which would provide Africans with employment-opportunities adjacent to their tribal lands instead of in the 'White' cities. The special inducements devised for border-area factories together with IDC capital participation persuaded a well-known British Lancashire cotton-textile industrialist (conveniently the recipient of the British Government's benefit-payments for elimination of excess, out-dated mill capacity in Lancashire) to 'ship' his poplin mill to a site near East London. This site, although within twelve miles of the 'White' city of East London, was nonetheless designated as qualifying for the benefits of border-area decentralization in accordance with the canons of Apartheid.

Anticipating the imposition of tariffs on their poplin-shirtings, the shirt-manufacturers stockpiled great yardages of imported poplins. This in turn resulted in financial difficulties for the under-capacity operations of the new poplin mill. Furthermore intense opposition to a scheme of specially-exclusive protection (by way of rebates) to this particular IDC poplin mill from other potential poplin manufacturers (with existing vast interests in the textile industry and also supporters of decentralized, border-area Government policy but in other border areas) created embarrassment. The requisite protection on poplin-shirtings, to safeguard both the IDC investment in the new mill and the prestige-showplace of Government border-area industrial policy in race relations, will assuredly be forthcoming. Nonetheless shirt manufacturers forsee that high-cost poplins will mean higher-priced shirts (or increased non-poplin shirts) for their customers among the Africans.

Despite some of the complexities and niceties of such forced industrialization, the facts of achievement are impressive and not readily denied. There has been a significant structural change in the South African economy in the last twenty-five years, when an increasing share of the domestic market has been secured to domestic manufacturers as a deliberate objective of state policy. The instruments employed – ranging from tariff-duty protection at higher rates, advance guarantees of tariff protection to induce large-scale, otherwise high-risk investments, import-controls to compel foreign manufacturer-exporters to franchise or participate in South African plants, state finance and other inducement-aids for strategic, import-substitution, heavily-capitalized enterprises – have helped industrialize the country.

There has been a sophistication of South African manufacturing industry. Consumer-goods manufacture has grown in categories and capacity to the point where more than ninety per cent of counter-goods bought and sold in the mass-price multiple stores are 'Made in South Africa'. Oil refining, where foreign capital and advanced technology are the critical inputs, has in 1966 a total fuel products output of about 5,000,000 a day – virtually the total demand for the country's petroleum fuels. The state-financed South African Coal, Oil and Gas Corporation Ltd or Sasol [36] produces oil-from-coal and, together with other private enterprise projects, has enabled a substantial petro-chemical industry to be brought into being. All the major activities in the petrochemical field – fertilizers and detergents, surface coatings and solvents, and the sector of the high polymers, including plastics and resin, synthetic fibres and synthetic rubber – are actually or prospectively under way [37].

The transformation of the institutional and structural framework of a dormant economy, as noted at the beginning of this chapter, was launched by and through the goldmining industry. It was revolutionized by and through manufacturing industry. This seems a fair claim to make for the policy of forced industrialization. What of capital formation – that other fundamental vitalizing instrument for economic development?

The manner in which foreign capital was attracted to exploit the mineral discoveries has already been related, and also the extent to which re-investment of profits and development-finance through the mining-finance group system ensured that lack of capital was only a temporary obstacle. One of the objections raised against the 'artificial stimulation' of manufacturing industry was that not only would it mean increased costs and reduced profitability in gold-mining – thereby inhibiting it as a source of capital formation, but that it would 'divert' scarce capital away from mineral exploitation to industrial development.

But it is doubtful, certainly in South African experience, whether capital is or has been so non-specific and so mobile as the 'diversion' argument implies. Much of mining capital came from a specialist class of investor-speculators, who were not at that historical stage interested in supplying capital for manufacturing industry. By the reverse token, manufacturing-industrialists were much more disposed to invest accumulated capital from their own earlier manufacturing activities in expansion and diversification of manufacturing rather than mining ventures.

In respect of South African manufacturing or so-called secondary industries, the initial smallness of the market-demand could not be overcome so long as the polity's mystical, traditional and legally entrenched land-labour policies imposed an unmovable immobility on the great mass of the population, the Non-Whites. The enlargement of the market through the rise in productivity which, as discussed by Ragnar Nurske in his *Problems of Capital Formation in Underdeveloped Countries* [38], would result from increased capital-intensity of production, was inhibited by the imposed smallness of the market down until the outbreak of the Second World War. The War not only reduced immobilities by the *de facto* breaches in the colour bar in employment and in the contrived scarcities of work-categories, it also ensured Nurske's key consideration 'that composition of the increased consumable output should correspond to the pattern of consumers' demands' [39].

Not only did Say's Law work but Alfred Marshall's external economies took on the wider significance of an enlargement of the total size of the market, following a wave of simultaneous investments in a whole range of complementary industries 'to break the bonds of the stationary equilibrium' [40]. Until the war-time expansion of manufacturing industry following on the erosion of the colour bar on employment, and the consequent increased geographical and social mobility of the Non-Whites generally and the Africans particularly, very little capital formation took place within manufacturing industry itself. But from then on, even many small under-capitalized manufacturers attained rates of profitability which served as a source of re-invested capital. Non-distribution of profits was encouraged by the operation of the excess profits duty, while the war-time non-availability of consumer-durables did not facilitate conspicuous expenditure by the *nouveau riche* among industrialists and farmers.

Inflationary gains and earnings were channeled into the flood of new industrial equities, beginning as a trickle in 1940 but continuing as a wave from 1945. Institutional finance – especially the insurance companies easily selling millions of new policies in an inflationary situation – became a large source of capital formation, more readily available perhaps to the public sector and for housing-mortgages than to the private sector of industrial enterprise.

Import-exchange control after 1948 and a conscious, concentrated programme of import-substitution after the 1961 declaration of the Republic (and increased United Nations threats of boycotts) significantly promoted a flow of foreign capital. Where such capital was forthcoming from foreign companies to enlarge or establish South African factories to make within the domestic market what had hitherto been exported by such foreign firms, the capital was available only for the very specific purpose of such manufacturing activity. It was not capital available for investment in mining or other alternatives – in that respect it was not a diversion of capital. Much industrial capital is available for industrial enterprises only and a policy of protection of 'forced industrialization' does not necessarily or merely divert scarce capital from higher marginal returns in, say, mining.

The psychological effect of inflation on the investment climate is to stimulate the so-called cult of the equity. A growing volume of investment funds, both from institutional sources and a widening number of private savers of middle-incomes, is readily available for public company ordinary shares. The 'reverse-yield gap' between government-gilt-edge stocks and ordinary shares also encourages public flotation of private companies, while the characteristic Johannesburg share market periods of speculative excitement that favoured capital-raising for the mining industry spread from 1945 into industrial shares. The table below is self-explanatory and reveals the extent of public interest in industrialization.

Data Relating to Company Capital – J'burg Share Market

	Mining Cos. No. (I)	Non-mining Cos. No. (II)	Total Market Value (I) Rm.	Total Market Value (II) Rm.
Sept. 1939	142	93	450	338
Sept. 1945	124	172	972	754
Sept. 1950	158	459	1,484	1,362
Sept. 1955	144	544	2,056	1,712
Sept. 1960	146	511	2,262	1,810
Mar. 1965	131	521	3,664	5,399
Sept. 1965	130	525	3,531	5,038

Profit retention as a source of capital formation has already been noted, more especially in relation to mining investment. A study [41] of a sample of quoted industrial and commercial companies for a nine-year period showed, on the average, a re-investment of 38·4 per cent of profits after providing for taxation. This sample of companies from 1 January 1949 to 30 September 1953 raised some £63 millions of capital by public subscription and during the same period, some £76 millions of new money through profit retentions. Another sample of 128 companies in the Industrial List of the Johannesburg Stock Exchange showed that, between 1946 to 1953, their aggregate net worth increased from £97·7 millions to £210·2 millions – of the increase of £112·5 millions, £55·6 millions resulted from profit re-investment – being almost equal to newly subscribed capital to the growth in the aggregate net worth [42]. Ignoring the immediate post-war boom years which facilitated new subscription capital, the same sample of companies from 1949 to 1953 showed that profit plough-back contributed almost twice as much as new capital from shareholders [43].

The general conclusion is that by 1949 (when the return to power of the Nationalist Government and other factors ended for a period the post-war boom) industrialization was sufficiently mature to generate an important volume of self-financing for capital formation and consequent continued growth.

The strategic variable of capital formation for economic development was also examined by the Viljoen Commission on Policy Relating to the Protection of Industry of 1958. It reported that one of the outstanding features of South Africa's post-1948 economic development had been the high rate of capital formation. It found that for the period 1946 to 1957, total gross domestic capital formation amounted to about £4,319 million, representing about 26 per cent of Gross National Product of the related period. Allowing for price changes, the value of gross capital formation increased by about 54 per cent between 1946 and 1957 [44].

Gross Saving and Capital Formation in South Africa – £ Millions

	1946–9 ave.	1950–3 ave.	1954	1955	1956
Gross domestic capital formation-investment (I)	242	352	485	504	479
Gross domestic saving (II)	113	285	440	453	464
(II) as %age of (I)	46·7%	81·0%	90·7%	89·9%	96·9%
Net foreign borrowing* (III)	129	67	45	51	15
(III) as %age of (I)	53·3%	19·0%	9·3%	10·1%	3·1%

(*Net foreign borrowing incl. realization gold and foreign exchange)

359

The Viljoen Commission Report noted a calculation of the South African Reserve Bank in respect of capital-output ratios that to maintain an increase of between 2 per cent to 3 per cent per annum (as at circa 1957) in *per capita* income, about one-quarter of the Gross National Product would have to be devoted to gross capital formation. The Viljoen Commission itself concluded that from about 1918 to 1958, the capital-output ratio had shown a consistent downward tendency and, if this trend persisted, then a declining percentage of income would have to be devoted to capital formation to achieve the same overall result. The Viljoen Commission believed that the main factors in this decline of the capital-output ratio were that the public sector had a relatively high capital-output ratio (for example, the South African Railways) but that the proportion of public sector to total was perhaps declining, while within the public sector, again for example the South African Railways, the ratio was declining.

The Commission also made very rough calculations of capital output ratios in respect of agriculture (3), mining (2) and private manufacturing ($1\frac{3}{4}$), and concluded that with the growing shift towards manufacturing, the overall capital output ratio would fall[46]. It may be questioned whether much reliance may be placed on such estimates of capital-output ratios derived from basic data of doubtful accuracy. Still less weight can be given to future projections in the light of continuing technological change.

It is claimed that (White) South Africans have from 1945 shown a high propensity to save, encouraged by a well-developed system of financial institutions. The table below gives informative data on the growth of total assets of certain of these institutions[47].

A: Growth of total Assets of Certain Financial and Savings Institutions (Rand millions)

PRIVATE SECTOR	1945	1950	1955	1960	1965*
1. Commercial Banks	668	810	1035	1299	2116
2. Building Societies	241	472	817	1266	1900
3. Deposit-receiving Institutions	40	61	92	253	758
4. Insurance cos. – long/short term	265	406	636	978	1562
5. Pension funds	—	—	228	511	1017
	1214	1749	2808	4267	7353

	1945	1950	1955	1960	1965
PUBLIC SECTOR					
6. Land-Agricultural Bank	54	95	177	295	354
7. Post Office Savings Bank	145	161	172	150	136
8. National Savings Certificates	71	46	34	60	111
	270	302	383	505	601
	1484	2051	3191	4772	7954
B: Net National Income	1227	1866	3025	4060	6170
C: 1. Gross Domestic Capital Formation	406	554	980	1134	1710
2. Personal Saving (Ave. – 5 year)	—	76	236	303	495
D: Indices (1955 = 100)					
1. Growth of Assets of Private Sector	43	62	100	152	262
2. Growth of Assets of Public Sector	70	79	100	132	157
3. Net National Income	41	62	100	134	204
4. Gross Domestic Capital Formation	41	56	100	116	174
5. Personal Savings	—	32	100	128	210

*1965 figures estimates throughout

Interpretation of the table above should take into account that in some instances investment by one institution in another inflates the figures in some instances; not all investment institutions, such as the mining houses and the money-market in the narrow sense, are included. Over the twenty-year period, 1945–65, the total increase in the funds of the 'private sector' and the 'public sector' was from R1,484 millions to R7,954 millions, or over 400 per cent, which is an impressive growth rate.

Small-savings for non-risk investment are mainly reflected in the figures for the building societies, life assurance societies, pension funds and certain deposit-receiving institutions. In 1955 the combined funds of such 'institutional finance' (excluding short-term business of the insurance companies) amounted to R1,707 millions or 53 per cent of the grand total of R3,191 millions for all institutions;

in 1965 the related figure for 'institutional finance' was R5,048 millions or 63 per cent of the grand total of R7,954 millions. Such a rate of growth in small savings is strategically significant for economic development. Although 'institutional finance' is traditionally available – apart from holdings of legally prescribed government assets – for mortgage loans, its relationship to risk-investment is exemplified in the case of mining investment. New goldmining fields, notably in the Free State, require the establishment of new townships of housing for White miners. 'Institutional finance' provides the great bulk of the mortgage money for such new townships, without which the mining development could not take place.

There are two other aspects of capital accumulation for economic development that merit brief comment – the sophistication of financial institutions and the relationship of domestic to foreign capital.

It might be fairly said that a money-market in the narrow sense marks an advanced stage of economic maturity. This money-market of merchant banks and discount houses, related to the central bank and the commercial banks, performs the task of optimizing the liquidity of the total money market of finance-capitalism. It mobilizes temporary idle funds at the short-end of the market, which in turn gives more economic deployment of funds at the long-end of the market. The money-market in the narrow sense, which developed in South Africa from 1955, depended much on the borrowed expertise of the City of London, and had by 1965 achieved all the sophistication of the City's famed money-mechanism[48].

In earlier chapters, the indispensible, distinctive part played by foreign capital investment in launching South Africa into economic development has been emphasized. Without such aid, the great mining wealth would never have come to fruition nor been fructified decade after decade. If the exploitation of mineral wealth was fundamental to the emergence of the economy from the stagnation of under-development, then the availability of foreign capital was cardinal as a strategic variable. Although domestic capital formation acquired an entirely new order of importance from about the time of the Second World War and played a growing role, it was only after the crucial decision to declare South Africa a Republic outside the Commonwealth in 1961 that the future role of foreign capital investment became highly problematical.

The break with the Commonwealth was followed within weeks

by the break with the City of London. The official controls on capital movements, announced by the Minister of Finance Dr Dönges on 17 June, 1961, severed the vital interconnections between the Johannesburg share market and the London share market by no longer permitting the unrestricted transferability of scrip between the two markets. This was a highly damaging but not yet mortal blow to further foreign capital investment in South Africa. A continued investment of foreign funds had not only to overcome the technical disruption between the two share markets but the great and growing hostility towards South Africa and its Apartheid, engendered or engineered in the United Nations.

The instrument used by the South African Government was the import-exchange control system itself. From the introduction of import-exchange controls in 1948, foreign firms had been faced with the alternative of further investment of funds in South African manufacturing facilities or withdrawing from the South African market. Many foreign firms with long-established market positions in South Africa, either by way of exporting from their home-based plants or from subsidiary manufacturing facilities already set up inside South Africa, elected to expand in South Africa. Some of these firms took advantage of liquid capital market-conditions in South Africa to use South African capital for financing their development projects, but others – often including the great names of British and American industry – were prepared to invest substantial additional funds from their own resources.

The scale of foreign investment fluctuated from year to year from 1948 onwards. After the tragedy of Sharpeville and the tragedy, at least to a minority of opinion, of withdrawal from the Commonwealth, the haemorrhage of the capital flight was stopped by the 1961 capital-movement controls. The political squeeze on foreign enterprises was now intensified by an import-substitution programme, fanned with all the propaganda and fervour of economic nationalism. The method and its foreign-capital inducement significance is exemplified on its most significant scale in the motor-automotive industry, as partly recounted in the previous chapter. The bigger the existing scale of investment and hence commitment of resources, the stronger the compulsion to further investment in order to protect the commitment.

Although the major motor-assembly plants chose to present their massive post-1963 capital investment projects as 'justified by the volume of sales-potential of the South African market, a far more potent form of persuasion was the new mechanism of import-permits for the automotive industry that the Board of Trade and Industries announced in 1961. In effect it 'lifted' import control in respect of what was defined as a 'South African-made car'; while allowing such derisory import permits to cars that could not come within this definition as to mean the latter's virtual total disappearance from the market. A car assembled in a South African plant qualified as a car made in a South African factory, provided a prescribed, upward-revised, minimum weight-content of the final car was of South African manufacture.

Although the early assembly facilities were established as far back as 1923 by Ford Motor Company and by 1926 by General Motors, as late as 1961 the imported content of cars assembled on South African lines was no less than 82 per cent by value or 87·5 per cent by weight. After 1961, the prescribed minimum weight-content ensured a substantial expansion of component-part manufacture by South African factories but these accessories or 'hang-on parts' did not necessarily involve the increase in South African weight-content to the critical minimum of the new import-exchange permit policy. This critical minimum depended on local engine manufacturing – the more complex, expensive, primary parts of the vehicle – by the foreign, parent company itself. Hence Ford, General Motors, SAMAD (in effect Mercedes-Volkswagen), British Motor Corporation – the Big Four plus subsequently Chrysler, Renault, Fiat and others – had to introduce their own, foreign capital on a massive scale.

Foreign capital investment in excess of an estimated R100 millions was required to meet the July 1964 import control formula. By that formula, a car model to be declared 'manufactured' in South Africa, and hence exempt from import control permits, had from a starting point of 45 per cent local content to guarantee that, within $3\frac{1}{2}$ years from declaration of intent, the model would reach 55 per cent South African content by weight [49].

The automotive industry is perhaps the most significant in terms of the scale of foreign investment that can be and was induced by Government policy, which in essence guarantees the industrialist a critical share of the domestic market. Indirectly the example gives substance to the theoretical proposition that market-demand is the key determinant for bringing about the crucial shift from economic underdevelopment to economic development. Although the example underlines that protection can secure co-operant (foreign) capital for underemployed (domestic) resources of labour, it must be stressed that the car manufacturers – and the Board of Trade itself – have justified their greatly expanded scale of production by projections of the growth of the demand for cars, which explicitly envisages a steady, substantial increase in car ownership by Africans. At very least, the new car market rate of absorption will require rising numbers of African buyers of second-hand cars.

It is also significant that the greatly enlarged plants of the major car assembler-manufacturers considerably expanded their employment of initially unskilled Africans. Appropriate revision of job categories and job specifications enabled an increasing range of assembly-line jobs to be brought within the competence of rapidly-trained African workers. The extent and possibilities of such work re-organization led, as previously detailed in an earlier chapter, to successful pressure by White trade unionists on the Industrial Tribunal to introduce job-reservation into the industry.

A complete study of import-exchange control in South Africa from 1948, though lengthy, would be necessary to bring out the full subtleties and extent to which such controls can induce capital investment through market-guarantees. Another interesting example is in respect of paper manufacture. Paper and especially newsprint was a large consumer of foreign exchange. In a significant diversification beyond goldmining, one of the major mining groups, Union Corporation, established South African Pulp and Paper Industries (Sappi) to utilize considerable resources of home-grown timber for paper manufacture, including newsprint. Paper and newsprint manufacture is exceptionally capital-intensive and the scale of capital investment will, from the investor's viewpoint, give mandatory importance to the certainty of future market demand.

In this instance war and post-war limitations on newsprint-usage by the newspaper publishers, at that stage entirely dependent on foreign-imported newsprint, provided a business incentive to such publishers to help in launching domestic newsprint-manufacture. Such publishers consequently co-operated with the import control authorities in an undertaking to take up the current output from Sappi before requesting import permits. The import control authorities, as output from Sappi mills was extended both of newsprint and all other types of paper, would not issue import permits to any end-users of paper (including a rapidly growing packaging industry) until the full, available output of the Sappi mills had been absorbed. Furthermore, any planned increases in capacity by Sappi – in accordance with paper-manufacturing technology requiring lump-sum jumps in scale of output and in inputs of capital – could be undertaken by the company in the certainty that foreign competition would be excluded as such plant-extensions came on stream.

From 1961 onwards, after the initial collapse of confidence by domestic and foreign investors following Sharpeville and the declaration of the Republic, the re-establishment of such confidence was accomplished to a degree surprising to contemporary observers. The instrument of the polity was not only an appeal to 'patrotism', which became increasingly effective as United Nations' pressures and the threat of armed intervention by the rest of Africa became more vociferous and unrestrained, but a general notification that import permits would not be available until importers had 'assured' themselves that no South African supplies of similar or satisfactory substitute materials were available. Import control authorities insisted on positive evidence that potential South African suppliers had been fully resourced before import permits were granted, and this technique was applied not only to consumer-goods imports but no less to intermediate industrial materials and capital goods.

The Industrial Development Corporation, IDC, took full advantage of this method of applying import-substitution in its programme of helping establish 'strategic' industries, more particularly in negotiations with foreign industrialists to supply both the capital and the no less important know-how technology for South African plants. In some instances IDC co-operation was with domestic capital – particularly Afrikaner finance houses – and in other instances with foreign capital; sometimes domestic and foreign capital were linked. Thus the Synthetic Rubber Company to produce synthetic rubber (styrene-butadiene rubber from Sasol raw materials) brought together South African capital and foreign capital, the latter coming from the tyre-manufacturers. An IDC link with foreign capital only – the Phillips Petroleum of the United States – enabled a carbon black plant to be set up [50].

It has already been remarked that foreign capital investment was crucial to mining development and has undoubtedly been strategic to maufacturing development. The customary debate, both responsibly economic and irresponsibly chauvanistic, over the 'proper' role of foreign capital investment has for a number of years been conducted in South Africa. At times when the country came under particularly strong external criticism of its race relations policies, patriotism has tended to insist that South Africans could save for themselves all the capital that could be effectively employed for the country's economic development. More experienced and more objective entrepreneurs, of no less patriotism but less myopic vision of the ultimate potential of continuing development, have insisted that dependence on substantial foreign capital investment will continue for the foreseeable future[51]. Recurrent crises in the balance-of-payments suggest the validity of the latter's arguments.

Ever since 1948 and no less markedly since 1961, when the Union became the Republic of South Africa, either an actual withdrawal of foreign investments or a diminished inflow of foreign capital has brought about such a diminution in foreign exchange reserves as to threaten a curtailment of the rate of economic development. Without doubt, domestic capital formation will enable some rate of economic development to continue[52]. But, hardly less unquestionably, a higher rate of economic development is not achievable without continuing foreign capital investment.

The first Economic Development Programme for South Africa 1964–9[53] makes a careful analysis of the rate of capital formation and of the supply of money and near-money to sustain different target rates of economic growth[54]. A $4\frac{1}{2}$ per cent rate of growth for the period of 1964–9 was held to result in a probable underemployment of the capital becoming available. Presumably the National Plan as programmed by EDP on a $4\frac{1}{2}$ per cent growth rate could be achieved from domestic capital formation alone without significant inputs of foreign capital. At a rate of growth in excess of 5 per cent per annum, EDP calculations (made at the end of 1964) suggested a small surplus on balance of payments on current account with the proviso 'if a fair inflow of capital can be secured to balance out the contractual outflow to which South Africa is already committed'.

It would seem that a considered viewpoint, as at the end of 1965, would be that for South Africa to maintain a $5\frac{1}{2}$ per cent rate of growth large amounts of foreign capital investment will be necessary. A $5\frac{1}{2}$ per cent growth rate may seem a fairly ambitious target but it must be remembered, despite the arguments of this chapter that South Africa has reached close to the stage of economic maturity, that this achievement is more of technical significance than a measure of the real standards of living of the very great majority of the Non-White population. International comparisons – no less than inter-African comparisons – of standards of living are, in the author's opinion, of highly dubious validity, In no other field of comparative statistics could comparisons be more invidious or more subjective. The very great majority of Non-Whites, and particularly Africans, in South Africa are, again in the author's opinion, very poor. A majority of rural Africans in South Africa are poverty-striken. Whatever the magnitudes, a rate of growth in excess of 5 per cent per annum would almost certainly demand a sustained inflow of foreign capital [55].

Foreign capital investment sets up, of course, its own needs for foreign exchange to meet the payments due to foreign investors of contractual interest or earnings from profits. The capital sums must also be amortised or repaid at some time in foreign exchange. Such repayment is contractually real in respect of loan-capital by Government or private enterprise but in respect of equity investments by foreign enterprise such capital is not generally repatriated unless alternative opportunities become more attractive than continued maintenance of the investment in the country to which it was first committed. Great car-manufacturing, chemical and engineering companies, for instance, rarely sell their non-domestic plant-investment to withdraw their original investments stakes. Such investments may sometimes be locked-in and then irretrievably lost in the event of violent political unheaval, in which unfortunate event no question of foreign exchange provision for repatriation arises. More relevantly in the case of a country like South Africa, the initial investment continues to be supported by not only re-investment of a substantial share of earned profits but also fresh inputs of foreign capital – and consequentially no real commitment for foreign exchange for redemption arises.

Nonetheless a country's rate of economic development, of course, necessitates exports in some relation to imports. The great, and often insuperable, difficulty in much development planning for under-developed countries is that exports cannot be generated at a level to sustain the scale of foreign aid, whether private investment or international assistance. In the case of South Africa, it has already been noted that it was the country's unique good fortune that massive foreign investment in goldmining produced as its product gold – the very medium of international money. One of the strongest arguments against 'forced' or 'artificial' development of South African manufacturing or secondary industry was that such industry was dependent on imported foreign materials and plant, and that the 'burden' of payment for the imports of manufacturing industry fell on the goldmines.

An earlier section of the text has also examined the extent to which the development of intermediate and basic raw-material industries led to an increasing portion of South African 'raw materials' being used in the later stages of South African manufacturing. Much of this argument seems artificial in the sense that economic development as it proceeds within the country sets up a correlated development of imports. It has repeatedly been observed that, for instance, the protection of South African industry has changed the character but not diminished the volume of imports, as is surely to be expected unless the crude version of the 'work-fund' is applied to the quantum of economic development. This increased demand for imports has been most notable in the contemporary exercise by South Africa of import-substitution programmes. This is reflected in some figures below. Only the most unsophisticated of economic nationalists believes in 'self-sufficiency', though it may be that in times of national peril such 'self-sufficiency' will support a siege economy at a tolerable level.

One of the critical variables for South African economic development is without doubt the volume of its exports. For decades – for three-quarters of a century now – the rising volume and value of gold output has made its vitalizing contribution to exports, launching the economy from stagnation through the take-off stage of growth into the final stages of maturity. Repeatedly over the years, warnings have been made of the pending end of this golden stream but, again and again, the 'miracles' of price-rises in gold and new gold discoveries have extended the marginal ores and the total output. The first mine of the Orange Free State goldfield began actual gold production as recently as 1954 but within ten years, the Free State goldfields had become the country's major mining area, producing 36 per cent of the gold output involving a capital investment of more than R520 millions. In 1910, gold contributed more than 80 per cent of the total value of South African exports; in 1965 the value of gold and uranium exported was nearly half the total value of all exports.

The critical factor in gold exports is the fixed price of gold. Ever since the last Cripps devaluation of British sterling in 1950, which brought the sterling price of gold to its current proximate 250s. a fine oz, South African Governments and the Chamber of Mines have deployed all the persuasiveness of the most elegant economic and monetary analysis (plus some less elegant propagandist public relations) to convince the key influences of the world – more especially the makers-of-policy in the United States of America – that only a substantial increase in the world gold-price could restore 'international liquidity'. The case for a higher gold price was that it alone could alleviate the perennial (or at least post Second World War perennial) crises in balance of payments that so much of the second half of the twentieth century appears to be heir to. The inexhaustible analyses and nuances of this endless debate are beyond the compass of this text. Patently a substantial increase in the world price of gold, though not without its cost-inflationary problems for the South African economy, would yet again carry the country's economic development another major stride forward. Nonetheless the benefits from absolute assurance of the sale of the total output at a fixed price, year after year, of the country's greatest 'raw material' and 'export crop' should not be overlooked. Least of all, should it be overlooked by any country on the African continent, the economies of which suffer so substantially from the wide fluctuations of prices in every other kind of mineral, raw material and agricultural export.

The stability which gold sales contributes to the production function of the South African economy is perhaps illustrated by the experience of the four-year period, 1957 to 1961. In 1957, the value of all South African exports, other than gold, was R903 millions. Following price falls in nearly all world markets for commodities, the total value of these non-gold exports dropped in 1958 to R783 millions and only in 1961 did the value of non-gold exports recover to the 1957 figure.

As at the year 1966, the Chamber of Mines believes that gold production in South Africa has reached its zenith and a gradual decline will set in. Price increases in gold will obviously off-set the decline but on the other hand, the second half of the twentieth century appears to have in-built inflationary factors that inexorably advance working costs of mining. It is also perhaps significant that the great mining finance house of the Oppenheimers, Anglo-American Corporation, has in recent times stepped up a strategical diversification of investments. The plough-back of its golden profits is more and more into non-gold ventures, such as the great steel-vanadium project, property development and other industrial ventures.

The significance of the gold output quantum as a key variable in all the econometric projections is underlined by the export-import experience of South Africa from 1961 onwards. It will be recollected that 1961 marks the critical political event of the constitution of the Republic of South Africa not only as a polity but as a political economy outside the Commonwealth and the number one target of United Nations hostility. Despite the near-heroic efforts at import-substitution (exemplified in the text above), imports into South Africa from 1962 increased by the startling figure of 22·2 per cent per annum. Despite still-increasing gold exports, the South African balance of payments, which showed a surplus in 1964 of R158·3 millions, had swung in 1965 to an estimated deficit of about R300 millions. In short, expansion of non-gold exports must be given a very high priority in all economic planning.

Exports of South African Goods and Re-exports (excluding gold) in R Millions [56]

	1963	1964	1965*	1966*
Food	289·9	272·3	203·3	250·0
Beverages/Tobacco	8·5	9·5	12·0	14·0
Crude Materials**	317·4	330·9	305·4	325·0
Mineral fuels	17·2	29·8	27·0	30·0
Mineral vegetables, oils, fats	6·9	9·3	10·0	10·0
Chemicals	32·3	33·8	38·0	42·0
Manufactured goods	201·2	212·7	275·0	330·0
Machinery & Transport	25·6	27·9	35·0	35·0
Misc. Manufactured goods	13·2	10·4	14·0	16·0
Not classified	3·7	19·7	6·0	10·0
Total (adjusted)	915·8	954·2	925·0	1072·0
Re-exports	80·5	84·0	115·0	150·0
	996·3	1038·2	1040·0	1222·0

*Estimates   **Primarily uranium

It is true that before 1939 manufactured goods provided only 3 per cent of South African exports, while for the first nine months of the latest year, 1966, this had increased to 27 per cent. It is substantial growth but it is clear that the achievement of export volumes for non-gold exports, on a salutary assumption of a decline in gold output over the not-distant future, remains one of the critical problems of South African economic strategy and development. It is patently not made easier by the philosophy and practices of the South African polity, by the political factor of Afrikanerdom, by an Apartheid which, aiming to separate the development of White South Africans and Black South Africans, might impose upon the Republic separate development outside an expanding world economy.

Economic development remains, as always, not an exercise in econometric manipulation but the wise deployment of political economy.

REPUBLICAN HERITAGE

In May, 1961 an Act of Parliament buried the Union of South Africa and brought into being the Republic of South Africa. Afrikanerdom had triumphed[1]. The political factor had after more than a century vanquished the imperial factor. The sovereignty of the polity was constitutionally unchallengeable[2] and the Africans, numbering at the 1960 census almost 11,000,000 out of a total population of 16,000,000, had no representation whatsoever in the Parliament of the Republic. The Asiatics were similarly unrepresented and the Coloureds, more rapidly increasing than any other section, had lost their century-old franchise rights on the common roll and were reduced to electing three members of Parliament of White skin.

Politically, the 'volkswil' was in total control of the polity and had moved far towards a totalitarian concept of the role of the polity. The unchanging objective of the political factor – the unalterable control of South African society in general and the South African economy in particular by its White peoples, as represented by Afrikanerdom – had been accomplished. The status relationships of White and Black, which the ethos of Afrikanerdom believed to be pre-ordained, had been made determinate in so far as the market could be legally subjugated to the polity.

Afrikanerdom believed passionately that it had constituted order in South Africa and in so doing, world opinion to the contrary, had secured the liberty of all its peoples, White and Non-White. Though Afrikanerdom denied any right whatsoever to world opinion to interfere in South Africa, it did not refuse to acknowledge that the world, and Africa, had changed. In relation to South Africa, Dr Verwoerd, as Minister of Native Affairs even before he inevitably became Prime Minister, had recognized that Smuts's old concept of trusteeship for the Natives was dead, that Hertzogite and Malanite

373

ideas of segregation were being over-run by economic development, and that the *realpolitik* of Strijdom's *baasskap*[3] was, however much the harsh reality of the South African social system, a potentially disastrous defiance of world, and African, forces.

A constitution of a new order and a concomitant re-orientation of the country's economic development was, in the ideals and ideologies of Afrikaner intellectuals under the inspiration of Dr Verwoerd as newly appointed Minister of Native Affairs and his academic colleague Dr W. W. M. Eiselen, newly summoned Secretary for Native Affairs, vital. Almost ten years before the proclamation of the Republic, Dr Verwoerd and Dr Eiselen had appointed *The Commission for the Socio-Economic Development of the Bantu Areas within the Union of South Africa*. The Commission under the chairmanship of Prof. F. R. Tomlinson, and known as the Tomlinson Commission, was 'to conduct an exhaustive inquiry into and to report on a comprehensive scheme for the rehabilitation of the Native Areas with a view to developing within them a social structure in keeping with the culture of the Native and based on effective socio-economic planning.'

The Tomlinson Commission was, in effect, to traverse once more the paths of a dozen of its predecessors but above all to refute the cardinal finding of the Fagan Commission: that the ideas of total segregation is utterly impracticable and that the movement from country to town has a background of economic necessity . . . that cannot be stopped or turned in the opposite direction . . . and that in our urban areas there are not only Native migrant labourers but there is also a settled, permanent Native population.

The labours of the Tomlinson Commission were herculean[4]. Almost four years of exhaustive evidence produced a Report of 51 chapters comprising 3,755 pages, 598 tables, and an atlas of 66 large-scale maps. So formidable was the cost of printing this Report in both official languages and, apparently, so improbable that anyone would read the unabridged version, that the full Report was never printed for general readership. Instead the Commission prepared an abridged Tomlinson Report, U.G. 61–1955, which is the one for general reference.

The Tomlinson Report was to provide the heritage for the Republic, pregnant in the Nationalist Party victory-consummation of the 1948 General Election. The Report looked into the demographic future[5]. On its Projection A, that the four population groups of Whites, African (Bantu), Coloureds and Asiatics would continue to grow from 1946 at the respective rates of increase prevailing from 1936 to 1946 but that additionally the Whites would be supplemented by an annual number of 5000 net immigrants, there would be 6,150,000 Whites, 16,337,000 Africans, 2,560,000 Coloureds and 1,120,000 Asiatics living in South Africa by the year 2000. An alternative extrapolation, Projection B, providing for steady declines in birth- and death-rates and no White immigration, gave the probable population at 2000 as: 4,588,000 Whites, 21,361,000 Africans, 3,917,000 Coloureds and 1,382,000 Asiatics – a total of 31,248,000 persons[6].

On the critical trend of urbanization of the Africans, the Report said that in the absence of government policy to check the tempo more than 10,000,000 of the estimated 21,000,000 Africans would be established in urban areas in the non-Bantu areas, that is in 'White South Africa's cities. This figure might readily rise to 15,000,000 if the present absorbent capacity of the Bantu areas, European farms and other rural areas is not raised . . .' The Report also anticipated that 'the vast majority of these Bantu will be concentrated at the four existing industrial complexes'[7].

These trends – the growth in numbers and the rising rate of urbanization – the Report recognized as the pattern of economic development of underdeveloped peoples.

Patently to the Tomlinson Commission the only possible solution to such a degree of integration of the Africans into White South Africa was the socio-economic development of the Native Reserves or, as they were now re-named, the Bantu Homelands[8]. It examined in exhaustive detail the environmental facts of these Bantu Homelands of some 260 separate areas, chiefly situated in the eastern parts of South Africa 'which, taken together form a rough horseshoe in shape, curving round the Orange Free State and the Transvaal.' The total extent of these Areas, always subject to the fact of final acquisition at *some* date in South African history of the additional land provided for in the 1936 Native Trust and Land Act (in itself intended to 'implement' the promises of the 1913 Act), would represent 13·7 per cent of the whole area of the Union. The Report found that this indefensible proportion would become more justifiable if the Protectorates of Basutoland, Swaziland, and Bechuanaland ('essentially Bantu Areas of Greater South Africa') were also included in the proportionate distribution of land-ownership between Europeans and Africans in Greater South Africa. In that

375

event 45 per cent of the land of 'South Africa' would belong to the Bantu[9].

According to the Report, the south-eastern sector of the Bantu Areas is very favourably situated as regards water sources but in the north-western sector, arid and even desert-like conditions are encountered. It claimed that in regard to the country's sources of power, coal and electricity, the Bantu Areas are relatively favourably situated; that though the Union's four chief minerals of gold, diamonds, coal and copper fell outside the Areas, there were present less important minerals; that the principal economic activities of commerce and industry were concentrated outside the Bantu Areas and 'as far as industries are concerned, the Bantu areas are in fact a desert . . .' Finally, the transport network of the Union, especially the railways, by-passed the Bantu Homelands[10].

As at 1951, the Bantu Areas with 3·6 million Africans were the most densely populated section of South Africa, apart from the major cities. The Commission believed that to the 1951 census *de facto* population of 3·6 millions, there were 569,000 Africans temporarily absent from their 'Homelands' giving a *de jure* total of 4,202,000. More than half the indigenous Bantu of the Union, the Tomlinson Report claimed, regard the Bantu Areas as their home[11].

The Tomlinson Commission accepted, as almost all 'White' historical opinion believes, that it was only the good faith of the Europeans which had secured the Bantu their homelands rather than that the White polity had imposed the territorial division on an unrepresented African population. It recognised that the agricultural development of these Areas had received a minimum of State aid. In 1945, it noted only £90,000 had been made available for technical agricultural services but by 1953 this had increased to £1,385,000. It found that current land settlement policy with its communal ownership and other traditional practices was in no way alleviating the agricultural poverty of the Africans[12]:

The present system thus fails entirely to bring into being an efficient, self-supporting agricultural community in the Reserves; it will have to be changed for a system in which the farming allotments on completed betterment areas can supply the families occupying them, with all their reasonable requirements.

Progressive deterioration could only be stopped and reversed, either by enlarging the Bantu Areas commensurate with the livestock they carry, or by limiting the human and farm animal population of the Areas. Though the Africans in their Areas cultivated some 23 per cent of the Union's total crop-area in 1949–50, the Bantu Area production was only about 10 per cent of the Union's total crop products in that year. And although the Commission estimated that agriculture contributed at least 62 per cent of the income of the Bantu Areas, no more than 25 per cent of the agricultural products of the Reserves were sold. The Bantu Areas remained essentially a subsistence economy, some 95 per cent of the agricultural and 60 per cent of the livestock being home-consumed. The development of marketing had by the middle of the twentieth century hardly begun in these Territories [13].

In brief, the major economic product of the Native Reserves or Bantu Homelands was the export of labour into the White Man's economy. The Report calculated that within the Bantu Areas, the Bantu man was economically active for a total of only 42 per cent of his working life and 'actually occupied in wage-earning employment for only 38 per cent of it' [14].

The Commission attempted to establish data for Bantu Area 'national income' and personal incomes. It calculated that in 1950–51, the Bantu Areas provided only 3·7 per cent of the total geographic income ('adjusted') of the Union and that *per capita* production of the Bantu Areas of £12·9 contrasted with £99·4 for the Union as a whole. Though geographic income of the Areas had, calculated at ruling prices, risen, the share of the generation of the Union's national income had 'declined considerably'. 'Real' income produced in the Reserves had remained unchanged from 1936 to the 1950's, while *per capita* income had fallen.

There was not the slightest doubt, therefore, in the Commission's view, that the politico-economic realities made the intensive development of the Bantu Areas essential. Furthermore, it was equally essential that such development should be planned. It was, however, a basic principle that the development of the Bantu Areas should be linked up with that of the Union as a whole:

It is essential that the economic unity of the country, and the free participation of the Bantu Areas in the total economic activity of the Union, should be preserved; moreover, economic barriers or divergent directions of development would not promote development, while different price structures, or a division of the national market area by customs barriers, would be unthinkable. . .[16].

It was a further basic principle that the Africans and their institutions should be regarded as the principal instruments for development; but as the chief source of the organizing ability, technical knowledge and capital required for initiating development as well as maintaining it for a considerable time, the participation of the Whites would be essential [17].

What then should be the lines of development? The Commission's investigations had 'shown conclusively that the Bantu Areas cannot carry their present population as full-time farmers' [18]. In trying to determine the size of farm-income in relation to the size of farming unit, the Report calculated that if £120 (as at 1951) was to be adopted as the standard, 'then at least 80 per cent of the present number of families in the Bantu Areas would have to be removed from the land' [19]. Such a population-shift would be impossible to carry out so the Commission adopted a figure of £60 gross income per farm-unit at 1951/52 prices. On that basis and other agro-economic assumptions, 'the Bantu Areas can carry about 307,000 farming families or about 51 per cent of the (Area's) population as recorded in the 1951 census' [20].

The necessity for the development of other income-earning activities needed no emphasis. Although the Commission held out hopes for sugar-cane planting, fibre and timber production and mining, the development of manufacturing industries was identified as clearly of the greatest significance. A programme of industrial development would, it said, therefore, occupy a central position in the general programme of development of the Bantu Areas.

The fundamental objective of the Nationalist Government, and the recently appointed Minister of Native Affairs Dr Verwoerd, was to prove that the process of integration of the Africans into the South African social system was not irreversible and that the 'ultimate ideal of complete segregation' could reasonably and realistically be pursued. Since it was never envisaged that the 1913 division of land, as amended in 1936, as between White and Black should be altered from its proportion of 86·3 per cent in perpetuity for White ownership and 13·7 per cent for Black ownership, it became the key task of the Tomlinson Commission to establish the 'carrying capacity' of the Bantu Homelands [21].

The Commission calculated that its programme of intensive development with its major dynamic of industrialization and urbanization within the Bantu Homelands might, after 25–30 years, achieve a carrying capacity of about 8 million people based on the employment opportunities provided by the Bantu Areas themselves. The residential carrying capacity might be an additional 1·5 millions of dependants and retired, maintained by breadwinners working outside the Areas. Adding again another half-million migratory workers, the final *de jure* potential population of the Bantu Homelands after a 25–30 year development programme would be 10,000,000 [22].

For the first ten years of the development programme, the Commission estimated the financial requirements to be £104·486 millions i.e. for the complete ten-year period. About £55,256,000 of this sum 'would be of a private economic nature, which will be a paying concern and which will be recoverable; and expenditure of £49,230,000 which is of a socio-economic nature' [23].

At the Commission's planned rate of development, it believed that the Bantu Areas would accommodate about 60 per cent of the African or Bantu population of South Africa by 1981, and about 70 per cent by the year 2000. 'The Commission thinks that as far as possible the tempo in future plans of development ought even to be raised. The ideal should be that the non-Bantu areas house a swiftly shrinking portion of the total Bantu population' [24].

The 'ideal' thus to be sought and accomplished was Apartheid or Separate Development or, even, Separate Freedoms as the intellectuals of Afrikanerdom named the policy of the White Man's polity towards the Black Man. Was the policy magic or myth? Perhaps Ernst Cassirer in *The Myth of the State*[25] provides the insight:

[This] description of the role of magic and mythology in primitive society applies equally well to highly advanced stages of man's political life . . . if modern man no longer believes in a natural magic, he has by no means given up the belief in a sort of 'social magic'. If a collective wish is felt in its whole strength and intensity, people can easily be persuaded that it only needs the right man to satisfy it. . . . It has been reserved for the twentieth century, our own great technical age, to develop a new technique of myth. Henceforth myths can be manufactured . . . the first step that had to be taken was a change in the function of language. . . . If we study our modern political myths and the use that has been made of them we find in them, to our great surprise, not only a transformation of all ethical values but also a transformation of human speech. The magic word takes the precedence of the semantic word. . . . New words have been coined; and even the old ones

are used in a new sense; they have undergone a deep change of meaning. . . .
Our ordinary words are charged with meanings; but these new-fangled
words are charged with feelings and violent passions. . . .

In the previous chapter, *Springs of Development*, the assertion was
made that, however strikingly Apartheid has evinced the avowed
purpose of Afrikanerdom, the real expression of White South
Africa's will has been an expanding bureaucratization of the direction
of economic resources. African labour at least as much as goldiferous
ore has been the country's major economic resource and it is on the
direction of African labour by the White polity, that the process of
state control has approached totalitarianism. Such a totalitarian
exercise of bureaucratic authority over the utilization of African
labour has not in fact aimed at Apartheid in the sense of 'separate
development'. As has already been shown, an administered market
for African labour completely eliminated contractual freedom for
Africans, and indirectly for employers of such labour. The fundamental motivation of the policy in administering this labour market
has been to preserve status relationships between the different
racial groups, and more particularly a permanent superiority of
White status and permanent inferiority of Black status.

This thesis – that the entrenchment of status relationships and
not separate development of viable Bantu sovereignties in their own
Homelands is the reality of social process in the Republic of South
Africa as it was in the Union of South Africa – emerges from the
Tomlinson Commission Report itself. More precisely, it emerges from
the manner of implementation by the Republican Government of
the Tomlinson recommendations.

The Commission said it wished to emphasize that while the
economy of South Africa is *essentially a single whole* with inter-
dependent and complementary parts, it was of great importance to
create *diversified means of livelihood* within the Bantu Areas [26]. It
consequentially examined two key policy issues in regard to industrialization of the Bantu Areas – the participation of White entrepreneurship and capital, and the actual location of industrial plants.

On the conclusive evidence that the necessary entrepreneurial
abilities were not currently available among the Bantu and that
capital formation by the Bantu themselves was far too meagre to
launch enterprises of any scale, the Commission reported that
'Europeans, either individually or through Government action, will

have to play a considerable part in providing the necessary stimulus to development' [27]. As far as possible 'the development of industry should be undertaken by private enterprise' but 'European entrepreneurs must aim at allowing the Bantu to participate progressively in the management of, as well as in investment in undertakings'.

The Commission then turned briefly to the question whether industrial development inside the Bantu Areas or in European areas adjacent to Bantu Areas should receive preference. The latter, known as border or perimeter areas, were defined as development in a European area situated so closely to the Bantu Areas, that families of Bantu employees engaged in that development could lead a full family life inside the Bantu Area.

Industrial development of such border areas could be viewed as part of the general decentralization of industry with the standard arguments in favour of decentralization and, in addition, that such border-industries would serve as growth points for urbanization and related tertiary occupations inside the Bantu Area adjacent. The tendency for the Africans to 'proceed to distant European areas will be counteracted, and, if the development of border areas is sufficiently extensive, the flow of immigrants from the Bantu Areas, may be reversed, with a corresponding alleviation of the social and political problems which arise as a result of the presence of the Bantu in the distant European industrial centres' [28].

But the Commission also noted the 'serious disadvantages'. It would not remove the 'ceiling' for the Bantu – the limitations in the industrial sphere, which apply to them in all other European areas, will also be in force here, and under such circumstances it will be particularly difficult to create a class of skilled workers and entrepreneurs among the Bantu'. Furthermore, continued the Commission, the population of the Bantu Areas will tend to congregate increasingly on the boundaries near the Europeans 'which will give rise to the feeling that they are an appendage of the European community' and 'in itself it does not necessarily stem the tide of integration with the Europeans' [29].

Industrial development inside the Bantu Areas, the Commission insisted, was necessary

because it is an integral part of an economic structure which wishes to achieve the maximum socio-economic development for the people, to provide the largest possible Bantu population in these Areas with a lasting livelihood, and to remove the 'ceiling' over its head in all spheres of social life. . . . Moreover, a class of Bantu skilled workers and entrepreneurs will only have the opportunity of developing fully if there are industries in the Bantu Areas, since there alone all restrictions on such development will be removed . . .

Apart from the broad advantages it has for the Bantu residents in these Areas, inside development has particular advantages for the entrepreneur, and the most important of these is the fact that the potential abilities of the Bantu population can be fully utilized for industrial purposes. They can also be freely employed in technical and administrative posts of all grades. . . [30].

The Commission is clear, if circumspect. A more fundamental and forthright observation is pertinent.

The White electorate, the governing Nationalist Party insisted, had again and again given its endorsement to the policy of Apartheid and a mandate for 'separate development'. Mr M. D. C. de Wet Nel, as Minister of Bantu Administration and Development in introducing the second reading of the Promotion of Bantu Self-Government Bill (Act No 46 of 1959), elaborated Government policy and Afrikanerdom's philosophy:

Mr Speaker, I want to say frankly that I believe in the existence of nationalism on the part of the Bantu population groups. We cannot deny it; it is there . . . I grant them that nationalism. . . . Moreover, nationalism is one of the forces which puts into motion the best things in the spirit of the human being. Nationalism is one of the forces which has led to the most beautiful deeds of idealism and sacrifice and inspiration. Should the Bantu not have it? . . . It is my honest conviction that these Bantu population groups can best be guided on the road to progress if their whole development is Bantu orientated, which means that all the administrative bodies from the highest to the lowest should be linked up and the whole of the Bantu population should be concerned in them. . . .

But the most important consideration is that this Bill makes it possible for the [Government] to transfer [its] legislative powers systematically to those Territorial Authorities . . . . If we extend the present system [of Bantu representation in Parliament] . . . it would create a racial hatred which South Africa simply cannot afford, because, in the course of years, we would then have a bitter struggle on the part of the White man to ensure that he is not ploughed under politically by the non-White groups of the population. . . [31].

This Act, together with the Bantu Investment Corporation Act No 34 of 1958, and the Bantu Homelands Development Corporation

Act No 86 of 1965, were to give legislative structure to the recommendations of the Tomlinson Commission Report[32].

The Promotion of Bantu Self-government Act of 1959 aimed to provide 'for the gradual development of self-governing Bantu national units and for direct consultation between the Government of the Union and the said national units in matters affecting the interests of such national units'. Whereas, said the preamble, the Bantu peoples of the Union of South Africa do not constitute a homogeneous people, but form separate national units on the basis of language and culture and whereas it is desirable . . . to afford recognition to the various national units and to provide for their gradual development within their own areas to self-governing units on the basis of Bantu systems of government . . . , the Act divides the Bantu population into eight national units. These separate national units are (a) North-Sotho (b) South Sotho (c) Swazi (d) Tsonga (e) Tswana (f) Venda (g) Xhosa and (h) Zulu.

Although the Government's Information Department has publicly stated that this Act 'contains an unequivocal assurance of the South African Government's intention to create self-governing Bantu national units', the Act in fact confers no significant powers of sovereign rights at all but 'for the gradual development [with] the tempo . . . determined on the one hand by the inherent vigour of the young Bantu communities and on the other hand depends upon responsible guidance by the White guardian who will gradually withdraw from his trusteeship'[33]. A territorial authority for the national unit may be established to which strictly limited, specific powers may be transferred. The first such territorial authority (and to date, 1966, only one) established the Transkeian Legislative Assembly in 1963.

This Transkei Legislative Assembly, together with the State President of the Republic, may legislate on all matters entrusted to the Transkei and which have not been reserved for the Government of the Republic of South Africa. Currently the responsibility for legislation on matters such as defence, foreign affairs, postal affairs, internal security, railways, national roads and harbours is retained by the Government of the Republic. Apart from these cardinal aspects of sovereignty for which constitutional authority is withheld from the Transkei Assembly, such Assembly may not legislate to obtain external capital investment or external technical aid. No investment of private capital, whether from Whites in South

Africa or from other non-South African sources, is permitted; nor has the Transkei Assembly authority to invite immigrants to enter its 'national territory'.

The Promotion of Bantu Self-Government Act confers no self-determination rights in regard to economic development on these Bantu national units. Such powers and authority for economic development are the legislative prerogative of the White polity. The Bantu Investment Corporation Act No 34 of 1959 established a Bantu Investment Corporation with a field of operation confined exclusively to Bantu persons and Bantu undertakings in the Bantu Areas. The objects of the Corporation are to promote and encourage the economic development of Bantu persons in the Bantu Areas through capital-technical aid, encouragement of industrial, financial and other undertakings, the promotion and planning of capital accumulation by the Bantu.

The directors of the Corporation are appointed by the Minister of Bantu Administration and Development and the share capital of £500,000 (or R1m) is provided by the Government of the Republic. All the shareholding is alloted to the South African Native Trust, originally established by the Hertzogite Acts of 1936, and this government-appointed Native Trust alone is capable of becoming a shareholder in the Bantu Investment Corporation. The Minister has the sole authority to increase the share capital to such extent as he deems expedient.

While this Investment Corporation, capitalized at R1 million, was intended to promote the economic development of the Bantu Areas as a whole, the Bantu Homelands Development Corporation Act No 86 of 1965 provides for a development corporation to be established at the discretion of the Minister of Bantu Administration and Development in respect of a particular Bantu Homeland i.e. a Homeland being a portion of the Bantu Areas occupied by one of the eight national units, created by the Bantu Promotion of Self-Government Act of 1959. The Corporation established under the Homelands Development Act of 1965 shall confine its activities to the particular Bantu Homeland and to Bantu persons and economic activities within such national unit. The objects of the Corporation are 'to plan and to promote in all spheres the economic development of the Bantu Homeland in respect of which it has been established' and its tasks include the determination of the general economic position and methods for acceleration of economic growth, of the nature and extent of the natural resources, the planning and carrying out of development projects, the envisaging and promotion of industrial, financial and other undertakings, giving technical and expert assistance, training Bantu persons in industrial, business and financial fields.

The Bantu Homeland Corporation has powers to acquire undertakings from non-Bantu persons in the Homeland and sell such to Bantu persons, to establish or help existing Bantu companies for industrial, business or financial purposes, and to provide capital. The Corporation's directors are appointed by the Minister of Bantu Administration and Development and the share capital of the Corporation shall consist of a sum of money determined by the Minister in consultation with the Minister of Finance. As in the case of the Bantu Investment Corporation, the shares of the Bantu Homeland Development Corporation may be held exclusively by the South African (Native) Trust.

Over the decades the economic deterioration of the tribal territories of the Africans or Bantu or Natives has been the subject of repeated examination and dire warnings of disaster, as evidenced in the numerous official commissions. Modern economic development theory and modern sociological analysis would have no difficulty in accounting for the decline of the tribal economy and the disintegration of the tribal social system. In briefest outline, once the extensive land-use by nomadic peoples under communal land-tenure had been halted partly by the inherent obstructions of such an organizational pattern and, more decisively, by the land-containment prohibitions imposed by the White polity, a population shift became an inevitable social process. This process was given enormous impetus by economic growth outside the original tribal land-areas, more especially the great and continuing input of capital into mining the diamonds and gold of the hitherto barren veldt. Export of labour from its declining productivity in the tribal land-areas was encouraged by taxes imposed by the White polity, which compelled self-sufficient, non-monetary minded tribesmen to enter the exchange economy, dominated by the White polity, to obtain the monetary cash to discharge tax-obligations.

As the exchange-economy inspired by the mineral discoveries increasingly developed the characteristic specialisation of market-orientated, resource-utilization, so the hitherto stagnant land-use by White land-occupiers came under capitalistic compulsions. These simultaneously intensified the demands for African labour on the White-owned farms and the pressures to exclude and expel African tenant-farmers, not contributing appropriate labour-dues, from the White-owned farms.

Foreign capital investment and domestic capital formation took economic growth a further stage forwards, after the world-wide gold-price increase in the early 1930's added a new dimension of profitability to goldmining with its spread effects on industrialization and urbanization. The Second World War and its aftermath extended industrialization to a point of structural change, while a soaring gold output financed a tremendous increase in imports.

This whole process of economic expansion centred on the four major industrial regions, which attracted the overwhelming proportion of capital investment and re-investment. The gap between the opportunities of capital- and labour-employment in these industrial, urban centres and the capital-starved, fixed territorial land of the old Native Reserves (or new Bantu Areas) had of human necessity to be bridged by the influx of Poor Blacks into the towns, just as it had at another stage by the trek of the Poor Whites away from their rural poverty.

The data on urbanizing trends until the latest, 1960, census lend conviction to the Fagan Commission contention 'that the movement from country to town has a background of economic necessity . . . that cannot be stopped or turned in the opposite direction' rather than to the socio-economic planning aspirations of the Tomlinson Commission to start a counter-migration back to the Homelands.

These are the figures of geographical mobility which, in the case of South Africa are also the figures of that occupational shift from nil, or even negative, productivity in agrarian sterility to positive productivity in mining-industrial, expanding urbanization. They mark the trend of genuine economic development of the population

No. of Africans in Regional Areas—Census 1911 to 1960
(1000's)

Regional Area	1960	1951	1946	1936	1921	1911
South Africa	10,927·9	8,560·0	7,830·5	6,595·6	4,697·3	4,018·8
Transkei	1,407·8	1,269·3	1,250·8	1,154·0	939·0	871·6
Ciskei	424·4	335·0	322·4	292·4	240·9	245·0
Zululand	550·2	409·3	387·2	352·8	250·8	215·0
Witwatersrand	1,296·5	1,008·3	870·9	611·4	297·7	274·6
O. F. S. Goldfield	121·7	34·1	—	—	—	—

*Population in Urban Areas as Percentage of Total—South Africa
by Racial Groups*

1960	1951	1946	1936	1921	1911	1904
			All Races			
46·7	43·4	39·3	33·6	28·2	25·9	23·6
			Whites			
83·6	79·1	75·6	68·2	59·7	53·0	53·6
			Coloureds			
68·3	66·2	62·5	58·0	52·4	50·4	49·2
			Asiatics			
83·2	77·6	72·8	69·5	60·4	52·8	36·5
			Africans			
31·8	27·9	24·3	19·0	14·0	13·0	10·4

as a whole and of each racial group separately. They also underline the complementarity of racial employment in a growth economy in disproof of alleged destructive racial competition for a share in an unchanging work-fund.

Population of Principal Urban Areas—1960 and 1951

	1960			1951		
	All Races	Whites	Africans	All Races	Whites	Africans
Jo'burg	1,152,525	413,153	650,912	918,700	365,657	491,818
Cape Town	807,211	305,155	75,200	632,013	266,715	59,937
Durban	681,492	196,398	221,535	498,047	152,859	162,120
Pretoria	422,590	207,202	199,890	285,379	151,100	122,407
P/Elizabeth	290,693	94,931	123,183	199,201	79,328	70,082

The Nationalist Party came back to power in 1948 on the old cry of 'Segregation' and from the assumption of office proclaimed the Government's absolute determination to reverse the tide of African influx into the 'White' cities and the 'White' areas. From 1951 to 1960, the tide had clearly not been stemmed let alone reversed. But the table below, more than perhaps any other set of figures, reveals that socio-economic process was not to be denied by legislative assertions.

Urban Population by Size Groups, All Races, 1960

Size Groups	No. of Centres	Total Pop.	Whites	Africans
500,000 & over	3	2,641,228	914,706	947,647
200,000–499,999	3	927,676	388,447	444,569
100,000–199,999	5	672,660	232,615	379,571
50,000– 99,999	8	645,690	220,820	395,185
20,000– 49,999	24	770,016	261,099	406,649
10,000– 19,999	34	461,298	154,190	232,914
5,000– 9,999	63	450,097	138,547	234,971
2,000– 4,999	202	610,850	173,248	300,493
1,000– 1,999	130	189,498	58,423	83,163
500– 999	116	85,024	27,555	34,785
200– 499	68	25,921	11,222	11,139

In every category of urban area from the major city to the village or dorp with some form of local authority, the Whites were outnumbered by the Africans. The above two tables do not give data for the other Non-White groups of Coloureds and Asiatics but it is clear that in every category the non-Whites substantially outnumbered the Whites.

It was, of course, the contention of the Tomlinson Commission, repeated and emphasised by the Cabinet, that the flow of the Africans into the White cities and regions would necessarily continue for a time until the new administrative measures of influx controls and more basic separate development policies could reverse the stream of Black Bantu out of White South Africa. The precise turning-date was put at 1978. The Prime Minister, Dr Verwoerd, told Parliament that 'with mechanization and automation, it was expected that by 1978 a decreasing number of Bantu would be required in industries situated in and around White urban areas. If the number of Bantu in White areas continued to increase in the White areas in the meantime, it was not in conflict with the Nationalist Party's ultimate goal of turning the flow back to Bantu homelands [34].

Dr Verwoerd's Government had rejected, however, those Tomlinson recommendations, which were cardinal to the technical strategy of economic development of the Homelands.

Private White capital and entrepreneurship was absolutely excluded from the Bantu Homelands [35]. The Minister of Finance, Dr Donges, explained to Parliament that if the Government did not refuse to allow 'White capital' into the Bantu Homelands for their development, the Government would be accused 'of the economic colonization of the Bantu Homelands'. The way of Government help, said Dr Donges, was through assistance by the Bantu Investment Corporation [36]. Even the subtleties of the fertile imagination of Dr Donges do not persuade that such an accusation of economic colonialism by White capitalists would be made by anyone other than the communistic.

A similar theme, with its curious stylized communist vocabulary, had been the subject of a speech by Dr Verwoerd, when opening the Transvaal Congress of the Nationalist Party in September, 1964:

The South African Government would not allow interference in the Transkei (the only Bantu Homeland to date), nor would it allow, as had recently been suggested, White investors to invest money in the Transkei and take profits from the territory in the period that the Bantu were still unable fully to do so themselves. South Africa helped the Transkei as a guardian. If industrialists were allowed to exploit the Bantu areas, the Bantu would resent it all the more when they realized what had been taken from them.

Opposed to this South African policy was the Oppenheimer Capitalist Policy. Mr. Oppenheimer mixes his Progressive Party political policies with his financial policies and advocates what amounts to international colonial capitalism, when he says that White capitalists should be allowed to operate in the Bantu areas. . . [37].

The Minister of Bantu Administration and Development, Mr de Wet Nel, took the opportunity, when addressing the Transkei Assembly, to warn against the 'White wolves of capitalists'.

The economic development theorist might question what development could be accomplished in industry and tertiary diversification by a capital sum of £500,000 or R1,000,000, voted for the state-owned Bantu Investment Corporation. This was not, of course, the total amount of Goverment endorsement of the Tomlinson development expenditure proposals of some £104·5 or R209 millions for the first ten years of creative financing of the Homelands. It is not easy to get a clear or accurate statement of what sums have been voted and spent by the Government in relation to this Tomlinson sum. But the short-fall gap is certainly a chasm.

Reporting in 1965, Dr J. Adendorff, general manager of the Bantu Investment Corporation, said that since the Corporation's establishment, it had investigated 2,900 applications for financial aid and 442 loans amounting to R1,450,000 had been granted; in early 1966

Dr Adendorff claimed an increased tempo with 182 loans amounting to R1,040,000. But these figures taken from the official Ministry of Information, South African Digest, appear to be confused – the figure reported in its issue of 14 Jan 1966 apparently re-capitulating the figure reported a year earlier in its issue of 26 February 1965.

The Minister, Mr de Wet Nel, claimed that the first five-year plan for the development of the Bantu Areas to end in April 1966 had achieved: from 1960 to December 1964, 950,000 acres of land had been bought for the Bantu by the S.A. Native Trust Fund (with 3,905,000 acres still to be bought in accordance with the 1936 legislation); one-third of the land previously destroyed by over-cropping had already been saved; plantations covering 130,000 acres of timberland had produced R16 min 1963; annual income for Bantu from fibre projects had reached R300,000. Furthermore, the Minister (March, 1965) said 'his Department was engaged in the planning and development of 94 Bantu towns in Bantu Areas ... of which 37 were wholly or partly inhabited [with] phenomenal success' [38].

No reference to any achievements in establishing industrial enterprises was made by the Minister, at least within the Bantu Homelands. If the 'White wolves' of capitalism were to be rigidly excluded from the Homelands, they received an open-handed invitation to join in the industrial development of the border areas – a programme which received much more enthusiastic Government support.

Indeed it is clear that Government policy had decisively, if not totally, rejected the Tomlinson Commission's strongly-expressed preference for industrial development within the Homelands rather than on the borders of these Homelands. It will be recollected that the Tomlinson Commission had reported that only internal development placed 'no ceilings' on the Bantu, whereas border-area industrialization still brought the Bantu workers within the orbit of all the restrictive industrial legislation and job-reservations policies.

Textile industry development, particularly in the border areas, was allocated a capital sum of R45,000,000 through a vote to the IDC, the Industrial Development Corporation. The IDC proposed to spend R20m. on erection of border-area factories to be rented to textile industrialists who would have the option to purchase, and the remaining R25m. was to be available for helping such industrialists in financing machinery and equipment. The capital assistance was to be available to both local and foreign investors.

A Report of the Permanent Committee for the Location of Industry and Border Area Development (March, 1965) claimed that more than R65m had been invested in areas bordering on Bantu Homelands during the past 4½ years, representing the cost of establishing 60 new manufacturing enterprises with extensions to 33 existing undertakings. Through these undertakings, an additional 24,000 persons including 19,000 Bantu had found employment. Financial assistance in the form of loans, share capital and factory installations had reached a total figure of R22·5m., of which R13m had been offered to industrialists in 1964.

A later Report from the same source (March, 1966) said 91 new projects had been established since the inception of the Border Areas Development Scheme only five years ago with 52 old-established firms extending activities. Capital in excess of R60m. was invested in 1965 alone and border-area industrialization had created jobs for 41,000 Non-Whites, the great majority being Bantu.

Such development projects are significant, though a Dr Rautenbach, the director of the Natural Resources Development Council, was perhaps a little excessive in his expressed view that the border industrial development had a moral and philosphical basis as sound and unimpeachable as any that human thought and reasoning had devised and crystallized for practical application [39].

Border industrial encouragement had, in addition to its 'mora and philosophical basis', a highly attractive capitalistic set of incentives offered to South African and foreign industrialists. Such industrialists (not, of course, to be labelled the White wolves of capitalism unless they put their factories down inside the Homelands, which was in any event illegal) were given capital grants, loans, cheap finance, guarantees against loss, tax-reductions, rented factories and, not least, substantially lower wage-rates for African workers than prescribed by the relevant industrial-wage legislation for such categories of jobs (even when performed by urban Africans) in the main (White) industrial regions [40]. In 1964 to speed up the rate of development of these border area industries, further concessions included doubling of the allowance on machinery, exclusion of the capital cost of water supply services from water-rates charged, low-interests funds for shunting-railway sidings, special road transport exemptions, an additional 10 per cent tax rebate on the cost of power, water and transport in the case of new undertakings to be deducted for a minimum period of five years from the taxable income of companies concerned. New industrialists were to be allowed accelerated write-off provisions – the investment allowance to be increased to 25 per cent on factory buildings and 35 per cent on machinery. The 20 per cent direct-grant refund of the cost of building a border-area factory was extended to buildings erected by the IDC, which is permitted to pass this on to industrialists hiring or buying such buildings. To encourage the border-area of the Ciskei, industrial products manufactured in that particular area and consigned to destinations outside would qualify for a 10 per cent rebate on rail-road charges [41].

The counterpart of such induced decentralization can be found in the experience of a number of countries. The theory is that such inducements off-set the hidden social costs, falling on the state, from 'excessive centralization' of economic activities. In respect of South Africa, it is by no means certain that the centralization of economic activities in the four major industrial-regions is 'uneconomic'. It may indeed be doubted whether the case would have such ardent supporters of decentralization, if all workers were White. It is difficult to credit, for instance, that it is 'economic' to allow industrialists putting up a new plant on a border-area site to write off – or capitalize – twice the difference between what it actually costs to produce their goods in the border-area factory than what it would have cost in their existing urban-area site [42].

The presentation of the case, and particularly official propaganda by the Ministry of Information, for border-area industrialization argues that it is an essential part of the policy of Apartheid or Separate Development or, even, of sovereign Bantu national units. The objective facts give no support whatsoever for such contentions.

Where are the major border-area industrial centres located in relation not to the Bantu Homelands *but to the White urbanized complexes*? The industrial township of Rosslyn, heavily financed by IDC, is 12 miles from the Republic's administrative capital of Pretoria. A larger industrial estate, also heavily backed by IDC-finance, known as the Elangeni Industrial Estate at Hammarsdale lies midway between Durban and Maritzburg within 20 miles from exclusive White residential surburbia. Rossyln is in fact within a couple of miles of a major concentration of 'White' industry at Pretoria West; Hammarsdale similarly is a few miles from the old industrial region of Pinetown. The much-proclaimed Cyril Lord textile mill – demonstration-model of a border-area industry – is located within the 'stamping-ground' of the Border (or Eastern Province) Rugby Football Union.

In a public address[43], Dr S. P. du T. Viljoen, chairman of the Board of Trade with special responsibility for implementing border-area industrialization, spoke of the Government's attempts to decentralize economic activity so as to form smaller concentrations to compete effectively with existing metropolitan centres for industrial locations. He described one of these types of 'smaller concentrations' as extensions of the existing metropolitan areas 'such as Rossyln, to the north of Pretoria, or Rustenburg, to the north of Johannesburg, which are natural extensions of the Southern Transvaal industrial complex. In Natal, again, Hammarsdale and even Pietermaritzburg are natural extensions of the Durban-Pinetown complex to the west, Tongaat to the north, and Umbogintwinini, Umkomaas and other centres to the south'[43].

Dr Viljoen went on:

These Border areas have the advantages of deriving all the external economies generated by the metropolitan centres of which they are the natural extensions, but, because the Bantu live in their own homelands, the concomitant economies and social disadvantages are largely eliminated.

In the words of the Tomlinson Commission, which for that very reason had favoured the socio-economic development through industrialization within the Bantu Homelands, such border-areas are the 'appendages' of the White areas. In sociological terminology, such border-area industrialization is an integral part of a single social system of White and Black South Africa. Indeed no instance of individual enterprise so mirrors the pattern of overall growth in South Africa – the combination of foreign capital and foreign management and imported skilled workers with unskilled migrant African workers at low wage-costs – than the Cyril Lord cotton-textile project.

This poplin-mill, with dismantled Lancashire machinery valued at R4m and new plant from Britain and Germany, is initially employing 300 immigrant skilled workers from Lancashire alongside 1,000 unskilled African workers, who migrate daily from their Bantu Homeland into the environs of East London. It is the old-established structural relationship of White and Black. It differs in no fundamental from the manner of development of mining and manufacturing industry in the rest of South Africa from the last quarter of the nineteenth century. Only the minutiae vary in that in this instance of 'pioneering' enterprise, the massive help of the State, and tax-payers' money, has been provided through capital cost contributions, a state-financed training school for the Bantu operative labour, state financial aid for the Lancashire immigrants, the full complement of cost concessions and tax-incentives for border-area enterprises and the presence in person of the Minister of Economic Affairs, supported by a civic luncheon for 300 White dignataries, 'to press a button to start the first Bantu border areas factory' [44].

While Minister Diederichs was pressing the button for the first of the border-area factories, it strains all credibility to see in it the inauguration of a meaningful policy of 'separate development' of structural significance to the integrated social system of the Republic of South Africa.

While border-area industrialization, therefore, is the continuation of the integrating process of economic growth, its highly publicized spectaculars tend to obscure the rapidly rising tempo of that process of economic growth in 'White South Africa' and the indissoluble integrating consequences of such expanding industrialization.

Goldmining output grew year by year: 1952 R294·3m; 1953 R295·1m; 1954 R329·4m; 1955 R365·5m; 1956 R397·0m; 1957 R425·2m; 1958 R440·1m; 1959 R500·3m; 1960 R536·0m; 1961 R574·9m; 1962 R636·6m; 1963 R686·3m; 1964 R731·1m. Concomitantly the labour force of African mineworkers grew to a new peak of nearly 400,000 of which a major part – some 60 per cent – was labour coming from without the borders of the Republic. The old problem of labour relationship and labour reservation between White and Black on the mining industry, as costs once more mounted against the fixed gold-price, yet again caused unrest and inquiry, as related below.

From 1948 to 1964, the gross value of output of manufacturing industry increased from about R600,000,000m. to an estimated R3,600,000,000 – all but a fraction from the 'White' industrial regions. In the last quarter-century in which net national income increased seven-fold to an estimated current R5,600m. a year, the contribution attributed to manufacturing industry now is as much as mining and agriculture combined.

There is no doubt as to where the overwhelming weight of capital generation and capital investment is made – in 'White' South Africa or the Bantu Homelands. The value of building plans approved in 1964 for 18 principal municipalities and 45 principal towns, all in 'White' South Africa, reached R344m., an increase of R110m. over the previous year. The Orange River Project, a vast irrigation-reclamation project with an envisaged capital investment of R450m. over thirty years, was launched to irrigate and reclaim a million acres of semi-desert land in White South Africa. This great scheme is to be in six phases with a first phase of R85m capital expenditure already under way.

A single centre-city redevelopment project in Johannesburg, announced in December 1965, comprising an office tower, international class hotel and shopping centre known as Carlton Centre and financed as part of a diversification programme by Anglo-American Corporation and South African Breweries at a capital cost of R50m., will exceed the real amount of capital invested in the Bantu Homelands during the ten years following the Tomlinson Commission Report.

The Government itself has given the full weight of legislative and administrative compulsion and encouragement to the massive re-housing of Africans employed in Johannesburg. In 19 years, from 1945, a 26 square mile complex, known as the South-Western Bantu Townships, houses almost half-a-million Africans. More than R60·5m. has been spent by the Johannesburg City Council on services and nearly 60,000 houses built.

This by far the largest African-inhabited city in South Africa started as Orlando Township, when the influx of tens of thousands of Africans into war-time factories began. The squatters' camps of corrugated iron and sacking proliferated out of control with 1947 as the year of potential breakdown of all social order. A tentative Smuts-Government plan was vigorously pursued by the incoming Nationalist Government. The key measure was the passage of the Native Building Workers Act No 27 of 1951, which provided for training and registration of African building workers, for the regulation of their conditions of employment and for their employment in building houses for occupation by Africans. This Act, subsequently more liberally amended by Act No 38 of 1953 and No 60 of 1955, made a breach in the hitherto complete job-reservation, job-restriction applied by White building trade unions. This – perhaps the most indefensible example of restrictive practice – had insisted that all building workers, other than unskilled labourers, should be Whites [46]. In consequence houses for Africans, financed from public funds, had to be built even in African townships by White artisans paid at wage-rates some five to seven times as much as the wage-rates of the African-occupiers of such housing. No artisan-training or even employment as erectors of industrial-type, prefabri-cated housing units was open to Africans. After fierce trade union opposition, the Government passed the legislation of 1951 that opened the way to employment of African building artisans on strictly-defined African housing.

This change, together with the Native Services Levy Act No 64 of 1952 that provided for contributions by employers of per African-employee levies towards the cost of certain services for the health, safety and transport of such employees, enabled the physical task and financial cost of African slum-clearance and re-housing to be pursued with energetic success. On the other side, all Africans who had enjoyed freehold-ownership rights in Sophiatown and Alexandra Township were deprived of such rights. While undoubtedly there has been much improvement in African urban housing as compared to the squatters' camps, all ownership rights have been forfeited and the vast mass-housing projects have a dreariness of drab uniformity that seem highly likely to produce their own brand of social prob-lems in the future.

Outside these African townships, job reservation restricting artisan work in the building trades to Whites (with certain exemp-tions for Coloureds in the Cape) has been rigidly extended. The critical point is, however, that the South-Western Bantu Township of Johannesburg ('the largest housing scheme of its kind in the world', according to the Ministry of Information Digest of August 21, 1964) and similar schemes in other metropolitan centres is vastly greater than any effort, or capital, applied in the Bantu Homelands.

Such housing is the complete *de facto* recognition by the Nationa-list Government of the permanence of the African urbanized-industrialized population in 'White' South Africa. It is the reality of the Fagan Commission as against the aspirant dreams of the Tomlinson Commission. Indeed, the Republic's Secretary of the Interior announced that during 1964 the labour authority of the Bantu Homeland of the Transkei 'has had to cope with an almost phenomenal expansion in the past year . . . latest figures show that during that period 15,000 Bantu were placed in employment through-out the Republic by the Labour Bureau – against 6,500 in 1963, which was then an all-time record'. These figures related only to some of the official recruiting labour organizations. The total number of workseekers, from this one Homeland, for work in 'White' South Africa probably exceeded 100,000 and a majority of these were for the Western Cape, which official Government policy had declared to be a region in which the Cape Coloureds would have preferential employment opportunities.

This process of African migration from rural-agriculture is similarly reflected in the continuing movement of the White population from the 'Platteland', the farms and villages of the country-side. The White population on the Platteland has declined absolutely by 200,000 between 1939 and 1964. The largest decline occurred from 1943–5 to the end of the Second World War. In the mid-sixties, it is estimated that the total White rural population was 496,000 out of a total White population of 4,000,000. The number of Whites occupationally engaged in agriculture decreased from 179,000 in 1936 to 118,000 in 1960 with an anticipated further decline to 94,000 in 1968 from a 1963 figure of 106,000. Yet, despite mechanization of White farming, the number of Non-Whites employed on or resident on White farms has been absolutely increasing.

According to a 1964 breakdown of the geographical distribution of the African population, 42 per cent were domiciled in the Homelands, 34 per cent on farms in White areas and 24 per cent in White urban areas. The total output of the (White) farm industry increased by some 75 per cent from 1940 to 1965 – White farmers are estimated at about 100,000 and Non-White farm workers at about 1,500,000 in the mid-sixties. Whether or not South African farming can double its output during the years to 2000 so as to provide the food and raw materials of the estimated population at that date [47], what seems unquestionable is that almost the entire farm-working force (as distinct from farm ownership) will be Non-White and predominantly African.

What degree of reality attaches to Apartheid or Separate Development in a social system in which the Whites' food and agricultural raw materials are produced almost entirely by a Non-White labour force employed on White-owned farms?

It is true that Dr Verwoerd at an early stage of his policy-thinking, when Minister of Native Affairs, declared that there was no need to apply Apartheid to farming – on the farms there was no 'mixing' of the races. This, probably unconscious, revelation that the functional purpose of Apartheid is not 'separation of the races' but of the preservation of status relationships between White and Black has been emphasized more than ever by the course of the Republic's political economy since 1961.

After the June 1961 shock of capital-controls to business confidence, Government policy swung into the most concentrated, contrived boom. It was instrumented by a cheap-money, liberal-credit, capital-expansionist, public expenditure, forced industrialization programme unparalleled in South African history. With capital locked-in and the constitution of order over-ruling every aspect of personal liberties of the Africans, capital investment had every inducement. This was especially marked, as previously related, in the case of manufacturing industry, whose gross output rose from about R1,051m. in 1959–60 to R1,800m. in 1965. Such a rate of contrived growth could not be maintained without balance-of-payments problems. Imports increased by about 60 per cent from R1,127m in 1960 to about R1,800 in 1965.

The most pronounced impact of this expansionist phase was on the labour market. White labour became scarce in all categories of skill and semi-skill with earnings reaching levels not previously attained. The Government gave enthusiastic support to state-aided (White) immigration, although the Nationalist Party had opposed all such immigration as evilly-intentioned 'to plough under the Afrikaner' until the Republic was achieved. The actual numbers of Africans entering the main urban-industrial centres were at an unexceeded rate, while job-reclassification overtly and tacitly expanded job-opportunities for Africans.

The Government's attitude to this last aspect was expressed by the Deputy Minister of Labour, Mr Marais Viljoen in these terms:

The present agitation for the removal of the colour bar in industry would fail, just as previous attempts had failed, for the simple reason that the Government was determined to maintain the traditional way of life in this country. . . . We are determined to continue maintaining order in the labour field. We are not prepared to create chaos just to satisfy a handful of un-South African fanatics.

This attitude did not mean that no Non-Whites would be employed in jobs previously filled by Whites. Such an attitude would be totally unrealistic and nonsensical. Anyone who looks round him in the industrial field will see Non-Whites doing work today that was done by Whites 10 or 20 years ago. It was for this reason that Mr Schoeman [Minister of Railways] had remarked as a result of the employment of 40 Bantu as locomotive cleaners, that it was nothing new – it happens from time to time that Non-Whites are used to take over certain types of work previously done by Whites[48].

What the deputy Minister of Labour (after the 1966 General Election appointed Minister of Labour) was stating was that the 'traditional way of life' was to make absolutely certain that Non-White, and African, labour was available to take on those jobs which the Whites were relinquishing for better rewards as economic development continued its expansionist career. Though the policy has brought material gains in due course to Africans, it is not possible to maintain that it is in any way dedicated to 'Separate Development'.

During these hectic years of contrived development, with even soberminded commentators claiming world-championship in the international growth-rate competition for the Republic's economy, only the rare, dedicated Afrikaner leader-writer questioned the implications. *Die Burger* was moved to write:

And now it is strange but true that one important aspect of South Africa's prosperity may itself become the worm in the apple. If prosperity means that the Whites are making themselves irrevocably more and more dependent on Black labour in the White territory, then doubt about the future would grow with the development. . . .

What many people, unfortunately, do not realize equally well is that increasing dependence on Black labour carries its own germ of destruction. . . . For a process which on the one hand strengthens the Black urge to 'break into' the power structure of the Whites, and is on the other hand constantly increasing the Whites' resistance to it, is a terrible and near evil, whatever ephemeral economic advantages it may bring.

It is necessary that especially supporters of the Government should understand the nature of the problem, and that each one will in his own circle do his utmost to limit the proportions of it. Otherwise we are still going to see the day when we will curse our highly-praised prosperity.

And well might another leader-writer, J. P. Scholtz of the Prime Minister's own *Die Transvaler* piteously cry: Where are the sacrifices of Apartheid? They were gone, all gone, sunk by the new wave of economic development.

REPUBLICAN HERITAGE
continued

The factual evidence seems irresistible that the continuing objective of the Government of the Republic, as it had been of all previous governments of the Union of South Africa, was to exercise political control over the employment of African labour. For a hundred years at least, compulsion and inducement had been exercised to increase the supply of African workers as agricultural labourers, domestic servants, mine workers, unskilled labour in industry, commerce and government and local authority services. Though increasingly vociferous lip-service had been given to diminishing the dependence on such Black labour, no serious legislative or administrative effort has ever been made to curtail the demand by White 'masters' for Black 'servants'. The heavily propagandized and publicized border-area industrial development has been shown on critical examination to preserve the identical status relationships that prevail in every other type of economic activity. The total legislative exclusion of private White investment in the Bantu Homelands (and the derisory scale of Goverment-controlled capital injections) alongside the extraordinarily generous 'incentives' to such private White capital to invest in border-area industries, which remain entirely within the legislative and administrative dominance of the White polity, can hardly be interpreted as any other economic strategy but that of White control of the entire economy of the geographical territory of South Africa [1].

While every Keynesian-type multiplier-acceleration technique was adopted by the Republic, together with sophisticated variations of economic nationalism, to stimulate economic growth to new peaks of pride, the White polity's control over the market for African labour was brought to the ultimate, legally-unchallengeable, direction of such labour.

The final legal consummation was the Bantu Laws Amendment

Act No 42 of 1964.* This Act supplements and takes further the detailed control of the polity over the African labour market, described in the earlier chapter *The Polity versus the Market* on urban area legislative controls.

Under the Bantu Laws Amendment Act of 1964 (and also Act No 76 of 1963) the definition of 'workseeker' is deleted so that the regulations governing the movement of Bantu persons apply to all Bantu persons and not only to 'workseekers', while the geographical range of movement is all movement except movement within the Bantu Homelands. For the control of such Bantu, a series of labour bureaux are provided. There is a local labour bureau for 'every prescribed area' or, in other words every urban area or municipality, under the authority of the municipal labour officer; a district labour bureau for every magisterial district and the jurisdictional district of every Bantu affairs commissioner, managed by a regional labour commissioner; a central labour bureau in the office of the Director of Bantu labour. These labour bureaux cover the entire country with subtly complicated demarcations of jurisdiction. The labour

---

*This Act is of an almost unique complexity. It amends the Native Labour Regulation, 1911; repeals the Native Services Contract Act, 1932; amends the Native Trust and Land Act, 1936, the Natives (Urban Areas) Consolidation Act, 1945; the Bantu Authorities Act, 1951; the Native Services Levy Act, 1952; the Natives (Abolition of Passes and Co-ordination of Documents) Act, 1952; the Natives (Prohibition of Interdicts) Act, 1956; the Native Transport Services Act, 1957; the Bantu Beer Act, 1962; and the Better Administration of Designated Areas Act, 1963; and substitutes the word 'native' and derivatives thereof in all laws.

Although the Government took the unusual step of publishing an interpretative White Paper W. P. 9 – '63 in an attempt to relate the amendments to the original Acts, the further complication for the commentator was introduced in that the White Paper refers to a Bill introduced in 1963. This aroused such a storm of protest against the reduction of the human status of the African worker to a 'labour unit' that this 1963 Bill was withdrawn. The legislation was then passed in two sections, one in an Act of 1963 and the other in Act 38 of 1964. The White Paper's identifications of clause, sub-clause, section and sub-section no longer relate to the numbering of clauses, sub-clauses, sections and sub-sections of the 1964 Act.

It is virtually impossible, in consequence to guarantee the absolute accuracy of the interpretations of the changes introduced by the new legislation, as made in the text that follows. The author has, however, made every effort to ascertain the facts of the legal position.

bureaux will be the only machinery to control all aspects of Bantu employment outside the Bantu areas.

The labour bureau grants or refuses permission to a Bantu, in terms of the Urban Areas Act No 25 of 1945, to be in a prescribed or, in other words, urban area. The labour bureau may refuse to sanction the employment or continued employment of any Bantu in its area and, by written notice to the employer concerned, cancel any contract of employment entered into with such Bantu, if the labour officer is satisfied (i) the contract of service is not *bona fide* or (ii) that the Bantu is not permitted under any law to be in the area or, in other words, has not obtained permission to take up employment in the area or (iii) when the Bantu has not been released from a previous service or labour contract or (iv) when the Bantu has not obtained the necessary permission to take up employment or (v) when the Bantu is not certified as medically fit or refuses to submit himself to a medical examination or (vi) when the labour bureau is of the opinion that it is not in the public interest that the contract of employment should be entered into or that it should be allowed to continue and the Secretary for Bantu Administration agrees or (vii) when an order of removal has been made under any law [2].

Any Bantu refused permission to take up or be in employment or whose employment has been terminated by the labour bureau may be referred to an 'aid centre' (the name substituted in the new version of the Act for the depot in which the Bantu might be ordered to be detained in the original version) and the official in charge 'may offer such Bantu suitable work either in his area or in any other area or may, with due regard to the family ties or other obligations or commitments of such Bantu, require such Bantu and his dependants to leave such area within a period determined' by that official.

The labour bureau's authority, that is, the authority for employment or ejection in certain cases, also applies to (a) Bantu born in the area concerned and who have lived there uninterruptedly (b) Bantu who have worked for say fifteen years and who have been with one employer for ten years and who have a clean criminal record and (c) the dependants of such Bantu who live with them. In other words, neither birth in the area nor long criminal-free service nor employment establish – as they did previously – the right of a Bantu (and his dependants) against the labour bureau to continue to be or to work in the area. Confirmation of endorsement out of the area in such instances in required from the chief Bantu affairs commissioner.

The new Bantu Administration Act also attempted to legislate for the old stubborn problem of farm labour tendency. No owner of land shall allow Bantu to congregate or reside on his land, except with the written approval of the Secretary for Bantu Administration who may at any time withdraw his approval. No Bantu shall congregate or reside on such land. These prohibitions do not apply to *bona fide* Bantu farm workers nor registered labour tenants nor registered squatters and the wives and dependants of such permitted persons. Bantu unlawfully occupying land may be ejected and removed elsewhere.

Once any particular land is free of farm labour tenants, no such tenants may subsequently be registered in respect of such land, while the Minister of Bantu Administration may if he considers it in the public interest abolish the labour tenant system in specified areas. The Minister may establish a Bantu labour tenants control board and a Bantu labour control board, apparently with interchangeable membership and authority. Such control boards may, or shall at the request of one owner of land or a labour liaison officer, make an inquiry into and a determination in respect of the appropriate number of Bantu labour or labour tenants required by a land-owner. It is an offence to retain any excess number after a stipulated period not to exceed twelve months.

Every Bantu affairs commissioner is required to keep a register of squatters resident in his area and prescribed fees are payable in respect of each licensed squatter. The fee per squatter rises from an initial R2 to R32 in the ninth year. This licence shall be issued by the Bantu affairs commissioner each year on payment of the increasing fee but no licence shall be renewed after the expiration of fifteen years.

There are general provisions tightening up the reporting to the Bantu affairs commissioner or the labour control or labour tenants' control board details of numbers and names of all Bantu residing on the owner's land, with penalties imposed on the owner for negligence or failure to make accurate returns. No labour tenant contract may be entered into for a period in excess of three years. An employer land-owner may terminate a labour tenant contract, if the Bantu tenant is absent from the land without permission when called upon to perform such labour service.

A new land-owner employer may within three months of assuming ownership of the land bought by him terminate a labour tenant contract on giving three months' notice. The labour tenant may also on such transfer of ownership of the land terminate his contract with the new owner. Whenever two or more Bantu belonging to the same household or family are bound under any labour tenant contract, entered into by them or on their behalf, to render service to any one employer, a failure of any one such Bantu to fulfill any of his obligations under such contract, which entitles the employer to terminate such contract as against that one Bantu, also entitles the employer to terminate the contract against all or any of the Bantu labour tenants concerned.

The Minister is empowered, if, in his opinion, the congregation of any Bantu on any land or the situation of the accomodation provided for Bantu on any land or the presence of Bantu in any area traversed by them for the purpose of congregating upon any land is causing a nuisance to persons resident in the vicinity, or it is undesirable – having regard to the locality of any land – that Bantu should congregate on such land, to prohibit the owner of the land from allowing such congregation of Bantu.

Under another section, the Minister may prohibit what are known as labour farms i.e. a farm or portion of farm exclusively or primarily used for the accommodation or housing of Bantu and not for *bona fide* farming operations.

It is clear that the Act makes a determined attempt to reduce the numbers of Africans residing on non-urban land in White ownership, and to limit such numbers to full-time, wage-remunerated farm labourers. Much more drastic extension of governmental–administrative powers over the *de jure* rights of White land-owners is provided for than in the many previous measures to cope with the 'problem' of Bantu labour tenants and squatters. As White agriculture becomes more capital-intensive and market-conscious, the incentives to use cash-remunerated labour are keener. Nevertheless, the minimisation of farm-labour wages is so entrenched a feature of South African farming that the new *de jure* provisions to replace payment-in-kind labour tenants and squatters may yet again prove a *de facto* dead-letter. Every time a major drought, such as in 1965, starkly reveals the precarious profitability of a large section of under-capitalized, state-aided, non-scientific farming, so the advantages from the land-owner-farmer's viewpoint of a substantial reserve of available

Africans on his own lands for unremunerated labour service become as attractive as they have been for a century.

The new Act of 1964 also amplifies other legislation to diminish the number of African domestic servants for White urban households. Only one full-time domestic servant may be accommodated without a licence on the premises of a private householder. When more than one domestic servant is to be accommodated, the owner or occupier of the house must first obtain a licence from the local authority. In the case of flats, a so-called locations-in-the-sky provision aims ultimately to exclude all resident African domestic servants from living-in such blocks of flats and to travel daily from the segregated township – or location on the outskirts of the municipality – to the employer-flat.

Though diminution or elimination of African domestic servants would be widely seen as a 'progressive' sign, the menial nature of the domestic servant's services rather unfortunately inhibits recognition of the positive contribution of domestic labour to economic development. In many societies, both in quantitative and qualitative terms, domestic service labour has promoted social change and mobility. For generations in the case of South Africa, domestic service has been the transition route from tribal society to participation in the exchange economy. Furthermore, however desirable the regulation of working conditions, no specific wage-fixing measures have been necessary to increase earnings. Competition has increased domestic wages of Non-Whites at perhaps a greater rate than in any other field of their employment since 1948.

It was noted in the preceding text that the labour bureau's authority for employment or ejection from employment extended to Bantu born in the areas and Bantu who had long-period uninterrupted employment in the area. This appears to conflict with a later section of the Bantu Laws Amendment Act No 38 of 1964 in the clause governing 'Influx Control'. An amendment to section ten of the Urban Areas Act 25 of 1945 substitutes for sub-section (1) the following:

No Bantu shall remain for more than 72 hours in a prescribed area unless he produces proof that (a) he has, since birth, resided continuously in such area; or (b) he has worked continuously in such area for one employer for a period of not less than ten years or has lawfully resided continuously in such area for a period of not less than fifteen years, and has thereafter continued to reside in such area and is not employed outside such area and has not during either period or thereafter been sentenced to a fine exceeding R100 or to imprisonment for a period exceeding six months, or such Bantu is the wife, unmarried daughter or son under the age at which he would become liable for payment of general tax . . . and, after lawful entry into such prescribed area, ordinarily resides with that Bantu in such area, or in the case of any other Bantu, permission so to remain has been granted by an officer appointed to manage a labour bureau. . . .

A further section creates a presumption in a criminal case that a Bantu has not obtained the necessary permission to be in the prescribed area. The new Act confirms in more rigid terms that only a labour bureau may place a Bantu, including a Bantu born in the area concerned, in employment. In addition, heavier penalties against an employer are provided – a second offence by an employer within two years carrying a minimum fine of R50 or imprisonment for a period of not less than three months or to both or imprisonment without the option. Burden of proof is transferred to the employer. Similarly no employer may bring in a Bantu worker from outside the prescribed area. The introduction of such worker is the pre-rogative of the labour bureau.

Any Bantu illegally in the prescribed or urban area may be removed, together with his dependants, to his home or last place of settlement or to a rural village, settlement, rehabilitation scheme, institution or other place indicated by the Secretary for Bantu Administration within a scheduled area or a released area i.e. a Bantu Homeland, or in the case of a foreign Bantu to the country from which he entered the Republic.

The Act amends section 28 of the Urban Areas Act No 25 of 1945 in such manner that the Minister may order the removal of 'redun-dant Bantu' from a prescribed or urban area when he is satisfied from statistics maintained by the labour bureaux and having regard to a labour quota, that the number of Bantu in the area or in a portion thereof exceeds the reasonable requirements of that area. The original version of the Bill provided that Bantu, and their dependants, who have the right to be in an area by reason of birth or long residence-employment might be removed from the area as surplus labour but only after all the other surplus labour had been removed. This was dropped from the Act of 1964 but the section of the Act covering the removal of idle or undesirable Bantu does not protect any rights of Bantu born or of long residence in the pre-scribed area. Under this section, when any authorized officer who 'has reason to believe that any Bantu (outside the Bantu Homelands) is an idle or undesirable person, he may, notwithstanding the provisions of any other law, without warrant arrest that Bantu . . . and take him before a Bantu affairs commissioner to be dealt with in accordance with the provisions of this section'.

Such provisions are as follows: An 'idle person' means a Bantu, other than a *bona fide* Bantu housewife, between 15 and 60 in the case of a female and 65 in the case of a male, who, whether or not in receipt of adequate maintenance from parent or guardian, though capable of being employed is normally unemployed; or has on three consecutive occasions refused or failed without lawful cause to accept suitable employment offered to him by a labour bureau; or has on more than two occasions during any period of six months . . . failed due to his own misconduct . . . to keep such employment for at least one month; or has on more than three occasions over any period of one year been discharged from employment due to his own misconduct.

'Idle or undesirable' extends to a Bantu who, because of his misconduct or default, fails to provide for his own support or his dependants; or who is addicted to drink; or who has been legally required to leave and not return for a specified period from the area and has not complied; or has even been guilty of a number of offences specified including violence or damage to public property.

The arrested 'idle or undesirable' Bantu is brought before a Bantu affairs commissioner, who exercises unchallengeable powers of deportation including detention for a period not exceeding two years for compulsory labour in a 'farm prison'. The powers of the Bantu affairs commissioner include permanent exclusion for life from a specified area (i.e. the place from which he is deported even though his birth-place) with no right of return, except with the written permission of the Secretary for Bantu Administration.

Finally, it may be noted that 'notwithstanding anything to the contrary in any law contained', no Bantu may unless he has obtained the required permission carry on in any prescribed area any trade or business including that of hawker or pedlar.

The moral justification of this draconian Bantu Law Amendment Act, offered by the Government, is that no Bantu has any citizenship rights whatsoever in 'White' South Africa – not political, nor social, nor economic rights – because he is free to enjoy all such rights in his own Bantu Homelands. It is not intended here to examine further the ethics or the credibility of the Government argument. But rather to examine the implications of this ultimate legislative control over the economic mobility of the African population of South Africa – not merely the economic mobility of individual Africans but of the entire African population.

Almost every theory of economic development gives central or strategic significance to geographical and occupational mobility. It is accepted as a cardinal social-structural change relating to economic development [4]. It is the major contribution of the innovating entrepreneur or 'social deviant' that he powerfully stimulates such mobility among tradition-bound masses bringing about the transformation of social behaviour [5]. This was, of course, the contribution of the pioneer Rand mining capitalists, the 'uitlanders' or foreigners – Rhodes, Beit, Wernher, Phillips and others – who aroused such passionate hostility among Afrikanerdom. The later generation of immigrants, frequently from Eastern Europe, who pioneered manufacturing industry [6], also aroused keen hostility. To Afrikanerdom, these were the Hoggenheimers, the profiteering foreigners and un-nationalist-minded whose 'social deviancy' was responsible for introducing streams of Africans into the cities to 'plough under' the Afrikaners.

It is striking from 1948 onwards, when capital formation among Afrikaners went ahead rapidly often aided by the interconnections with political Afrikanerdom now in indisputable command of the polity, that industrialization and profit-making capitalistic enterprise became not only highly respectable but patriotic. But capital investment, whether by mining 'uitlanders', Jewish industrialists, or Afrikaner institutional finance, or even the State-financed IDC, pushed and pulled the tribal Africans out of their environment of self-subsistence and isolation into the shattering changes of diversified wage employment in a cosmopolitanising urbanization. Despite the highly effective identification of the 'foreign money-power' of Hoggenheimer with the imperialist-lackey Smuts in its party political propaganda, Afrikaner nationalism never had any real worries about the effective influence in politics of the 'money-power'. As Schumpeter wrote:

A genius in the business office may be, and often is, unable outside of it to say boo to a goose – both in the drawing room and on the platform. Knowing this, he wants to be left alone and to leave politics alone. . . . In contrast to the political naiveté of the bourgeoisie, there is the professional skill of the opinion-maker, i.e. the politician. The ways in which issues and the popular will on any issue are being manufactured is exactly analagous to the ways of commercial advertising. . . . We find the same technique of creating unfavourable associations, which are the more effective the less rational they are. We find the . . . same trick of producing opinion by re-iterated assertion that is successful precisely to the extent to which it avoids rational argument and the dangers of awakening the critical faculties of the people[7].

Only Smuts and the Second World War briefly interrupted the political hegemony of Afrikanerdom. But Afrikanerdom's control of government was never seriously intended – except among a few unworldly academics and churchmen – to be used to hold back economic development. The Afrikaner Poor Whites were too poor, too white and too Afrikaner not to call upon their polity to advance their material standards. In pushing and pulling the Poor Whites out of their rural isolation into the urbanized exchange economy, inevitably and irresistibly the Poor Blacks were also magnetized by the same impulses.

The polity of Afrikanerdom most deeply and fiercely resented the latter consequence and, increasingly from 1948 onwards, forged a totalitarian bureaucracy to control it. But however eloquently Dr Verwoerd might assure his supporters and dramatically defy his opponents by proclaiming 'We would rather be poor but White than rich and multi-racial', no attempt whatsoever was made by his Republican Government to hold up or reverse the tide of economic development.

Indeed, increasingly, Government spokesmen and economists have stressed the rising market-demand among Africans for consumer-goods as manufacturing industry's profit potential[8]. The relationship of productive opportunity to consumption targets is, however, such that the massive restrictions on the geographical and economic mobility of the entire African population, as well as the minutiae of restraints on social contacts, must inhibit African consumption expenditures. What Arthur Lewis called 'limited horizons' applied, of course, most rigorously to Africans in their tribal territories. But Africans in mining compounds, peri-urban slum-locations and, even, working in border-area factories by day to return to Homeland huts by night could hardly be inspired by 'emulative consumption'.

Where Africans have had effective exposure to urban ways of

living and consumption patterns – in industrial-commercial employment and domestic service in towns – there is nothing to suggest that such Africans are not highly responsive in terms of work-effort to the wants of an urbanized culture. Indeed much of the Africans' assumed leisure-preference, the so-called backward-sloping demand curve for money-wages on the mines, may well be explained by lack of the amenities or satisfactions in tribal territories, mining compounds and on farms[9].

One of the most striking illustrations of how urbanization has established consumer demands and behaviour, which Africans potentially share with White South Africans, is through the extraordinary rise in circulation of popular weeklies which enterprising publishers launched for urban Africans. Editorial and advertising content are essentially the same as in the millions-circulation weeklies of Britain[10].

It may well prove that a future sociologist will see the first five years of the Republic of South Africa, when the most absolute legislative-administrative mechanism of immobilization of the African peoples was given formal codification, as the period in which the tempo of African urbanization and integration into the economy of White South Africa rose fastest. It was also unquestionably the period when what is known as 'klein apartheid', the rigidities of separation in social life, was most completely clamped down. Africans were prohibited from attending as spectators at 'White' sporting events, the Cape Coloured lost admission-rights to concert and theatrical performances and even to hire of municipal halls for their own separate functions, mixed libraries were no longer allowed, almost every contact-association that might imply an 'equality of status' between White and Non-White was proscribed. It was as if the guilt-complex of the bureaucratic machine which turned a blinder and blinder eye to economic integration was driven to proclaim publicly and with maximum ostentation that social segregation was never to be breached[11].

From the outbreak of the Second World War, the opportunities for making money in South Africa proliferated in an manner which Arthur Lewis attributed to be the fundamental explanation of 'any industrial revolution'[12]. The Afrikaans-speaking élite were no less stimulated to participate and exhilarated by the snowball of success as English-speaking capitalists. Despite or because of the rising clamour of Africa against South Africa, and despite or because of the increasing breakdown of stability in newly-independent Africa, the political security of capital in the Republic of South Africa seemed more guaranteed. Dr Verwoerd's Republic had deliberately preferred the constitution of order for White capital against the constitution of liberty for Black labour. Such security for capital intensified the demands for such Black labour. The bureaucratic direction of labour controls over Africans[13] has produced a kind of revolving fund for African labour supply. In 1964, for instance, over 122,000 African men were allowed into the Witwatersrand-Pretoria urban-complex to take up allocated employment and some 66,000 were endorsed out of the area; in Durban nearly 14,000 were endorsed in and over 10,000 endorsed out; in Martizburg over 12,000 were admitted and over 9,000 excluded[14]. An increasing proportion of such admitted workers were 'bachelor' males unaccompanied by wives or children. This rising employment is effect and cause of the intensified rate of economic growth.

From 1948 to 1963, the average increase in South Africa's gross national product was estimated at 4·9 per cent. In each of the three years, 1962 to 1964, the average increase is put at 7·5 per cent and the Economic Development Programme accepted by the Government proposed a growth rate of 5·5 per cent for 1964–9[15]. In the five years, from 1960 to 1965, African employment in industry grew by 100,000 alone and the numbers of Africans in every major industrial region (including the Western Cape, from which it is declared Government policy eventually to remove all Africans) rose by tens of thousands.

Ministerial statements, and actions, no longer conceal the realities. Mr de Wet Nel, the Minister of Bantu Administration, told Parliament: 'Millions of Bantu will still come here to work in the White areas. We will continue to make use of Bantu labour and, to a very large extent, they will supplement our own labour force in our economy'[16]. The Deputy Minister of Bantu Administration (from April 1966, the new Minister) stated: 'In terms of our policy we say that Bantu may be present in the White areas to offer labour but not for the sake of enjoying all sorts of privileges such as citizenship rights, political rights, social integration etc.; we are adamant on that. And if the number of Bantu increase on this basis under our policy, their presence will not constitute a danger to us'[17].

The distinction between African employment in the White's economy and the economic integration of the Africans into White

South Africa was recently rationalized by a Nationalist M.P. in debate:

The Bantu are not being incorporated in our economy. They will only have become integrated when they have a joint say in regard to the way in which our economy must be run, but so long as the Bantu are only allowed to sell their labour in the White area, they are not integrated in our economy. . . . All we are doing is to import labour into South Africa, and when those labourers have completed their work here, they return to their homeland, where they have their roots, where their future lies, where they can realise their ideals and where they can get their rights. They only come here to supply labour. They are only supplying a commodity, the commodity of labour. . . . As soon as the Opposition understands this principle that it is labour we are importing and not labourers as individuals, the question of numbers will not worry them either. As far as principle is concerned, it makes no difference whether one or 5000 or 5 million Bantu come here to supply labour and then return to their homeland again[18].

As hewers of wood and drawers of water, the Bantu are units of labour. As hewers of wood and drawers of water, they are not integrated. As the Deputy Minister of Bantu Administration and Development (presently Minister) declared:

[Economic integration would mean that the Bantu] is potentially equal and will gradually become increasingly more equal to the Whites in that same economy. In other words, those Bantu should not just do unskilled work; they must be able to become apprentices in a trade, and when they have completed their apprenticeship they must be able to become artisans, and then must be able to make progress and become foremen and managers. . . . Then, because it will be dishonest to throw down the boom at managership, you must allow him also to become an entrepreneur. . . . The ownership of land is intimately linked with this economic integration . . . because the man who becomes an apprentice and then becomes an artisan and a manager will, if he becomes an entrepreneur, surely want to own the land on which his factory is built. Surely it is logical that he should want to own the land on which the factory of his company is built. That is denied to the Bantu here. It cannot happen here. All this is part of the chain constituting economic integration[19].

The chain of logic may lead the Deputy Minister to his irrefutable vindication of admitting Africans as hewers of wood and drawers of water. The chain of economic development, unfortunately for the Deputy Minister, appears to obey its own rules of logic – and development. As the money-managed boom of the Republic generated higher and higher rates of investment, private and public, and larger and larger earnings for consumers, so the economy's demand for labour grew. It expanded in numbers and in functional differentiation. The economy wanted more manpower and changing combinations of manpower, more skills and more sub-divisions of semi-skills. It wanted a maximum of flexibility.

The Government strove to manage the tensions, while maintaining the patterns of the past[20]. A survey of the Department of Labour in April 1963 reported a shortage of 28,662 White workers in all sectors with the greatest shortages among professional and semi-professional, technical and skilled workers. The Economic Development Programme forecast a shortage by 1969 of 47,000 White workers. Among 101,200 graded White posts on the S.A. Railways, there were in March 1965 7,500 vacancies; in June 1965, according to the Minister of Mines, there was a shortage of over 2,000 White miners. The Director of the Steel and Engineering Industries Federation early in 1965 said: 'the acute shortage of technical and skilled labour continues, and even operator classes and unskilled labour is not freely available in certain instances'. The official journal of the Building Trade Employers, January 1965, wrote: 'the time has come when the building industry has virtually reached a dead end in its endeavours to recruit and train adequate skilled labour supplies in accordance with the requirements of the traditional labour pattern'[21].

State-supported immigration efforts were intensified with recruiting teams from the major nationalized industries and large private undertakings on special visits to find White skills. There was a big increase of immigrants in 1963 and 1964, many coming from the disturbed, recently independent African territories of Central and East Africa. A recruiting mission of the S.A. Railways to Europe in search of 1200 skilled White workers is reported to have succeeded in engaging 118 only.

The colour barriers began tacitly to be modified. On the railways and in the post office, where shortages of workers threatened near-breakdown, increasing numbers of Non-White Workers were admitted to jobs previously the preserve of Whites. White workers' associations agreed to such release of 'inferior' gradings of jobs, subject to rigid rules of social separation at work places and undertakings of the 'temporary' concessions. In the building industry, as in others, exemptions from job-reservation determinations were granted by the Minister of Labour. In the building industry, also, attempts were made to extend the range of pre-fabricated parts and equipment items assembled in factories where job reservations did not apply – Africans were employed in such assembly lines in place of White craftsmen in 'reserved occupations' on the building sites.

In the engineering industry, considerable dilution of skilled-category jobs was achieved by management so that substantial numbers of Africans were taken on for rapid training as operative class workers. The non-existence of trade unions among the Africans minimised the training problems and the flexibility with which management could apply working arrangements was not inhibited by any 'bargaining power' of African workers. This was by no means a disadvantage to such African workers, since job-opportunities were more readily increased and earnings were generally higher than in previous underemployment.

The existence of White trade unions was, of course, a much more formidably complicated obstacle. The complexity had been compounded by the splintering confusion facilitated by the Industrial Conciliation Act, with its encouragement of rival unions. The Trade Union Council of South Africa with affiliated recognised White, Coloured and Indian unions and a few non-recognised African unions opposed job reservation but favoured 'equal pay for equal work', in its own way hardly less of a colour bar to African job-opportunities than legal colour bars. The South African Confederation of Labour, representative almost exclusively of White trade unionists, adopted in January 1965 the following resolution:

That reservation of work is essential to preserve industrial peace and equity, and supports the application of work reservation determinations as flexible measures which are subject to adjustment whenever the circumstances demand; that fragmentation of work should not be permitted unless agreed to by the trade union representing the workers or industry concerned;

that such fragmentation should be associated with rates of pay commensurate with the responsibility and requirements of the work[22].

As White political attitudes in South Africa reacted to the growing troubles in Central Africa, the tendency has been for the multiracial Trade Union Council to lose some of its most powerful affiliating organizations. Yet in manufacturing industry generally, the technical factors in the production function were not entirely frustrated by White trade-union politics from changing combinations which increased the contribution of the Non-Whites. Resistance to new and modified production techniques with consequential dilution of skills has not stultified South African manufacturing during the recent years of rapid economic development. It has been in the goldmining industry that the tradition-bound obscurantism of White trade-unionism allied to the most deep-rooted political-racial prejudices have proved completely unyielding – though even here some leading trade unionists have shown a willingness to change.

Early in 1964 the Gold Producers' Committee of the Chamber of Mines began a highly discreet move to bring about a change in the minutiae of mine-work regulations, which had been the immediate cause of the 1922 Rand Strike. It will be recollected[23] that the Chamber of Mines won the syndicalist battle and for a brief year or two modified the regulations that (*a*) reduced the effective working-time of the African work-force by more than one-third of the time actually spent underground and (*b*) compelled White supervisory-miners to be paid at pay-rates twelve or more times as large as the Africans for certain supervisory jobs often, tacitly and illegally, actually performed by the Africans. Then came the Nationalist Party victory in the 1924 General Election and the reversion to the absolute rigidities of the old colour-bar regulations.

Now forty years later, when once again the profit marginality had been squeezed by inflationary working costs and a continued American refusal to increase the world gold-price, another effort was made. The 1964 Gold Producers' Committee reported:

A joint committee (with the Mine Workers' Union) was appointed to examine the details and to discuss with the Government Mining Engineer exemption from certain regulations to enable the proposals to be tested on certain mines on an experimental basis. Under temporary exemptions granted by the Government Mining Engineer a reorganisation of work has been undertaken on certain mines as an experiment. Miners engaged in this experiment are not relieved of any responsibility but the amount of physical supervision previously required of them under the Mining Regulations has been decreased by the allocation of trained Bantu, still under their charge, to certain supervisory tasks. The experiments are to continue until the end of June, 1965, when the results will be closely examined.

This experiment was, as noted, an attempt to revive the work-procedures of the 1922–4 inter-regnum, when the 1911 Mines and

Works Regulations were declared invalid and then re-imposed by the incoming Pact Government of Nationalists and Labour Party. It provided for Africans 'boss-boys', re-named in 1965 Competent Non-Scheduled Persons (CNSP's), to undertake preliminary work-safety inspections so that labouring operations by the African mine-workers might begin without waiting the regulation pre-shift visit by the White supervisor, and subsequent visits by the latter for checking that again caused considerable idle time by labour gangs.

With labour gangs working at distances apart and on different levels, the overall supervisory function compulsorily carried out by the White supervisor meant major lost-time. In recent years, apart from the extra labour costs involved, supervision problems have been aggravated by difficulties in finding Whites willing to work underground. In the 1960's, mining no longer represented the 'aristocracy' of White employment in South Africa as it had in decades past [24]. Sons no longer follow fathers into mining and alternative job-opportunities are more attractive.

The experiment had the strong support of the official leadership of the Mineworker's Union, more particularly its General Secretary, as it promised that daily-paid White miners would become monthly salaried personnel with additional fringe-benefits. Higher earnings for CNSP's, or boss-boys, would also follow. Their fitness to discharge the duties of work-safety supervision had already been evidenced at the beginning of the century, so that this aspect of the 'experiment' was not especially adventurous or experimental.

Despite these favourable conditions and despite the official blessing of the Government Mining Inspector, it was probably naïve of the Chamber of Mines to believe that the politicians would not hasten to exacerbate an old sore-spot. In due course a Nationalist Party member embarrassed the Minister of Mines by asking questions. The Minister disclaimed knowledge of the experiment – or at least goverment approval for an experiment which the Government Mining Engineer had seemingly not told his Minister about; and when a breakaway, dissident group opposed the official Union leadership threatening both strikes and personal violence, the Minister instructed the Industrial Tribunal to investigate and report. The Mine Inquiry was 'to examine the matter from a much wider point of view than merely according to financial benefits or safety factors'. The Inquiry Commission concluded that 'there is no doubt that any reorganization which is aimed at the more efficient use of manpower will be to the direct advantage of the industry'. But it also concluded: 'If this experiment is an attempt to solve the problem of labour shortage, it must necessarily serve as an encouragement to other industries, some of which have more serious labour problems than the mining industry, to conduct similar experiments'. The question-begging nature of this observation hardly merits comment. Apart from all relevant considerations of cost-reductions to improve marginal profitability of declining ore-reserves, of increased benefits for White miners and increased wages for a small group of African miners, the Government had repeatedly allowed work-reorganization in manufacturing industries and in its own controlled-enterprises to extend operative and semi-skilled jobs for Non-Whites in the absence of Whites to fill vacancies. Nevertheless the Government shied away from this most explosive of all industrial-relations issues in South African experience and ordered the discontinuation of the mining-industry experiment 'in view of the detrimental implications involved' [25].

The most 'detrimental' of the implications, from the criteria of economic development, is, of course, the loss of gold output. Despite the undoubted broadening of the country's economic activities and the contemporary diversification of the income stream, optimum gold output remains of strategic importance to gross national product. South Africa's balance of payments cannot be indifferent to the shift in the margin of goldmining profitability that merely awaits a modification of work-regulations which were of doubtful justification in the early 1900's. It may well be that the Government itself will finally accept the challenge of the right-wing element in the Mineworkers' Union and insist on the resumption of the 'experiment'. There is a continuing instability about South Africa's balance of payments that must make it increasingly burdensome to treat the deliberate cost-inflation in goldmining as less 'detrimental' to the nation than the appeasement of a declining minority of White miners. Foreign exchange reserves which reached an all-time peak of R525m. in September 1963 fell away rapidly from early in 1964 to a low of R306m in September 1965 and only stringent measures of credit restraints, tighter capital controls and a renewed, induced capital inflow brought reserves back to R442m. in early 1966.

The goldmining industry has for so long played the role of economic frontier in South African economic history, analagous to the West in American history, that it may still be extended. Mining technology in South Africa today probably leads the world and ultra-deep mining has shown dramatic achievements [26]. Furthermore, with the world's largest uranium reserves as a joint-product of gold production, a nuclear-powered era holds out stimulating prospects. What, finally, can be said about the imposed immobilities on African labour? It probably defies econometric calculation to establish even an estimate of its past, present and future consequence to South African economic development. Arthur Lewis, as many others, places great weight on the dependence of economic growth on a high degree of vertical mobility:

Economic growth is usually associated with a high degree of vertical mobility, upward and downward. . . . In the first place, if the upper classes – in business, government, science and other spheres – are not continually refreshed from below, they degenerate, both biologically and culturally. . . .

In South Africa a total barrier has been placed on vertical mobility as between White and Black. During the entire course of legislation and administration from the formation of the Union, and with rising rigidity from the establishment of the Republic, every action of the political factor has striven to ensure that no White man should fall in status below a Black man and that no Black man should rise in status above a White man. But economic forces, more precisely the development of capitalism, have brought about in South Africa the same decay of feudalism as they did in medieval Europe. Even the Land Act of 1911, that led to a concentration of land ownership in fewer and fewer White hands (as market-demand added its values to unutilized resources), might from a broad standpoint be interpreted as similar in ultimate significance as the enclosure of the commons in Britain. Thus, in due course, sheep and maize-farming did come to yield – especially after the 1940's – large profits, that became a key source of capital formation among the Afrikaners and over the decades forced mobility on the Africans.

The total barrier to the extension of land ownership among tribal Africans, and the legal restraints on labour tenancy in White agriculture, slowly broke up the undivided family and opened up the incentives that come from individualization of effort and reward. In the Native Reserves high birth rates were off-set by high death rates; there was no technological progress and no resource discovery, no capital accumulation and no set savings. There was, in the terms of Higgins[27], a truly stagnant economy. The migration of labour from these tribal territories in search of monetary rewards as wage-paid workers in mining and in manufacturing industry began a vital move. Mining discoveries at Kimberley and on the Witwatersrand favoured private capital investment and hence the whole scale of autonomous, as distinct from induced, investment.

Furthermore, world technological progress from after the Second World War provided new technical plant in industry that greatly favoured operative-class or semi-skilled labour. The Non-Whites of South Africa were a very large supply of such labour and more than any other change, this increased the geographical and social mobility of the Non-Whites. Though totally denied any place or real promise (other than in a non-existent separate economic development) of leadership, such prohibition on the Non-Whites has not in fact prevented economic growth. Arthur Lewis shrewdly discerned that so long as vertical mobility was possible within White South Africa, the fact that the Whites represented one-fifth of the country's total population was perhaps sufficient to maintain fresh leadership for the whole society[28].

Within the White population, there has indeed been an almost complete absence of class or social distinction to inhibit abilities or capitalistic mores and drives. White supremacy has, moreover, guaranteed political security of capital. In the context of an increasingly turbulent Africa, the Republic has assured capitalists from arbitrary despoliation by communism, socialism or even excessively regressive taxation systems. At least the security has seemed to be for the time-span, which an ebullient class of capitalists has interpreted as within their life-times. *Après moi, le déluge* has comforted the White profit-makers of South Africa no less than the Bourbons.

Yet labour does remain a limiting factor in economic development. The Economic Development Programme, 1964–9, believed that a growth rate of $5\frac{1}{2}$ per cent per annum could be maintained. This would result in 47,400 vacancies for Whites but, it argued, if the current, 1963, rate of immigration could be maintained or increased, 'a shortage of White (skilled) labour will, generally speaking, not cause a serious bottleneck'[29]. Immigration has in the years 1963 to 1965 exceeded the estimated 20,000 of the EDP calculation by a large margin – probably by about 10,000 in each year[30]. What is difficult to understand, however, is that the EDP should ignore the incontestable evidence that increased White immigration increases the demands for Non-White labour and *for Non-White labour of rising grades of skill.*

EDP's further analysis of trends in labour demand and labour supply, made 'within the broad framework of the Government's policy', was that the labour bottleneck was in reality a dearth of White skills and that total unemployment for 1969 would be in excess of 190,000. There would, in other words, be available a very substantial number of unemployed Non-Whites who, Government policy permitting, constituted a resource for a rate of growth in excess of 5½ per cent per annum.

The immobilites imposed on the Non-Whites were the real bottle neck to economic growth and not the 'dearth' of White skills. It is in the nature of macro-economic planning to treat labour as a 'resource' or 'magnitude'. The dehumanizing aspect of this approach becomes only too evident in the case of the Republic of South Africa, where the African is at once a 'unit of labour' in relation to his rights to participate in the economic activities of the country and Africans are an 'aggregate of labour' in establishing economic development programmes for a society, in which they have no political rights of any kind.

The absence of such rights has unquestionably entrenched the differentials in earnings and incomes between Whites and Non-Whites, and more particularly between Whites and Africans.

Economically Active Population, Males only, Republic of South Africa by Some Categories – Official Census 1960

	Total	Whites	Coloureds	Asiatics	Africans
Professional, tech- nical, related*	116,576	81,901	7,297	3,909	23,469
Administrative, execu- tive, managerial	59,871	51,714	1,129	2,410	4,528
Clerical	167,793	135,346	6,026	7,867	18,554
Farm workers	1,096,103	11,643	109,675	9,241	965,541
Miner, quarryman	558,676	31,563	3,237	182	523,694
Transport:					
Driver, fireman (Rly)	11,398	11,398	—	—	—
Driver (road)	66,270	18,483	12,472	6,025	29,290

*In respect of the Non-Whites, this classification consists overwhelmingly of teachers and nurses. As at 1960, no African and indeed no Non-Whites appeared as architects, engineers, surveyors, veterinarians, scientists or even as medical doctors. This last seems, however, an error as there are known to be Coloured and Asiatic doctors and a few Africans in training.

When the further breakdown of the classification of 'Craftsman, production worker, labourer' is made, the status relationships emerge in even starker contrast.

	All Races	Whites	Coloured	Asiatic	Africans
Craftsman, production, labourer	1,147,591	254,381	155,421	33,766	704,023
Fitter/turner/ boilermaker	33,775	32,628	1,147	—	—
Mechanic (non-electrical)	31,112	28,615	1,849	648	—
Plumber, steel metal worker	10,275	8,677	1,598	—	—
Other metal worker	16,276	15,189	1,087	—	—
Electrician	28,218	27,294	924	—	—
Carpenter	36,425	23,028	8,000	1,757	3,640
Painter	20,897	7,982	7,703	836	4,376
Bricklayer, plasterer	10,505	7,258	2,094	1,153	—
Labourer	758,721	14,119	90,631	10,386	643,585

Income Groups, 1960, Whites and Coloureds—Male/Female

(1964 Year Book)

Annual Income in Rands	White male	White female	Annual Income in Rands	Coloureds male	Coloureds female
No income*	627,034	1,132,288	No income	400,377	578,785
Under 200	18,065	29,533	Under 200	147,484	114,544
200—	47,313	73,376	200—	92,207	27,790
400—	37,966	44,600	400—	40,561	16,448
600—	57,447	74,829	600—	22,231	5,871
800—	47,862	52,221	800—	11,912	1,727
1000—	51,785	38,532	1000—	8,293	696
1200—	116,729	43,904	1200—	8,907	332
1600—	153,517	18,206	1600—	4,228	247
2000—	213,838	14,118	2000—	1,577	—
3000—	65,535	4,178	3000+	261	—
4000—	31,085	1,840			
5000—	14,630	791			
6000—	14,719	862			
8000—	6,554	311			
10,000—	5,893	352			
15,000+	3,751	290			
No return	15,380	19,158	No return	12,794	11,986
	1,539,103	1,549,389		750,832	758,426

(*No income group would be mainly children and elderly persons)

The economic colour barriers are, of course, reflected in earnings and income structure. The table above gives income group classifications for Whites and Coloureds from the official statistical yearbook for 1964. No figures for Africans are published but African incomes are known to be substantially less than those for Coloured, as is indeed obvious from the overwhelming proportion of Africans working as farm-workers and unskilled labourers.

Excluding the no income (that is, children and elderly) and the no return groups, there were, in 1960, 734,162 Whites (male and female) out of a total of 1,294,632 income-earning who received less than R1200 or £600 in that year; there were 499,003 Coloureds (male and female) out of a total of 505,316 income-earning who received less than R1200 or £600 in that year. That is, 64 per cent of Whites earned less than R1200, and 99 per cent of Coloureds earned less than R1200. No figures for Africans are available.

In the goldmining industry, relative earnings are reflected in:

	Nos. Employed		Salaries/Wages Total R000's		Earnings per capita	
	Whites	Africans	Whites	Africans	Whites	Africans
1945	43,425	331,108	43,358	28,578	R1000	R86
1963	48,686	395,762	130,317	60,622	R2676	R153

(Source – South African Year Book 1964)

In 1945, the earnings per White miner were R1000 as compared with R86 per African miner. By 1963 the earnings of the African miner had increased by R67 per year, the earnings of the White miner by R1676 per year. The earnings of the African miner increased by nearly 80 per cent from 1945 to 1963 but, whereas the White miner earned eleven times as much as the African miner in 1945, by 1963 the White miner was earning over 17 times as much. Earnings for Africans are cash only and exclude compound-living and food.

The author is most doubtful of the validity of all calculations of the proportion of White and African shares in the national income. No real statistical facts are available. Nonetheless the chairman of the Board of Trade and Industries, Dr S. P. du T. Viljoen in an address in October 1964 said: Estimates of Bantu (African) income are usually based on the assumption that the Bantu get approximately one-quarter of the total net domestic product. Recent investigations would seem to indicate however that this proportion is too high, and that one-fifth would probably be a more realistic figure.

Prof. Enke in his macro-economic analysis of the South African economy accepted a figure of allocating the total wage income within the modern sector (i.e. excluding the Bantu Homelands) between Whites and Non-Whites in the ratio of five to one. Dr J. de V. Graaff in an alternative model of South African growth, while noting that the great difference in productivity between European and Non-European labour is in part due to restrictions on vertical and geographical mobility imposed by law, makes the legitimate point that the difference is also due to profound cultural differences. How rapidly these differences will disappear is, he says, a matter of conjecture [31].

It is the thesis of this book that both the rate of economic development and the income relationships of White and Non-White have been crucially influenced by the political factor of Afrikanerdom. This political factor with its fundamental aim of White supremacy progressively disenfranchised the Africans totally and the Coloureds to a nullity (the Asiatics have never had any kind of parliamentary representation). The absolute and the relative poverty of the Coloureds, the Asiatics and the Africans is, in the author's contention, inescapably involved in such disenfranchisement.

Bernard Crick writes in his *Defence of Politics*:

Perhaps it all comes down to the fact that there are two great enemies of politics: indifference to human suffering and the passionate quest for certainty in matters which are essentially political. Indifference to human suffering discredits free regimes which are unable, or which fear, to extend the habits and possibility of freedom from the few to the many. The quest for certainty scorns the political virtues – of prudence, of conciliation, of compromise, of variety, of adaptability, of liveliness – in favour of some pseudo-science of government, some absolute-sounding ethic, or some ideology, some world-picture in terms of either race or economics[32].

The ethos of Afrikanerdom saw and sees it differently. In the opening chapter of his *The Afrikaner's Interpretation of South African History* Prof. F. A. van Jaarsveld writes that the belief of the Afrikaner people, that they have been assigned a place in the southern corner of Africa for a 'purpose' and to 'fulfil a mission', lies deep-rooted in South African history. Further, he says, the idea of divine election, purpose or calling has ties with the process of self-assertion of the

Afrikaner and with his nationalism[33]. The Afrikaner, with Old Testament inspiration and Calvanistic conviction, saw himself 'Sheltered by God; bringing light to the benighted.'

The threat of 'equalization' to 'self-preservation' moved the editor of *Die Transvaler* to a passionate defence:

Here, at the southern point of Africa, just over 3,000,000 Whites are acting in a way that incurs the censure of a very large portion of the rest of the world. . . . Not only do the detractors believe that no such thing as racial differences exist, but they also hold the view when it comes to politics, matters such as differences in culture and civilization should not be taken into account. The question here concerns one of the most important manifestations of the great process of equalization which is threatening to engulf the world. Attempting to check this process is a task demanding superhuman exertion. Yet this is exactly what the Whites of the Republic will have to do. . . . The wise Creator has endowed every living organism, however small or weak, with the urge for self-preservation. An animal threatened with death will fight to the last. . . . It finds expression also in a nation. . . . In this period of equalization, to which everything must be sacrificed the people of South Africa are now faced with a challenge. . . . The people know that if they were to yield to the ultimatum, it would be their end.

Every nation has a life philosophy of its own. This life philosophy is based primarily on certain principles which for a particular nation are life itself. It is these principles – and not the skin colour – which in the past have induced nations to fight to the bitter end for the maintenance of their life philosophy, their principles, their culture and their civilization. . . .

The handful of Whites know that if they were to yield to the pressures from abroad and start with a process of equalization, they would have to sacrifice everything that had made life worth living for them. As the position is at present, the process of equalization will not result in the uncivilized non-Whites (who are in the majority) being raised to the level of the Whites; the latter will be forced down to the level of the non-Whites. And this is a level where all the big principles of life – principles with which the Whites can manage as little as fish can do without water – are not recognized[34].

But Afrikanerdom faced not only world forces of equalization. It faced a rapid rate of economic development generated from within. A dynamic capitalism was in the long run no less an integrating force of equalitarianism. In the years when Afrikanerdom was in political opposition, in the decades past when it fought the Imperial Factor, it saw no less clearly the dangers from capitalistic growth and conceived the answer in Aparthied – in separate development. But when Afrkikanerdom came to power, it determined to welcome and promote economic development – not least because only a powerful economy might offer successful resistance to those external forces of equalization.

What mattered was political power and the crux of Apartheid became political separation. Territorial separation was downgraded to secondary significance, while the increasing use of African labour in the White man's economic domain no longer constituted integration. The Prime Minister, Dr Verwoerd, pronounced:

The crux of the policy of separation is political separation. The basic standpoint is that the Bantu and the Whites will have their political future apart from one another. . . . Territorial separation is not the crux of the policy of separation. Territorial separation is important in the sense that the further one can develop it, the greater are the chances of having good relations and of avoiding conflict. . . . While the territorial separation is not complete, while many Bantu are still in our midst and work here – we admit this will be the position for a long time still – care should be taken that the other forms of separation are maintained here. These forms of separation are residential separation, educational separation and social separation in all spheres, including sport and amusement. . . .

The next allegation is that prosperity is the result of accelerated integration . . . we always stated very clearly that there was a difference between the presence of people and the employment of workers on the one hand and the integration or incorporation with your nation and its life on the other.

Integration in respect of the Bantu exists in the economics phere only when . . . one accepts him everywhere as equal in the economic sphere. . . . They would then be able to become skilled workers and rise to any level, equal to that of the Whites, and they would be able to compete on an equal basis with the Whites, and they would be able to have White apprentices under them if they were more highly skilled. If such a total absorption of the Bantu on a basis of equalism comes about in the industrial sphere, then integration takes place there. But the policy of the Nationalist Party does not allow of that. According to our policy there is in fact employment, and therefore the presence, of the non-Whites, but then all the principles of separation in industry (as elsewhere) come into operation[35].

In the introductory chapter, it was suggested that social process in South African experience was the account of a political economy in action and the technique of recording events might appropriately be related to that of network analysis with an ultimate objective in view. The account that has been given in these pages of the country's economic development shows no programming, no scheduling and little planning of such development. But the self-expression of market forces, of individual capitalistic profit-making, has had to come to terms with the motivations and ethos of the polity.

The peculiar dynamism and imperatives of the political factor in South African society, of Afrikanerdom, were to impose the pattern of status relationships through, firstly, complete control of the polity by the Whites and, secondly, total exclusion of Non-Whites from the polity of power. Until the attainment of the Republic, the Imperial Factor had invariably been represented as the enemy of Afrikanerdom. But even before the triumph of the Republic, a new imperial factor had in Afrikaner eyes emerged as the enemy of its existence. It was Afro-Asian imperialism and world equalitarianism, centring in the United Nations.

Once more, Afrikanerdom faced the extinction of its national soul – the preservation of its Whiteness. Again the characteristic reaction of Afrikanerdom to outside interference was to trek away into the laager of self-sustaining effort. Economic development was not only desirable for the increased material benefits it brought to all, Whites and Non-Whites, but vital to a siege society confronted by the threat of a United Nations-imposed boycott.

Escapism, by way of economic development, from the growing involvement of the Non-Whites in the economy of the Whites nevertheless proves more and more a mirage. However vehemently the Architect of Apartheid, Dr Verwoerd himself, may have protested that the presence of the Non-Whites, and of millions of Africans, in 'White South Africa' did not constitute their integration, no serious student of social systems nor objective observer of contemporary South Africa would deny the realities of acculturization.

The very numbers of demography are overwhelming. By the year 2000, just over thirty years ahead, the population of the country is estimated to reach at least 42 millions. Of that 42 millions, only 6·75 millions will be White and 35·25 millions Non-White[36]. Yet the political will of the Whites to retain unchallengeable, unalterable control is also undeniable. In the May 1966 General Election, in which of course Whites alone voted, the Nationalist Party was returned to power for a record fifth term. Afrikanerdom, in uninterrupted control of office for eighteen years, in 1966 holds the biggest majority – about three to one – in the fifty-six years of the South African House of Assembly. Nor are the 126 parliamentary seats of the Nationalist Party the complete measure of the electorate's will to White supremacy. The United Party minority of 39 is if anything even more committed to 'maintaining White control over the whole of South Africa'.

Only the single Progressive Party member stood for and won on an appeal for a multi-racial society and a common, qualified franchise. A record 83 per cent of the total White electorate polled. Of 1,325,000 voters, 1,267,737 favoured the Nationalist-United Party ideal of White supremacy and 41,065 a Progressive Party ideal of multi-racialism.

White South Africa has never more completely voted to perpetuate the differentials of racial status. Whatever theories of Apartheid or Separate Development in Bantu Homelands are propounded and sincerely sought, the *raison d'être* of the political factor remains that economic development should never be allowed to alter White-Black relationships advantageously to the politico-social status of the Non-Whites and disadvantageously to the politico-social status of the Whites. But the South African economy is inescapably integrated in the pursuit of productivity. Economic rationality urges the polity forward beyond its ideology.

NOTES

CHAPTER 1

1 See C. S. Richards, *S.A. Journal of Economics*, Vol. 30, No. 1. March 1962.
2 The Treaty of Vereeniging, May 1902, concluded the South African or Anglo-Boer War, in which General Smuts had fought so gallantly and so unyieldingly against the British. Smuts, the author of *A Century of Wrong*, from being a national hero of his Boer people, was henceforth increasingly denounced as a traitor and betrayer.
3 'Volkswil' is literally translated as 'will of the people' but it is a mystical concept of an expression of nationalism of Teutonic origin and emulation.

CHAPTER 2

1 F. A. van Jaarsveld, *The Awakening of Afrikaner Nationalism* (translated by F. R. Metrowich) (Cape Town: Human & Rousseau) 1961.
2 Prof. H. M. Robertson has most painstakingly and percipiently identified the realities of land in the early economic development of South Africa.
3 De Kiewiet in his chapter 'New Frontiers for Old' in his *History of South Africa*, already cited, gives an excellent account of the peculiar – and even unique – character of land colonization and settlement in South Africa during the same period when countries like Australia, the American West and Canada were being settled. 'Thought and life and land were inseparably involved in the Boer mind', p. 57 *et seq.*
4 D. M. Goodfellow, *Economic History of South Africa* (London: Routledge) 1931, p. 52 *et seq.* This study of land utilization has been drawn on substantially in the account which follows.
5 The best documented account of the early development of confrontation and conflict is H. M. Robertson's, '150 Years of Economic Contact Between Black and White: a preliminary survey' (*S.A. Journal of Economics*, Vol. 3, No. 1 and Vol. 2, No. 4).
6 Goodfellow, already cited, pp. 120–1. Goodfellow also writes that the exception were the Fingos, a tribe who showed an aptitude for trade – 'the Jews of the Bantu' – and who began to develop a commercial agriculture including maize for sale to a market.
7 *ibid.*, p. 67.

8   *A History of South Africa* by the noted South African historian, Eric A. Walker (London: Longmans, Green & Co. – various editions) is the most informed, detailed account of land-ownership and land-rights as the focus of South African political history.

De Kiewiet, already cited, in his chapter 'New Frontiers for Old' gives a perceptive and sympathetic interpretation to both White and Black of the struggle for land as the conditioning factor which ended in binding White and Black together in the closest dependence upon each other.

9   Goodfellow, *passim.*

10 *ibid., passim.*

11 *ibid.,* p. 103.

12 Goodfellow notes that the natural conditions in the Orange Free State were relatively favourable and with the African population concentrated in the neighbouring tribal territory of Basutoland, there did not develop the same pressures on the land that were creating endless difficulties and growing indigency in the Transvaal, p.129. Agricultural skills had been lost in the Transvaal and sheep farming was primitive in the extreme.

13 *ibid.,* p. 132.

14 *ibid.,* p. 119.

15 The famous Glen Grey Act of 1894, identified with the premiership of Cecil John Rhodes in the Cape Colony whose extraordinarily developed sense of innovation extended far beyond financial entrepreneurship, aimed to encourage the growth of individual tenure of land ownership and related improvement of agricultural methods in the Transkei. See Goodfellow, p. 155.

16 *ibid.,* pp. 144–5.

17 *ibid.,* p. 146.

18 Cecil John Rhodes inevitably came to be one of the most controversial figures in South African and imperial history. Rhodes, par excellence, is the innovator-entrepreneur, whose personal influence on 'the rise of economic individualism' makes him perhaps the most decisive figure in the history of economic development in South Africa.

19 The detailed account of early competition and subsequent co-ordination of recruitment of native mine labour is given by Dr. S. T. van der Horst in *Native Labour in South Africa*, pp. 128–36, 191–7 and Goodfellow, *Economic History of South Africa*, pp. 139 *et seq.* The primary sources of information are the annual reports of the Chamber of Mines 1889 on and of the related recruiting organizations. In addition there were a number of official commissions of enquiry, cf. Transvaal Labour Commission 1897, Industrial Commission of Inquiry 1897, Cape Labour Commission Report G.3, 1894.

20 For the operation of the 'maximum average' system, see S. T. van der

Horst, *Native Labour in S.A.*, p. 165, pp. 208 *et seq*: also H. M. Robertson, '150 Years of Economic Contact between Black and White', already cited *S.A. Journal of Economics*, March 1935, p. 19.

21 S. T. van der Horst, p. 210.

22 J. Schumpeter, *Theory of Economic Development* (Harvard U.P. 1934) p. 63.

CHAPTER 3

1 Transvaal Indigency Commission T.G. 13–1908, pp. 11–12. Rationalization of war, and therefore of the enemy, as the source of the demoralization of a part of the defeated nation is one of the most well-established examples of nationalizing history.

2 De Kiewiet in his *History of South Africa*, already cited, traces this most firmly rooted value orientation or pattern of belief as follows: 'Slaves and droughts, Hottentots and isolation, cheap labour and land, combined to create the institutions and habits of South African society. The sons and daughters born to sturdy Hollanders and Huguenots learned to look upon the labour of the field and upon all hard physical toil as the functions of a servile race.' p. 21.

3 Transvaal Indigency Report, pp. 21–2.

4 *ibid.*, p. 24. It must be strongly emphasized that this statement of the Afrikaner's attitude to manual work as 'kaffir's work' is in no sense the view of those opposed or hostile to the Afrikaner. Thus witnesses to the Transvaal Indigency Commission such as Afrikaans-speaking predikants and political leaders repeatedly referred to the refusal to undertake 'menial work'.

5 Transvaal Indigency Commission, p. 38. 'A qualified artisan in England earns . . . 35/– to 40/– a week. . . . The labouring classes in England such as bricklayer's assistants earn from 20/– to 25/– a week. . . . Many unskilled workers in England are paid less than 21/– a week. The ordinary qualified artisan in Johannesburg, however, expects a wage of at least £26 a month. . . .' Note these figures refer to the years around 1905.

6 See p. 83 of *The Theory of Idle Resources* by W. H. Hutt (London: Jonathan Cape, 1939).

7 Transvaal Indigency Commission, pp. 44–6.

8 The Blankewerkersbeskermingsbond or White Workers' Protection Union was established by the National Council of Trustees, in itself an organ of Christian-Nationalism, as part of Christian National Trade-Unionism in the late 1930's.

9 According to Marxist analysis, the emergence of the proletariat is essentially bound up with the development of modern capitalistic methods of production. See articles on Proletariat in *Encyclopaedia*

Britannica, 1961 edition, Vol. 18, pp. 576/576A, and *Encyclopaedia of Social Sciences*, Vol. 12, pp. 510–518 (author Alfred Meusel is patently sympathetic to Marxist interpretation).

10 Professor Edgar Brookes in his *History of Native Policy in South Africa* described the members 'as one of the most brilliant gatherings of Native Administrators ever brought together in South Africa'. In his book, *Shadow and Substance in South Africa*, C. M. Tatz claims that the essential value of the Commission's Report is that the very foundations of Union Native policy were laid down in its recommendations.

11 Report South African Native Affairs Commission, par. 75.

12 *ibid.*, par. 147.

13 *ibid.*, par. 189–91.

14 *ibid.*, par. 192.

15 This is not strictly true of the Progressive Party and the Liberal Party, which were established after 1955 and whose views on landownership are more flexible.

16 Par. 193. One of the Commissioners, Col. Stanford, dissented on grounds of principle, while the Natal Commissioners dissented on grounds that it would be stopping the possibilities of lucrative land sales by Europeans to Natives.

It did not seem to occur to the Commission that if 'free traffic in land' were permitted and the Natives did not maximize the market potentiality of the land they acquired, it would always have been open to the Europeans to re-acquire the land by subsequent market purchase.

17 It has already been noted – note 10 – that the members were all highly experienced *administrators*. Repeatedly in South African economic history in respect of race relations especially, the crucial decisions have been made by administrators. The politicians have translated such decisions into policies, often fatally undermining sound administrative principles but very rarely have economists exercised influence on either decisions or policies.

18 *ibid.*—see table, par. 361.

19 *ibid.*, pars. 378–9.

20 See C. M. Tatz, *Shadow and Substance in South Africa*, already cited.

21 *Encyclopaedia of Social Sciences*, article by Alfred Meusel, already cited.

22 See *Capitalism and the Historians*, ed. by F. A. von Hayek.

CHAPTER 4

1 'Die kaffer in sy plek' is the Afrikaans version of the servant's position is below the stairs.

2 S. T. van der Horst, *Native Labour*, p. 50 and *passim*.

3 Transvaal Labour Commission Report of 1903, par. 70.

4 *ibid.*, par. 71. The whole tone of these statements bear a quite remark
able similarity to the analysis of Sombart of proletarianization under
declining medievalism and rising urbanization-industrialization.

5 The limitations of the arguments in respect of bargaining advantage
and disadvantage, and the resultant indeterminateness of the wage
'bargain', are fully analysed in respect of labour by W. H. Hutt in his
The Theory of Collective Bargaining (Illinois: The Free Press, Glencoe,
1954 edition). Virtually the identical case can be applied to market
determination of the price of land – with due recognition of the element
of psychic satisfaction that an individual may derive from land-
ownership or farming as a 'way of life' similar to psychic satisfactions
derived in other occupational preferences.

6 Transvaal Labour Commission, 1903, pars. 88–9.

7 *ibid.*, par. 17.

8 Transvaal Labour Commission, 1903, par. 80. See also the informed
and interesting discussion of this tenaciously-held view of the gold-
mining industry in S. T. van der Horst, *Native Labour . . .*, pp. 197–9
under section: *The Strength of the Natives' Desire for Income.*

The Lansdowne Report – Witwatersrand Natives' Wages Commission U.G.21, 1944 – noted the earlier views, including those of the
South African Native Affairs Commission, on the common belief that
the tribal natives returned home 'as soon as they had earned enough
money to satisfy those definite needs which could not be met from
production in the Reserves. The Lansdowne Report found the Chamber of Mines evidence that the mine work period of 14 months followed
by a 12-month 'holiday' in the Reserves to be inaccurate. A test
carried out at the Commission's request by the Director of Native
Labour on 31 days during October and November, 1943, in respect
of 10,000 natives showed 7·6 months to be average period at home in
Reserves. '. . . Thus in all 16·8% (20·66% of 81·3%) of the total
British South African labour force have returned to work after what
may be regarded as no more than a holiday visit to the Reserves'.
Pars. 207–9. This evidence casts considerable doubt on the backward-
sloping demand curve.

9, 10 Transvaal Labour Commission, Minority Report, par. 17 and par.
25. This minority report also records the answer of Mr Wm. Grant, a
man of 50 years' experience of African Natives and from 1893 to 1897
Native Labour Commissioner to the Chamber of Mines. Q: Under any
system some mines will be short of labour. Why? A: Failure in control,
just as some ladies are always changing their servants.

11 The Minority Commissioners, already cited, found the shortage of
supply of Native labour in the gold mines at the time to be due to
abnormal post-war circumstances and 'the ill-advised reduction in
wages [of Native mine labourers] carried out in 1900, [for which] the

Chamber of Mines must be held directly responsible', par. 62. Other contemporary evidence suggests that this wage-reduction had a wide and long-lasting effect on the attitude of Native workers towards employment in the gold mines.

12　Report of the Mining Industry Commission, 1907–1908 (T.G. 2–08).

13　*ibid* . . . 'Whether the mass of coloured labour, actual and potential, in South Africa will encroach year by year upon the field of employment and the means of livelihood of white men, or whether the tide is to be turned so that white labour will enter into the entire field of industry in South Africa, and occupy it to a constantly increasing extent, is one issue. Upon this may be said to depend the other great issue, remote as it may appear to be to-day, namely, whether the vast expanses of South Africa, so eminently adapted to white occupation, shall be the home of a great white people or be the habitation and breeding-place of masses of natives and other coloured people of mixed races, in all degrees of semi-barbarism and semi-civilization'. p. 132.

14　*ibid.*, par. 255–6.

15　*ibid.*, par. 260–1. The Commission meant 'coloured' i.e. indentured Chinese and 'native' to apply *mutatis mutandis*.

16　*ibid.*, pars. 275/279/281.

17　*ibid.*, par. 267.

18　*ibid.*, par. 268.

19　*ibid.*, par. 270.

20　*ibid.*, par. 319–20.

21　*ibid.*, par. 481.

22　*ibid.*, par. 657.

23　*ibid.*, see whole section: A comparison of the effect on working, and of the consequences to the country, of the adoption of . . . pp. 28 *et seq.*

24　It is most interesting that certain witnesses of th Chamber of Mines clearly recognized that such calculation could not be a 'mere matter of arithmetic'. For the demolition of the whole body of cost-calculations by the Majority Commissioners, the Minority Commissioner C. H. Spencer is entertainingly convincing – see pp. 136–8.

25　*ibid.*, pars. 629–711 for details of Mr Ross Browne's assumptions.

26　Par. 725. Q.19,542 – Suppose you were to take one of these mines – the Crown Deep for example – in a balloon over to America (California), and worked it, with the labour you have there, would you get the work done with about one quarter the number of individuals?

A. (Mr C. J. Price, general manager of Messrs Ecksteins) I quite agree with that – I have no hesitation in agreeing. I would go further, and say that if you could take your balloon and transfer all the natives out of South Africa, and work the mines entirely by whites, you would accomplish the same results.

27　Minority Report *ibid.*, p. 136.

28 *ibid.*, p. 137. Mr Spencer then went on to make the empirical proposal that the Government take over one or two typical mines, say a large low-grade deep-level proposition and a smaller out-crop mine . . . and to work these for a period with white labour on the lines, and under the restrictions, suggested in the Majority Report'. Mr Spencer appeared quite happy to base the future of the whole industry on the test.

29 *ibid.*, par. 797.

30 *ibid.*, pars. 810 to 867.

31 Some of the most interesting views on the colour bar are expressed in the evidence of trade unionists. Thus: Mr A. H. Andrews, secretary of the Amalgamated Society of Engineers (the most notable communist-labour leader of his day in South Africa) said: The upper strata of society in all countries is constantly being replenished by recruits from the lower: in some States the process is more rapid than in others, but the tendency is always present. This results in nothing but benefit to a State composed of one race and one colour, but the same tendency applies in a mixed population, and the coloured man will inevitably force his way towards the top in time, and then his numbers, his vitality, and his low standard of living will cause him to become a danger to the very existence, not only of the workers, but the very State itself. This is the answer we give to the cry of unfair competition of white unskilled labour (with white skilled labour). We say it is at its worst infinitely preferable and more natural than the far more serious and unfair competition of the coloured races. par. 599.

32 Mining Industry Commission, par. 912. It also believed that in the absence of the Pass Laws, the mining companies would have no legal control over their native workers from within British South Africa whose prompt desertion would take place in such numbers as to make place for the balance of its recommended all-White work-force.

33 The ending of the long post-war depression that had persisted since 1903 and reached its lowest point just about the time of the Commission's enquiry (1907–8) was also no doubt empirically persuasive. South African imports had declined from £48,761,000 in 1903 to £24,366,000 in 1908, but early in 1908 the shortage of African labour on the mines ended and – perhaps coincidentally – a rapid recovery began with the gold industry 'advancing by leaps and bounds', p. 126, *Economic History of South Africa* by M. H. de Kock (Cape Town: Juta & Co Ltd, 1924).

In his biography of Smuts, W. K. Hancock, after noting the strong trade revival in 1908 almost coincident with Het Volk taking office in the newly constituted responsible government of the Transvaal Colony, writes: 'Smuts soon discovered Hoggenheimer to be a fictitious animal. Within a month of taking office, he told Merriman that he had

435

received a deputation from the Chamber of Mines and had discovered
in their reasoning "a sound substratum of fact". Within twelve months,
if not sooner, he had established frank and cordial relations with
Lionel Phillips, who was perhaps the brightest intelligence in the
Chamber of Mines. But the growth of his intimacy with Phillips was
accompanied by the decline of his intimacy with Creswell', p. 237,
Smuts, Vol. 1 by W. K. Hancock (Cambridge U.P., 1962).

34   U.G. 12-'14, par. 43.

CHAPTER 5

1   Quoted by J. S. Marais in his *The Fall of Kruger's Republic* (Oxford:
Clarendon Press, 1961), p. 325.

2   *ibid.*, p. 325.

3   In his *The Fall of Kruger's Republic*, Professor J. S. Marais makes such
an exhaustive analysis, and in her *Railways and Customs Policies in South
Africa, 1885–1910* (London: Longmans, Green, 1933) Dr Jean van der
Poel undertakes such a critical examination. R. H. Brand, subsequently
Lord Brand, a distinguished British financier, who was a key member
of the famous Milner Kindergarten who contributed so much to the
preparation and achievement of the Act of Union 1910, wrote a most
valuable account of the National Convention that led to Union. In
his *The Union of South Africa* (Oxford: Clarendon Press, 1909) he wrote:
'In a community whose main object is to develop resources hitherto
untouched, and where the government's main work is to foster such
development, freedom to adapt customs dues and railway rates to the
rapidly changing needs of the community is a matter of life and death',
p. 15.

4   J. S. Marais, *op cit.*, p. 327. He dismisses the superficiality that the
mining magnates engineered the war for the sake of their dividends.

5   Jean van der Poel, *Railways and Customs Policies*, already cited. See
especially the preface.

6   *ibid.*, p. 10.

7   *ibid.*, p. 72.

8   The Netherlands Railway Company under the authority of the Transvaal Government controlled the rail lines and revenues within the
territory of the Transvaal Republic itself.

9   '. . . but the Transvaal Government had, in 1898, consented to a
substantial reduction in the [Netherlands] Company's railway rates,
and the route via Delagoa Bay continued to draw away traffic from
both colonial lines. . . . In the south the Cape sank towards the
financial nadir . . . in 1898 the railways paid their expenses and very
little more, and the Treasury prepared to face a deficit of £620,000 on
the general revenue of 1899. . . . Even Natal saw her share of the

Transvaal trade fall steadily from the maximum of one-half recognized in her agreement with the republic and approximate to the minimum of one-third. In 1897 her railway revenue decresed by 8 per cent: in 1898 by 17 per cent. As for the Free State her railways shared in the ill-fortune of the Cape lines to which they were linked. . . . Thus the discontent of all South Africa clamoured at the door of the Transvaal Government – surged up from the South against its tariff walls and its protected railways: cried loudly from the Rand against its autocratic conservatism, its inexpert administration of the gold-mining industry, its excessive rates and duties. . . .' Jean van der Poel, *Railway Policy in South Africa*, pp. 104–5.

10 See S. T. van der Horst, *Native Labour in South Africa, passim.*

11 The speed with which the vital market-mining heart of South Africa was restored by Milner, when he secured the necessary plenary powers after the first phase of Lord Roberts' campaign enabled him to assume office in Pretoria, illustrate the great administrative abilities of Milner. His biographer, Sir Evelyn Wrench, regards him as perhaps the greatest administrative mind in Britain in the first part of this century.

12 *Railway Policy*, pp. 136–7.

13 L. M. Thompson, *The Unification of South Africa: 1902–1910* (Oxford: Clarendon Press, 1960). General Botha with Smuts as his *éminence grise* was Prime Minister of the Transvaal Colony, John X. Merriman was Premier of the Cape Colony.

14 According to Thompson (*ibid.*) of those attending the National Convention, 'The dominant economic interest represented in the convention was, of course, farming . . . in addition to these ten [farmers pure and simple), four of the lawyers had abandoned their profession for farming and politics and there were at least another six who owned farms, so that not less than twenty delegates were in some sense farmers. . . . However significant the inter-racial and inter-colonial rivalries may have been, therefore, the Convention could be counted on not to neglect the interests or ignore the prejudices of the white farmers of South Africa, pp. 174–5.

15 Bernard Crick, *In Defence of Politics* (London: Weidenfeld & Nicolson, 1962), p. 14.

16 *ibid.*, p. 19.

17 Thompson, *Unification of South Africa*, p. 94.

18 Olive Schreiner in her booklet *Closer Union:* A letter on the South African Union and the Principles of Government (London, 1909) shrewdly recognized the merits of a loose federation in permitting 'More personal freedom, more individuality and a higher social vitality'.

19 See Thompson, *Unification of South Africa*, pp. 284–94. It is also not without interest and significance that the committee appointed by

the National Convention to make the recommendations on finance and trade consisting of Merriman (subsequently relieved by Sauer), Jagger, Hyslop, Greene, Hull, Farrar, Fischer, Browne and Mitchell, had seven English-speaking delegates to one Afrikaans-speaking. This underlines the identification of English-speaking South Africans even as politicians with 'economic rationality' rather than 'ideology'.

20 Graham Wallas in his *Human Nature in Politics* (London: Constable, 1927) makes the penetrating observation that the creation of an independent civil service 'with the right and duty of making their voice heard, without the necessity of making their will, by fair means or foul, prevail' was 'the one great political invention in nineteenth-century England. . . .' Such an independent civil service, says Wallas, provides the real Second Chamber, the real constitutional check in Britain and not the House of Lords or the Monarchy, p. 249.

The Milner Kindergarten is the most powerful example of the contribution of such a civil service to the making of a constitution and the principles of the British civil service adopted for the Union of South Africa served such a constitutional function most admirably until unfortunately political jobbery after the advent of the first Hertzog Government slowly eroded the South African civil service as 'a second base in politics, consisting of persons independent of the tactics by which electoral opinion is formed . . .', Wallas, p. 248.

CHAPTER 6

1 The Cape principle of non-racial citizenship goes back or derives from Dr John Phillip's famous nin-discriminatory Extension of Hottentot Liberties, Ordinance No. 50 of 1828.

2 The full detail of the discussions regarding the franchise qualifications is given in L. M. Thompson, *The Unification of South Africa 1902–1910* (Oxford: Clarendon Press, 1960), pp. 212 *et seq*. The general impression of Thompson's full and careful examinaiton of the proceedings is that within the Convention there was no really strong fight made to extend the Cape's colour-blind franchise. Botha's amendment that any change should be by a two-thirds majority of both Houses sitting together, as against the Committee recommendation of a two-thirds majority of each House sitting separately, was adopted without its significance apparently being appreciated.

3 In recent years the view has been accepted – or assiduously fostered – that the Uitlanders' demands for the vote in Kruger's Republic were largely propaganda and that most Uitlanders would never have accepted a citizenship or nationality that deprived them of, for instance, the status of British subject. In the light of very recent history (the 1950's) which also attempts to 'prove' that the Africans are – apart

from Communistic and liberalistic agitators – not interested in the vote, Uitlander grievances over their non-enfranchisement in the 1890's became perhaps more rather than less real. Professor Thompson notes that the 1889 constituency arrangement for the first Volksraad of the Transvaal meant that Johannesburg with 76,500 white inhabitants returned one member and Lydenburg, with 3500 white – rural – inhabitants returned two. It was after all some sixty years since Birmingham had gone unrepresented in the House of Commons with Old Sarum returning two M.P.s. Reform in South Africa had to wait.

4 Thompson in his study of the National Convention, already cited, pp. 227 *et seq.* has a full discussion of what in time proved to be a highly significant set of rules and procedures for constituency delimitation. The Cape Premier, John X. Merriman, though a staunch liberal, had an intense dislike of large cities and above all of that 'sink of iniquity, Johannesburg'. His influence strongly operated against one vote, one value which Sir Percy Fitzpatrick as leader of the Transvaal Progressives (in effect mining Johannesburg) with his Uitlander experience regarded as the crux of the constitution.

The manipulation of representations to the periodic delimitation commissions was soon developed as a fine art by the paid organizers of the political parties and undoubtedly many a seat was lost and won at the initial delimitation stage. Some students of politics consider that General Smuts lost the fateful 1948 general election because of his negligence to correct the constituency loadings that had developed by then.

5 Thompson, already cited, p. 478.

5a House of Assembly Debates, First Session, First Parliament 1910–19, col. 1122 *et seq.*

6 See Chapter: The South African Way of Life, Part 1.

7 See Chapter: Neither Squatter Nor Skilled.

8 W. K. Hancock, *Smuts 1870–1919* Vol. 1, (Cambridge U.P., 1962), p. 320. It is not quite clear why Hancock refers to clause 15 as the potentially explosive one. This clause provided for a penalty for fraudulently obtaining a certificate of competency. The crucial clause was clause 4 (1) (n) governing regulations for issue of certificates of competency for approved categories of work.

9 Low Grade Mines Commission, Final Report U.G. 34-1920, par. 164. See also S. T. Van Der Horst *Native Labour in South Africa*, pp. 179/180.

10 See Chapter: Poor Whites and Black Proletariat.

11 It is interesting that the last-minute introduction of a major bill affecting the destiny of the African people, which was to become a feature of so much subsequent Native legislation, should have provoked the kind of argument to be heard repeatedly down the years. The

member for Castle (Cape Town) M. Alexander, protested that this important Bill, not even mentioned in the Speech from the Throne, was introduced in the dying stages of the session. J. X. Merriman appealed against proceeding in haste and T. L. Schreiner (Tembuland) queries 'this deplorably premature Bill'. From Government supporters and Cabinet Ministers came the counter-declarations that the vital urgency of the matter brooked no delay.

Like in so many later instances, too, of this type of legislation affecting African rights, the Government was seriously challenged on matters of factual accuracy which were simply ignored by the responsible Minister in his reply.

12 House of Assembly Debates, Third Session, First Parliament, cols. 2270 *et seq.*, 2482 *et seq.*, 2530 *et seq.*, 2825 *et seq.*

13 Debate, already cited, col. 2285.

14 Debate, col. 2477.

15 Debates, already cited, col. 2290.

16 Quoted from C. M. Van den Heever, *General J. B. M. Hertzog* (Johannesburg; A.P.B. 1946 English translation), p. 148. His biographer, van den Heever, claims for General Hertzog that the latter's 'Afrikaner' included both Afrikaans-speaking and English-speaking persons whose roots were in South Africa as opposed to 'foreign fortune-seekers'. English-speaking South Africans, Hertzog said, consciously or unconsciously cling to England and its interests, although claiming to love South Africa as much as the Afrikaners, who knew no other homeland. 'There was thus clearly an Afrikaans stream, distinguished by the Afrikaans language. It must remain separate. Beside it flowed the English stream . . . they flowed in the same country, but they were different'. Here, says van den Heever, was the famous two-stream policy – General Hertzog's greatest contribution to South African thought. His later actions followed logically from it. pp. 147–8.

17 Debates, already cited, col. 2494 *et seq.* C. M. Tatz in his excellent analysis of the relationship between land provisions and representation in South African Native policy between 1910 and 1960, *Shadow and Substance in South Africa* (Maritzburg: Natal U.P., 1962) claims that Hertzog was the true author of the Native Lands Bill. See Tatz, Chapter 11, pp. 13 *et seq.*

18 The Native Land Act of 1913 applied only to the land in rural areas. The tenure and occupation of land in urban townships was not considered, perhaps because this was a 'farmers' parliament' and because there was little African ownership of urban land in 1910.

19 C. M. Tatz, already cited, traces in great and exhaustive detail the full story between the foundations of the Union's land policy by the South African Native Affairs Commission of 1905 and Hertzog's twin Native Bills of 1936 – see the first six chapters of *Shadow and Substance.*

CHAPTER 7

1 Dominions Royal Commission on Natural Resources, South Africa, Part II, 1914, col. 7707, No. 2040.

2 Witwatersrand Disturbances Commission U.G. 55 – 1913, chairman Sir Johannes Wessels. The Commission found that the original trouble was due to the tactlessness of a new manager at the New Kleinfontein Mine, which was seized upon by the Amalgamated Society of Engineers to make a political demand for an Eight Hours Bill and then to threaten a general strike. This was followed by intimidation of Africans who were incited to strike and were threatened with being blown up by dynamite if they, the natives, worked with strike-breakers. The Commission found there was 'a downright general class war incitement to violence', that in effect the Strike Committee took over control of Benoni and the police were virtually powerless. There was general intimidation at the other mines with a daily increase in violence, assaults and shootings.

The Commission further found: There can be no doubt whatever that the effect of the meeting of the 29th was disastrous to the Witwatersrand, for after it the strike spread like wild fire. The mob lost all self-restraint, and within a few days after this fateful meeting they perpetrated repulsive acts of cowardice, cruelty and barbarism. The scum of the Benoni population gained the upper hand, and lawlessness and ruffianism reached such a pitch that the town was in a state of anarchy.

The Commission quotes from an article in a paper called *The Worker*, July 3, describing itself as the official organ of the South African Labour Party: 'War having been declared in the shape of a general strike on the Rand . . . [it] has to be fought . . . to victory . . .. For victory means bringing the South African public, and in particular the Union Parliament, to its senses and its knees, and extorting substantial legislation in the workers' interest. . . . We can still be "constitutional" . . . but now it is "war" . . . until they cry for mercy and really, once it is war, the things usually called murder, arson, destruction of property, and so on become the principal occupation of armies, and there is no reason of principle, but only in tactics, why they should not be included in the various forms of acute pressure which have to be exercised in industrial war', p. XXXIII.

This was followed shortly by rioting mobs in Johannesburg, an attempt to wreck Park Station, and the power station. The *Star* newspaper office was totally destroyed in an incendiary fire and then a similar attempt made on the 'Corner House'. There was continuous stone-throwing, gunshops were looted and indiscriminate firing on the police and military. On the next day there were rumours of a march on Johannesburg from the East Rand, of an attack on the Rand Club and regular exchanges of shots between soldiers and mob.

Read fifty years later and allowing for the temper of unrest at that time, the Commission's Report still reflects a real revolutionary violence – far in excess of any civil disobedience campaigns or protest meetings of Africans against pass laws in the 1950's.

3   An interesting, brief account appears in Eric A. Walker, *History of South Africa* (Longmans, Green & Co., 1935 ed.), pp. 557–60.

4   The novelist-biographer Sarah G. Millin in her biography, *General Smuts* (London: Faber & Faber, 1936) gives a very readable though not analytical account of the extraordinary bitterness and effectiveness with which Smuts was pursued and undermined by his political opponents. As 'character-assassinators', his detractors were unrelenting and Smuts's increasing imperiousness made him more and more remote from electoral realities.

5   The Black Peril cry was raised in the first session of Parliament in 1910 by the Labour Party member, Mr Madeley, who asked questions about sexual outrages against White women with such obvious propaganda intent as to draw a rebuke from the Minister of Justice, General Hertzog – Hansard, col. 1084. In his Native Lands Bill of 1913, Hertzog – now in opposition – in his speech felt that the Black Peril had reached such significance as to be a factor justifying land separation – Hansard, 1913, col. 2495.

6   S. G. Millin, *Smuts*, already cited, p. 307.

7   Transvaal Indigency Commission Report, already cited, pp. 197–8.

8   Unemployment Commission – 2nd Interim Report, U.G. 34–21, par. 3.

9   Carnegie Commission on Poor Whites, Parts I–V (Stellenbosch: Pro Ecclesia, 1932), Joint Findings and Recommendations, Part I, p. VII, No. 9.

10 *ibid.*, p. XXX, par. 109.

11 *ibid.*, par. 110. In the 1960's this may sound a trifle pre-Beveridge but it must be emphasized there was never any question of these recipients of State aid ever paying taxes or insurance contributions.

12 Carnegie Commission on Poor Whites: Professor J. F. W. Grosskopf, Economic Report, Part I, pp. 99–100.

13 Already cited, Rev. J. R. Albertyn Sociological Report, Part V, pp. 73–4.

14 O. Pirow, *J. B. M. Hertzog* (Cape Town: Howard Immins, c. 1956). Mr Pirow, one-time member of Hertzog's Cabinet was for twenty years one of General Hertzog's closest political and personal friends. His biography though partial is lively and informative, p. 96.

15 U.G. 21–'14, p. 9.

16 S. G. Millin, *Smuts*, already quoted. See Chapters XXXVIII and XXXIX, pp. 359 to 389 entitled 'The Hob-Nailed Boot and The Rand Revolution'. The vivid description suggests the author was resident in Johannesburg at the time: On February 27 there were clashes and some strikers gaoled. Outside the gaol the Red Flag was sung and after refusing to disperse, shots were fired, and three strikers killed. A two-mile long procession followed the coffins with great banners such as that of the Industrial Federation 'Remember Our Comrades Murdered in 1913'. A classically tactless decision by the Chamber of Mines that the mines would be worked without strikers was followed by a general strike by all trades affiliated to the South African Industrial Federation – light, power and transportation stopped. The revolutionaries seized every Reef town and controlled the whole of Johannesburg except the station, law courts and a few central streets. 'There was no reason why the revolutionaries should not have completely taken Johannesburg, and so held the gold mines and the whole country to ransom. There was nothing to stop them. They attacked women and children, murdered running frightened people and isolated mine officials . . . it was not until March 10 that Martial Law was proclaimed in Johannesburg when Smuts announced "This morning, from practically one side of the Reef to the other, the commandos attacked and fighting has been going on over a large part of the Rand . . . all essential services have been brought to a standstill and the natives from one end of the Reef to another are in a state of wild turmoil. . . ." ', p. 375.

17 Martial Law Inquiry Judicial Committee U.G. 35–22.

18 *ibid.*, par. 27.

19 *ibid.*, par. 29/31.

20 *ibid.*, par. 33.

21 *ibid.*, par. 51.

22 *ibid.*, par. 52.

23 *ibid.*, pars. 96/97.

24 *ibid.*, par. 97.

25 *ibid.*, par. 97.

26 *ibid.*, par. 278.

27 See Eric Walker, *History of South Africa*, pp. 570–1. A version more sympathetic to the Trade Unions appears in Ivan L. Walker and Ben Weinbren, *2000 Casualties – A History of the South African Labour Movement, 1961*.

28 Unemployment Commission, 1921, U.G. 34–'21, already cited, pars. 9–10.

29 *ibid.*, par. 10. Later in the Report, '. . . the more successful farmers turn from them [the bywoners], not so much from want of sympathy, but because, as a rule, they can spare neither the time nor the means to

come to their assistance. With no encouragement, no sympathy, and regarded more as a burden than any assistance to their neighbourhood, with no hope or prospect and used to failure, they have lost heart and given up hope and the struggle in despair . . .', par. 30.

30 At this time of intense political excitement and with the clear prospect of victory, General Hertzog made a major series of political speeches.

31 Quoted in Martial Law Inquiry Commission, already cited.

32 This however was the 1920's and not the 1960's in the South African record of 'the safety of the State'; so when Prime Minister Smuts asked for a parliamentary indemnity for his declaration of martial law, the Nationalist Party leader Hertzog – then in opposition – opposed and said: 'The Premier sat still and incited the men. He shot them down with one object – that he might sit behind the tortoise to stick his fork into his head when it should put that head out – did the Prime Minister in his statement display any sense of justice? . . . he was totally unconcerned about innocent people being killed . . . . The Prime Minister's footsteps drip with blood. His footsteps will go down in history in that manner . . .', quoted by S. G. Millin in her biography of Smuts, already cited. Other times, other parliamentary manners.

33 Grosskopf, Economic Report, Part I, Carnegie Commission, cited, pp. 99–100.

34 Pirow, J. B. M. Hertzog, already cited, p. 97.

35 See Chapter: The Political Economy of Labour.

36 Although the Prime Minister was able to accept 'Comrade' Bill Andrews to the extent of recognizing his appointment to the well-known Economic and Wage Commission of 1925, the Nationalist Party leader was not so well disposed (nor was 'Comrade' Bill) to 'Comrade' Clements Kadalie. Kadalie developed the ICU, the Industrial and Commercial Workers' Union, into by far the most powerful and effective African trade union in South African history. Kadalie's admixture of Black nationalism to international socialism was not acceptable.

37 Some account of the quarrels and ultimate split in the South African Labour Party is given in Margaret Creswell's personal memoir of her husband: *Frederic Hugh Creswell, an Epoch of the Political History of South Africa* (Cape Town: A. A. Balkema [n.d.]), see pp. 133 *et seq.*

CHAPTER 8

1 The Royal Commission on the Natural Resources, Trade and Legislation of Certain Portions of His Majesty's Dominions. This – more familiarly the Dominions Royal Commission of 1914 – issued two volumes of evidence, Part I Cd. 7706, Part II Cd. 7707 – and the Third Interim Report Cd. 7505.

2 Dominions Royal Commission Report, Part I, No. 97 *et seq.*

3 *ibid.*, Part I, No. 238 *et seq.*

4 *ibid.*, Part II. Evidence of W. J. Laite, general secretary to the S.A. Manufacturers' Association, No. 3193 *et seq.*

5 *ibid.*, Part II, No. 83/85. Sir Alfred Bateman to Union Secretary for Mines and Industries: The estimate you give of 12 to 15 hundred millions is the amount of gold still to be got from the Rand? – Yes, in pounds sterling.

   85. It is no estimate at all – it is almost waste paper, is it not? Well, it must have been arrived at, I take it, on certain rough but ascertained figures.

6 Dominions Royal Commission, Part II, No. 2271. Sir Alfred Bateman to Director of Census, J. B. Moffat, 'I have been simply thirsting for statistics ever since I came to this country. Wherever we have been they have told us there is only the Census, and that is said not to be accurate, but you propose, I understand, to get statistics in regard to other branches?' – Yes.

7 Schumpeter, *Theory of Economic Development*, already cited, p. 63.

8 *ibid.*, p. 63.

9 *ibid.*, p. 66. In a footnote to p. 80 Schumpeter emphasizes that the Central European peasant 'calculates: there is no deficiency of the "economic way of thinking" in him. Yet he cannot take a step out of the beaten path; his economy has not changed at all for centuries, except perhaps through the exercise of external force and influence. Why? Because the choice of new methods is not simply an element in the concept of rational economic action, not a matter of course, but a distinct process which stands in need of special explanation'. The relevance of this passage to land utilization by most African tribesmen and most White pastoralist-agriculturists in South Africa as late as 1910 hardly needs underlining.

10 Goodfellow, *Economic History of S.A.* already cited, pp. 103–8.

11 S. H. Frankel, *Co-operation and Competition in the Marketing of Maize in South Africa* (London: P. S. King, 1926), p. 22 *et seq.*

12 Alfred Beit, who with Cecil John Rhodes ranks as one of the decisive entrepreneurial minds of Southern African history, in his will provided for the establishment of a Railway Trust endowed with an initial capital sum of £1,200,000 and clause 18 of his will reads: 'I believe that by the promotion and construction of railways, telegraphs (including wireless telegraphy), and telephones, civilization will be best advanced in Africa, for the benefit of the inhabitants thereof, whether native, or immigrant'. Beit was, of course, thinking of a railway-communication system for Rhodesia but it demonstrates the thinking of a key figure in the development of the great Rand goldmining industry.

13   S. H. Frankel, *The Railway Policy of South Africa* (Johannesburg: Hortors, 1928).

14   *ibid.*, pp. 78–89.

15   Frankel claimed that from 1912–13 to 1926–7, a total gross expenditure on new rolling stock of £14½ million was met from the Renewals Fund though only £1,670,000 of rolling stock was actually withdrawn, pp. 84–98.

16   *ibid.*, pp. 112–124.

17   The literature on this subject is extensive. The case for overhead-spreading and differential rating was argued in respect of the S.A. Railways in the Departmental Railway Tariffs Inquiry Committee Report U.G. 56–'29.

18   Pigou, *Economics of Welfare* (Macmillan, 3rd ed), pp. 297–9.

19   See Ralph Horwitz, *Competition between Road and Rail Transport in South Africa*, unpublished M.A. thesis.

20   Dominions Royal Commission, already cited, Third Interim Report Cd. 7505, 1914, par. 102.

21   Dominions Royal Commission, already cited, Third Interim Report, par. 130.

22   *ibid.*, par. 131.

23   The most interesting, in economic theory and subsequent political significance, development rate was in respect of maize. Some aspects of this key-crop, below-cost rate are considered in the next chapter.

24   R. A. Lehfeldt, *The National Resources of South Africa* (London: Longmans, Green & Co., 1922), p. 11. In an interpolated note, page 25, for the year 1921, Lehfeldt said, 'the net yield of farming is now much less than in 1917–18'.

25   *ibid.*, pp. 35–6 *et seq.*

26   W. M. MacMillan, *The South African Agrarian Problem and Its Historical Development* (C.N.A. Johannesburg, 1919) gives a graphic and penetrating analysis of South Africa's sociological malaise that was the consequence of the failure of the country to diversify its economy as late as the nineteen-twenties.

27   See the Appendix to R. A. Lehfeldt's *The National Resources of S.A.* already cited, on pp. 71–3 for detail of his calculations in respect of the agricultural sector.

28   See W. M. MacMillan *The South African Agrarian Problem*, already cited, pp. 95 *et seq.*

CHAPTER 9

1   W. W. Rostow, *The Process of Economic Growth* (O.U.P., 1953).

2   Benjamin Higgins in *Economic Development* (London: Constable, 1959)

derives from Harrod's model his own truly stagnant economy: High
birth rates are offset by equally high death rates . . ., p. 162.

3   F. B. Smith, *Some Observations upon the probable Effect of the Closer Union
of South Africa upon Agriculture* (Pretoria, Government Printer, 1908).
The extracts here given are all from this paper. F. B. Smith was one of
the Milner Kindergarten, appointed by Lord Milner, to organize a
desperately needed scientific expertise for agriculture.

4   F. B. Smith expressed his hope that a central department of agriculture
would be free from the 'petty jealousies and intrigues . . . the undue
pressure of local politicians . . . the danger of nepotism and of political
appointments . . . the short-sighted and unreasonable feeling against
the introduction of specialists from abroad. . .' Until 1891 in the
Cape Colony and 1897 in Natal there had been no provision for
veterinary research, although cattle diseases had been endemic in the
country for more than a hundred years.

5   The Transvaal Indigency Commission of 1908, already cited, had
drawn the perhaps unduly prejudiced comparison between '*poor* Boer
and German farmers'. 'The system of farming of the Boer is still that
of the voortrekker. It cannot really be called farming at all. It is
unsystematic, primitive and wasteful. It consists merely of tending a
few cattle and a flock of sheep and goats. . . . Agriculture is limited
to scratching a patch of ground in which to grow mealies . . . the
whole existence of the backward Boer farmer is arranged on a hand to
mouth basis . . . mealie porridge is cooked in large quantities one or
two days a week and left in a bowl on the table and the children come
in and take a piece when they feel hungry without ever sitting down to a
proper meal. The clothing is usually old and dirty . . .

The German homestead on the other hand is clean and substantial,
though built almost entirely by the farmer with his own hands . . . there
is a fully stocked vegetable garden and farm usually planted with
trees . . . the whole family look clean and neatly dressed, and they
have plenty of wholesome, if plain, food raised from the land by the
farmer himself. In every way these people appear to be admirable
settlers . . .', p. 62.

6   See C. S. Richards, 'Subsidies, Quotas, Tariffs and the Excess Cost of
Agriculture in South Africa' (*S.A. Journal of Economics*, Vol. 3, 1935),
p. 365 *et seq.* A footnote on pp. 371–3 gives the titles of these acts.
This legislation does not include the very numerous enactments to
give 'special' or 'temporary' assistance, more especially in respect of
marketing. This latter aspect is discussed in the next chapter: The
Political Economy of Food. Eric Davis in 'Some Aspects of Marketing
Farm Produce in South Africa' (*S.A. Journal of Economics*, Vol. 1, 1933,
pp. 167–187) grouped the 'hotch-potch of measures large and small,
general and specific' into six classes but asserts there has been no clear

trend of explicit policy in the four-score Acts. Between 1910 and 1922, the legislation was mainly concerned with supply of seed, stock registration, pest and disease eradication, fencing and drought relief. There were two major measures for export marketing and increasingly legislation concerned itself with financial and marketing problems and help.

7 De Kiewiet in his *History of South Africa*, already cited, gives some of the detail with characteristic crispness.

8 The 1913 Commission, known as the Beaumont Commission, recommended The Beaumont areas. Subsequently these recommendations were incorporated in the Native Affairs Administration Bill of 1917, introduced by the then Prime Minister and Minister of Native Affairs, General Botha. This Bill was however abandoned when it became clear that it involved a conflict with the entrenched provisions of the Act of Union in respect of the Cape Native franchise. Five Local Committees for the Cape (U.G. 8–1918), Natal (U.G. 34–1918), Orange Free State (U.G. 22–1918), Eastern Transvaal (U.G. 31–1918), Western Transvaal (U.G. 23–1918) were however appointed to examine and recommend on the suitability of the scheduled areas, the setting apart of other demarcated areas where scheduled areas appeared to be inadequate and the exclusion from the scheduled areas of such areas not required for the purpose of African areas. These local Committees radically altered the recommendations of the Beaumont Commission and African opinion, especially, believed for the worse. General dissatisfaction with all the reports of these Local Committees in effect resulted in no significant action being implemented until the 1936 legislation.

9 Natives Land Commission – the Beaumont Minute U.G. 26–'16.

10 Beaumont Minute, already cited, pars. 17/18/21/22.

11 *ibid.*, par. 24.

12 *ibid.*, par. 25.

13 *ibid.*, par. 26. In par. 31, Beaumont added his famous, oft-quoted conclusion: 'It is, in fact, too late in the day to define large compact Native areas or to draw bold lines of demarcation; for reserves, mission lands, Native farms and other lands solely occupied by Natives are, with the exception of the Transkeian Territories, scattered in all directions and hopelessly intermixed with the lands owned and occupied by Europeans, whose vested interests have to be considered; and any attempt to deal with this matter in a drastic fashion, involving wholesale removals, would not only entail enormous expenditure but would create wide-spread dissatisfaction'.

14 W. M. MacMillan, *Complex South Africa* (London: Faber & Faber, 1940).

15 *ibid.*, p. 118.

16 *ibid.*, p. 120: '. . . For if in the end the real original cause of the

economic ill-health of the rural European is, in a word, that it has too much land for efficiency, the state of the Natives is the extreme opposite, that they are grossly over-crowded and certainly have far too little – too little to allow for their living as they once did, and too little even for mere subsistence. With little direct help from Europeans, the Bantu millions have had to face a prodigious social revolution. They have been called upon, in the space of three generations or less, to adapt themselves, somehow or other, to live on what may be put at a rough estimate at about one-fifth of the land they lately held'.

17 In 1927 the Secretary for Native Affairs gave a Select Committee (S.C. 10–'27) figures, collected from magistrates, of 4,250,000 rural Natives (i.e. excluding Natives on mines and in towns) of which 2,527,000 were in the scheduled Native areas or Reserves, 375,000 on *proposed* 'released areas' (i.e. land mostly owned by Europeans under consideration for potential Native purchase) and 1,618,000 on European farms – quoted by MacMillan, *Complex South Africa*, already cited, p. 119.

18 *ibid.*, MacMillan, pp. 127 *et seq.*; also Appendix, pp. 281 *et seq.*

19 'The consensus of opinion in this country is that the White race and its civilization cannot be preserved unless the White man owns and farms the land. Furthermore, his proximity to Native influence makes it necessary that while so owning and farming the land he must achieve a standard of living commensurate with the requirements of the civilization he must preserve. That achievement is not possible in South Africa unless the burden is assumed by the nation as a whole' – J. R. McLoughlin, general secretary of the Livestock and Meat Industries Control Board in 'Control in the Marketing of Agricultural Products', *S.A. Journal of Economics*, Vol. 6, 1938, p. 295.

20 S. H. Frankel, *Capital Investment in Africa* (O.U.P., 1938), p. 119.

21 Lord Hailey, *An African Survey* (O.U.P., 1938 ed.), p. 807.

22 W. M. MacMillan, *Complex South Africa*, already cited, p. 133.

23 Drought Investigation Commission, Interim Report, U.G. 20–'22, par. 3.

24 *ibid.*, par. 26.

25 *ibid.*, *passim.*

26 See Chapter 8.

27 See Frankel, *Railway Policy in South Africa*, already cited, pp. 182 *et seq.* Even on the basis of the S.A. Railway's value-of-service rating principles, the export maize rate is illuminating evidence of the minutiae of voting-jobbery. Export coal worth about 18/– per ton was charged a rail rate of 13/8½ per ton for 332 miles transport to port of shipment, while export maize valued at from £5 to £6 per ton was charged a rail rate of 15/– per ton (in fact including a 6/8 maize elevator charge so that the rail rate was 8/4 per ton).

28 Not only did these heavily-capitalized elevators incur current losses

but during the years extremely large new capital investment has had to be made by the S.A. Railways to handle the ever-increasing maize-crops. The consequences in turn that have flowed from the political necessity of the S.A. Railways protecting its total revenues to justify this kind of capital investment provide a fascinating example of the endless side-complications from an initial below-cost development policy. Many tens of millions of rands of investment in obsolescent rail transport in place of competitive road motor transport as well as tens of millions of rands of foregone export revenues from undeliverable base minerals can be traced to the interconnections of the maize rail-rate and the party political influence of the Orange Free State and Transvaal maize-farmers.

29 See the writings, in particular, of A. G. B. Fisher, *The Clash of Progress and Security* and *Economic Progress and Social Security* (London: Macmillan, 1946) especially 'Back to the Land', pp. 171 *et seq*. Also Benjamin Higgins in *Economic Development*, already cited, repeatedly observes that a declining proportion of agriculturists with increasing agricultural productivity is of the essence of economic development – *passim*.

30 H. A. Shannon, 'Urbanization 1904–1936', *S.A. Journal of Economics*, Vol. 5, 1937, pp. 164–90. He stresses the dangers of translating the technical distinction between 'urban' and 'rural' into 'town' and 'country', and the even more dangerous identification of 'town' and 'country' with non-agricultural and agricultural.

31 See Tatz, *Shadow and Substance in South Africa*, already cited, pp. 46–8.

32 *ibid*. 'The "shadow" of the vote, the snare, hypocrisy and "Nessus-shirt", in Hertzog's terms, was to be replaced by the solid "substance" of the land, forever a burning question in African life. In a sense the Land Act was ideal for Hertzog's purposes: in one respect it was clear that something concrete had to be done about the land question, as the 1913 Act had imposed restrictions and disabilities on Africans for a far longer period than had been promised. In another respect it provided Hertzog with a convenient bargaining point: a major grant of land rights in exchange for the surrender of the vote', pp. 48/49.

33 Members of the Native Affairs Commission (which had been established by Smuts in his Native Affairs Act, 1920) gave evidence to these Select Committees as follows: Dr Loram – Natives regarded the franchise as the most sacred thing politically that they possessed; Senator Roberts – I think the case made out for more land for the Native is so overwhelming that it will overcome any political bargaining capacity that the Land Bill possesses. (Tatz, *ibid*., pp. 57–8.)

34 'I at once asked myself what those (Cape) qualifications had to prove, what object we wanted to attain by them. I could see no other reply than that we wanted the education test and the proof of civilization; but I want at once to say that to fix a civilization test for the White

woman and man in South Africa would be equivalent to denying the civilization of the White man. I maintain that there is no White man or woman from whom we could expect anything else but that they should be considered as properly civilized' – Hertzog in House of Assembly Debates, Sixth Parliament, 17 January–31 May, col. 1520.

35 The Franchise Laws Amendment Act of 1931 enfranchised another 10,000 White males in the Cape and in Natal. Once again Hertzog said: 'the European has a tradition of 1000 years behind him and has, for a long time, lived under compulsory education. Owing to tradition and legislation, we have for years been able to take it that every European is civilized and complies with certain elementary qualifications. This Bill, therefore, follows the principle which was adopted by the two Northern Provinces that every White man is a civilized person who ought to have the franchise'.

36 Senator Nicholls's own proposed Bill would have secured the total exclusion of Native voters in the House of Assembly as 'the House of Democracy . . . the mere right to vote is recognition of the existence of democratic institutions, and I hold that these democratic institutions are alien to the Bantu race . . . to ensure European dominance it is essential that there should be no vote of any kind cast except by the European. . . .' Nicholls as quoted by Tatz, *Shadow and Substance*, already cited, p. 69.

37 It is exceptionally complex to get an absolutely accurate statement of areas scheduled, proposed for release and actually released over all the decades. The table below appears in Lord Hailey, *An African Survey*, already cited, p. 723.

ALLOCATION OF NATIVE AREAS IN ACRES (000'S OMITTED)

	Province			
	Cape	Natal	Transvaal	O.F.S.
1. Areas Scheduled by Act 27 of 1913 .	12,791	5,880	2,256	157
2. Scheduled Areas as extended by subsequent Acts	12,925	6,343	2,608	157
3. Additional Areas recommended by Beaumont Commission (1916) .	2,779	3,940	10,673	314
4. Revised Areas recommended by the Local Committees of 1918 . .	3,404	911	9,921	alternative suggestions
5. Maximum Areas to be 'released' under the Act of 1936 . .	3,420	1,113	10,642	169
6. Total of Scheduled and Released Areas (Cols. 2 and 5) . .	16,346	7,456	13,249	327
7. Percentage of Col. 6 to total land area of province . . .	9·2	33·0	18·7	1·0
8. Native rural population 1936 (000)	1,826	1,426	1,747	449
9. European rural population 1936 (000)	287	45	255	109

According to Professor J. Lewin (*Cape Times*, March 1, 1965), by 1949 the Native Affairs Commission reported that acquisition of further land from willing White settlers was 'almost hopeless'. Professor Lewin in the same article also claims that the full text of the Tomlinson Commission confirms that 'no less than two million morgen of promised land were missing from the areas released under the 1936 Land Act' and that Hertzog's 1936 land promises remain unfulfilled as of 1965.

38 The value-orientations which lay behind the White polity were strikingly evidenced in the prolonged debates over Hertzog's 1936 legislation. Hertzog in his second reading speech on the Representation Bill said there were two things which caused anxiety to White South African: The danger of 'intermingling of blood' and the danger of being 'dominated' by Africans. The Prime Minister could not accept the continuation of the Cape Africans on the common roll because

'. . . there was also a measure of social intercourse with each other, social intercourse which was inevitably caused by the way in which candidates were out to get the vote of the electors . . . it was a thing which went against the grain, and against the will of the Europeans, and I say it is against the ideals of the English-speaking as well as Dutch-speaking people that they should vote together, should vote jointly, be on the same voters' roll, that they should go together to the same ballot box . . . that was a thing which offended the feelings, because this free association caused by the joint voting allowed the position of the White man in his opposition to miscegenation in South Africa to be weakened. Inevitably the easy intercourse was bound to lead to a considerable amount of social intercourse . . .'.

Strijdom (then in the Nationalist Opposition and subsequently postwar Nationalist Prime Minister) after the Native Representation Act had been passed objected that there was no immediate reason for proceeding with the Native Trust and Land Bill as there were some 500,000 Poor Whites in South Africa 'who needed the land much more' – quoted by Tatz, already cited, in Chapter VI.

CHAPTER 10

1 There is of course a very large literature on this highly controversial subject. F. A. Hayek's *The Road to Serfdom* (London: Routledge, 1944) remains the most readable and the same author's *The Constitution of Liberty* perhaps the most profound.

2 Unless the votes of the farmers are so significant that the polity must *pay* them *not* to produce, as in the United States of America. The other end-stage may be when the votes of consumers become so significant

that the polity must compensate the individual farmer and take his farm away from him, as in the United Kingdom.

Although the account above suggests a segregation only between domestic market and export markets, the polity may have sufficient sovereignty to segregate a number of distinct domestic markets according to their estimated capacity to pay different polity-prices in a manner analogous to a railway-rating policy of 'value-of-service' principle or charging what the traffic will bear.

3 So long as rail-transport had a virtual technological monopoly in transport, no competitive-market price-system for transport could evolve. When road motor transport became sufficiently significant to bring about such a competitive transport market and related pricing mechanism, it was the determination of farmers to maintain their below-cost, polity-fixed rail rates which as much as any other influence secured the entrenchment of the S.A. Railways' monopoly by passage of restrictive legislation on road motor transport in the Motor Carrier Transportation Act No. 39 of 1930.

4 J. G. van der Horst, 'Two Conferences', in *S.A. Journal of Economics*, Vol. 1, 1933, pp. 1–23. It is of particular interest that both conferences were called by the Minister of Justice – the first was called a legal conference and the second an economic conference.

5 *ibid.*, p. 13.

6 See detail and criticism of the Van der Horst Plan in a discussion of the problem of farming indebtedness in E. H. D. Arndt 'Die Landboukrediet en Landbouskuldvraagstuk', *S.A. Journal of Economics*, Vol. 1, 1933, p. 161.

The van der Horst proposals indicate the gravity of the problem as they appeared to a candid friend of the farmer. A variation of it whereby the State assumed portion of the debt charges was subsequently enacted.

7 Commission on Co-operation and Agricultural Credit U.G. 16–'34, pp. 153 *et seq*. It must of course be recognized that total and average figures do not disclose the actual number of virtually insolvent farmers.

8 See Vol. 6, 1938, of the *S.A. Journal of Economics* with two Economists' Protests – pp. 24 *et seq*. and pp. 186 *et seq*.; H. M. Robertson, 'The Cabinet Committee and the Control Boards', p. 44; P. R. Viljoen, 'Planned Agriculture in South Africa', p. 280; J. R. McLoughlin, 'A Defence of Control in the Marketing of Agricultural Products', p. 293; 'A Comment' by R. W. Anderson, p. 418; and 'A Reply' and 'A Rejoinder' by C. S. Richards, p. 303 and p. 427. In addition the daily and periodical press carried their own quotas of controversy.

9 Co-operation and Agricultural Credit Commission U.G. 16–'34, p. 197. An informed assessment of this Commission was made by

T. H. Kelly, 'Report of the Commission on Agricultural Co-operation', *S.A. Journal of Economics*, Vol. 2, 1934, p. 195.

Though the Commission had chosen tobacco and wine as warning examples of the dangers of maintaining artificial price-levels, it has – perhaps discreetly – avoided the even more painful instance of the operations of the dairy industry control board. The earlier operations of 'orderly marketing' in the dairy industry with particular reference to Control Board's export marketing of butter were examined by J. G. Kneen, in 'The Dairy Industry in South Africa', *S.A. Journal of Economics*, Vol. 3, 1935, pp. 202–28 and 441–7. He showed how the board giving scant, if any, consideration to technological and environmental difficulties of infertile soil, uncertain rainfall, primitive irrigation systems, transport of cream over very long distances by cart or train through hot, dusty weather promoting acidity and bacteria, nonetheless followed a marketing policy giving maximum incentive to production of butter as a sideline by general farmers.

See also E. Davis, 'Some Aspects of the Marketing of Farm Products in S.A.', *S.A. Journal of Economics*, Vol. 1, 1933, pp. 167 *et seq.*, which has some shrewd and informed comments on the possibilities and limitations of controlled marketing in relation to specific technical and market situations for different products.

10 For an entertaining account of how Dr Viljoen reversed himself in his evidence to the Select Committee on the Marketing Bill (S.C.6, 1936) see C. S. Richards, 'The "New Despotism" in Agriculture', *S.A. Journal of Economics*, Vol. 4, 1936, pp. 470–80. It is worth noting that in five days of evidence as principal witness the Secretary of Agriculture was putting forward in detail the enabling powers to be conferred on him by the proposed legislation as Chairman of the National Marketing Council. It is an instructive example of the workings of the sincere but passionate bureaucratic mind.

11 See *S.A. Journal of Economics*, Vol. 6, 1938 – already cited. H. M. Robertson in 'The Cabinet Committee and the Control Boards', an economic historian of austerely academic impartiality, was moved to an unusual asperity by 'bureaucracy' in action.

12 '. . . Must we ask the Native and the poor Europeans we are striving to raise from their poverty to pay for the feed for our cattle? They cannot do it. The mine compounds may be considered fair game, but the mines are a powerful adversary for a control board inexperienced in its new functions! As for the Natives who must find their own food or starve – they starve . . .'. Economists' Protest, already cited, pp. 41–2.

13 S. H. Frankel *Capital Investment in Africa*, already cited, p. 122.

14 C. S. Richards, 'Subsidies, Quotas, Tariffs and the Excess Cost of Agriculture in S.A.', *S.A. Journal of Economics*, Vol. 3, 1935, pp. 365–403, pp. 607–9.

15 *Reconstruction of Agriculture*, Report of the Reconstruction Committee of the Department of Agriculture and Forestry, G.P.-S. 9278, 1943/4. Three members of the Committee were currently members of the National Marketing Council, in particular P. R. Viljoen, Secretary for Agriculture, and C. H. Neveling, Under Secretary for Agriculture. The exceptional interest that attaches to this Report is not in its economic authority but in its revelations of the ultimate concepts of 'planned agriculture'.

16 *ibid.*, par. 17.

17 *ibid.*, pars. 16 and 18.

18 *ibid.*, pars. 35/6. The Report was highly critical of State land-settlement policies which had granted land 'to persons who do not possess anything like the requisite knowledge, training, outlook and perseverance to make a success of farming, persons who have failed in farming or other walks of life (and who) often lack those personal qualities such as an inborn love of soil and stock . . .', par. 41.

19 *ibid.*, pars. 43/4.

20 *ibid.*, Section III, 'The Disabilities of Farming', pars. 22–61, is a section of unrelieved woe.

21 *ibid.*, par. 62.

22 *ibid.*, par. 161.

23 *ibid.*, par. 84.

24 *ibid.* The continuous passage that follows is in the actual words of the Report though the original text is at much greater length and more elaboration. The quotation is however not out of context and is a fair reflection of the exposition of viewpoint and recommendation.

25 *ibid.*, pars. 94–104 elaborate the 'irreparable damage' that has been done by sacrificing grazing land to the plough in areas that are totally unsuited to crop production.

The Report builds up a truly fearsome picture of loss of natural fertility of the land but nowhere is there a word of recognition that the polity-price system evolved by the control boards and the National Marketing Council were in any way a factor encouraging land-utilization contrary to 'natural controls'.

26 *ibid.*, pars. 130/1.

27 *ibid.*, par. 156.

28 *ibid.*, par. 161.

29 *ibid.*, par. 166.

30 *ibid.*, par. 169. In respect of perishable-product distribution, the Report favoured a national policy by establishing centralized control over municipal markets: '. . . even in the best-run municipalities the market has often been the play-ball of parish politics, equally at the mercy of rank amateurs, as of interested parties' (sic!).

31 See Von Mises, *Socialism* (Jonathan Cape, 1932) and Hayek, *Road to*

Serfdom, already cited, Lionel Robbins, *Economic Planning and International Order*.

32 Report of Reconstruction Committee – section XI from which the extended reference that follows in the text is taken.

33 *ibid.*, pars. 276–82.

34 See J. M. Tinley, *South African Food and Agriculture in World War II* (California: Stanford U.P., 1953).

35 The appointment of Dr R. P. Viljoen, already a highly controversial figure with his commitments to food producers, as the guardian of the interests of food consumers shows the farmer-influence and departmental power. Even when the Food Controller was separated from the Department of Agriculture in 1944, he continued to operate under the general supervision of the Minister of Agriculture. Only the continued deterioration in food-marketing in the immediate post-war years finally compelled the appointment of Dr van Eck as Director of Food Supplies and Distribution with direct responsibility to the Minister of Finance in late 1946, after which the position markedly improved.

36 Early in 1946 the South African Government appealed to the British Ministry of Food for the expert advice of Sir Henry French, whose report was published as U.G. 31, 1946.

37 See Report No. 4 of the Social and Economic Planning Council: *The Future of Farming in South Africa*, including comments on the Report of the Reconstruction Committee of the Department of Agriculture. U.G. 10–'45. For students of behind-the-scenes, red-claw, interdepartmental rivalry papered over for all to see, the Introduction to this Report is a prize exhibit. Tables are taken from pp. 2–3 of this Report.

Subsequently the Smuts Government attempted the inevitable reconciliation of policy conflicts and produced the equally inevitable meaningless compromise in the Prime Minister's White Paper on Agricultural Policy W.P. 10–'46. The Smuts Government gave way, of course, in the 1948 general election to the Nationalist Party Government under Dr D. F. Malan.

CHAPTER 11

1 The significance of the 'colour-blind' market is the theme of *The Economics of the Colour Bar* by W. H. Hutt (Andre Deutsch, 1964).

2 In the first phase of the Dutch East India Company's operation of the Cape as a supply port-of-call, the Company's opposition to European colonization compelled the manual labour needs to be met by slaves imported from the East to supplement unsatisfactory tribal Hottentots and Bushmen. When the British on occupation of the Cape prohibited the importation of slaves and then made slavery illegal, the progeny

of intermarriage between Hottentots, slaves and Whites – the Cape Coloureds – largely constituted the labour supply for a non-industrial, near-stationary economy in the Western Cape.

Where British settlers (and subsequently German immigrants) were introduced into the Eastern Cape and wool-farming became increasingly commercialized, conflicts over land between White colonists and African tribesmen and among tribes themselves eventually compelled abandonment of the British Colonial Office policy of limiting all contacts between the races to a minimum. When the self-destruction of the Xhosa cattle-killing tragedy broke the tribal economy, many tens of thousands of African tribesmen were left with nothing but their labour to sell.

In the Natal Colony, after the withdrawal of the Voortrekkers and colonization by British settlers, commercial cultivation of cotton, sugar and tea required plantation labour. The early years of such commercial farming precluded sufficiently effective cash wages to be offered to African tribesmen, whose title to their own land holdings in locations and tribal homelands was supported by British Colonial Office policy. The failure to induce African tribesmen to enter wage-employment in the needed numbers led to the indenture of Indian labour with official sanction.

The labour-needs of White land-owners in the Voortrekker Republics of the Transvaal and the Orange Free State, where commercial agriculture was rudimentary, were met by the labour-tenant system. Africans dwelling on the land, alienated to White occupiers, might as required have to contribute labour-services of indeterminate character but only rarely in return for a cash payment.

For this pre-mineral period of labour utilization, see the early chapters of *Native Labour in South Africa* by S. T. van der Horst and *150 Years Contact Between Black and White* by H. M. Robertson, already cited. Also *Bantu, Boer and Briton* and *Complex South Africa* by W. M. MacMillan.

3   See previous chapters – especially chapters 4 and 6. See also S. T. van der Horst *Native Labour in South Africa*, already cited, pp. 126 *et seq.*, and 186 *et seq.* Also G. V. Doxey, *The Industrial Colour Bar* (O.U.P., 1961), pp. 39 *et seq.*

4   Doxey, *ibid.*, p. 44 quoting Chamber of Mines Annual Report for 1894.

5   The most authoritative documentation of trade unionism in South Africa is by Muriel Horrell, *South African Trade Unionism* (Johannesburg: S.A. Institute of Race Relations, 1961). Its sub-title, 'A Study of Divided Working Class' is not only fully reflected in the informative text but is a major element in the complex organizational factors influencing the South African labour-market and wage-structure.

457

The *2000 Casualties – A History of the South African Labour Movement* (Walker and Weinbren, 1961) is unfortunately mainly shibboleth.

6 Economic Commission U.G. 12–'14 – Chairman Professor S. J. Chapman of Manchester University.

7 *ibid.*, pars. 23–4.

8 *ibid.*, par. 27.

9 *ibid.*, par. 18.

10 *ibid.*, par. 36.

11 Economic and Wage Commission (Mills-Clay) U.G. 14–'26, par. 46.

12 Thus: Mining Industry Commission 1907–8, T.G.2; Low Grade Mines Commission 1919/20 U.G. 24–'20; Low Grade Ore Commission U.G. 16–'32.

13 See S. T. van der Horst, *Native Labour in S.A.*, already cited, pp. 192 *et seq.*

14 Specific working conditions such as the compound system, food provision and family quarters have a significance impossible to evaluate.

15 If it was practicably impossible to establish an alternative to monopsony (because of the power of the Chamber of Mines to enforce it for decades), there is no 'lost opportunity', whose cost can be empirically established.

16 Economic and Wage Commission Report, U.G. 14–'26, par. 58.

17 See previous Chapter 6 – 'Neither Squatter nor Skilled' for earlier views on African labour 'scarcity' and leisure-preference. Later references to this crucial variable follow in this chapter. The Chamber of Mines was not, of course, arguing that wage-competition *between* the mining companies would not result in a shift of African labour from one mine to another, but that the *total* labour supplied would be reduced by a higher wage-level for *all* such labour.

18 The absence of a response by the tribalized Africans (at this time the vast majority) to money-incentives would seem to have made it much easier for the White polity to have restrained economic development and thereby maintained the consequent 'traditional' segregation or apartheid between the Whites and Africans. By ensuring that the Africans were confirmed in the appropriate share of land as the fundamental of their institutionalized culture, based on a non-exchange or non-market social system, the Africans would not have been drawn into (or integrated into) the exchange economy and social system of the White man. Then as now there was little evidence of the willingness of the White man to make the so-called 'sacrifices for Apartheid'.

19 Such restraint-of-competition attempts are reported by Hatch and Chalmers in their *The Gold Mines of the Rand*, 1895, and of course culminated in centralized recruiting, which was facilitated by one of

the first enactments of the new Union Parliament. P. T. Bauer in his *Economic Analysis and Policy in Underdeveloped Countries* gives an interesting account of how 'custom-dominated and caste-bound' people respond to economic incentives in India. There are interesting parallels with the response of tribal Africans throughout Southern Africa to the discovery of the gold mines in 1886 as the continent's richest resource.

20 Report of the Native Grievances Inquiry, U.G. 37–'14.

21 *ibid.*, par. 65, pars. 71–2.

22 *ibid.*, par. 83.

23 For many years, as late as 1913 and after, almost all the mine developing and stoping was done under a 'contract system'. There were many variations but in essence the so-called flat contract with guaranteed wage meant that the 'contractor', i.e. the White miner, was given a price per, say, fathom of machine stoping and was charged by the mine management at set rates for African labour and stores with the mining company supplying tools, compressed air and other necessaries. The White miner-contractor received the surplus of gross earnings over costs charged, however big the margin while almost invariably a 'contractor' who had bad luck and who would have earned little or nothing under the contract had his earnings made up to, say, a day's pay rate. This meant very wide fluctuation in the monthly-received total remuneration and hence a considerable factor in instability and unrest of White miners. It also patently encouraged the unscrupulous White miner-contractor, hard-pressed for immediate earnings, to increase the surplus over costs by non-marking the 'tickets' of his African work-gang and thereby obtaining for himself the benefit of the gang's unremunerated work-shift. As the Economic Commission, U.G. 12–'14 noted, it was difficult to think of a system, which originated in the early days of unorganized recruiting when the 'contractor' assembled his own African labour and had no working capital, more likely to create unfavourable labour-relations.

24 Under prevailing conditions of compound 'bachelor' living and underground work, the 'leisure-preference' of the African which motivated him to periodic return to his tribal home and either marriage to secure tribal rights to land or to his family seems not unusual. The 'backward-sloping' supply curve for labour, including African unskilled labour, seems more realistically to be related to contemporary working conditions.

25 *ibid.*, par. 254.

26 *ibid.*, par. 280. 'Under the present Mining Regulations, certain provisions of responsibility must be filled, in the Cape and Natal, by a "competent man", whether White or Coloured. In the Transvaal and Orange Free State, they must be filled by a "White" man, whether competent or incompetent. If my life ever depends upon these people's

care and skill, as many lives do to-day, I hope it will be in one of the former Provinces', par. 281.

27 The 1918 Annual Report of the Transvaal Chamber of Mines said: It is impossible to deny that the colour bar as laid down in the Government Mining Regulations imposes an artificial restriction on the advancement of the coloured and native population. But much more important than the Government Mining Regulations is the force of custom. Public opinion is not prepared to see the substitution of coloured or native workers for white skilled and semi-skilled workers, and any attempt to employ the non-white workman on mining work at present occupied by white men would cause a strike of white employees on the mines, who would be supported by the great bulk of the white population of the Rand, p. 92.

28 Low Grade Mines Commission issued an Interim Report, U.G. 45–'19 in September 1919 and a Final Report 34–'20. Between the two reports some relaxation was afforded by a new agreement of July 24, 1919, between the Chamber of Mines and their new agents, Messrs Rothschilds, to pass on any premium in price through the creation in London of a free market for producers' gold. The relief was temporary but became 'permanent' when the gold price was raised.

29 Interim Report, *ibid.*, par. 6.

30 *ibid.*, U.G. 34–'20. Pars. 155–7. In pars. 162 *et seq.* the Commission detailed the specific provisions of Section 4 (1), under which regulations establishing 'competency' for specified jobs operated as a *de facto* colour bar. 'Custom and the constant effort of the trade unions have secured a considerable extension of the White man's prerogative. In annexure H we give a list of 51 occupations on the mines . . . in 32 of these, comprising 7,057 persons, the employment of white men is prescribed by the Regulations, but not in 19 others, comprising 4,020 persons. Yet the colour bar is as rigorously applied in these as in the others. . . . Customs, public opinion and Trades Unions are therefore at least as powerful as doubtful legal provisions in establishing and maintaining an effective colour bar. . . .'

31 *ibid.*, par. 167.

32 *ibid.*, *passim.*

33 See earlier discussion in text on the 'extra-economic' and the 'economic' as concepts justified by exposition rather than by 'rigour'.

34 U.G. 34–'20, pars. 178–9.

35 U.G. 34–'20, par. 2 of Minority Report.

36 See S. T. van der Horst *Native Labour in South Africa*, already cited, pp. 201–5, for discussion of relationship of labour supplied to the individual mine's gold-production capacity.

37 Low Grade Mines Commission, Final Report, U.G. 34–'20, pars. 193–6.

38 *ibid.*, par. 196. This Commission seems to have accepted that a revised regulation by the Chamber of Mines of February 11, 1914 abolished the maximum average clause (as condemned by the Economic Commission of 1914). But the replacement with a 'sliding scale' and a discretionary application of the penalty clause to a black-leg mine does not in fact alter the Chamber's monopsonistic position in relation to African mine-labour – nor indeed, as will subsequently appear, made much impact on the average earnings of Africans on the gold mines through at least another two decades.

39 Low Grade Mines Commission, Interim Report, U.G. 45–'19, par. 41.

40 *ibid.*, pars. 41 *et seq.* This recommendation was not in fact accepted by the Government, which maintained the prohibition.

41 See C. G. W. Schumann, *Structural Changes and Business Cycles in South Africa, 1806–1936* (London: Staples Press, 1938), Graph V, facing p. 230.

42 Working profit was of course affected by the strike. In 1923, following work re-organization, working profit rose again to £12·6 millions.

43 Quoted in Low Grade Mines Commission, Final Report, 1920, par. 64.

44 Low Grade Ore Commission Report, U.G. 16–'32, par. 9.

	1921	1923
Average number White employees	20,825	17,666
Average income p.a. –do–	£495	£370
Average rate per shift –do–	30/33	20/11
Tonnage milled	23,437,196	26,765,126
Working costs per ton milled	25/8	20/–

A judgement in *Rex v. Hildick Smith* (1923) T.P.D. had declared the 'colour-bar' provision in the Mines and Works Act, 1911, to be *ultra vires*.

CHAPTER 12

1 Mining Regulations Commission, U.G. 36–'25. The members of the Commission were Wm. Pittman, J. H. Munnik, R. B. Waterston and J. J. Wessels.

2 *ibid.*, par. 8.

3 *ibid.*, pars. 24–8.

4 *ibid.*, pars. 52–4.

5 *ibid.*, pars. 68–9.

6 *ibid.*, par. 90.

7 *ibid.*, par. 91.

8 *ibid.*, par. 92.

9 *ibid.*, pars. 93–4.

10 *ibid.*, par. 95.

11 *ibid.*, pars. 97–8.

12 *ibid.*, pars. 112–5.

13 *ibid.*, par. 119.

14 See pp. 122–4 of the Economic and Wage Commission Report, U.G. 14–'26.

15 The passage of this Bill, originally introduced in 1925 and rejected by the Senate (in which the Pact Ministry was in a minority), eventually necessitated a joint sitting of both Houses of Parliament. It was one of the measures that led to the situation rather like that forced on the Asquith Liberal Government to propose a creation of an appropriate number of Liberal peers. In South Africa it was resolved by Act No. 77 of 1926, which ensured that the eight nominated senatorships were at all times at the disposal of the incoming Prime Minister. This sufficed to ensure Government control of the Senate and of Parliament, except in respect of those entrenched provisions of the Act of Union requiring a two-thirds majority in a joint sitting. This obstacle was faced by the Malan Government of 1955 and surmounted by increasing the number of government-controlled senators from 44 to 89, which inflated total was subsequently deflated after its purpose of eliminating the Coloured roll common franchise had been achieved.

16 The regulations framed under the 1926 Act did not indeed establish all the specific Luddite make-work recommendations of the Mining Regulations Commission. The essence of such regulations was however to ensure that in the collective bargaining between the Chamber of Mines and the White miners' unions, the Chamber never challenged demarcated White job categories.

17 To this day, 1966 Nationalist Party (i.e. Government or Afrikanerdom) explanation and exposition accepts only the 'inter-dependence' of White and Non-White in the labour market and denies the existence of an integrated labour market.

18 The Population Register was established by the Population Registration Act, No. 30 of 1950 and as subsequently amended. Essentially it provided for the legal classification of all South Africans as White, Coloured, Asiatic or Native (Bantu), with identification to be a matter of administrative decision. See *Civil Liberty in South Africa* by E. H. Brookes and J. B. Macaulay (O.U.P., 1958), pp. 15–7, 45.

19 See Chapters 6 and 7: 'Neither Squatter Nor Skilled' and 'The White Polity Takes Charge'. Creswell believed passionately that this alone could secure South Africa as 'the home of a great White people'.

20 S. T. van der Horst, *Native Labour in South Africa*, already cited; G. V. Doxey, *The Industrial Colour Bar in South Africa*, already cited; W. H. Hutt, *Economics of the Colour Bar*, already cited; W. H. Hutt, 'Logical Issues in the Study of Industrial Legislation in the Union' in *S.A. Journal of Economics*, Vol. 3, 1934, pp. 26 *et seq.* S. T. van der Horst, *Some Effects of Industrial legislation on the Market for Native Labour* in *South Africa*, Vol. 3, 1953, pp. 481 *et seq.*

21 Economic and Wage Commission (1925), U.G. 14–'26 still recognized as one of the classic reports on the fundamentals of the South African economy. There was a 'Majority' Report signed by Mills (chairman), Clay and Martin and a 'Minority' Report signed by Andrews, Lucas and Rood.

22 *ibid.*, Majority Report, pars. 221–3.

23 The Industrial Conciliation Act No. 11 of 1924 was in fact the legislation of the Smuts Government just prior to its fall. The industrial conciliation law is however 'attributed' to the later 1924 Pact Government as part of the 'myth-making process' to present Smuts as the 'villain of the piece' on the side of the Chamber of Mines against the 'defenceless workers' and, therefore, to obscure his contribution to the creation of industrial conciliation. The Industrial Conciliation Act of 1924 was redrafted as Act No. 36 of 1937 and Act No. 28 of 1956 – see G. V. Doxey *Industrial Colour Bar in South Africa*, already cited, pp. 135 *et seq*. See also later discussion under Chapters 15–7.

24 It is noteworthy that the printing industry in South Africa, with its exceptional record of 'industrial peace' is probably the most highly organized of the 'bilateral monopolies'. See 'A Review of the Board of Trade and Industries Report on the Printing Industry' in the *S.A. Journal of Economics*, Vol. 25, No. 1, 1957 by Ralph Horwitz. The Industrial Conciliation Act of 1924 was in fact largely modelled on the National Council for the Printing Industry that had been established in 1919 and Ivan L. Walker, secretary of the S.A. Typographical Union was later to become Secretary for Labour in the Ministry and as such a key official in the administration of industrial legislation.

25 See S. T. van der Horst, already cited, pp. 245 *et seq*.; G. V. Doxey, already cited, pp. 135 *et seq*.

26 The position of Coloured and Indian workers is, of course, part of the complex least-cost substitutions but their significance grew with technological change favouring the growth of operatives. It is more properly part of the post World War II phase.

27 Unemployment Commission, U.G. 34–'21, par. 15.

28 A small number of Coloured youths were apprenticed in Cape Town but during the years of slow industrial growth, their numbers were a fraction only of the number of White youths. In three years from 1932 to 1935, out of 641 apprenticeship contracts in Cape Town only 36 were Cape Coloured. Virtually no Africans obtained apprenticeships.

29 See both *South African Trade Unionism* by Muriel Horrell, already cited, later chapters on right-wing and left-wing trade unions, and *2000 Casualties* by Walker and Weinbren, already cited, Chapters 39 and 43 including the incident that led to the murder in 1939 of Charles Harris, secretary of the South African Mineworkers' Union by a

fanatical devotee of the campaign for Afrikaans Christian-National Trade Unionism.

30 From the viewpoint of the Chamber of Mines, from 1924 onwards, it was no longer 'economically rational' to pursue productivity beyond the 'boundary condition' of the colour bar. For econometric calculation the colour bar on labour-categories was a 'boundary condition' for the Chamber of Mines in their determination of rational economic policy of mine management from 1924. Cf. J. Tinbergen *Economic Policy: Principles and Design* (Amsterdam: North Holland Publishing Company, 1956), p. 25.

31 Department of Labour, Circular No. 5 of October 31, 1924.

32 See S. T. van der Horst, already cited, p. 251.

33 Economic and Wage Commssion Report, Clay-Martin-Mills, Chapter VIII – *The Fostering of Maniufacturing Industry*, pars. 290 *et seq.*

34 House of Assembly Debates, 1925, Vol. 3, col. 1589/1590/1593.

35 S. T. van der Horst, *Native Labour in South Africa*, already cited, pp. 253 *et seq.*

36 The Native Economic Commission of 1932 reported that the Bantu masses were becoming poorer and in the Reserves in some parts were facing 'mass starvation'; while the Carnegie Commission on Poor Whites, 1932, had estimated the numbers of White indigents at 300,000.

37 The United Party was formally constituted out of the Fusion-Coalition Cabinet, at the end of 1934. Creswell had not been appointed to the Coalition Cabinet. According to the version in the biography by Margaret Creswell, already cited, 'Just before the new (Coalition) Cabinet was formed, however, General Hertzog journeyed to Kuils River to have a talk with Creswell. He told him he had wished to include him in the coalition ministry as Minister of Labour but that General Smuts had refused to include him in the Cabinet'. Mr A. P. J. Fourie became Minister of Labour – no Labour Party member was given a Cabinet seat.

38 Industrial Legislation Commission, U.G. 37-'35ll

39 *ibid.*, par. 10.

40 *ibid.*, par. 12:

Wage-level Relationships Based on Wage-Regulation as at 1935

	Skilled	Semi-skilled	Unskilled
Baking/Confectionary, Durban . .	100	66–60	30–27
Baking/Confectionary, Witwatersrand .	100	—	25
Building, Cape Peninsula . . .	100	—	31–24
Building, Rand/Pretoria . . .	100	30–29	11–10
Furniture, Rand/Pretoria . . .	100	28–65	24–18
Furniture, Main Industrial Centres .	100	30–56	22
Motor Engineering, Rand/Pretoria .	100	47–63	14–30

A Board of Trade and Industries Report No. 282, Annexure F, provided a chart of nominal unskilled and skilled wage rates in a number of countries for the year 1938. The chart showed that South Africa had the lowest nominal unskilled wage rate but the second highest skilled wage rate of the countries listed.

41 *ibid.*, par. 20.

42 *ibid.*, par. 23.

43 *ibid.*, par. 93.

44 *ibid.*, par. 113.

45 *ibid.*, par. 728.

46 The Commission found its 'solution of the white labour problem' in essentially social welfare measures. It summarized:

(1) Improving the living conditions of the lower grades of labour through education and constructive social welfare work.

(2) Improving the general level of wages for workers in the lower paid occupations.

(3) State aid in connection with social services including housing and transportation.

(4) Schemes for improving the mental outlook and physical fitness of individuals and in this way helping them to fend for themselves, and

(5) The provision of consumptive credit facilities on reasonable terms under general Government supervision, par. 192.

47 *ibid.*, par. 258.

48 Such persons excluded by statutory definition were now extended to persons whose contracts of employment were subject to the Native (Urban Areas) Act of 1923. This meant virtually all Africans, including those in the Cape Province.

49 S. T. van der Horst, already cited, p. 248.

50 For a discussion of effects of 1937 legislation see S. T. van der Horst, already cited, pp. 258 *et seq.*

51 Industrial Legislation Commission, U.G. 37-'35, par. 102.

CHAPTER 13

1 The 'Squatters' laws to induce a supply of labour and related land legislation with similar purpose have already been discussed in earlier chapters. See also Chapter XV of MacMillan, *Complex South Africa*, already cited, for an account of 'Farm' Natives at the period c. 1930. He notes the general absence of factual information about their numbers, conditions of employment or even public notice of their existence in ministerial speeches.

2 See Economic and Wage Commission Report, U.G. 14-'26, pars. 60-4, for a view that these Acts provided some protection for Non-White

'servants' in that although subjecting them to criminal penalties for breach of contract, they also permitted action by 'servants' against 'masters' for recovery of wages or supply of food.

3   S. T. van der Horst, already cited, writing of the growing competition from the Rand in the period 1886–1899, records: The increase in the competition for the services of Natives led to many complaints from farmers. In Natal farmers and landlords complained, and magistrates reported, that labour-tenants evaded their obligations by going to the Rand where wages were 'exorbitant'. The report for 1897 of the Magistrate of Weenen gives a typical description of the exodus to Johannesburg. He wrote:

> The sole cause of the trouble continues to be the constant exodus of Natives to Johannesburg, where, attracted by the high wages paid them there, they persist in going, despite damages sued for by their landlords under their contracts and prosecution and punishment under the Master and Servants (Natives) Act, on their return. p. 145.

4   Wage-paid farm labourers were not necessarily 'better-off' than farm labour-tenants. As W. M. MacMillan observed in his *Complex South Africa*, already cited, 'from the nature of the case social information about the conditions on private farms is peculiarly inaccessible, varying from Province to Province and even from farm to farm'. A study by the S.A. Institute of Race Relations, *Farm Labour in the Orange Free State* (Monograph series No. 2, April 1939), said 'anything in the nature of reliable statistical evidence . . . could not be obtained . . . due . . . to the . . . employers themselves are not often aware of the true facts . . . and the conditions vary so greatly, almost from farm to farm . . . for statistical generalization'. This study reported cash wages in the Winburg district (1939) of 10/– per month per male worker, 5/– per month per domestic female worker, shepherds at 5/– per month. In addition there were wages in kind – rations of ½ bag of mealie meal per month, separated milk, salt, very occasionally meat. Remuneration in Bloemfontein district was about 15 per cent higher but lower in areas more remote from urban Bloemfontein.

See especially a gallant attempt to establish data on 'The Economic Status of the Cape Province Farm Native' by E. S. Haines (*S.A Journal of Economics*, Vol. 3, 1935, pp. 57 *et seq.*) which arrived at an estimate of total real wage for the heads of fifty-six families at 27/6 per month and 'a very strong impression that total real wages in this area (of investigation) amount to something under 30/- per month . . . a cash wage of 10/– per month, for instance, if of very general occurrence'.

5   Taxation imposed on African males, such as the poll tax or the hut tax, compelled *some* cash income to be earned. The objective was indeed to induce Africans to enter the money-economy of employment

but in many Transvaal farming areas, no cash wage was paid.

6 In introducing the second reading, the Minister of Justice, Mr. O. Pirow, said on clause 11: '. . . in its original form it stated that corporal punishment (on a breach of contract) could be given to any native, adult or juvenile. The select committee has thought fit to alter the clause so that it will not apply to youthful natives. I do not agree with this alteration and, for the most part, in the interests of the natives themselves. However we disguise the matter, the fact remains that not only in the Transvaal and Natal, but right through the Union, the farmers themselves inflict corporal punishment on natives. The general maltreatment of which we sometimes read in certain newspapers does not take place at all. It is imaginary. But there is not the least doubt that throughout South Africa – one can almost say by traditional law – corporal punishment is applied not only to youthful natives' – House of Assembly Debates, Vol. 18, 1932, col. 640.

7 The Native Farm Labour Committee, 1937, 1939 (G.P. 9523, 1940), par. 45. This Committee incidentally acknowledged that it did not find opportunity to make close contact with native labour tenants and farm labourers themselves. Indeed some farmer-witnesses objected to evidence being given or heard from Africans. The Committee recommended that farmers' associations should combine in an organization to keep their labour problem under continuing study with consultation among employers, local Native chiefs and the Native Commissioner – this was not acceptable to the farmers, who refused to contemplate any form of consultation with African labour even through chiefs and recognized leaders. This Committee was not appointed by nor did it report to the Minister of Labour but to the Minister of Native Affairs.

8 *ibid.*, par. 16 says perhaps more than it intended: 'The evidence of representatives of farmers at almost all the centres . . . was unanimous that there was a general shortage of Native farm labourers. Many of these representatives, on being questioned as to whether their own farming operations were being hampered by such a shortage, had to admit that this was not the case, but that they were able to meet all their requirements. They, however, assured the Committee that the vast majority of farmers in the areas represented by them were not so fortunate. This assurance your Committee is prepared to accept, as it is clear that the persons who experience no difficulty in regard to labour are, in the majority of cases, the leaders of the farming community in their areas, large land-owners or financially strong farmers, who are able to offer such conditions of employment as would attract labour'.

9 *ibid.*, par. 26.

10 *ibid.*, par. 26.

11 *ibid.*, par. 29.

12 The analogy to the selective employment tax introduced in Britain in the sixties to stop firms 'hogging' labour is interesting. In the South African context, however, the use of a penal fiscal measure to bring to an end the continuing reality of land-ownership, land-occupation and land-utilization has not yet succeeded. Squatting and labour-tenancy preserved for some Africans some of the factual ownership of land which they had always occupied but from which they had been legally deprived and legally excluded; while White farmers who had not in fact developed a market agriculture and fully entered into the exchange economy of the twentieth century could obtain 'rent' from African squatters and/or labour service for little or no cash wage.

It is noteworthy that the Committee a quarter-century after the passage of the Native Land Act of 1913 reported: 'We have also noted a general feeling of dissatisfaction amongst the rural Natives with the policy of the Native Land Act, 1913. They trace all their present troubles back to this legislation, and cannot yet understand why it was necessary to break up the position then existing, and so deprive them of the benefits to be derived from the use of land in agreement with the farmers. Here the social system still strongly rooted in the rural Natives was brought into conflict with the economy which Government saw fit to impose on all landowners', par. 42.

13 *ibid.*, Chapter III, pars. 56 *et seq.*

14 *ibid.*, par. 12.

15 *ibid.*, pars. 467–8.

16 The 'choice' however was already evident in the credit-expansionist boom, which official monetary management had induced.

17 Schumpeter *Economic Doctrine and Method*, p. 142.

CHAPTER 14

1 For the elementary production function of an economic development plan model $O = f(L,K,Q)$, aimed at raising productivity per unit of factor of production employed, see Higgins *Economic Development*, already cited, pp. 631 *et seq.* Here O is output; L is size of total labour force (employed or unemployed); K is the quantity of natural resources or 'land'; Q is the amount of plant and equipment or 'capital'.

2 These are the names of some of the more prominent early individuals, out of whose competitive-combinations the later group system evolved.

3 S. H. Frankel, *Capital Investment in Africa* (O.U.P., 1938).

4 Apart from the great Cecil John Rhodes – financier, prime minister, founder of companies and of a country – himself, there was his associate Alfred Beit whose contribution seems not fully recognized by the present generation. In *Alfred Beit, A Study* (London: Ivor Nicholson &

Watson, 1932), his biographer G. S. Fort quotes an early Rand pioneer J. B. Taylor for this appreciation: Beit's was the master-mind in making a success of the gold-mining industry on the Rand. From the first he resolved that the mines under his firm's control were not to be run for share-making and marketing purposes. For in no instance did the firm issue a prospectus. The working capital was always found by the firm and the companies financed until they became dividend-paying. The shareholders were informed monthly of everything that happened on the mines – nothing was hidden. It was a complete revolution in mining history, and his lead compelled all other mining companies to follow suit, pp. 92–3. Beit's name is identified with the 'Corner House', one of the great early names of the mining-finance houses.

Another great name of no lesser stature as a financier in more recent times is Sir Ernest Oppenheimer of Anglo-American Corporation. Sir Ernest Oppenheimer might well qualify as one of the greatest of twentieth century financiers, whose contribution to the economic development of Southern Africa as an entrepreneur possibly is as great as that of any man. See later reference in text.

5   Most of the factual data of this section is taken from S. H. Frankel's *Capital Investment in Africa*, already cited, pp. 75 *et seq.*

6   Higgins, already cited, p. 238.

7   See *Ernest Oppenheimer and the Economic Development of Southern Africa* by Sir Theodore Gregory (Cape Town: O.U.P., 1962): It is not the case that Kimberley was the sole source of finance, whether for the Barberton area or subsequently for the Rand. . . . What is true is that at Kimberley was to be found a unique combination of factors which made for leadership: men of great individual wealth and great ability, enjoying international prestige and with connections with the great finance houses of Europe; there was experience of large-scale organization: and there was also appreciation of the importance of technology and of technical experts. It was the *qualitative* and not merely the *quantitative* advantages Kimberley men possessed which made them the leaders of the new era in the Transvaal, pp. 76–7.

8   Frankel, already cited, p. 53.

9   Frankel, already cited, pp. 89 *et seq.* Frankel calculated the mean or average annual yield to capital invested in the gold-mining industry for the period 1887 to 1932 to be no more than 4·1 per cent p.a. 'In other words, the sometimes very large yields in particular mines have been counter-balanced by absolute losses or very low yields in others', p. 91.

10 Dividend payments amounted to £248,000,000 plus another £7m. of so-called liquidation dividends or capital-return distribution.

11 See *Structural Changes and Business Cycles in South Africa, 1806–1936* by C. G. W. Schumann (London: Staples Press, 1938), *passim* for problems and availability of statistical data. Schumann, though not

personally over-sympathetic to the value-orientations of the immigrant capitalists after the discovery of minerals, notes that during the period of the European Industrial Revolution, the South African economy generally stagnated, where it did not revert to pre-capitalistic forms—see pp. 31 *et seq.*

12 See 'The Gross Domestic Product of South Africa, 1911–1959' by Dr J. J. Stadler in *S.A. Journal of Economics*, Vol. 31, No. 3, September, 1963, pp. 185 *et seq.*

13 For figures, source is S. T. van der Horst, *Native Labour*, already cited, *passim.*

14 Table taken from S. T. van der Horst, already cited, pp. 216/217. Note figures do not exactly agree with those quoted in earlier chapter on Political Economy of Labour. It is unfortunate that South African statistical sources rarely adopt such rigid classification-identification as to permit reconciliation of data wthout elaborate examination that is normally unjustified by the meaningfulness of their context.

15 For both such an econometric and a social system analysis, the article 'Economic Development with Unlimited Supplies of Labour' by Arthur Lewis in the *Manchester School*, Vol. 22, 1954, and Vol. 26, 1958, is fundamental.

16 See article by H. Myint in Oxford Economic Papers, Vol. 6, 1954, pp. 132 *et seq.*

17 Quoted in Higgins, *Economic Development*, already cited, p. 676.

18 It was about this time that certain politicians, members of the Nationalist Party then in opposition, began an attempt to capture leadership control of key trade-unions. A particular target was the Mineworkers' Union, the aim being to convert it into 'an Afrikaans Christian-National Trade Union', which would indoctrinate 'Afrikaaner workers with the belief that traditional forms of trade unionism were hostile to their traditions, unfaithful to their church, and disloyal to their country'. An influential figure in this Blankewerkers-Beskermingsbond, i.e. White Workers Protection Movement, was Dr Albert Hertzog, who incidentally has never disavowed his approval of nationalization of the goldmines. It was the internecine struggle that resulted in sporadic strikes for higher wages.

The 53rd Annual Report of the Chamber of Mines for 1942 carried this statement: 'During the year our relations with (White) employees on the mines remained on the satisfactory basis which we have come to regard as a tradition'. South Africans' 'traditions' have a delightful capacity for undergoing metamorphoses.

19 An econometric model might indeed be devised on certain assumptions which are not inhibited by the compulsion to treat the 'colour bar' as an unalterable parameter or condition. The task is commended to an econometrician, who has no political inhibitions. In 1936 the Chamber

NOTES

of Mines President on giving details of the dramatic expansionist effects of the gold price increase from 85/– per oz to 142/– per oz, said, 'The higher exchange value of gold or, in other words, the fall of 1·842 dwts in the cost of mining and treating one ton of ore, has had a result similar to what would have been the case if, under the 1942 conditions, working costs had fallen by approximately 7/– per ton'. The econometric calculation would involve how close to such a 7/– per ton reduction, working costs might have been brought in the absence of all rigidities.

20 See Arthur Lewis article in *Manchester School*, already cited.

21 Though there was an increase in money-wages in 1943 for the first time since almost the beginning of the century, the price index rise suggests no significant increase in real wages. This is more fully examined in a later chapter.

22 It is present-day South African Government contention that such 'illegal' entry is evidence that its Republic cannot be a 'slave-labour' state, suggested by its Afro-Asian opponents. The more realistic considerations seem to be that the mineral resources of the Rand-Free State are the greatest natural resource of Southern Africa, exercising a most powerful centripetal force on tribal-subsistence labour from those parts of Southern Africa where environmental conditions result in zero or negative productivity in their homelands. Labour from such economies is the only form of export. Restrictions on entry of such labour by the South African Governments are in effect a form of import control against its neighbours.

23 On this occasion, though leading figures of the mining industry were undoubtedly influential in bringing about the replacement of the Nationalist Government by the Coalition Government and the related sterling adjustment of the gold price, the extremities of the farmers in consequence of the Nationalist Government's refusal to follow 'the British pound' were at least as strong a political influence. Indeed the Government by a special impost tried to ensure that the whole 'windfall gain' to the mining shareholders accrued to the State. In so far as the Chamber of Mines secured government acquiescence for the migrant-labour policy this, too, was largely because it coincided with the interests of the much more politically effective farmers.

24 Explosives for the Rand mines loaded as full-truck loads from Firgrove, Cape Province, paid a railage rate of £13 15s per ton, as compared with 32/– per ton of cattle dip and 15/– per ton of artificial manure also from Firgrove to the Rand.

RAILAGE RATES PER TON IN PENCE (1930)

	400 miles	500 miles	1000 miles
Agricultural machinery	704	820	1260
Industrial machinery	1340	1520	2140

471

25 See Committee Report of Gold Mining Taxation U.G.16—1946, more particularly para. 78 *et seq.* on the distinction between primary risk-takers (i.e. the sponsoring mining-finance house) and secondary risk-takers (i.e. the 'public' buying shares at premium on flotation) and how taxes on profits exercise continuing influence on opening of new mines. The general problem is that taxation should not discourage the exploitation currently or prospectively of marginal ore, while on the other side from the State's revenue derived from taxation of a wasting asset new income-generating assets should be developed.

26 See *The Theory of Gold Supply* by W. J. Busschau (London: O.U.P., 1936) for a standard, authoritative treatment, more particularly from page 38 onwards.

27 'We (the Chamber of Mines) feel convinced that unless, in the near future, working costs can be brought down to 16s. a ton for the producing mines, the profitable life of the mines of the Witwatersrand will be comparatively short, and the foundations of the structure of the State and municipal finance which has been erected on the output of the Witwatersrand will crumble.' T.G. 2–'08, par. 169.

28 T.G. 2–'08, par. 189. And in par. 190: 'The true function of the mining industry in the economy of the State is not primarily to yield the greatest possible profit to those whose capital has been embarked in mining enterprises . . . The mines might conceivably be yielding large profits, and the exploitation of the mineral wealth of the country might be proceeding at a great rate under conditions which would contribute but little to the maintenance and growth of a white population, and not at all to the growth of a white working population.'

29 Low Grade Ore Commission U.G. 16–'32 (Interim and Final Reports) par. 14.

30 *ibid.*, par. 20.

31 *ibid.*, par. 46. This Commission also had submitted to it certain radical proposals by Dr Hans Pirow, the Government Mining Engineer and a Mr Allen of the S.A. Labour Party. The Pirow proposal was for a drastic reduction of the numbers of White underground workers with a related increase in White surface workers to maintain the overall race ratio; the Allen proposal was to reduce underground time for White workers to 6 hours daily. Both were motivated by serious concern at incidence of miner's phthisis, to which the African was said to be far less susceptible than the White miner because the African did not spend more than a year continuously underground.

While this Commission did not accept either of these proposals, it did commend to the Government in its main conclusions: We are definitely of the opinion that some operations underground at present reserved for the White man could be carried out by specially trained Africans without detriment to safety and health (No. 28); that the

Mines and Works Regulations should be amended in such a manner as will permit trained Africans to perform such underground operations as they are capable of performing without detrimentally affecting the safety and health of all underground employees (No. 32). Neither recommendation was implemented by the Government.

32   In the context of African mine labour, 'British South Africa' meant the territories of the Union of South Africa and the Protectorates of Bechuanaland, Basutoland and Swaziland.

33   A major technological change should, however, be noted. As the Low Grade Ore Commission of 1930 recorded: 'Owing chiefly to the use of the jackhammer drill, 18,577 Africans employed in stoping during the first six months of 1930 were able to break 14,800,000 tons of rock as compared with 10,900,000 tons broken by 44,392 Africans during the last six months of 1914. The fathoms per African shift employed on machine-work were ·538 as compared in 1930 with ·190 in 1914' (par. 47).

This technical improvement had been a replacement of the heavy reciprocating type of machine drill by the light jackhammer type which, with an improved better-shaped steel drill, almost eliminated hand stoping. But this substantial productivity gain in African man-shift from 1914 to 1929 was offset by increased White wages and phthisis compensation so that the benefits of mechanization went almost entirely to White workers acting as supervisors and not to the Africans as the actual miners.

34   Low Grade Ore Commission U.G. 16-'32 par. 25.

35   It will be recollected that with the previous Low Grade Mines Commission of 1919, there had been a similar reversal of prospects and fortune between the interim and final reports. South African historians also like to recall the occasions when a drought-distress commission has had to convert itself into a flood-relief authority.

36   For the academic controversy with political overtones, see Report of the Select Committee on the Gold Standard S.C. 9-'32. Much of the heat of the controversy among non-academic but highly partial opinion arose, firstly, from the belief that South Africa in 'abandoning the gold standard' by devaluation was in fact repudiating gold as a monetary medium and thereby proposing to commit suicide (if not immediately then sometime) and, secondly, that for the South African pound to be devalued by aligning its exchange-rate with the British pound was another typical Smuts act of tying South Africa to Britain's coat-tails and a repudiation of Hertzog's long-avowed goal of sovereign national independence.

37   One of the best inside-accounts of the political drama of the gold-standard crisis is given in Oswald Pirow's biography of General Hertzog, already cited. Sir Abe Bailey, a leading mining-financier,

played a key role in bringing about the totally unexpected coalition of General Hertzog and General Smuts, which led through Fusion to the United Party. Though there is no reason to believe that Bailey's influence was fundamental, it is one of few reliable instances of effective exercise of political intervention by the Chamber of Mines. The lack of real political power of the Chamber of Mines is however demonstrated by the near-confiscatory special taxation imposed by Havenga, still Finance Minister in the reconstituted Government, on devaluation gains. Though Havenga subsequently adopted a more 'conciliatory' taxation policy towards the gold-mining industry, neither his nor his successors' clearly discriminatory taxation of gold-mining profits give evidence of the 'political domination', allegedly exercised by the mining-capitalists.

38 Transvaal Chamber of Mines, 1931, Proceedings pp. 141–53, address by Mr John Martin.

39 In an article 'Gold Mining Investment' in the *S.A. Journal of Economics*, Vol. 5, 1937, pp. 11–27, W. J. Busschau writing on price levels and mining costs says that any rise in commodity prices (consequent on major re-armament programmes by powers) would primarily affect stores rather than wages. Stores items, he puts at roughly 5s. per ton for 1936 so that even a 20 percent increase in cost of stores would add only 1s. per ton. Moreover because of controlled prices of major products like maize, he anticipated a much smaller rise in the cost of living and in the cost of mining stores.

As at October, 1936, the index number of wholesale prices with 1929 = 100 was South Africa 85, United Kingdom 81, United States 85, France 75, Germany 76.

40 See C. G. W. Schumann, *Structural Changes . . .*, already cited, pp. 288–97, for remarks on 'The Abandonment of the Gold Standard in 1932.' Also the Board of Trade and Industries Report No. 282, par. 150.

41 See 'The Gross Domestic Product of South Africa, 1911–1959' by Dr J. J. Stadler in *S.A. Journal of Economics*, Vol. 31, No. 3, pp. 185–208.

CHAPTER 15

1 Economic and Wage Commission Report, already cited, par. 294 *et seq.* The six Commissioners split evenly, each group of three submitting a separate report.

2 See the article so entitled in the *S.A. Journal of Economics*, Vol. 12, 1944, pp. 112–38, from which the data in the text are taken.

3 Frankel, *Analysis of National Income*, already cited, p. 118.

4 A social system may be regarded as the sum of any particular set of human interactions. The American sociologist, Talcott Parsons, has elaborated a general theory of social systems with great sophistication,

perhaps over-sophistication, in a number of writings. Two works of particular theoretical interest for a study of South African social process are: Talcott Parsons and Edwin A. Shils eds., *Towards a General Theory of Action* and Talcott Parsons and Neil J. Smelser, *Economy and Society* (London: Routledge and Kegan Paul, 1957).

5   In a personal comment to the author, Prof. Frankel stated his reservations about national income calculation were clear and explicit.

6   The author argued such a special case in 'Is there a special case for the Protection of South African Industry?' in the *South African Bankers' Journal*, January 1958. What follows is taken largely from it.

7   For a modern well-formulated statement see Enka and Salera, *International Economics* (London: Denis Dobson). Also *The Theory of International Trade* by Gottfried von Haberler (English edition published by William Hodge & Co., London, 1950).

8   Britain, of course, both adopted protection and devalued so that the significance of protection on post-1930 British employment cannot be isolated.

9   See article 'Industry's Early Struggle—The Battle for Protection' in the Golden Jubilee number of *South African Industry and Trade*, May 1957, p. 129 *et seq.* (ed: Ralph Horwitz).

10 For a succinct history of 'Customs Tariff Protection and Other Forms of State Assistance to Encourage Industrial Development', see Chapter XI of the Board of Trade and Industries Report No. 282: *Investigation into Manufacturing Industries in the Union of South Africa* (first interim report). Also the Memorandum submitted by the Board of Trade and Industries to the Tariff Commission, 1934, and published as annexure 6 to U.G.5-'36.

11 Customs Tariff Commission, 1934-35 U.G. 5-'36, pars. 13-14.

12 *ibid.*, pp. 7-8, and annexure 3.

13 *ibid.*, par. 37. See also Annexure 4, pp. 110-11 for detailed tables of White employment.

14 *ibid.*, par. 39.

15 *A Quarter Century of Industrial Progress in South Africa* by A. J. Norval (Cape Town: Juta, 1962). The book summarises much valuable data and inside experience, despite its naive enthusiasm which leads the author to chauvinist assertions of South Africa as potentially one of the greatest industrial nations of the world.

16 Norval, already cited, p. 115.

17 The significance of administrative-decision is well brought out in *The Economics of the Wholesale Clothing Industry of South Africa, 1907-1957* by H. A. F. Barker (Johannesburg: Pallas, 1962).

18 Board of Trade Report No. 282, already cited, par. 86. See also remarks of Customs Tariff Commission, 1934, already cited, pars. 73-4.

19 Tariff Commission, already cited, par. 215.

20 See contemporary articles in *S.A. Journal of Economics* on 'The Boom in Kaffirs' and press articles by Prof. C. S. Richards, particularly.

21 Tariff Commission, already cited, par. 232. It is a point of some political importance in the history of South African fiscal policy that though the Board of Trade and Industries had the administrative responsibility for the protection of industry and came under the Department of Commerce and Industries, the actual legislative enactment of tariff duties was the authority of the Minister of Finance. The influential decision-takers on customs tariffs for many years were Mr Havenga and his Secretary for Finance, Dr Holloway.

Mr Havenga in particular, to whom the unfailing announcement of a new 'record' annual budget surplus became as much the writ of financial conservatism as a personal triumph of his mastery of national book-keeping, was far too much concerned with customs duties as sources of revenue to impose protective duties at levels to exclude imports and thereby deny himself customs dues, which at one time amounted to one-third of total state revenue.

22 Tariff Commission, already cited, par. 205.

23 *ibid.*, par. 206.

24 *ibid.*, par. 224.

25 Tariff Commission, already cited, see Section VIII: 'The Effect of Protection of the Gold Mining Industry'. There is no mention that it was the post-1933 gold price which exposed the 'facts of the available reserves of low-grade ore'; perhaps the chairman, Dr Holloway, was not over-anxious to 'expose' his Minister's opposition to the increased gold-price.

26 *ibid.*, par. 126. This was echoed by the van Eck Commission on Agricultural and Industrial Requirements, U.G. 40-'41, which wrote: It is, therefore, indubitable that industrial protection is largely a protection of skilled wages at a level, which had its origin in the early part of this century when the Union had to rely on imported artisans and experienced an acute shortage of skilled workmen, par. 110.

27 G. S. Richards: *The Iron and Steel Industry in South Africa, with special reference to 'Iscor'* (Johannesburg: Witwatersrand U.P. 1940).

This massive study arouses interesting reflections on the empirical significance of monopolistic competition to the theory of international trade. It prompts serious consideration of the inherent difficulties in applying 'comparative costs' to real situations, when 'costs' are so patently what decision-takers of large-scale specific plants of multi-products choose to make them. In the times before the Second World War, when excess capacity in steel plants throughout the world made export prices depend entirely on the strategy of combinations of board-rooms, Iscor was totally unable to compete and 'hopelessly uneconomic'.

In post-war times it is Iscor's proud boast, and oft-claimed justification of the 'far-sighted Nationalist Government' decision to give South Africa 'its own iron and steel industry', that Iscor provides 'South Africa with the cheapest steel in the world'. Patently the administered prices of steel permit of conflicting interpretations of theory and practice.

28 See Richards, already cited, p. 293 *et seq.* pars. 501–11. It is of interest to note that it was the Labour Ministers in the Pact Cabinet who pressed most insistently for the vital state-operation clauses in the Iron and Steel Industry Bill, that had previously been introduced on a private enterprise basis by the Smuts Government. Hence Iscor gave Creswell his long-sought opportunity to 'prove' his all-White labour policy and, more particularly, that the White man's productivity on labouring work was so superior to the African's that 'civilized rates of pay' would not involve increased costs. The experience of Iscor proved otherwise to the Arbitration Boards that had subsequently to be appointed in 1936–7 to bring about Iscor's withdrawal from the Creswellian commitment – after the Minister of Labour had departed from office.

29 These figures are for 'Private Industrial Establishments' only and are taken from the Jubilee issue of *Union Statistics*. This is perhaps an appropriate point to warn readers that statistics quoted throughout this text will often not 'tie-up'. Statistical definition in South Africa is far from precise or homogeneous so that different authorities often give divergent data when they are apparently referring to the same thing. Definitions and classifications are a special hazard in the case of national income data and industrial censuses.

30 The Industrial and Agricultural Requirements Commission is familiarly known as the van Eck Commission. Its first, U.G. 33–'40, and second, U.G. 49–'40, interim reports devoted attention exclusively to emergency questions. The third interim report looked backwards and forwards to fundamentals and was published as U.G. 40–'41. The references which follow are to this third interim report.

31 *ibid.*, par. 15.

32 Van Eck Report, already cited, *passim*.

33 *ibid.*, p. 82 – see Conclusions and Recommendations 11.

34 Statistical investigation after the war suggests that the size of individual manufacturing units grew and that such larger-size units contributed more to the growth of gross output than the increase in the number of manufacturing units. It is also a fact that necessity proved to be the mother of considerable innovation, and that the war years resulted in significant technological advance and resource-exploitation. It was a period of Schumpeterian 'development from within'.

35 The long-standing taunt that 'infant industries never grow up' does

not necessarily dispose of the infant industry argument. Protected industries will inevitably expand output and increase costs to the new margin set by the tariffs. The expansion will take place up to that margin by both the 'low-cost' factories and the 'high-cost' factories. So that, at any given time, the tariff is always necessary to protect the existing output. If the 'infant' tariff is withdrawn, there will be a withdrawal from that marginal output. Certain high-cost factories will reduce their output, but the industry as a whole will not necessarily stop production or go out of production altogether on the removal of the 'infant' tariff.

In a real political economy, of course, operating conditions will generally preclude the reduction or elimination of the tariff. But the considerations are political rather than economic.

36   *The Economics of Under-developed Countries* by Bauer and Yamey (London: Nisbet, 1957) does not, indeed, except in a passing footnote make reference to South Africa.

37   See chapter: 'The Springs of Development.'

38   Thus the golden goslings of the Orange Free State extension of the gold-bearing reef were producing in 1963 about one-quarter of the Free World's gold output and more than one-third of South African gold production. At the end of the Second World War, they were no more than a glitter in some financier's eye – but Sir Ernest Oppenheimer had great faith in Mother Goose.

39   See *Apartheid* by N. J. Rhoodie and H. J. Venter (Cape Town: Haum, 1959), *passim*.

CHAPTER 16

1   See *The Awakening of Afrikaner Nationalism* by F. A. van Jaarsveld (Cape Town: Human & Rousseau, 1961). In his resumé, Professor van Jaarsveld declares that Afrikaner nationalism began in 1877 as a reaction to the challenge of British Imperialism in South Africa and specifically to Lord Carnarvon's attempt at federation, which led to the First Transvaal War of Independence (1881). From the Great Trek in the 1830s until 1868, there was little to give the widely scattered Afrikaners even spiritual unity but when the long, strong arm of the British Government again began to intervene in the lives of the Republican Afrikaners, national consciousness grew.

'The development of Afrikaans nationalism . . . brought certain characteristics to the fore . . . that can now be analysed. In essence, Afrikaans nationalism was a question of the heart . . . there was (also) a sense of suppression and subjection that led to indignation and grievances . . . in the second place the emphasis began to fall strongly on the entity "nation" and the term "fatherland". . . . In the "suppression", the scattered individuals discovered one another as "brothers" and colleagues whose joys and sorrows were shared by all. Loyalty was now displayed to one another and continual reference made to the bonds of blood, race and ancestors. The "nation" became a sort of mystical whole, which was more than the individual. . . . In contrast with the "true" or "genuine" Afrikaners there were the "people's enemies" and "traitors" of their nation, namely the English-minded Afrikaners, who were looked upon as despicable. . . .

In the fourth place, there was in Afrikaans nationalism a sense of having been called and chosen, that brought with it an element of religion. There was a belief in a kind of supernatural or mystic creation of the Afrikaner nation. . . . The idea that they had been chosen, made its appearance strongly in the nation's nationalism. . . . The Afrikaans-speaking people had a "task", "mission", or "calling". It was presented as the opening up of the interior for civilization and Christianity and the propaganda of the Gospel among the heathen. . . .

In the fifth place, love for the nation's past became a major characteristic of Afrikaans nationalism. The "pious" ancestors, whose memory was "sacred", had given the example of sacrificial love and had shown the road to the future . . . the youth should be bound to them and should draw inspirations from them. . . . History "was" the nation, and he who spoke disparagingly of the past was guilty of sacrilege. . . . The writing of history itself, which was inspired by nationalism, was to be a defensive art. . . . History had to defend and justify the national existence. . . . History became a series of object lessons for the politics of the day, and in this way a political affair. The content was interpreted as a struggle between Boer and Briton. . . . The struggle of the past was the struggle of the present, and the struggle of the present the same as that of the past . . .' pp. 214 *et seq.*

This sympathetic account of the origins of Afrikaner nationalism by the Professor of History at the University of South Africa achieves a perceptive professionalism.

2 In a radio broadcast preceding the 1953 General Election, Dr D. F. Malan used the striking final appeal (in Afrikaans): Look into the depths of your Afrikaner heart, and you will know which way to vote.

3 General Smuts was defeated in his own constituency, Standerton, by W. C. du Plessis in the 1938 election. In December, 1944, in the middle of the Second World War, Smuts had accused the Broederbond of being 'a sort of Gestapo . . . a dangerous, cunning, political Fascist organization of which no civil servant, if he is to retain his loyalty to the State and the Administration, can be allowed to be a member'.

4 Just as van Jaarsveld's *The Awakening of Afrikaner Nationalism* provides the source-book for its origins, so Prof. Gwendolin M. Carter's *The*

Politics of Inequality (London: Thames & Hudson, 1959), is a professionally percipient analysis by an American political scientist of 'South Africa since 1948'. Prof. Carter's work is the more valuable in that not only does it sift and present the data of 'political science', unique in South African academic analysis of politics, but its subjective judgments are made by a non-South African, which permits an admirable degree of objectivity.

5   Carter, *ibid.*, pp. 36–7.

6   *ibid.*, p. 250. For a broad account see chapter 10 of that study – 'Nationalist Groups and Influences'. There are other sources but the value of Prof. Carter's survey is that it is by a non-South African.

7   See 'Is Separation Practicable?' in Sabra's *Journal of Racial Affairs*, January 1950, p. 13 *et seq.*

8   In 1964, following a parliamentary attack on 'secret societies' by the Opposition Leader, the Prime Minister, Dr Verwoerd, appointed a one-man commission to inquire into all 'secret societies' including the Broederbond, the proceedings to be held *in camera*. The Opposition subsequently refused to appear before such a commission. The Report, published in February, 1965, of its one-man Judicial Commissioner, found no evidence that the Broederbond had put the interests of its exclusive, secret membership before those of the State.

9   Quoted from Carter, already cited, pp. 252–3. Carter also quotes from a circular of the Broederbond, January 16, 1934, in which the chairman and secretary wrote:

> Let us focus attention on the fact that the primary consideration is: whether Afrikanerdom will reach its ultimate destiny of domination (baasskap) in South Africa. Brothers, our solution of South Africa's ailments is not whether one Party or another shall obtain the whip-hand, but that the Afrikaner-Broederbond shall govern South Africa.

10   Carter, already cited, pp. 255–6.

11   In 1937 Dr N. J. van der Merwe, opening the annual F.A.K. Congress declared that: 'The FAK is born of strife, and is even a product of a conflict of soul, in which the Afrikaner is searching for a united front against hostile forces which divide him, and smother his soul,' quoted in Carter, *ibid.*, p. 256.

12   The official exposition of C.N.E. education as applied to Afrikaans-speaking children and students denotes 'Christian' as a view of life and the world 'based on Holy Scripture and formulated in the Articles of Faith of our three Afrikaans churches'; 'National' as a 'love for everything that is our own, with special reference to our country, our language, our history and our culture' with the 'National principle' under the guidance of the fundamentalist and authoritarian doctrine of the Dutch Reformed Churches. Education is defined as 'the controlling guidance

and formation of a child's development into an adult in submission to the Word of God in all things'. Civics aims 'to rear Christian and National citizens'; geography to develop 'a love for our own native country, also in comparison and in contrast with other countries'. While accepting the essential unity of history, C.N.E. history emphasizes that God 'willed separate nations and peoples, and has given to each separate nation and people its special calling and task and talents'. 'Christian-oriented science' is sharply contrasted with 'non-Christain science'. See Carter already cited, pp. 262–6.

13 *ibid.*, p. 250.

14 'The unparalleled upsurge of Afrikaner nationalism after the Second World War had a deciding effect on the crystallization and consolidation of the apartheid idea. The National(ist) Party, the Afrikaans Churches, the Universities, individual Afrikaner intellectuals and SABRA (the latter after 1948) were the most important instruments and moving spirits behind this process of 'ideological nationalization'. As the Afrikaners were ready for this process of nationalization they were able to associate the crystallization of the apartheid idea with a national movement.

Nationalism is always inclined to stimulate a group's instinct of self-preservation, and as this instinct is one of the fundamental principles of the apartheid idea, the new apartheid synthesis was the more acceptable to the Afrikaner people,' p. 160, *Apartheid* by Rhoodie & Venter, already cited.

15 While Apartheid legislation dominated, there was much immediate concentration on entrenching the parliamentary majority of Afrikaner-dom. The South-West Africa Affairs Amendment Act of 1949 gave representation in the Union Parliament on the basis of six seats for a total registered number of 24,000 voters, i.e. from one-half to one-third of the average electorate in Union constituencies. The South African Citizenship Act, 1949, required five years domicile for British Common-wealth immigrants (six years for non-Commonwealth) in place of the previous two years. Furthermore, in place of automatic qualification for citizenship by Commonwealth immigrants after two years domicile, citizenship even after the extended domicile was no longer automatic but subject to absolute ministerial discretion. In the debate the Minister of Justice, C. R. Swart, declared that United-Party imported immi-grants would vote 'against the nationalist-minded' and Dr A. J. R. van Rhijn, subsequently a Cabinet Minister, said that immigrants might determine 'which Government is going to govern the country'. *Die Transvaler*, Nationalist Party newspaper, responded to a plea for 'balanced and selective immigration' with the reply that 'it threatened to plough the Afrikaner under'.

16 The Appeal Court decision became the *cause célèbre* of the 1953 General

Election proving no less a contest-winner than the Black Manifesto of 1924.

17   Debate speeches are informative. P. W. Botha, Secretary of the Cape Nationalist Party and subsequently Minister of Community Development, said: 'To gain a clear view regarding fair treatment and the rights of non-Europeans, we should first answer another question and this is: do we stand for the domination and supremacy of the European or not? . . . For if you stand for the domination and supremacy of the European, then everything you do must in the first place be calculated to ensure that domination' (Hansard, Vol. 82, col. 2086). C. R. Swart, Minister of Justice, said: '. . . necessary for a nation to be educated in colour sense in order to maintain proper behaviour.' This debate in Hansard, Vol. 82, second reading, col. 1052 *et seq.* and cols. 2064–401 is instructive on the value-orientations of White South Africa.

In the author's personal knowledge, a Factory Inspector's ruling that a separate fire-escape for Non-Whites must be provided at a cost of £60,000 at that stage of construction was only set aside on ministerial intervention. In February 1965, it became compulsory for all cultural organizations such as theatre and concert managements and sporting bodies to obtain a permit for 'mixed-audiences', otherwise prohibited.

18   In the related debate, the Opposition Party member, Dr Bernard Friedman, said: '. . . the epoch of the witch-hunt is upon us. The search for the taint in the blood has become a major political pre-occupation in this country . . . in the end, in order to avoid infinite trouble and vexation, it will be far more convenient to have some distinguishing mark tattoed on your forehead like some oriental caste . . .'

19   See *Hofmeyr* by Alan Paton (O.U.P., 1964) – especially chapter 34: 'Hofmeyr Must be Destroyed,' In an address as Chancellor of Witwatersrand University in 1946, Hofmeyr said: 'The plain truth, whether we like it or not, is that the dominant mentality in South Africa is a Herrenvolk mentality—the essential feature of our race problems must be found in that fact. . . . Ten years ago (in 1936) it was announced with a great flourish of trumpets that we had found a solution to our Native problem—but there was no change in our Herrenvolk mentality', p. 422.

20   See Debate in Hansard, Vol. 73, cols. 7433–826.

21   *ibid.* The phrase was used by J. E. Potgieter, M.P.

22   *ibid.* The phrase was used by D. H. Uys, M.P.

23   The model or paradigm of a social system, elaborated by Talcott Parsons and Smelser in *Economy and Society* is especially suggestive for this post-1948 phase of social process in South Africa.

24 The Bantu Education Act of 1953 has generated some of the most violently opposed views. Nationalists have insisted that the aim is to increase the numbers of Africans given the benefit of education and to provide a distinctive education 'more in line with the needs of their community and tradition.' Opponents have seen in this administrative measure, that transferred education from the till then overwhelmingly state-aided mission schools to the central government within the Department of Native Affairs, a specific intent to restrict Africans to a permanently subordinate status. Special significance was attached to such allegedly discriminatory education to restrict the employment potential of Non-Whites in the special Committee Report on Questions concerning South Africa that led to the expulsion of South Africa from the International Labour Office.

In the violent controversy over the Native Laws Amendment Act of 1957, which gave the Government powers to prevent the mixing of races at all meetings and gatherings including church attendance, *Die Transvaler*, the Government newspaper wrote (Feb. 27, 1957): It is not so much the overwhelming numbers of the non-Europeans but the destruction of the feeling of difference and otherness, which is the greater danger for the preservation of the European and his civilization in this multi-racial land. As long as liberalistic bishops and canons, professors, students and politicians can freely attend church and hold meetings and socials together, apartheid will be infringed in its marrow (quoted by Carter, already cited, p. 118).

The Bantu Authorities Act, 1951, aimed to re-establish the authority of the tribal chiefs, abolishing the Native Representatives Council with a new pattern of local administration based on tribal councils.

25 See C. M. Tatz, *Shadow and Substance in South Africa*, already cited, section 'Definitions of Apartheid' in Chapter VIII, pp. 130 *et seq.*; Dr Malan: 'If one could attain total territorial apartheid, if it were practicable, everybody would admit that it would be an ideal state of affairs. It would be an ideal state, but that is not the policy of the party. . . . It is nowhere to be found in our official declaration of policy. On the contrary . . . when we were accused of aiming at total social separation, I clearly stated . . . that total territory separation was impracticable under present circumstances in South Africa, where our whole economic structure is to a large extent based on Native labour. It is not practicable and it does not pay any party to endeavour to achieve the impossible. . . .'

Mr Strijdom, successor to Dr Malan as prime minister: 'If the European loses his colour sense he cannot remain a White man. . . . On the basis of unity you cannot retain your sense of colour if there is no Apartheid in the everyday social life, in the political sphere or whatever sphere it may be, and if there is no residential separation. . . .

South Africa can only remain a White country if we continue to see that the Europeans remain the dominant nation; and we can only remain the dominant nation if we have the power to govern the country and if the Europeans, by means of their efforts, remain the dominant section. . . .'

Dr Verwoerd's re-interpretations of his philosophy do not permit of brief statement.

26   In the course of bitter parliamentary debate on the constitutional issues, two Government backbenchers expressed the ethos of Afrikanerdom. D. J. Potgieter: 'I see in it [the High Court of Parliament Bill] the safeguarding and the perpetuation of the White Christian trusteeship in the interests of the Whites as well as Non-Whites in so far as it protects one of the most important foundations of Christian trusteeship, namely the political influence of the Whites'—Hansard, Vol. 78, col. 5090. S. M. Loubser: 'The United Party comes and whines "the Constitution". Anyone would think the Constitution was of greater importance than the maintenance of White civilization in our country' —Hansard, Vol. 78, col. 5003.

27   The Board of Trade & Industries in its Report No. 282 noted that the outstanding trend of its table of European employment is that between 1921 and 1941, the number of Europeans engaged in agriculture showed a slight increase, while the numbers engaged in manufacturing increased from 66,500 to 190,300 or by nearly 200 per cent. 'The shift of the working population was especially rapid during the period 1936–1941, when the numbers engaged in agriculture showed an annual average rate of decrease of 1·32 per cent as compared with a similar *increase* of 7·49 per cent in manufacturing.' par. 49.

28   Source of data is *Union Statistics for 50 Years*—Bureau of Census & Statistics.

29   U.G. 36–'58, par. 136(2).

30   The most dramatic example of world-demand stimulating hitherto unexploited fertility is in respect of South African sea-fisheries. The rapid post-war rise of this booming industry is instructive of many aspects of 'micro-economic development'.

31   The rising wealth of Afrikaner farmers brought a subtle change into the significance of the 'farm-vote' in politics. The influence on party politics was henceforth exerted not so much directly by appeal to the declining number of rural Poor Whites but by the fighting-fund contribution of wealthy farmers to the political parties.

32   See an interesting review article by Dr Marcus Arkin 'The Jewish Share in S.A. Economic Development', *S.A. Journal of Economics*, Vol. 24, 1956. The Jewish population in South Africa from the time of the mineral discoveries to 1910 increased from 4,000 to over 40,000. The early immigrants came from Lithuania and as such were not the

urbanized factory-workers from Germany–Poland, who went to the U.S.A. The stream to South Africa were mainly shopkeepers, itinerant pedlars and petty craftsmen by occupational origin. Two of the most notable examples of entrepreneurial development are: the Mosenthal brothers who during the 1840's and 1850's set up a series of trading stations in the Eastern and Central Cape, which became entrepots for the marketing of merino fleeces and whose 'unofficial' bank-notes enjoyed unquestioned confidence and were freely negotiable; and the famed Sammy Marks who arrived in 1868 beginning as a *smous* and during 1886–95 'helped by concessions from President Kruger' and anticipating the rise of a market on the Rand established a brick and tile works, a glass factory, a brewery and distillery, fruit and meat preserving plants, a tannery and boot factory. Together with his partner, Isaac Lewis, the firm launched the embryo iron and steel industry – the precursor to Iscor.

33 This is an appropriate point to stress again the formidable difficulties in ensuring strict comparability of statistical data. The frequent changes in basic definition are such that to trace back quoted figures in various sources to a common definition is practically impossible. Thus in respect of data for manufacturing industry, there have been major changes in the definition of 'industrial establishment', in classification of categories in manufacturing industry. One of the large over-statements of South African industrial statistics arises from its basic unit of 'industrial establishment'. In the early years in particular, the numbers of 'factories' was grossly exaggerated by the inclusion of such 'processes' as icecream-making in cafes, alterations to customers' clothing in retail stores and like operations. At one time 'construction', i.e. building activities, was included in 'manufacturing industry' and later excluded.

In 1950–51, a fundamental change in classifications was the adoption of the 'International Standard Industrial Classification of all Economic Activities'.

A study of the Notes that appear on page M.65 of the *Statistical Year Book for 1965*, published by the Bureau of Statistics, Pretoria, will make only too obvious the dangers of interpreting reported figures in any-thing more than the broadest trends.

34 See chapter 18: 'Springs of Development'—for further account of post-War industrialization.

35 See A. J. Norval, already cited, pp. 116 *et seq.*

36 The post-War exchange controls which the Nationalist Government imposed almost immediately on taking office could indeed only have been avoided by a more resolute deflationary policy on the part of the preceding Smuts Government. Though there is no evidence, there is some suspicion that General Smuts himself had resisted tougher

deflationary measures which the more austere Jan Hofmeyr, as Minister of Finance, would have regarded as not too much 'sacrifice' from wartime profits and incomes. Smuts, the pragmatist, was perhaps more conscious than Hofmeyr, the principled, that his slender pro-war majority might be encouraged by adding profits to patriotism. The Smuts Government had indeed taken the decision on exchange control that the Malan Government was forced to impose.

37 The regularity of the solemn ministerial 'warnings' to industry of the 'early end of exchange control that must not be confused with protection' could possibly be correlated with the lunar phases – and with equal relevance to actual industrial experience.

38 See an article on 'The Output of Manufacturing Industry' by O. P. F. Horwood in the golden jubilee number, *South African Industry & Trade* (ed. Ralph Horwitz), March 1960.

39 June 17, 1961.

40 Commission of Enquiry into Policy Relating to the Protection of Industries U.G. 36/1958. The chairman was Dr S. P. du Toit Viljoen, subsequent chairman of the Board of Trade & Industries, and its membership was exceptionally strong in economic analysis. The Viljoen Report is of strategic significance to an understanding of the *actual* Government policy pursued after the Sharpeville and Langa crisis in race relations.

41 Viljoen Commission, already cited, pars. 38 and 41. Dr Viljoen was subsequently as chairman of the Board of Trade to be the main author of the import-permit incentive system to induce a multi-million rand capital investment programme to increase 'local-content' in motor assembly with the ultimate aim of the South African-made car – for fuller account, see later text.

42 *ibid.*, par. 135(2).

43 *ibid.*, par. 142(3). The Committee said in conclusion: There does not appear to be any single article used directly by the mining industry in respect of which the existing tariff can be said to impose an unreasonably heavy burden on the mining industry.

A particular case of interest in the infant industry or guaranteed market-share argument is that of newsprint manufacture in South Africa – for further details, see chapter: 'Springs of Development.'

44 The fluctuating record of the balance-of-payments problem and the response of the monetary authorities is best read in the regular reviews of the *Quarterly Bulletin of Statistics*, published by the South African Reserve Bank. During the latter part of 1957, external factors again caused a deterioration in the balance of payments due to (*a*) a considerable deterioration in the Union's terms of trade as world prices of raw materials declined and (*b*) higher interest rates and the related credit squeeze in Britain so that there was an outflow of private capital from

486

the Union of South Africa. In the first half of 1958 the Union's monetary authorities adopted a tighter internal monetary policy and raised interest rates to curtail internal demand. For the first time, too, the newly acquired power of the Reserve Bank to apply supplementary reserve requirements to the commercial banks was applied.

In the second half of 1958, following on the restricted imports, the adverse balance of payments on current account diminished and there was a substantial net inflow of capital, when interest rates were reduced and the credit squeeze was relaxed in Britain. However South African exports, particularly of the values of non-gold exports, further declined and in the second half of 1958 there were distinct signs of recession in South Africa.

At the beginning of 1959 the South African monetary authorities eased monetary policy with a reduction in interest rates, a reduction in supplementary reserve requirements of the commercial banks from 8 per cent in October 1958 to 4 per cent in February 1959 and 'a number of other expansionist measures taken by Government with a view to stimulating development in certain branches of the economy'. During 1959 there was a considerable improvement in merchandise exports and a substantial increase in gold output so that 'an exceptional improvement occurred in the country's net current account balance with the outside world, allowing for substantial repayments of foreign debt, as well as a considerable increase in gold and foreign exchange reserves'. Towards the end of 1959, it was decided to suspend the remaining supplementary reserve requirements for the commercial banks and the March 1960 Budget was specifically expansionist to stimulate both private investment and consumption.

Just after the Budget, towards the end of March 1960, the Sharpeville–Langa riots led to the Government declaring a state of emergency that lasted until September 1960. This, together with intensified troubles in the Congo and Africa generally, led to unease inside South Africa, while in June 1960 higher interest rates and tightening of credit in Britain accentuated the outflow of funds from South Africa.

Although the S.A. Reserve Bank was anxious to avoid monetary policy contributing to the growing recession, the S.A. bank rate was raised to 4½ per cent in August 1960.

During 1960 there was a large net outflow of capital in all forms from South Africa amounting to about R162 millions – the outflow of private capital of about R194 millions being partly off-set by official and bank borrowings abroad of about R32 millions. The estimated net outflow of Union-resident capital was about R28 million and the net outflow of foreign capital amounted to about R148 millions, of which no less than R78 millions was accounted for by net purchases by

Union residents from foreigners of securities listed on the Johannesburg Stock Exchange.

In the first quarter of 1961 there was a further net outflow of capital of about R20 millions despite official and banking institutions borrowing R25 millions in support of the Rand from abroad – mainly drawings from the I.M.F. The overall outflow of R45 millions was again mainly due to foreigners selling securities on the Johannesburg Stock Exchange. Furthermore the net outflow of South African-resident capital amounted in this quarter to about R20 millions compared with a quarterly average of about R7 millions in 1960.

During April and May 1961 gold and foreign exchange reserves of the S.A. Reserve Bank continued their decline. In December 1959 they had totalled R303·8 millions; in December 1960 they had fallen uninterruptedly to R171·6 millions – recovered briefly with foreign borrowings in March 1961 at R184·8 millions, April R162·9 millions, May R152·7 millions and R153.4 millions at end June 1961.

It was evident that the Minister of Finance, Dr Donges, had been most reluctant to take the essential action that signalled the gravity of the country's *financial* (not economic) weakness as the magic date of declaration of the Republic of South Africa, May 31, 1961, approached. In the third week of May, forward exchange dealings to cover stock exchange transactions as well as importation of consumer goods were suspended while, at the request of the Reserve Bank, commercial banks restricted credit for stock exchange purposes and refused to grant to foreign-controlled branches and subsidiaries such loan facilities as would enable them to repatriate funds from South Africa.

The S.A. Reserve Bank, with the Republic's birthday over, relates the final decision to 'break' with the 'City': 'During the month of May 1961, import control was intensified and extended, and as from June 17, South African residents were prohibited from remitting funds abroad for the purchase of South African and Rhodesian securities, as is the case of foreign securities generally. While non-residents were permitted to continue selling securities on the Johannesburg Stock Exchange, the proceeds of such sales were to be blocked and could be re-invested only in securities quoted on this exchange.'

The Republican era had arrived – but for this see the last chapter.

45   Bantustans were the old Native Territories or Native Reserves – they now became known as the homelands of the Bantu in official policy-statements; 'border-areas' were the areas bordering geographically on these Bantustans or Bantu homelands – border areas are also known as the perimeter areas of the policy of industrialization decentralization.

46 The Johannesburg Stock Exchange duly reflected the contemporary climate and anticipated the unlimited future:

New Issues of Marketable Securities–Rm.*

Year	Public sector	Private sector	Total
1955	117	23	140
1956	90	53	143
1957	140	47	188
1958	127	74	200
1959	224	97	321
1960	175	55	229
1961	120	76	196
1962	342	84	425
1963	280	106	386
1964**	171	120	291

* Figures represent cash flows, except issues by private sector prior to 1963.
** First half 1963.
(Source: *S.A. Reserve Bank Quarterly Bulletin*, September 1964, p. xiv.)

47 Published by O.U.P. (1962). This biography by Sir Theodore Gregory is not only a fascinating contribution to entrepreneurial history but a mine of informative decision-taking practice and invaluable guidance for the theory and practice of business administration.

48 See Gregory, already cited, Chapter V: 'The Diamond Story—World Crisis and World Leadership'. It was the essential changes in the marketing-structure of world diamonds, that was not only to preserve enormous invested capitalization in diamonds owned by individuals but the future of diamond-mining in South Africa, for which Sir Ernest Oppenheimer was primarily responsible. Although Gregory suggests that Solly Joel had the original idea, it was Sir Ernest who converted the Diamond Syndicate as a buying organization into the Diamond Corporation as a 'buying and selling' organization and relationships between all diamond producers (including the South African Government) were made reconcilable by the foundation of the Diamond Producers' Association. A genuine cost-reducing rationalization of De Beers mining and administration was carried out and Sir Ernest also took the initiative in the technological development of industrial diamonds, which led in turn to the major cost-reducing diamond-drills for breaking of mine-ore.

A later generation of more timid South African business men might with benefit read the account of the open confrontation between the Minister of Mines, ever-mindful of the Poor Whites votes, and the capitalist Sir Ernest Oppenheimer with the responsibility of the present and future livelihood of a considerable fraction of South Africa – see pp. 265 *et seq.*

49 Gregory, already cited, p. 37. If to this signal entrepreneurial record is added the achievements in the Rhodesian Copperbelt, which in Gregory's view may yet outrank in significance the diamonds-gold exploitation of South Africa, it seems no exaggeration of language to claim for Sir Ernest Oppenheimer the status of a Schumpeterian Colossus and one of the makers of modern Southern Africa. It was he who conceived the economy of development of the Free State gold as a mine-field and not as a series of mines. Welkom from a 'dorp' or village of less than 10,000 population had by 1958 become the Union's seventh largest city with a population of 90,000. In ten years of develop-ment of the Free State gold fields, between 1945 and 1955, some £200,000,000 had been raised 'to enable the development of the gold-field to proceed unchecked by any shortage of finance, and perhaps the most remarkable aspect of the whole development has been the fact that it was always possible to provide capital as and when called for'. Contrast this with the interrupted vicissitudes of financing the original Rand gold field.

CHAPTER 17

1 See Introduction

2 See *Economic Development in a Plural Society* by D. Hobart Houghton (Cape Town: O.U.P., 1960) for a most detailed study of a dual economy in the Border Region of the Cape Province.

3 See *Reaction to Conquest* by Monica Hunter (O.U.P.). The second edition of 1961 of this book originally written in 1936 as a study of the effects of contact with Europeans on the Pondo peoples, generally regarded as among the more backward of the tribal societies and only annexed to the Cape in 1894, indicates the change brought about by 25 years of diminishing self-sufficiency of the Reserves and increasing individuali-zation of employment in a cash economy. See also the same author's study of an urbanizing, detribalizing community—*Langa* by Monica Wilson and Archie Mafeje (O.U.P., 1963).

4 Quoted in Native Laws Commission Report (Fagan Commission) U.G. 38, 1948 par. 2.

5 The memorandum is set out in detail in the Fagan Commission Report, *ibid.*, par. 2(c). The Bill based on this was passed into law as the Natives (Urban Areas) Act No. 21 of 1923. This remained for many years the basis of legislation on urbanized Africans, being extensively amended in 1930, 1934, 1937, 1941, 1942 and 1944. These Acts were subsequently superseded by the Natives (Urban Areas) Consolidation Act No. 25 of 1945, in turn amplified by amendments in Act No. 38 of

1945, Act No. 43 of 1945, Act No. 42 of 1946 and Act No. 45 of 1947. With the advent of the new Nationalist Government in 1948, further legislation followed.

6 Transvaal Local Government Commission of 1921 (Stallard Commission) T.P. 1–'22, par. 42. It is worth noting that Col Stallard, one of the founders of the ultra-British Dominion Party, became identified in party political history as a leading British 'jingo' at the other end of the spectrum from Afrikanerdom, i.e. the spectrum of English–Afrikaans relationships and not White–Black relationships.

7 While a single medium of exchange will evolve as the only money of a sovereign polity, no one city or market-area will eliminate all other cities or market-areas within the polity's economy but there will be powerful factors favouring the dominating superiority of a relatively few cities or market areas, even in the largest territorial and most populous country.

8 By the end of the Second World War, a situation of frightening chaos in the living conditions of urban Africans had developed. In the War and immediate post-war years building was very tightly controlled and during this period, there was an exceptionally large influx of Africans into urbanized employment. Denied legal admission into municipal locations, which themselves became grossly over-crowded, thousands of Africans established themselves just beyond the municipal boundaries in any form of habitation. The shanty towns of squatters around the major cities grew to unmanageable proportions. When post-War building became more possible, the great increase in building costs based on white skilled wages implied a financial burden of future indebtedness, that became a continuous haggle between the central government and local government.

When the Nationalist Government came to power, action had become imperative. Full employment of White workers on post-war building and constructional projects in 'White' areas enabled the Government to insist that 'Africans should be allowed to build for Africans' in conformity with its general policy of 'each race serving the needs of itself'. Large new African townships were planned under site-and-service schemes in which local authorities made provision for water, light and sewerage services and sites were rented to Africans. No ownership of site or house was permitted or could ever be acquired by Africans, whose permanent status as urban citizens was totally abrogated. But Africans could rent sites on which they could then build their own houses with their own labour or have them built cheaply on government-borrowed money.

Since these townships were generally situated at maximum distance from employment or work-places in the 'White' cities, additional and subsidized transport was provided. Transport costs, however, still take an exceptionally high fraction of the African worker's wage-earnings.

In 1959, the Minister of Bantu Administration and Development announced that in the previous eight years 500,000 Africans had been housed in 100,000 family units and building was still proceeding steadily. A major slum-clearance programme had been completed. The Government throughout has maintained that such re-housing is still no more than satisfactory accommodation-provision for a 'temporary' population, whose ultimate residential rights and domicile must be in the Native Territories of future Bantustans. (See L. Marquard: *The Peoples and Policies of South Africa*—O.U.P., 3rd ed., pp. 46–54).

9 See Chapter 4.

10 Native Economic Commission, 1930–32, known as the Holloway Commission U.G. 22, 1932, par. 16. In the very next paragraph, the Commission went on: 'On its European side no useful approach can be found by allowing an undermining of the standards which the White community has built up by centuries of effort. The European is the bearer of civilization in South Africa, and anything which retards his civilization will ultimately react detrimentally on the Native as well.' This, of course, ignored the reality that the 'centuries of effort' had by 1870 and even by 1910 produced at the earlier date a largely stagnant economy, while the progress achieved from mining exploitation by 1910 had been made possible only with the co-operation of labour obtained, by every kind of pressure, from the tribal societies in Southern Africa.

11 *ibid.*, pars. 68–95.

12 See *The Economics of Bantu Education in South Africa* in S.A. Institute of Race Relations (Johannesburg, 1964) by N. Hurwitz and *A Decade of Bantu Education* in S.A. Institute of Race Relations (Johannesburg, 1964) by M. Horrell.

13 Holloway Commission, pars. 83–5.

14 *ibid.*, par. 92.

15 *ibid.*, par. 96.

16 It should be observed that Commissioners Dr Roberts and Mr Lucas, sometimes jointly and sometimes severally, frequently excepted to the interpretations and recommendations of the majority commissioners. On many fundamental aspects of control of mobility and the pass-system, diametrically opposed views were expressed.

17 *ibid.*, par. 529.

18 *ibid.*, pars. 544–58.

19 *ibid.*, par. 845, But (par. 847) Dr Roberts wishes to state that there are two cardinal principles which should govern the movement and employment of all citizens of the Union, namely freedom of movement, and freedom of occupation; and that to endeavour to limit the occupa-

tion or the movement of Natives is therefore an infringement of their rights as citizens of the land. And (pars. 849–50) Mr Lucas: 'The exclusion of Natives on the grounds of colour from certain occupations, by law or custom, or by Government or by Trade union action, has served to embitter the attitude of Natives towards the administration. . . . The opposition to a colour bar in the sense here described is very widespread. It was shown before the Commission in every part of the country. The colour bar undoubtedly plays a great part in creating illfeeling towards Europeans in the minds of Natives [and] is looked upon by the Natives as depriving them of a fundamental right to develop their own powers and to employ them lawfully as they please. . . .' It is of interest that F. A. W. Lucas, who had been the first Chairman of the Wage Board, showed considerable disillusionment with the manner in which industrial legislation has been administered to extend the effective colour barriers to employment opportunities and higher earnings for Africans.

20 This was the description given to the public feeling by the Fagan Commission in U.G. 28—1948 par. 3.

21 Relevant extracts of the Young-Barrett Departmental Committee Report are published as appendix 5, pp. 61 *et seq.* of the Fagan Commission, already cited. They provide much illumination on the feelings of White opinion and of the strongly opposed value-orientations towards the civil rights of Africans in the cities and on the human rights and obligations in a multi-racial society.

22 This was the 'pass' to end all other passes issued in terms of the Natives (Abolition of Passes and Co-ordination of Documents) Act No. 67 of 1952. In place of all the manifold passes issued by numerous authorities under bewildering regulations of different laws, all male Africans after the fixed date Feb. 1, 1958 and all female Africans after the fixed date Dec. 1, 1960, born in South Africa and South-West Africa, had to possess a reference book. (Africans in South Africa, born outside, are required to possess a virtually identical document known as an identity document.)

The reference book contains the individual's identity card, issued in terms of the Population Registration Act No. 30 of 1950, bearing personal photograph, identity number, name, group, tribe; Section A stating address of permanent residence and with spaces for efflux and influx control and registration endorsements; Section B giving details of all employment facts and changes; Section C for tax-stamp payments; Section D for Bantu-Authorities tax payments and Section E for additional personal particulars.

African chiefs, headmen, professors, lecturers, ministers of religion, advocates, attorneys, medical practitioners, dentists and some others who furnish specimen signatures in place of finger-prints may request a green-covered reference book in all other respects identical with the standard brown-covered reference book.

23   For further details of the legal facts of movement controls and related rights and obligations of Africans, see *The 'Pass' Laws*, compiled by Muriel Horrell for the S.A. Institute of Race Relations No. 7–1960. The restrictions and rights here mentioned, as of 1960, were further tightened and limited by the Bantu Laws Amendment Act No. 76, 1963 & No. 47 of 1964 for which see the last chapter, 'Republican Heritage.'

24   While Africans are not prohibited from forming their own separate trade unions, such trade unions are prohibited from recognition and the right to strike is generally prohibited. Whether collective bargaining rights increase or diminish the individual's bargaining rights, the labour market for African labour in South Africa bears only the slightest resemblance to the competitive market of theoretical analysis.

25   While the law deprived the African work-seeker of any real bargaining rights and *apparently* in consequence placed his wage- and working-conditions in the unfettered power of the employer, the employer's demand for labour in the face of administrative arbitrary interference with the supply has occasionally made the bargaining realities of the controlled market favour the work-seeker. This is notably the case in domestic service employemnt which, though never subject to any form of industrial legislation, has with the years shown a total turn-round of 'bargaining power' from master to servant.

26   Thus in the year 1957, legal statistics showed just over 1,000 Africans were convicted *per day* for offences against laws and regulations controlling their freedom of movement. In addition, extremely large numbers of admissions of guilt are paid that are not recorded in such statistics. More than 400,000 Africans per year were regularly contravening movement-laws.

27   It is of interest that Chief Justice Fagan, a man of notable courtesy and humanity and a life-long Hertzogite, after his retirement from the Bench and the accession of Dr Verwoerd to the premiership, felt himself morally compelled (at an advanced age) to return to active politics as an active anti-Nationalist. In a private conversation with the author, he in a moment of depressed candour confessed 'that I never thought to live to the day when I would see my fellow-Afrikaners behave as they have'.

28   U.G. 28–'48, already cited, par. 28.

29   See *Apartheid* by N. J. Rhoodie and H. J. Venter, already cited.

30   From *Apartheid*, already cited, *passim*.

31   U.G. 62—1951.

32   *ibid.* See chapter 2: 'The Labour Force of the Union.' Note this

Report introduces its own amended and more realistic definitions of 'urban' and 'rural' into its figures, which appear here.

33 It is of relevance that the official Department of Labour publication, published in 1960 for external information, on Work Reservation has a section on Operatives' Work. It says: 'The Non-White was rapidly entrenching himself not only in operative work but also in trades, which were hitherto considered the prerogative of the White worker. The usual process is for employers to start their factories with White labour and then gradually to train Non-Whites, who eventually replace the Whites. This process is usually assisted by the dilution of skilled work which results in portions of the journeyman's work being classified as operatives' work. Technological progress in industry and especially in mechanization has changed production methods. This has resulted in a re-evaluation and a regrouping of abilities and skills . . . the reclassification is usually coupled with a revision of the wage scales . . . only too often fixed on a level unacceptable to White employees.

34 For a legal analysis, with occasional reference to industrial relations' implications, see *Industrial Laws of South Africa* by A. de Kock (Cape Town: Juta, 1956).

35 The Commission recorded (par. 1040): 'the evidence presented to the Commission was overwhelmingly against the introduction of legislation compelling the segregation of the various races into separate unions, and the witnesses who advocated the retention of mixed unions included employers and employees.' The Commission, itself, however rejected such evidence (par. 1075): 'Admittedly the majority of witnesses favoured the retention of mixed organizations. It does not follow, however, that they should remain because the majority supported them; truth is not necessarily based on the number of witnesses holding a certain view. Some witnesses who were in favour of mixed-unions were so for ideological reasons; they were either communists or communistically-inclined. A second group desiring the perpetuation of multi-racial unions were swayed by political reasons, believing or fearing that, if they supported racial separation, this would be tantamount to supporting the present Government's Apartheid policy. A third category of witnesses, again, did not express the views and sentiments of the people, or the majority of the people, they claimed to represent.'

It must be left to the reader to assess to what extent the Commission itself was swayed by 'ideological reasons,' 'political reasons' or even representative in their recommendations of the evidence presented to it!

36 See de Kock, already cited, p. 79.

37 Party political interference in trade unionism by the Nationalist Party and its instrument, the Blankewerkers Beskermingsbond (White-Workers Protection-Society), though it began before the Second

495

World War was much intensified by the decision of the S.A. Labour Party to support South Africa's entry into the War, and that Labour Party's subsequent adoption of a more 'liberal' policy towards African aspirations.

38 See *South African Trade Unionism* by Muriel Horrell, already cited, pp. 21–6.

39 It will be observed that the only 'protection' of the interests of African workers, prohibited from striking or from registering a trade union, is a Government official. Nor does any African in person appear before the Industrial Tribunal to state a case in respect of either existing or future employment rights or prospects.

40 See official release by Dept. of Labour: *Work Reservation*.

41 The following text from Determination No. 8 C.G. June 2, 1961, will illustrate the legalistic complexity – a complexity that is reported to have so defied interpretation by *anybody*, including the Department of Labour, that the Reservation Order is in practice a nullity:

> Any reference in this determination to a percentage of White employees or Coloured employees or White employees and Coloured employees of an employer or new employer, in proportion to the total number of the employees of such employer or new employer, shall be read and construed as a reference to the percentage of White employees or Coloured employees or White employees and Coloured employees, as the case may be, employed by such employer or new employer in relation to any particular factory, in proportion to the total number of employees employed by such employer or new employer in relation to such particular factory.

42 The key figure in this Garment Workers Union was E. S. Sachs. He was almost the archetype of British militant trade unionist, 'educated' by the social miseries of unemployment and sweated labour-conditions (themselves the consequence of under-capitalized factories in the circumstances of intensive competition). Though 'alien' to the whole cultural and religious background of Afrikaans-speaking clothing workers, Sachs's tremendous personal efforts on their behalf as members of a multi-racial union in negotiating wages-working conditions from reluctant employers won for him a unique loyalty from such Afrikaans-speaking workers, especially women. Their loyalty withstood the most vicious 'splitting' tactics – including physical violence – by a 'rival' White garment workers body, organized by 'Afrikanerdom'. Sachs won a notable libel action against accusations of being a communist. He was, however, one of the early targets of subsequent Nationalist Government legislation against Communism, and forced to leave South Africa for residence in Britain. Many of the Afrikaans-speaking women, whom he had trained in trade unionism, continued the fight to

keep the old multi-racial Garment Workers Union in being but were finally defeated by the mechanism and machinations of the Industrial Conciliation Amendment Act.

43 The Report Recommendation by the Industrial Tribunal on Work Reservation in the Motor Assembly Industry is the source of factual data given. It is instructive that the employer-assessors make a formidable case against job-reservation, emphasizing that the initiative in instigating the enquiry was the S.A. Yster-en Staal-bedryfsvereniging. This Union, not recognized by the employers, had obtained recognition as a registered union of White employees for the Port Elizabeth area only in terms of the (amended) Industrial Conciliation Act of 1956. This Whites-only union made strong representations for work-reservation for Whites in order to protect themselves against competition from Coloureds. The Coloured workers organized, and recognized by the employer-organization in the area, in the Western Province Motor Assembly Workers' Union, specifically opposed job-reservation in evidence. Employee assessors on the Industrial Tribunal appeared to have represented only the White union.

44 It is also an industry of obvious importance for military independence.

45 The whole subject would provide fascinating empirical material for games-theory. In evidence to the Industrial Tribunal the motor assembly industry employers said: 'Employers have been required to render statistics regarding the racial complement of their employee strengths on a number of occasions in recent years. Such employers have been well aware of the interest of the Government in ensuring that inter-racial competition does not take place . . . the employers have thus been careful to see that no criticism can be levelled against them in this regard.'

46 The most interesting example is the textile mill in the border area near East London established by Cyril Lord, for details of which see later text.

47 Quoted in Rhoodie and Venter *Apartheid*, already cited p. 194. See their whole Chapter XI for 'The Practical Application of Apartheid'.

48 U.G. 36-'58, already cited, par. 15.

CHAPTER 18

1 'The organizer of industry, who thinks he has "made" himself and his business, has found a whole social system ready to his hand in skilled workers, machinery, a market, peace and order – a vast apparatus and a pervasive atmosphere, the joint creation of millions of men and scores of generations.' L. T. Hobhouse *The Elements of Social Justice*, quoted by Paul A. Samuelson in *Economics* (McGraw-Hill, 4th ed.), p. 445.

2 At this period, Governor Grey, the historian Froude, and Lord Carnarvon attempted to impose their ideas and plans for federation on the quarrelsome territorial divisions of a country that seemed never-destined to achieve the framework and impulse of a progressive society – or, in modern terms, to escape from underdevelopment.

3 Essay by Henry J. Bruton 'Contemporary Theorizing on Economic Growth' in *Theories of Economic Growth*, ed. by Hoselitz, already cited, p. 267: 'It must therefore be emphasized that the growth process must be viewed in a larger context than simply the arithmetic of capital-output ratios, savings-income ratios, and population growth rates. Of greater relevance is an understanding of the mechanism by which the general environment, within which the ecomony functions, changes in response to those forces immediately responsible for a rising per capita income.'

4 *ibid.*, p. 267 – more especially W. W. Rostow though also Schumpeter, Hansen and Robertson.

5 See Higgins *Economic Development*, already cited, pp. 188–93.

6 'When the industry is being prosecuted with an adequate labour supply and without interruption from industrial troubles, its immense volume of production and spending power acts like a great flywheel in the economic life of the country . . .' from Sir Robert Kotze's Departmental Committee of the Mines Dept. on the Mineral Resources of the Union, Report Jan. 1925, par. 6.

7 The only major mining-management to propose and press for a permanent, family-based African mine-labour force was Anglo-American Corporation, when developing the new Orange Free State mine-complex in the 1950's. But the Oppenheimers' innovation in labour-organization was rejected by Dr Verwoerd as Minister of Native Affairs – see Chapter 16.

8 The real extent to which tribal Africans returned from the mines to rot and die from silicosis in their tribal homelands (and to spread the incidence of this terrible disease) is the subject of keen, and acrimonious, controversy.

9 U.G. 21–'44.

10 '. . . the Commission has been surprised at the evidence of a number of witnesses who appear to have accepted some of the conclusions of the (Van Eck) 1941 Third Interim Report on the decline of the gold-mining industry, without a sufficiently careful study of the premises on which they are based, and who are apparently prepared to accelerate such decline in the belief that thereby the attainment by the Union of a greater and sounder prosperity will be expedited . . .' *ibid.*, par. 11.

11 *ibid.*, par. 13.

12 *ibid.*, pars. 70–71.

13 *Economic Development with Unlimited Supplies of Labour* by Arthur Lewis, already cited.

14 *ibid.*, p. 149.

15 *ibid.*, p. 158.

16 Although the conspicuous expenditure of some of the early Randlords or mining magnates made an impression in Edwardian England, it was only a very minor fraction of mining profits that went into personal consumption. Plough-back of profits by both mining capitalists and later manufacturing capitalists in South African history has been a major source of high rates of domestic capital formation especially since the Second World War.

In an article 'Some Aspects of Profit Re-investment in the Union' (*S.A. Journal of Economics*', Vol. 23, 1955) P. K. Lomas writes: 'Until the post-war years profit retention was, for indigenous industrial and commercial companies as distinct from subsidiaries and branches of overseas concerns, the main if not the only source of funds for expansion and many public companies which, in recent years, have been able to make public issues of securities, owe their present size and status to the abstentions of their founders.'

17 Lansdown Commission U.G. 21–'44 par. 68 *et seq.*

18 It is interesting that the Lansdown Commission reported that from this then record figure, there had been a substantial decline in 1943 when some 105,000 Union and High Commission Territory Africans 'enlisted for military service'. Any external activity offering more favourable alternatives rapidly diminished the numbers of African mine workers, again suggesting a keen awareness of market wages and casting doubt on the 'backward-sloping' demand curve.

19 *ibid.*, par. 68.

20 *ibid.*, par. 78.

21 *ibid.*, par. 80. There was no overtime pay, no holiday pay, only Christmas and Good-Friday being regarded as paid holidays. There was no scheme of automatic pay increase but length of service and experience might be recognized by an extra penny per shift. Deductions from wages during the first few months covered repayment of advance at time of recruitment, purchase of boots, 'buying of a cheap mattress or sacking which he can use upon his concrete bunk for sleeping purposes' and usually some essential clothing and the replacement of the first free issue of miner's lamp and protective jacket, often lost or stolen. Pars. 87–8.

It is difficult for any private enquirer to obtain current details of African mine-workers' remuneration and, in particular, the extent to which the maximum-average, monopsonistic practice still applies in 1966.

22 *ibid.*, par. 101.

23 The counter-figures submitted by the Chamber of Mines are of some interest. According to the Chamber's evidence: the economic requirements of the tribal native must be divided into: (*a*) that part of the upkeep of the home in the Native Reserves which is obtained from his land; (*b*) the articles required by the native and his family (wife and three children) while in the Reserves in addition to these included under (*a*); and (*c*) necessary additional expenditure of the native while he is on the Witwatersrand. For (*a*) the Chamber relied on evidence of the Native Affairs Commission of 1939/40 and adopted the average annual income of a native family in a Reserve at £30 per year or £2 10s 0d per month; for (*b*) manufactured food – tea, sugar, coffee – and other needs such as paraffin, matches etc. were put at 10/6 per month and clothing at 12/10 per month at 1943 price level, this total figure of 23/4 per month being reduced by one-third since while the male worker was away at the mine the Reserve family needs were thereby reduced; for (*c*) the Chamber's estimate was per year taxes 25/–, three pairs boots 43/6; lamp (if lost) 7/–; cost of repatriation 50/– and other expenses 40/–, giving a total of £7 0s 6d per year or 11/9 per month 'at an outside estimate'.

Hence the Chamber of Mines arrived at the total cash requirements of the average married mine native, less its estimate of the value of the surplus produce of the native from his land of £3 p.a., at £12 for a 26-month period on the basis of 1939 prices. The Chamber claimed that no adjustment to new price-levels was necessary because the native 'grows his own food and sold the surplus at the new price-level'. The Chamber gave the minimum cash earnings of a labourer for 14 months at £35 14s 0d for underground and £31 4s 9d for surface workers. 'On these data, therefore, it was argued that, on the basis of the 1939 cost of living, the native labourer is able to earn in fourteen months sufficient not only to maintain himself and his family during his absence of 14 months at the mines and to keep him in idleness for a further period of 12 months, but that he actually has a large margin with which to purchase stock and improve his standard of living. It was also contended that he could easily augment this surplus by extending his period of work on the mines without detriment to his tribal life, and increase his income by the adoption of improved methods of agriculture.' Pars. 103–10.

24 Lansdown Commission, already cited, par. 101.

25 The Lansdown Commission briefly noted many representations made to it from persons in favour of the removal of the colour bar but that the Chamber of Mines itself had made no representations. The Commission itself believed that 'only some few natives' might be affected and 'the issue being partly political and deeply rooted in tradition and custom', it contented itself with 'stating the facts'.

26 *ibid.*, par. 102.

27 *ibid.*, par. 267. The comparative figures of wage-earnings of White miners are illuminating. In 1933 the average income of White miners (excluding officials, apprentices and learners) was £367 14s od per year; in June 1942 the average was £383 5s od per year plus fringe benefits of £60 17s od per year. Par. 276.

27 *ibid.*, par. 211–12.

28 'The emergence of a market or exchange economy in place of the previous subsistence economy is an essential condition of economic progress beyond a most primitive level . . .' Bauer and Yamey *The Economics of Under-developed Countries*, p. 182.

29 Van Eck Commission U.G. 40–'41, already cited. par. 61.

30 Benjamin Higgins in his *Economic Development*, already cited, emphasizes the importance of the increasing *rate* of discovery of new natural resources and of the increase in the *rate* of technological progress for producing continuing economic expansion (see p. 244 *et seq.*). The South African goldmining industry provides powerful confirmation of these arguments both in respect of the secular discoveries of profitable goldiferous ore (related of course, in part, to gold price increases and to technological progress in mining and ore-extraction).

31 Gunnar Myrdal in his *Economic Theory and Under-developed Regions* (London: Duckworth, 1957) most directly relates the 'self-interest' aspect in international trade theory to the particular context of regional development.

32 Myrdal, already cited, p. 16, draws attention to South Italy's continued deterioration after the removal of internal tariff barriers following Italian unification and stresses that economic analysis disregards the non-economic factors, which in terms of circular causation often results in the vicious-circle situations.

33 See Higgins *Economic Development*, already cited, Chapter 16.

34 'Industrialization of Eastern and South Eastern Europe' by P. N. Rosenstein–Rhodan in the *Economic Journal*, 1943.

35 See A. J. Norval, already cited.

36 For a good account of this strategic, commanding-heights, state-financed Corporation's activities, see the supplement on Sasol in the *Financial Mail*, issue of April 3, 1964. It is worth noting, though this is not fully reflected in the Supplement or in any other public account, that the basic oil-from-coal project eventually required more than four times the original capitalization before any oil flowed.

Only the State probably could make available the never-ending demands for capital (supplied by more or less ignorant and acquiescent tax-payers). Whether Sasol does or does not prove the merits of nationalized projects, and whether or not it is an example of forced industrialization that has made an undeniable contribution to economic development, must await a full, impartial investigation. It may well be that the diversion of scarce capital substantiates the classical case for free trade rather than the 'modern' case for protection.

37   For a factual account of industrialization, from which much of this text-material has been based, see the *Annual Review of the South African Economy*, supplement to the *Cape Times*—1965 issue of Feb. 20, 1965; 1966 issue of Feb. 12, 1966 (consulting editor – Ralph Horwitz).

38   See Ragnar Nurske, already cited, p. 10.

39   *ibid.*, p. 12.

40   *ibid.*, p. 15.

41   Articles by P. K. Lomas in *S.A. Journal of Economics*, Vol. 23, 1955, already cited.

42   *ibid.*

43   *ibid.*

44   U.G. 36–'58, already cited, par. 288.

45   Table extracted from the Viljoen Commission U.G. 36–'58, already cited, table IX. Further statistical data on capital formation appear in the *Quarterly Bulletin of S.A. Reserve Bank* – see especially article 'Capital Formation in Post-war Period in South Africa', No. 65, Sept. 1962 by J. C. du Plessis.

    An unpublished thesis, 1955, by J. J. D. Willers *Kapitaalvorming en Kapitaalbasis in die Unie, 1910–1953*, according to a letter to the author, gave figures for annual gross domestic capital formation and net domestic capital formation in the Union of South Africa, 1910–1953, and also estimates of total value of capital assets in S.A.

46   U.G. 36–'58, pars, 296/297.

47   See *Annual Review of S.A. Economy* (Cape Times), 1965, already cited – article by Dr M. S. Louw: 'Size and Significance of Institutional Finance.' Dr M. S. Louw is one of the most highly respected figures in the 'Afrikaans' financial movement. His career is interesting and significant. One of the first Afrikaans-speaking actuaries, he helped to establish the first 'Afrikaans' life assurance company, Sanlam. Sanlam, originally basing its marketing appeal on 'support fellow-Afrikaners', grew especially in the post-war period into the country's second largest life-assurance company. It has unquestionably played a notable part in encouraging small-savings among rural and urban Afrikaners, who for many years regarded even the most uneconomic piece of 'land' as the only acceptable form of savings.

    From Sanlam there grew up a complex of 'Afrikaans' financial institutions in all fields – building societies, deposit-receiving institutions, savings-banks, commercial banks. Their personnel had very close links with political and cultural Afrikanerdom and their 'mutual aid' financial support and interlocking investments powerfully aided the post-1948 rise of Afrikaner-dominated industrial and, later, mining companies.

The whole story of the rise of Afrikaner-finance and its contribution to Afrikaner-participation in commerce and manufacturing, though it includes questionable abuse of political power at every level of central and local authority, is in itself a highly interesting example of Talcott Parson's social system theory. Undoubtedly it greatly helped to push Afrikanerdom out of stagnant, rural-based, cultural isolationism into a more flexible, more modern-minded assimilation of twentieth-century capitalistic achievements and ambitions.

48 It is of interest that the first institution of the money market was Union Acceptances Ltd, established in 1955 and acting both as a merchant bank and a discount house until 1957, at which later date its discount department was separated and taken over by The Discount House of South Africa Ltd. These initiating institutions were established by Anglo-American Corporation, the mining finance house, associated with the entrepreneurial genius of Sir Ernest Oppenheimer. Not long after, the Afrikaans-based financial organization also launched into the merchant banking-discount house business.

49 Some of the marketing-finance consequences of this import-substitution policy are of interest. It was very evident that, far from the existing or potential market-sales justifying the enormous capital investments, the car manufacturers would (a) have drastically to reduce the variety of models offered to car-buyers and (b) exert themselves to achieve as soon as possible a substantially increased sale of such specific models by providing massive consumer-finance directly or indirectly through the various financial institutions. There followed for a time not only a stretching to the legal limit of the terms of hire-purchase selling but novel schemes of leasing and open-credit terms, which undoubtedly contributed towards a crisis in banking liquidity in 1965. The S.A. Reserve Bank was 'forced' to introduce a freezing scheme on interest-rates in an attempt to maintain an appropriate distribution of liquid funds throughout the money market, especially to the commercial banks for their normal trade-financing and to the building societies for their mortgage-financing. The resultant credit controls for car-buying brought about a significant drop in car sales. The reduced volume of sales exposed the 'uneconomic' scale of capital investment in the 'South African Made' car; but from the viewpoint of the Government, a substantial volume of foreign investment had been induced from the foreign car-manufacturers at a critical time in the country's balance-of-payments.

50 A good account, though perhaps too uncritical and unenquiring into the high-cost character of some of the ventures of the Industrial

Development Corporation over 25 years appears in a supplement 'Cash, Counsel & Courage' to the *Financial Mail*, May, 28, 1966.

51 The heads of the great mining-finance groups, notably Mr Harry Oppenheimer of the Anglo-American Corporation, have never doubted that foreign capital is indispensable. Mr Oppenheimer publicly declared his grave concern at the June, 1961 decision which imposed restrictions on capital movements between South Africa and the outside world, more particularly the City of London. Although his enormous expertise as a financier and the tremendous prestige of Anglo-American and De Beers have repeatedly been deployed to obtain massive foreign capital support (not only from the traditional source of the City of London but also from newer sources such as the American, Swiss and West German banks), often to an extent which the South African Government itself could not command, Mr Oppenheimer has had to face political attacks from the extreme wing of Afrikaner nationalism.

The political factor has not over-graciously acknowledged nor accepted the contributions of the Oppenheimers, as financiers and entrepreneurs to economic development.

On the other side, it should be noted that an increasing number of influential Afrikaner financiers would welcome foreign capital and recognize its critical contribution to a high rate of development – see the article by P. R. Rorich, successor to Dr M. S. Louw as managing director of Bonuscor, in the *Annual Review of the S.A. Economy*, Cape Times, Feb. 12, 1966.

52 A valuable academic analysis of the significance of capital investment, domestic and foreign, to South African economic development was made by a visiting American econometrician, Prof. Stephen Enke. In his article 'South African Growth: A Macro-Economic Analysis' (*S.A. Journal of Economics*, Vol. 30, No. 1, March, 1962), he concluded: It would seem that the South African economy has a considerable long-term growth potential despite a complete cessation of foreign capital inflows . . . of course, capital inflows would increase this rate of growth, the contribution of each R100 million of extra foreign capital a year being roughly 0·28 of 1 per cent extra increase in gross domestic output.

53 This document carries no identifying U.G. number but was duplicated and released by the Department of Planning – Prime Minister's Office in Nov/Dec. 1964.

54 See E.D.P., already cited, pars. 94 *et seq.*

55 P. R. Rorich in an article in the *Annual Review of the S.A. Economy*, Cape Times – Feb. 12, 1966, suggested that a target rate of $5\frac{1}{2}$ per cent growth in Gross Domestic Product requires a related gross capital formation increase from R1,563 million in 1965 to R2,112 million in

1969. Depreciation, he writes, accounts for about 40 per cent of gross capital formation, requiring about 60 per cent to be found from savings and foreign investment. His conclusion, after assumptions of investment requirements in various categories of activity, is that, while it is not possible to make a reasoned estimate of the amounts of foreign capital required for different rates of growth, 'at most I would hazard that between a growth of 5 per cent and $5\frac{1}{2}$ per cent large amounts of foreign investment would be required'. His final conclusion – coming from the managing director of Bonuscor, a key stronghold of Afrikaner venture-finance – is perhaps worth noting: 'I have noticed that where overseas companies have a financial interest in South Africa, their office-bearers invariably have an understanding of our South African problems. They may not agree with us but at least they try to understand us and this in itself justifies attempts at obtaining overseas capital.'

56 Abstracted from article in *Annual Review of S.A. Economy* (Cape Times— Feb. 12, 1966) on 'The Role of Exports in our Economic Future' by J. J. Williams.

CHAPTER 19

1 The figures of votes cast at the special referendum on republican status for the Union of South Africa were: In favour 850,458; Not in favour 775,878.

2 The Act constituting the Republic

3 Dr Strijdom was prime minister after Dr Malan's resignation for a brief period until his death. He openly declared his native policy to be 'baasskap:' 'Call it paramountcy, baasskap or what you will, it is still domination. I am being as blunt as I can. I am making no excuses. Either the White man dominates or the Black man takes over. I say that the non-European will not accept leadership – if he has a choice. The only way the European can maintain supremacy is by domination . . . It is because the voting power is in the hands of the White man that the White man is able to govern South Africa today. Under the existing law it is not possible for the Natives, through merit or any other means, to get the domination into their hands. The government of the country is in the hands of the White man as the result of the franchise laws, and for that reason the White man is *baas* in South Africa . . . A speech by Dr Strijdom to Parliament, April, 1955. Quoted by L. E. Neame in *The History of Apartheid*.
No other prime minister has been so candid—or perhaps so truthful.

4 The Tomlinson Commission in terms of its labours was exceeded only by the famed Press Commission appointed to inquire into the alleged misrepresentations of the English-language press journalists. The

Press Commission, which took more than twelve years over its labours, duplicated a few copies of a report so long that nobody is known to have read it *in toto*.

5 Tomlinson Report U.G. 61–1955, pp. 28–9 pars. 28–31.

6 A projection by the S. A. Bureau of Census and Statistics (March 1966) gave a total population for South Africa in the year 2000 of 42,000,000 with the most startling growth predicted for the Coloureds – an increase of 300 per cent to 5,831,000 in year 2000.

7 Tomlinsom Report, p. 29, par. 32.

8 *ibid.* Chapter 11 – 'the Bantu Areas' p. 42, *et seq.*, gives useful summary of these Native Territories – subsequently known as Bantu Homelands or Bantustans.

9 The relationship of these British Protectorates to the Union of South Africa is, of course, one of the key geopolitical facts of South African history. From 1966 onwards the former Protectorates will become independent, self-governing sovereignties but bound by virtually indissoluble economic ties to the Republic.

10 Tomlinson Report, p. 49, pars. 25 *et seq.*

11 *ibid.*, p. 53, par. 4. 'What the majority of the non-White organizations thought of the Tomlinson Commission was shown at a conference held in Bloemfontein in October 1955, sponsored by the Inter-denominational African Ministers' Federation, presided over by Chief A. J. Luthuli, president of the African National Congress. Some 400 delegates attended, claimed to be representatives of all shades of African opinion.

Prof. Z. K. Matthews, vice-president of the ANC, said the life of the Black man in South Africa consisted of one crisis after another. It rejected the recommendations of the Tomlinson Commission *in toto*: '(1) Nothing in this Report remotely resembling a satisfactory arrangement with regard to the political aspect; (2) could not accept Commission's view of only two alternatives – "complete integration" or "complete segregation" but that 'a proper reading of the South African situation calls for co-operation and interdependence between the various races comprising the South African nation and denies that this arrangement would constitute a threat to the survival of the White man in South Africa; (3) the net result of the implementation of the Tomlinson Report would be 'a continuation of the *status quo* and indeed an aggravation of the worst evils of the present system including their extension to the Protectorates".' Quoted in L. E. Neame *The History of Apartheid*, p. 127.

12 *ibid.* (Tomlinson Report), p. 77, par. 47.

13 *ibid.*, p. 86, pars. 135 *et seq.*

14 *ibid.*, p. 95, pars. 17 *et seq.*

15 *ibid.*, pp. 98–9, pars. 10 *et seq.*

16 *ibid.*, p. 111, par. 5.

17 *ibid.*, p. 112, pars. 6–7.

18 *ibid.* Chapter 28. As in most developments 'plans' for under-developed territories, the Tomlinson Commission saw the need both to promote agricultural development and to achieve a decisive shift out of agriculture.

19 *ibid.*, p. 113, par. 8 *et seq.*

20 *ibid.*, p. 114, par. 20.

21 *ibid.*, see Chapter 45 and following chapters.

22 *ibid.*, p. 179, par. 12.

23 *ibid.*, p. 206, section 'Financial Requirements' gives summarized details. The government's response on the financial proposals came from Dr Verwoerd, as Minister of Native Affairs (Hansard, Vol. 94, 1957); 'For secondary and tertiary development £30,000,000 has been calculated [by Tomlinson Report]. That is the amount which is really intended for the development of White industries in the Native areas with State assistance. That can help kill the White industries now existing in the White areas . . .. I think it would be catastrophic for the present economic development of South Africa for the State to spend £30,000,000 over the next ten years to establish subsidized White industries in Native areas in competition with the existing White industries. Therefore that £30,000,000 falls away' (Hansard, Vol. 94, 1957, col. 3749).

It was the same Dr Verwoerd who as prime minister introduced the special incentives to encourage border-area industries (see later text) involving State assistance far in excess of £30m and with numerous highly favourable discriminatory provisions in direct competition with private industry not located on the perimeters of the Bantu Homelands.

24 *ibid.*, p. 184, par. 10.

25 *The Myth of the State* by Ernst Cassirer (Yale U.P.,1946), see pp. 277–96 on 'The Technique of the Modern Political Myths'.

26 Tomlinson Report, p. 132, par. 17.

27 *ibid.*, p. 133, par. 25.

28 *ibid.*, p. 140, par. 11.

29 *ibid.*, p. 141, pars. 13–14.

30 *ibid.*, p. 141, pars. 16–17.

31 Speech of May 18, 1959, by M. D. C. de Wet Nel from *South African Parties and Policies, 1910–1960* (ed. by Prof. D. W. Kruger; Cape Town: Human & Rousseau, 1960) pp. 441–52.

32 The Government published a White Paper on the Tomlinson Report. The White Paper endorsed the Government's acceptance of the major principle of the Tomlinson Report that the only acceptable policy was 'separate development'. It rejected, however, the crucial recommendation on industrialization by White private enterprise inside the

Bantu Homelands and also drastically modified the recommendations for new urbanized communities.

33 See *The Progress of the Bantu Peoples towards Nationhood*, a publication of the Ministry of Information, p. 10.

34 Quoted in *South African Digest*, Ministry of Information weekly, issue of April 16, 1965.

35 The majority of the Tomlinson Commission had, as already elaborated in the text, recommended such private enterprise interest as essential though under safeguards. Two Commission members, Messrs Young and Prinsloo, had opposed such White private interest. Mr M. C. de Wet Nel, member of the Commission and of Parliament but not yet Minister of Bantu Administration and Development, had accepted the majority recommendation – which, when he became Minister, he most vehemently denounced.

36 House of Assembly Debates, 3rd reading Part Appropriation Bill, March 1965.

37 *South African Digest*, Sept. 11, 1964 issue.

38 *ibid.*, March 19, 1965 and March 26, 1965.

39 *ibid.*, December 4, 1964.

40 For the consolidated 'Measures for the Encouragement of Industrial Development in the Border Areas' see p. 17 *et seq.* of: *Decentralized Industrial Development in South Africa*, a booklet of the Ministry of Information.

41 Statement by Dr Diederichs, Minister of Economic Affairs, April 30, 1965.

42 See *Financial Mail*, May 8, 1964 for *Border Pastures Grow Greener*.

43 Address by Dr S. P. du T. Viljoen, chairman of Board of Trade and Industries to National Management and Development Foundation, October 1964.

44 For an entertaining and instructive account of this venture, see 'The High Cost of Cyril Lord', article in *Financial Mail*, August 23, 1964. Despite the heavily sponsored nature of this demonstration model of Government border-area policy, the company almost immediately found itself in need of substantial protection. The form proposed was a complete rebate of duty imposed on imported loomstate cloth – the rebate to be available for five years from September 1963 to a maximum in any one year of 30m. square yards. The Lord mills would finish off the process. In order, however, that this most generous concession should not be available to other textile manufacturers, who had used their own capital without adventitious aids to set in being their enterprises, the proposed rebate was to be conditional on the applicant setting up an integrated spinning, weaving and finishing plant with a balanced capacity of at least 7·5m. square yards a year and giving an undertaking to expand to 15m. square yards by June 30, 1968. Finally,

this installation must have been put in after June 30, 1963. Curiously enough only Cyril Lord's venture could qualify to meet these conditions.

45   In the Senate, June 5, 1964, Dr Verwoerd said: 'In the case of the Orange River scheme there must not be this blackening process . . . I believe it [the Orange River settlements] must be for Whites alone who farm there with mechanization alone. . . .' The R450m. project was to establish a White heartland.

46   This strictly refers to the Transvaal and the Orange Free State. In the Cape Province most building artisans are, and have been for generations, Cape Coloured.

47   See article 'South African Farming Will Have to Double its Output' by Dr F. J. van Biljon in *Annual Review of the S.A. Economy*, Cape Times, Feb. 12, 1966, already cited.

48   Address by Mr Marais Viljoen, Deputy Minister of Labour, to Rapportryersklub (a right-wing cultural association of Afrikanerdom), *Cape Argus* report, Nov. 28, 1964.

CHAPTER 20

1   It is noteworthy that the former British Protectorates of Basutoland, Swaziland and Bechuanaland, with their newly constituted Black Governments, are welcoming private capital investment from all sources. There is no indication that such Black Governments regard such capital investment as 'economic neo-colonialism'.

2   The White Paper W.P.9–63 on the original Bill made it clear that the powers of the labour bureaux to refuse employment or cancel existing service contracts extended to 'when the Bantu is regarded as surplus to the labour requirements in that region; that the labour bureaux might regulate concerning the classes of employers to whom Bantu may be made available for employment and the manner and conditions of such employment; when the work to be performed is of a class or is to be performed in an area gazetted as being one in which no Bantu may be taken into employment; when the employment will exceed a labour quota fixed for a certain area or class of work.'

These powers do not specifically appear in the Act of 1964. Presumably it was recognized that the labour bureaux were being authorized to administer on their authority an unfettered job-reservation jurisdiction, the 'proper' authority for which lay with the Industrial Tribunal set up under Industrial Conciliation legislation. On the other hand, the power of the labour bureaux to refuse to sanction employment or cancel existing employment 'if he [the official] is satisfied it is not in the public interest', an authority conferred by the Act of 1964, is broad enough to cover the application of any interpretation of 'public interest', including surplus labour etc.

Further, in the White Paper, the original version of the Bill authorized the Minister of Bantu Administration to establish a class of work or an area in which no Bantu or further Bantu might be employed, or to determine a quota of such labour subject to consultation with the Minister of Labour and of Economic Affairs, the urban local authority and taking into account the availability of non-Bantu labour or the proportion which Bantu labour has to non-Bantu labour, and to giving a month's notice of intention to the public. Again these provisions appear to have been dropped from the final Act of 1964 but the powers in general of the Minister of Bantu Administration to control the numbers of Bantu seeking work are complete and unfettered.

3   In blocks of flats in the main cities, it has been customary to provide servants' accommodation in rooms on the top floor of the building (sometimes incidentally and accidentally giving the best views). Such 'locations-in-the-sky' have proved a major source of friction between Africans and the police, as police raids are carried out to remove friends of the domestic who have – illegally – been given shelter in such rooms.

4   See Benjamin Higgins *Economic Development*, Bauer & Yamey *Economics of Underdeveloped Countries*, Arthur Lewis *Economic Growth, passim*.

5   See essay by Bert Hoselitz 'A Sociological Approach to Economic Development' in his *Sociological Aspects of Economic Growth* (Free Press of Glencoe, 1960).

6   See *Economic Analysis and Policy in Underdeveloped Countries* by P. T. Bauer (Durham U.P., 1957), on Migrants pp. 72 *et seq*: 'Even where the migrants have entered the country without capital, they have, in the aggregate, often created capital on a massive scale by spending less than their incomes. . . . This type of capital formation is often overlooked . . . it is generally managed and invested by those who have accumulated it.' This point is strikingly and repeatedly illustrated from South African experience, the latest instance being the emigrés from Hitler's Europe who, arriving with no resources in the 1930's formed capital and pioneered new industries with remarkable success from after the War.

7   See *Capitalism, Socialism & Democracy* by Joseph A. Schumpeter (London: George Allen and Unwin, 1943) pp. 137–8.

8   See studies conducted by the Bureau of Market Research of the University of South Africa under Prof. de Comay.

9   Arthur Lewis in *Economic Growth*, already cited, writes: 'The expansibility of wants increases as physical equipment increases, as the culture becomes more complex, as the hold of convention weakens, and as knowledge of new goods is spread. This last is naturally the key to the expansion of wants, since it is the knowledge of new goods which sets in motion the forces that destroy convention or change the physical

environment,' p. 31. All this certainly applied to tribal Africans but no less to the rural Afrikaner bywoners.

10 See the book *Drum* by Antony Sampson. Sampson, an Oxbridge product, was engaged as editor of *Drum*, most successful of the African-orientated weeklies, and gave it a unique character reflecting all the colour, zest and violence of the Africans who in one or two generations had left tribalism behind for the excitement and struggles of urban Johannesburg. *Drum* mirrors remarkably the speed of acceptance of modern urbanized values from beauty queens to night life.

11 The limits of the bureaucratic mind may be illustrated from a few instances: (1) a Cape Coloured operatic group known as the Eoan Group performed before a distinguished White audience including the State President but the Cape Coloureds as an audience had to be accommodated at their own entirely separate performance; (2) the South African rugby Springboks were permitted to play against Maoris on a visit to New Zealand but a return visit of New Zealanders which was to include Maori players has been banned. This kind of incident can be repeated almost without end.

12 See Arthur Lewis, *Economic Growth*, already cited, pp. 234–7: 'The British, the Japanese and the Russian industrial revolutions all fit into this pattern. . . . In each case the immediate result is that the benefits of raising productivity go not to the classes who would increase their consumption – peasants, wage-earners – but into private profits or public taxation, where the proceeds are used for further capital formation. . . .

13 The detailed administrative code of regulations governing African labour employment appears in Bantu Labour Regulations, 1965, Govt. Notice No. R. 1892 of 1965.

14 Hansard, House of Assembly Debates, 1965, No. 14, col. 4430.

15 See Economic Development Programme, Dept. of Planning, already cited.

16 Hansard, House of Assembly Debates No. 14, col. 5618.

17 *ibid.*, col. 5571.

18 *ibid.*, cols. 5460–61, speech by Mr Froneman.

19 *ibid.*, No. 11, cols. 4206–7.

20 The interactions between the polity and the economy once more conform realistically to Talcott Parsons social system schema.

21 See International Labour Office, *Second Special Report on the Application of the Declaration concerning Apartheid* (1966) *passim*.

22 *The South African Worker*, Feb., 1965, quoted in ILO special report, already cited.

23 See Chapter 7: 'The White Polity Takes Control.'

24 According to a figure quoted by Dr L. J. E. Beyers, counsel for the dissident, breakaway members of the Mineworkers Union opposed to the Union's official leadership, the Union's membership had dropped

from 28,800 to 13,000 in 20 years. These figures do not tie in with actual number of Whites employed by the goldmines.

25 See Industrial Tribunal Report.

26 One of the last acts of entrepreneurship of Sir Ernest Oppenheimer was to initiate ultra-deep level goldmining. Western Deep Levels, which cost substantially more to open than any other mine, promises to be one of South Africa's greatest gold producers.

27 See Benjamin Higgins, *Economic Development*, already cited, p. 162.

28 Arthur Lewis, *Economic Growth*, already cited, p. 86.

29 Economic Development Programme already cited, par. 279.

30 The figures for gross immigration are (in '000s)

	Total	Africa	U.K.	Europe	Rest
1963	37·9	20·1	10·1	6·3	1·4
1964	40·8	17·1	12·8	8·9	1·9
1965	38·2	10·7	12·0	13·1	2·4

These are offset through emigration by about 10,000 a year.

31 See articles by S. Enke and J. de V. Graaff in *S.A. Journal of Economics*, Vol. 3), No. 1 March 1962, already cited.

See also an article of Prof. L. H. Samuels in the Golden Jubilee Number of *South African Industry and Trade*, May 1957, in which he refers to productivity studies in the United States where 'it has been found that possibly one-fifth or less of the increase per capita product can be explained by availability of additional labour, capital and other resources; the remaining four-fifths seem to have come about because of "improvements in national efficiency".'

If the production function of an economic development plan is $O = f$ (L.K.Q), where and what influence does 'national efficiency' exert? Is 'national efficiency' a function of the polity and of the value-orientations of the people? What is patriotism – is it a product of education, individual participation and identification with national aspirations? Does patriotism produce an upsurge of national energy? This may be so for the Afrikaners but what of the Africans?

32 Bernard Crick *In Defence of Politics*, already cited, p. 155.

33 See *The Afrikaners Interpretation of History* by F. A. van Jaarsveld, already cited, Chapter 1. Prof. van Jaarsveld specifically disclaims ideas of superior and inferior races but shows how Calvinism, isolationalism and the Old Testament together with historical experience moulded the Afrikaner and Afrikanerdom.

34 Leading article in *Die Transvaler*, August 1963.

35 Hansard, House of Assembly Debates, Vol. 13, 1965, cols. 625–6.

36 Estimate used by the Bureau of Standards, 1965, in a study of future water needs of South Africa, which disclosed that water resources might prove an obstacle to growth.

INDEX

513

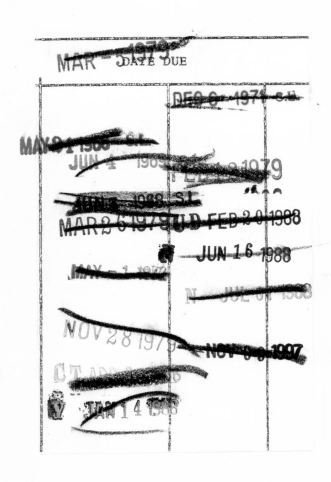